Brothers and Strangers

BROTHERS AND STRANGERS

Black Zion,

Black Slavery,

1914–1940

Ibrahim Sundiata

DUKE UNIVERSITY PRESS

Durham and London

2003

Printed in the United States of

America on acid-free paper ∞

Designed by C. H. Westmoreland

Typeset in Carter & Cone Galliard

with Jaeger Daily News display

by Keystone Typesetting, Inc.

*Library of Congress Cataloging-
in-Publication Data*

Sundiata, Ibrahim K.

Brothers and strangers : Black Zion,

Black slavery, 1914–1940 /

Ibrahim Sundiata.

p. cm.

Includes bibliographical references

(p.) and index.

ISBN 0-8223-3233-7 (cloth : alk. paper)

ISBN 0-8223-3247-7 (pbk. : alk. paper)

1. Back to Africa movement. 2. African

Americans—Colonization—Liberia.

3. African Americans—Colonization—

Africa. 4. Liberia—History—1847–1944.

5. Garvey, Marcus, 1887–1940. I. Title.

DT634.386 2003

966.62′00496073—dc22

2003016058

FOR

MY MOTHER

IN MEMORIAM

Contents

List of Illustrations

Acknowledgments

This study has had a long gestation, from research long ago to insights gained over the last few years. Initially I published a study of the crisis surrounding accusations of slavery against Liberia in 1929. Several years later, I was a contributing editor to *The Marcus Garvey and Universal Negro Improvement Association Papers*. I knew Liberia the place; I knew less of Garvey and the circumstances that had produced him. The editor of the papers, Robert A. Hill, sent me tons of material whetting my appetite to know more. I thank him very much for that impetus. My growing interest in the Diaspora led me to wonder why African American emigrationism had been seen by many as an impractical, if glorious, detour on the road toward participation in a multiracial society. Ten years ago Randall Kennedy of the Harvard Law School suggested to me that I pursue the question. Time and other projects pulled me in other directions, but the questions remained. This book is my answer to some of them, and it hopes to raise other questions, especially with regard to human rights and the frameworks in which we view them.

I conducted research in Liberia, Great Britain, the United States, and Spain. In Liberia I went through the National Archives before the overthrow of the Tolbert regime and have not retraced my steps. The same is true of the United Kingdom. I have returned to Spain several times. The Archivo General de la Administración Civil del Estado in Alcalá de Henares, which was closed to me earlier, is now open. In the late 1980s I was also given access to previously closed archives in the Republic of Equatorial Guinea.

I thank all those who aided my early efforts, especially Joel Jutkowitz who helped me first get into print on Liberia and labor. As an Africanist who has "drifted" toward the Diaspora, I want to thank all of those who have helped me along the way. African American collections have been invaluable in bridging that "middle passage" between the formerly artificially separated fields of Africa and its Diaspora. The Moorland-Spingarn Research Center at Howard University was more than helpful. I thank chief librarian Jean Church and Ida Jones, Donna Wells, and Clifford Muse for their assistance, especially with my insistent requests for photographs. I thank Leila Torres of the center for her moral support. The Schomburg Center for Research in Black Culture in New York gave me a whole new insight through its Lester Walton Papers, and a short return trip to the Chicago Historical Society provided valuable insights into the ongoing relationship between Walton and his confidant, Claude Barnett of the Associated Negro Press. I thank Lonnie Bunch for expediting my visit to the Historical Society archives. Walter Hill of the National Archives very kindly supplied me with the complete guide to the archives's Liberian and Garvey material compiled by Jacquelyn A. Kyles.

I have been able to count on Wilson Jeremiah Moses, Pan-Africanist scholar par excellence, who acted as an example and moral support. Some old friends have remained a constant in this evolving work. Among other things, it is to Hans Panofsky, bibliophile and unintentional mentor, that I owe my knowledge of the fate of the Liberian diplomat Antoine Sotille. I very much appreciate that it was Arnold Taylor, professor emeritus of Howard University, who long ago lent me photocopies of the J. P. Moffat Papers. Joseph Harris, Taylor's colleague and mine, has been an inspiration as he persisted with hard questions on how we speak about *Diaspora*. Elliott Skinner, emeritus professor at Columbia University, and I had interesting conversations about sources, and I look forward to his forthcoming volume on African Americans and foreign policy since the mid-1920s. Jane Martin, emerita of Boston University, has been steadfast over the years in providing valuable information and contacts. Indeed, she kept me aware of the Liberian dimension of the story. Elizabeth Elderedge, former student and fellow Africanist, was incredibly steadfast in those times when it was most needed. John Yoder, whom I knew as a graduate student, was more than generous in supplying me with his manuscript on current conditions in Liberia. Svend Holsoe, a man with a long association with Liberia and founder of the Liberian Studies Association, was marvelous in letting me use his photographs, which are now at the University of Indiana. Adele Logan Alexander of George Washington University offered her time and contacts for obtaining papers. She went the extra mile; I am obliged to her for gaining access to the journal of William H. Hunt, and I thank Phyllis Gibbs Fauntleroy for letting me use the Hunt journal.

I am very fortunate to have been at the W. E. B. Du Bois Institute in 2003 as a Du Bois Research Fellow. As one colleague described it, it is an "intellectual playground" in which people from various disciplines meet, mingle, and challenge disciplinary boundaries. Kudos go to Henry Louis Gates and his wonderful team. The business of preparing a manuscript is a daunting one, at least for this writer. At Harvard I had an incredibly efficient and hardworking fact checker and factotum in Ashley Aull. Reference librarian Barbara Burg's electronic wizardry at the Widener Library was invaluable. I want to thank Milagros Denis, my research assistant at Howard University. Also, typing is not done by automatons; many thanks to Geraldine Shearod, my typist at Howard. A special thanks to Bessie Hill, administrator of the History Department at Howard University. Her steadfastness and efficiency left me with the time to produce this work.

More than thanks, more than anything, I acknowledge the support of Eleanor Stewart, who oversaw this project as if it were her own. She critiqued, she edited, and she mailed. She made it happen.

Introduction

What is Africa to me:

Copper sun or scarlet sea,

Jungle star or jungle track,

Strong bronze men, or regal black

Women from whose loins I sprang

When the birds of Eden sang?

One three centuries removed

From the scenes his fathers loved.

Spicy grove, cinnamon tree,

What is Africa to me?

— Countee Cullen

"What is Africa to me?" This too oft quoted line by a New World black man still interrogates. To many, the continent signifies the home of the black race, the iconic antipode of Europe, the home of the white. Indeed, Africa in the American popular perception continues to be either an edenic mother/fatherland or the barbarous home of famine, disease, and civil war. With an acknowledgment of this dual vision we begin our investigation of how two constructs — the image of Africa and the image of slavery — have mediated, and continue to mediate, relations between the Black Diaspora and the peoples of the African continent.

In the years immediately preceding Countee Cullen's rhapsodic question, the immigrant Jamaican Pan-Africanist Marcus Garvey created a mass movement bent on transforming inchoate longings into a modern nation state. In the year World War I began, he founded the Universal Negro Improvement Association. Liberia was eventually chosen as the black Zion, and between 1920 and 1924, millions of African Americans were briefly caught up in the thrill of having a nation of their own, a nation on the ancestral continent. Haiti existed, but it was not African.

Ethiopia was independent, but too feudal to present a blueprint for the future. Liberia, "founded" by returnees from the African Diaspora in the early nineteenth century, seemed to meet all the desiderata of a national home, a land of "strong bronze men, or regal black." However, sadly, it was in the Black Republic that the poesy of trans-Atlantic longing ran headlong into African sociopolitical reality—including slavery. Garvey's plan to merge the image and the reality of Africa foundered in a sea of disillusionment. The planned return of millions of the scattered sons and daughters of Africa to their ancestral continent failed, and Liberia, long touted as the black Zion, proved to be a "bitter Canaan," to use Charles S. Johnson's phrasing. This book is partially an account of the rise and fall of the twentieth century's most potent African dream.

Four short years after the collapse of Garvey's dream, the United States officially accused the Black Republic of the most heinous of black-on-black crimes—slavery. Racists excoriated the small state, while Pan-Africanists, like Du Bois, and other anti-imperialists mounted a campaign of defense. Moral certainties became cloudy. White newspapers called for reform. At the same time, many of them screamed, in hardly masked contempt, of how a state "founded" by black returnees to Africa was enslaving fellow blacks. A Brooklyn newspaper remarked on its editorial page in 1931, "It is strange that in a country, founded as a haven for escaped American Negroes long before the Civil War, and ruled ever since that time by the Negro race, slavery still rears its horrid head."[1] Many commentators argued that Liberia, like Haiti, had failed as a nation. The forced labor scandal quickly became part of a revived debate on "the Negro's place in nature." One writer in *Current History* declared, "In a real sense the Negro race in Liberia is on trial before the world."[2]

Africa in the diasporic imagination represents many things—things imaged, things recorded, and things suppressed. African Americans are perpetually left with Cullen's question and the specter of slavery and the Middle Passage that stands behind it. We may begin by asking: What *is* the relationship to ancestral Africa? We do know, of course, that from the fifteenth century onward, approximately 15 million forced migrants left the African continent to people both of the Americas and the islands of the Caribbean. At the point of egress, captured women and men were phenotypically and culturally African, but much has happened since then. Their culture was never static; it went through syncretistic reformation, subsumption/transmogrification and reintegration/reassertion. In the United States, persons of African descent form a minority, but perhaps nowhere else is the sense of diaspora greater. As Elliott Skinner has noted, African Americans "remain . . . structurally linked to Africa whether they had any emotional bonds to that 'mysterious' continent or not. . . . Whenever African Americans sought equality with Americans of European descent, they were reminded that their Africaness precluded such aspirations."[3] *Blackness* has been defined by rigidly imposed endogamy and residential segregation. African Americans have a corporate identity that has arisen in the context of white political and ideological hegemony. For the 10 percent of the population that is "black," the future is seen as one of separate but equal communities, each with equal access to the economic and social benefits of the society at large. The gradual construction of whiteness in the North American context has made blacks operate as the perpetual Other in a society with no common myth of origin nor any national myth of eventual fusion. Africa operates as a fixed point, the loadstone of ethnic identity, an identity often analyzed so as to diffuse issues of hybridization and creolization. Whether the locus of collective origin lies in ancient Egypt or among the Yoruba, a core Africanity is posited because societal constructs so clearly set off the black community from the white in a Manichaean worldview governing everything from politics to the music industry.

Where "race" has been enforced for over nine generations, as in the United States, we must take that construct very seriously. The fact that by the 1990s, the term *African American* had displaced most others is, by itself, very indicative. The black population, by its very name, asserts its Africanity. As Sterling Stuckey has pointed out:

> The final gift of African "tribalism" in the nineteenth century was its life as a lingering memory in the minds of American slaves. That memory enabled them to go back to the sense of community in the traditional African setting and to include all Africans in their common experience of oppression in North America. It is greatly ironic, therefore, that African ethnicity, an obstacle to African nationalism in the twentieth century, was in this way the principal avenue to black unity in antebellum America. Whether free black or slave, whether in the North or in the South, the ultimate impact of that development was profound.[4]

Hypodescent, the "one drop rule," has molded discussions of the culture and delimitation of the Black Diaspora. It is within this context that Pan-Africanism developed and a sense of kindredhood with the peoples of Africa and the Anglophone Caribbean emerged. While often focused on parochial issues, American blacks could never forget and were never allowed to forget that they constituted a separate people, one with roots on an alien continent. However creolized their culture, they were consciously reminded at every turn that they were a distinct folk, regardless of class position. Never numbering more than 20 percent of the population, African Americans made for the permanent minority, whose exact place within the polity was never fully spelled out. Under segregation, separate but equal became the law of the land and, by a queer transmogrification, separate but equal remains the ideal for all but public spaces after integration.[5]

The image of Africa and the image of slavery are inextricably bound. In early 1998, President Bill Clinton visited Africa. The trip was a triumphal one, focused on trade, international security, and the ties that bind Africa and African Americans. Howard French, an African American writer for the *New York Times,* mused over whether the United States should apologize for the Atlantic Slave Trade. He said, "In the end, appropriately solemn Mr. Clinton stopped short of an outright apology for America's part in the slave trade, finding other ways to express his regret as he focused on the future."[6] When the president did express regret, he spoke at a school in Uganda. The act was unintentionally symbolic, the equivalent of apologizing for the Irish Potato Famine in Slovakia. Perhaps most telling, in the president's discussion of the evils of slavery, nothing was said of present-day bondage across the border in neighboring Sudan. "In what seems to be a recurring political ritual," in 2003 George W. Bush went to Goree Island in Senegal and "talked about Frederick Douglass and Sojourner Truth, Harriet Beecher Stowe and Abraham Lincoln." As the *New York Times* noted, the American president "traveled to an island off the coast of Africa to give a speech on slavery in America."[7]

In the Diaspora, the subject of slavery can produce either rage or shame. The latter is especially true of slavery in Africa. Commenting on President Clinton's decision to express official regret for the historic slave trade, the *New York Times* writer mentioned what we may call the *slavers' canard*: "Weren't Africans engaging in slavery themselves well before the first Europeans came and carried off their first human cargoes? Didn't African chiefs themselves conduct . . . slaving raids on neighboring tribes and march their harvest to the shores for sale?"[8] The charge is an old one. Beginning in the eighteenth century, defenders of Atlantic slavery maintained that Africa itself was rife with the institution; Europeans only took away the surplus produced by semipermanent warfare. In 1734, Thomas Snelgrave, a trader, remarked: "It is evident, that abundance of captives, taken in war, would be inhumanly destroyed, was there not an opportunity of disposing of them to the Europeans. So that at least many lives are saved, and great numbers of useful persons kept in being."[9]

The canard has been around for more than two centuries and continues to mold much of the North American discussion of slaving. Nineteenth-century abolitionists responded to the slavers' canard by painting an image of a bucolic Africa in which slaves were part of the family, a status hardly comparable to chattel status in the American South. In the twentieth century, Maulana Karenga maintains that bondspeople in Africa "often lived as members of the family, married their masters' daughters and rose to political and economic prominence and did not face the brutalization and dehumanization which defined European chattel slavery."[10] From the right of the political spectrum, polemicists continue to hammer away. The conservative ideologue Dinesh D'Souza decries attempts to "downplay African slavery." Any claims "of the benign quality of African slavery are hard to square with such reports as slaves being tortured at the discretion of their owners, or executed en masse to publicly commemorate the deaths of the kings of Dahomey."[11] Perhaps the most bizarre version of the canard appeared in *Harper's* in the late 1970s. Lewis Latham, miffed at Andrew Young's stance in the United Nations, let off a broadside. Latham accused Young of forgetting "to mention that the tribes of Africa speak as many as 700 languages and that in a disturbingly large number of those languages the verb 'to eat' has the further and metaphorical meaning of 'win,' 'conquer,' or 'gain.'" In seeking to inform himself about African history, Latham lamented that he could only read "extensively about the slave trade, cannibalism, tribal wars, woodcarving, raffia waving, and the steady state of Stone Age cultures that had survived for possibly as long as 250,000 years." Of slavery itself, according to the journalist, the record was dismal: "Its success depended on the eagerness of the African tribes to sell their enemies, their wives, their friends, and their children at whatever price was offered."[12] This racist fantasy of Africa as a Hobbesian nightmare persists, deforming the continent's image among both whites and blacks.

If *Africa* is simply the metonym for *Black Man's Land,* a place without nations, ethnicities, or languages, the charge of slavery is devastating. Zora Neale Hurston lamented, "But the inescapable fact that stuck in my craw was: my people had sold me. . . . My own people had exterminated whole nations and torn families apart for profit before the strangers got their chance at a cut."[13] Richard Wright was bedeviled by similar thoughts. "Had some of my ancestors," he mused, "sold their relatives to white men?" The writer wondered: "What would my feelings be when I looked into the black face of an African, feeling that maybe his great-great-great-grandfather had sold my great-great-great-grandfather into slavery?"[14] Recently, Henry Louis Gates Jr., the doyen of African American studies, has commented, "The image of slavery we had when I was kid was that the Europeans showed up with these fish nets and swept all the Africans away." He is startled. "Rubbish. It's like they went to a shopping mall. Without the Africans there wouldn't have been a slave trade."[15] The indictment is particularly blistering:

> For African Americans the most painful truth concerning the extraordinary complex phenomenon that was the African slave trade is the role of black Africans themselves in its origins, its operation, and its perpetuation. It was an uneasiness and anger about this truth that fueled Richard Wright's barely concealed contempt for his Ghanaian kinsman in *Black Power* and that led many African Americans to view their New World culture as *sui generis,* connected only tenuously to its African antecedents, if at all. Western images of African barbarism and savagery, of course, did not endear us to our native land [*sic*]. But for many of my countrymen, the African role in the slave trade of other Africans is both a horrific surprise and the ultimate betrayal, something akin to fratricide and soricide. Imagine the impact of a revelation that Sephardic Jews had served as the middlemen in the capture and incarceration of Ashkenazi Jews during the Holocaust, and you can perhaps begin to understand Richard Wright's disgust.[16]

This raises the question of who is a "brother" and a "kinsman." Of course, if the African continent is the "nation," an equivalent would be to view the Holocaust as a *Mittel-Europaische* family feud of particular ferocity — Europeans exterminating their own people while in league with an alien race from the other end of the world.[17] Pearl-Alice Marsh, executive director of the Africa Policy Information, laments, "There are millions of Americans who still think Africa is a country, not a continent."[18] The idea of an Africa composed of competing ethnicities and polities is irrelevant in the face of the metonym. Unfortunately, in the popular American imagination, the fifty-odd African states still remain an irrelevant hodgepodge. The continent remains largely featureless; languages are "dialects" and ethnicities are "tribes." If Africa — three times the size of the United States and containing 748 million people speaking some 1,500 languages — is reduced to simply a mythic homeland, confusion is sure to follow. And worse than confusion, a basic lack of understanding or sympathy for Africans as they exist will ensue.

The North American image of slavery in Africa has historically stood as a distortion, either a magnification or diminution, of the image of American slavery. Trans-Atlantic bondage is the absolute before which all other manifestations are held as relative. In the United States, slavery is the cause of the essential national fissure. The national (white) image of the institution has gone through various permutations, without questioning basic assumptions. Early in the twentieth century, Southern historians like Ulrich B. Phillips painted a rosy picture of bondage in Dixie; indeed, slavery was a benign "school" for blacks. D. W. Griffith's *Birth of a Nation* contained images of both "faithful darkies" and "ferocious bucks." The popular image of kindly slavery perhaps reached its apogee in Margaret Mitchell's *Gone with the Wind*.

The African American view of slavery has changed drastically in the years since emancipation. Various nineteenth-century black thinkers, among them Martin Delany, Henry M. Turner, Alexander Crummell, and Edward Blyden, saw the Middle Passage as providential, even if highly painful. Turner maintained that the world might one day be thankful for slavery, as it would eventuate in the evangelization of Africa. To Blyden, Africans were people who "had been carried away, in the providence of God, . . . carried away from heathenism into slavery among civilized and Christian peoples."[19] Booker T. Washington, the leader of African American opinion at the end of the nineteenth century, wrote, "Notwithstanding the cruelty and moral wrong of slavery, the ten million Negroes . . ., who themselves or whose ancestors went through the school of American slavery, are in a stronger and more hopeful condition, materially, intellectually, morally, and religiously, than is true of an equal number of black people in any other portion of the globe."[20] Later, the Nation of Islam preached, "Our slavery . . . was actually all for a Divine purpose, that Almighty Allah (God) might make Himself known through us to our enemies and let the world know the Truth that He alone is God."[21] An echo of these earlier sentiments comes in journalist Keith Richburg's 1997 assertion that "condemning slavery should not inhibit us from recognizing mankind's ability to make something good arise often in the aftermath of the most horrible evil. . . . In short, thank God that I am an American."[22]

By the time of the civil rights movement, providential slavery had all but disappeared from most African American discourse on slavery and the slave trade. The image of slavery emerged not so much as a labor system, but as a systematic torture of millions rooted in innate racial antagonism. In this scenario, sexual exploitation and gross barbarity fueled by raging hatred characterized every day of slave existence. The plantation resembled not so much Booker T. Washington's "school" as it did Stanley Elkins's later comparison with a concentration camp.[23] The Jamaican-born sociologist Orlando Patterson has elaborated on "social death" and dishonor as the essential features of slavery. Slavery is, in his psychodynamic view, "the permanent, violent domination of natally alienated and generally dishonored persons."[24] In the realm of high art, the chief proponent of this view is the Nobel laureate Toni Morrison. Reflecting a sea change since *Gone with the Wind,* she provides an antidote in the terminally bleak *Beloved*. The book is dedicated to the "60 million" people she estimates perished in the slave trade. The number, a significant multiple of 6 million, holds power.[25]

An Old Dixie Narrative had emerged. Simply stated, this view of history says: Slavery was confined to Dixie and slaves grew cotton. Nowhere else in the history of humanity has slavery existed and nowhere else were human beings chattel. Africans, in this version of history, were selected slaves because they were black. Racism drove a slave trade and slavery, which existed as the ultimate form of psychosexual torture. The numbers immolated in the holocaust of the Middle Passage and in the cotton fields ran into the hundreds of millions. At the popular level, the Old Dixie Narrative floats in the American collective consciousness, even among those who have never given it much thought.

For many African Americans, looking back through the prism of Jim Crow and lynch law, a view of slavery as the ultimate horror provides ample proof of the ultimate fixity of human nature. Racism was as alive in fifteenth-century Lisbon as it was in nineteenth-century Louisville. History becomes one long version of *Up from Slavery*, and always a struggle against the Manichaean "Other." Blacks remain the ultimate out-group, one that erases European division and suffering. But Morrison rightly notes, "If there were no black people here in this country, it would have been Balkanized. The immigrants would have torn each other's throats out, as they have done everywhere else."[26] Or, as Cornel West puts it: "White supremacy dictates the limits of the operation of American democracy—with black folk the indispensable sacrificial lamb vital to its sustenance." Thus "black subordination constitutes the necessary condition for the flourishing of American democracy, the tragic prerequisite for America itself."[27] In the Old Dixie Narrative, both sides of the racial divide agree that blacks have always been drawers of water and hewers of wood. Class becomes eternally raced. It constitutes a mythos above and beyond all empirical analysis or comparison. It may be true, as David Brion Davis points out, that "some of the privileged 'Atlantic creole' slaves in the seventeenth-century Chesapeake and in Carolina clearly possessed more de facto freedom and range of choice than did the later Chinese indentured servants who shoveled guano, or seafowl excrement, off the coast of Peru."[28] In terms of the Old Dixie Narrative, however filthy this work, it becomes irrelevant.

If slavery were only about race, then Africans could not have engaged in slave traffic in Liberia or anywhere else. Indeed, the charge itself constitutes racial calumny. However, long ago, the Trinidadian historian Eric Williams sounded a cautionary note. Best known for maintaining that white humanitarianism did not abolish the slave trade, the scholar made a subsidiary, and often overlooked, point: capitalism and slavery are no great respecters of persons. Writing from beyond the confines of the Old Dixie Narrative, he observed, "The 'horrors' of the Middle Passage have been exaggerated. For this the British abolitionists are in large part responsible." Furthermore, "A racial twist has . . . been given to what is basically an economic phenomenon. Slavery was not born of racism; rather, racism was the consequence of slavery. Bound labor in the New World was brown, white, black, and yellow; Catholic, Protestant and pagan."[29] Orlando Patterson notes that "slavery has existed from the dawn of human history right down to the 20th century, in the most primitive of human societies and in the most civilized." Moreover, "There is no region on earth that has not at some time harbored the institution. Probably there is no group of people whose ancestors were not at one time slaves or slaveholders."[30] What is remarkable about slavery in the United States is not that it existed, but its long afterbirth— legalized segregation and a caste society. North American racial theorists noted that the country's "peculiar institution" was not very peculiar at all. What they boasted about was American "race feeling," a phenomenon that kept the United States from descending into the Latin American "coffee-colored comprise" of race amalgamation. The United States *is* the most racially organized society in the Americas.

Unfortunately, few could think in terms of C. L. R. James's dictum: "The race question is subsidiary to the class question in politics. . . . But to neglect the racial factor as merely incidental is error only less grave than to make it fundamental."[31] We should go a bit further and "put . . . slave systems in the context of unfree labor in general, and its role in the evolution of the modern world." In this broader context, "American slavery—and New World slavery in general—is a part of what can be termed the 'labor question': who should work for whom, under what terms should work be performed, and how should it be compelled or rewarded?"[32] If we follow this tact, we end up with somewhat different conclusions. Slavery, like marriage, emerges as a fairly universal institution. Most societies have had some form of it. Slavery, at base, rests on the ability to coerce labor and/or sexual reproduction. Charging a peculiar black guilt for slavery makes for an ahistorical and presentist trap. However, denial of slavery in Africa, like a denial of the existence of prostitution in Africa, is no more than a flight from reality. Like the flight from the acknowledgment of AIDS and prostitution, it is also dangerous.

Slavery need not be raced. It could exist in ancient Rome, medieval Kosovo, nineteenth-century Korea, and in the Liberia of the interwar years. This brings us to the central question: How do we confront social oppression in black-ruled Africa? Liberia provides a test case of the limits of Pan-Africanism. Whole libraries have been written on the movement as anticolonialist ideology. These range from the congresses organized by Du Bois to the activism inspired by Garvey in places as disparate as South Africa and Brazil. My aim here differs. I look at "Pan-Africanism in one country," a specific African place. In crisis, Liberia stretched forth her hands to the Black Diaspora. The appeal affected both those who viewed the Black Republic as the symbol of black independence and those who viewed it as a field for black capitalism. The question subtly became: What is Liberia to me? If the oligarchy in Monrovia was corrupt, it should be condemned. Yet condemnation fell in very nicely with the charges of white racists and might threaten black independence. The deep desire of many blacks in the Diaspora to keep Liberia open as a "Black Man's Country" encouraged apologetics, even in the face of festering doubts about the country's rulers. This ambiguity of the erstwhile black Zion in the interwar period raises the continuing question of whether racial solidarity calls for solidarity with unrepresentative present-day African regimes — or the people made to suffer under them. More broadly, it raises the question of how American minorities are to react to conflicts in the "old country," be it Northern Ireland or the West Bank.

Liberia, a country that operated more or less as an American protectorate from the First World War through the cold war, is today beyond the range of major United States foreign policy interests. Seventy years ago, in the name of human rights, a Republican administration stood on the verge of using military force to secure a material deemed essential to national defense. Today, amid the slaughter of thousands, another Republican administration is timorous of all but token involvement. Interventions proceed, but perceived national interests have shifted elsewhere. This is the most cautionary part of this tale.

1 Confronting the Motherland

The Negro is an American. We know nothing of Africa.

— Martin Luther King Jr.

For many generations, slaves and the descendants of slaves in America invented a homeland called "Africa" — a land before slave ships, a prelapsarian savanna whereupon the provocatively dressed gazelle could stroll safely after dark. Perhaps someday Africa will exist, in which case it will have been patented by African Americans in the U.S.A. from the example of the American Civil Rights movement.

— Richard Rodriguez

People from the African Diaspora have often been at the forefront of the movement for African liberation. Their contribution to anticolonial Pan-Africanism has been immense. In 1947, W. E. B. Du Bois (1868–1963) observed, "The idea of one Africa to unite the thought and ideals of all native peoples of the dark continent belongs to the twentieth century and stems naturally from the West Indies and the United States." In these two places, "various groups of Africans, quite separate in origin, became so united in experience and so exposed to the impact of new cultures that they began to think of Africa as one idea and one land."[1] Thinkers and activists such as Alexander Crummell, Edward Blyden, Du Bois, Marcus Garvey, George Padmore, and Malcolm X have all formed part of a long tradition. Vis-à-vis European colonialism and racism, they have been the proverbial miner's canary. Diasporic blacks have borne witness to and warned of the full meaning of white supremacy. They have known (and continue to know) that whatever differences of ethnicity or language may exist among blacks, white supremacy posits the subordination of all blacks. As Malcolm X told the Organization of African States in 1964, "Your problems will never be fully solved until and unless ours are solved. You will never be fully respected until and unless we are also respected." He reminded his listeners, "Our problem is your problem. It is not a Negro problem, nor an American problem. . . . It is not a problem of civil rights, but a problem of human rights."[2]

Identity in the Diaspora has assumed tremendous importance. Du Bois struggled with the issue for the more than seventy years of his adult life. The intellectual, educated at Fisk, Harvard, and The University of Berlin, was one of the founders of the National Association for the Advancement pf Colored People (NAACP) in 1909 and, until 1934, the editor of its journal, the *Crisis*. He has emerged as a central figure in twentieth-century Pan-Africanism; Du Bois was at the forefront of organizing a series of Pan-African conferences held in Europe in the years following World War I. In his ninety-five years, the African American polymath moved from a rather genteel late-Victorian emphasis on the transformative power of the liberal bourgeoisie to Marxist-Leninism and membership in the Communist Party.

On the question of identity, the Massachusetts-born Du Bois was an early multiculturalist. In the address "The Conservation of Races," delivered in 1897, he spoke of what Africa meant to him and his folk. Races, not individuals, were the motive force in history. His people had a racial message they had not yet been able to give to the world. Because of the uniqueness of their gift, "the advance guard of the Negro people — the 8,000,000 people of Negro blood in the United States of America — must soon come to realize that if they are to take their just place in the van of Pan-Negroism, then their destiny is *not* absorption by the white Americans."[3]

African Americans were just that, one branch of the great and ramifying Negro race whose seat was Africa. Du Bois makes a virtue of necessity in the face of white American psychosexual hysteria surrounding "mongrelization." A year after *Plessy v. Ferguson,* and in a country in which many states had miscegenation laws, Du Bois's minatory tone on absorption was unneeded. His defensive conceptualization of what black folk had to offer American society was a spirituality that harkened back to Africa. His ideas resemble those of an earlier Pan-African thinker, Edward Blyden (1832–1912). The older man had elaborated the idea of the "African Personality," which stressed warmth, communality, and spirituality in opposition to European coolness, individualism, and materialism. Such dichotomizations formed part of a more general late-nineteenth-century pattern. As in Slavophilism and Hindutsva, "spirituality" constituted a counterweight to the values of the successfully imperialist West.

In 1897, Du Bois called African Americans a nation, but he avoided nationalist appeals. Blacks were distinct and should perpetually remain so, but without a political state of their own. Instead, they should seek entrance into the civic sphere in a secular and race-neutral state. At the turn of the twentieth century, Du Bois advocated a politically engaged version of "separate but equal." Whereas Booker T. Washington, the dominant spokesman in contemporary black political life, publicly eschewed political participation, Du Bois demanded access to full civil rights within a pluralistic sociopolitical order. He felt that, "if . . . there is substantial agreement in laws, language and religion; if there is a satisfactory adjustment of economic life, then there is no reason why, in the same country and on the same street, two or three great nation ideals might not thrive and develop, that men of different races might not strive together for their race ideals as well, perhaps even better, than in isolation."[4] Over his long lifespan, Du Bois remained insistent on a core of African American rights. Much else changed and shifted. The man who could see danger in amalgamation in 1897 could write in 1920 that he saw no reason to exclude blacks from social, including sexual, equality.[5] Fourteen years later, in one of the greatest shifts of his life, Du Bois embraced black self-segregation and self-development as the answer to the problems of Depression-weary black America. Perhaps unintentionally, Du Bois's most lasting contribution to the ongoing debate on race was his early enunciation of the liberal modus vivendi, which had become part of the American consensus on race relations by the 1960s. What is most significant is that his lifelong commitment to the advancement of his folk at all times remained consistent with a general concern for social justice. His quest for the latter was never ending, although he seldom took a straight path.

Throughout Du Bois's adult life, Africa remained important. He first visited the continent in 1923; he died there some thirty years later. David Levering Lewis notes:

> In Du Bois, the Pan-African idea found an intellectual temperament and organizational audacity enabling it to advance beyond the evangelical and literary to become an embryonic movement whose cultural, political, and economic potential would assume, in the long term, worldwide significance. No other person of color then living, with the significant and calamitous exception of Marcus Garvey, was more capable of articulating the idea and mobilizing others in its service.[6]

Africa, however enveloped in mythopoeic projections, was necessary. While whites posited exclusion because of the inferiority of Negro blood, Du Bois retorted with the claim of a specific gift contained within that blood. Hence the two races might remain separate together, to their mutual benefit. In his 1903 collection of essays, *The Souls of Black Folk*, he assures his audience that the black man "would not Africanize America, for America has too much to teach the world and Africa. He would not bleach his Negro soul in a flood of white Americanism, for he knows that Negro blood has a message for the world."[7] The Negro derived his gift from Africa. Of his people, Du Bois said, "We are Americans, not only by birth and by citizenship, but by our political ideals, our language, our religion. Farther than that, our Americanism does not go." To the obvious question of why, he responds, "We are Negroes, members of a vast historic race that from the very dawn of creation has slept but half awakening in the dark forests of its African fatherland."[8] Du Bois's Africa is totemic, a *lieu de mémoire*; it gives the eternal social separation of North American blacks a rationale. It is a lyrical conception, a construct that transmutes exclusion into conservation. It is not a geographical expression, but a spiritual pedigree. As such it proves essential to Du Bois's American project, but it is an Africa projected from without, from the Diaspora. It is the Black Man's Land, a peaceful *Volksgemeinschaft* (national/folk community). Totemic Africa long preceded Du Bois's encounter with Africa as a geographical place. He later remarked, "I did not myself become actively interested in Africa until 1908 or 1910. Franz Boas really influenced me to begin studying this subject and I began really to get into it only after 1915."[9] By this time, Africa the totem was firmly in place, filtering all information from Africa the place.

Admittedly, Du Bois did eventually move away from assertions of grand spiritual affinities and conceived of the link between Africa and the Diaspora as one of shared oppression. In 1940, he proclaimed, "But one thing is sure and that is the fact that since the fifteenth century these ancestors of mine and their descendants have had a common history; have suffered a common disaster and have one long memory." Phenotype was no cardinal point. What provided a connection was the "social heritage of slavery; the discrimination and insult, and this heritage binds together not simply the children of Africa, but extends through yellow Asia and into the South Seas. It is this unity that draws me to Africa."[10] The slave trade, slavery, and its heritage of discrimination thus prove central to the linkage between Africa and its Diaspora. However, what happens if we look backward and inward? Are class, ethnicity, and gender so easily trumped? Do all African social classes become linked to the forced migrants? Did the Middle Passage really bind together a cane cutter in Jamaica and King Gezo of Dahomey? If we succumb to the Manichaean binary of an exploiting West and a passive and undifferentiated "rest," we are left with no critique of multiple forms of social oppression found among this rest.

Enter Garvey

Marcus Garvey (1887–1940) stands out as the most programmatic of diasporic Pan-Africanists. Malcolm X credited Garvey and his Universal Negro Improvement Association (UNIA) with starting "the entire freedom movement, which brought about the independence of African nations."[11] The Trinidadian historian Tony Martin says Garvey "demonstrated the underlying unity of the African world, despite its regional diversities. He showed that Africans from Canada to South Africa and from Australia to Panama could be appealed to and mobilized around a common program of race first, self-reliance and nationhood."[12] Garvey linked the disparate parts of the Diaspora—the Caribbean, the United States, and Africa—in a great arc of black suffering, which was, in turn, linked by a future of racial greatness. Combined with this notion of common cultural affinity, but not always coterminous with it, was the idea of a unified political destiny.

Garvey continues to be endlessly analyzed and critiqued, his person and thought often caught between the opposing perceptions of hagiographers and detractors. Recently, looking at the evolution of Caribbean radicalism, Winston James has argued that Garvey's non-American background proves particularly important:

It is almost unthinkable ... that an African American leader at the time would have adopted the high profile, noisy, confrontational posture adopted by the Garvey movement in the early part of the century—the Universal African Legions, a proto-military wing of the UNIA, even had a cavalry unit which paraded on the streets of New York on horseback, in full military regalia; it is almost unthinkable, because the historical experience of Afro-America would certainly have ruled out such an option. It was too much of an obvious high-risk gamble.

Given the later career of the Black Panthers, one might question this assertion. Some critics dismiss Garvey as simply the leader of an ephemeral and doomed back-to-Africa scheme. More than forty years ago, George Padmore, a doyen of Pan-Africanism, compared Garvey and his rival Du Bois: "Garvey's bombastic broadsides against the white man, coupled with his garish showmanship, had an hypnotic effect upon the unlettered, unsophisticated West Indian immigrants and Southern Negroes." The reason for the UNIA's success was that "Du Bois could not compete with Garvey's appeal to these under-privileged people. He was too intelligent, too honest to play on their ignorance of the real situation in Africa."[13] In the mid-1980s, Judith Stein came to just the opposite conclusion. Seeking to place the UNIA within a non-Marxist class critique, she maintained that Garveyism represented the yearnings of a would-be black bourgeoisie whose aims diverged in significant ways from those of the black masses. For her, it constituted a movement of urbanized strivers enamored of black capitalism. "Because the class structure of the black community was different from that of the Anglo-Saxon, Jewish, Italian, and Chinese communities did not mean that it was nonexistent." Furthermore, "the class structure of the black community in Gary, Indiana, was different from the ones in Macon County, Alabama, in Kingston, Jamaica, and in Monrovia, Liberia. The lives of black farmers, factory workers, and teachers were not identical. It would be surprising if their politics were."[14]

The abortion of Garveyism has been attributed to many causes: the narrowness of its class aims; the opposition of the established African American elite; the interference of the European colonial powers; the opposition of the Liberian oligarchy; the harassment by the FBI. All of these played a part in the subversion of Marcus Garvey and the UNIA. None of them, in and of itself, suffices as an explanation. The defeat (rather than the failure) of Garveyism does not rest on the inherent illogic of its program. It rests on a failure to disentangle the claims of a national minority from those of pan-ethnicity. In Liberia, the site of the proposed experiment, the UNIA ran into issues of class and ethnicity, which belied the very unity it proclaimed as its raison d'être.

The lineaments of Marcus Mosiah Garvey's biography are well known and oft repeated. A considerable literature has already accumulated, much of it focused on the rise and fall of Garvey's movement within the United States. Other writings have assessed the impact of his anti-colonial rhetoric in the broad African and Caribbean contexts. I intend neither of these approaches here. My purpose is to examine Garveyism and its aftermath in Liberia, the "national centre" which Garvey promised his followers and the world.

Briefly summarized, Garvey's life was truly international, moving as it did between the Caribbean, North America, and Europe. The future leader was born at St. Ann's Bay, in northern Jamaica, on August 17, 1887, the son of a mason and a seamstress. The youth left school at the age of fourteen and became a printer's apprentice in Kingston. Garvey subsequently achieved the status of master printer and foreman at the large P. A. Benjamin Company. In 1907, the young foreman supported a strike and lost his position as a result. He went to work in the Government Printing Office and founded a short-lived newspaper, *Garvey's Watchman*. Subsequently, he joined the political and literary National Club and published a bimonthly newspaper called *Our Own*. Garvey also made the acquaintance of Dr. J. Robert Love, a British-trained Bahamian political critic, who published the *Advocate*. The future black nationalist left Jamaica in 1910 for Costa Rica, where he worked for the United Fruit Company. Outraged by the treatment of his fellow West Indians on the plantations, Garvey went to Port Limón, where he demanded that the British consul protect black workers. In Costa Rica, the young ex-printer established yet another ephemeral publication, *La Nacional,* before moving on to Panama, where he started *La Prensa*.

The politically awakened Garvey returned to Jamaica in 1911. His sojourn was brief; he left for London the following year. In the imperial capital, he came into contact with a wide range of black opinion. One of his contacts was the journalist and Pan-Africanist Duse Mohammed Ali, the publisher of the *African Times and Orient Review,* who gave him employment. In October of 1913, Garvey observed, "As one who knows the people well, I make no apology for prophesying that there will soon be a turning point in the history of the West Indies." He predicted that "the people who inhabit that portion of the Western Hemisphere [i.e., the West Indies] will be the instruments of uniting a scattered Race, who before the close of many centuries will found an Empire on which the sun shall shine as ceaseless as it shines on the Empire of the North today."[15]

At the same time that he espoused a triumphant vision of black imperialism, Garvey was also drawn to the moral uplift and economic self-sufficiency preached by Booker T. Washington. Washington's book, *Up from Slavery,* inspired the Jamaican to plan a program of vocational education in his homeland. Garvey returned to Jamaica in July of 1914 determined to do something "Washingtonian" for his people. The outgrowth of this striving was the Universal Negro Improvement and Conservation Association and the African Communities League. On the face of it, he pursued a conservative aim. "The bulk of our people," he observed, "are in darkness and are really unfit for good society." The new association proposed "to go among the people and help them up to a better state of appreciation among the cultured classes, and raise them to the standard of civilized approval."[16] In March of 1916, Garvey traveled to the United States to see Washington for the purpose of raising money for a school in Jamaica. Unfortunately, his arrival came several months after the Sage of Tuskegee's death.

Garvey's arrival proved a turning point. In the wider ambit of North

American society, he very quickly came to the conclusion that the organization of black business must supersede his original plan to establish an educational institution. Garvey, once an optimist about the prospects of education and uplift in the Diaspora, was deeply affected by the wave of racial violence during and after the First World War. Lynching and riots convinced him that the United States was essentially a white man's country. The Jamaican immigrant moved his headquarters to New York's Harlem after spending about fifteen months lecturing and fund-raising across the United States. Within a few years, his UNIA had emerged as the most dynamic group in Harlem.

Garvey's advent coincided with the Great Migration of African Americans from the South. Seeking better conditions, thousands left. Between 1910 and 1920, the first wave (300,000) arrived in the North. In the next decade, a huge number (1,300,000) arrived. Northern cities saw the expansion of urban ghettoes. Chicago's black population went from 44,103 to 233,903 between 1910 and 1930, Detroit's from 5,741 to 120,066. New York, the nation's largest urban area, had a black population that grew from 91,709 to 327,796.[17] In the black metropolis, migrants from the agrarian American South both warily viewed and mixed with immigrants from the Anglophone West Indies. Whatever their differences, both were caught on the wrong side of the color line, sharing a common language and a heritage of Protestant evangelization.

It was to these people that Garvey revived many of the emigrationist hopes of the nineteenth century which he promised to give concrete form. In May of 1919, he announced the formation of the Black Star Line, a steamship company linking the scattered sons and daughters of Africa and supported by their investment. The flagship of the line was the *Yarmouth*, which was bought to enter the produce trade with the West Indies. The company also purchased the *Shadyside*, a fifty-year-old ferryboat and the *Kanawha*, a steam yacht. The shipping concern was to constitute the centerpiece of a commercial empire envisioned to include stores, factories, and a host of retail enterprises (a mail-order business, steam and electric laundry, and the Negro Factories Corporation). The association also owned a restaurant and a newspaper, the *Negro World*. Efforts toward economic self-sufficiency included the purchase of Liberty Hall, the UNIA's Harlem headquarters. The organization ramified to include the African Black Cross nurses, the African Legion, and a motor corps. The association held its national convention in August of 1920 and, for a month, Madison Square Garden was filled with 25,000 delegates. They approved the fifty-four-article "Declaration of Negro Rights." A number of offices were created: Supreme Potentate, Provisional President of Africa, American Leader, and leaders of the Eastern and Western Caribbean. The potentate and his deputy were required to be African-born and to reside on the African continent. Garvey became Provisional President of Africa. The association pursued bold and broad general aims:

> To establish a universal confraternity among the race; to promote the spirit of pride and love; to reclaim the fallen, to administer to and assist the needy; to assist in civilizing the backward tribes of Africa; to assist in the development of independent Negro nations and communities; to establish a central nation for the race; to establish commissaries or agencies in the principal countries and cities of the world for the representation of all Negroes; to promote a conscientious spiritual worship among the native tribes of Africa; to establish universities, colleges, academies and schools for the racial education and culture of the people; to work for better conditions among Negroes everywhere.[18]

Writing in the early 1960s, the Nigerian analyst E. U. Essien-Udom said of the Nation of Islam, "It is . . . extraordinary that its belief in itself as a definite nation of people has produced absolutely no political program for the establishment of a national home." Furthermore, "the final national homeland is guaranteed solely through eschatological beliefs taken from Old Testament prophecies."[19] This is certainly not true of Garveyism. As one commentator has noted, "Garvey's proposal of a separatist solution cannot be dismissed as a superficial *deus ex machina* or delusory *non sequitur*." Whether it was correct or not, "apropos the specific dilemma of the minority black community within the United States, he discerns no democratic remedy for black genocide in a regime which, by its very nature, is controlled by a prejudiced white majority."[20]

Some have portrayed the UNIA as simply a back-to-Africa movement bent on provoking an uncontrollable mass exodus from the Western Hemisphere. This was not the case; Garvey himself quite explicitly said so. In 1921 he explained, "It is a mistake to suppose that I want to take the Negroes to Africa. I believe that the American Negroes have helped to establish the North American civilization and, therefore, have a perfect right to live in the U.S. and to aspire to equality of opportunities and treatment." Indeed, "Each Negro can be a citizen of the nation in which he was born or that he has chosen. But I foresee the building of a great state in Africa which, featuring in the concert of the great nations, will make the Negro race as respectable as the others."[21] Emigration would occur, but it would be spread out over a half century. The head of the UNIA believed that an "overwhelming majority [is] in favor of the plan of returning the race to Africa by careful and proper arrangements and methods, whereby the somewhat settled national equilibrium, industrially and generally, would not be disturbed."[22] White immigration would eventually provide the labor the South and other sections of the United States depended on.

Garvey's political blueprint for the future was vague. By the end of 1919, the UNIA had set its sights on Liberia in West Africa. Beyond this, the conceptualization of the future "central nation for the race" always remained sketchy and a bit naive. The envisioned polity was to be capitalist and authoritarian; socialism and trade unionism represented anathemas. However, capital would not go unchecked. Individual investments over 1 million dollars and corporate investments over 5 million dollars would be prohibited, with the government controlling capital above this limit. An elite, bound together by love of race, would occupy positions of trust. The creation of titles and honorifics, derided by Garvey's enemies, foreshadowed the black meritocracy that would govern after the nation's creation. In that polity, the president would be elected, but would also have absolute power to appoint all subordinate officers. Should the chief executive or any of his subordinates prove corrupt, they were to be put to death. Love of race would supposedly prevent malfeasance, even among officials holding unbridled power.

The Universal Negro Improvement Association reached its apogee in 1919–20. Its message struck a chord with large numbers of African Americans, many of whom had migrated from the Deep South only to find their dreams of a better life cruelly betrayed. The UNIA spoke to this constituency. For thirty-five cents a month, black women and men experienced solidarity and received a message that promised an end to socioeconomic subordination. "Liberty Halls" were set up in every town where the association had a chapter. Within them, the social mingled with the political — there were concerts, dances, public meetings, and religious services.

August of 1920 became the climacteric. Membership was affected by a downturn in the economy in 1920–21, and sales of stock in the Black Star Line fell off. The UNIA received only $4,000 in membership fees in 1921 from a claimed membership of 4 million.[23] In addition to financial problems, the movement found itself attacked from both the political right and left. Garvey had gained an enemy in Du Bois. The intellectual had initially maintained a rather neutral stance toward the association; he had made contact in 1915 during a trip to Jamaica. However, Du Bois could not help but realize that Garveyism directly opposed his integrationism. Also, he had developed his own elite version of Pan-Africanism; he organized congresses in 1919, 1921, and 1923, which directly competed for attention with the UNIA's annual conventions. In the pages of the *Crisis,* he increasingly questioned Garvey's methods. In his view, Garvey was as foolish as he was impolitic: "And finally, without arms, money, effective organization or base of operations, Mr. Garvey openly and wildly talks of 'Conquest' and of telling white Europeans in Africa to 'get out!' and of becoming himself a black Napoleon!"[24] The black socialist A. Philip Randolph voiced similar sentiments when he announced in his *Messenger* publication that "the whole scheme of a black empire, in the raging sea of imperialism would make it impossible to maintain power, nor would it bring liberation to Africa, for Negro exploiters and tyrants are as bad as white ones."[25] Eventually Randolph and William Pickens of the NAACP, calling themselves the Friends of Negro Freedom, held four meetings with a central aim—Marcus Garvey must go! From a completely different angle, J. Edgar Hoover of the Federal Bureau of Investigation (FBI) was convinced that Garvey was, as Martin Luther King Jr. was later to be, "a notorious Negro agitator." Hoover aimed to speed "the prosecution . . . in order that he [Garvey] may be once and for all put where he can peruse his past activities behind the four walls in the Atlanta clime."[26]

A number of UNIA officials left the association in 1921 and 1922, and a number of prominent African Americans distanced themselves from the organization. This held especially true after a June 1922 meeting between Garvey and Edward Young Clarke, the second in command of the Ku Klux Klan. Events now moved toward their tragic denouement. Garvey purged his leadership in August 1922, but dissension continued. At the beginning of 1923, James Eason, a former UNIA official and later vitriolic Garvey critic, was murdered in New Orleans. On May 21, 1923, Garvey was tried for mail fraud in federal court in New York; almost a month later the court declared him guilty. His second wife, Amy Jacques Garvey, estimated that the movement had taken in $10 million between 1919 and 1921, leaving no assets and running a deficit of $700,000.[27] Garvey was given a $1,000 fine, made to pay court costs, and sentenced to five years in prison. The Provisional President of Africa was jailed and then released on bond pending appeal. The organization was battered, but still intact. Membership numbers were still impressive: New York City, 30,000; Chicago, 9,000; Philadelphia, 6,000; Cincinnati, 5,600; Detroit, 4,000; Washington, D.C., 7000; Jamaica, 5,000; Guatemala, 3,000.[28]

Garvey's judicial appeals proved futile, and in February of 1925 he was remanded to Atlanta Federal Penitentiary. In the final act of the U.S. phase of the Garvey drama, President Calvin Coolidge commuted the sentence in November of 1927. Less than a month later, on December 2, Marcus Garvey was deported from the United States, never to return. The UNIA in the United States fell victim to factionalism and lost its cohesion, and Garvey's attempts to reestablish himself in Jamaica

W. E. B. Du Bois.
Photo from Prints and
Photographs Department,
Moorland-Spingarn Research
Center, Howard University.

Marcus Garvey
in plumed hat.
Photo from
*The Philosophy and
Opinions of Marcus
Garvey.*

amounted to little. In 1935, he took up residence in London, the capital of the empire he had once hoped to topple. Garvey, who had constantly predicted race war, died in 1940 during a different kind of war, but one that would begin to shake the foundations of imperialism. Although Garveyism has been analyzed as a religious movement, its significance lies in its rejection of chiliastic solutions.[29] In his modernist project, Garvey, unlike many later black nationalists, eschewed eschatology.[30] What others would later promise to do through divine intervention, he would do with tractors and cement. James Weldon Johnson, a one-time secretary of the NAACP remarked that Garvey "might have succeeded with more than moderate success. He had energy and daring and the Napoleonic personality, the personality that draws masses of followers." Furthermore, "He stirred the imagination of the Negro masses as no Negro ever had."[31] One might ask: How could a conservative, antisocialist, and segregationist organization fail in an era of increasing xenophobia and racism? Garvey's aim of throwing white imperialism out of Africa, while complementary to white supremacy in America, ran counter to the wider claims of white imperial hegemony. Garvey's anticolonialism, seen as antiwhite bombast by his critics, obscured the accommodationist racial modus vivendi contained in his message.

One can envision, perhaps, a counter-historical Garvey, the leader of an organization stressing Christian proselytization and white support. Perhaps he could have initially renounced the title of provisional president of Africa. Fascinatingly, Du Bois essentially proposed this scheme in 1922. As the Black Star Line's fortunes seemed to be ebbing, Du Bois wrote the American secretary of state to suggest that the government take it over. The professor suggested a "small company in which colored people had representation" to open up direct trade between Liberia and the United States. The government owned ships, and Du Bois requested to know if there was any legal way for them to be diverted to linking the United States and Liberia. Such an undertaking would restore the faith of the "mass of American Negroes in commercial enterprise with Africa, possibly having a private company headed by men of highest integrity, both white and colored, to take up and hold in trust the Black Star Line certificates."[32] Du Bois's appeal proved futile.

A Black Mother/Fatherland

In the nineteenth century, Liberia, the state "founded" by refugees from the Diaspora, was touted by some race men as a place where the despised black man of the Diaspora might truly feel at home. Early Liberia had received settlements of African Americans under the auspices of the white American Colonization Society. Monrovia, the capital of Liberia, was founded in 1822. The Maryland State Colonization Society established a colony at Cape Palmas (Harper) in 1833; the Louisiana and Mississippi Colonization Societies founded a settlement at Sinoe in the year 1837. Ten years later, the settlers, except those in the Maryland settlement, proclaimed their independence. By 1850, the coast between the Gallinas and San Pedro Rivers (except for one small enclave), was claimed either by Liberia or by the independent Maryland County. The latter joined the republic in 1857. The coastal settlements came to be grouped into five counties (Grand Cape Mount, Montserrado, Grand Bassa, Sinoe, and Maryland). Many toponymns were redolent of Dixie (e.g., Clay-Ashland, Virginia, Greenville, and Maryland), and the settler elite aspired to a lifestyle echoic of the Old South. By the late 1920s, 12,000 to 15,000 "Americo-Liberians" lived surrounded by an indigenous population of perhaps 1.5 million.[33]

In the early days, many of the Americo-Liberians took to commerce rather than agriculture, developing a good trade in fish and rice with indigenous villages. Cloth, rum, and tobacco were also exchanged for cam wood, cane sugar, palm kernels, rice, and some ivory. Agriculture went in fits and starts. In 1835, black Quakers established farms near the mouth of the Saint John River. Three years later, an agricultural settlement was founded at the entrance to the Sinoe River by freedmen sent out by the Mississippi Colonization Society. In the same year, Lewis Sheridan, a North Carolina freedman, was granted a long lease on six hundred acres. In spite of this early start, however, farming experienced continuing problems. Local food crops proved unattractive to the settlers, and the market for cash crops appeared limited. In the second half of the century, coffee cultivation promised to be the mainstay of a prosperous export agriculture. By the 1870s, production was in full swing, and by 1892, the country grew well over a million pounds. The boom did not last, however. Liberian producers suffered from competition with Indonesia and Brazil and from failure to rationalize marketing. By the early twentieth century, world prices for coffee had greatly declined, and Liberia's coffee exports sank to a level of under 500,000 pounds.[34] The dearth of labor, laterite soils, and competition in international markets all helped retard export-oriented agriculture.

The desire to emigrate to somewhere, be it Liberia or the Caribbean, has always had as an impetus the marginal status of blacks in the American republic. We face the fact that the Herrenvolk Democracy of the founding fathers was premised on the creation of the White through the exclusion of the Black. In the 1850s, Martin Delany proclaimed: "I am not in favor of caste, nor a separation of the brotherhood of mankind and would as willingly live among white men as black, if I had an *equal possession and enjoyment of privileges*; but shall never be reconciled to live among them, subservient to their will."[35] For many whites, the central challenge of Delany's statement lay in the "equal possession and enjoyment of privileges." For much of the history of the United States, African Americans have existed as a species of the permanent alien, either de facto or de jure. The attraction of the Universal Negro Improvement Association lay in the promise of carving out a place and location to be somebody. The legal end of slavery did not shatter the carapace of caste. Under legalized segregation, blacks remained economically discriminated against, endogamous, and residentially segregated. It is this perpetually liminal state that black nationalists before and after Garvey have found unacceptable. Delany referred to African Americans as a "nation within a nation." They were as much a nation as "the Poles in Russia, the Hungarians in Austria; the Welsh, Irish and Scotch in the British Dominions."[36]

Delany did not favor Liberia as a destination. His contemporary, Edward Blyden, did. He is the Pan-African thinker who most clearly foreshadows Garvey. Blyden was born in the Danish Virgin Islands, lived briefly in the United States, and then spent more than sixty years in West Africa, principally in Liberia. He became a Presbyterian minister, served as president of Liberia College, and headed the Liberian diplomatic corps. To him, black people, both in Africa and abroad, possessed the "African Personality," a bundle of traits centered on communalism and spirituality. These would serve the world, in Blyden's formulation, as an antidote to the materialism and rampant individualism of the industrial West.

Beyond elaborating his theory of cultural vitalism, Blyden looked forward to a time when those blacks with Western skills would return to the African continent, beginning with Liberia. In the 1860s, Blyden struck a note that the UNIA would later echo:

> We need some African power, some great centre of the race where our physical pecuniary, and intellectual strength may be collected. We need some spot whence such an influence may go forth in behalf of the race as shall be felt by the nations. We are now so scattered and divided that we can do nothing. . . . So long as we remain thus divided, we may expect impositions. So long as we live simply by the sufferance of the nations, we must expect to be subject to their caprices.[37]

More than half a century later, Garvey asked himself, "Where is the black man's Government? Where is his King and his kingdom? Where is his President, his country, and his ambassador, his army, his navy, his men of big affairs?" He responded, "I could not find them, and then I declared, 'I will help to make them.'"[38] In Africa, the Word would be made Flesh. In Africa, specifically Liberia, the idea of a place to be somebody combined with the promise of untapped riches. The promise may have seemed utopian, but the same could have been said of the Irish nationalist proposal to divide the British Isles after eight centuries of union. Equally unrealistic to many was the Zionist proposal to create a homeland in the Middle East after nearly two millennia of absence. At times, Garvey and his movement saw themselves as parallel to the later movement in many ways. Robert Hill, the editor of the Garvey Papers, cogently notes: "The redemption of Africa, which Garvey took to mean that Africa must be for the Africans, and them exclusively, was thus on a par, ideologically, with the Zionist goal of restoring Palestine for the Jews. The goal of Jewish restoration also served as the key political paradigm for the sense of unity that the leaders and supporters of the scattered Garvey movement sought to communicate."[39]

Garveyism, infused with a deep and homegrown African American pessimism, offered a most logical way out of the specifically American dilemma. Blacks in North America were a minority surrounded by enemies in perpetuity; the only permanent refuge was emigration. Rent strikes, unionization, cooperative buying, and the establishment of small businesses did not address the central problem of national minority status. Electoral politics, while not entirely dismissed, could provide no permanent solutions. As with Theodor Herzl and his Zionist colleagues, coalition politics in situ could only provide palliatives. While sometimes suspicious of its aims, Garvey noted the Zionist precedent: "Thanks to Zionism, a very recent growth considering the age of the Jew, they can betake themselves to a national home in Palestine." He observed further that "this is a good object lesson for the Negro."[40] In 1920, at the height of his powers, the leader of the UNIA chided the previous generation of leaders: "Because Washington did not prepare us, because Moton did not prepare us there is no Africa for the Negro as there is a Palestine for the Jew, a Poland for the Poles, but what they did not do in the years past we're going to do now."[41]

The foundation of a Jewish state cannot be truly compared with Pan-Africanism—the latter encompasses a far greater number and diversity of peoples. However, if we think only in terms of African American nationalism, there are apparent points of conjuncture. David Brion Davis observes the similarities: "The Zionists ideal is to create a national center that will radiate pride, dignity, and standards of conduct for those Jews (or African-Americans) who remain in the Diaspora (and it should be stressed that many Jews and peoples of African descent have long believed that they live in a Diaspora.)"[42] He reminds us that "countless times, in various kinds of societies from Moorish Spain to Weimar Germany, Jews have 'succeeded' and won 'acceptance' only to encounter a sudden pogrom or outburst of ancient anti-Semitic canards." Remembering this, it is possible that "like Jews (to say nothing of Kosovars, Serbs and Tutsis), African-Americans might seem more accepted and then face a revival of the kind of anti-black racism that had supposedly disappeared . . . we have no reason for complacency about having conquered such feelings here."[43]

But of course differences exist. The rise of fin de siècle anti-Semitism had its roots in the real and imagined growth of Jewish power in the Western world. Proscription of African Americans was aimed at keeping what Booker T. Washington referred to as the "world's most complacent peasantry" exactly that—a peasantry. In 1924, a communist writer for the *Daily Worker* decried "Negro Zionism," despite all the superficial resemblance, as "the wildest folly": "The Great Powers and the League of Nations can cheerfully give a few thousand Jews a chance to settle in Palestine," but "the Great Powers cannot tolerate for one instant the propaganda for Negro independent nationalism in any quarter of Africa—not even in the Negro states of Abyssinia and Liberia, especially not in the "fanatical" form in which alone this movement is found."[44] Superficially, Zionism and Garveyism have some resemblance. However, and very importantly, the former represented an exclusive minority nationalism seeking to be the bulwark of the West. The latter was a "pan" movement seeing to include peoples who had never been united and to mold them into worldwide resistance to Western imperialism. There is no Pan-Semitism analogous to Pan-Africanism.

To some Garveyism represents just one more example of a peculiar, paranoid style in American political culture. For these persons, the Liberia plan marks a flight into a world of make believe: "The 'Back to Africa' slogan was particularly disturbing. In essence, it was a form of escapism. There was no possibility of transporting millions of Negroes across the Atlantic to a strange and inhospitable environment guarded by a half-dozen European powers."[45] One must be careful here, separating out the impediments imposed by "an inhospitable climate" and those imposed by hostile interests. By the 1920s, major epidemiological hurdles to African emigration had been removed. Malaria prophylaxis, steam transportation, and motor transport made the prospect of movement far different from what it had been one hundred years earlier. At the time of Garvey's movement, hundreds of Lebanese traders (Syrians) were already well ensconced in West Africa. Indeed, in 1919, riots broke out in Freetown, Sierra Leone, against their supposed lock on small-scale retail trade.[46]

The generalized American hostility to black emigration remains somewhat puzzling. The United States itself was a place of both entrance and exit in the period 1880–1920. One-fourth to one-third of all entrées returned to their country of origin. And, interestingly, elsewhere in the Americas, black repatriation was neither novel nor threatening. Hundreds of Afro-Brazilian returnees, mainly of Yoruba descent, left for the areas of present-day southern Nigeria, Togo, and Benin. African Americans had also migrated. German colonialists used African American agronomists in Togo before the First World War, and the Stalinist regime used them for the same purpose in Central Asia in the 1930s. In one sad irony, the United States, the government which squelched the back-to-Africa scheme, shipped over a thousand African Americans to Liberia during World War II — as soldiers.

Garvey was not the first twentieth-century emigrationist. Hope sprang eternally and ephemerally. Emigrationism was a mixed bag, arising as it did from the desire of some to flee persecution and the desire of others to benefit from the supposed riches of the "motherland." One of the foremost boosters of turn-of-the-century emigration, Bishop Turner, saw Liberia as a place where fortunes could be made. He was far too optimistic. But his message had appeal to people ground down by poverty and proscription. Between 1890 and 1910, approximately 1,000 African Americans emigrated to the Black Republic.[47] For more than a generation before Garvey, ephemeral emigration societies had come and gone. In 1900, the African Jubilee Emigration Society promised to provide passage to Liberia for less than $20 and grant each emigrant twenty-five acres of land. In October of 1901, Bishop Turner helped unite various independent emigration societies into the Colored National Emigration and Commercial Association (CNECA). The CNECA planned to raise a capital of $100,000 through the sale of stock to purchase a ship to travel to Africa, "especially the Republic of Liberia." The initiative flopped, much to Turner's chagrin. He demanded to know, "Had all of us rather remain in this country and be disfranchised, uncivilized, shot, hunted, burnt and skinned alive, without judge or jury, than build up a nation of our own outside of this devil-ridden country"?[48] A few years later, two organizers proposed the New York and Liberia Steamship Company. It offered $5 shares of stocks in blocks of the five through fifty. The company received the endorsement of Arthur Barclay, the Liberian president, and his entire cabinet. Unfortunately, by 1905, the company had disappeared. Another enterprise, the Ethiopian American Steamship Freight and Passenger Colonization Company, was capitalized at $500,000 and promised to carry mail, freight, and passengers between San Pedro, California, and Monrovia. It failed. In 1905 a Mrs. M. French-Sheldon visited Liberia on behalf of the Americo-Liberian Industrial Company. She was "a native of the United States of America . . . some of whose greatest men [are] moved by their love of Africa and just desire for the welfare of the Negro race."[49] French-Sheldon initially got the Liberian legislature and the president to agree to her commercial plans. In a move that adumbrated the later treatment of the Garvey movement, President Arthur Barclay reneged on promises made.

On the eve of the Great War, yet another venture, the African Union Company (AUC), appeared. It was organized in December of 1913 and incorporated in March of 1914 in New York. Capitalized at $500,000, it looked to trade with Africa generally. The firm announced holdings in mahogany and timberlands, as well as palm oil plantations. Although the organizers claimed that several "kings" and "chiefs" had bought stock, it did not give their names. As many of its predecessors had, the company vanished like a will-'o-the-wisp. One African chief did present himself, however. In 1912 in Oklahoma, Chief Alfred Sam, a Gold Coaster interested in U.S.–West African trade, struck a cord with several hundred land-hungry farmers. In 1915, his Akim Trading Company venture managed to take men, women, and children not to Liberia, but to the Gold Coast. Unfortunately, Chief Sam disappeared, and many of the emigrants eventually returned to the United States.

Liberia was the cynosure of emigrationist interest, but many people just wanted to get away, be it to a British colony like the Gold Coast or elsewhere. One example, which adumbrates Garveyism, occurred in 1912. Issac B. Atkinson, the sixty-three-year-old editor of *Atkinson's Monthly Magazine,* published in Louisville, Kentucky, appealed for an "On-to Africa Congress." Atkinson, an Arkansan, had been a successful farmer, schoolteacher, and small-time politician. He also presided over the Ethiopian Afro-American Franchise Protective League, headquartered in St. Louis. Atkinson's planned On-to-Africa Congress planned to send commissioners to England, Germany, France, and Belgium to secure lands. Treaties with the colonial governments would guarantee "the right to select the location for the colonies, to build railroads, and public highways, to develop [*sic*] and protect the waterways to develop farming and commerce, the right to have and maintain any army for the protection of the colonies, etc." The African American colonies would have the same relationship with the metropole as did Canada or Australia. Atkinson was not planning to set up a steamship company. Instead, "The [colonial] governments will be asked to furnish ships. . . . Money to be loaned on 20, 40, and 60 years time with reasonable interest."[50] Atkinson's appeal, which was sent to George V, was not answered by the British Foreign Office.

Garvey's own interest in Liberia formed part of a general quickening of outside interest in Africa during the period around the First World War. Liberia seemed to offer entry to Africa even as other schemes, including the possibility that the United States might acquire former German colonies, faded. However, there were both political barriers and inducements. The country was de jure independent when Garveyism burst on the scene. However, this independence was far from unfettered. Liberia exemplified a case of neocolonialism before the invention of the term. Nineteenth-century debt had enmeshed the country in a financial tangle which only grew worse with time. An 1871 loan had proven disastrous; most of the money never arrived in the hands of the Liberian government. A British-engineered loan of 1906 promised to repay the debt, but it also brought undue British influence into Liberian affairs. In 1909, the black government sent a commission to the United States to ask for financial and other aid. The following year, an American commission visited the African country and recommended reforms and financial assistance. In 1912, the Liberians succeeded in obtaining a new loan overseen by customs receivers from the United States, Great Britain, France, and Germany. In 1918, the United States converted the receivership into an all-American one, and the Liberian Frontier Force received training by American officers.

Thus by the time Garvey became interested in Liberia, the country had turned into a semiprotectorate of the United States. However, it was not a protectorate the Americans were willing to pay for. Between 1918 and 1922, the U.S. State Department attempted to secure an intergovernmental loan for the Black Republic. At first this was to happen under the terms of wartime measures, which allowed the extension of credits to allied nations. Although Liberia declared war on Germany in 1917, no loan had been authorized by the time of the armistice in November of 1918. The State Department then tried to get Congressional approval for the loan of 5 million dollars. The effort remained unsuccessful, and the Liberian loan was defeated in the Senate in November of 1922.

In its attempts to procure American aid, Liberia had long had important trans-Atlantic collaborators. For instance, in 1909, Booker T. Washington was instrumental in securing a successful hearing for the Liberian commission. The group, headed by Vice President James Dossen, was squired around the capital by Washington, who wrote to Theodore

Roosevelt that this was the first "Commission, composed of Negroes" to pay an official visit. The educator "was most anxious that they be treated with just as much courtesy as the custom by the United States will allow even if an exception has [to be] made, I think it will be a fine thing."[51] As expected, the visitors asked for financial aid. In addition, they asked for help with industrial education, Washington's great achievement. The Liberians maintained that the country should be kept "intact for all Negroes in America who might, in the future, desire to go to the fatherland."[52] Dossen and his colleagues went on a subsequent tour of Tuskegee, and the following year an American mission visited Monrovia. It included Washington's personal secretary, Emmett Scott, as its only black member.

A decade later, Garvey chose to emulate his hero and step in to aid the Black Republic. The UNIA approached president-elect of Liberia, C. D. B. King, while he stayed in Paris for the 1919 peace conference. In September of 1919, King came to New York, and a group of Garveyites, among them John E. Bruce and Reverend F. Wilcom Ellegor, approached him on the subject of assistance to the Black Republic. Hilary Johnson, the son of the mayor of Monrovia, appeared at Liberty Hall in November and encouraged UNIA members to visit Liberia.

Reverend Dr. Lewis G. Jordan, secretary of the National Baptist Convention, informed a Liberty Hall audience in April of 1920 that conditions were ripe. Jordan had just returned from Liberia, where President King had supposedly told him that the UNIA was indeed welcome.[53] The UNIA hoped that, finally, the rhetoric of Pan-Africanism would see realization. Garvey declared, "We of the UNIA at this moment have a solemn duty to perform and that is to free Liberia of any debt that she owes to any white government."[54] In 1920, a group of Liberians paid mayor Gabriel Johnson's passage to the United States. Importantly, Johnson was a member of a Liberian faction that opposed the American loan.

Plans concretized with the first association mission to Liberia. It set out in May of 1920, headed by Elie Garcia, a striving Haitian entrepreneur. The immigrant had come to the United States to pursue trade in logwood. Later he worked for the United States government at a laboratory in Nitro, West Virginia. He met Garvey in Philadelphia in 1919 and became the local representative of the Black Star Line. Once in Liberia, Garcia was outwardly effusive about prospects. He also succeeded in recruiting several prominent Liberians to the cause. Gabriel Johnson was proclaimed supreme potentate — titular head of the world's black peoples. The UNIA's coup in co-opting a prominent African politician promised to insure close collaboration between Harlem and Monrovia.

The promise would prove hard to fulfill, however. Garcia confidentially informed Garvey that the Americo-Liberians were, in his judgment, rapacious and that the parent UNIA should keep control in money matters. Garcia had hit on a thorny problem which neither Garveyism nor later Pan-Africanism successfully surmounted: How did differences of class and culture fit within the conceptualization of a Black World pursuing a common destiny?

The 1920 convention voted to raise 2 million dollars for development projects. The UNIA contemplated following Garcia's suggestions: steamer service along the Liberian coast; the construction of a small railroad of thirty or forty miles; and the construction of about a hundred miles of good roads. Garvey planned to send out a Black Star vessel with the trade goods and machinery. In January of 1921, the UNIA in Liberia was incorporated under an act of the Liberian legislature, and the following month a second UNIA mission arrived. The mission included, among others, Cyril Henry (an agricultural expert), Cyril Critchlow (owner of a secretarial school and a director of the Black Star Line), and George Marke (a former civil servant from Sierra Leone and supreme deputy of the UNIA). The emissaries met with the acting president of Liberia, Edwin Barclay, and the Liberian cabinet on March 22, 1921. Barclay claimed that the government would gladly have the association occupy certain settlements which had already been laid out. The Liberians set a number of restrictions. For one, even though money for the Black Star Line had largely been raised in the United States, the UNIA men were informed that vessels flying the Liberian flag had to be manned and owned by Liberians. The Garveyites were also prohibited from setting up their own settlements. Since by law only Liberians could own real property, the parent body of the UNIA in New York could not directly purchase land. Under these somewhat onerous conditions, the UNIA team began work. However, dissension between Gabriel Johnson and Critchlow soon erupted; the latter charged that Johnson only wanted to further his private business interests. The mission stopped its work after two months because of lack of funds, and by July of 1923, all of its members had returned home.

Late in 1923 the UNIA sent a third mission to Liberia. An area of some five hundred square miles in Maryland County was selected as the site of a settlement. Representatives of the local UNIA and three delegates from overseas (Robert L. Poston, Henrietta Vinton Davis, and Milton Van Lowe) agreed on provisions regarding the prospective UNIA base in February of 1924. Five hundred settlers were to emigrate from the United States later that year. It was agreed that settlers would subscribe to an oath before departing from the United States, declaring that they

Second group of officials and first group of experts sent to Liberia in 1921. Bottom row (l. to r.): G. O. Marke, Supreme Deputy Potentate of the U.N.I.A.; Cyril Critchlow, Resident Secretary of Legation of the U.N.I.A. Top row (r. to l.): McLeod, Surveyor; Henry, Agriculturalist; Laurence, Pharmacist; Jamott, Builder. Photo from *The Philosophy and Opinions of Marcus Garvey*.

would respect the authority of the Liberian government. It was also agreed that each family would possess at least $1,500 and that each single person would have at least $500.

Like its predecessors, the third Garveyite mission was plagued by bad luck. The Liberian president later maintained that he had spoken to it only unofficially. Unfortunately, after the mission, personnel either died or deserted. The mission head, Robert Lincoln Poston, the UNIA assistant president general, passed away on the return voyage. Chief Justice Dossen died on August 30, 1924. Milton J. Marshall, head of the Liberian UNIA, was murdered by an unknown assailant, and Gabriel Johnson had already been deprived of his post as mayor of Monrovia.

In May of 1924, a final team of experts was sent to prepare the projected UNIA settlement. On their arrival in Liberia in June, they were seized and detained. On July 31, 1924, they were deported. The following month, the Liberian *News,* supporting the official line, published a stinging repudiation of Garvey's Pan-Negro assumptions:

Group of Commissioners of U.N.I.A. sent to Liberia in 1924 in company
with local Liberian Committee at Monrovia. Front row: W. Dennis and Ex-
President Howard (whom King succeeded). Second row: Van Lowe, Lady
Davis, R. L. Poston, and Chief Justice Dossen. Rear: Ex-President Barclay
(Comptroller of Customs), Dixon Brown, and D. C. Carranda (a govern-
ment employee). Photo from *The Philosophy and Opinions of Marcus Garvey.*

The History of Liberia is the history of a community developing along lines
of peaceful endeavour; and this community both by tradition and incli-
nation, is influenced rather by considerations which tend to secure and
strengthen *national* existence, progress and stability than by *racial* Utopias.

It is recognized that the future of Liberia is dependent upon amicable
cooperation with all the forces which are at work for the uplift of the
African peoples. This is a fundamental idea underlying Liberian national
thought. Primarily, however, the practical aspects of Negro development
and emancipation are limited in Liberia to making Liberia. Every other
consideration is subordinate. The Negro race will achieve its place beside
the other races by the inevitable processes of evolution. But this achievement will and can only be realized along the ways of progressive peaceful
effort. And so it is unthinkable to a Liberian, influenced as he must be by
the facts of his national environment and traditions, when he comes to
realize their potentialities for national evil, that Liberia can be used as the
point d'appui, whence the grandiose schemes of the "Negro Moses" may find
their genesis.[55]

In January of 1925 the Liberian legislature ratified president C. D. B. King's exclusion of the UNIA. Garveyism in Liberia was dead.

Anatomy of Betrayal

What killed the UNIA's chances in Liberia? Was it the blandishments of Du Bois and his American backers that shifted the balance against the hope for any real emigration? Did the association's rabid anti-imperialism result in overwhelming pressure on the small black state? Indeed, some have sought to exculpate the Monrovia government by arguing just this point.[56] In his 1921 meeting with the UNIA delegation, Liberian secretary of state Barclay did announce that the British and the French had inquired as to the Liberian attitude toward the UNIA. While agreeing that "there isn't a Negro in the world who, if given the opportunity and the power to do certain things, will not do them," he urged caution. He told the UNIA men, "It is not always advisable nor politic to openly expose our secret thoughts." In words pregnant with future meaning for the UNIA, he noted, "We don't tell them what we think; we only tell them what we like them to hear—what, in fact, they like to hear."[57] In September of 1924, the Liberian consul general in the United States told the State Department that the UNIA's anti-imperialism had brought forth complaints from the French in Ivory Coast and the British in Sierra Leone.[58]

No doubt Liberia knew of European hostility to Garveyism. Members of the association experienced difficulties receiving clearance to travel about the colonial empires. The UNIA paper, the *Negro World,* was banned in many colonies and mere possession of it was often treated as a criminal offense. Yet it was not pressure from Britain or France that sealed the fate of the UNIA venture in Liberia. Almost thirty years ago, Robert Weisbond found that there existed little documentary evidence to argue that the British served as the motive force behind the derailment of Garveyism in Liberia.[59] American and French documents also indicate that these governments were willing to let Monrovia itself dispose of Garvey. In September of 1921, a draft memorandum in the State Department's Division of Western European Affairs observed that "officially the Liberian Government is not disposed to favor the political aspirations of the movement." The reason for this attitude seemed "to be largely based on fear that the UNIA might become powerful enough to take control of the Republic's government from the little group of Americo-Liberians who have run things for seventy-five years."[60] Two months later, R. Pêtre, French chargé d'affaires in Monrovia, wrote to his government that "the men currently in power have not failed to understand that the arrival here of partisans of MARCUS GARVEY would be the signal, not only of their rapid downfall, but of the disappearance from the political scene of representatives of all the old Liberian families."[61] The chargé seemed confident the oligarchy was capable of destroying Garvey and Garveyism on its own. A year later, he reiterated that "Marcus Garvey has never had and cannot have influence in Liberia. The tiny oligarchy which holds power is too jealous to give any of it up."[62] In his analysis, chargé Pêtre saw Gabriel Johnson as the only real link between Liberian citizens and the American UNIA. Of Johnson's continued involvement, the French diplomat opined, "it is a matter of business and not of feeling." These sentiments were maintained by Pêtre's successor, who maintained that "the arrival here of colored people likely one day to take the power jealously held by a few Liberian families could not be agreeable to this country's statement."[63] The diplomat also reported that the government was offering Johnson the post of consul in the Spanish colony of Fernando Po, but on condition he abandon the UNIA. On July 4, 1924, as the Liberia scheme foundered, chargé Georges Bouet exulted, informing his superiors, "I might remind you that I foresaw, a long time ago, the pan-African maneuvers in this region of the black continent would fail."[64] When the Liberians hustled the last of UNIA personnel out of the country, the British were caught off guard. A member of the British Colonial Office remarked in a minute, "I am rather surprised at the Liberians being so prompt to get rid of them. I suppose they were afraid of rivals in their running and exploiting of the 'broke' nation."[65]

The Garvey plan in Liberia failed not because it was illogical or unfeasible, but because key members of the Liberian political class opposed it from the outset. The causes were both economic and psychological. In a world dominated by white supremacy, a little bit of status goes a very long way. The Liberian ruling families were simultaneously members of a despised race and an internationally recognized polity. In a world that subjected the majority of black people to imperialism and/or racial segregation, the oligarchy was deeply conscious of its relatively privileged position within the world schema. The settlement of Liberia, whatever gloss was later put on it, was not part of the Pan-African project. To Martin Delany, the nineteenth-century abolitionist, Liberia was a "poor miserable mockery — a burlesque on a government . . . a mere dependency of Southern slave-holders."[66] Pan-Negroism might have had rhetorical value, but the elite avidly sought the prestige and economic contacts available from the white world. Far from constituting the vanguard of the forces of African liberation, they were initially the grateful servitors of whites. The Americo-Liberian elite was closed, conservative, and imbued with many of the values of Old Dixie. Separated by law from the "native" masses, the Americo-Liberians' diasporic origins, rather than their color, defined them. Their reality was the diversity that was West Africa. Power meant the manipulation of congeries of ethnolinguistic units, all of them black.

Settler economic survival depended on squeezing benefit from a decrepit economy built on the backs of a disenfranchised native majority. Many Liberians attracted to the UNIA apparently saw it as a way out of their individual financial difficulties. One example will do. In 1921, Garvey urged Critchlow to prevent Gabriel Johnson from mixing his multiform business interests with those of the association. The mayor of Monrovia planned to lease a dilapidated building to the UNIA for its drugstore, in addition to having the association rent inhospitable land from a female friend. Johnson also attempted to put his son, Hilary, an American-trained architect and builder, in charge of the Monrovia UNIA office.

A 1921 statement by the Sierra Leonean George O. Marke to Cyril Critchlow summed up the contradictions in the relationship between the Diaspora and independent Africa. "The American and West Indian Negroes could control things on their side of the water; we Africans will run things over here. We hold the trump cards," Marke told Critchlow.[67] Earlier, Elie Garcia had written to Garvey, "The Liberian politicians understand clearly that they are degenerated and weak morally and they know that if any number of honest Negroes with brains, energy and experience come to Liberia and are permitted to take part in the ruling of the nation they will be absorbed and ousted in a very short while."[68]

The Monrovia elite was small, closed, heavily intermarried, and divided on the American loan, immigration, and "native policy." Several prominent and interrelated families dominated Liberian politics: the Shermans and Watsons in Grand Cape Mount; the Barclays, Colemans, Coopers, Dennises, Grimeses, Howards, Kings, Johnsons, and Morrises in Montserrado; the Harmons and Horaces in Grand Bassa; the Grisbys and Rosses in Sinoe; the Dossens, Gibsons, and Tubmans in Maryland County.[69] At the time of the Garvey initiative, president Charles Burgess Dunbar King (1920–30), a man wary of emigration from America, increasingly held the political apparatus in his hands. Unfortunately for the Garveyites, King's authority expanded during the very period in which the association's plan was floated. The president managed to assert his control over the only viable political party, the True Whigs, and to create an impressive patronage machine. Dissatisfied

C. D. B. King.
Photo from the Liberian
Collections Project, Indiana
University.

with this course of events, King's predecessor, Daniel Howard, broke with him and organized the People's Party in 1922. Various factions and families opposed to King's policies, including his seeming vacillation on immigration, coalesced in the new organization. Preceding the election of 1923, the American receiver of customs analyzed the constellation of forces: "The Barclay faction is the most powerful political faction here. Actually the line up may be said to have been, Cape Palmas — that is the Dossen faction. Next the Howard-Cooper-Walker faction. Then the King faction and finally the Barclay faction." The white official believed that "Dossen was won over by King early in the game, but the combined Howard-Barclay crowds could have beaten him."[70] In the election, the People's Party candidate was defeated 7,000 votes to 40,000 votes. Significantly, the number of votes cast far exceeded the number of registered voters.

After the Liberian debacle, the provisional president of Africa looked back and lamented, "And in the year 1925, when Africa is waking from her slumber, and it is becoming increasingly difficult to fool even the most simple-minded. . . . Surely Charles Dunbar King will go down unhonored and unsung by black men."[71] Garvey was correct in his suspicions that King had proven his nemesis. A decade older than the Jamaican, the Liberian president was a scion of the Kings of Montserrado County, some of whom hailed from Barbados. A lawyer, King had taken up the post of attorney general in 1906 and progressed on to secretary of state in 1912. While president-elect, he chaired the Liberian delegation to the Paris peace conference in 1919. One African American visitor to Liberia left a penetrating character sketch of the chief of state, a man, who, "behind quiet eyes, alive to every word, gesture, and intonation was, without doubt, the most astute political intelligence in the republic, indeed one of the shrewdest minds in Africa. Nothing escaped him, either of subtle flattery or subtler intrigue."[72] The Liberian was a diplomatic chameleon:

The president had an uncanny aptitude for sensing and achieving expression in homely language of the precise sentiment for the occasion, however difficult the situation. . . . To an American in Liberia, he could say that America was traditionally Liberia's best friend. To the Firestone [Rubber Company] people, he could say, as he did in a speech at the opening of a new development: "Liberia must have something. The Gold Coast is the greatest cocoa-producing country in the world. Why cannot Liberia be the greatest rubber-producing country in the world?" . . . To the British, he could say . . : "The one thing that has struck me about England is its extraordinary sense of justice. . . ." To his colonial neighbors who feared a general awakening of Africa's Blacks: "I am working for the Liberian nation and not for the Black race. The Black race was there before Liberia." . . . To Blacks: "God must have had plans for a people who could survive so long in Africa, and when uprooted and transplanted to America keep alive and flourish." Native chiefs upon whom he wished to impress the need of cooperation with the government could at least understand his pleas for cooperation when he used their own proverb: "One finger cannot pick a louse."[73]

Even before the UNIA proffered its loan, the Liberian leader was deeply biased against the racial ideology it embodied. The Garveyites first approached King while he was in Paris in February of 1919. The UNIA high commissioner in France, Eliezer Cadet, interviewed him; King supposedly said that if conditions in America were so bad, African Americans might want to emigrate.[74] King repeated this sentiment again during a visit to the United States in September 1919.[75] As Tony Martin, the most thorough of Garvey scholars, notes, "Yet, if these statements seemed favorable to UNIA aspiration, there were other indications to the contrary."[76] British intelligence sources reported that the Liberian president claimed not to feel any affinity with the struggles waged by black people in the United States.[77] More tellingly, on September 25, 1919, King visited the United States State Department and spoke candidly and off the record. He reportedly "felt that in view of the tendency of the American Negroes to look on problems from a local point of view and to fail to grasp international view points, it would be inadvisable to have an American Negro as minister of Liberia in Washington." The Liberian "observed that this was said without desire to criticize the American Negro, but this opinion was formed as a result of his observations while in the United States."[78] King's confidences somehow became known to a group of African Americans (Emmett Scott, Louis Cobb, and William Lewis) who threatened that unless King adopted a different attitude, African Americans would not interest themselves in the fate of the Black Republic.[79] King's apparent vacillations must be seen against the background of his anti–Pan-Africanism. In June of 1921, three months after he had received a UNIA delegation in New York, he wrote an open letter to Du Bois's *Crisis,* promising that under "no circumstances" would Liberia "allow her territory to be made a center of aggression or conspiracy against other sovereign states."[80] There is a grandly duplicitous quality in the pronouncements emanating from Monrovia. In July, Edwin Barclay wrote the British consul, "Mr. Marcus Garvey's movements and activities are . . . of no practical interest to this Government as they have not given and will not give endorsement to his fantastic schemes. Steps have already been taken by President King to put an end [to] Mr. Garvey's unauthorized and unwarranted exploitation of Liberia."[81]

In 1923, the American receiver of customs wrote that King felt very strongly on the subject of settlement by American blacks. "King to this day wants a loan and, if he could get the personnel from [white] men of Haitian, Dominican, Philippine and Mexican experience, he would again be perfectly satisfied to let the [State] Department select them, provided no Negroes were sent." The receiver continued, "Back in the Department you have no idea of how the American Negro is despised and hated by the Liberian, but he is." In his view, the Liberians were constrained from saying so, "because of the wrath of the Negroes in America and of the Negro American missionaries who are trying to bring our American race problem out here and embarrass the Liberian in his dealings with the white nations." If Liberian sentiments were known, "it would raise the devil in the churches and stop missionary funds from coming."[82]

Garvey accused King of servile Anglophilia. The president had been educated in British Sierra Leone and did, indeed, accept a colonial commendation in 1925, after the UNIA debacle. The British governor praised King for "slamming the door on spurious patriots from across the Atlantic, men who sought to make Liberia a focus for racial animosity on this Continent." Seeing King as allied to stable government (identified with colonial rule), the governor thought the Liberian president "deservedly earned the gratitude not only of every West African Government, but of all who have the true welfare of the African at heart."[83] King, for his part, spoke to the Freetown Grammar School in tones reminiscent of Garvey: "A few of the people on the West Coast of Africa have assumed the responsibility of at least 400 millions of people; it is a very great responsibility." He continued, noting, "The criticisms that may be leveled upon the Liberian Administration will not be confined to Liberians only but on every black man, whether he be of Sierra Leone, the Gold Coast, Nigeria, the West Indies or the United States of America."[84] Having just vanquished the specter of Garveyism, King wrapped himself in the language of Garveyism to ward off any continuing Garveyite attacks.

In spite of the public rhetoric of Pan-Negroism, King clung to his private animadversions. In 1934, the American chargé in Monrovia asked ex-president King if he felt that foreign financial aid officers should be black. King, echoing his previous sentiments, replied that he felt white men would be preferable because they would be more detached and because it would be easier to find suitable white candidates.[85] In the same year, Ernest Lyon, the African American who served as Liberian consul general in Baltimore, wrote to the Liberian secretary of state, saying that "it is commonly rumored that Ex-President King opposed the employment of American colored men by the Firestone Corporation."[86] Still later, a white Southerner observed, "Monrovia is the capital of a Negro nation and has long since ceased to declaim about it." Writing of the arrival of Liberian envoys in the United States at the end of the Second World War, he remarked that they were greeted by representatives of "the radical Negro press and the Communist press" to whom they announced, "We are here to represent a nation — not a race."[87] The cynical pragmatism of the ruling group remained intact.

Conclusion: The Diasporic Dilemma

To Harold Cruse, Garveyism "was not an Afro-American nationalist movement engaged in an historical confrontation with the realities of the American situation out of which it sprung." Instead, "Garveyism was Afro-British nationalism functioning outside its historical British empire context, hence avoiding British confrontation."[88] This is a narrow view. Garveyism in America was not a *deraciné* West Indian movement. Garvey had far greater success in Northern ghettoes than he ever experienced in Jamaican politics. His problem was the continual conflation of *race* and *nation,* a problem that bedevils diasporic rhetoric and ideology to this day. What unit is the "nation"? Is it some version of the Black Atlantic? Or is it African American?

Several critics have said that Garvey's failure was related to his ignorance of African American concerns. Theodore Draper commented in 1969, "There was something both real and fantastic about Garvey's movement." Draper acknowledged that the UNIA's ideology appealed to the black masses, "but, these ideas had little or nothing to do with their immediate lives, with their own time and place." According to Draper, "more than anything else, this was Garvey's undoing."[89] Taking a different tack, Judith Stein discounts Garvey's mass appeal and sees him as basically a representative of petty strivers enamored of capitalism. She also discounts racism as the basis for African American mobilization. "Racial politics," she maintains, "does not originate inevitably in an immediate experience of racial discrimination or oppression. It is not dependent upon the existence of formal racial proscription, such as Jim Crow laws."[90] In this analysis, Garveyism did not work because it could not provide jobs for the black masses. More successful, in her view, were the strategies of the 1930s, when "the popular, often Communist-led or -inspired, politics . . . won jobs, relief, and tenant protections for numerous blacks."[91] This interpretation, interestingly, does not fundamentally challenge the economic order, but, instead, recommends that blacks should have been more militant in gaining entrance to it. Shorn of its radical rhetoric, it recommends militant protest policies aimed at integrating capitalism. This line of reasoning can inspire a range of policies, ranging from the Urban League's program through the labor unionism of A. Phillip Randolph and on to the liberal integrationism of the modern Democratic Party.

In the United States, the limited economic opportunities open to blacks and their continued social subordination created the conditions from which unity arose. Few African Americans in the first half of the twentieth century would have found it possible to escape the strictures of "race," however logically or illogically construed. Racism had compressed the African American class structure in particular ways. Anglo-Saxons might include Andrew Carnegie and the Hatfields and the McCoys, but it would be naive, to say the least, to look for anything approaching this spread among blacks. It is important to remember that race and class are not two contrasting social constructs. Race interdigitates with class in that it serves as a means to position individuals in a class hierarchy. Certainly, at the opening of the nineteenth century, the vast majority of blacks were illiterate predial laborers confined to the South. At the opening of the twentieth century, most blacks found themselves in the same position, although without the legal strictures of slavery. The group continued to be physically, socially, and economically removed from the rest of the population. Behind the color line, a small group of professionals, clergy, and small business owners served the community. Stein would have had black migrants in the North abandon any thought of business and, instead, organize and agitate for entrance in the wider labor market. This many did. However, attempts to breach the color barrier economically did not change the nature of either caste or capitalism. What liberal integrationism urged was the opening of the job market and the civic arena. At the same time, it assumed no fundamental change in the American class structure. Stein avers that "Garvey's question of why Africa should not give to the world its black Rockefeller, Rothschild, and Henry Ford was not located in African social reality."[92] Perhaps not, but the inference here proves troubling. It implies that in both the United States and Africa, come what may, blacks would have to continue to work for the white man. In 1925, one observer caught the core of Garvey's appeal: "Marcus Garvey argues when the colored man needs a suit of clothes, there should be a colored tailor competent to fit him, a colored wholesale store from which the goods can be procured, colored factory for the preparation of the raw material, colored producers for this raw material and ships manned and owned by men of his race to transport the goods." In this view, Garvey "would close up the whole economic circle with agents and agencies of his own people."[93]

A simplistic reductionism which limits race to an epiphenomenon of class seriously misses the issue. One should remember that in 1928 the Communist Party in the United States itself endorsed a program for self-determination in the Black Belt of the South. Trotskyists also adopted this position. Although no more possible to realize than was socialist revolution in the United States, such positions do acknowledge the existence of blacks as a "people," not just white workers in blackface. The creation of minority congressional districts, the debates over Lani Guinier's nonmajoritarian proposals, and demands for reparations all indicate a reality far more complex than any that could simply be addressed by the provision of fair employment. Economic exclusion, endogamy, and residential segregation maintain caste. This fact makes it difficult to assert the primacy of any one class in the ongoing evolution of black nationalism from Garvey to Malcolm X and beyond. The class composition of the African American group shifts; the consciousness of separateness, internally as well as externally maintained, remains. In the present situation, impressive numbers of African Americans continue to respond to events like the Million Man March and to calls for ethnic autarky. It would be hard to argue seriously that this simply constitutes a manifestation of the ideology of the African American haute bourgeoisie. From the underclass to the ensconced figures of the academic elite, the call to "Do for Self" continues to exert an attraction. Stein has said that "so long as Pan-Africanists sought Rockefellers, not Lenins or Gandhis, the elites of Afro-American and Africa became competitors, both of them divorced from the masses they aspired to speak for."[94] In terms of African Americans, the advice to produce a Lenin or a Gandhi instead of business persons seems ingenuous, at best. Gandhian cottage industry never provided an answer to the conundrum of African American existence; a command economy on the Marxist-Lenist model proved even more of a flight from reality, especially given the position of the white working class.

Nationalism, in its many varieties, offers an ideological way out of the dilemma of African American existence. There is nothing very remarkable in Stein's rediscovery of what was once termed petty bourgeois nationalism. Nationalism among African Americans may well have the same class base as it does in places as disparate as Moldova and Malaysia. Nationalism triumphed almost everywhere in the world as an elite movement, which, through the manipulation of common symbols and broad grievances, was able to appeal to a rural and agrarian majority. "Back-to-Africa" attracted, at various times, land-hungry farmers as well as undertakers, teachers, and Pullman porters.

Critiquing Pan-Africanism in general, Stanley Crouch has said, "This German-derived idea of fusing genetics and cultural vision declares that race transcends place, which means that black Americans are but one segment of an international black world and should shape their allegiances accordingly." He adds that, in this view, "all black people are essentially the same, unless their identities have been distorted by Eurocentric influences."[95] Kwame Appiah makes the same point. Speaking of Blyden's fellow Liberian immigrant and intellectual colleague Alexander Crummell, he notes an underlying assumption of commonality. In 1862, Crummell wrote a text entitled the *Future of Africa,* in which he urged his readers to labor for the uplift of the continent, a work in which the scattered sons and daughters of Africa had a special role. Appiah notes that

> at the core of Crummell's vision is a single guiding concept: race. Crummell's "Africa" is the motherland of the Negro race, and his right to act in it, to speak for it, to plot its future, derived—in his conception—from the fact that he too was a Negro. More than this, Crummell held that there was a common destiny for the people of Africa—by which we are always to understand the black people—not because they shared a common ecology, nor because they had a common historical experience or faced a common threat from imperial Europe, but because they belonged to this one race. What made Africa one for him was that it was the home of the Negro, as

England was the home of the Anglo-Saxon, or Germany the home of the Teuton. Crummell was one of the first people to speak as a Negro in Africa, and his writing effectively inaugurated the discourse of Pan-Africanism.[96]

Such thinkers "left us, through the linking of race and Pan-Africanism, with a burdensome legacy."[97] Appiah is highly skeptical of any ideology that would put the chimera of race first. He argues that the perception of race differs in the Diaspora and in Africa. In the latter place, "where black people were in the majority and where lives continued to be largely controlled by indigenous moral and cognitive conceptions, they had no reason to believe that they were inferior to white people and they had, correspondingly, less reason to resent them."[98] For the sake of argument one might note that a supranational black identity is no more a mirage than a supranational Hispanic identity transcending region, race, and class. Both are imagined communities, which become real as congeries of individuals come to use them for political mobilization within the context of a Diaspora.

Appiah's much-mentioned criticism of Pan-Africanism does raise a point. What is the specific telos of African American collective existence? What are African Americans? A group? A category? A minority? A "national" minority? The eternal Other? We should begin by saying that Garvey, for all of his vagueness as to the borders of the nation, was one of the most concrete of diasporic thinkers. Black nationalism is many things to many people; indeed, it is one of the most protean terms in the American political lexicon. For example, Malcolm X was asked at one point: "Is there a Negro movement in the United States that wishes to form a Negro state with the Africans?" Malcolm answered:

> Yes, they are important. There are an increasing number of Afro-Americans who want to migrate back to Africa. Now if it were to take place tomorrow you would probably have a limited number. So, in my opinion, if you wanted to solve the problem you would have to make the problem more digestible to a greater number of Afro-Americans. The idea is good but those who propagated the idea in the past put it to the public in the wrong way and because of this didn't get the desired result. The one who made the greatest impact was the honorable Marcus Garvey. And the United States government put him in prison and charged him with fraud.[99]

Here, political nationalism can only emerge as a last resort. To most of the world's nationalists, from East Timor to Kalistan, this would seem very bizarre as a political stance indeed. In spite of his rhetoric, Malcolm's prescriptions remain amazingly vague.

Garvey was clearer. However, while appealing to African American nationalist longings, Garvey could never disentangle the national minority from the pan-ethnicity. Given the diasporic worldview, he, like Du Bois, was, perforce, a Pan-Africanist. One commentator has noted that "at various points, Garvey refers to a black republic, a black empire, a collection of 'African Communities,' and a 'political superstate'; indeed, one statement outlining the objectives of the u.n.i.a. schizophrenically pledges [to] . . . develop 'Independent Negro Nations and Communities' and establish 'a central nation for the race.'"[100] Pan-Negroism was never replaced by a neater vision of the political community. In the mid-1970s, an elderly African American Garveyite in Accra, Ghana, was asked if she had any regrets. She said: "Oh no. . . . He [Garvey] knew nothing about Africa, not like I now know it is, and really you know, it all had nothing to do with Africa." The woman continued, "But he made the black people of the world, America, the West Indies, Africa, feel they were all one."[101] The problem is that, at some point, such a concept becomes geographically so broad as to turn politically meaningless. However, it is not necessary to argue that black people in Accra and Atlanta belong to a trans-Atlantic ecumene. This in no way addresses the central question of whether or not African Americans, per se, constitute a "people." Indeed, based on commonality of language, religion, and shared historical experience, they may well experience peoplehood in a way Ghanaians never can.

Garveyite Pan-Africanism was a Black Diaspora echo of the grand nineteenth-century pan-movements: Pan-Slavism, Pan-Teutonism, Pan-Islamism, Pan-Hellenism, Pan-Arabism, Pan-Turanianism, among others. Garveyism failed not because it was Afro-Caribbean, but because it could not delimit its ambitions. Establishing an African American homeland and uniting all of Africa in one superstate do not constitute the same aim. Although Garvey was influenced by the cry of self-determination after the Great War, he seems to have failed to notice that the creation of Czechoslovakia, Poland, and Yugoslavia militated against the raison d'être of Pan-Slavism, one of the main pan-movements of the prewar period. An even more telling example would have been Turkey, which in 1923 turned its back on both Pan-Islamism and Pan-Turanianism and opted for a smaller, more compact definition of itself.

One of the strangest things about the continuing career of black nationalism in America is its avoidance of *African American* national feeling. Indeed, as the years have moved on, studies of the African Diaspora have mushroomed. Many maintain that blacks everywhere have a commonality that should somehow translate into political power on the world stage. So far, this has failed to happen. African American nationalism usually eschews anything approaching the Irish nationalist motto

Sinn Fein (We, Ourselves). Instead, it continues to elide into a Pan-Africanism around which it is very hard to construct a political program. I contend here that African Americans do indeed have many of the essential components usually constituting a nation. Far more than colonial creations like Congo or Ghana, they have a shared historical experience going back at least two centuries; the ancestors of most African Americans had arrived in North America by at least 1750. Indeed, as an *ethnie*, they are older than many African groups — the Baule or Ndebele, for instance. As Daryl Scott has noted, however, this usually has not given rise to political minority nationalism.[102]

Garvey's problem was how to delimit his Negro world. Unfortunately, his Pan-Negroism, placing a political agenda on perceived phenotypical and cultural similarities, remained unwieldy. Like many today who speak of a Black Atlantic, Garvey spoke most strongly to elements of the Anglophone Diaspora in the Americas. In Liberia, he confronted a national elite very conscious of its peculiar position *outside* that Diaspora. And it betrayed him.

2 The Black Zion

Africa remains the heritage of Black people, as Palestine is of the Jews.

— Marcus Garvey

I'm an African American, which means that somebody in my family came from Africa — someplace — most probably somewhere between Senegal and Angola. Because we don't know where we came from, we are the first truly Pan-African people. And it means that therefore we can claim all of Africa — as a homeland — as well as none of Africa.

— Henry Louis Gates Jr.

In 1936, the American anthropologist Melville Herskovits wrote of Africa and what he referred to as the American Negro, opining that "studies in the scientific problems of the Negro made by those coming from this side of the Atlantic should be concentrated, for purposes of scientific strategy, on the peoples of West Africa." Of the peoples of West Africa, he remarked: "We know relatively little of their manner of living; we know even less of their history."[1] A decade and a half earlier, a government informer attending a Garvey rally remarked: "Most of these people haven't any idea of the geographical location of Africa or under what conditions Africa [is] governed by the several European countries. Some of these people really believe that after this convention they will have elected a president for Africa and all they will have to do is to go over there and set up their government."[2] Garvey's image of Africa was as mythic as Du Bois's, although it was meant to serve different purposes. In 1920, he told his Liberty Hall followers: "Men, it is a dream now; it is a vision now; but do you not know that you can make this dream, this vision, a reality?" It was

the vision, not of America, but of a greater country, the vision of Africa, the greatest country in the world; the country wherein the black man first saw the light of day; the country where it is destined that the black man shall meet his judgment in common with other men when Gabriel blows his horn. . . .Tonight you see Africa a great forest country, a great wilderness, and 400,000,000 people saying: "It shall be a wilderness, it shall be a forest, no longer. Where there are forests, we will build cities. Where the wilderness is, we will build great townships. Where there is no place of human abode, we will make great settlements. Where there is not even the semblance of government, we will make a great nation."[3]

The "real" Africa represented by Liberia remained far removed from any imagined edenic past or messianic future. It was inhabited by congeries of peoples who sometimes collaborated and who sometimes warred. Diasporic thought, especially of the emigrationist orientation, remained vague as to exactly who were to be the hewers of wood and the drawers of water in the new black folk community. In the Manichaean world of the Diaspora, the question had not come up. Yet when asked in the context of an independent African state, it was insistent. The Diaspora's conjuncture with an African state raised questions about the very premises on which Pan-Africanism rested. In Liberia, the rhetoric of an international black folk community met the reality of an African state ruled by a self-conscious ethnic minority — a situation repeated in many parts of Africa today.

Even as Du Bois argued that a veil separated white and black America, some visitors found a barrier between the brethren from beyond the sea and those at home. Cyril Henry, who helped the second UNIA mission to Liberia, wrote in July of 1921 of the contradictions in the Liberian national experiment. He concluded that "you will not be surpri[s]ed when you imagine a mere handful of partly Westernized Negroes as compared with the millions of aboriginal inhabitants seeking to establish a government with all the virtues and defects of European and African ideals to contend with."[4] Henry, commenting on the culture shock he was sure awaited immigrants from the Americas, concluded that "Africa, is more Oriental than Occidental." The Garveyite thought that "the Liberian as an off-shoot of the Westernized American in this conflict of ideas [and] strives to maintain himself in a class separate and distinct; but he either draws [away] entirely from his brother native in sympathy or, given time, reverts to his ways."[5]

The Place and the People

Liberia, the intended home for millions of future Garveyite returnees from the Americas, is about the size of Pennsylvania or Ohio (43,000 square miles). Bordered by the Ivory Coast, Guinea, and Sierra Leone, it has coastline of 350 miles stretching between the Cavalla and Mano Rivers. The coastal zone contains mangrove swamps and shallow lagoons, as well as beaches of sand. Behind this, there is a rain forest belt which rises to an elevation of 1,000 feet above sea level. Further inland, a plateau climbs to an altitude of 2,000 feet and features the Nimba and Walo Mountains. The country has six major rivers, none of which is navigable beyond a few miles; lagoons and sandbars block their mouths. Like most of West Africa, the area has a dry and a rainy season, with the latter running from roughly April to October. Along the coast, where rainfall is the greatest, precipitation reaches two hundred inches per annum. As in much of Africa, vegetational "tropical exuberance" belies a sad fact: the soils are laterite and easy leached of their nutrients. Only 2 percent of the country's soil is ideal for agriculture, and this is the alluvial soil constituted by deposits of sand, loam, and clay along the banks of watercourses. Rice makes for the staple crop in the northern and western parts of the country. In the southeast, yams and other tubers predominate as staples. Other cultigens are eggplant, cassava, corn, pumpkin, and cotton. Women cultivate most of the foods, with the exception of rice.

The bare-bones facts of Liberia's geography do little to excite the vision of an edenic mother- or fatherland. Imagination is needed. When Du Bois made his first trip to Liberia in the mid-1920s, he wrote:

> Africa is vegetation. It is the riotous, unbridled bursting life of leaf and limb. It is sunshine—pitiless shine of blue rising from morning mists and sinking to hot night shadows. . . . Nothing is more beautiful than an African village—its harmonious colorings—its cleanliness, its dainty houses with the kitchen palaver place of entertainment, its careful delicate decorations and then the people. I believe that the African form in color and curve is the most beautiful thing on earth—the face is not so lovely—though often comely with perfect teeth and shining eyes,—but form of the slim limb, the muscled torso, the deep full breasts![6]

This is not ethnography; this is not reportage. It is an Africa full of features, yet strangely nonspecific. That social oppression might lurk in those dainty villages was not Du Bois's main concern. When ethnography did come into play, it still came through the filter of the image of the "primitive." In 1926, James Sibley and Dietrich Westermann published an anthropological work that managed to combine alien notions of socioeconomic relations with on-the-spot observation. They asserted that "the paramount chief or 'king' is the owner of all the land belonging to his territory, and of its natural products." Having said this, they quickly acknowledged that, "this ownership is, however, limited by the regulation that the king can only dispose of the soil in agreement with his elders and for the benefit of the community."[7] In reality, the term *ownership* does not adequately describe the system. Ownership of land was not an indigenous concept. Land allocation was made on the basis of membership in a patrilineage. Non-kin could also use land; strangers could attach themselves to an existing patrilineage or ask the political authorities for land on which to farm. Gifts or the prospect of continued tribute usually accompanied such requests.

In Liberia, other activities, such as stock raising, supplement agriculture. Livestock include cattle, sheep, and goats. Along the southeastern coast, fishing constitutes a major economic activity. Male household members of a particular age set perform the fishing under the tutelage of household members of an older age set. The care and repair of fishing equipment is men's responsibility, while the women prepare and preserve the fish.

Indigenous life, in and of itself, held little interest for the settlers. No Liberian W. E. B. Du Bois or Zora Neale Hurston emerged to evoke the folkways of *these* black folk. To outsiders, the customs and names seemed strange, the mentality hard to penetrate. Yet this constituted the black majority. Graham Greene, writing in the mid-1930s, may have captured a glimpse of the core of indigenous life, but no more than that:

> But though nearly all the villages at which I stayed had these common properties — a hill, a stream, palaver-house and forge, the burning ember carried around at dark, the cows and goats standing between the huts, the little grove of banana-trees like clusters of tall green feathers gathering dust — not one quite the same. . . . I never wearied of the villages in which I spent the night: the sense of a small courageous community barely existing above the desert of trees, hemmed in by a sun too fierce to work under and a darkness filled with evil spirits — love was an arm around the neck, a cramped embrace in the smoke, wealth a little pile of palm-nuts, old age sores and leprosy, religion a few stones in the centre of the village where the dead chiefs lay, a grove of trees where the rice-birds, like yellow and green canaries, built their nests, a man in a mask with raffia skirts dancing at burials. This never varied, only their kindness to strangers, the extent of their poverty and the immediacy of their terrors.[8]

Liberia contains at least sixteen separate ethnic groups. Most of these peoples had migrated from the interior of Africa in the last several hundred years. The various groups belong to three linguistic units — the Mel-, Mande-, and Kwa-speaking peoples, and arrived in what is now Liberia at different times. The Mel and Mande predominate in the west and northwest. There are two Mel groups: the Gola and the Kissi. One of their most outstanding characteristics is the development of the Poro society. This all-male society was responsible for rites of passage and sacred functions. Poro members could also punish threats to the social order such as murder, incest, arson, and looting. A similar institution, the Sande society, existed among women for the initiation of young girls, a process which included clitoridectomy. The Mande-speaking peoples constitute the largest ethnolinguistic group in the subregion. It includes the Vai, Mandingo (Malinke), Mende, Gbande, Kpelle, Loma, Mah (Mano), and Dan (Gio). The Mande-speaking peoples developed a sophisticated long-distance trade network linking the coast with the savanna region. Some of these Mande-speakers may have introduced the slash-and-burn method of upland farming into the tropical rain forest region. It is also believed that the Mande-speaking peoples, as a result of interaction in the savanna region, introduced the chieftaincy system of political order into the forest. Some of the migrants may have been Muslim by the time of their entrance into the forest.

The Kwa-speaking peoples belong to a language family that stretches eastward to the Niger Delta. Six ethnic groups form the Kwa family: the Dei, Belle, Bassa, Kru, Grebo, and Krahn. Between the late fifteenth century and the mid-seventeenth century, waves of Kwa-speaking peoples migrated to the coast and came to inhabit what now constitutes the central area of the coastal belt. Subsequent migrations by way of the St. John and Cavalla Rivers formed communities within the eastern coastal region and its interior. In all of these communities, the patrilineal, polygynous family, the "household," formed the basic unit of social organization. Surrounding this unit was an extended family of relatives, clients, and other dependents. The household constituted the most important unit of production, especially in agriculture. Each household operated a farm that provided its sustenance, and every member farmed under the control of the heads of household, who often had more than one plot, each one worked by a wife and her children. Individual status depended on relationship to the male head. The senior wife was the most deferred to, and her oldest son was usually the designated heir.

The household existed within a wider social context. A group of related households made up a quarter. Among the Mande and the Mel, the quarter was a lineage segment; it contained within it the sentimental attachment of relatives bonded by a presumed kinship derived from a common patrilineage. Among the Kwa, the quarter was a group of related patrilineal households with shared sentiments, allegiances, and history, which might connect with clusters of related patrilineal households in other polities. It was more common, however, for the term *quarter* to refer to a section of a village inhabited by any recognized group. A quarter could be made up of distant relatives, non-kin clients, slaves, servants, wards, or strangers. Half-towns, or satellite villages, emerged when quarters became too large. In Mande- and Mel-speaking communities, the influence of the quarter depended on its connection to the main patrilineage. Rule was gerontocratic; the eldest male of the quarter served as the leader, whom elderly male relatives advised. In the quarter, family rites were conducted, family disputes resolved, and sociopolitical duties to the larger society carried out. Most importantly, the quarter apportioned land.

A cluster of quarters constituted the village. This made up the political community. Among the Mande and the Mel, the elder of the quarter of the founding ancestor had to hold the post of chief or head of the political community. A council of elders representing the quarters sought to reach decisions by consensus. In case of failure to reach a decision, the matter was taken to the Poro for resolution. The Kwa-speaking peoples exhibited a greater tendency to put such matters before a broader group. Often this included women and youngsters if the issue was not a matter of war and peace.

Beyond the village level, there existed a number of political arrangements, some resulting in the construction of fairly large-scale kingdoms and confederations. Warren d'Azevedo has stressed that the polities of the Liberian region developed "on the basis of intricate ethnic and structural compromises among participating groups"[9] He has identified four types of political arrangements in the region during the nineteenth century. The migrant band consisted of a leader, a group of his kinsmen, and a number of clients or followers, as well as those held in domestic servitude. In the conservative village chiefdom, authority reposed in a founding patrilineage. There were also secondary lineages and other affiliates, sometimes included through putative kinship. Such chiefdoms usually remained small and were ruled by ascription. The typology names as its third case the exploitative expanding chiefdom. Although organized around principles of kinship and descent, it differed from the conserva tive village chiefdom in that it did not aspire to keep an equilibrium; it sought to take over other units. Its core ideology rested on the mythopoeic lore of a founding patrilineage. Leaders of such systems generally designated themselves by military prowess and wealth. D'Azevedo's final type is the confederation, a mix of the previous three types under the control of a powerful chief or despotic warrior. "Essentially an aristocracy of powerful leaders representing diverse and unrelated groups held together by opportunistic fealty to a supreme ruler" wielded political authority.[10] The ruler accumulated vast wealth, which he used to create a loyal entourage and control not only the vassal groups but also traditional institutions. In the early nineteenth century, Sao Boso, a Mandingo, became the most successful head of a confederation in Liberia and ruled over people drawn from the Loma, Gola, Bassa, Dei, Kpelle, Vai, and Gbande peoples. Sao Boso had been raised by a Gbande chief and, at one point, was employed by British traders. His polity was not a "tribe"; many of the settlements under his control were made up of pawns whose parents or chiefs had donated them as signs of loyalty, clients seeking refuge, slaves collected through raiding, and wives received through payment of a dowry or through exchange.[11]

Power rested in the hands of males, yet as in cases in Nigeria (Madame Tinubu) and neighboring Sierra Leone (Mammy Yoko), some women could accumulate political and economic power. In 1904, the African American secretary to the Monrovia legation, George Ellis, visited the Vai country and wrote one of the first anthropological accounts of indigenous Liberia. His eyewitness record shows keen observation mixed with a sense of the diachronic:

> A Vai man by the name of Gonda was made king. For this kingship for more than a century there have been two rival families, — the Bessy and Sandfish houses. . . . No female can occupy the throne, according to customary law. Yet a woman has ruled over a portion of the Vai country. Taradoba was the favorite wife of King Arma, who died from a wound received in battle [twenty-five to thirty years ago]. . . . By the new king of the Vais three attempts were made to subdue her, but she successfully repelled each invasion. . . . She ruled for many years, and her son, Momulu Massaquoi, educated at Central Tennessee College, is now king over the Gallinas.[12]

Ellis said little of forced labor in the Gallinas region, although this constituted one of the central pillars of its nineteenth- and early-twentieth-century economy.

Slavery on the Windward Coast

An example from the Liberia/Sierra Leone frontier may help demonstrate the complexity of our conceptions and narratives of enslavement. When Steven Spielberg released his film *Amistad* in late 1997, a tie-in novel by Alex Pate accompanied it. The work centers on the capture and enslavement of a Mende farmer, Sengbe Pieh (later Joseph Cinque). In the novel's account of the protagonist's capture, it notes, "Slavery had existed for generations in many tribes in Africa, but when the white man turned it into big business, it was suddenly changed." With this change, "the black body was a symbol of dumb, cheap labor, work animals."

Sengbe Pieh's captor, Birmaja, "knew what they were doing was wrong. But it was the way now." In the novel, a hostile white American asks Sengbe Pieh if it is not true that "certain tribes in Africa, for hundreds of years—thousands, perhaps—have owned slaves." The answer from Sengbe Pieh's translator in the novel is—"It's different."[13]

Different, but how different? In the nineteenth century, several unfree statuses existed in what is now Liberia. First was what might be called the indentured laborer. This was an individual who made his labor available to his creditors until he compensated them for a debt. The services of indentured laborers' offspring were also available. In general practice, the social distance between indentured servants and free people did not become readily noticeable. Only rarely were indentured servants sold into the Atlantic slave trade, although they could be. Looking at traditional society, one commentator says:

> Not only political conditions, but also the social landscape of Liberia was fluid and dynamic. As in most parts of Africa, wealth was measured in terms of labor not land. A wealthy man was one with numerous clients, pawns, slaves, wives, and children. Wives and children could cultivate gardens to provide food for the men and their clients and guests. Pawns, clients, and slaves generated booty, farm produce, dowry items and commercial products such as kola nuts, ivory, hides, cotton cloth, salt, malaqueta pepper, palm oil, or camwood. In addition, slaves could be exchanged for important trade goods that earned powerful leaders and invading ethnic groups further income. The household of a truly big man positioned near a major trade route or coastal port numbered in the dozens, scores, or hundreds of people.[14]

Indenture elided into the practice know as pawning. A man had the right to pawn his children or other dependents to a creditor until his debts were paid. Usually, pawns who remained within their society of origin kept the right to maintain kinship and ritual ties with their kin. They might also have the right to marry within the household of the master. In societies that had already developed considerable social stratification, like that of the Vai, pawns from other ethnic groups faced severe hardships and were likely to be sold for export. Domestic slaves were obtained in a variety of ways: as a result of warfare; by outright purchase; as punishment for a crime. A fourth situation would be the birth into slavery of the children of domestic slaves or of the offspring of freemen and slave women.

This brings us back to the *Amistad* and the transatlantic vision of African slavery. Charles Johnson remarked, "The Mandingos and Vais were most harsh in their treatment of slaves. Averse to agriculture, they had greater need of slaves and of a rigid decorum to govern the relationship of master and slave."[15] The historical Sengbe was captured by a fellow Mende, who claimed Sengbe Pieh for debt. The man handed him over to one Bamadha, son of Siaka of the Genduma of the Vai country. The Vai were divided into freeborn persons, *manja dennu* (chief's children) and *jonnu* (persons without full kinship status and rights). The jonnu included individuals who had fallen under an economic obligation and who, in certain instances, retained certain kinship rights. Individuals captured or traded from the interior, like Sengbe, constituted another group of jonnu — export slaves. Most were Kpelle and Bassa.

When speaking of serfdom, pawnship of any other status, we must be careful to avoid the historicist trap of seeing these statuses as part of a lineal movement toward "freedom." The trade in human beings from the Vai area waxed and waned with overseas demand. The Liberia–Sierra Leone border remained fairly unimportant in the Atlantic trade until after 1807. Thereafter, slaving became dominant, and jonnu of all categories probably constituted the majority of the slave population. One expert estimates that between 1840 and 1850, Vai middlemen annually sold up to 15,000 domestic slaves, indentured servants, and pawns.[16] Also, increased produce trading with the interior in return for European trade goods in part supported the growing population. In the 1840s, in the aftermath of the destruction of the slave barracoons of Pedro Blanco on the Gallinas River, the combined actions of the American and British squadrons and the Liberian government interdicted slaving. The network of labor supply continued, however. In 1853, a British firm contracted to supply "free" labor to the Caribbean and Guyana. Vai chiefs were paid to produce workers for two-year contracts, and the political leaders responded with alacrity. Four years later, the French obtained labor for Réunion using the same methods. Such recruiting was discouraged by the 1860s, and the number of jonnu taken in and exported probably declined. This decline did not, however, mark a reduction in labor coercion. The Vai used some of their domestic slaves in palm kernel, palm oil, and coffee production. Importantly, they also sent their slaves out as long-distance porters. The intervention of the Liberian state in the third quarter of the nineteenth century brought new economic consequences. Monrovia's demand for taxes and other exactions led more and more interior peoples to pawn kinsfolk to Vai middlemen. When in the 1890s the Liberian government permitted the shipment of contract labor to Spanish Guinea and the French and Belgian Congos, the free Vai (*manja dennu*) responded again. Initially, the persons sent abroad were domestic servants, individuals of low status, and pawns. As the twentieth century continued, the system underwent modifications. Increasingly "pawns" from peoples such as the Kpelle were produced as contract laborers. In 1903, a Briton noted that workers from Liberia employed in the Nigeria-Cameroon area came mainly from the Vai, Mandingo, and Kissi areas.[17] In many cases, these groups were passing on individuals obtained from interior groups. The traditional laborers up and down the coast, the Kru and Grebo, were less inclined to go to areas with reportedly extremely poor labor conditions.

Early in the twentieth century among the Kpelle, wealthy men took many wives who engaged in farming. The women also produced more offspring for the wealthy man and seduced unmarried men required to reimburse the "big man" through labor and the payment of fines. Control of women was essential to the accumulation of wealth.[18] Wealth could become an avenue to sociopolitical power; in Kpelle society the powerful and wealthy were called *loi-kalon* (uncles). Less fortunate men were treated as subordinate nephews.[19]

Looking at the situation, one specialist notes:

> The Kpelle example is replicated in other regions of Liberia. In all traditional societies, older men and women monopolize wealth, power, and knowledge. Young men seeking wives, barren women desirous of having children, individuals wanting to know the future, and law-breakers or people involved in conflict must go to the powerful, wise, and wealthy elders for help in receiving a wife, improving fertility, learning an answer, or gaining redress. By this system, the established authorities are able to appropriate the labor and the loyalty of the less powerful. A dowry, payment to a healer or seer, and court judgments generally involve compensation in the form of labor or trade goods purchased through wage labor. In a complex hierarchical system, the labor of the young, the outsider, the client, or the slave, benefit the more privileged elite.[20]

Even the Kru and Grebo societies, viewed as freer than others in Liberia, exhibited mechanisms of coercion and a fluidity of categories undermining any attempt to create universal taxonomies of labor systems. In the early 1840s, a British missionary observed a group of Krumen being shipped down to Fernando Po and noted:

> I was a passenger in a vessel which carried 80 wood cutters . . . and I saw the manner in which they were obtained. There were 89 in all brought on board the vessel; and though it was not by force yet there was something very like it. They had no voice in the matter; they came upon the deck in a state of nudity, very few having as much as a piece of cloth about their middle. The man who brought them received for each person, certain pieces of cloth or other articles, according to his choice. Two of them had been disposed of as slaves; not for life, but for the time being . . . I should mention that six

of these men, to manifest their unwillingness to leave their own country, jumped overboard, got into their canoes by night, and made their escape.[21]

What are we to make of this? It indicates that many ties of dependency could provide labor. Early in the nineteenth century, slaves may have been the men chosen for overseas employment. As time went on, such employment became a rite of passage for young men, although it would be wrong to see it as the simple or quick elimination of the participation of pawns and captives. Also, it was never an egalitarian arrangement. Claude Meillassoux sees the development of bondage in subsistence economies as the result of competition between elders and their juniors.[22] Pierre-Phillipe Rey believes slavery to have its genesis in the pawning of younger males. This served as the source of the power for the gerontocrats who controlled access to marriageable women. Elders could expand their lineages while, at the same time, removing trouble-some youngsters from the society.[23] In the case of the Kru Coast, this appears to have been the case. In the 1820s, an outsider described how a seasoned Kru worker would take "with him some raw, inexperienced youngster, whom he initiates into his own profession, taking no small portion of the wages of the *elève* for his trouble."[24] The protégé would, in time, with patience and obedience, earn enough to take more and more wives. By 1906, Henry Nevinson, a critic of colonial labor policies, saw the outflow of manpower as free. "When they [i.e., the laborers] return, they give the chief a share of their earnings as a tribute. . . .This is a kind of feudalism but it has nothing to do with slavery, especially as there is a keen competition among the boys to serve."[25] By the 1920s, in addition to the exactions of local elders, those of the Liberian state created new burdens, burdens which eventuated in conditions analogous to slavery.

It is easy, looking at the conflict generated between the Americo-Liberians and the indigenes, to think of it as a settler-versus-native scenario. The reality proved far more complex; settlers simply added to the mix. In the 1930s, a German medical expert opined that "the Mandingo has no love for the native peoples of the forest region. He is a Mohammedan and despises them as heathens." However, the Mandingo had "long since learned to appreciate the fruits of the earth; and this led to the introduction of slavery. . . . Even to-day, when the former slaves have been set free . . . the Mandingos are quite good at defrauding and exploiting natives."[26]

In the 1960s, a researcher asked Gola informants to describe the other peoples of Liberia. The nearby Mandingos were described both negatively and positively. Their negative traits, from the Gola point of view, were ruthlessness in war, conceit, and contempt for others. In addition, they were said to irresponsibly sell dangerous magic to the highest bidder. Their positive qualities were their devotion to prayer, their wealth, and their commercial acumen. The Vai and Dei groups were described in mildly derogatory terms. Groups farther away were perceived even more negatively. The Grebo, Kru, and Bassa were accused of stealing children for ritual murder or adoption, of being irreligious groups who did not have Poro, of smelling bad, of being poor farmers, of being sexually vulgar, of wearing strange tattoos, of being unfriendly. The distant Kissi were described as cannibals with pointed teeth.[27]

The Civilizing Mission

The Americo-Liberians, backed up, however feebly, by the power of the United States, added a new ingredient to the mix. In the 1930s, a European observed: "Strange to say, almost all of the tribes in this region have the same word for a civilized man, *kui*." The term was used for black and white (although some peoples referred to the latter as *kui pu*). The female traveler noted that "in so far as they are there to order him, the native, about, they are a burden to him, and he does not care a bit what colour his tormenter is."[28] Americo-Liberians were, until the present century, largely confined to a coastal strip thirty to forty miles wide. Even there, their presence was contested and relations abrasive. In the 1880s, an American visitor noted,

> Until within the past ten years, the relation between the native and the Negro emigrant from America has been that of master and slave. The former American slave treated the African freeman as if he had no rights which were worthy of respect! . . . This fact of the ill-treatment of the natives by the emigrants is not so strange after all; for the oppressed, when given an opportunity, generally become oppressors. The natives of Liberia have been to the emigrants from America just what these ex-slaves were to the whites of the South. They have been defrauded, beaten with stripes, and made to feel that they were inferior beings. . . . I have seen a civilized native boy . . . frequently enter a house on a business errand by the back way and the mistress of the house, a woman who cooked and washed in the United States for a living, wanted it to be distinctly understood, that her "front do'" was not to be used by "country people," as the natives are sometimes called. One Sabbath morning several natives came into a church in Liberia. They were shown into back pews. . . . But a thin-skinned female emigrant flounced out of the pew and out of the door with the air that an ill-bred white American woman would exhibit on changing her seat in a street-car because she was too near a "nigger."[29]

The African reality threatened to destroy diasporic unity. There existed, even at its best, an ambivalence in the Liberian civilizing mission. In 1870, Alexander Crummell advised his compeers to "give up the idle notion of dragging hither a nation from America, and go to work at once in the great endeavour to construct a vast national existence out of the native material about us."[30] At the same time, he remarked on "the childhood of the natives and, consequently, our responsibility of guardianship over them." Guardianship brought with it a responsibility — the use of force. Crummell ardently argued for its necessity. It "should be the force of restoration and progress — the force which anticipates the insensate ferocity of the pagan, by demonstrating the blessedness of permanent habitation and lasting peace; which forestalls a degrading ignorance and superstition, by the enlightenment of schools and training which neutralizes the bareness of a native rusticity by the creation of new wants and the stimulation of old ones."[31] Crummell's colleague, Blyden, blamed the problem of immigrant and indigene on the republic's mulatto ruling strata. However, this group had been swept away by the 1880s. Political power henceforth rested firmly in the hands of the all-black True Whig Party, but hierarchy remained. Culture replaced color, and law enshrined the difference between the "civilized" and the "natives." The latter did not participate directly in the state's political apparatus. Each "tribal" group was represented in the national legislature by one or two chiefs designated as delegates after paying the government a hundred dollars per head. The delegates could speak through interpreters only on matters of concern to their particular group, and they could not vote.

It is easy to be censorious of what has traditionally been called the Americo-Liberian settler elite. Indeed, one scion of a Jamaican immigrant family has written a spirited defense of the group, arguing that their power has been greatly overemphasized and that their critics never clearly delineated whether they were a class, an elite, or an ethnicity: "The notion that the Americo-Liberian ethnic group was coterminous with the ruling class is a myth akin to such phrases as 'the Jewish banking cabal' or 'the white ruling class of the world.'" To the defender, the idea "retains a ring of truth so long as some members of the stereotyped group remain engaged in the disreputed [*sic*] activity."[32] Animadversion "is sustained by invented quotes, by generalization of individual wrongdoings onto an entire group, and, most of all, imposing ethnicity as an explanatory factor where this is not supported by the evidence." Perhaps most importantly, what were the settlers to do?

Nations, after all, do not result full-blown from people's heads but rather out of social relations which, in Liberia of the early 1800s, included clientship, slavery, serfdom, etc. . . . Had the repatriates jettisoned African-American culture (the only one they know), whose should they have taken? The Vai? The Kru? Had they opted for Vai culture, which set of values should they have adopted, the local slaves or the slave-holders? Furthermore, why should the settlers have magically forged a national culture or a "dynamic nationalism" when local ethnic groups, in contact for hundreds of years, had not done so?[33]

One can argue that the Americo-Liberians were no worse than settler groups elsewhere. Indeed, the group did assimilate at its fringes a number of indigenous peoples who increasingly held interstitial power in the Liberian state. This would have been out of the question in Rhodesia or South Africa. There was intermarriage, both formal and informal, between settler and indigene. Maurice Delafosse, French consul in Monrovia in the late 1890s, observed, "A number of indigenous people Christianized by American missionaries — Vai, Bassa, Kru and especially Grebo — have contracted unions with Liberians [i.e., Americo-Liberians]. Furthermore, the latter have slaves or semi-slaves whose children (by settler fathers) become Liberians. The unions of Liberians with indigenous women, although not legalized, are excessively frequent."[34] The Harvard African Expedition of 1926–27 estimated that as many as 50,000 persons were affected by unions of this type. People drawn into this cultural web had "some knowledge of the English language and [were] regarded as civilized." The expedition team concluded that there was "no clear cut distinction between the Americo-Liberian and many of the subjects over whom they rule."[35] Du Bois later repeated this sentiment almost verbatim. What is important to remember is that most of these unions were hypogamous and that the children born of them usually held subordinate places within the Americo-Liberian community. As Latin America has long shown, sexual interbreeding serves as no indicator of the lack of social hierarchy based on ethnicity.

Liberia belied its own rhetoric. Settlers demanded land and/or labor. The people landing from America and the Caribbean needed both and had to obtain them from the congeries of often competing African groups they found in situ. Competition *and* collaboration marked the contact. The fulsome language of African redemption meant little in practicality. Indeed, because the Americo-Liberians, the Vai, the Kpelle, the Gola, the Grebo, the Kissi, the Bassa, the Kru, and the other groups inhabiting what became Liberia did not form a national culture, one of the chief premises on which various Pan-African projects were based, foundered. Liberia, because of its very nature, could never be what its defenders such as Crummell and Blyden wanted it to be. The Pan-

Negro folk community emanating from the African Personality proved a chimera. In the Liberian reality, this became increasingly obvious.

The World War I period, the period which saw the birth of Garveyism, also witnessed the emergence of Americo-Liberian military/political supremacy over indigenous Liberia. In 1912, Monrovia set up Indirect Rule in the hinterland. The indigenous population was supposed to be ruled through their traditional leaders, but, as elsewhere in colonial Africa, trustees of the regime were often installed in power. Under Indirect Rule, the "natives" were to provide labor for the construction of roads, rest homes, barracks, and district commissioners' quarters. They were also to work on government farms (holdings sometimes indistinguishable from the private farms of the commissioners and other government officials). In 1914, the hinterland administration underwent further refinement. The government created a new position, commissioner general, and redrew the boundaries between districts. Monrovia also attempted to define the separation of civilian and military authority. A commissioner constituted the highest authority in a district, but he could not command troops without the approval of the officer serving in his district. Military and civilian courts were instituted; the latter were to have authority over the indigenes. Only civilian authority could conduct trials of chiefs and other indigenes. On paper, instructions were set down for the recruitment and payment of native labor.

Paper provisions for good governance soon fell by the wayside. The Frontier Force continued to exercise its military and civilian roles. By the eve of the First World War, the government and its officials felt strong enough to dispense with efforts to cajole and coax their hinterland subjects. Increasingly, Americo-Liberian officials oversaw a system in which chiefs were confined to obeying these officials' wishes and carrying out their directives. District boundaries were often arbitrarily drawn with the aim of *divide et impera*. Clans from different groups were placed in the same unit with the aim of exploiting their differences and impeding any coordinated action. Two years after this general reorganization, the government introduced an annual hut tax payable by adult African men on each tenanted native dwelling. In 1922, in the midst of Garvey's emigration plans, the hut tax represented approximately one-third of gross government revenues.[36]

In the 1920s, further efforts to open up the interior added to the distress of the population. Extensive road building using corvée labor began. About 6,000 natives were set to work here. Indigenous men were required to purchase their own food and tools and, in addition, were often subject to authorized and unauthorized fees and fines. As no trained Liberian engineers existed, the roads were often poorly thought out and planned. Once built, they quickly reverted to bush. Soon, charges of abuse and extortion began to trickle out of the hinterland. One glaring example comes from the career of James W. Cooper, who was appointed secretary of war and acting secretary of the interior in 1920. Almost immediately, Cooper began an inland plantation; the estate used local inhabitants and the concubines of Frontier Force troops in conditions that approached slavery.[37] Within a period of twenty-one months, the official transferred payments totaling $20,000 to his private account with the Bank of British West Africa.

There were other abuses too. In the interior, torture was sometimes an adjunct of extortion. Two of the more ingenious were "smoked in the kitchen" and "No. 1 basket." In the first, a recalcitrant tribesman was set on the roof of a hut that was then set on fire. According to an observer, "The discomfort of slow suffocation inevitably changed the victim's attitude towards work."[38] In the second technique, a double-woven container of about two feet in diameter and fifteen inches deep was filled with dirt and stones. It was placed on the refractory indigene's head and given a spin. Alternatively, the victim might be told to walk around, with the burden supported by his head and neck. The spine could be injured or the neck broken.

Although military supremacy arrived, its impact varied. The Vai area saw little immigrant settlement. In the nineteenth century, the use of force was largely avoided and government taxes were not imposed until 1916. Few missionaries entered the isolated area. Many Vai had become Muslim, and by the opening of the twentieth century, a few individuals like Momolu Massaquoi had entered the Americo-Liberian power structure. Relations with the Kru and Grebo of the southern coast proved much more abrasive. While many individuals from these groups entered the charmed circle of the governing elite, Americo-Liberian settlement and desire to control trade generated armed conflict that ran on intermittently for three decades. In general, the Liberian Frontier Force's abuse of Indirect Rule was often flagrant, and revolts by indigenous peoples marked the early years of the century: Grebo (1910), Kru (1915), Gola (1918), Joquelle Kpelle (1920). Illegal requisitions and the destruction of property, along with forced concubinage of hinterland women, were frequently reported. In one case, in Barrabo, women spoke up during a council:

> We stand here and listen to the men to see if they tell all. If they leave out anything, we tell it. They have told almost everything, but one thing we want to say. They took us women to the barracks against our will. Yes. They

took us in groups . . . and we were there for nine months. The soldiers used us as their wives, we who had husbands and children. They had guns and we could not protect ourselves and our husbands could not protect us. Now it is a country custom that when a woman conceives, she must prove her child [its paternity]. We have not been able to prove these children of the soldiers, and this has made much trouble for us at home, although we could not help ourselves, and the men who were there could not help us. It has been necessary for us to kill the children [before they were born]. We pray to have us stopped from having to go to the barracks.[39]

Down in Maryland

In March of 1924, Garvey wrote to President King "that we approve and agree to the suggestions of the local advisory committee that the first settlement of colonists be established on the Cavella River, in Maryland county, near Cape Palmas, and to inform you that we are making arrangements for the first group of colonists of about four hundred (400) or five hundred (500) to sail from New York."[40] One of Maryland County's chief political figures, former vice president, now chief justice, James Dossen, emerged as the UNIA's staunchest high-level supporter. He reassured Garvey that "it was a pleasure to the friends of emigration to note the general enthusiasm shown by our people in the program to send to Liberia colonists of the race in other lands to help build up this nation."[41] Well before the advent of Garveyism, Dossen had cherished his own development schemes. In 1921, he had asked King, while in the United States, to publicize one of his defunct projects, the Excelsior Mining Company. He also bargained with a German company to develop mining in Maryland County. Immigration would dovetail with his larger vision. Colonists would bring capital and skills to bolster the Maryland Americo-Liberian minority. As wageworkers, new settlers would perform as the local subsistence farmers could not. In spite of Dossen's roseate projections, conditions on the coast did not warrant optimism. Harper, the largest Americo-Liberian settlement in Maryland, had no named streets, no census, nor record of births and deaths. The five hundred or so descendants of immigrants lived off of government jobs or as middlemen trading in palm oil, cassava, and rice.

The Garveyites needed to go to a real place in real time. Maryland County was to be the home of the UNIA's new experiment in the tropics. Neither Garvey nor his adherents seemed aware of the political maelstrom into which they were casting their fortunes. All had not been well between the settlers and the local Americo-Liberian political class. Indeed, in 1910, while Garvey was toiling away in Central America and formulating his vision of Pan-Africa, Maryland became the site of a small-scale war in which Dossen played a prominent part in putting down native resistance. The idea of an Africa of "one blood" was at least three thousand miles removed from the realities of southern Liberia. The indigenous peoples of Liberia had little feeling of black unity, but they were greatly concerned about the local distribution of goods and political power. The concerns of Liberty Hall lost much in trans-Atlantic translation.

The Grebo of Maryland, often designated as "Kruboys" or "Krumen," along with their northern neighbors, the Kru of Sinoe County, were proud, if somewhat fractious. They were divided into those who lived on the coast, called Grebo, and those who lived approximately thirty miles inland, known as Half-Grebo or Bush Grebo. Trade competition eventuated in long-lasting feuds and permanent division. Within the small Grebo villages themselves, political leaders held little continuous power; authority was gerontocratic, running through a system of age sets. The *kinkbo* (youngest age set) was composed of young, unmarried men. The eldest age set provided the *bodio,* a chief religious official, and the *wodaba* (or *worabanh*), the leader in time of war. The bodio had final authority in time of peace; under his leadership a village met to pass judgment and levy fines.

Americo-Liberian attempts to control trade from time to time erupted in violence. This held especially true at the end of the first decade of the twentieth century. The Grebo and Kru had, since at least the late eighteenth century, worked as wage laborers. Although it was maintained that they neither experienced enslavement nor ever kept slaves themselves, they were, at various times, involved in the slave trade as intermediaries, pilots, and interpreters. Many also served on the vessels of the British antislaving squadrons or worked as stevedores in ports such as Freetown in Sierra Leone. British steamers alone recruited as many as 20,000 workers from the Kru Coast each year in the late 1860s.[42] Later Krumen found employment in a variety of onshore tasks: mining, lumbering, porterage, and plantation agriculture. Laborers from the Kru Coast accompanied David Livingstone on his trek across central Africa, the British Niger Expedition of 1841, and Ferdinand de Lesseps in both his Suez and Panama Canal projects. By the end of the nineteenth century, Krumen had been employed as far away as the Congo Basin, Namibia, and South Africa.

Beginning in the nineteenth century, Americo-Liberians steadily destroyed the indigenous domination of coastal trade. In the 1870s, the Grebo formed the Gedebo Reunited Kingdom modeled after the Fanti

Confederation on the Gold Coast. This attempt at unity proved abortive, and Americo-Liberian control increasingly encroached. It is possible to see the conflict in Maryland as one between the Americo-Liberians and the Grebo, but this seems too simplistic. The Grebo were divided among themselves and seldom presented a united front to the interlopers. The conflict on the coast was also not one between the "civilized" and the "primitive." The semiliterate community huddled along the coast was not, ipso facto, more cosmopolitan or enlightened than elements of the indigenous population. Indeed, travel up and down the coast had created a worldview considerably more cosmopolitan than that of many of the settlers from Dixie. Episcopal missionaries aided in the creation of a Western-educated Grebo elite which chafed at the glass ceiling imposed by Americo-Liberian control of the governmental struggle. Many Grebo entered the service of the Liberian state, yet the co-optation of individuals could not hide the fact that the area now called Maryland had been superimposed on a proud, seafaring people who, whatever their internal divisions, believed that they had the right to run their own affairs. One source of friction was the extortion experienced by migrant workers at the hands of Liberian officials. In 1908, President Arthur Barclay had tried to allay some of these tensions by creating a commission to investigate and deal with complaints of Grebo migrants on the payment of customs. The commission decided that certain goods brought in by returnees should be duty-free. As a further concession, an educated Grebo was appointed to assist in assessing duties in Harper.[43] The 1908–9 session of the Liberian legislature reduced the tax on exported labor from five to four dollars per person.[44] Unfortunately, Maryland officials ignored this act, and Grebo migrants continued to pay both the old tax and duties on all goods brought into the country. Customs officials reportedly also charged excessive duties on desirable articles, keeping them for themselves when workers were unable to pay. Reportedly, customs inspectors also pilfered workers' belongings ordered left overnight on wharves.

A prophet emerged to denounce the abuses. The thunder before the storm came in the form of Prophet William Waddy Harris. The Grebo preacher had been born to non-Christian parents at Half-Graway (Glogbale) around 1865, made several voyages as a "Kruboy," and served as an interpreter for the Liberian government. In 1909, the future holy man publicly desecrated the Liberian flag and raised the Union Jack. A group of his followers played brass instruments and drums while yelling invectives at watching Americo-Liberians.[45] Revolt did not come; Harris was quietly arrested and imprisoned for more than a year. His religious conversion supposedly came through the Archangel Gabriel while the prophet was kept in a Liberian prison. Harris abandoned Liberia and gained his greatest fame as an itinerant evangelist in the Ivory and Gold Coasts in the years 1913–14. He made an impressive sight as he marched hundreds of miles barefoot "with a white sheep's skin rolled in his hand and his cross and Bible in the other."[46] Dressed in white, with a white turban, and accompanied by two women of his church, he quickly spread his gospel. Thousands flocked to hear his message and destroy the symbols of their old faith.

Violence in Harris's homeland erupted the year after his abortive call to arms. Conflict partially resulted from festering land disputes among the Grebo themselves. Although the case was adjudicated by President Barclay, one group, the Kudernowe, refused to accept the judgment. In 1909, they appealed to the head of the local Frontier Force for redress, and violence followed. Rivals of the Kudernowe received the blame, and the local authority in Harper accused them of disrupting trade in the Cavalla River region. The same year, Monrovia sent a commission, accompanied by a military unit, to investigate intraethnic conflict. Instead of settling the matter, the commission's arrival provoked more violence. Many educated Grebo feared that they, as well as their unlettered compatriots, might become targets. Rumors circulated that mission-educated men had been killed by the force sent out from Monrovia. Some Grebo living among Americo-Liberians were indeed murdered by their neighbors. One, referred to as Tailor Kilbu, was pursued into the ocean and drowned. Another, the Episcopal priest B. K. Speare, was shot to death on his front porch. Educated Grebo residents in Harper fled, among them the commissioner's secretary. The commission sent from Monrovia made matters worse by insisting that loyal Grebo register with the government in Harper. By February of 1910, full-scale war had erupted between the Nyomowe Grebo of Cape Palmas and the Americo-Liberians. Chief Gyude and a group of Grebo leaders wrote to the American Colonization Society and complained, "Since the incorporation of the colony . . . we and our fathers have always befriended the Liberian Republic as a struggling nation of our race." Proffered friendship had born bitter fruit, for the Americo-Liberians "soon began to despise us, placing us in their [place] and they in their masters', just as in the same fashion as in their slavery days in America."[47] He also complained that Cape Palmas Grebos remained targets of "unjust exactions."

As the uprising continued, a Liberian gunboat threatened the recalcitrant villages and trade languished. The indigenes appealed to their traditional trading partners, the British, for aid. None arrived. Instead, the USS *Birmingham* arrived off the coast carrying vice president Dossen and attorney general C. D. B. King. The Monrovia government received a loan from a German firm and sent an additional 250 troops to Cape Palmas in mid-May 1910. By August, the "revolt" was over; armed forces returning to the capital took eight chiefs with them as living trophies.

Vice president Dossen, the future patron of the UNIA, derided the Grebos' attempt at resistance. The political activity of Kede Bla Seton, a Western-educated Grebo who widely protested the treatment of his people, particularly incensed him. Dossen wrote:

> The story which Mr. Kede Bla Seton has striven to build in his letter published in Lagos, Nigeria, in the Lagos Record as well as in the one to the American Colonization Society purporting to have emanated from King Gyude, and which has appeared in several leading American journals, is as malicious as it is misleading and, by persons conversant with Liberian affairs and her benevolent, tolerant policy towards her native population particularly the Cape Palmas Greboes—will be read with disappointment and disgust. Where else in Western Africa is the native accorded the same political, civil and educational advantages, as are provided him in Liberia? Seton, himself a graduate of our State College and the son of a heathen Grebo rescued from Heathenism, educated, Christianized and fitted for civilization and citizenship, and who held several prominent positions in the State, such as a member of the National Legislature, Public School Commissioner (which post he held for fully a decade) and lastly judge of the Probate Court, which office he filled up to the time of his death, unblushing arraigns Liberia for "shutting the door of political and civil privileges to competent Greboes and of being negligent in providing the means for their education." To both of these charges I enter on behalf of Liberia the plea of "Not Guilty," and I challenge Mr. Seton and his compatriots to make good these malicious, wicked shameful accusations by an array of solid facts in support.[48]

The aged Blyden looked on in dismay. By the time of the Grebo War of 1910, he had come to condemn the Americo-Liberian elite as decadent— unfit for the great task of African redemption that history had thrust on it. In 1909, he acerbically observed that "unfortunately, as soon as the Liberians were placed upon what they believed was a sure international footing, they began to infringe the treaties they had made with the natives when they obtained the cession of their country, assuming what the natives regarded as an oppressive attitude." The settlers interfered with indigenous rights in order to foster "[as the Liberians alleged] the

Gospel of peace and good will, which they believed themselves to have brought from America."[49] President Arthur Barclay blamed the Grebo revolt on "Dr. Blyden . . . who received recently a stipend from the British Government in recognition for services rendered."[50] An Americo-Liberian newspaper said sedition was the work of "one who is called Liberia's greatest and most learned man — a man who spends more time in England than he does in Liberia . . . who it is believed is a member of the British diplomatic corps not withstanding his pretended Liberian citizenship."[51] The grand old man of Pan-Africanism ended his days accused by a settler minority of inciting an African majority in order to further the aims of outside imperialism.

Up in Sinoe

The West African nationalist J. E. Casely Hayford opined that "the Kroo man is the scavenger of the world . . . Mammon has used the Kroo man all these years. And now God has need of him."[52] Like their Grebo neighbors to the south, the Kru of Sinoe did not present a common front to their Americo-Liberian neighbors. Power was decentralized. The Kru were organized into loose sociocultural alliances called *dako*. The basic social unit was the *panton*, or patrilineage. It was headed by a *nyefue,* its eldest capable male member. It was his job to settle disputes within the lineage. A *kroba*, or "father of the town" was selected by the heads of the various pantons (*nyefei* in the plural). In time of war, the kroba's authority was superseded by that of the *gbaubi*, or "father of the army." The society contained age sets which were formed every eight to twelve years and which included members of all lineages.

Settler-indigene tension did not remain confined to Maryland; in the adjoining county of Sinoe, similar conditions and practices prevailed. By the opening of the twentieth century, it had already become evident that certain local politicians viewed the county as a satrapy, geographically and politically removed from close supervision by Monrovia. The political head of Sinoe was Samuel Alford Ross, the son of Georgia-born J. J. Ross, the county's dominant political figure in the late nineteenth century.[53] The younger Ross was described as the "huge, black and genial political boss in Sinoe County" who had "at various times, been lawyer, preacher, and merchant and at all times a shrewd politician."[54] Samuel Ross sought not only to derive profit from the preexisting flow of labor but also to use the police power at his command to coerce an increasingly reluctant labor force to migrate. Ross's policies were not always consonant with national policy. At times when politicians in the northern counties attempted to prohibit the outflow of native manpower, Ross doggedly persisted in attempts to maximize the outflow of labor from the area under his control.

An underlying source of tension between the administrator and the local people was a 1905 order from Monrovia making the town of Settra Kru a port of entry. The superintendent, apparently fearing that expansion of local trade options would divert part of the labor traffic and the produce trade from his control, blocked the central government's decision. Liberian officials on their way to Settra Kru were detained in Greenville when they arrived, and no further effort was made to open that town to trade. The residents were enraged and engaged in acts of defiance. In response, Ross, now a senator, fined Settra Kru some three thousand dollars in 1910. Because the people could not pay, a detachment of the Frontier Force sacked the town, taking payment in the forms of produce, cattle, and women. In 1911, Ross lynched a Kru chief for supposedly aiding rebels; then he hanged five other local officials without trial.[55]

In order to obtain redress for a number of grievances, the Kru sent a long petition to the United States government in 1912. The Kru of Settra Kru asked the United States to intervene on their behalf to put an end to Ross's imposed trade embargo. In November of 1912, disturbances broke out at River Cess, also in Sinoe County. A year later, the American minister in Monrovia warned, "The Krus have profound contempt for Liberian Officers and know of their lack of skill and military stamina. . . . The Kru Coast is destined to give the Liberian Government a great deal of trouble in the near future."[56] Two years later the minister said, "The natives despise the Americo-Liberians and feel fully capable of defeating the armed forces of the government if American . . . support is withheld. They keep well informed of the conditions of the government at all times."[57] In 1915, sporadic fighting was reported on the Kru Coast; in June, the towns of Grand Cess and Picaninny Cess fought each other; in September, Kru from River Cess to Betu rose in revolt. Their grievances included resentment against the exactions of Liberian officials and the imposition of a hut tax at a time of trade depression (World War I), but the immediate cause of the rebellion, according to Kru interviewed by American commissioners, was Ross's decision to enlarge the labor pool.[58]

The Kru hoped the British would aid them in their struggle against Americo-Liberian rule, but the British consulate tersely discouraged this idea. "You have been told by me before," said the consul, "to live peacefully and do your duty to the Liberian Government whose subjects you are. . . . I have told you that when trouble or misunderstanding came you should come to Monrovia quietly and respectfully and ask the Liberian Government to put things right for you." The rebels were told that they should expect no aid from the British government and that the consulate would receive no more letters from them.[59] Without modern arms, the Kru proved no match for the Frontier Force, backed as it was by an American war vessel. The Kru were defeated, the chiefs of the warring tribes hanged, and a number of prisoners killed. The government then tried and sentenced at least sixty-two Kru leaders to death for treason. President Howard commuted forty-seven of the sentences, but his clemency (life imprisonment) did not become known in Greenville until all but twenty of the men had been executed. A Kru later testified that all "natives" on the coast at the time of the revolt became suspect. "In the land of the Kru chiefs the principal question was 'where were you — were you in Sierra Leone, or Lagos, or where? That was the principal question. If he said, 'Yes, I was in Liberia!,' then he was pretty guilty."[60] In Sinoe County the reprisals caused considerable alarm. The people appealed to Colonel James F. Cooper for leniency. President D. E. Howard supposedly was dissuaded from such a course by secretary of state C. D. B. King, who advised that "bad sore requires hard medicine."[61]

The punishment of the Kru was completed by disarming them, a regulation later extended to all tribes within the republic. At the end of 1916, the American minister observed that "the [Kru] coast is now in the hands of and under the control of the [Liberian] Government for the first time since its existence."[62] This breaking of Kru resistance marked the last major outbreak of violence before Ross's death in 1929. However, the end of the Kru War of 1915 did not bring any lessening of exactions; on the contrary, it paved the way for their increase, so much so that it eventuated in scandal. It was this atmosphere of exaction and resistance that Du Bois and Garvey inadvertently entered in the 1920s.

Africa and Pan-Africa

In January of 1924, Du Bois wrote from Liberia of a visit to Monrovia's Kru section. He found himself entranced:

> And the people! Last night I went to Kru-town and saw a Christmas masque. There were young women and men of the color of warm ripe horse chestnuts, clothed, in white robes and turbaned. They played the Christ story with sincerity, naivete and verve. Conceive "Silent Night" sung in Kru by this dark white procession with flaming candles; the little black mother of Christ crossing with her baby, figured blue, with Joseph in Mandigan fez

and multi-colored cloak and beside them on her worshiping knees the white wreathed figure of a solemn dark angel. The shepherds watched their flocks by night, the angels sang; and Simeon, raising the baby high in his black arms, sang . . . Kru-wise, "Lord now lettest thou thy servant depart in peace for mine eyes have seen they salvation!"[63]

While Du Bois went to Liberia, Garvey never did. In August of 1923, the editor of the *Crisis* announced that the Third Pan-African Congress would take place in November, with meetings in London and Lisbon. He also planned his first visit to the motherland. Given his running ideological and political battle with Garvey, he was anxious to be officially received by the Monrovia government at the time of president King's second inauguration. He offered his services to the State Department, but it rebuffed him.[64] Several individuals lobbied on his behalf, most notably William H. Lewis, a black Republican attorney. The lawyer assured the administration that naming Du Bois an envoy would assure "the support of *The Crisis*, the most widely read publication among the colored people, or stultify it, if it should come out against us."[65] Eventually, after he had left for Europe, Du Bois received confirmation that he had been named Calvin Coolidge's envoy extraordinary and minister plenipotentiary — without salary.

Du Bois arrived in Monrovia in December. As an official representative at the January ceremony, the envoy's remarks to the Liberian president were eloquent: "In America live eleven million persons of African descent; they are citizens, legally invested with every right that inheres in American citizenship. . . . [President Coolidge] knows how proud they are of the hundred [*sic*] years of independence which you have maintained by force of arms and by brawn and brain upon the edge of this mighty continent; he knows that in the great battle against color caste in America, the ability of Negroes to rule in Africa has been and ever will be a great and encouraging reenforcement."[66] President King reposited that Liberia was "a Republic founded by Black Men, maintained by Black Men and [one] which holds out the highest hopes and aspirations for Black Men."[67]

At the age of fifty-five, Du Bois finally consummated his long love affair with the motherland. Given the pomp and circumstance of his mission, he saw the occasion as adding to the dignity of the Negro race. Liberia stood as a palimpsest for the history of that race. Africa was essential to the race concept, but it was a mythic Africa visualized from the Diaspora and projected back onto the continental reality. Du Bois, a sixth-generation descendant of Africa, could never be American in the same way as men who left Smyrna, Trieste, Genoa, and Ostend. He remained caught on the horns of a dilemma, one which Garvey over-leapt by emigration. Du Bois looked forward to both civic participation in the United States and an African American role in a distant and highly idealized Africa, the fountainhead of the Negro race. Neither phenotype nor culture made Du Bois a Pan-Africanist. According to him, "the real essence of this kinship is its social heritage of slavery. . . . It is this unity that draws me to Africa."[68] Africa proved essential to the problem of the color line. However, in this Black Man's Land, where are the Hausa or the Yoruba? More importantly, where are the Kru and the Grebo? As isomorphs of *Negro,* they became swallowed up in ancestral blackness and emerge as irrelevant to the Du Boisian project.

Echoing Blyden, Du Bois resuscitated the image of a spiritual noble savage.

> And there and elsewhere in two long months I began to learn: primitive men were not following us afar, frantically waving and seeking our goals; primitive men were not behind us in some swift foot-race. Primitive men have already arrived. They are abreast, and in places ahead of us; in others behind. But all their curving advance line is contemporary, not prehistoric. They have used other paths and these paths have led them by scenes sometimes fairer, sometimes uglier than ours, but always toward the Pools of Happiness. Or, to put it otherwise, these folk have the leisure for sleep and laughter.[69]

Unlike Blyden, however, Du Bois seldom engages the "native" as more than a foil for the Occident. He visits, and the natives remain invisible. Speaking of his landing, he wrote:

> We climbed the upright shore to a senator's home and received his wide and kindly hospitality—curious blend of feudal lord and modern farmers—sandwiches, cake, and champagne. Again we glided up the drowsy river—five, ten, twenty miles and came to our hostess, a mansion of five generations with a compound of endless native servants and cows under the palm thatches. The daughters of the family wore, on the beautiful black skin of their necks, the exquisite pale gold chains of the Liberian artisan and the slim, black little granddaughter of the house had a wide pink ribbon on the thick curls of her dark hair, that lay like sudden sunlight on the shadows. Double porches, one above the other, welcomed us to ease. A native man, gay with Christmas and a dash of gin, sang and danced in the road.[70]

With the commander of the Liberian Frontier Force as his special aide, Du Bois saw nothing amiss, observed nothing amiss. His Africa is the good, the polite, and the leisurely. Hunger, exploitation and want cannot mar the portrait of the Black Republic. David Levering Lewis observes that a seventy-five-year remove from these African effusions invites a certain amount of amusement at Du Bois's expense, and, perhaps, for some, even disappointment bordering on reproach. Pan-Africanism's origins in the Black Diaspora elite were never more evident than during his performance in Liberia and Sierra Leone, where a tone of unconscious cultural superiority permeated Du Bois's carefully crafted statements proclaiming the solidarity of darker peoples. Too many gestures and phrases bore the stamp of the classic European in Africa, as though Cecil Rhodes and Kipling were shaking hands with Delany and Alexander Crummell. . . . Exhilarated as seldom before in life by what he saw as the significance of being in Africa, puffed up by Ethiopianist presumptions and conceits embedded in his uplift ideology, Du Bois came perilously close to imagining himself a pan-African proconsul empowered to redirect the political course of the continent. No longer the result of a cynical White House favor arranged at his own request by a powerful GOP stalwart, the mission to Monrovia took on unprecedented historic and political valence as Du Bois moved among the Liberians.[71]

What did Du Bois see as he moved among the Liberians? According to the distinguished visitor, indigenous Liberians "have time for their children — such well-trained, beautified children with perfect, unhidden bodies. . . . Come to Africa, and see well-bred and courteous children, playing happily and never sniffling and whining."[72] Six years later, the black sociologist Charles Johnson received the opposite impression. "The large number of children with open sores on their faces and bodies was conspicuous. . . . Several of these children's faces were a mass of sores. . . . A favorite game was 'soldiers catch men and beat them.'"[73] Two African Americans, observing many of the same things, could paint very different pictures. Du Bois said, exulted, "I am riding on the singing heads of black boys swinging in a hammock. The smooth black bodies swing and sing, the neck set square, the hips sway. Oh, lovely voices and sweet young souls of Africa!"[74] Charles Johnson wrote, "An hour's walk from Soloken is the town site of Kordor, hard hit by the [government] raids. Forty-one huts had been inhabited. . . . The rotting thatch and crumbling mud walls of the dwellings, the rampant vegetation, the toadstools, decaying bread-fruit everywhere, the reptiles scampering through the shells of the huts, all gave it the aspect of a city of the dead."[75] Wherein lies the truth?

Du Bois reportedly felt that "it was absolutely necessary for the [Liberian] government to take a high hand . . . [with the indigenes] in order to assure them that it really was a government, otherwise the tribal chiefs would take matters into their own hands."[76] But why? Why were African polities illegitimate? Why did a group descended from largely illiterate Southern peasants take precedence? Charles Johnson remarked that there was "something fantastic about the spectacle of a group of 12,000 to 15,000 American Liberians, concentrated in six small towns on the coast, presuming to control an area of 43,000 square miles and an unknown native population of about 1.5 million."[77] The irony of the situation was lost on Du Bois. The reason lies in an understandable and deeply ingrained Western bias. In December of 1918, Du Bois had written that "the principle of self-determination . . . cannot be wholly applied to semi-civilized peoples."[78] Unlike Blyden, Du Bois could never quite abandon the idea of a diasporic civilizing mission.

The issue proves complex; did the indigenes have any right to choose their government, or was the overriding issue the preservation of Africa's only "republic." Blyden and Du Bois came to quite opposite conclusions. What stands out most clearly in the latter's thought is its mythic abstraction. A contrast can be made with Casely Hayford. Indeed, the Gold Coaster faulted Du Bois for his seeming belief in the Diaspora as the vanguard of African liberation. The African also opined that African Americans might need specific instruction from Africans on aspects of the continent's culture. In 1923, Casely Hayford's *Gold Coast Leader* contrasted Garvey's program favorably with Du Bois's.[79] Ideologically, Garvey was as much a "civilizationist" as Du Bois. However, the obstructionism of the Liberian elite made him look, perforce, beneath the facade embodied in the Black Republic. In 1924, Garvey declared, in an oblique reference to Du Bois, that the oligarchy in Monrovia was afraid of him, "for they realized that they have no colleague in me to exploit the labor of the unfortunate blacks and build up class distinctions."[80] Earlier Garvey had tried to make his position plain. "It will be useless, as stated, for bombastic Negroes to leave America and the West Indies to go to Africa, thinking that they will have privileged positions to inflict upon the race that bastard aristocracy that they have tried to maintain in this Western world at the expense of the masses." Garvey, the emigrationist, proclaimed, "Africa shall develop an aristocracy of its own, but it shall be based upon service and loyalty to race."[81]

Garvey's vision was as grand and poetic in its sweep as Du Bois's. It differed in that Garvey wanted to "Make the Word Flesh." In Garveyism, Africa-as-Totem meets Africa-as-Future. As in the Du Boisian formulation, the continent provided the Diaspora's pedigree. At the same time, for Garvey, it was something more. The UNIA's Pan-Africanism took on the task of nation building in the real world. It was here that Garveyism faced the suspicions of both the white world and the Liberian oligarchy. More centrally, to be successful, it would have to move from simple anticolonialism and confront the very nature of the continent itself. Although Garvey might maintain that there was "not even the semblance of government" in Africa, its leaders and peoples might fear otherwise. Early in 1921, one African, Madarikan Deniyi, expressed his dismay: "How can Marcus Garvey and the U.N.I.A redeem Africa without the consent and cooperation of the black kings, chiefs and presidents who were born and elected to rule the natives in Africa?"[82] In the following year another African, the Basuto M. Mokete Manoedi, critiqued the whole Garveyite enterprise in similar terms: "It is about as sensible and logical to speak of a president of Africa as it is to speak of a president or king of Europe or of all the Americas." He noted that Africa contained a multitude of polities and cultures that were not "always at peace merely because they occupy the same continent. Witness the recent world war between nations, such as France and Germany, both European nations." Manoedi pointed out that not all of the inhabitants of Africa considered themselves Negroes. In a pointed critique of the tendency to use *Africa* as a metonym for *Black Man's Land,* the African wrote that the continent was composed of diverse nations, races, religions, and colors:

> The term African is a composite one like Asia or Europe. It does not denote a nation or race. But the fallacy of calling a continent a nation or of calling a nation a race is a small matter with this blatant, superficial braggart. His erroneous terminology is of a piece with his fantastic mathematics. For instance, he shouts about liberating 400,000,000 Negroes. Where are they? In his imagination, of course! He assumes that by adding the population of Africa to the population of Negroes in the United States, the West Indies, South and Central America, it will give that sum, which, of course, is not true even if we grant that all of the population of Africa are Negroes, which [they] are not. . . .Thus you see, it is the height of insanity and suicidal folly for one, with the air of omniscience and omnipotence to rant and fulminate about what he is going to do to, for or with Africa without taking into consideration the fact of differences in race, religion and nationality, together with multifarious tribal distinctions.[83]

A diasporic response from Pan-Africanists of either the Garvey or Du Bois camps would have held that these diverse populations were bound together by the heritage of slavery and the ravages of imperialism. They were Negroes because whites considered them Negroes. This reply worked in the Diaspora, but it proved less obvious in the African context. Imperialism did not fuse the Tutsi and Hutu or the Fulani and the Yoruba. Nor did it always treat all Africans peoples as equal; *tribe* and *ethnicity* were quite capable of colonialist manipulation. Administrators could be very inventive in their search for favored peoples, warrior races with Hamitic affinities. All colonials were subject, but some subjects were superior to others.

In the case of Liberia, the rulers were very aware of their position as rulers and of their uniqueness in a sea of colonialism. Garveyism, wedded to the idea of folk community, was eventually stymied by their self-interest. Whatever the idea of universal black unity, the UNIA had to face the distinction between "native" and "civilized." Elie Garcia's 1921 letter to Garvey observed:

> Class distinctions—This question is also a great hindrance to the develop-
> ment of Liberia. There are at this present time two classes of people: the
> Americo-Liberians also called "sons of the soil" and the natives. The first
> class, although the educated one, constitutes the most despicable element in
> Liberia. Because of their very education, they are self-conceited and believe
> that the only honorable way for them to make a living is by having a "Gov-
> ernment job." The men of this class having places, are used to a life, which the
> salaries paid by the Government do not suffice to maintain. Therefore,
> dishonesty is prevalent. . . . Another important fact is the attitude of the
> Americo-Liberian towards enlightening the native tribes. . . . As it is, the
> Americo-Liberians are using the natives as slaves, and human chattel slavery
> still exists there. . . . They buy men or women to serve them, and the least
> little insignificant Americo-Liberian has half a dozen boys at his service. . . . It
> is also deplorable to state that the highest Liberian official lives in a state
> of polygamy, which is highly detrimental to the improvement of morality
> among the natives as well as to social development among themselves.[84]

It was the UNIA's potential impact on the delicate balance between the settlers and the indigenes that made it an anathema in Monrovia. In March of 1922, the London-based colonial organ, *African World*, published a purloined copy of Garcia's secret report. The expected happened. The government-controlled *Liberian News* later claimed that the report "gave a clear picture of the revolutionary purposes of the UNIA in Liberia, and determined the Government's irrevocable attitude of opposition."[85] Seeking to placate Monrovia, Garvey was willing, for a time, to temporize. Late in 1923, he criticized Critchlow and Garcia, who had both fallen afoul of the King government. They had done "a great deal of harm with their indiscretions, which caused us to have delayed, and in other words, suspended the efforts we started to make in carrying out of our industrial program in Liberia."[86] Once finally betrayed, Garvey attacked "the Negroes of the Barclay and King type" who kept "the natives poor, hungry, shelterless and naked." Indeed, "in Liberia the Negroes of the Barclay and King type treat the natives like dogs, and with greater inhumanity than some of the most selfish whites."[87]

Historically, the UNIA's criticism of the Liberian class structure constituted its finest hour. After the betrayal of the Liberian scheme, Garveyites conducted a steady propaganda to expose the Monrovia regime. In 1929, C. D. B. King, the favorite of the American State Department, was implicated in a slavery scandal; the following year he was forced to resign. After King, three subsequent presidents successfully maintained Americo-Liberian rule for another half-century. In 1980, a group of young indigenous army personnel bloodily swept away the Americo-Liberian elite. The leader of the coup, Samuel K. Doe, had attended a secondary school named for the founder of the UNIA. This was perhaps Marcus Garvey's most unintended vindication.

3 Abuse

My skinfolks, but not my kinfolks

— Zora Neale Hurston

Oppressors talking about oppressors

Oppressing their oppressors

Where are the oppressed?

— Mutabaruka

More than twenty years ago, this writer spoke to several veterans of the Universal Negro Improvement Association in Philadelphia.[1] These aging members of the vestigial organization vociferously maintained that the real culprit in the demise of the UNIA's grand design was none other than Charles Burgess Dunbar King. Indeed, of all Pan-Africanists, the Garveyites most consistently condemned social oppression in the ancestral homeland. Unlike many of their Pan-Africanist colleagues, they placed blame on Monrovia, as well as on London and Washington. Unlike those who attempted to exculpate the ruling clique in the Black Republic, the Garveyites excoriated it. We must remember that Garvey spoke bluntly and broke the ideal of the folk community when he said, "They keep the Natives poor, hungry, shelterless and naked, while they parade themselves in the tropical sun in English frock coats and evening dress." Worse still, "They work and tax the natives to death while they, themselves, impugn the dignity of labor and pay no taxes."[2]

The Traffic and Traffickers

While Marcus Garvey sat on his throne in High Harlem and talked of the redemption of a continent, events on the Windward Coast were working against him. Over three thousand miles away, a contest was underway, which, while exotic in Harlem, Detroit, or Atlanta, held burning importance to the future of African American return. The indigenes were restless. People in preexisting subordinate statuses, such as young male mariners among the Kru and Grebo, increasingly felt the pressure of labor demands by the Liberian state. In the Garveyites' view, both they and the native peoples had been betrayed by the African American elite and by white American capital, represented by the newly introduced Firestone Rubber. In 1925, the UNIA blasted the King-Barclay group as labor procurers and abusers of the worst type—the agents of "a new slavery":

> Listen to the language of the selfish, "ignorant intellectual" heartless black Negro exploiter and "Statesman" from Liberia typical of the King Administration of that country: This man is without any apology an agent and subject of the new slavery imposed upon African natives, whose labor is sold by this type of the race for twenty-five cents and less per diem for producing rubber, etc., for a white exploiting corporation—another Belgian Leopold outrage. Can you see the reason why Barclay and King and their kind in Liberia hate and oppose me? They can sell the labor of "husky" black men and women for twenty-five cents and make the profits. Garvey sought to standardize the wages of the black race and dignify the social life of the people. They sought to exploit the people and keep them in "their places" for themselves and the unreasonable capitalistic systems of Africa. Must the two million blacks of Liberia perish at the hands of such men? Must wide-awake and right thinking American and West Indian Negroes, be kept out of Liberia and prevented from helping in the honorable development of their ancestral country? . . . Oh, Government! How many crimes are committed in thy name?[3]

Labor appeared to be Liberia's most important export. The voracious demand for it abroad encouraged the ruthless labor recruitment policies followed in Sinoe and Maryland counties. Liberia's lack of an important export crop also fostered the export of manpower itself. Attempting to maintain a place for its coffee in the international market, the Liberian government could not avoid an awareness that the colonial powers valued Liberia's labor far more than the declining product of its soil. In 1914, the year in which the UNIA was formed, Liberia had agreed to supply laborers to a white colonial government in Spanish Guinea. The colony, comprising the island of Fernando Po and the enclave of Rio Muni, was particularly starved of labor. The insular portion of the colony amounted to roughly eight hundred square miles in area; the island lies about twenty-five miles from the Cameroonian coast and fifty miles from the Nigerian port of Calabar. Fernando Po's indigenous population, the Bantu-speaking Bubi, had avoided much contact with outsiders until the end of the nineteenth century. When European colonialism finally enveloped them in the twentieth century, they experienced precipitate population decline. Spain now had a colony with a rapidly shrinking labor supply.

A Briton in Liberia, commenting shortly after the agreement with the Spanish went into effect, said that the government had "without giving any notice, pounced upon the tribal Chiefs for hut and other taxes." Because the indigenous people had "had no time to prepare payment for these claims in kind, the officials sent up [other officials], under escort of a detachment of the Liberian Frontier Force, [and] not only confiscated their cattle, grain, etc., but brought down as hostages numbers of their boys who were relegated to work, for no payment, on the Liberian Coffee Estates for some time, then shipped [them] to Fernando Po." In this transaction, "the Liberian Government received £5 per head headmoney from the Spanish Government.[4]

The 1914 accord offered the Liberian government head monies for laborers shipped to the cocoa plantations and promised as well to safeguard the workers' well-being. The agreement with Spain provided for a Liberian consul in Santa Isabel, the capital of the island. It authorized labor recruitment in selected Liberian ports by agents under the supervision of the Spanish consul in Monrovia.[5] Liberia would select four recruiting agents and planters from Fernando Po who could go to Monrovia to make arrangements with the Liberian authorities. Copies of the labor contracts would be given to the Liberian customs, the Liberian secretary of state, and the Liberian consul general on Fernando Po. Each statement would contain the worker's name, county, town, district, tribe, chief, and period of contracted labor. The statement was to be presented to the labor agent in Liberia three days before the transportation of the laborer to Fernando Po. The maximum period of a contract came to two years, the minimum one year; workers were to be refused to employers not approved by the governor of Fernando Po and the Liberian authorities. Labor was not to go to insolvent farmers; contracts would not be subject to extension, and wages were to be paid in English money, one half on Fernando Po and one half through the Spanish consul on the worker's return to Liberia. The labor agreement itself was subject to termination by either country on six months' notice.

For the agriculturists of Fernando Po, the agreement proved economically burdensome, but as long as it delivered labor, the island's black and white planters stood to gain. Thousands of laborers were shipped under the 1914 convention; between 1919 and 1926, a known 4,268 were recruited and employed on the island. A 1930 investigatory commission calculated that, averaging 600 a year, the total number from 1914 to 1927 was at least 7,268 (a calculation that seems to fall well below the number one would expect).[6] Imported labor was dear, especially for the smaller producers. In 1915 English missionaries on Fernando Po reported acute economic conditions and that "the cost of each worker has increased alarmingly during the recent years both in Government demands and standard of wage, together with increase in rations."[7] Moreover, the exigencies of the First World War endangered the shipment of laborers from Liberian ports. A decree of July 15, 1918, authorized a two-year reengagement of workers who had completed their contracts.[8] But early the next year, Liberia proposed to terminate the agreement entirely after six months. The American minister in Monrovia noted, "A well defined feeling among Liberian officials that most of the complaints of the laborers have some foundation in fact."[9] There existed another defect in the working of the convention — the unwillingness of Spanish ships to land laborers at any place other than Monrovia. In addition, many also viewed the agreement as depriving Liberian planters and tribal farms of labor. The minister observed that the agreement's termination would lead to Liberia's loss of about $10,000 per year.[10]

Who were the managers of the labor flow both within and without Liberia? One was Allen Yancy, the superintendent of Maryland County (1920–28). The Liberian politician ruthlessly exploited disputes between indigenous groups to his own advantage. He was described as "a small ferretlike individual." The superintendent "talked always with the air of a proprietor, gesturing at the town of Harper after the manner of one referring to his private farm. . . . His restless energy, his Napoleonic complex, the cold cunning of his tiny bright eyes, gave some credibility to the reports [of forced labor]."[11] Yancy was born in Cape Palmas (Harper) in 1881, the son of a Georgia preacher. As a resourceful son of immigrant parents, he had a variegated career that can serve as a study in upward mobility. His political life began in 1905, when he was appointed justice of the peace. In the 1910 Grebo War, Yancy chose neutrality even though he was a captain in the Liberian Guard, a stance which allowed him to repair guns for the Grebo (he had married a Grebo woman in 1902) and make a healthy profit. He was later persuaded to take up his duties as an officer, but he expressed an unwillingness to participate in warfare; his company mutinied and fled in the face of a Grebo attack. Finding himself opposed by both his fellow Americo-Liberians and the Grebo, he reportedly attempted to leave the country for the Gold Coast and narrowly evaded execution. Yancy then devoted himself to business, managing a store for the English trading firm Woodin and Company. He became a good friend of future president Edwin Barclay, and in 1918, with Barclay's aid, he was appointed county attorney of Maryland. Two years afterward, he became superintendent of Maryland; seven years later he was elected vice president.

In 1930, the British consulate in Monrovia sanguinely analyzed Yancy's prospects: "Said to be active, intelligent and fairly honest in his commercial transactions . . . . Will probably run for President at the next election as the official candidate of the True Whig party."[12] In the late 1920s, Yancy exploited disputes between indigenous groups to his own advantage in the labor trade. Head monies were collected from European shippers for Yancy's benefit and that of his colleagues. By 1929, he reportedly had spread the profits of his activities to several prominent citizens: County superintendent Brooks, senator (and future president) William Tubman, senator Dossen, and three members of the House of Representatives. The district commissioner of District Five in the Maryland hinterland also benefited from Yancy's export of labor.[13]

How was labor procured? Perhaps one in-depth example will do. It most clearly shows the perversion of the legal system for the purpose of public and private gain. In 1924, the Wedabo (Webbo) people became caught in the web of coerced labor recruitment. Early in the century, the Wedabo had been involved in a disagreement with the Po River people, a small group of Kru origin living between the Garawe people and a shore-living section of the Wedabo.[14] After the turn of the century, the Po River and Wedabo peoples had agreed on a modus vivendi that provided the Wedabo, most of whom lived inland, with access to the sea and the seaport of Harper. In 1908, this accord received the legal sanction of the "civilized" courts, as well as traditional reconfirmation. However, the pact was not always observed; between 1908 and 1923, seven Wedabo were killed while en route to or from the sea. The Wedabo appealed to Yancy, but received little aid; supposedly he told them, "You Wedabo people are damn fools. When you see people are killing you why don't you do something to them instead of always complaining?"[15]

When three Po River people were killed in a 1923 dispute, the Wedabo took their first step toward entanglement in Yancy's labor recruitment net. A district commissioner summoned Wedabo paramount chief Tuweley Jeh, described by one observer as "tall, bronzed, and magnificent."[16] Sixty subchiefs were detained while Chief Jeh was sent home to collect £100. After the payment to the district commissioner, superintendent Yancy heard of the affair and ordered the matter referred to him. Jeh was told he needed legal counsel, and three lawyers were recommended, among them Senator Tubman. The superintendent reportedly told Jeh to "go back and bring [the] lawyers £100."[17] However, when the matter reached court, Yancy allegedly said the sum already delivered (£100) would not cover the fees. Again the paramount chief returned home, and it was resolved to borrow the required funds from a European trading firm. The Wedabo borrowed £300 and turned it over to Yancy. Jeh was then informed he had won his case. However, Yancy demanded and received a further £60 for his good offices.

But the Wedabo matter had not concluded. The dissatisfied Po River people sent a delegation to president C. D. B. King, who ordered Jeh to Monrovia. To defray his travel expenses, the chief approached the Woodin company for £100; Yancy intervened to negotiate the loan. The chief received only £20. Among other things, £40 had been given to senator Tubman for his legal services, and £5 had been paid to an Americo-Liberian interpreter. In Monrovia, Chief Jeh was subject to further exactions. The president of the republic demanded the payment of a fine of £100, plus the surrender of the murderers of the Po River people. To insure payment, the Wedabo paramount was retained as a hostage. Again Yancy intervened, offering to advance the money if the Wedabo would produce men for shipment to the Spanish colony of Fernando Po. A council of chiefs balked at the suggestion, but it was ultimately forced to comply with Yancy's threat to saddle the group with still another fine. A consignment of five hundred men was demanded and a Spanish ship sent to Wedabo Beach. Unfortunately, the men requested were not present on the vessel's arrival, and Yancy threatened to burn two towns if the workers were not produced. He took townspeople as hostages, and by daybreak, 316 men presented themselves for shipment. Later, after the Wedabo had supplied the full complement, Jeh's ransom was paid, and he was permitted to return home with the proviso that those guilty of clashing with the Po River people be bound over to Yancy.[18] Jeh's return coincided with a new demand for two hundred workers. The Wedabo leader demurred, and Yancy dispatched a force to take the men and discipline the chief. The Liberian Frontier Force attacked the town of Julucan, where they seized twelve old men, flogged and tied them, slaughtered animals, and demanded a payment of £10. The elders were marched to a neighboring town and then delivered to Yancy in Harper, where they were held pending the delivery of two hundred laborers. Later, they were taken to the superintendent's farm, where he set them to work cleaning coffee and cassava, carrying sticks, and making lines for rubber trees. The hostages remained on Yancy's estate for approximately two months, by which time a full labor contingent had surrendered. Later, the black sociologist Charles Johnson remarked:

> When Jeh returned from Monrovia, he found great consternation and grief in his towns. His women were weeping, his elders in melancholy council,

and his strong men had been carried away. "What!" he exclaimed, "they break our country." They told him of the demand for 500 more. "They cannot go. It will destroy our country," he shouted desperately and as it turned out, fatally. The protest so vexed the superintendent that he sent his soldiers into the land of the Webbos to chastise this insolence and capture the men he needed. . . . The Frontier soldiers, who lived chiefly by plunder, being them more than nine years in arrears in pay, helped themselves to the town's cattle, fowl and rice, while the commander imposed arbitrary fines as his share of the spoils . . . leaving women and children panic-stricken and weeping in their trail. . . . To impress the old men, the soldiers flogged them and required them to carry the captured goats on the long march until their arms were paralyzed with fatigue. These old men then were held hostage and required to work on the private farms of government officials until the younger men for exportation returned from the bush and surrendered.[19]

Labor recruitment under the auspices of Yancy and his subordinates had a marked effect on the Wedabo people. Of seven hundred Wedabo men shipped in 1924–25, a League of Nations report said that many died and others returned with very little money. In 1930 in Soloken, the major Wedabo town, there were 30 percent more females than males in a population of 650.[20] Of the families remaining, ninety-one had members who either had died on the Spanish island of Fernando Po or for some reason had failed to communicate with or return to their homeland. Of the returnees, two were ill and one had gone insane. Notably, in spite of the reduced population, the hut tax assessment on the village did not decrease.[21]

Samuel Ross, who ran Sinoe County, also employed the Liberian Frontier Force and the taxation system to coerce labor, even in situations where the indigenous economy clearly could not support his demands. Because public and private interests overlapped, labor procurement often bore the stamp of semilegality. For instance, in the late summer of 1927, Edward Blackett, a quartermaster for the commissioner of Liberian District Four in the hinterland of Sinoe County, was ordered by his superior to procure and deliver to Ross a large number of workers. Each man was to carry, in addition to his own food, a hamper of rice for sale. The quartermaster arrived with three hundred laborers, who were confined in a barracoon in Greenville, awaiting shipment to Fernando Po the following day. Despite the vigilance of the shippers, ten of the "boys" escaped during the night.[22]

In September of 1927, Ross's recruitment methods created an incident which attracted national and, then, international attention. On September 21, 1927, the district commissioner ordered Blackett to take soldiers and capture up to 250 men for delivery to Greenville. In the Sinoe

Members of the Liberian Frontier Force. Photo from the Liberian Collections Project, Indiana University.

interior, Blackett, according to the testimony of a chief, flogged and bound all who refused to accompany him. On October 5, the quartermaster and his labor contingent arrived on the coast. By chance, Blackett's arrival coincided with that of Reginald Sherman, postmaster general of Liberia. Ross requested that Sherman forward a radiogram for him, asking permission to send workers by a German steamer instead of the usual Spanish vessel. The message was transmitted, but Sherman, even in the face of a proffered bribe, refused to countenance the forced shipment of men. After inspecting the compound where the workers were kept, he sent an indignant radiogram to the attorney general in Monrovia. Ross, for his part, radiogrammed the secretary of state Edwin Barclay, then acting president:

> Sorry P.M.G. [i.e., postmaster general] visited compound without even Superintendent['s] knowledge and alleges an insult was offered him by one Blackett [,] District Quartermaster, who accompanied boys down. Will have each boy over this morning before Superintendent and P.M.G. and let each boy express his willingness, or not to go to Fernandipo [*sic*]. Boys all agree to go to Fernandipo rather than return to bush. Local prejudice led by Rev. Cooper Claudius Major and few others are trying to create disturbances. All satisfaction will be given P.M.G. Revoke decision and let boys go. Ross.[23]

The central government ordered the release of all workers who did not agree to go to Fernando Po, but the Sinoe Incident betrayed the ambivalence of the Liberian ruling circle on the export of labor. The event's outcome followed an existing pattern: abuses when exposed were verbally condemned, but their perpetrators remained in government service. Sherman's denunciation of the labor shipments did result in a court action by certain residents of Greenville, and the subsequent investigation did reveal forced recruitment. Quartermaster Blackett also testified that the rice taken to the coast was sold and the proceeds given to his superior, district commissioner Watson. It was revealed that Watson had shared part of the payment for the "boys" with Ross. These disclosures, however, did not lead to Ross's indictment; indeed, a 1930 investigation surmised that Ross had powerful friends in Monrovia and that interference in his recruiting activities would have proven politically unwise.[24] An attempt was made to indict Blackett, but a grand jury refused unless the same was done to Ross. In 1928, with the case still pending, Ross was appointed postmaster general to succeed Sherman, the complainant. The county attorney who investigated the case was deprived of office, while the district commissioner involved remained at a post in the hinterland administration.[25]

The Climax of the Liberian Traffic

The traffic in "boys" from Liberia does not provide the greatest example of forced labor in Africa. It was also not the longest lasting or the example with the greatest repercussions. Because of the relative weakness of the Liberian state and the charge of black-on-black crime, the "slavery" issue did emerge as a signal challenge to Pan-Africanists and antiracists. Internal and external abuse of workers peaked in the late 1920s and then, through a confluence of forces, came to a halt. Importantly, as the Hispano-Liberian labor convention continued, so did stories of labor abuse. As early as 1920, the British consul on Fernando Po noted that "the law is carried out in a very slack way."[26] In 1921, an act of the Liberian legislature directed the Liberian president to give six months' notice that shipment of laborers from Montserrado County and the territories of Grand Cape Mount and Marshall would be prohibited.[27] Although the next year saw the full-scale labor traffic to Fernando Po renewed, the supply of labor continued to be sporadically interdicted. An upswing in the Liberian economy in the latter part of 1923 perhaps made it possible for Monrovia to adopt a more critical attitude to the labor convention. Tariff revenues were up, and the import-export balance began to shift in the republic's favor, although government customs revenues did not reach their prewar level.[28] In 1925, the Liberian legislature prohibited the shipment of laborers from the county of Grand Bassa. Early in the same year, the *Agricultural World,* commenting on the visit to Liberia of the governor-general of Spanish Guinea, said, "We would drop this hint just here . . . , that unless we see more of our boys returning home when the time for which they [were] shipped is out . . . certain steps will be taken to put an end to the labor shipping contract, if this part of the Agreement is not satisfied."[29]

On Fernando Po, the Spanish colonial authorities frustrated efforts to monitor the treatment of labor. Early in 1925, in an incident tinged with racial overtones, Liberia and Spain fell into a diplomatic wrangle. In February, the Liberian consul went to the western side of Fernando Po, where a large number of Liberian farmers and workers lived. After visiting the regional subgovernor, he asked for permission to inspect the jail and the hospital. During the evening, the consul also visited J. Sharpe, sometime Liberian secretary of state, and more of his countrymen. While this meeting was taking place, African policemen, who declared the gathering illegal and against colonial law, interrupted it. In spite of the Liberian official and his friend's protests, the two black men were confined in a small hut attached to the jail. In the morning, consul Coleman was brought to Santa Isabel and questioned by the governor-general.[30] In response to the detention of its consul, Liberia demanded £500 sterling, one half of which was to be paid by July 18, 1925. The island's planters themselves collected the indemnity and gave it to their government for transmission to Liberia. The affair played havoc with the island's precarious economy; no laborers were sent to Fernando Po in 1925, and only forty came in the first six months of 1926.[31] In 1926, the *Liberian News* both assured and threatened the planters of Fernando Po that the labor demands of the American Firestone Company would have no effect on the shipment of workers as long as "our boys are treated more humanly [*sic*] than heretofore by the authorities at Fernando Po."[32] In March of 1926, C. D. B. King visited the island and explained to its planters' association that Liberia was about to embark on a vast program of internal development, a message amplified in an address to the Liberian legislature the following October. The president's statements implied a future termination of the labor traffic; again the island faced the prospect of uncollected cocoa harvests and financial ruin. This bleak future seemed real when in late 1927 the Liberian secretary of state terminated the labor agreement of 1914 without six months' notice.[33]

This rupture, like its predecessors, caused consternation in Spanish

Guinea. Liberia apparently had Fernando Po at its mercy, and before agreeing to a new convention, it sought a preferential tariff for its coffee and other produce. The Spanish colonial regime, for its part, attempted to escape from its predicament by attracting permanent Liberian settlement. Liberian secretary of state Edwin Barclay heard of this maneuver and commented to the Liberian consul on Fernando Po, "It would seem to me to argue a very low estimate of the Liberian Government's intelligence if the Spanish Government have the slightest idea that they could put such a [worker settlement] scheme over."[34] In defense of their interests, the planters of Fernando Po hung on tenaciously. Two representatives, one black and one white, were sent to Monrovia to arrange for the continuance of some sort of labor flow.[35] At first the prospects for a private agreement did not appear bright. The Liberian secretary of state took the position that he "could not negotiate with a private organization on a question of this nature unless there existed a general treaty of amity between the two States which would guarantee the rights of our citizens laboring in the Spanish possession."[36] But the Fernando Po interests were desperate for labor and willing to pay well, a fact appreciated by senator Ross. A private agreement was soon entered into between a group calling itself the Sindicato Agrícola de Guinea and a group of Liberian citizens headed by Ross.[37] The Liberian group included the brother of president C. D. B. King (E. G. W. King), as well as two of Ross's sons-in-law.[38] The sindicato promised to pay the Liberian recruiting agents for 3,000 laborers at £9 each. It also promised to provide transportation and a bonus of £1,000 for each 1,500 laborers shipped. A Spanish ship would call at Greenville and Harper to pick up laborers. Ross and his associates were to use the £9 to pay various imposts (head monies, taxes, etc.).[39] The agreement went into effect April 12, 1928, and it emerged as fraught with difficulties as the previous 1914 accord.[40] The Spanish consul complained that Ross demanded the payment of £900 for the transportation of certain workers from Monrovia to Greenville, since such transport was prohibited from Montserrado County. Ross, for his part, maintained that he previously had paid out of his own pocket for the transshipment of workers and threatened that no more workers would be forthcoming unless the Spaniards made payment.[41]

Ross paid $2.50 per head into the Liberian treasury, which gave the national government an interest in the Greenville labor operation at a time when it was experiencing great difficulty in controlling and profiting from the migration of laborers.[42] In March of 1928, the secretary of the interior had attempted to regulate recruitment in Monrovia, an effort that had backfired. By then, almost all headmen for ships and most Kru ship laborers were recruited in Monrovia or Freetown. In an effort to ward off a threatened strike over wages, working conditions, and dishonest headmen, the secretary told the agents of steamship lines that they must supply lists of headmen they were willing to employ. From this list the Liberian government would solicit those allowed to work. The government also offered to blacklist any headman who might foment a strike. But the proposal met with opposition from the shippers, who jealously guarded their right to choose headmen who would not question company policies and rates of pay. The Holland Line, the American West African Line, and the Elder Dempster Line all agreed to recruit their headmen in Freetown. The German Woermann Line, the largest employer of Liberian ship labor, joined the boycott in May.[43] The shippers' boycott encouraged the national government to look to Ross's activities as a source of compensatory revenue, a step that was soon to have severe international repercussions.

Samuel Ross was not alone in the 1928 labor shipments; Allen Yancy became a subcontractor. The two men, their associates, and their subordinates had reached their heyday in the years immediately preceding investigation in 1930. The lucrative nature of the labor export created some jostling between them. In 1929, the American chargé in Liberia reported, "I have to admit that Ross and Yancy don't get on well together . . . Ross has tried to corner the market. The Spanish consul has told me he does not like Ross, but thinks Yancy a gentleman."[44] Yancy widened his labor-exporting activities by sending laborers to French Gabon. Charles Johnson later reported, "It is understood that a group of French men offered more than Fernando Po to Yancy and many of the men who, on the Ross agreement should have gone to Fernando Po, were sent to Libreville [Gabon]."[45] Evidently, shipments from Harper were very much in progress in 1929. In June, Washington was informed that according to the Monrovia representative of the Barber Line, that company's agent at Harper was booking one hundred Liberians as deck passengers for Libreville. The American minister told the Liberian government of this proposed shipment and threatened criminal proceedings against the steamship company.[46] On October 24, 1929, some twenty-four laborers found themselves placed in a surfboat at Monrovia to be carried first to Harper and then to Fernando Po. Secretary of state Edwin Barclay intervened and asked the laborers whether or not they wanted to go. Some did, while some did not. Nonetheless, a few days later, a full contingent of laborers was shipped.[47]

Between them, Ross and Yancy, along with associates and subordinates, managed to ship over 2,000 workers to Fernando Po.[48] Between the autumn of 1928 and December 31, 1929, 2,431 workers were sent to the island, 1,005 from Harper and 1,426 from Greenville.[49] In 1930, with the practice under international attack in the League of Nations, shipments from Maryland County remained in progress.[50] The labor traffic benefited not only Yancy, Ross, and their colleagues; some Frontier Force officers, district commissioners, chiefs, and headmen also profited. In addition, itinerant labor canvassers and subagents got their share of business. Lawyers gained from the preparation of legal documents for each worker; some did a booming business in connection with European shippers and consulates. Women in Monrovia were paid to operate hostels for the accommodation of workers before their departure; they received five shillings per head.

Later investigation paid scant attention to the issue of labor abuse on Fernando Po even though testimony before a 1930 commission of inquiry indicated that labor conditions in the European colony left much to be desired. Chief Hoto of Manohlu testified:

Now after I got too close to Cape Palmas, Mr. Yancy called me and said why did my boys object to go to Fernando Po, and that Fernando Po was an altogether good place, they were not fighting war down there. To satisfy myself, he suggested that he pay my passage and I go down and see what the work the boys were doing was like. It was not my will and pleasure to do this. I went down there through the same process of forcing. I went down there, and was not at all satisfied with the conditions of the boys at Fernando Po. The Spanish people would not allow us to see the boys. On that occasion we were two chiefs sent down by Mr. Yancy to see our boys. Only Doblah happened to see two of his accidentally one day, and when they were asked about the treatment, his tale was that of woe. He stopped with a Liberian down there. The name of the Liberian Consul at this time was one Mr. Johns. He did not give us any help.

On my return I told Mr. Yancy that I did not like the idea of my boys going to Fernando Po because they were not being treated at all good down there, but he would not listen to me. When I came back, he gave me £12. But I was not satisfied and still I am not satisfied with the whole Fernando Po business.[51]

The wage paid on Fernando Po amounted to £1.10 per month and a food ration. One half of the worker's salary was paid to him on the island in Spanish currency, while he supposedly received the other half on his return to Liberia. Many returned workers complained of insufficient payment or none at all.[52] The workers were usually illiterate and rarely retained payment slips; only in one case was the commission able to see such a slip. The laborer had been on Fernando Po for fourteen months, and the slip called for the paltry sum of £12.13. The commission also noted that when workers changed employers on the island, only the last employer paid them, and only for the time they worked for him. Later investigation reported the testimony of Samuel Togba, appearing as a representative of the Sasstown chief, who "complained that of the 500 or more boys who had been sent away through the agency of one Robert Bro, a Recruiting Agent for the Maryland County Recruiting Company [Yancy's group], those who returned had little to show for their two years of service and to demonstrate gave the particular case of his brother, who spent his entire amount received on his return in the purchase of 20 heads of tobacco and one cloth."[53]

The government of Liberia formally prohibited labor export in October 1930, but it itself inadvertently mentioned a case of robbery perpetrated on a worker returned from Fernando Po in 1931.[54] Visiting Liberia in that year, George Schuyler, an African American journalist, reported, "The Spanish steamships do not call at Liberian ports with the frequency that they did before the slave scandal broke, but I note that they do call at Monrovia once a month. Whether they call at other Liberian ports I cannot say. Certainly, it is no more difficult now to crowd a score of 'boys' into a Kru surf boat and carry them out to a waiting steamer than it was before the traffic was outlawed."[55] The journalist interviewed Liberian laborers and found evidence of abuse at the Fernando Po terminus of the traffic:

> In addition to the weekly rice-and-fish ration, they received also a kilo of coffee and a cup of palm oil. They revealed that on Fernando Po they were put to work at 6 a.m., worked until 11 a.m., went to work again at 1 p.m. and quit at 6. . . . They lived in warehouses, fifty "boys" being packed close together on beds of cocoa staves and banana leaves. Women were difficult to get and those available were diseased. If the "boys" contracted sleeping sickness, venereal disease or any of the other numerous maladies to be caught there, the Spanish sent them to the hospital, but they received no pay during their illness, whether or not they were at fault. These conditions prevail in Fernando Po today.[56]

Abuse in Context

As we shall see, the actions of the Liberian regime eventually came under particular scrutiny and opprobrium from the international community. It is easy to see that the actions of Yancy and Ross constituted gross abuses of power and, divorced of its context, the Black Republic's labor traffic seems particularly repellent. It *was* to its victims. However, when compared with the tremendous abuses perpetuated throughout Africa by the colonial powers, the operations of Yancy and Ross appear puny. In the early 1930s, looking back at the Liberia of the previous decade, W. E. B. Du Bois noted: "There was only one thing that Liberia had left, and that was her native labor. She could not use it herself because she had no capital. She was beset by England, France and Spain to allow them to use it. . . . She was guilty but she was not nearly as guilty as Spain, Belgium, France and England."[57]

Did labor abuse in Liberia seem more egregious because it was black — and poor? The European powers that Barclay believed would look away from labor abuse in Liberia, were ideologically committed to both the eradication of slavery and to economic "development." The latter all too often involved coercion, and often it was extreme. Adam Hochschild notes:

> If you were to ask most Americans or Europeans what were the great totalitarian systems of the century just ended, almost all would be likely to say: Communism and Fascism. But the violent 20th century was home not to two great totalitarian systems, but to three: Communism, Fascism, and European colonialism — the latter imposed in its deadliest form in Africa. Each of the three systems asserted the right to control its subjects' lives; each was buttressed by an elaborate ideology; each perverted language in an Orwellian way; and each caused tens of millions of deaths. In all three cases we are still living with the consequences.[58]

The Swedish author Sven Lindqvist, in his *Exterminate All the Brutes,* sees Europe's own twentieth-century genocides as having their origins in attitudes forged during the scramble for Africa: "Auschwitz was the modern industrial application of a policy of extermination on which European world domination had long rested."[59] One does not have to see the whole of colonial Africa as a Conradian Heart of Darkness to recognize that at some time and in some places, the European powers destroyed millions in the name of progress and development, just as Stalin, Mao, and Pol Pot were later to do in their respective spheres.

Under European colonialism, traditional slavery was attacked as backward and unmodern; in its place came various types of labor procurement, ranging from corvée drafts to the imposition of hut, dog, and poll taxes as ways of forcing men into the colonial economies. Slavery came under official attack; coerced labor proved another matter. The late nineteenth and early twentieth centuries saw a number of cases of serious labor abuse: in the Congo Free State from the 1880s to 1908, on Portuguese São Tomé at the turn of the century, in Kenya in the years following World War I. In addition, there was the ongoing outflow of labor from Portuguese-ruled Mozambique to the gold fields of British

South Africa. These East Coast boys were sent to the Witwatersrand in numbers that dwarfed the miniscule traffic out of Liberia. For shear barbarity, little can equal the German attempt to "pacify" Namibia (German Southwest Africa) through a calculated policy of genocide against the Herero people in the years 1904–5.

More than a generation before the Liberian scandal, the "Congo atrocities" had broken in on the conscience of the world. Operating through a series of humanitarian front organizations, Leopold II of Belgium had gained control of the Congo Free State in 1885. Thereafter, rubber and ivory became state monopolies, and the government proclaimed all vacant lands state property. In 1896, Leopold proclaimed a huge area (more than 112,000 square miles) the *domaine de la couronne* (crown's domain); this was to serve as his private property. As the Free State continued, Africans were increasingly forced to fill ivory and rubber quotas. When indigenous people failed more and more to find these diminishing products, they were sometimes shot, sometimes mutilated. Hands, breasts, and feet were amputated. Eventually an international commission of inquiry was established to investigate. In 1908, the Congo was taken from Leopold and given to the Belgian government. By this time, the colonial administration is conservatively believed to have cost the lives of between 5 and 10 million people.[60] Even after the Belgian government stepped in, forced labor continued into the late 1920s.[61] Belgium did not ratify the Antislavery Convention itself until 1944. Looking at the carnage in the Congo Basin, Adam Hochschild reminds us, "Refugee flight, uprisings, and the conscription of most able-bodied men as forced laborers meant few Africans were able to cultivate crops and go hunting or fishing. Famine spread throughout the territory, and millions of traumatized, half-starved people died of diseases they otherwise would have survived."[62]

The Belgians were not the only offenders. At the time that Yancy, Ross, and their confederates were engaged in sending several thousand men to the Bight of Biafra, the nearby Portuguese islands of São Tomé and Príncipe had imported a far greater number of laborers at far greater human cost. The islands produced cocoa, and early in the twentieth century an average of 4,000 laborers per year were imported to keep the labor force at between 30,000 and 40,000. In 1902, the British became very concerned about reports of the continuation of the Angolan slave trade and the export of labor to the islands. Press reports denounced a "modern slavery," and health reports noted mortality rates from sleeping sickness of up to two hundred per thousand — five times the normal average.[63] For many Africans laboring on the Portuguese possessions, their "contracts" turned into a death sentence. In 1908, the Quaker chocolate manufacturer William Cadbury visited São Tomé and subsequently agreed to a boycott of the island's cocoa. The Portuguese colonial regime was embarrassed; no Angolan laborers came from Angola between 1910 and 1912. Recruitment in Mozambique and the Cape Verde Islands made up for the dearth of labor. The government continued to use penal labor throughout the period of the First World War. Only in 1921 were provisions made for the abolition recontracting laborers and for their repatriation. In 1928, on the eve of the Liberian troubles, the colonial rulers officially outlawed government involvement in recruitment for private purposes. Nevertheless, workers still faced coerced new contracts. Only the decline of cocoa production eased the demand for labor; the number of workers fell from a peak of 38,000 in 1921 to 10,000 less than nineteen years later.[64]

There were still other colonial offenders. One horrendous example comes from Central Africa. In the French Congo, the French built a rail line parallel to one in the Belgian Congo. Enormously expensive in terms of human life, the rail line served no essential economic need. It was begun in 1921 and did not see completion until 1934. By the time it was completed, 127,000 individuals had labored on it for at least a short period. Conditions were terrible. Many of the laborers came from savanna areas and were unused to the tropical areas in which they were obliged to work. The overall mortality rate reached a yearly 100 per thousand; it reached as high as 240 per thousand at the peak of mortality. There were a total of forty-five dead for each mile of track on the 317-mile run.[65]

Conditions in French West Africa did not prove much better. Brutal tax collection and forced labor went hand in hand. British anthropologist Geoffrey Gorer recorded conditions in the 1930s:

When a village fails to pay its taxes the administration steps in brutally and ruthlessly. When punitive measures are taken, as they frequently are, the administrator himself is never present, and therefore has a complete alibi; he sends his Negro soldiers—naturally always of a different race [i.e., ethnic group] to the people they are sent out against . . . with instructions to collect the money. . . . The employment of Negroes for the dirty work serves a double aim; it keeps lively the interracial [intertribal] hatred which is so essential for colonies where the subject races are more numerous than the colonizers, and it enables the administration to deny forthright the more inhuman practices in which they tacitly acquiesce, or should the facts be irrefutable, to lay the blame on the excessive zeal of their subordinates. . . . A village in the southern Sudan [Mali] was unable to pay the taxes, the native guards were sent, took all the women and children of the village, put them into a compound in the center, burned the huts, and told the men they could have their families back when the taxes were paid. In north Dahomey two men who had not paid their taxes fully . . . were flogged with the chacoute (a heavy leather whip) in front of the assembled village until they fainted, were taken to prison with medical attention where they had to work for fifty days, and were then sent back with the remainder of the tax still owing. I spoke to one of the men in question and saw his back covered with suppurating sores. In a village in the northern Ivory Coast, the chief's son had been taken as hostage until the tax was paid. The chief had not seen his son for nearly two years. Incidentally, the practice of hostage taking is very common.[66]

Among the imperial powers, the British were often in the vanguard of those denouncing traditional slavery and colonial forced labor in Africa. In 1924, they had threatened to bring Liberia before the League on the slavery question, but Secretary Barclay soundly rebuffed them. The Liberians were able to point out that slavery persisted even in areas of British control. For instance, slavery was only abolished in Sierra Leone, on the borders of Liberia, in 1928. Importantly, British denunciation of slavery did not question the raison d'être of colonialism, but aimed at rationalizing and husbanding the use of colonial manpower. As Frederick Cooper has observed in an East African case, "a crisis over forced labor erupted in 1919, provoked by the order of the Government of Kenya for official 'encouragement' of African labor for settler farms. All concerned knew quite well that 'encouragement' was a euphemism for coercion, pressure brought to bear by District Officers and African headsmen." The paradox Cooper notes is that "in labeling as slavery — and hence archaic and un-British — the policy of 'encouragement,' the Christian critics were making the underlying structure of settler economy appear all the more British and moral. The encouragement issue was easily papered over by better-phrased memoranda. As the crisis passed more and more Kenyans were going to work."[67]

By standards of the great colonial labor scandals, one could almost call the Liberian abuses jejune. Defenders of Liberia had good reason to believe that the country was under attack because it was poor and black in a world dominated by white imperialism. At the same time, even as it rallied Pan-African support, the scandal threatened to explode the long-cherished notion of a universal black folk community. Few noticed the paradox. In 1924, Gabriel Johnson sent his letter of resignation to the UNIA. In a cruel irony, Johnson wrote his letter from Fernando Po, where he had been sent as consul to oversee traffic in migrant labor. What galls is that the titular head of all the Negroes of the world left his post to become a trafficker in black "boys" to a white colony.

4 Investigation of an Investigation

> This gesture of the Yankee slave masters in the role of "champions" of
> human rights is enough to make the proverbial cat laugh.
>
> — George Padmore

> I believe that Africa is important for North American imperialism,
> especially as a reserve. . . . if Africa . . . calmly develops its system of neo-
> colonialism, with no great commotion, investments could be transferred
> there — it has already begun — as a way of ensuring survival. For that
> vast and immensely rich continent has hardly yet been tapped
> by imperialism. — Ernesto "Che" Guevara

In June of 1929, years after Elie Garcia's denunciation of Liberian labor
conditions, the U.S. State Department told the Liberian government
that there had come to its attention disturbing reports of "the so-called
'export' of labor from Liberia to Fernando Po." The reports indicated
that the labor system in question was "hardly distinguishable from [an]
organized slave trade, and that in the enforcement of this system the
services of the Liberian Frontier Force, and the services and influences
of certain high Government officials, are constantly and systematically
used."[1] One must ask: How did the United States come to involve itself
in the affairs of Samuel Ross and Allen Yancy? In 1928, observers could
say that "from the standpoint of international affairs Liberia's outlook
was never better than it is today. She has always shown a desire to meet
her responsibilities and as soon as funds became available paid up her
obligations to the United States and to other groups."[2] A year later, this
sanguine view of the Liberian scene would appear totally false. The
United States, Liberia's "best friend," was breathing heavily down the
neck of the small republic, and a British magazine felt compelled to note,
"No one who follows the question would be surprised if . . . the United
States were invited to take a more definite administrative interest in
Liberia. It is thought that America may be prepared to enter upon an

extension of a colonial policy in West Africa."[3] Indeed, with its note of protest of June 8, 1929, the United States thrust itself directly into West African politics. Many since have seen American interest as part of a series of machinations designed to promote an American protectorate. The Spanish dismissed the international outcry as an attempt to sabotage the development of Fernando Po and pointed to international silence on abuses elsewhere.

The question has never been adequately answered — why did the United States intervene diplomatically in Liberia? Those who have interpreted this intervention as economically motivated have pointed to the heavy investment of American capital by the Firestone Rubber Company. They have painted Harvey Firestone Sr. as the driving force behind the American entrance in Liberia. Born in the same year as W. E. B. Du Bois, Firestone, a self-made rubber tycoon, had followed a career path blocked to all people of color, no matter how well educated. He had started his company in the first year of the twentieth century, after spending some time in the rubber business in Chicago. He returned to his native Ohio and began marketing bicycle tires, rubber horseshoe pads, and solid rubber tires for carriages in Akron. In 1902, Firestone began to manufacture its own products, and within two years became the largest producer of tires in the world. Firestone began to manufacture pneumatic automobile tires in 1905, receiving its first contract from the Ford Motor Company. This relationship was to endure into scandals in the twenty-first century. In 1909, the rubber company started to make its own steel rims for pneumatic tires and began to expand into the production of household supplies, reclaimed rubber, and fabrics. Vis-à-vis its workers, Firestone pursued a highly paternalistic policy. It provided insurance plans and subsidized housing to its workers but would not tolerate any union activity. In 1913, the Industrial Workers of the World (IWW) led strikes in Akron's rubber industry in which 15,000 of the city's 22,500 workers walked out. The IWW eventually collapsed, and unionization failed until the late 1930s. In addition to union/management issues, racial segregation was the order of the day. In the plant "white men were still white and black men were still black, a difference often painfully evident in Akron's factories."[4] Black workers were given the worst jobs. They cleaned the spittoons, scrubbed the toilets, and swept the floors, or they worked in hot pits or the soot of the mill room.

To this day, the Firestone archives remain closed to researchers. Doubtless, they have much to tell us about the concern's business and political maneuverings. We do know that, like his compeer, Henry Ford, Harvey Firestone had imbibed a rock-ribbed Republicanism tinctured with a high degree of economic nationalism. The company's interest in West

Harvey Firestone Sr.
Photo from the Free Library
of Philadelphia.

Africa arose out of the U.S. need for some alternative to British and
Dutch control of the major sources of natural rubber. In 1922, when
Great Britain's colonies produced 75 percent of the world's rubber and
Americans used 70 percent of it, the British enacted the Stevenson Act,
restricting the production of their Asian rubber plantations. This situation created concern in the U.S. Congress, and a bill was unanimously
passed assigning $500,000 for an investigation of rubber resources. Har-
vey Firestone commenced an independent, worldwide search, and in
late 1923, he sent an expert to Liberia to explore the possibility of rubber
exploitation. The rubber company head enthusiastically advocated aggressive American economic nationalism. He opined, "We are trapped
by a maneuver for British imperial advantage, we can minimize the
immediate cost to America . . . by meeting an invading nationalism with
a defending nationalism."[5] And this could best be achieved by proving
that Americans could produce their own rubber.

After study, the company concluded that Liberia offered "the best
natural advantages." The labor supply is indigenous and practically inexhaustible.[6] On November 18, 1926, after two years negotiation, the
Liberian legislature agreed to "grant, demise, and farmlet unto the
Lessee (Firestone Plantations Company, incorporated in the state of
Delaware, U.S.A., with principal offices in Akron, Ohio) for the period
of ninety-nine years . . . land . . . suitable for the production of rubber or
other agricultural products."[7] The agreement provided for a maximum

lease of a million acres. The Firestone Company agreed to pay an annual rent of six cents an acre on land actually under development, with a proviso to pay rent on no less than 20,000 acres in five years. Plans called for an investment of 1 million dollars and the employment of 350,000 Liberians. (These grandiose expectations were not met; in 1930 only about 55,000 acres had been cleared and Firestone had not employed more than 18,000 laborers.)[8]

By the end of 1926, the Firestone Company had arranged to supplement this plantation agreement with a sizable loan to the Liberian treasury. But the relationship between the company and the Liberian government was an uneasy one. Firestone soon accused the Liberians of hindering the development of its investment, and Liberia accused Firestone of attempting to dominate a sovereign nation. By 1933, relations had become so acrimonious that W. E. B. Du Bois was prompted to ask whether the company was attempting to protect its capital by urging the United States to invade the republic. "Are we starting the United States Army towards Liberia to guarantee the Firestone Company's profits in a falling rubber market or smash another Haiti in the attempt?"[9]

But invasion never came. If the investigation of Liberia was prompted by economic imperialism, how do we explain the absence of colonial expansion? Does this rule out, as some commentators have argued, imperialistic motives in United States diplomatic intervention? Critics have charged that "well-meaning enemies of imperialism . . . tend to overlook the scandalous social conditions in Liberia, the government's toleration of an almost grotesque degree of corruption among its officials, and perhaps most important, the lack of evidence, at least in the beginning stages of the crisis, of other than humanitarian motives for America's diplomatic intervention."[10] One can maintain that the American protest represented only one manifestation of the generally stricter scrutiny of African working conditions in the 1920s. It has been said that public opinion in Europe and America in this period had turned against forced labor, and that this found ultimate expression in the International Labor Organization's Forced Labor Convention of 1930.[11] M. B. Akpan has posited that "the international crisis in which Liberia was involved in 1930 was essentially the result of a realization by the powers, particularly the United States of America, that given whatever length of time or opportunity, the oligarchy in Liberia would not of its own volition put its house in order and must be forced to do so by international pressure."[12]

Those suspicious of U.S. motives pointed out that labor abuse was rife in both colonial Africa and Dixie. Many blacks pointed to the double standard involved in the American government's denunciation of Liberia. Indeed, the 1920s had seen a resurgence of slavelike conditions within the United States itself. "The Justice Department continued to pay scant attention to peonage complaints, and federal apathy, local customs, and community acquiescence allowed peonage to exist almost as unhindered in the 1920s as it had a generation earlier." The institution "was so deeply rooted that it could not be dislodged by the efforts of either the NAACP, U.S. attorneys in the field, or the victims." In Dixie, "life ground on inexorably, filled with pain. Far removed from the excitement of Garveyism, the Harlem Renaissance and jazz, these black Southerners had their own sad theme, the weary blues."[13]

The Nigerian Benjamin Nnamdi Azikiwe wrote, "One wonders at the hypocrisy of the United States which, after failing to curb forced labor for private purposes within her territory, as was pointed out by the International Labor Conference, yet had the audacity to sign the Slavery Convention with [a] reservation on Article V, Section 2, which [imposes] sanctions [on] the very practices indulged [in] by the United States." The Nigerian pointedly noted, "If peonage is slavery and forced labor is slavery, the United States has no right to charge Liberia with slavery because the United States itself is a slave state."[14] Besides Jim Crow and the periodic outbreak of lynching, labor conditions in the Deep South often remained appalling. Tenant farmers were often intimidated into working for landowners who cheated them. In 1921, the governor of Georgia reported that one planter had killed eleven African Americans in order to stop them from revealing conditions on his plantation.[15] The same source reported that

A Negro worked for a farmer in County No. 7 for the last six or seven years. The contract called for a certain wage, but the employer would pay him what he chose. The Negro left three or four times, but was always brought back.

The year 1920, he was to receive $25 a month and board. At Christmas, the Negro asked his employer how much the employer owed him. The man told him $65, and paid him $10. The Negro left and came to Atlanta where he was arrested and carried back, January 26, 1921.

Another Negro was arrested in Atlanta and fined $25 for keeping late hours. The same white man paid the fine in April, 1920, and carried the Negro to the farm to work upon a promise of $40 per month, board and lodging. Three other Negroes were carried there at the same time. He remained for four months, when he escaped. He was caught and carried back, severely whipped and locked up.

He was whipped twice. He claims to have seen another Negro beaten and then shot by a Negro for running away, at the instance of the white.[16]

Prisoner labor was degraded and often procured on very flimsy pretexts. At the turn of the twentieth century, one investigator observed that penal servitude "had the worst aspects of slavery without any of its redeeming features." Vast numbers of human beings were caught up in the net of a skewed Southern justice. "The innocent, the guilty, and the depraved were herded together, children and adults, men and women, given into complete control of practically irresponsible men, whose sole object was to make the most money possible."[17] At the time at which the State Department denounced Liberian labor conditions, an investigator for the Russell Sage Foundation visited Mississippi's chief prison farm and concluded "that their cotton was very profitable but that profit was secured by reducing the men to a condition of abject slavery."[18] The following year, another observer remarked, "The convict's condition [following the Civil War] was much worse than slavery. The life of the slave was valuable to his master, but there was no financial loss . . . if a convict died."[19] In 1935, a Southerner noted that, "On the whole, the conditions under which prisoners live . . . their occupation and routine of living are closer by far to the methods of the large antebellum plantation worked by numbers of slaves than to those of the typical prison."[20] And the system proved profitable; at the end of the First World War, "the most profitable prison farming on record . . . [was] in the State of Mississippi . . . which received in 1918 a net revenue of $825,000. . . . Given its total of 1,200 prisoners — and subtracting invalids, cripples, or incompetents — it made a profit over $800 for each working prisoner."[21] "Free" labor was little better off. In the Mississippi Delta, labor camps "were often isolated, surrounded by jungle, where one or two white men controlled a hundred 'Of the most reckless meanest niggers in the world.' . . . On the levees mules were worth more than blacks."[22]

During the great Mississippi flood of 1927, hundreds of black men were terrorized and forced to unpaid labor in efforts to control the rising waters. A black clergyman in Greenville, Mississippi, wrote to the American president, praying for help. African American males were "being made to work under the gun, [whites] just bossing the colored men with big guns buckled to them. . . . All of this mean and brutish treatment of the colored people is nothing but downright slavery."[23] A wave of lynching followed in the wake of the flood. In one case, in Little Rock, Arkansas, a black man "was tied to an automobile and dragged

Nnamdi Azikiwe.
Photo from Prints and
Photographs Department,
Moorland-Spingarn
Research Center, Howard
University.

through downtown streets crowded at rush hour, trailed by a dozen cars blowing their horns like celebrants at a football victory." The victim was "thrown onto a pyre and incinerated; photographs showed police officers watching."[24]

The horrors attendant on Mississippi flood control did not end with the 1920s. In 1932, senator Robert Wagner of New York introduced a bill to investigate continuing reports of forced labor in the construction of levees. In the fall of that year, the NAACP launched an undercover investigation by assistant secretary Roy Wilkins and the muckraking journalist George Schuyler, which showed that workers were beaten, underpaid, and overcharged. In addition, they suffered atrocious living conditions — workers often had no proper facilities for sewage disposal, and some areas were rife with malaria. Early in 1933, the NAACP published a pamphlet entitled "Mississippi River Slavery — 1932." George Schuyler reported, "The whole matter of the treatment of Negroes on the plantation, and public works, including government projects . . . borders on peonage and there should be a congressional investigation so as to bring out the truth in such a manner that the public can understand."[25] The black journalist, also one of the most vociferous critics of the True Whig regime, declared, "From what I have seen in the last three weeks, I have no hesitancy in declaring that the Mississippi Negro laborers are worse off in many respects than the natives in the hinterland of Liberia."[26]

Such outrages made the Pan-Africanist George Padmore marvel at the insolent hypocrisy involved in the State Department's note to Liberia. The Trinidadian noted that "within the very borders of the United States — 'the land of the free and the home of the brave' — twelve million Negroes are held enslaved under the most vicious and brutal system of peonage and Jim Crowism, segregation and Mob [Rule]." Furthermore, "hundreds of thousands of Negro workers are [reduced] to virtual slavery on the cotton and tobacco plantations and Turpentine Camps in the Southern states." Specifically, "on the very day that [Secretary of State] Stimson [handed] his note to the Liberian Minister in Washington one of the most bestial lynchings occurred."[27]

The Haitian Precedent

When the Liberian scandal broke in 1929, Dantes Bellegarde, Haitian delegate to the League of Nations, emerged as one of its chief defenders. From Geneva he thundered against the usurping of the rights of small and poverty-stricken nations. Many African Americans were struck by the similarities between the position of Liberia in the early 1930s and that of Haiti fifteen years before. African American observers were keenly aware of the racist attitudes occupiers had carried to Haiti. Even before the occupation, one white traveler had opined, "The term 'Black Republic,' by which it is commonly known, is far from apropos, for while it certainly is black in morals, instincts, conditions, and the colour of its people, yet it cannot with truth be considered a 'republic,' save in theory."[28] Official circles were not immune to such animadversions. One high commissioner, General John B. Russell, the de facto head of the occupation government, believed that the average Haitian had a mental age of seven.[29] Secretary of state Robert Lansing believed that both Haitians and Liberians shared an "inherent tendency to revert to savagery."[30] One member of the State Department was not even sure that Haitians should be compared with children, "since they have had no ancestry of intelligence as a foundation."[31] In the early 1930s, a marine published an account in which he stated his aversion to the people he had promised to "protect" in the strongest racist terms possible. "The Cuban calls the Haitian, 'the animal nearest resembling man.'" It was the American's "personal opinion that the Cuban pays the Haitian a high compliment. Dumb! . . . There's no answer, because there isn't anything that dumb."[32] Some officers of the occupying force referred to Haitians as "wretched people," "damned liars," "miserable cockroaches," and "grasping niggers."[33]

In 1915, the first step after the restoration of order in the Haitian capital had been to legitimize the American presence. A defiant legislature was cajoled into acceptance of intervention, and a new president was put into office. A convention was approved which made Haiti an American protectorate for ten years, a status later extended to 1936. A new constitution, which increased the power of the president over the legislature, was approved in 1918. Importantly, it left out the requirement that land ownership be restricted to citizens. As might be expected, the Haitian economy was so ordered as to benefit American capital. Especially after 1922, the most important expenditure went toward servicing the external debt owed to the United States.[34] Five years later, the Haitian government spent 40 percent of its budget on debt repayment.

Revolt among the rural peasantry flared as the United States extended its authority. By the time the campaign of pacification had ended, 3,000 Haitians were dead. The American military also enforced corvée labor. James Weldon Johnson of the NAACP wrote, "no able-bodied Haitian was safe . . . slavery it was—though temporary."[35] Weldon Johnson noted that American racism was no respecter of class:

> Brutalities and atrocities on the part of American marines have occurred with sufficient frequency to be the cause of deep resentment and terror. Marines talk freely of what they "did" to some Haitians in the outlying districts. Familiar methods of torture to make captives reveal what they often do not know are nonchalantly discussed. Just before I left Port-au-Prince, an American Marine had caught a Haitian boy stealing sugar off the wharf and, instead of arresting him, battered his brains out with the butt of his rifle. I learned from the lips of American Marines themselves of rape of Haitian women by marines. . . . I heard another, a captain of marines, relate how he, at a fire in Port-au-Prince ordered a "rather dressed up Haitian," standing on the sidewalk, to "get in there" and take a hand at the pumps. It appears that the Haitian merely shrugged his shoulders. The captain of marines then laughingly said, "I had on a pretty heavy pair of boots and I let him have a kick that landed him in the middle of the street. Someone ran up and told me that the man was an ex-member of the Haitian Assembly." The fact that the man had been a member of the Haitian Assembly made the whole incident more laughable to the captain of marines.[36]

Weldon Johnson, an indefatigable worker on behalf of Haitian independence, observed these abuses in 1920 while investigating for the NAACP. On the island, he helped to found the Patriotic Union, an organization based on the NAACP's civil rights strategy. In the United States, he sought to build up anti-imperialist sentiment among a diverse group of white and black groups. One expression of such sentiment resulted in the Haiti–Santo Domingo Independence Society, which functioned until American troops withdrew from the Dominican Republic in 1924.

In 1920, Weldon Johnson wrote Garvey, telling him, "it was exceedingly necessary that the colored people of America unite with their brothers in Haiti."[37] The UNIA, with its large Caribbean constituency, needed little prodding. A year before Weldon Johnson's appeal, the UNIA delegate to the Paris Peace Conference had been the Haitian, Eliezer Cadet. Cadet attacked "the infamous persons slandering the Haitian people and their best statesmen in order to attract the good will of the implacable enemies of our color."[38] Thomas Fortune, editorial writer for the *Negro World,* came out strongly in support of the little republic, charging that the occupation was a "farce and a lie."[39] Other Garveyites also championed the small state. Among them were a prominent émigré, Jean-Joseph Adam, and Theodora Holly, daughter of a famous nineteenth-century emigrationist. Garvey himself was not loath to condemn the collaboration of military might and capital, which held Haiti in thrall. To Garvey, "Wall Street has gone down to Haiti and has taken control of the government of Haiti." With which result? "The National City Bank of New York controls Haiti." And why? "The directors of the National City Bank never had a nickel for themselves. You went to work and saved your money and cast it into the repository of the National City Bank, and they took that money and bought concessions in Haiti and placed your own race in slavery in Haiti."[40] In his 1928 petition to the League of Nations, Garvey stressed the importance of maintaining the independence of both Haiti and Liberia.

The black right and left sometimes agreed on the Haitian question, even if they could agree on nothing else. In 1921, socialist union organizer A. Philip Randolph's *Messenger* announced that "Santo Domingo and Haiti are the Ireland of America."[41] Three years later, the National Colored Republican Conference voted strongly against the occupation, a sentiment echoed by the communist-inspired American Negro Labor Conference a year later. In 1929, Captain Napoleon B. Marshall of Harlem organized the Save Haiti League to urge the restoration of the republic's independence. Marshall was a Harvard-educated lawyer and a World War I veteran who had spent several years in Haiti as an American legation employee. The New York–based league worked closely with the Union Patriotique d'Haiti. In 1930, the same year as the League of Nations Liberian investigation, the American government, in an effort to calm critics of the "dollar diplomacy," sent two commissions to Haiti, one white and one black. The former was charged with reviewing general policy options. The latter, headed by Robert Moton of Tuskegee, was charged with looking into "negro education."

To Pan-Africanists the defense of the two black republics were linked. In October of 1934, the NAACP's Walter White wrote to the Haitian president:

> We are strongly of the opinion that Haiti should stand firm and refuse to accept half-way measures which in the long run can result only in further throttling of Haitian liberty. The Republic of Liberia has refused to submit to an ultimatum from the League of Nations and the United States and British Government. Friends of Liberia, who are also friends of Haiti, have vigorously supported Liberia's position and we learn that protest has already resulted in a marked change in the attitude of the American State Department. Courage and refusal to compromise by Haiti can and will bring about similar results.[42]

In the same year, for a complex series of reasons, the United States withdrew from Haiti.

The Role of Firestone

While concern with human rights abroad can no doubt make for a potent force in mobilizing public sentiment, it is nowhere more obvious than in the Liberian crisis that disinterested concern with black lives did not motivate intervention. Within the United States, the American-based International Missionary Association did successfully lobby for Senate ratification of the League of Nation's 1926 Anti-Slavery Convention. Success in this case may have resulted from more than just goodwill. According to one analyst, "State Department officials decided to push for ratification of the antislavery convention on their own terms in collaboration with an elite segment of the American religious establishment."[43] Ratification diffused the issue raised by labor unions "of the relationship between imported cheap goods and the forced labor system which produced the goods."[44]

The U.S. State Department had long received reports of labor abuse in Liberia and paid them little attention; only when labor abuse threatened to taint American investment did the department choose to act. Nine years before the scandal broke, for example, the American minister in Monrovia had sent the State Department reports of the involvement of government officials in the purchase of human beings.[45] In February of 1928, sixteen months before the United States issued its note to Liberia, the leader of the Harvard African Expedition to Liberia complained to the American president that Liberian Frontier Force troops committed atrocities. Also in 1928, William T. Francis, American minister to Liberia, informed the State Department of conditions surrounding the shipment of labor to Fernando Po and voiced his fear that conditions might "cause considerable trouble for Liberia and incidentally embarrass Firestone interests."[46] Response to Francis's intelligence was slow. A State Department official recoded in his minutes that "Francis' letter seems rather vague, and I cannot see that the 'slavery' business concerns either us or Firestone."[47]

American diplomatic intervention did not target labor abuse per se. Some critics have charged that those "who have dealt with the subject . . . have yielded to the temptation of seeing this episode as nothing more than a last flagrant manifestation of Dollar Diplomacy, and have painted a simplified moralistic picture of an innocent small country under attack by greedy imperialists."[48] Much Pan-Africanist and leftist writing did indeed adopt this position. To the UNIA, the entrance of Firestone in Liberia constituted one of the greatest betrayals of all time. Garvey lamented:

> All well informed and keen business men and statesmen knew years ago, that the re-action in the immediate rubber industry would come, bringing a sudden change in the supply and markets, affecting the whole world, and especially America, with its limited and circumscribed field of supply. This afforded Liberia a wonderful chance to have pushed herself forward, and by proper co-operation and management among Negroes, force an entry into the rubber market and practically corner the trade, the revenue from which could have been used for national development and for placing the Country in an enviable position among the progressive nations of the world. . . . After entering into agreements and understandings . . . the dishonorable, racially unpatriotic officials of the country, were, no doubt, influenced to double-cross us, as they did, and give away the concessions and country to white exploiting capitalists and thus deprive the race of the opportunity and glorious chance to make good under its own direction. . . . This treachery to the race out-does that of Benedict Arnold . . . the King and Barclay group in Liberia had no confidence in their race and had no patience in our "getting there." They were, no doubt, dazzled by the glittering and attractive Gold Dollars of the Firestone Rubber Company, and as Lucifer — they fell.[49]

Garveyites followed the 1924 negotiations between Firestone and the King regime with trepidation. They viewed a visit by Edwin Barclay to the United States as a journey to collect the proverbial thirty pieces of silver. The *Pittsburgh American* reported that the Liberian secretary of state did not oppose black emigration, but "said that neither Garvey nor any one identified with him would be welcome to Liberia."[50] The UNIA saw Du Bois as part of the pro-white capitalist cabal fighting against the organization. At the time of Du Bois's sojourn in Liberia, John E. Bruce of the UNIA cabled J. E. Casely Hayford and warned, "Du Bois — Crisis — on trip to Africa, bent on mischief due to failure of his Pan-African congress scheme." The Garveyite noted that the professor was backed "by Joel Spingarn, a Jew, and other interests (white) inimical to African independence. Watch him."[51] Du Bois was later to deny any role in the abortion of the UNIA's plans. Indeed, we have Du Bois's categorical denial of any pro-white capitalist and anti-Garveyite machinations in Monrovia. When the communist *Daily Worker* attacked him, he reacted with righteous indignation. He informed the paper that "I was not sent to Liberia. I was attending the third Pan-African Congress in Lisbon and visited West Africa on my own initiative. I had had no consultation with the President or any official before I went on Garvey or any other matter. While there I was appointed by cable to represent President Coolidge at the inauguration of President King." Furthermore, Du Bois said that he "did not mention Garvey or his movement to President King of Liberia or any of his officials." The professor stoutly maintained that he did not "represent capitalists, imperialists or anyone else but my own fairly well-know views on race matters."[52] In 1932, Du Bois repeated his denial in a letter to Azikiwe. He maintained that he "had nothing to do at all with the relations of Garvey and the Republic of Liberia. Garvey's colonization scheme had already been rejected by Liberia before I went there and before there was the slightest intimation of my appointment."[53] Judith Stein sees the affair as a nonissue:

> There is no evidence to support the view that Du Bois convinced a friendly Liberia to expel the UNIA. . . . His position on Garvey was clear and publicly recorded in his *Crisis* editorials before his trip. . . . King's judgement of Garvey was more negative than that of Du Bois. To attribute the exclusion to Du Bois ignores the history of the Liberians' relations with Garvey and makes the shrewd Liberians pliant puppets of Afro-American publicists, roles they never played.[54]

Levering Lewis holds another view: "If his Liberian stay had actually overlapped the arrival of the UNIA mission in the first week of February 1924 (as might be mistakenly assumed due to Du Bois's own inaccuracy), it would demand the faith of the gullible to credit Du Bois's repeated denials that he never even discussed Garvey with his host." Furthermore, even if "his denials benefit from the fact of his absence from Monrovia, there is an overwhelming probability, nevertheless, that understandings about preventing a UNIA beachhead in the republic would already have been reached between Du Bois and the Liberians."[55] Levering Lewis is doubtlessly correct. King was, as we have seen, suspicious of Garveyism well before Du Bois made his appearance in Monrovia; the intellectual was not the motive force behind the abortion of the UNIA's plans. Importantly, that is not to say that Du Bois remained neutral or uninvolved. Almost all evidence strongly points to his involvement.[56] Indeed, the doctor was, despite his protestations, an eloquent booster of white American capital, the obvious counterweight to Garveyism and its threat of subversion. In January of 1924, Du Bois, along with the United States minister and a white Firestone rubber expert, D. A. Ross, traveled to inspect potential rubber lands for the company. On his return, the editor of the *Crisis* sought to reconcile profit with enlightened philanthropy when he wrote the U.S. secretary of state suggesting that "the United States should send a small commission of experts to Liberia to examine and report on her agricultural and industrial possibilities and the best methods of realizing them." The commission "should include not simply business men, but men also trained in anthropology and economics, who have in mind not simply the possible profits to exploiters of the country, but the ultimate welfare of the Liberian State, its people and its native races." The men sent out should "be colored American citizens."[57] In 1933, Du Bois remembered:

> On my return to the United States I wrote to him [Firestone]. I know what modern capital does to poor and colored peoples. I know what European imperialism has done to Asia and Africa; but, nevertheless, I had not then lost faith in the capitalistic system, and I believed that it was possible for a great corporation, headed by a man of vision, to go into a country with something more than the mere ideal of profit. . . . I tried to point out that by using trained American Negroes he might avoid this situation [i.e., exploitation] in Liberia and have a more normal development by putting in the hands of people of the same race, local and immigrant, such power over the invested capital as would divert it, at least to some extent, towards ends of social welfare as well as towards profit.[58]

Du Bois appears to have been dimly aware at this time of the danger of black-on-black exploitation; in 1921, he had already pointed out the "danger to black France . . . that its educated and voting leaders will join in the industrial robbery of Africa rather than lead its masses to education and culture."[59] But not even Du Bois remained immune to the tendency of seeing Africa as a zone for economic penetration by black Americans, a tendency that could, as in the Firestone case, be manipulated by white America. For example, during his visit to Monrovia, Du Bois met the American receiver of customs, Sidney De La Rue, a man who soon felt that it would prove most useful to rally "the negro element" in support of the Firestone concession. He advised the State Department that such support would be increased if the American company would grant posts to black graduates of technical schools. If this were done, he asserted, "we should have all the radical press controlled by Du Bois also on our side."[60] Du Bois's proposal for the entrance of "integrated" capital met with little or no real response. However, it came at a stage when it proved a useful counterweight to the appeal of Garvey and his followers.

United States attitudes and actions toward Liberia were demonstrably molded by the presence of American capital. It does not follow that the American aim was to incorporate Liberia formally into its colonial empire. In fact, the United States assiduously avoided open absorption of the West African republic, not wishing to create another Haitian situation. Rather, American policy wanted to promote the dominance of its capital behind the facade of an independent state managed by the national elite. On occasion, the United States specifically backed away from direct control of Liberian affairs. At the same time, it did take actions short of military intervention to foster the interests of the major American investor. Thus the United States encouraged investment in West Africa, but it did not want to assume the burden of policing that investment. It was quite willing to see the Firestone Company circumscribe the independence of the Black Republic, but it was unwilling to administer the coup de grâce. Certain members of the Foreign Service bureaucracy urged a forward policy of imperialism and the diminution or termination of Liberian independence, but the State Department was reluctant to make such a commitment; instead it hoped that private enterprise would be able to construct its own imperium.

Initially, the Firestone Company agreements had contained no mention of a loan; when a company representative visited Monrovia and negotiated three draft accords in June of 1924, none mentioned lending.[61] The idea seems to have germinated among the American officials of the existing customs receivership. The general receiver, Sidney De La Rue, saw a new loan as a means of tightening U.S. control and increasing the amount of revenue he handled.[62] For the American official and his assistant, C. R. Bussell, the loan concept became an idée fixe. The latter advised Washington that the success of Firestone's venture would "ultimately necessitate either his [Firestone] obtaining a very strong voice in the Government by means of a private loan or otherwise, or the supervision of a more advanced Government over the Liberian Government until such time as the latter has become more highly developed."[63] In July of 1924, the receiver himself traveled to the United States and visited Firestone, on whom he strongly urged the desirability of a loan—one coming under the purview of the receivership rather than that of the company.[64] Firestone did not accept the receiver's position in toto; indeed, Firestone's actions were largely aimed at supplanting the financial apparatus bequeathed by the loan of 1912. However, the rubber company did take up with alacrity the idea that a loan, guaranteed by governmental revenues and administered by foreigners, was necessary in light of Liberian "instability." The firm insisted that Liberia accept a loan, especially as the United States refused to revive any proposal for intergovernmental lending.[65] The company felt that liens on Liberian revenue, overseen by white officials, provided security for the Firestone investment.[66]

Initially the Liberian government, through the secretary of state, expressed disapproval of any such arrangement. The Firestone Company then sought to circumvent Liberian scruples by establishing a subsidiary, the Finance Corporation of America, to handle the loan agreement. The corporation agreed to make a forty-year maximum loan of five million dollars to refund the 1912 loan held by European and American bankers and to promote internal development.[67] The basic loan agreement, as finally negotiated, dispensed with the already nominal provisions for three European receivers contained in the 1912 agreement; instead Liberia was given eight new officials, led by a financial adviser designated by the American president. Five were to manage fiscal matters, and two, U.S. army officers, were to administer the Liberian Frontier Force.[68]

The U.S. State Department adopted an attitude of interested but less than aggressive solicitude toward the Firestone Company's proposals. After some procedural reservations, the assistant secretary of state advised that the department "lend appropriate support to the Company in order that it might have a fair and equal opportunity to carry out its project in Liberia."[69] Washington wanted American investment in Liberia, but remained timorous about future political involvement. In December of 1924, therefore, when the rubber company allowed the State Department to examine drafts of its agreements, the department noted divergences from the tentative accords of June 1924; the insertion of "certain allusions to protection and support in the future" caused concern that the rubber interest was attempting to gain military guarantees for its capital. The State Department, having smiled favorably on the concession, now made efforts to insure that it had issued no carte blanche, warning that it could offer "no different assurance in the case of Liberia than . . . in a similar case with respect to any other country." However, after some minor emendations, the department gave the "appropriate moral support" to the venture.[70] In practice, this meant that considerable pressure was to be used against the African state.

Although some American officials actively encouraged the diminution of Liberian sovereignty, others cautioned restraint. In early 1925, a U.S. Foreign Service inspector visited Liberia and reported that one of the Firestone Company's own experts did not see the necessity of a loan. The latter reportedly believed that Liberia's independence "should not now be taken away from it by a loan. It would be wrongful to place [the Liberians] in such bondage as would be brought about by a loan."[71] The inspector later reported that the American receiver viewed a loan as "only necessary to give [the receivership] control of the country" and that the receiver's assistant admitted working "with the idea of making this country an American colony." The inspector was "most reluctantly compelled to conclude that [the] question of a loan has been allowed to jeopardize the [rubber] concession scheme [and that] Mr. De La Rue has made [the loan] the prime and sole consideration of his activities."[72] The official attitude toward the machinations of the general receivership and the Firestone Company proved contradictory. The State Department discouraged schemes to broaden the scope of the existing receivership while at the same time consenting to a Firestone loan which would financially hobble the Black Republic. Early in 1925, the department warned the receiver that the United States had "never taken the stand that a loan was an essential part of [the Firestone] agreement." It added that if "Liberia does not actually need a loan and if Mr. Firestone does not want to make a loan of any size, the Department could hardly urge him to do so."[73]

But Mr. Firestone did want to make a loan. The United States government thus made itself the agent of a company decision, using its influence to fasten new financial arrangements on Liberia. In May of 1925, the U.S. secretary of state wrote the Liberians, saying that his government believed "that the successful establishment of the rubber industry in Liberia will tend to promote the country's welfare. . . . Mr. Firestone has assured the Department that as soon as the contracts are in effect there will be money available for necessary public works such as roads and ports." The secretary added that it would be "most unfortunate should a disagreement as to the exact terms of a loan prevent or delay the conclusion of a contract which will in all probability be of immense advantage to Liberia."[74] The secretary repeated his advice several times, but it was not easily taken. Throughout most of 1926, the Liberian government and the Firestone Company engaged in a heated controversy on the terms of Firestone's entry into Liberia. The legislature in Monrovia, hoping to avoid another "Haiti affair," approved a loan agreement altered by some twenty-four amendments. Harvey Firestone would not accept such a solution and wired the State Department, "They must accept agreement without a single change if we go into Liberia."[75] Monrovia and Firestone also came to an impasse on the resolution of future disputes. Finally, in the fall of 1926, they achieved a compromise: routine disagreements were to be settled between two arbitrators, one from each side. In the event these two could not reach an agreement, the U.S. secretary of state would appoint a third arbiter, neither American nor Liberian, and the majority would decide on the dispute.[76]

The Liberian government eventually came around, but only after American officialdom had cajoled Liberian officials on behalf of the company. The U.S. consul general in Monrovia, for example, informed the Liberians that the State Department, "having carefully gone over the Firestone contract, felt that all that had been previously contemplated in [the] loan of 1921 might be accomplished through these Firestone Agreements.[77] After much deliberation, Liberia finally ratified the loan agreement on December 7, 1926.

Firestone got both its plantations and its loan agreement. Exploiting these took years of jostling with the Monrovia government. The first rubber site was on the Du River, about forty miles east of Monrovia. It later expanded to the Farmington River. The principal location on the Du was given the name Harbel, after Harvey Firestone Sr.'s mansion in Ohio. Eventually the Harbel concession would consist of 60,000 acres of mature trees and constitute the largest rubber plantation in the world. A second site was located 240 miles south of Monrovia, on the Cavalla River near Cape Palmas. The plantations were divided into divisions of from 1,500 to 2,500 acres. Harbel consisted of forty-five divisions, Cavalla of one. Each division had a white American or European super-intendent living near a central headquarters. By law the concessionaire was limited to employing no more than 1,500 white men, plus their dependents. The majority of the "native" workers came from the Kpelle, Loma, Dan, Mano, and Bassa groups. Liberian tappers dwelt in villages with a divisional store and earned a basic wage of thirty cents per day. Although thought of as unskilled, their work demanded considerable expertise. Tappers had to be careful to make one-millimeter cuts into the outer bark of the rubber trees; if they counted too lightly, the latex would not bleed sufficiently. If the tree was cut too deeply, on the other hand, it could suffer damage. Firestone's man in the field, Donald Ross, thought that Firestone would save $300,000 in labor costs in 1927 by using an African force of 6,000 rather than having to pay a wage rate comparable to that paid in the Far East.[78] By the end of 1928, Firestone had cleared 15,000 acres on the Du and Cavalla estates. The senior Firestone estimated the cost was a hundred dollars per acre for clearing and planting. This was a bargain when compared with costs in Southeast Asia. In the four years after 1926, Firestone employed about 18,000 men. By 1928, Firestone had 23,000 acres under cultivation in Montserrado County and 12,000 acres in Maryland. Firestone used an average of 8,262 unskilled workers and 530 skilled workers at the Du estates. President King reported that Firestone paid Africans $1,024,050 in wages.[79] In February of 1928, Harvey Firestone Jr. visited and was greeted by a double line of from 8,000 to 9,000 workers gathered to meet the "Great White Chief."[80]

Firestone's beginnings showed the possibilities of labor abuse. In 1926, the government revived its Labor Bureau originally established in 1912. A British plantation manager in Firestone's employ commented:

I arrived in Monrovia in the middle of November, 1925 and early in December proceeded 30 miles up the Du River and commenced felling operations. A start was made with the few available voluntary laborers, but as recruiting by the Company's officials was not allowed, the labour force soon dwindled until work was practically at a stand still. To meet the situation a Government Labour Bureau was formed with the concurrence of Firestone and gangs of forced labour under armed guards began to arrive on the Plantations. In many cases these men had been herded from their villages hundreds of miles away and, as no food was provided on the march by the Government, many arrived in an exhausted and emaciated condition. Out of the first batch of 150 men I saw arrive twelve died within a week of arrival.[81]

As a result of the agreements of 1926, Firestone had acquired the right to enter Liberia, but it was obvious that certain government officials, who found the existing uses of labor, including its export, a far more readily tappable source of revenue than incipient rubber plantations, balked at the actual exploitation of Liberian rubber. The promise of future national revenue held little allure for them counterpoised against the opportunity for immediate personal gain. If Firestone wanted to prosper, it appeared that certain Liberians would have to be coerced into abandoning this lucrative export of labor.

At the inception of its concession, the Firestone Company had made its need for labor clear, and the Liberian government had agreed to assist in its procurement.[82] Firestone agreed not to import unskilled labor unless the local supply proved inadequate, in which case the Liberian government would have to approve the labor importation. But as Spanish and other critics of American policy later charged, the American company's demand for labor conflicted with the preexisting export of labor to Spanish Fernando Po; this then may have constituted one of the factors in American scrutiny of labor export to that island.[83] In 1926, the American receiver of customs noted that "with the increased demand for labor on Liberian [Firestone] plantations, those who have customarily sought employment at Fernando Po, Gold Coast, and other places have, to a large extent, stayed at home."[84] Soon reports of conflicting demands for labor emerged from the Liberian hinterland. "Chiefs are complaining that they have found it more difficult to find men for the roads. Likewise natives who hitherto have sought work in Fernando Po can now find employment at home [on the Firestone plantations]."[85] The vying demands of the Liberian government, the Firestone plantations, and the Fernando Po traffic became increasingly manifest. In 1927, the American legation in Monrovia reported that "Firestone is experiencing some difficulty in recruiting labor.[86] There was talk that the Liberian government, unhappy about the terms of Firestone's concession, was deliberately impeding the company's search for manpower. In October of 1928, the *Liberian Express and Agricultural World* intimated as much, only to print a retraction the following month.[87]

American interests were alive to the danger existing conditions presented to investment. A visitor noting that the Firestone holdings in the southern part of the country might be seriously threatened, wrote, "Since . . . a good proportion of the men sent into serfdom to the Fernando Po Plantations have come from Districts No. 4 and 5, the supply of labor available for the Cape Palmas Plantations will to some extent depend upon what the future policy of the Government will be towards the furnishing of workers for Fernando Po."[88] In late 1929, Donald A. Ross, the young Scottish manager of the Firestone plantations, personally complained to the Liberian secretary of state about the labor shortage in Maryland County.[89] Later in the same year, a district commissioner informed a Firestone manager that there were three hundred laborers who wanted employment with the company, but that unless he received a personal payment, he would send them to Fernando Po.[90]

The American financial adviser predicted that in the future "the rubber industry here will be in active competition with Fernando Po for a supply of labor, unless some powerful influence is brought to bear that will separate by compulsion the traffic from actual government support."[91] Commenting on a meeting of the International Labor Conference in Geneva in the spring of 1929, an American memorandum clearly touched on the dangers inherent in the Liberian situation:

The United States Government from a political point of view and American manufacturers from an economic point of view are interested in the extent to which their competitors are using forced labor. If American owners of rubber plantations and oil nut concessions in Africa, the Dutch East Indies, and other such countries are forced to compete with competitors using forced labor, the disadvantage they will suffer is obvious. An instance, however, may be cited in the case of Liberia where, according to published reports of the Firestone Company, approximately 300,000 men will be needed when the proposed rubber plantations come to fruition. The contract labor which is being shipped yearly out of the country to a Spanish concession along the coast may have serious effects upon American enterprise in limiting the available labor supply in that part of Africa unless a similar system of forced or contract labor is used by an American company.[92]

Doubtless, the U.S. State Department was aware of Firestone's labor difficulties; whether it took direct action to remove those difficulties is hard to determine. The State Department did note that the loss of labor might itself provide clear cause for complaint: "It would seem that Firestone or any other American Company doing business in Liberia and requiring considerable native labor might properly protest at the gradual reduction in the labor supply by these shipments to Fernando Po."[93] In 1930, the American chargé d'affaires blamed Liberia's parlous economic state not on the worldwide economic depression, but on the "curtailment of the Firestone operations and reduction of their expenditures due largely to the Government's labor policy and the Fernando Po traffic."[94] The interconnection between Firestone's labor needs and American action was underlined in 1931, when Harvey Firestone wrote to the secretary of state "to express my appreciation of the firm stand which our Government is taking in demanding that Liberia take effective measures to abolish enforced labor. . . . As you know [this] has seriously interfered with our obtaining free labor."[95] It is reasonable to suppose that concern for the labor supply played a substantial role in American intervention.

The Critics

The Firestone Company's problems also prompted U.S. government action in a more obvious way. Not only did the export traffic compete with Firestone for manpower, it also threatened to draw adverse criticism to American investment. Professor Raymond Leslie Buell emerged as one of the most consistent of Firestone's critics. In 1925, Harvard

University, in conjunction with the Rockefeller Foundation, selected the twenty-nine-year-old Buell of the Bureau of International Research of Harvard and Radcliffe to undertake an exhaustive research tour of working conditions in colonial Africa. The research took fifteen months in 1925 and 1926 and compiled a wealth of social and economic data. In 1927, the young academic became director of the Foreign Policy Association and a year later published *The Native Problem in Africa*. In his book, Buell maintained that Firestone had already entered into arrangements with the Liberian Labor Bureau whereby the company was paying district commissioners to procure labor through chiefs. "Thus, under this system, which is similar to that which has produced wholesale compulsory labor in other parts of Africa, the Firestone Plantations Company is making it financially worthwhile for the government and for the chiefs to keep the plantations supplied."[96] In Buell's eyes, the preexisting system of labor recruitment for Fernando Po was being used for the rubber plantations.

Buell's criticism has been discussed, but its importance has been dismissed:

> [A] weak explanation [of U.S. diplomatic intervention] . . . is that the State Department's note, which after all amounted to unusual interference in the internal affairs of a sovereign nation, reflected a sudden public interest in Liberian conditions, aroused by the publication of several books and articles. . . . Of the books usually mentioned, only Reeve's *The Black Republic* appeared before June, 1929. It is difficult to see why this work, which deals with Liberian conditions only up to 1922, should suddenly be the cause for diplomatic intervention seven years later. Raymond Buell's volume, *The Native Problem in Africa*, although published in 1928, was not designed, in view of its sympathetic attitude toward Liberia, to arouse the ire of the State Department.[97]

But such dismissal of the influence of published works on American policy proves an egregious error. Although State Department intervention arose from dissatisfaction with Liberian obstructionism, Buell's book in fact constituted its immediate catalyst. Buell, although somewhat sympathetic to Liberia, was, most importantly, highly censorious of Firestone. In 1928, in print and from the platform, Buell attacked the Firestone Company and the State Department for callous economic imperialism in Africa. In *The Native Problem in Africa*, he charged that his government had "apparently thrown its influence against the native farmer in favor of the outside capitalist."[98] Furthermore,

> the experience in other parts of Africa shows that the development of large-scale European industry inevitably outruns the local labor supply — a condi-

tion which leads employers to invoke the aid of governments in scouring the surrounding territory for men. Inevitably the system has led . . . to forms of compulsion, to the disorganization of native village life, a high death rate in labor compounds and depopulation in the villages. . . . Mr. Firestone has declared that the labor supply of Liberia is "practically inexhaustible — and that his development will require three hundred thousand or three hundred and fifty thousand men. Now the total able-bodied male population of Liberia is only between three hundred thousand and four hundred thousand and it is difficult to believe that, despite the persuasive powers of the Firestone recruiters and of the Liberian Government, Mr. Firestone will be able to place under his employ . . . the entire adult male population of the country.[99]

Buell also claimed that the United States had promised to protect Liberia from French border encroachments in return for Liberian acceptance of the Firestone agreements.[100] Liberia had thus saved itself, but at the price of sacrificing its people to exploitation by American capital. Buell maintained that American economic interest in Liberia would lead the United States to shield Liberia from outside questioning on the matter of labor abuse.

Buell's statements, which portrayed the United States as the fosterer of forced labor in Africa, received extraordinary attention in official U.S. circles. In the summer of 1927, the State Department received a portion of the soon to be published manuscript of Buell's book. A memorandum from a staff member to William Castle, undersecretary of state, succinctly stated the department's fears, warning that "the Department must be prepared to meet misstatement of facts in order that the distinction may be made clear as to how much of Mr. Buell's conclusions are based on fact and how far they are to be attributed to his personal bias."[101] The following year, Buell continued his attacks unabated. In May he wrote in the *Nation*, "As long as the Firestone Company makes it financially profitable for the chiefs to supply labor, the available men must work whether they like it or not. This is the system which prevails in regard to labor for the Spanish plantations in Fernando [Po]."[102]

It was obvious that at this point any revelation of abuse would redound to the detriment of American capital. In June of 1928, William Castle of the State Department wrote the American minister in Monrovia, after discussions with Sidney De La Rue, Harvey Firestone, and others, outlining the means by which U.S. involvement in any possible scandal could be evaded:

I agree with you thoroughly that it would be unfortunate from many points of view if the question were to be aired at this time in the League of Nations or in other quarters, particularly in view of the critical attitude taken by Professor Buell in his recent book on the Native Problem in Africa. It is far from unlikely that any attempt may be made to shoulder Firestone and even the Department with the responsibility for undesirable conditions now existing in Liberia, both with reference to commercialized slave trading of the nature reported in your letter, but more particularly in connection with the forced labor exacted from the natives by the District Commissioners and other Liberian officials and by their friends. It appears that the methods of the Liberian Labor Bureau in recruiting labor for Firestone have a tendency to result in conditions analogous to those of forced labor and are likely at some time to draw the well-merited censure of civilized opinion. When that day comes it seems highly important that the Department and the Legation may be in a position to show beyond question where the responsibility for such conditions rests and be able to show that American influence has been exerted so far as has proved possible against such conditions. As a first step it would be desirable to secure a clear and succinct statement of the present conditions and to that end I am going to ask you to prepare a strictly confidential memorandum for the use of the Department. For obvious reasons the fact that you are preparing such a memorandum must remain absolutely secret and accordingly you will have to depend almost entirely upon your general knowledge of conditions and upon such specific information as may come to your attention in the ordinary course of conversation, correspondence, et cetera. . . . For the sake of the record the Department is sending you a formal instruction asking you to report upon the attitude of the Liberian Government toward ratifying the Slavery Convention.[103]

The State Department's hypersensitivity no doubt resulted from the accuracy of Buell's indictment. He had predicted labor abuse if Harvey Firestone carried out his grandiose scheme, and even though the scheme itself did not soon come to fruition, Buell's predictions appeared correct. In the past, the Liberian government had shown itself less than scrupulous in the recruitment of labor and, in the case of Firestone, it continued to make demands for labor with little regard for the details of recruitment, including whether or not coercion was used. For example, in early 1930, an aide to president King wrote to a district commissioner, "The General Manager of the Firestone Company, having represented to me that there is a shortage in their labor employ, as it is important that the Government should render such assistance as lies in its power to promote the industry of said Company, you are authorized to use your good offices in order to facilitate the recruitment within your district [of] one thousand laborers by the Representative of the above named company."[104]

Recruitment for the Firestone plantations did not differ significantly from other types of labor procurement. Both the Liberian government and chiefs received monetary inducements to procure as much labor as possible, an arrangement which obviously lent itself to abuse. Firestone and the Liberian Labor Bureau had agreed that the company would pay one cent to the Liberian government, one half-cent to the paramount chief, and one half-cent to the chief for each day's work. The company later claimed that recruitment through the Labor Bureau lasted only about four months in 1927 and accounted for only ten percent of its labor supply. Other laborers were reportedly recruited "voluntarily or through their [Firestone's] own American staff."[105] But in any case, many workers complained that they had not received pay for company work. The company explained that it had recontracted workers to private individuals, who then had failed to pay the workers. Firestone also parried allegations of unpaid labor by asserting that this problem resulted from misunderstanding of the task system, under which failure to accomplish a set task resulted in a decrease of the daily wage.[106]

In July of 1928, the American secretary of state cabled the U.S. consul in Geneva and expressed fear that because of Buell's book, Henri de Junod of the International Society for the Protection of Natives would attack Firestone's concession and call it to the attention of the League of Nations.[107] The consul replied that American activities in Liberia did not fall within the League's purview. The State Department remained uneasy, however. In August, a department official warned the American legation in Monrovia that the "Department anticipates that Buell will shortly repeat his charges regarding the American loan and the Firestone concession in lectures which he is planning to deliver at the Williamstown [Massachusetts] Institute of Politics."[108] The department understood that W. D. Hines, representative of Harvey Firestone in Liberia, was discussing with President King a rebuttal to any statement Buell might make. Such a reply would be "along lines recently sent Firestone by Hines." American officials appear to have been quite willing to orchestrate a publicity campaign, with Liberians playing subsidiary roles. The American minister replied that King was absent from Monrovia, but "if publication imperative this week advise and I will find a way."[109] The State Department urged that a rebuttal to Buell's intended remarks be sent directly to the Associated Press before American papers had time for editorial comment.[110]

Buell's speech, when delivered, forcefully reiterated his previous points. He warned, "The State Department gladly accepted obligations which may sooner or later make Liberia into another Haiti or Nicaragua. It is difficult to find in the history of international relations a better example of secret diplomacy in the worst sense of the word."[111] President King dutifully replied to Buell's charges through the Associated Press after receiving two cables from the State Department. In the matter of labor abuse, he strenuously defended the Firestone record; the rubber company, he insisted, was the answer to the republic's unemployment problem: "The Government has had no occasion whatever to coerce labor and reports seem to indicate that far from suffering from a dearth of laborers, the Firestone plantations are suffering from an embarrassment of riches in this respect." Portentously he added, "On this point [i.e., labor abuse] the Government of Liberia would welcome an investigation on the spot by an impartial commission."[112] The State Department itself responded to Buell's speech at a press conference, claiming the lecture contained "an enormous number of inconsistencies and untruths."[113]

Despite attempts to discredit Buell, the Firestone investment continued to arouse criticism in the United States and elsewhere. The American foreign policy apparatus wished to avoid the impression of playing "Caribbean" politics in West Africa or of conniving at labor abuse. Even before the conclusion of the Firestone agreements, a State Department official had warned, "It would be nuts for the people who are always smelling out imperialistic schemes to be able to say that we forced a loan on the Republic for the purpose of getting control."[114] Indeed, Marcus Garvey was traveling in Europe and, in early September 1928, addressed a plea to Sir Eric Drummond, secretary-general of the League of Nations in Geneva. He condemned "One Harvey Firestone, a white rubber magnate" who had grabbed "one million acres of Liberian lands, for the exclusive use of the Firestone interests . . . thereby depriving the natives . . . from settling on the lands that were intended for them by the persons and governments and powers that helped create Liberia a free Negro State." The head of the UNIA continued:

> We further believe that the President of the Republic, Mr. Charles Dunbar King, profited by the agreement, and that the very act of forcing himself upon the people of Liberia for a third consecutive term as President after undertaking this affair, is indicative of questionable purpose. There is no doubt that the act of granting this concession to the Firestone interests was against the best interests of Liberia, and the natives thereof, and the Negro race at large, for whom the Republic of Liberia was intended. Since the granting of this concession to Firestone the natives of Liberia have been forced to contribute free labor to the building of roads, etc., for the convenience of the Firestone interests, and in many instances they have been treated as virtual slaves. This is respectfully brought to the attention of your Excellencies to show how wealthy white capitalists do bribe and influence[,] with the assistance of their governments, Negroes, to act against their own interests, thereby occasioning great suffering among the black people.[115]

In March of 1929, the department received a detailed review of the labor situation in Liberia in the form of an eighty-six-page confidential memorandum from the legation in Monrovia.[116] The following month, William Castle warned of the dangers of continued inaction. He suggested that the Reverend Anson Phelps-Stokes, as one connected with missionary interests in Liberia, be briefed on the State Department's concern.[117] In early May, he wrote to Dr. Robert W. Patton, bishop of the Episcopal Church, asking for a copy of a report the bishop had prepared on the Liberian situation.[118] Soon afterward, Castle told the department that if the situation in Liberia became widely known, the department might "be terribly criticized." He advised the secretary of state that the time for self-justification had arrived: "The telegram [to Liberia], if you decide to send it, would not be given out now. . . . But when and if the story gets out in this country and there is a row in the press, we should be able to say that we have acted and what we have done.[119]

The dominant motive behind the diplomatic note of June 1929, was the Department of State's burning desire to distance itself and the American investor from any revelations of labor abuse. As the department had feared, the story of Liberian conditions soon reached the press. In the same month, Thomas J. R. Faulkner, defeated candidate for the Liberian presidency, wrote the League of Nations charging rampant labor abuse in Liberia. The North Carolina–born Liberian legislator and entrepreneur raised the question and would not let it rest. In addressing the secretary-general of the League of Nations, Faulkner was quite clear in his indictment:

The natives of Liberia are forced to work on the roads under the following conditions: 1) They are forced to work nine months of the year. 2) They are compelled to furnish their own tools. 3) They receive no compensation whatever for roadwork. 4) They are compelled to furnish their own food. 5) They are compelled to furnish food, i.e. rice and palm oil, to the commissioner and to the soldiers who act as overseers. 6) Upon failure of the chief of a tribe to supply the demanded number of men, he is at once heavily fined and forced to pay cash forthwith or go to jail. Often these men are compelled to pawn their wives and children to get the money to pay these fines. 7) For the most trivial thing the laborers are fined small sums and forced to pay in cash, which is quite an impossibility. They often have to sell their food, which they have brought long distances, to get the money to meet these fines. 8) It is said that men on the roads are whipped so severely that they die.[120]

In July of 1929, Faulkner repeated his charges in the *Baltimore Afro-American*. Importantly, the businessman was sympathetic to Garveyism. In 1924, supplies sent out by Garvey had been consigned to Faulkner, and when Faulkner's wife died in 1925, the *Negro World* memorialized her. A fearless opponent of the True Whig oligarchy, Faulkner had been defeated in an outrageously fraudulent election. He continued to raise his voice against internal abuses and came to the United States to raise money for internal improvements and, more importantly, to expose the gross abuses of the ruling clique in Monrovia. The latter were well aware of the threat Faulkner represented. In August of 1929, after investigation of slavery was announced the chargé in Monrovia noted, "President [King] asks no selection of Garvey man or one in sympathy with United States Negro Improvement Association [*sic*]." He "reiterated [that the] Department had in mind [a] man [of the] type of [Emmett] Scott and I assured [King] he should have no apprehension."[121]

The American secretary of state wrote to the chargé in Monrovia that further pressure should be put on the Liberians, "for it is likely that . . . article[s] will be followed by other public discussion in this country."[122] A British paper printed an article ("Tyre Firm's Slave Trade Outrage") which caused consternation among State Department officials. The department nervously asked for reports on conditions in Liberia and was told by the chargé that the Firestone Company had contracted with certain Americo-Liberians (including Allen Yancy) to have lands cleared in Maryland County. Firestone's representative in Liberia, Walter Hines, fuzzily replied that he had no idea how the workers were procured.[123]

The close collaboration between the Firestone Company and the State Department, plus the latter's fear of the existence of actual labor abuse, made it imperative to disavow collusion in any such practices. The American-inspired investigation constituted a preemptive strike designed to ward off criticism of U.S. officialdom and American business. In the month preceding the American note, the Monrovia legation expressed its apprehension that a scandal would break before the department could hurl its accusation at the Liberians:

> It was thought by some here that the British Foreign Office would lay the matter before the League of Nations, but the Minister does not share in that belief. He thinks that the attitude of the British Government will be to keep its hands off in the hope that conditions may grow worse and thus have an adverse effect upon the Republic, interfere with the development of American Rubber Interest, and reflect on America when the stench which must sooner or later arise from this mess, reaches the nostrils of the civilized world. It is to be expected that our Government and its people[,] having fostered and nurtured the Liberian Republic in its infancy (and in many ways after its maturity) standing between it an [*sic*] absorption by the British and French Governments cannot escape severe criticism for the shortcomings of its protegé in a backward step into barbarism.[124]

Once the preemptive strike had been launched, Harvey Firestone enthusiastically supported it.[125] A State Department official, Henry Carter, noted, "Firestone is of course keenly interested in the whole situation and has asked that we keep him informed of all the developments which might affect his interests." He added, "this should be done by telephone or personal interview except in matters of routine, in order to keep the Department off the record."[126]

The generally negative attitude of both the Firestone Company and the State Department toward the Black Republic aided diplomatic intervention in Liberia. After 1926, the Liberian government had shown a marked resistance to the demands of Firestone and its patrons in Washington. The American minister reported Liberia's attempt, through casual letters, to annul part of the loan agreement. The president of Liberia failed to answer American letters on the status of foreign fiscal officers, while the American legation continued to press rights considered existing under the Firestone agreements.[127] By 1929, many of the unresolved issues between the Liberian elite and American business had come to a head. The Liberians complained of Firestone's reduction of the company's labor force and of attendant economic hardship. The American minister retorted that the reduction was in part attributable to Monrovia's obstructionism.[128] Further trouble resulted from President King's request that the receiver of customs, an American, issue permits for the shipment of eight laborers from Monrovia for overseas employment. The receiver maintained that he had no authority to do so, precipitating disagreement on the receivership's independence.[129] In September of 1929, a Liberian, Albert Porte, complained of the high-handedness of American loan officials. "We are unofficially informed that recently when a Government Official, in conversation with one of the White employees, disagreed with the views of the latter, he [the American] intimated to him that he [the Liberian] was only an employee of the Liberian Government . . . under the dictatorship of America."[130] At the end of the year, Harvey Firestone Jr., son of the rubber baron, heard "that the high executive officers of the Government of Liberia are either engaged in or acquiescing in a program for defeating full enforcement of the terms of the Loan Agreement by the Financial Advisor."[131] Firestone Jr. was advised that "the bondholders should complain to the State Department, which complaint is a proper subject for their representations to the Government of the Republic of Liberia."[132]

There was also displeasure at the conduct of a Liberian customs cashier. After being dismissed by his American supervisor, the cashier appealed to the Liberian acting secretary of the treasury, who supported his stand. The U.S. State Department accepted this as proof positive of a

Liberian desire to ignore its agreements. "Not only has the Government of Liberia no desire to cooperate with the American fiscal officers but on the other hand shows positive opposition."[133] The Liberians, for the most part, viewed the American fiscal officials as attempting to subvert both the constitution and sovereignty of the Black Republic. A Liberian secretary of the treasury later commented:

> Messrs. Loomis, McCaskey, Fitzsimmons and Homan were all reported to have been engaged at one time in the Philippines and other smaller countries where it is believed they gave the same series of trouble[s] as regards the smooth working of [the] inhabitants. It was Mr. Loomis who set forth the argument that the Fiscal Officers were not under the Treasury Department, and instilled this evil spirit into his collaborators which made them feel that they were a set of demagogues [sic], separate and distinct from the constitutionally appointed officials of the Republic.[134]

It would seem that the motives traditionally adduced for the American diplomatic intervention which prompted the Liberian inquiry do not fully fit the case. Neither positing an American scheme to yoke Liberia with formal colonial status nor asserting that the United States was moved by abstract humanitarianism, seems more to agree with the facts. As in parts of Latin America, the United States would have been quite content to exploit Liberia behind a facade of national sovereignty. In Liberia, however, the activities of American capital were balked at by an obstreperous national elite, which threatened, moreover, to attract adverse publicity at a time when American capital already saw itself under heavy attack. An inquiry into Liberian conditions not only provided the United States and its interests with an opportunity to disassociate itself from embarrassment but also promised to bludgeon the elite into a more cooperative attitude, while at the same time assuring American investment an adequate supply of labor. The Washington-inspired investigation of 1930, however, gave the United States a Pyrrhic victory. Liberia was exposed, abuses indicated, yet what should have marked the end of a period of tension between the Black Republic's national government and American investors was only the beginning of a protracted diplomatic struggle. The world asked what action would be taken in the wake of the various denunciations of Liberian conditions, and the United States found itself at a loss for an answer.

After years of rumored forced labor, little Liberia, under pressure, agreed to a League of Nations inquiry. From June to December 1929, the two governments debated its terms. By the end of the year, they had agreed that a three-man commission composed of an American, a European, and a Liberian would conduct the probe. The State Department knew what it wanted. One official wrote a memorandum urging the need for firm action and questioning the capacity of blacks to govern themselves. The nameless functionary opined, "At present, Liberia is attempting to prove that a country can be run by colored people and [they] are making a mess of it to the dissatisfaction of every man, white or colored, who has an interest in the interest of colored people." The solution to retarded development was greater investment. For instance, "encouragement might be extended to American capital for coffee cultivation." The law confining landownership to "Negroes" would have to be "so arranged that exploitation might be carried out by civilized peoples, white or colored." Another official, Henry Carter, believed that the report should damn the Liberians and lead to some kind of remedial action. Facts might be lacking because of a lack of competent witnesses and documents, but a good case could be made. What was most important was that "the commission would be able to make a series of stringent recommendations."[135] Liberia's need for American support would make it pay heed. A December 16 memorandum suggested that the commission of inquiry visit both the Liberian hinterland and the island of Fernando Po. The recruiting methods and books of the Liberian government should undergo scrutiny: "Even if such proof is not of a definite nature, it would seem that if the commission learns that by general repute, the 'graft' is divided among various officials, that fact should be mentioned in their report and given the prominence it deserves even if there is only a moral certainty."[136]

American policy on Africa seldom exists beyond the specter of race. Although the State Department sought to stress the dichotomy between national prejudice and national policy, its need for a stronger defense against the charge of racism was obvious. Early on, therefore, the department sought to involve African Americans in its indictment of the Black Republic. In 1931, the communist George Padmore warned, "It is important for every Negro worker to take note that, whenever the American or other white capitalists have some dirty task to perform in connection with Negro countries like Haiti and Liberia, they always secure the service of some black lickspittle who is supposed to be a 'big' leader of his race, pay him a few dollars or give him some petty office and thereby get him to do the job for them." Padmore added, "The usual policy in America is to have the President take his photo with the Negro in question or have a glass of tea, and the whole betrayal is settled."[137] To a certain extent, this held true. In selecting a member of the 1930 commission, such considerations played a signal part. The secretary of state himself wrote to President Hoover in the autumn of 1929, saying, "In considering the nature of the recommendation to be made to you in the premises, the Department has been inclined to believe that it would on the whole be preferable to recommend a colored man for the position, assuming that a suitably qualified colored man of sufficient standing and prominence and prominence was [sic] available."[138] Soon thereafter, undersecretary of state William Castle reiterated the advantages of a black candidate, saying the department "felt that, from many points of view, it would be better if we could get the right kind of colored man. . . . If the investigation proves that slavery, or something like it, exists with the connivance of the Government, it would make a much better impression among the Negroes of this country if the report were signed by a man of their own race."[139]

While the constitution of the commission was under discussion, the American minister in Monrovia nominated Emmett Scott, treasurer of Howard University. Scott, unlike other likely nominees, had had Liberian experience. He had been a member of the 1910 American commission to Liberia and, in addition, during the First World War, had been one of a group of African American leaders sent to France to counsel and caution black troops. During the summer and fall of 1929, State Department officials spent much effort trying to persuade the educator to take the position. The president of the United States himself intervened, but Scott avoided agreeing to the job. In October and November, when again asked, he declined, citing the burden of budgetary work at Howard. The State Department reassured Scott that he would not have to leave until after New Year's Day 1930, but the university official gave his final refusal on November 15.[140]

Scott would not take on a third mission abroad for his race and country. The refusal may have been related to his previous contact with the Liberian oligarchy. A rumor circulated in Monrovia that Scott may have been involved, along with Boston lawyer Charles Lewis, in accepting payments for lobbying the American government on behalf of the 1921 Liberian loan. On September 10, Clifton Wharton, African American chargé of the American legation in Monrovia, wrote, "Last night for the first time, President King while not raising objection to Scott, asked, in view of [the] probability [of] Scott's implication in scandal, 'what effect would this have on Scott's impartiality if he is recommended by the United States to serve on commission.'" On September 16, Wharton informed the secretary of state:

> I informed the President that I knew nothing about any scandal in connection with the 1921 loan and asked him what was the nature of the scandal. He replied that when it seemed that the 1921 loan would be granted to Liberia, certain colored American citizens attempted to obtain thousands of dollars from the Liberian government, claiming this money was due them for services rendered in getting the loan through Congress, for using their influence, lobbying, etc. He said that his government received a telegram from one colored [person], in plain English, claiming this money. He stated that it was rumored that Dr. Scott was one of the men who claimed a share. He said that such a charge was of utmost delicacy, that he was very hesitant to bring up the rumor, and indeed, did not know whether or not Dr. Scott was one of those involved.[141]

State Department officials sought to gain more information. On October 31, one State Department officer was able to report that nothing specific could be found on Scott's involvement.[142] After the American chargé defended Scott, the president reversed himself. Wharton in Monrovia was puzzled by King's vacillation and asked the State Department to investigate the charges further. Nothing turned up. This episode may be indicative of nothing more than the political savvy of C. D. B. King. The master politician, who would eventually lose office as a result of the commission's report, was, no doubt, playing for time and, before the fact, impugning the impartiality of the American sent out to judge him.

Scott's refusal to serve forced the State Department to turn to other "colored" candidates. An assistant secretary of state, probably William Castle, wrote late in November about Henry West, a white candidate, and Charles Lewis. The opinion was that West was "a pleasant little man, but . . . if a good colored man exists we ought to send him." The black lawyer, Lewis, was judged "a conceited person, but able."[143] In spite of the unknowing, backhanded compliment, Emmett Scott informed the State Department that Lewis was not interested.[144] With the need now more urgent than ever, another department official wrote to Castle, agreeing that "it would be preferable under the circumstances to send a colored man as investigator to Liberia assuming that one who is suitably qualified can be found without delay." However, prompt action was more "important than the appointment of a colored man as such." The official, J. P. Moffat, went on to run down the list of possible black candidates:

[Scott] previously suggested the name of Mr. Charles S. Johnson of Chicago, who might be a possible choice, but I do not think much of the other two suggestions that he made in his letter to you. Lewis has made himself very unpopular with certain missionary and colored elements and was involved to a certain extent in the attempt made in 1922 by certain individuals including the Liberian Consul General in Baltimore to secure a commission for their services in obtaining the 1922 loan. President King has already inquired whether Emmett Scott was not involved in this and would, I think be certain to do so in the case of Lewis.

Another suggestion which has been in the back of my mind for some time, has been the possible appointment of W. E. Burghart Du Bois. In spite of the radicalism and bitterness which marked him in previous years, I think he has calmed down very considerably and there can be little question as to his ability and distinction. He might prove somewhat difficult to handle, but I think that in the present circumstances it would be well to consider him seriously.[145]

The suggestion of Du Bois went nowhere. Secretary of state Stimson forwarded the names of the historian Charles H. Wesley of Howard University and the sociologist Charles S. Johnson on to the American president. The sociologist's curriculum vitae was far more detailed than that of the historian. (This perhaps reflected Scott's bias, for it was he who forwarded them.) Johnson became the prime candidate. Known for his work on African Americans during the Great Migration, the thirty-six-year-old Virginian had never set foot in Africa. Having earned a B.A. from Virginia Union University in 1917, Johnson had gone on to graduate work at the University of Chicago. After stopping his education for a stint in the military during the First World War, he returned to Chicago as a fellow in sociology. It was there that Johnson had written *The Negro in Chicago* (1922), a book spurred by the race riots of 1919. In 1927, Johnson had published *Ebony and Topaz*, an edited volume, and, in the same year as his Liberian service, *The Negro in American Civilization.* At the time of his appointment to the League of Nations commission, the sociologist was director of the department of social science at Fisk University in Nashville, Tennessee. In addition, Johnson was a member of the Advisory Committee on Interracial Policy of the Social Science Committee, a member of the editorial council of the *World Tomorrow,* and a member of the Industrial Division of the National Conference of Social Work. A year before he was considered for the Liberian post, the social scientist had collected extensive information from seventy-five cities for the Research Committee of the National Interracial Conference. In the autumn of 1929, Johnson was collecting race relations data for the Rockefeller Foundation.[146] Johnson was later to emerge as a moving force in the Commission on Interracial Cooperation and the Southern Regional Council, organizations attempting to ameliorate the conditions of Southern blacks within the framework of segregation. An admirer has written: "He led no mass movement. He shunned controversy. His name was far more likely to appear in a byline than a headline." Until his death in 1956, "he served as the consummate race diplomat in a hostile territory — the American South."[147]

In Johnson, the State Department had its "suitable colored man," although suspicion continued across the color line. The department's J. P. Moffat observed, "He is an intellectual Negro, quiet and unassuming on the surface, but I suspect him to be haughty and autocratic."[148] The State Department circulated the black sociologist's name to the white philanthropic establishment. Secretary of state Stimson sent a telegram to Trevor Arnett, president of the Rockefeller General Education Board and, on the strength of the word of Jackson Davis, his foundation's southern affairs program officer, Arnett recommended Johnson highly.[149]

On November 27, Castle decided to recommend Johnson's appointment. He wrote Jackson Davis for more information on the black social scientist and was informed that Johnson had "the objective attitude of the scientist and presents facts in such a way that they point to a logical conclusion. We found him very tactful and efficient and I believe he is discreet and entirely trustworthy." The foundation functionary added, "Certainly he is highly respected among the colored people of the South as a scholar and as a trained investigator of social and economic problems."[150] The Rockefeller recommendation was added to letters already received from Thomas Jesse Jones of the Phelps Stokes Fund and James Dillard of the Jeanes Fund and General Education Board. Johnson was officially invited to become the American member of the commission of inquiry on November 26, 1929.

On December 2, Johnson accepted the post by telegram; he reaffirmed his commitment six days later by letter. His government announced the appointment to the world seventeen days later. On the penultimate day of the year, Johnson presented his two choices for personal secretary, John Matheus of the West Virginia Collegiate Institute, and Arthur A. Schomburg of New York. He chose the younger Matheus.[151] The State Department wanted the commission to begin its work by the second week of February 1930, and to terminate before the Liberian rainy season began in June. According to the initial timetable, Johnson would have time to consult with American officials between the end of December and the middle of January. He would then confer with European experts on Africa before moving on to Monrovia to meet his League of Nations and Liberian colleagues. However, like much involved with the Liberian scandal, things moved much more slowly than originally envisioned. Johnson's duties at Fisk delayed his trip to Washington by several days. He did not arrive until mid-January. As it turned out, he was not able to leave Europe for Liberia until mid-February. The League's representative, Judge Meek of Norway, had already balked at the suggestion of so late a start and resigned. The league appointed Cuthbert Christy, a British medical expert, in the Scandinavian's stead.

Johnson arrived in Monrovia in early March. The members of the commission of inquiry made for an odd trio. The Liberian member was former president Arthur Barclay, the grand old man of Liberian politics. He had been married four times and was deeply immersed in the web of oligarchic family connections. He was the father-in-law of president King and the uncle of secretary of state Edwin Barclay. The former president was also the brother-in-law of Gabriel Johnson, formerly supreme potentate of the UNIA. In retirement, Barclay practiced law and had Firestone among his clients. Cuthbert Christy was a longtime colonial official whose résumé read like a travelogue of imperialism's high noon. He had been senior medical officer in Northern Nigeria (1898–1900); special medical officer in Bombay for the plague (1900–1901); member of the Uganda Sickness Commission (1902); assistant lecturer at the Liverpool School of Tropical Medicine (1903); researcher on sleeping sickness in the Congo (1903–4). He went on to work in Ceylon (1906), in Uganda and East Africa (1906–9), in Nigeria, the Gold Coast, and the Cameroons (1909–10). Christy had published a technical book on the African rubber industry in 1911 and spent the next three years in the Congo making a natural history collection on behalf of the Belgian government. During the Great War, the doctor had researched malaria and sleeping sickness in Mesopotamia, the Sudan, and the Congo. At the end of the war, Christy had been awarded the Royal Geographical Medal for his explorations in Central Africa. In the years immediately preceding his service in Liberia, he was employed in Tanganyika (1925–28) and in French Equatorial and West Africa (1928–29).[152]

The League of Nation's commission, after some hesitations, began its functions on April 8, 1930. It probed the export of labor to Fernando Po, in addition to the conditions of labor employed in road building and porterage. Evidence was also taken on the practice of pawning. Barclay, because of age and infirmity, did not accompany his colleagues on their trips beyond Monrovia. After six weeks, Christy and Johnson journeyed to Kataka and then to Cape Palmas, where they took the testimony of chiefs, subchiefs, and others. After Garawe, the two men took separate routes in order to observe a wider area. They returned to Monrovia on July 7 and continued to take evidence until August 8. At the conclusion of their fact-finding, the investigators had taken the testimony of 109 witnesses in Monrovia. In addition, they had heard 39 spokesmen for sections and towns at their Kataka meetings and 116 such spokesmen in Maryland County. Of the total number of persons giving evidence, 20 were paramount chiefs, 82 subchiefs, 103 indigenous civilians, 3 cabinet ministers, and 26 public officials, including justices of the supreme court, senators, county superintendents, and district commissioners. In all, the League's investigators took 264 dispositions.[153]

Although the commission produced a unified report, Johnson and Christy disagreed on many points of interpretation. In addition, the much younger Johnson felt that Christy, the official head of the group, depended on him for far too much; he especially resented the Englishman's "taking my drafts and calling them his own." On the issue at hand — slavery — the two men held widely varying opinions. According to Johnson, "His [Christy's] . . . hysterical, extreme statements in summary fashion [condemned] the whole government and [called] everything slavery, slave dealing, slave traffic, etc." Furthermore, the sociologist had two major criticisms of how the chairman handled the question of slavery. First, "we cannot make findings before knowing what we have — it would be better to state our observations and results of the testimony before beginning to plan a finding — psychologically this should come last, anyhow." In the second place, Johnson's elderly companion was "muddled on what is slavery." In the Virginian's opinion, "Capture and flogging need not be slave raiding, etc. We have seen no common slavery, but domestic slavery and pawning etc. Fernando Po cannot be regarded as slavery."[154]

Like many other things involving the Liberian matter, race intruded. Johnson said his colleague Christy felt Africans were "standing still and [were] 100 years behind England . . . and France . . . , that U. S. Negroes were 100 years behind whites." The black sociologist "suggested . . . that with all of Africa gone [under European domination] this little 40,000 square miles might well be an experiment in Negro self rule, citing the case of Ireland on the British Isle [*sic*] which was just as far behind England, and only in the last 10 or 15 years had started ahead."[155] The black American reminded his European colleague that "they [the Irish] have been trying even longer than the Liberians. Czecho-Slovokia [is] another illustration." The two men disagreed on how best to alleviate the problems found in Liberia; Johnson noted that "after mutual agreement on corruption and lack of standards, he [Christy] ventured it was a situation that could not correct itself now by American Negroes, because they could not have the standards." Christy favored administration by white men; Johnson thought black self-rule should not be imperiled and that American blacks might play a significant role in rehabilitation. At length Christy agreed that Liberia should remain independent, a change Johnson credited to his own example of personal achievement.[156]

When the commission's report was completed in September, it concluded that postmaster general Samuel Ross, vice president Allen Yancy, and others had connived at the forcible export of labor, although the actual presence of *slavery* (i.e., organized slave markets) was not found. The report noted the persistence of pawning in the hinterland. It characterized Liberia's road-building projects as not well thought out and stated that they proved wasteful of labor and demoralizing to the indigenous population. The commission recommended that Liberia: (1) abandon its policy of the "closed door" (the discouragement of foreign investment); (2) reestablish the authority of the chiefs; (3) appoint Americans to administrative positions in the government (commissioners, district officers, etc.); (4) declare domestic slavery and pawning illegal; (5) cease the shipment of laborers to Fernando Po and other foreign places; (6) increase discipline over military forces; and (7) encourage African American immigration.[157]

Some of the information collected by the 1930 commission begged for further investigation. The League of Nations investigation hastened the termination of the labor traffic, and it probably also hastened Ross's death in November of 1929. As the time of the inquiry approached, the labor exporter decided to visit Germany. His departure embarrassed the regime, and he was persuaded to return and write a letter absolving President King of complicity in the traffic. While in Monrovia, Ross died mysteriously. His body was then sent to Greenville by launch; the craft capsized, the body disappeared, and Ross's young son drowned.[158]

King's Fall

The findings of the 1930 commission of inquiry greatly embarrassed the regime of president C. D. B. King, whose administration was directly implicated. In addition, the commission's recommendation that Liberia employ outside administrators proved highly unpopular in the Black Republic. Caught between international censure and the demands and interests of his constituents, King attempted to satisfy both. On October 1, 1930, he issued decrees prohibiting the further export of labor and making the pawning of human beings illegal. On October 30, he submitted the League of Nations report to the legislature for action. In December, the thirteen-member House of Representatives expelled two members, P. F. Simpson and W. J. McBorrough, who were then indicted on charges of trafficking in forced labor. Former vice president Allen Yancy, senator (and future president) W. V. S. Tubman, Captain J. C. Phillips of the Frontier Force, former director of public works John L. Morris, and former county superintendent D. C. Watson all later faced indictment on similar charges.[159]

The revelations of the Christy-Johnson commission also began the political eclipse of King himself. The president, then fifty-seven, had served in office since 1920 and previously had appeared to enjoy good political health. On the eve of his expulsion from office, the British legation felt that he had "the reputation of being relatively honest," although he was "personally interested in the organized labor traffic with Fernando Po and the French Congo, and very anxious as to the outcome of the Commission of Enquiry."[160] But the investigation had produced a demand by King's opponents for a change of government. On June 17, 1930, a public meeting attended by about five hundred citizens adopted a resolution condemning the government for its complicity in the labor traffic and calling for the resignation and prosecution of culpable officials.[161] On September 25, after the Christy-Johnson commission's report had become public, this group met at Clay Ashland and formed itself into a citizens' league. The new league thanked the commission for its inquiry and publicly accepted its report.[162]

At the beginning of October, the citizens' league proposed installation of a provisional government until the regular elections in May of 1931. On October 14, a women's citizens' league held a meeting and agreed to accompany the men in their petition. The proposed interim government would be composed of a provisional president, the president pro tem of the Senate as vice president, and those members of the legislature not involved in the Fernando Po scandal. If expulsion of guilty members seriously depleted either house of the legislature, the provisional president would order a plenary election immediately to avoid delaying impeachment proceedings against King. The new government would begin reforming the administration of the hinterland forthwith, replacing the present hinterland officials and refunding all illegal exactions made during the King regime. Domestic slavery and pawning would be suppressed.

The citizens' league's program of reforms was submitted to the legislature in October of 1930 in a petition also demanding King's resignation. Attorney general Louis Grimes had cautioned the president against taking such a step: "I invite your Excellency's most careful consideration, not only in your own interest, nor of the present administration alone, but also because of the bad precedent that might be set, and the possibility of adversely affecting the prerogative of the President of Liberia for all time."[163] But by December, the rush of events was proving too strong. The British legation reported that the president's acceptance of the recommendations of the Christy-Johnson commission "aroused opposition . . . , and was highly unpopular with the masses of the people, who feared that it would bring about the complete domination of Liberia by the "white man."[164] Powers greater than the president intervened. In Monrovia, the Grand Lodge of Ancient Free and Accepted Masons met; their leader, W. O. D. Bright, urged King, a former grand master of masons, to do what was best for the political order. King said that he would resign on the condition that the vice president would precede him. The president also asked for immunity from prosecution for any acts committed during his administration. Vice president Allen Yancy resigned on the morning of December 2, 1930. King submitted his resignation to a joint session of the legislature on the following afternoon. The deed was done; King was out of office and the True Whig Party still formed the government.

The American note had in effect signaled the abandonment of a sometime protégé. In 1926, the State Department had urged Firestone to moderate its demands since the company's "best security [lay] in a continuation of the King regime . . . , to give King a chance to save face before his own people and not to hamper him by putting him in a *politically* indefensible position."[165] Belatedly the Liberian president reminded the United States of services rendered. The American legation wrote Washington: "The President, as previously reported, feels that the Legation's note of June 8, 1929 . . . was unnecessarily severe, and, if I remember correctly, the President intimated to the late Minister [Francis] that when Buell's charges were made the Liberian Government and the Department cooperated in refuting them."[166] King had in 1928 been the State Department's collaborator. When he stepped down in December of 1930, his successor promised to be less conciliatory. Thus, having sabotaged King, the Americans found themselves at a loss for a more pliable replacement. After his resignation, the disgraced president did receive some solace from the Firestone interests. The man under whose administration slavery had supposedly flourished, became one of the company's Liberian lawyers.

The furor that preceded the resignation of President King might have been the occasion for a bloodless coup. Opponents of King's True Whig Party, centered chiefly in the People's Party headed by Thomas Faulkner, saw a chance to unseat a corrupt regime that could not be upset through electoral politics. Faulkner owned and managed an ice and electric light plant, as well as a hotel. The immigrant, who hoped that a mass black exodus from the United States would follow him, was not content to confine himself to a business role. As mentioned, he was a member of the legislature, and in 1923, he became his party's candidate for vice president. In the flagrantly rigged election of 1927, Faulkner won 9,000 votes as the candidate of the People's Party, while 235,000 went to the candidate of the True Whig Party (King). Given the limited scope of the Liberian electorate, the results were farcical. For example, in Bassa County, with its no more than 3,000 legal voters, 32,000 persons were registered and 72,000 votes cast.[167] A protest was made in the courts, but the administration intimidated officers of the law by fining them. When the ballot boxes were examined, stacks of ballots were found unopened.

A British Foreign Office report opined that Faulkner was "one of the ablest men in Liberia"; although he was thought to be anti-British, the report remarked that he acted with "the courage of his conviction."[168] Charles Johnson wrote of Faulkner:

> The most hated and one of the most lonely men in the republic was Thomas J. R. Faulkner, leader of the People's Party, the Liberian citizen who first laid charges against his government at the door of the U.S. government and the League of Nations. Fearless, eternally active, of powerful physique despite his sixty years, he had been a relentless foe of the administration, a friend of the native, whose zeal for reform became almost an obsession . . . his business was destroyed by political prejudice, and through it all he opposed the dictatorship of King and the Whigs with ever-increasing fury. Indeed, it was difficult at times to distinguish between pure humanitarian sentiment and personal grievances. He could have justly been accused of intemperance in his charges against the administration, of stirring up native unrest against the government in his determination to air their grievances before the world, but although he held public office and was active in the country for over forty years, no one, not even his political enemies, ever accused him of dishonesty or of deliberate injustice. Because of his activities the government threatened to try him for treason; the most bitter pens of the administration attacked him, impugning his motives, even assassination was attempted, but Faulkner continued unabated, a painful, albeit salutatory, thorn in the body politic.[169]

In September of 1929, Joseph Johnson, an African American partisan of Faulkner's and a former American minister to Liberia, wrote the State Department, saying he felt that the League of Nation's commission of inquiry "might well be empowered to look into other conditions as well, particularly conditions surrounding general elections."[170] Faulkner visited the department in 1929 and spoke of the abuses being committed under the existing regime. An official observed, "If Faulkner is clever, he can exploit politically the clamor that is sure to arise over the slavery commission, but in the meantime, I think we should continue to impress upon him in his personal conversations . . . the desirability of working for an agreement between the two parties [True Whig and People's] by direct negotiations and an agreement which will not involve a recourse to our assistance."[171]

Two months before King's fall from power, Harvey Firestone sent a message to his representative in Liberia outlining a naive modus vivendi for King and his foes: the president might retire the members of his cabinet and appoint in their stead Faulkner and the other principal leaders of the opposition.[172] Men like Faulkner, ex-president Daniel Howard, former postmaster general Reginald Sherman, chief justice J. J. Johnson, associate justice Abayomi Karnga, N. H. Sie Brownell, and Doughba Carranda could participate in a new government set up on the ruins of the previous regime. But King's political eclipse did not pave the way for such a development; the president resigned, but his party continued. The opposition could rail against King, but they could not oust the party once it had decided to jettison him. The U.S. State Department was itself cool to the idea that a change of party government in Monrovia would bring amelioration of conditions. Early in 1930, the secretary of state observed, "It is true that there exists a number of coast negroes who are in opposition to the present government and take their stand that reforms are needed. It is not believed from the character of the opposition that should they be placed in power matters would mend."[173] The opposition, therefore, remained in opposition, and at the next election, history repeated itself: in May of 1931, Faulkner once again accused the True Whig Party of stuffing ballot boxes.

The continued dominance of the True Whig Party in part resulted from the remarkable tenacity of its new leader, Edwin Barclay, nephew of ex-president Arthur Barclay. The new president assumed his post with studied determination, and with each passing year he arrogated more power to himself. A sedition law and, later, an expanded presidential term of eight years cemented his grasp on the reins of power. His succession, like much of his career, had about it an air of studied calculation. On the resignation of King and Yancy, the presidency should have gone to the speaker of the House of Representatives, J. N. Lewis of Sinoe County. The speaker had, for some curious reason, decided to absent himself from the capital and return to Greenville as the presidential crisis came to a head. In the absence of the speaker, the office of chief of state went to the fourth in line, the secretary of state, who was to serve until January of 1932, the remainder of King's unexpired term.

Edwin Barclay, the illegitimate son of a prominent family, had risen through the ranks of Liberian politics. Born in Brewerville, Liberia, in 1882, he became an attorney in 1904 and a counselor of the Supreme Court in 1911. He also served as professor of mathematics at Liberia College. From 1910 to 1912, he served as secretary of public instruction; in the latter year, he became a judge of the circuit court of the first judicial circuit. He served as attorney general from 1916 to 1920, and as secretary of state from 1920 to 1930. In that year, the British consulate described him as "very touchy, hot-tempered and impulsive" and noted friction between Barclay and President King.[174] "Should he be elected in 1931," the consulate warned, "he is likely to make things very unpleasant for the foreign resident, and the British representative will have his hands full."[175] The Americans also had misgivings. The State Department viewed Barclay (who had visited the United States in 1925) as "anti-white" and questioned the constitutionality of his accession until assured by the legation that the transfer of power had been legitimate.[176]

Both the United States and Britain nevertheless refused to recognize the new regime officially (i.e., the American minister did not present his credentials). William H. Hunt, an African American diplomat with previous postings in Madagascar, France, and the Azores, arrived in Monrovia as King slid from power. "I discovered," he wrote "on arrival in Monrovia that the American Government and the President of Liberia were 'en politesse diplomatique' following the findings of the 'International Inquiry Commission.'" Hunt went on to note that "strange to say, although I met three of the former Presidents of the Republic, the Honorables Arthur Barclay, Howard and C. D. B. King, I never met President Edwin Barclay personally."[177] Little did he know that Barclay would long survive the Hoover administration or that Hoover's successor, Franklin D. Roosevelt, would one day visit Monrovia as Barclay's honored guest.

5 Dollar Diplomacy

Liberia has the world's largest rubber plantation in a place called Firestone.

The Americans use the rubber to make condoms and tires. They send

condoms and cars to Africa. . . . The condoms control the birthrate, and

the cars kill because the roads are so bad. So who's to blame?

— Williams Sassine to Manthia Diawara

In 1931 George Schuyler wrote, "There are times when the masses actually become better off when ruled by efficient foreign imperialists than by their own clique who are frequently more cruel and exacting."[1] Sixty-two years later, the *New York Times Magazine* published an article entitled "Colonialism's Back — and Not a Moment Too Soon." The subtitle of the piece read "Let's Face It: Some Countries Are Just Not Fit to Govern Themselves." The author, Paul Johnson, asserted:

> It is obvious that Africa, where normal government is breaking down in a score or more states, is the most likely theater for . . . action. The appeals for help come not so much from Africa's political elites, who are anxious to cling to the trappings of power, as from ordinary desperate citizens, who carry the burden of misrule. Recently in Liberia, where rival bands of heavily armed thugs have been struggling for mastery, a humble inhabitant of the capital, Monrovia, named after the fifth President of the United States, approached a marine guarding the United States Embassy and said, "For God's sake come and govern us!"[2]

The article reads more like 1933 than 1993. Indeed, it would be right at home with the "liberal imperialism" espoused in the 1930s by the likes of Lord Frederick Lugard and Margery Perham. Its aims are the general welfare, a welfare which can only be assured by honest and disciplined foreign administrators — backed up by military force. Johnson's suggestion is that

> the Security Council could commit a territory where authority has irretrievably broken down to one or more trustees. These would be empowered

not merely to impose order by force but to assume political functions. They would in effect be possessed of sovereign powers.

The mandate would usually be of limited duration—5,10, 20 years for example—and subject to supervision by the Security Council; and their ultimate object would be to take constitutional measures to insure a return to effective self-government with all deliberate speed. . . . So the mandate may last 50 years, or 100. . . .

[Misrule's] continued existence, and the violence and human degradation [it] breed[s], is a threat to the stability of their neighbors as well as an affront to our consciences. There is a moral issue here: the civilized world has a mission to go out to these desperate places and govern.[3]

Johnson, at the end of his plea for a return to colonialism, asserts, "The only satisfaction will be the unspoken gratitude of millions of misgoverned or ungoverned people who will find in this altruistic revival of colonialism the only way out of their present intractable miseries."[4] Ten years after Johnson's proposals, in the wake of the U.S. occupation of Iraq, Niall Ferguson advocated an even more forceful projection of American power in the Third World. Using the British Empire as a model, he chided Americans for not taking up the burden. Imperialism was good: "A striking number of the things currently recommended by economists to developing countries were in fact imposed by British rule." Indeed, "There was . . . a 'London consensus' not unlike the 'Washington consensus' of our own time, with the difference that the International Monetary Fund cannot rely on the services of the Royal Navy to enforce its recommendations."[5] The problem today is that "the American empire dare not speak its own name." In a world of failed regimes, "Americans need to go there. If the best and brightest insist on staying home, today's unspoken imperial project may end—unspeakably—tomorrow."[6] Iraq should be only the beginning of a rearrangement of the world, a rearrangement overseen by an honest and efficient foreign bureaucracy backed by an efficient and well-armed constabulary. Given the savage civil war in Liberia in the 1990s and the current misery rending Sierra Leone apart, outside occupation may seem called for. However, colonialism was not and is not an eleemosynary endeavor. The colonial powers always sought to derive more from their possessions than they put in. One must remember that it was not until 1940 that the British floated their first colonial "development" scheme. The questions remain the same: Who is to pay? And who is to give orders? Who is to be the trustee, and how are the ruled to have their views expressed? Simply put, what does the "trustee" get out of it. . . . Iraq differs greatly from Rwanda or Liberia.

In 1930, once Liberia, through U.S. initiative, had undergone investigation, Washington had several alternatives: (1) withdraw from Liberian affairs, leaving the country alone to contend with the European colonial powers; (2) accept a League of Nations mandate over the country; (3) exercise camouflaged control through the Firestone Company; (4) assist Liberia in its own program of reform; and (5) collaborate with the League of Nations in drafting and inaugurating a plan of reform.[7] There existed conflicting tendencies within the American foreign policy apparatus. The chargé in Monrovia, Henry Carter, earnestly attempted to involve his country in full-scale intervention. In September of 1929, he observed, "It will be noted that the idea of sending a battleship has been temporarily dropped, although the telegram has been so worded as to make it possible for us to revive the idea at any time."[8] In 1930, he warned that European financial interests might gain a foothold in Liberia and argued for unilateral American intervention.

When the Liberian secretary of state hinted that American fiscal officials should help the Liberian government obtain a loan from the Bank of British West Africa, Carter advised, after a consultation with the Firestone Company's general manager in Liberia and an American fiscal official, that the United States should press for control well beyond that already exercised under the 1926 loan agreement.[9] The American secretary of state strongly admonished Carter and informed the chargé that "this Government has no intention whatsoever, as you, of course, are aware, of 'intervening' in Liberia."[10] Carter was told that "the Department will instruct you; and meanwhile you will not make any commitments nor express any views on this Government's behalf in regard to important developments in the internal affairs of Liberia." Attempting to reconcile his position with the department's scruples, the chargé replied, "My intervention references envisaged a possible intensifying of American control, including a financial dictatorship, a reform of government machinery, and a reorganization by American officials of the hinterland administration. . . . The initiative for adopting such a program would have to come from the Liberian Government in the form of a request for the good offices of the United States."[11]

But the United States did not want the full "burden" of Liberia. The Liberia question arose during a hiatus in the American imperialist impulse. In the early twentieth century, American forces had occupied Cuba, Panama, Haiti, Nicaragua, and the Dominican Republic. By the mid-1930s, the United States was prepared to use more subtle means to protect its interests in the Third World. The occupation of the Dominican Republic in 1965 signaled a renewal of the policy of occupation, a policy that reached far-flung spheres of influence in the Middle East by the early twenty-first century.

In the early 1930s the United States did want economic and political dominance in Liberia. Trying to distinguish official policy from Carter's, J. P. Moffat of the State Department said, "I do not think that the word intervention as used by Mr. Carter and as we understand it in the Department, is the same." Rather fuzzily, Moffat concluded, "If by intervention is meant the use of a form of compulsion by this Government against Liberia it is quite correct to say that this Government has never intervened in the affairs of Liberia, but I do not think it is entirely correct to say that this Government has never considered intervening."[12] Undersecretary of state William Castle put forward the suggestion that American dominance might be maintained behind the facade of Firestone Company rule, "a case, although the world would not know it, similar to the old East India Company." The idea was advanced "as a suggestion, unsatisfactory perhaps, but with fewer inherent dangers than there would be in either turning Liberia over to the League of Nations or in accepting a mandate ourselves which would inevitably lead to military control of the country for a long time."[13]

In December of 1930, Harvey Firestone urged the department to take an actively imperialistic role in Liberia, basing his demand on the pessimistic assumption that Liberia was headed for anarchy. Secretary of state Henry Stimson agreed with Firestone's prognosis, but told the rubber baron that the United States was loath to undertake responsibilities in Africa and favored the League of Nations to handle the matter. Stimson told Firestone that he "saw no likelihood of the American Government being willing to assume responsibility in Liberia across the Atlantic" and that the problem of reform in Liberia "would have to be eventually handled by the League of Nations with such advice or help as [the United States] can give them, whatever that might be."[14] A few weeks later, a State Department official drafted a memorandum elucidating Stimson's policy. Control of Liberia by the U.S. government "would inevitably lead to active and long-continued participation in Africa, which, while doubtlessly justified by many on philanthropic or racial grounds, could not fail to arouse the hostility of others as imperialism."[15] He expressed fear of the "establishment of a virtual American colony in Africa. It would render the continued espousal of the Monroe Doctrine difficult to justify, and it would unquestionably arouse the suspicion of Europe and South America." Importantly, the memorandum noted that "no compensating gain, in profit or in prestige, would accrue to the United States if it took over Liberia." Soon after, Stimson reported that his president, Herbert Hoover, supported collaboration "with other nations in some form of joint international control for Liberia."[16]

Reaction among the American public at first remained relatively low-key. Racists screamed that Liberia was another Haiti or worse. Many African Americans, initially, willingly wanted to go along with some form of reform. *Opportunity,* the journal of the National Urban League, wrote that "since the United States government has acted in concert with the League of Nations in investigating slavery and conditions of forced labor in that country, there is no valid reason why it should not continue to act with the League until the distressing conditions revealed by the report have been completely eradicated."[17] In March of 1931, Alain Locke, professor of philosophy at Howard University, called for U.S. cooperation "in some international plan of supervision and assistance" which might demand "the modification of terms of the Firestone concession and the surrender of our present receivership" in Liberia.[18] In November of 1932, Rayford W. Logan, assistant to Carter C. Woodson of the Association for the Study of Negro Life and History, supported the original League of Nations proposals, "even if they implied a temporary curtailment of Liberian sovereignty."[19] In the same month, Walter White and W. E. B. Du Bois of the NAACP gave their support to what constituted, in Du Bois's words, "the excellent plan of reform drawn up by the League."[20] In March of 1931, a delegation of black clergymen representing the National Baptist Convention petitioned the secretary of state, asking the U.S. government "to do everything in its power, through the Committee of the League of Nations recently appointed to help Liberia, and also through the representatives of our Government in Liberia, to the end that all the unwholesome conditions of forced labor, slavery and other oppressions may be removed, that health conditions may be improved, and that the Republic of Liberia may retain its place as an independent self-governing nation."[21]

The League and Slavery

The League of Nations had to wrestle with the definition of slavery. It also had to tread lightly, knowing that many colonial governments looked the other way on the issue of slavery, especially where it could be described as "domestic." Slavery in neighboring Sierra Leone was only abolished in 1928. In many colonies, demands for corvée labor often drew on preexisting pools of slaves, a connection which from time to time burst forth in labor scandals. The impetus to do something in Liberia came at a time when the league, largely under British pressure, took on the general issue of slavery in the tropics. Sir John Harris of the British Anti-Slavery and Aborigines Protection Society continued to use his parliamentary contacts to both embarrass and prod the Foreign Office into taking a stand on colonial slavery. In the 1930s, both Ethiopia and Liberia attracted his interest. It was also helpful that Sir John Simon, foreign secretary until 1935, was the husband of Lady Kathleen Simon, the author of the 1929 work *Slavery,* a compendium of information on the state of the institution.

In 1932, while the Liberian situation was under consideration, the League established the Committee of Experts on Slavery. It constituted a weak instrument, largely charged with gathering information. All of the colonial powers were represented on the committee; few representatives remained independent of their government's colonial offices. The International Labor Organization received only observer status. The Committee of Experts was set up to operate for only one year and to look into the implementation of the 1926 convention. It met in private and could only consider reports submitted through or by governments. Unfavorable information submitted by one government about conditions in the territory of another had to be vetted with the supposed offender.

In her book *Slavery,* which sought to cover all the regions of the earth, Lady Simon drew her definition from the League's slavery convention itself:

> Slavery is the status or condition of a person over whom any or all of the powers attaching to the right of ownership were exercised. The slave trade includes all acts involved in the capture, acquisition or disposal of a person with intent to reduce him to slavery; all acts involved in the acquisition of a slave with a view to selling or exchanging him; all acts of disposal by sale or exchange of a slave acquired with a view to being sold or exchanged, and, in general, every act of trade or transport in slaves.[22]

The League's definition remained, perhaps of necessity, imprecise. The term *ownership,* as in the case of wives, was problematical. Colonial governments often winked at any such definitions. Some colonial officials fell back on the idea of "traditional" slavery as something familial and paternal. Of course, this simply raises the question of what was traditional? Many present-day discussions of the topic still center around this issue, with the slavers' canard looming in the background. In 1940, the African American minister in Monrovia averred, "There is no such slavery in Liberia as at one time existed in the United States."[23] This comment raises the issue of the image of slavery in Africa in general. A notable Nigerian scholar has correctly pointed out that what many have called slavery in Africa would be referred to as serfdom in Europe. Joseph Inikori concludes that

> given the sociology of knowledge which informed the study of slavery in Africa, it is understandable why very little attention has been paid to the terminological precision that characterizes the study of dependent social categories in the history of precapitalist Europe . . . while there were slaves in late-nineteenth century Africa, the bulk of the people hitherto so described were approximately serfs. The phenomenon of what scholars refer to as intergenerational mobility among the slave populations of Africa . . . [occurred] largely because the children of slaves normally did not remain in slavery. They either became free or became serfs.[24]

The writer concludes, "It is thus clear that the chattel slavery experienced by Africans in the Americas were [*sic*] something new for them . . . the vast majority of forced migrants from Africa were entirely legally free people captured in wars or raids, or kidnapped like Olaudah Equiano."[25] Inikori recognizes that there were "regions with high densities of servile populations . . . like Asante, Dahomey, and the Benin kingdom of south-western Nigeria." In these areas "a significant population of dependent people whose socioeconomic conditions approximated those of slaves, existed side by side with others, in greater number, whose conditions were closer to those of serfs" (in other words, bound, but nonsaleable labor).[26]

Some time ago, in comparing slavery in the Americas, the anthropologist Marvin Harris noted the "Myth of the Kindly Master," in which non-U.S. slavery was envisioned as somehow innately less harsh and burdensome than the North American variety.[27] If some African societies seemed to offer bondspersons more leeway than others, it was, in the logic of Harris's argument, because of the lower intensity of their economic production. It would be very hard to argue that the slave salt miners of Taodeni or the miners in the Asante gold mines participated in any form of "familial" slavery or predial serfdom. Even when using the kinship idiom, we must realize that folks can be awfully hard on their kin (for example, Roman fathers had the legal right to sell their spouses and children).

We must avoid trying to reify *slavery*. Indeed, in doing so, we run the risk of making the same mistake we do when we impose late-nineteenth-century anthropological terms on African social reality. *Slavery* implied a degree of dependence and the lack of a unilateral right to break the bond. Beyond these simple prerequisites, we run into a welter of statuses:

> Slaves might be menial field workers, downtrodden servants, cherished concubines, surrogate kin, trusted trading agents, high officials, army com-

manders, ostracized social groups dedicated to a deity, or a ready pool of candidates for human sacrifice. Owners might be corporate kin groups or individuals of either sex. A minority of individual owners and a majority of first-generation slaves were women, valued for their productive as well as their reproductive capacities, since women did much of the agricultural work in sub-Saharan Africa.[28]

"Slavery" thus existed (and exists) within a series of other labor relations. Paul Lovejoy notes that "besides slavery, there were other categories of dependency, including pawnship, in which persons were held for security for debts, and junior age-sets, in which younger kin were not allowed to participate fully in the decisions of the lineage. Even marriage and concubinage were institutions of dependency."[29] Orlando Patterson's psychodynamic view of slavery as "the permanent, violent domination of natally alienated and generally dishonored persons" calls up questions he does not pursue, especially as they pertain to gender and marriage.[30] It is possible to argue that a late-seventeenth-century Ottoman sultana of unfree Ukrainian origins ensconced in the Topkapi was less free than a French princess encased in the Escorial. Yet an examination of cases might find that any postpubescent female wrenched against her will from her home and family in return for a complex series of financial and territorial arrangements does not fit within the dichotomy of *slave* and *free woman*.[31] Females' status puts them at a complex juncture in patriarchies in which all women are subordinate, but some are more subordinate than others. Looking at work done among the Tonga in Nyasaland (Malawi), Roberts and Miers note that an investigator "found that freeborn women began to consider themselves to be the equivalent of slaves, because the departure of men as migrant wage labor not only increased their work load but changed male attitudes towards their wives, whom they came to regard, like slaves, as economic investments."[32]

Suzanne Miers and Igor Kopytoff argue that the key to understanding slavery in Africa is to recognize its fragmented nature and the functioning of concentric bands of otherness in African societies. Individuals existed within a web of kinship obligations and privileges. Within these, there existed rights-in-persons; these were "rights, usually mutual, but seldom equal, that exist in almost all social relationships."[33] Adults taken from other societies were seldom integrated into the new society; they often remained alien *durante vita* (for life). The bundle of rights-in-persons attached to newcomer individuals would be fairly extensive. She or he would have almost no recourse to kin for legal or physical protection. Children and grandchildren might, in some subsistence economies, be absorbed. Even so, the stigma of slave status might remain. Early in the twentieth century, British anthropologist R. S. Rattray remarked on the previous status of slaves among the Asante in present-day Ghana:

> Slavery in West Africa has been aptly described by Mary Kingsley as "a state of servitude guarded by rights." . . . To kill a slave without . . . permission was "murder," and the offence was liable to be punished as such. Even the powerful *Mpanyimfo* (Elders) in Kumasi had no power to kill their slaves. The mutilation of a slave without similar authority was forbidden. A slave might marry; own property; himself own a slave; swear an "oath"; be a competent witness; and ultimately might become heir to his master.[34]

With this description, we obviously find ourselves well outside the Old Dixie Narrative. We also find ourselves outside any picture of an edenic familial slavery. Rattray points out:

> The rights of a slave in an Ashanti family have . . . been examined and also the heaviest of his disabilities, i.e., the ever-imminent possibility of having his head cut off at funeral custom. There are several other disadvantages resulting from his inferior status which may be well to record. Apart from the especially fortunate position of some favourite slaves, an *odonko* (foreign-born slave) was never supposed to mix too familiarly with free men. . . . ("When a slave gets very familiar, we take him to a funeral custom"), grimly runs an Ashanti proverb. A slave might not go to a Chief's house (unless he were the slave of that Chief). . . . A slave was not allowed to wear any gold ornaments. . . . A slave generally wore a jerkin of blue and white material, called *koboaka,* drawers (*kadana*), and a metal or stone bangle on the right upper arm. Such dress was not compulsory. My Ashanti informant stated that even when an *odonko* dressed like an Ashanti he could always tell him by the way he wore his cloth.[35]

The slavery described here is not that described by Harriet Beecher Stowe or Toni Morrison. At the same time, it remains far removed from a system of "kindly masters." The foreign-born individual in servitude was permanently unequal and permanently insecure. This held true in many areas of Liberia, like the Vai country. The imposition of Liberian control made all Liberian ethnicities scramble to pay government exactions; the already coerced were among the first to suffer further coercion. The investigation of 1930 largely broke the chain of long-distance forced migration. Tied labor was left to slowly wither in the following decades. Firestone, like concessionaires in many other parts of Africa, wanted to pry a labor force away from its black masters in what was considered a primitive subsistence economy. By 1940, the process was far from over, but the rubber company had inserted itself as an alternative to the preexisting relations of labor.

Lady Simon believed that the Black Republic was salvageable and "would not lack friends who will be ready to watch her efforts with patience, and help her in any way possible to work out her own salvation."[36] According to Padmore, Du Bois, and Azikiwe, the interest of the League of Nations in Liberia reeked of hypocrisy. Many observers asked how Spanish Guinea and French Gabon, where some of the laborers had been sent, could escape blame. Azikiwe thought it odd that the "so-called commentators on Liberian affairs have failed to drag Spain, in unequivocal terms without mincing their words into this international debacle."[37] One American journal observed that "the Liberians do not export slaves without inducement, and in this case the inducement apparently comes from Spaniards at Fernando Po."[38] The Associated Negro Press questioned the absence of much concern over the European role and noted that "when the League delegates learned that France and Spain were the nations to be censured, the matter was dropped—there was not even a suggestion that Paris and Madrid be asked to explain."[39] The *Crisis* said that Spain and France deserved "quite as much censure as the Liberian Government." The journal felt that the Spaniards and their neighbors had "demanded the enslaved labor which was supplied."[40]

The United States went out of its way not to involve Spain in its accusations. Madrid, for its part, denied culpability, but an internal governmental report acknowledged infractions in the work code and coercion in the reengagement of workers.[41] In spite of this, abuse continued well past 1930. Spain adhered to the Forced Labor Convention of 1930, but it did not abolish forced labor (*prestación personal*) until the late thirties. In 1932, a Transmediterránea Company ship ran aground near Fernando Po with eight hundred passengers, of which six hundred were illegal African laborers. A French journal took up the issue and gave it wide publicity. Madrid denied wrongdoing, but, sensitive to the slavery scandal, the Dirección General de Marruecos y Colonias initiated an investigation.[42] Six years after the League of Nations investigation, the British Foreign Office ordered an on-the-spot report. It was discovered that Nigerian laborers continued to be smuggled. As in the past, many workers complained of insufficient payment. Conditions of labor were hard, especially at the higher elevations.[43] In the same year, two writers reported that illegal labor shipments continued from Liberia.[44] Pan-Africanists could not help but notice the double standard.

Only one state, Liberia, requested league aid on the slavery issue. A special committee of the council initially included representatives of the

United Kingdom, France, Germany, Italy, Spain, Poland, Venezuela, and Liberia. The United States, although not a member of the League of Nations, also sent a representative. The United Kingdom representative served as the chairman (first the secretary of state for foreign affairs and, later, Viscount Robert Cecil of Chelwood). As head of the Liberia Committee, Cecil adopted a paternalistic attitude toward the African republic, mixed with a highly legalistic belief in the sanctity of national sovereignty.

African Americans could not help but notice that race partially determined the paternalism whites intermittently displayed toward the Black Republic. Likewise, Washington and Monrovia were both aware that racial considerations impinged on their relations. Although the U.S. State Department sought to maintain the fiction that such considerations did not intrude, in actuality the racism permeating American life had a very definite effect on these relations. To most American officials, Liberia represented a "demigovernment" run by a race considered lacking in the requisite skills and capacities for national self-government. In the mid-1920s, a U.S. official in Liberia would express the opinion that all Liberians sensed their inferiority vis-à-vis white men; later an American customs receiver could say, "You never really know where you are with a negro."[45] In the mid-1930s, former Liberian president Howard told an American official that President Barclay wanted a deal, but that the attitude of the American officials working for the receivership was one of "starving out the dam [*sic*] niggers."[46] The Christy-Johnson commission only served to reinforce what many in the foreign policy apparatus already devoutly believed.

Admittedly, Liberia was a mess. In 1930, the Finance Corporation declined to make further payments on the 1927 loan beyond $18,000. Even before the Depression struck, Liberia had in fact accumulated a floating debt and was annually spending more than it received. The national deficit increased from $61,648 in the pre-Depression fiscal year 1927–28 to $220,000 in 1930–31.[47] The government's income declined from $1,276,438 in 1928 to $551,306 in 1931. The interest charges and the salaries of the American loan officials remained fixed. Monrovia estimated that whereas these costs (interest and American salaries) consumed only 20 percent of governmental revenue in 1928, they took up 54.9 percent in 1931.[48] The government went into default in the second half of 1931 and found it impossible to pay many of its employees.

The League of Nations took on not only economic and labor conditions but health conditions as well. In 1929, yellow fever appeared in Liberia and, in the course of the outbreak, William Francis, the American minister, and James L. Sibley, representative of the Advisory Committee on Education in Liberia, died. The plague reportedly threatened Liberia—endangering colonies up and down the West African coast.[49] The Monrovia branch of the Bank of British West Africa closed, ostensibly in protest against the Liberian government's lack of adequate health precautions.[50]

The Plans

When the United States called in the League of Nations to handle the Liberian affair, it remained to be seen whether the organization would lend itself to the aims of American government and capital. The league was suspicious of American big business, and Harvey Firestone was suspicious of the League of Nations as a blind for British imperialism (rubber interests particularly). The State Department's vacillation meant that no consistent pressure was applied to either the league or the company. In this situation, Liberia maneuvered with considerable skill, playing the league off against Firestone and vice versa. Firestone's insistence on firm American control (an insistence which went well beyond the State Department's) meant that Liberia could find shelter in the protective arms of the League of Nations. When the League finally grew tired of the Liberian "problem" and threatened Liberia with expulsion and worse, Firestone's vested interest proved an excellent counterweight to the threat of a European-imposed mandate. Liberia's experience with the League has an *opera bouffe* quality which stands in stark contrast to the tragic handling of the 1935 Ethiopian crisis. The Liberian affair finally smothered to death under the weight of its own paperwork. Committees followed commissions, which were in turn followed by other commissions. Data were accumulated and debated, so that further data could then be collected. All of this took time, and the Liberian administration used it to play off its adversaries, who spent most of their time debating plans that never came to fruition.

Hoping to draw up a plan of assistance, the Liberia Committee appointed three experts to investigate economic, labor, and health conditions: Charles Brunot of France, administrative expert and chairman; Theodorus Ligthart of the Netherlands, financial expert; and Melville Mackenzie of Great Britain, medical expert.[51] On September 25, 1931, after a six-week mission to Liberia, they completed their report, which was not published until the following May. They found it imperative that the sanitary and financial health of the republic be improved through international assistance. To this end, they urged that a mining and agricultural survey be made and an accurate census be taken. They called for the abolition of all compulsory labor except for communal labor on roads in tribal areas. They recommended an improved educational system, but felt no new taxes should be levied until an effective system of interior administration became operative. For this purpose, they proposed that the entire country be divided into three provinces. Most controversially, the Brunot commission recommended that Liberia hire twenty foreign technical assistants. The price of this assistance would amount to an estimated $398,000 per annum.[52] The question of how Liberia should pay this sum was left open.

Liberia reacted to the Brunot commission's report by asking for time. In January of 1932, Monrovia said that since the report had arrived there only in November, the government had not had a chance to peruse it. The Liberia Committee agreed that a final decision on the plan should be left until April. It did decide to undertake a preliminary examination of the document, over Liberian objections. The committee then concerned itself with three points of contention in the Brunot proposals: the number and status of the foreign administrators and specialists; the issuance of a new loan; and renegotiation of the Firestone contracts. The Liberia Committee disagreed with the experts' proposal that the Firestone Company issue the second half of the 1927 loan. It reasoned that if Firestone's presence was onerous, the extension of more money would make that presence all the more so.[53] The committee thought that reforms could be achieved if Firestone cooperated, since Monrovia had its internal revenue and the unspent balance of the 1927 loan. The committee proposed a moratorium on repayment of the loan until the annual national revenues reached $650,000; after the termination of the moratorium, the interest charges should be reduced and the Firestone rental on Liberian lands increased from six to approximately fifty cents an acre. In the end, the costs of assistance were to be met through economies in the Liberian national budget; the idea of a direct outside grant was not broached.

The Brunot commission sought to strengthen the Liberian administration by injecting foreign experts into the Liberian system. The Liberia Committee advocated neither as many officials as proposed by the commission nor as few as the Liberian government would have liked. The committee recommended that the Liberian hinterland be divided into three provinces — Eastern, Central, and Western.[54] Each of these divisions would have a provincial and a deputy commissioner. The League of Nations threw in an apple of discord when it proposed that the commissioner for the Western Province be French and that the commissioner for the Eastern Province be British. The Central Province was to be assigned a Dutch official.

Administratively the scheme constituted a complicated dyarchy. The commissioners would be responsible to the president of Liberia through the secretary of the interior. The League of Nations would nominate these six commissioners; Liberia would then appoint them, and their removal could be obtained only with the consent of the league. A chief adviser would oversee the work of the foreign administrators. He would be responsible to and removable by the League of Nations, although, like the commissioners, he would be attached to the Liberian government. In addition to coordinating the activities of the commissioners, the adviser would be empowered to request Liberian government documents, conduct investigations, and settle disputes between the American financial adviser and the Liberian government. If the chief adviser found that certain Liberian officials were delinquent in carrying out the league's plan of assistance, he would inform the Liberian government, advising them of what steps were to be taken. Should this prove ineffective, he would make written recommendations to the Liberian government. Should this, too, prove ineffective, he would submit the question to the Council of the League of Nations.

The plan to save little Liberia did not end here. Indeed, it had a Rube Goldberg aspect, which in retrospect makes the whole enterprise look slightly ridiculous. If Monrovia refused to carry out the council's recommendations, the council could declare its arrangement with Liberia terminated. This would void financial arrangements favorable to Liberia renegotiated with the Finance Corporation of America under the league's aegis. The council's decision on such matters would have to be unanimous, Liberia's vote not included. The president of the league council could act on behalf of the council in urgent cases, with the proviso that he refer to the council as soon as possible. The League's plan of assistance would run for a period of five years, unless the Liberian government wanted it to continue further. The league would have the right to discontinue collaboration before the end of five years if it saw fit. In addition to administrative personnel, the Liberia Committee proposed that Liberia take on two foreign medical officers and continue to appoint the five financial officials called for under the terms of the 1926 loan contract.[55]

The U.S. representative at Geneva objected to the League plan on the grounds that it was "thoroughly unworkable and impractical" and that the chief adviser had not received enough authority.[56] In May of 1932, the League of Nations council accepted the report of its committee, noting that the Americans had reservations. Already in January, Harvey Firestone had put forward his own plan of assistance to the Liberia Committee, proposing an American commissioner general with wide-ranging powers. The U.S. secretary of state supported the idea, but stuck to the fact that Liberian reform should be undertaken under the "juris-diction of the League through an international committee in which the United States would be represented." Otherwise, the American government was in full agreement with Firestone. The secretary of state maintained that unless "complete executive and administrative control is granted [an American] for a period of probably ten years no genuine reforms or rehabilitation could be achieved in Liberia."[57]

And what of the Liberians? The government perceived of itself as engaged in a David-and-Goliath struggle with the colonial powers. The Liberian delegation was small but astute. It included secretary of state Louis Grimes, Antoine Sottile (described by J. P. Moffat of the State Department as "the Italian Jew, who used to represent Nicaragua at the League until Liberia raised its ante and took him away from Nicaragua"),[58] plus Liberian consul general in Liverpool, Henry Ford Cooper, and later Liberian consul general in Hamburg, James S. Wiles. The permanent delegate for Liberia, Sottile, remarked, "You will . . . allow me perhaps to thank the journalists for the Press campaign they have conducted against Liberia." Sarcastically, he opined that all of the publicity was of benefit. "Liberia was an unknown country. She needed advertising and this campaign has therefore been useful to my country."[59] The Monrovia government saw itself as a victim, superior to its tormentors only in its ability to outwit them. Later, a Liberian diplomat wrote:

> The lobbying of the Liberian delegation among members of the Council found not a single delegate favorable to Liberia's predicament, or sympathetic to the seriousness of the attack on the sovereignty of the Nation. Even the Ethiopians, at that time, were indifferent and did not choose to be identified with black Africa. Hostile individuals in the streets of Geneva or when traveling in buses, openly castigated or stared in disgust at our representatives. The color of their skin made them conspicuously easy targets. Not a single friend, indeed. . . . The Liberian delegation could be only seated in the Gallery overlooking the Council chambers, and from that position listened to the fate of their Country being decided upon by the great colonial powers and other European countries. The Liberians were not only restricted from the floor of the chambers but were also told to conform with the decorum of the place if they wished to be permitted to retain their seats during the discussions.[60]

The Liberians did not stand entirely alone in the battle with the forces arrayed against them. They had several cards to play, and they played them well. Early on, while still secretary of state, Barclay maintained that the close examination of Liberian conditions constituted an anomaly and that other powers in Africa had far worse records. He told one American official that the "League of Nations representatives of Belgium, Portugal, Spain, and France do not want an investigation of the conditions in Liberia of compulsory labor for public purposes." The Liberian politician concluded, "These countries, therefore, are reluctant to have the League use its offices in such an investigation in Liberia . . . the French are very severe and hard with compulsory labor for public purposes in French colonies and also others."[61] Indeed, seven years before the league's investigation, the French member of the Temporary Slavery Commission, Delafosse, had defended Liberia. He stoutly asserted that during his sojourn in the country from 1897 to 1899, "there was no trace of slave-dealing, either open or disguised in the districts subject to the authority of the Liberian Government."[62]

As in Ethiopia's defense before the League of Nations five years later, Liberia sought to portray herself as the spokesperson for the rights of small states everywhere. Sottile asked his listeners, "Is there a single member of the League that would agree that, on the pretext of assistance, the administration of its country should form the subject of an arrangement between the League and a third State [i.e., the United States]? Such an admission would be a negation of the fundamental principles on which the League is based, and on account of which the small countries which form the great majority of the members of the League, have come to Geneva."[63] In addition, "the Committee does not consist only of a representative of the United States, but of eight members all on a footing of legal equality." Bearing this in mind, all should recognize that "the assistance of the League does not concern one specific member only, it concerns the eight members of the Committee, seeing that it is League assistance within the framework and limits of the Covenant." Sottile's appeal struck certain responsive chords. For a nation like Venezuela, the specter of Yankee imperialism, still ensconced in Haiti and only recently withdrawn from Nicaragua and the Dominican Republic, was very real. Poland was suspicious of any league attempt to oversee internal minority matters in light of its own "Jewish Question." The representative of the new Spanish Republic, Salvador de Madariaga, was no great admirer of the Monrovia regime; in 1930 he had archly observed, "Liberia . . . has a treaty with Spain whereby she provides Spain with black labor for Spanish cocoa plantations in Fernando Po at the rate of twenty-five dollars a head." In mock horror he asked, "Slavery? Oh dear no! All these laborers are free citizens of a free republic."[64] At the same time, the Spaniard was highly suspicious of Firestone's motives and emerged as one of the most consistent questioners of the company's ultimate political designs. Last but not least came the "race card" among Liberia's defenses. Early on in the investigation, many prominent African Americans had supported reform and reorganization in Liberia. Then, as events wore on, the Barclay regime ably wrapped itself in the mantle of racial patriotism; defense of Liberia became defense of the race.

In the Liberian view, the league's plans remained altogether too heedless of Liberian sovereignty. When the Brunot report was submitted, the Liberian representatives in Geneva maintained that Brunot and his colleagues had exceeded their investigation's terms of reference. In addition, they pointed out that any proposal for the concentration of executive and judicial authority in the same person contradicted the Liberian constitution.[65] On April 27, 1932, in a formal reply to the Brunot report, the Liberian government maintained that Liberia already had enough citizens who could serve as administrators. The Black Republic was willing to employ some foreign experts, but "it was never contemplated by the Government that proposals would be made to substitute the native organization wholly by foreigners, nor to withdraw its native population from under direct administration of Liberians and place them entirely under the direction of an alien race."[66] "To carry out the suggestion of the Brunot Commission," the Liberian government said, "would not only rob qualified citizens of a natural right to effectively participate in the Government of the Provinces, but would destroy the fealty which the population now displays toward the Government of the Republic; and would also work against the ideal of a homogeneous people."[67] The next month (May of 1932), Monrovia submitted to the League of Nations a statement stressing that the league had no power to tamper with the internal political management of Liberia. The country could not "accept any assistance, plan or suggestion relating to matters other than social, health, or finance reform."[68] Liberia would not accept staff from countries that held territory adjacent to Liberia (Britain and France), nor would it accept as foreign advisers members of the Christy-Johnson or Brunot commissions.

Instead of implementing the Brunot plan, Liberia offered to appoint for a period of five years three provincial commissioners recommended by the League of Nations. They would be responsible to the Liberian secretary of state, but copies of their reports would be supplied to the League. No doubt the Liberians reasoned that three commissioners would cost less than six. Also, if they were subordinate to the Liberian president through a cabinet member, there would be less likelihood of foreign subversion of the Liberian constitution. The financial officials called for under the 1926 loan agreement would remain, unless their number could be lessened by mutual accord. In addition to these officials, a director of sanitation and a health officer would be provided for.[69]

Hoping to placate American insistence on a strong presence, Barclay asked the U.S. State Department to nominate three Americans as commissioners in the Liberian hinterland. Although nominated by the Americans, they would operate under the purview of the Liberian government. Barclay said that if the United States would support his proposal, future policy would "be based upon close cooperation with the United States Government and legitimate American interests established in Liberia."[70] Secretary of state Stimson did not acknowledge the maneuver. Instead, he told Charles Mitchell, the American minister, that the Liberian administration had "brought the present difficulties upon itself by its own indifference to its responsibility to the country as such and to the native people . . . it [had] abused and exploited, and by its refusal to take advantage of the counsel of the American adviser."[71]

The American minister put a counteroffer to Barclay privately: the Liberian president should call his legislature and request authorization for the League of Nations to appoint a commissioner general, to whom Barclay "would delegate authority and control, administrative and executive, for him to effect the re-organization and rehabilitation of the country."[72] If the Liberian president would request that the commissioner general be an American, the U.S. government would use its influence to secure favorable modifications in Liberia's contract with the Finance Corporation of America. The American warned that the price for failing to take such a course would be heavy. The alternative was "a deadlock between Liberia and the League, leading to independent action toward Liberia by one or another of the powers whose interests in Africa [could] not fail to be affected by the continual disorders, social disintegration and health menace provided by Liberia in its present condition."[73] Mitchell told Barclay that the Americans would probably not object to such intervention. The Liberian president should act at once, before it was "too late."[74]

While the United States thus overtly collaborated with the League of Nations, it covertly sought to promote the policy advocated by American business. The American minister had an "informal confidential talk" with the Liberian president and presented secretary Stimson's plan. Barclay did not accept the suggestion, but instead offered his own compromise. Barclay would accept the League of Nations plan of reform with an American chief adviser (recommended by the president of the United States, nominated by the League, and accepted by the president of Liberia). The adviser would be a minister without portfolio in the Liberian cabinet.[75] This solution proved unacceptable to Stimson because it "would still further and very materially weaken the [League] plan, which was unacceptable . . . in its original form because of the basic weakness regarding the question of delegation of authority."[76]

In the summer of 1932, Gabriel Dennis, the Liberian secretary of state, met with Firestone and Stimson, without breaking the impasse. In July of 1932, the United States was pushed into a corner on the question of the nationality of the chief adviser. J. P. Moffat of the State Department wrote, "Crossing our telegram indicating that we are not going to yield without trying to have the Chief Adviser named an American, came in a telegram wherein Cecil told us that he would be pleased to support our position on nearly every other point if we would not press for an American Adviser."[77] Cecil implied that the matter could be settled by the League of Nations or by the United States, but not by both in competition. Faced with this choice, Stimson backed down.

On September 23, the U.S. government withdrew its strenuous insistence on an American adviser.[78] The State Department now stood between the Scylla and Charybdis of Firestone and the League of Nations. Once the department had withdrawn its insistence on an American adviser, Firestone pounced, and after "the talk was over and the smoke had cleared away, the Secretary went a long way toward meeting the Firestone wishes."[79] Stimson's feeble compromise was to tell the British and the French that the State Department would not force the American company to abandon its insistence on an American adviser, though the department itself would not insist. Battered from all sides, Stimson asked the British to ponder "whether, if the situation was reversed, [they] would not find great difficulty in putting pressure on a British corporation that was the only real influence for civilization in an ill-governed tropical community to modify its contracts and advance yet further money in support of a plan until they were fully satisfied that their interests would be adequately protected."[80]

The tone in the League already inclined toward suspicion of any such argument. The Brunot commission noted that the Firestone Company's rubber contract was "very favorable to the lessee." It observed that at the end of five years, the Liberian government would probably receive $40,320 from the rubber export tax and rent, "an amount which is not sufficient even to pay the officials responsible for the service of the loan."[81] To the commissioners, the financial arrangements made by Firestone appeared extremely burdensome. They reported that only the first installment of a five million dollar loan was put at the Liberian Government's disposal. Furthermore, "The second installment, which, including a balance of 300,000 dollars due on the first installment, was to amount to about 2,800,000 dollars, was, under the terms of the loan agreement, only to be paid out when the Customs revenue rose to almost double the present figures."[82] Naturally, such a level could only be reached after Liberia's economic recovery. The result was a vicious circle with no escape route except the modification of the loan terms, in agreement with the Finance Corporation of America.[83] The Brunot commission urged the negotiation of a new agreement between the Liberian government and the rubber company providing for a moratorium on repayment of the 1927 loan, so that the savings could be applied to Liberia's rehabilitation.[84]

Although the Christy-Johnson commission had cleared the Firestone Company of direct connivance in Liberian forced labor, Johnson reported that Christy saw the reason for Liberia's problems as "principally Firestone."[85] Suspicions concerning the company's role lingered after the submission of the 1930 report. Charles Brunot, head of the second commission, tended to be suspicious of business; in 1924, forestry concerns caused his recall as governor of the Ivory Coast because of his objection to forced recruitment.[86] At a session of the League of Nation's Liberia Committee, Ligthart, the Dutch financial expert, expressed the view that the Liberian concession to Firestone was "unfortunate." Because of the country's low population density, "all the labor employed by the plantation represented a dead loss to native growers who had need of it."[87] It was obviously better "for the normal development of Liberia, for the Firestone Company to leave the country, but that was impossible as the contract with that company had been concluded for a period of 99 years." Ultimately, the Brunot commission decided the large concessionaire and small native cultivation to be compatible if Firestone constructed model villages surrounded by cultivable land. And it expressed the view that "dancing and the cinema attract the African negro even more than high wages."[88]

The Liberia Committee's second report to the league council, in March of 1932, said that "in the opinion of certain members of the Committee, the coexistence in Liberia of a weak State and a powerful undertaking gives rise to disadvantages."[89] Those members considered it "indispensable that the rate of development of the plantations . . . be adapted to the economic and social conditions of Liberia" and that the burden of the loan agreement of 1926 be reduced. Salvador de Madariaga questioned not only the Firestone Company's interest in Liberia, but also the initial impetus for international diplomatic concern. The Christy-Johnson report "had obviously been prepared by men of undoubted honesty and good will, but it showed a lack of perspective, and, for that reason, was to some extent wanting in objectivity."[90] Looking at the present situation, de Madariaga acerbically questioned the good of obtaining money for Liberia if the Firestone Company was already having a deleterious effect on the population.[91]

At its sitting in May of 1932, the League council adopted a report asking that if the Liberians accepted the principle of the Liberia Committee's plan, negotiations on its adoption should take place in August. The result of these deliberations could then be confirmed at the council's September session. Since success hinged on modification of the Firestone Company's agreement with Liberia, in August the British embassy in Washington urged the State Department to pressure the company to send representatives to the September meeting.

J. P. Moffat confided in his diary, "I did not tell him [D. B. Osborne of the British embassy] that we were urging the Firestones not to send representatives, but did indicate that his request would be pretty difficult in view of the generally unsatisfactory nature of the report and Liberian acceptance."[92] In October, the State Department, following assurances from Geneva on Liberia's full acceptance and an adequate delegation of authority, endorsed the League of Nations plan and sent it on to Firestone.[93] But the company maintained its position of intransigence, and Moffat concluded that "for the sake of the record at least we shall have to send a fairly stiff letter to Firestone and then make clear to [Firestone] by telephone that what we are interested in is less the outcome of the negotiations than that such negotiations should be held."[94]

Soon afterward, acting secretary of state William Castle warned Harvey Firestone that his refusal to enter into direct negotiations brought on "a responsibility to public opinion both in [the United States] and abroad which the American Government [was] not prepared to assume on [his] behalf.[95] Firestone arrived the following day "in all his wrath" to demand that the department stand behind his refusal to negotiate. He was told that appearances had to be preserved. It was finally agreed that if the State Department "could so arrange that the negotiations could not take place until after the elections [i.e., the American presidential elections of 1932], he [Firestone] would inform the League of his willingness to cooperate."[96] Firestone apparently hoped that once the Hoover administration was assured of four more years in office, it would have greater freedom of action.

The State Department and the company then collaborated in Firestone's bid for time. The department told the League of Nations that a company representative could not sail before around November 1, and Harvey Firestone announced to the League that he was sending a representative to Liberia to collect direct information before beginning talks in Geneva.[97] November 1 came and passed, and still Firestone had not sent his representative. Only on November 13 did he announce to the

State Department that his emissary was departing and would arrive in Liberia on December 11.

Just before the Firestone representative arrived in Monrovia, the Liberian legislature took an action that further complicated the already embroiled relations between the company and the Black Republic. On December 17, 1932, the Liberian legislature passed a joint resolution that suspended all payments on the Firestone loan until governmental intake reached $700,000 per year. It also reduced the number of personnel working for the receivership and lowered the salaries of the remaining officials.[98] The action was a gamble, but Barclay surmised that he had accurately assessed the forces ranged against him.

Reaction in Black and White

As a Liberian diplomat said later, many in Liberia felt that Barclay "knew 'enough book' to outwit the white man." The triangular struggle between Monrovia, Washington, and Geneva "was a war of 'brains' being fought in a very subtle manner, because the world would decry any invasion by military force since Liberia was such a small and weak nation." Because the contest "continued in the strategy of words, everyone, even the smallest child, had the confidence that Liberia would win with the type of leadership she had."[99] Liberia appealed to the race. The NAACP was chief among those organizations that came to support the cause of Liberian independence as a symbol of black rule. As early as March of 1931, the organization showed interest in the findings of the Christy-Johnson commission.[100] But its concern for Liberia really began in earnest in early 1932.[101] In an effort to prod the State Department into a more conciliatory attitude toward the Barclay regime, the association early on attempted to enlist the aid of Charles S. Johnson as the black most intimately involved with the details of Liberian labor conditions. Johnson had already corresponded with Du Bois and others, whom he felt had not understood the import of the commission's condemnation of Liberian conditions.[102] The sociologist refused to make a public statement. "My assumption," he wrote, "whether or not completely founded in fact, has been that my services were originally sought primarily as an investigator and social student, and there is nothing more than consistency in my insistence that it not be made by me a matter of racial protest."[103] Another Fisk University sociologist, E. Franklin Frazier, thought Johnson could be involved in a public discussion of the Liberian matter by asking the State Department why he was not being consulted. Frazier reasoned, "It may be that this course of strategy will reveal any recommendations that Johnson might have made to the State Department which have not been made public."[104] The NAACP followed this course and was icily informed by the State Department that the sociologist was not being consulted at the present time but that, if he wanted to give the department his views, they would gladly receive them.[105] Privately Johnson asked Walter White if the Liberia Committee might work better if at least one black person sat on it. In keeping with the proposal for a just American adviser, White of the NAACP wrote to Liberian secretary of state Grimes, opposing the selection of a European (White suspected it would be a Belgian) and suggesting that a competent American be chosen.[106] Grimes rejected the idea of an American adviser, however well disposed, because he believed any American would ultimately reflect the position of the American State Department.[107] Nevertheless, the idea persisted, and in June of 1933, White cabled Grimes that Raymond Buell would be an ideal and impartial appointee.[108]

The NAACP was not alone in its combat with the State Department and the Firestone Company. Indeed, it sometimes played junior partner to the Women's International League for Peace and Freedom (WILPF), an anti-imperialist and internationalist organization. With Jane Addams as one of its leading spirits, the organization had long sought to bring white and black women together on the issue of peace and international cooperation.[109] At times, the WILP appeared less a lobbying group than a pressure group; it often sought to embarrass rather than cajole — a fact sometimes noted with displeasure by its black allies. The women of the WILP were often dismissed as a group of shrill hysterics, but no one could entirely deny their voice. Given its contacts in liberal circles with political access, any official hopes of excluding the women's group altogether were illusory. The WILP's interest in Liberia represented a kind of nonideological, liberal anti-imperialism, with all of the pitfalls such a stance entailed. Some members could sympathize with the plight of the indigenes in the Liberian hinterland, while others lobbied Washington not to intervene on their behalf. In its contest with the State Department, the WILPF constituted a feminist organization entering a bastion of WASP male privilege. In Washington, a provocative alliance of white women and black men confronted the racism and sexism embedded in the corridors of power. Given the times and its perceptions, the collaboration was remarkable; its subtlety contradicted race and gender hierarchies. Those individuals who planned strategy together would have been hard put to find a public place in which they could eat a meal together. At the same time, the somewhat genteel backgrounds of their white and black members united the organizations in a vague class alliance. Neither the NAACP nor the WILPF were mass organizations in the 1930s. And they made little effort to be.

Even before her association actively jumped into the Liberian fray, a WILPF officer, Emily Balch, expressed unhappiness about Firestone's loan; the terms of the plantation agreement were "perfectly inconceivable in their disregard for the most elementary protection of the negro population."[110] Balch discussed her views with Raymond Buell, Walter White, W. E. B. Du Bois, and Roger Baldwin of the American Civil Liberties Union. Direct involvement with the Liberian situation came about when Liberian secretary of state Grimes made contact with a representative of the WILPF in Geneva.[111] The woman, Anna M. Graves, was the daughter of a wealthy Southern family and had long been involved in anti-imperialist activities. She had taught in the Soviet Union in the 1920s, but eccentrically floated above all ideologies.[112] Grimes thought Graves an excellent asset to the Liberian cause; he credited her with persuading de Madariaga, to make a defense of Liberia in the League of Nations.[113] In July of 1932, the Liberian secretary of state wrote to Graves that the American government's fear of the black vote would restrain it from embarking on a Haiti-like adventure.[114]

By the fall of 1932, the WILP was in touch with the NAACP and Dorothy Detzer, the executive director of its American section, was radiogramming from Switzerland, "Negro protests against American plan needed."[115] White and Du Bois then telegraphed the secretary of state, warning him against a "destructive occupation" like the one in Haiti.[116] The two also stated, incorrectly, that the League of Nations would never accept American objections to its reform plans. The NAACP mailed copies of its telegram to Edwin Barclay, L. A. Grimes, and the *Journal de Genève*. The organization also included copies of a cable sent to the head of the Liberia Committee, Lord Cecil. An accompanying letter to Barclay noted, "The views expressed . . . represent the measured opinion of Negro Americans and of a considerable number of liberal white Americans."[117] In a separate communication, White sent Barclay the NAACP report on slavelike conditions on the federally funded Mississippi Flood Control Project. Barclay's representative in Geneva, Grimes, wrote to White, thanking him for the NAACP's interest "in the fate of Liberians, your own kith and kin, separated by thousands of miles across the sea."[118] During the fall election campaign of 1932, Du Bois urged blacks to vote for Roosevelt. Hoover could be faulted for "his attitude toward the 'Lily-White' movement in the South, and his attitude towards Liberia."[119]

The black church also weighed in. In March of 1932, Dr. J. E. East, executive secretary of the Foreign Mission Board of the National Baptist Convention and a former missionary, visited the State Department along with a colleague and stated that black Americans would oppose any plan of assistance unless its administrators were black. The black population in America would view the placement of whites in such positions as evidence that Liberia had been surrendered to white rule. Any such possibility would lead black citizens to call for American intervention to control the situation (with the presumed participation of black Americans).[120]

In September, Reverend W. H. Jernagin, pastor of the Mount Carmel Baptist Church in Washington, D.C., and three other black pastors delivered a letter to the State Department expressing grave concern for Liberia's sovereignty and indicating that the destruction of Liberian independence would constitute a great blow to black missionary enterprise in Africa, since most European powers restricted African American missionary activity. The State Department was urged to aid Liberia in carrying out its own program of reforms. Jernagin stressed black opposition to a white chief adviser and emphasized a strong desire that Liberia remain black-ruled.[121] On September 9, secretary of state Stimson wrote to E. H. Coit, chairman of the Foreign Missionary Board of the African Methodist Episcopal Church, disagreeing with the clergyman's assertion that Liberia had cooperated in reforming itself.[122]

If Barclay had his ties to Pan-Africanists and anti-imperialists, Firestone also had his network of boosters and allies. Many white missionary and educational organizations favored a firm American presence in Liberia and supported the Firestone family's version of the crisis. Harvey Firestone Jr. was a member of the Advisory Committee on Education in Liberia, and the Firestone Company contributed to various philanthropic and religious groups.[123] Opinion in many philanthropic quarters was that the Firestone investment was a godsend for Liberia. Thomas Jesse Jones, for example, educational adviser to the Phelps-Stokes Fund, believed strongly in the desirability of that investment.[124] During the crisis of Liberian independence, Jones tended to urge strong American initiatives, at the same time remaining aware that such a stance might jeopardize his position with the existing Liberian regime. In August of 1931, for instance, Jones wrote that in light of the division of opinion among groups active in Liberia, "the policy of the Advisory Committee on Education in Liberia and other organizations concerned in the welfare of the Republic seem[s] to require cooperative relationships with President Barclay, including as much friendly pressure as possible upon him so that he may request and encourage international participation in Liberian affairs."[125] In August of 1932, Dr. Robert Patton of the Episcopal Foreign Mission Association and Henry West of the American Colonization Association visited the State Department. West, described as a "hard-boiled newspaper man of some sixty years of age . . . [with] the hobby of African missions," was about to go off on an inspection tour of Liberia to determine what financial and other policies the missionary boards should maintain.[126] After his return, he remained one of Firestone's most vociferous champions.

Hoover's Last Days

Between the election of Franklin D. Roosevelt in November of 1932 and his inauguration in March of 1933, the Firestones redoubled their lobbying efforts. Harvey Firestone believed that Barclay was relying on the League of Nations and Great Britain to defy him. The rubber tycoon's "idée fixe [was] that all the resources of Great Britain, both Governmental and business, are directed toward displacing [his] interests in Liberia and toward doing so under the guise of international action."[127] Stimson thought the charge "ridiculous," but President Hoover took it seriously. The secretary observed that "the President himself had a fight against the British rubber interests some years ago when he was Secretary of Commerce and consequently he is rather inclined to believe one hundred percent Firestone's views."[128] Hoover's attitude had had a long genesis: "Though officially no more than Secretary of Commerce from 1921 to 1928, Hoover demanded, and received, a quasi-official veto over foreign policy as a condition of entering the cabinet. Armed with this authority, he exercised great influence on foreign affairs." Like Calvin Coolidge, in whose administration he had served, he believed that the business of America was business. Modern corporations had replaced banks as centers of capital. Based on this assumption, Hoover developed two themes: "First, all economic cooperation would center on the corporation; and second, the government, representing the populace at large, would cooperate with the corporation to insure national prosperity and democratic procedure." Abroad, the government should seek and encourage investment in vital raw materials.[129]

During a conference at the State Department in January of 1933, Firestone and his son, Harvey Firestone Jr., maintained that there existed "a vast British conspiracy to do away with [their] rubber plantations in Liberia.[130] Reading from pilfered Liberian cabinet meeting minutes, the elder Firestone charged Lord Cecil with being a party to the machinations. Stimson listened but dismissed Firestone's request for more than "a blanket promise of general support."[131] In January of 1933, the

United States told Lord Cecil that Liberia's actions amounted "in effect to the confiscation of moneys due to an American corporation and to destruction of the security on which funds were advanced."[132] Stimson suggested that the American "path would be much easier" if the League of Nations would tell the Liberians that it did not support the Liberian moratorium. Cecil conferred with the Foreign Office, which noted "the Americans are making heavy weather over what they profess to regard as a British commercial intrigue to oust Firestone." The Foreign Office agreed that the Liberia Committee could not put pressure on the Liberians "on the strength of a one-sided account of what has happened."[133] The head of the Liberia Committee informed the United States government of this position and strongly condemned the Firestone Company's previous dilatoriness in negotiation. Cecil told Stimson "that several members of the Committee have arrived at the conclusion that the object of the Firestone Company was, by insisting on the rigid execution of what was, after all, a very onerous agreement, to drive the Liberian Government into such straits that they would be at the mercy of the corporation."[134]

Stimson, caught in the middle again, reexamined the history of Firestone's relations with the League of Nations and heatedly told a company representative that the firm had been deliberately uncooperative. Only if the rubber company collaborated with the League would the State Department aid it around the present impasse.[135] Harvey Firestone gave way a little. He consented to deal with the league if the State Department could bring about a lifting of Liberia's moratorium and agreed to acknowledge a de facto moratorium on loan payments during direct negotiations. For its part, the Liberia Committee sent Barclay a cable asking for, but not strenuously demanding, a suspension of the moratorium resolution of December 17.[136]

In the waning days of the Hoover administration, the Liberian government remained recalcitrant while the League of Nations continued its path of caution. Harvey Firestone attempted to brush aside these impediments by demanding an armed invasion. Between January 24 and February 14, the Firestones or their lawyers visited the State Department at least six times to demand that a cruiser be sent to Monrovia. On January 21, 1933, the Liberians had added insult to injury (in the Firestone view) by demanding the resignations of all the officers employed by the receivership. The Liberians also dismissed the American supervisor of internal revenue and stopped depositing customs revenues in the official depository.

In response, a Firestone lawyer, Everett Sanders (also chairman of the Republican National Committee), demanded protection of American investment, putting considerable pressure on the outgoing administration. As a result, President Hoover reportedly informed his secretary of state "that if necessary he would go to extreme lengths to protect the rubber plantations, even to sending a naval force.[137] State Department officials J. P. Moffat and William Castle drafted a note protesting the dismissal of the fiscal officers and related actions. Later they saw Stimson, whose "final directions were to remember to be as strong as we could, but not to commit us to a situation where a naval ship would be necessary without letting him know."[138] Two days later Moffat reported that "the pressure from the Firestones is getting daily greater and they are more and more unmasking their designs to have this administration, during its forty days left, send a gunboat to Monrovia."[139] But a few days later, the rubber manufacturer's pressure apparently backfired. The secretary of state balked when Everett Sanders came to plead for a ship; the State Department would not intervene militarily. Moffat noted, "Mr. Sanders left rather crestfallen and we are left wondering anew why the Firestones should employ the Chairman of the Republican National Committee five weeks before the Democrats come in."[140]

Firestone also called in his philanthropic allies. In January of 1933, Henry West of the American Colonization Society visited again and stated that he entirely supported the State Department's policy in Liberia. Indeed, West was probably more "pro-American" than the department. He wrote a pamphlet in which he characterized the Firestone Company as a boon to the Black Republic and maintained that "an American pilot [chief adviser], insisted upon by the Department of State, could steer Liberia into a harbor of prosperity and security"[141] The British Foreign Office took notice of the pamphlet and its author to conclude that "the pamphlet is based on a mass of lies and might have been written by Mr. Firestone himself, so strong is its pro-Firestone bias."[142] Ellis Briggs of the State Department met with the Advisory Committee on Education in Liberia and received a similar impression. "It was an amusing experience . . . since the three representatives use almost word for word, gesture for gesture, the statements and motions executed interminably by the Firestones during recent interviews with the Secretary and with us at the Department."[143] Indeed, throughout the Liberian crisis, the Advisory Committee on Education listened to Harvey Firestone's version of his troubles. The Phelps-Stokes Fund's archives contain a memorandum on the situation that clearly mirrors Firestone's obsessions. "As a solution to the Liberian crisis," the memorandum, drafted during the Hoover administration's final days, "recommended that an agent of the United States Government proceed promptly to Monrovia to deal with the increasing serious conditions in

Liberia and that he be sent on an American navy vessel to ensure his timely arrival."[144] The next month J. P. Moffat had to write "a letter to the missionaries who are asking for more aggressive action toward Liberia [,] including a warship at Monrovia."[145]

In early February, the Harvey Firestones, Sr. and Jr., descended on the State Department and once again asked for direct intervention in Liberia. They were less insistent than usual. "The reason for their calm," Moffat said, "I think, may be summed up in one sentence, that they were convinced that events were forcing us around to their point of view and would, in a short while, force us to send a cruiser even though we might not agree with them as to the advisability of doing it at once."[146] But the State Department wished to avoid a drift in that direction. Stimson took some satisfaction in noting that the president "took the position that we had to make as good as possible paper record for [the Firestones], so that the coming administration would find it difficult to abandon good American interests out there; but that we should be very careful about sending a ship over." Hoover thought that "the new [Roosevelt] administration would like nothing better than to reverse that kind of action on our part."[147]

In the prevailing deadlock of conflicting motives and interests, the League of Nations took a small step away from an impasse when on February 7, 1933, it insisted that Liberia withdraw its repudiationist legislation. Soon after Stimson learned of this development, the Firestones entered his office with their old demands. They dismissed the league's recent action and suggested as an excuse for sending a battleship to ostensibly send out a mediator. Firestone Sr. reportedly maintained, "the only way in which Liberia could be convinced that America was prepared to stand up for its rights was to make a show of force and that this would give sufficient aid and comfort to Barclay's enemies, who were basically pro-American to take matters into their own hands."[148] Stimson objected on several grounds: (1) the United States was collaborating with the League; (2) Liberia was not the only country to repudiate her contractual obligations; (3) American lives were certainly not at their greatest peril in Liberia; (4) "the sending of a warship to another continent would be almost certainly open to misinterpretation, and would create political repercussions not only in world public opinion, but more immediately among the blacks and other elements in [the United States]"; (5) the Roosevelt administration would be coming in twenty-five days.[149]

Harvey Firestone, however, remained adamant in his insistence on American intervention. Not content with the State Department's reactions, he went over the agency's head and visited President Hoover.

Hoover, "remembering," according to J. P. Moffat, "that they [the Firestones] were among the largest Republican contributors and also that he personally played a large part in the initiation of their Liberian investment, tries in every way to please them and I rather gather the impression that he encourages them to put pressure on the Secretary while officially upholding the Secretary's hands.[150] The next time the two Firestones visited the State Department, the secretary refused to see them.

In its final days, the Hoover administration decided to send a commissioner to Liberia. The judge advocate of the United States Army, General Blanton Winship, a southern military gentleman, was dispatched in February of 1933, accompanied by Ellis Briggs of the State Department. The mission hoped to remove the deadlock created by Liberia's repudiationist legislation.[151] Winship had to persuade the Firestone Company to moderate its position; at the same time he had to encourage Barclay to recognize the legitimacy of the Firestone agreements. While they were in London in March of 1933, the British foreign secretary bluntly told the Americans that "it was, in actual fact, impossible to expect an administration which was budgeting for a revenue of under 500,000 dollars, to devote some 200,000 dollars to the service of the Firestone loan."[152]

The British thought the proposals put forward by the Firestone Company's representative in Liberia "monstrous." One official complained that "not even the Liberian Govt. could be expected to accept them [i.e., Firestone's proposals], for their acceptance would mean that in all matters financial, neither Parliament nor the Govt. would have a say."[153] As the clock ran out, Firestone seemed desperate. Indeed, Herbert Hoover, one of the least beloved American presidents, was on his way out and, in the process, the company lost its chief protector. The rubber giant and the Black Republic remained poised for the next stage of their battle before the bar of public opinion.

6 A New Deal for Liberia

If the American Negro could bring such a pressure upon things
politically in America, then the President would be in a quandary and
ultimately he would have to show his hand. We regard Mr. Roosevelt as a
friend, and would not like to embarrass him, but it is our duty to bring
to the attention of our race situations as they do arise and the
difficulties that they have to overcome.

— Marcus Garvey

"The Shroud of Color" is no longer the agonizing
spiritual cry of a thwarted intellectual with a Phi Beta Kappa key; it is
now the agonizing body cry of thousands of half starved sharecroppers
in the peonage belt. And to sum up facetiously, the deep jungle notes
of Duke Ellington's Mood Indigo in the 1920's have changed in the
1930's to the sharp shrill blasts of Louis Armstrong's trumpet.

— Randolph Edmonds

Franklin Delano Roosevelt became the thirty-second president of the
United States in March of 1933. The Hoover administration had begun
to pull back from gunboat diplomacy and military interventions. The
Roosevelt administration quickened the rhythm and the rhetoric. In
December of 1933 at the Seventh Pan-American Conference in Monte-
video the United States agreed to a convention that stated that "No state
has the right to intervene in the internal or external affairs of another."[1]
In the same month the new president made his position clear: "The
maintenance of constitutional government in other nations is not a
sacred obligation devolving upon the United States alone . . . the definite policy of the United States from now on is one opposed to armed

intervention."[2] In the case of Liberia, a reversal of policy was not immediately obvious, however. Roosevelt's accession brought no immediate solution to the Liberian crisis. In August, Raymond Buell attacked American policy in the *New Republic*: "Under the previous administration, one could not have expected the State Department to be firm with Mr. Firestone, because it was Mr. Hoover who joined with Mr. Firestone in a campaign against the British rubber 'monopoly,' and it was Mr. Firestone who contributed $20,396.74 to Mr. Hoover's 1932 campaign."[3] But looking at current policy, the political scientist had to conclude that "the only possible explanation is that pressed with more immediate duties, the political heads of the new administration have had no time for Liberia and have entrusted this question entirely to subordinate permanent officials who apparently have no understanding or sympathy with the New Deal."[4] Mauritz Hallgren had protested in the *Nation* that "Liberia, having already been reduced to helplessness through the financial dictatorship of the Firestone rubber interests, is now, with the aid of the League of Nations and consent of the American State Department about to be placed in complete servitude." He further argued that Liberia's government had lost its financial independence through the 1926 loan agreement, "which the State Department compelled it to accept against its will." Soon the Black Republic was "to be stripped of its administrative independence and cultural autonomy as well."[5]

The truth of the matter is probably that during his "First Hundred Days," FDR had far more on his plate than the matter of an impecunious tropical dependency well outside the American sphere of interest. In the spring of 1933, after five weeks of negotiations in Monrovia, Blanton Winship and Ellis Briggs did obtain certain modifications to the 1926 loan agreement. Winship reported this to the League of Nations, and in June he conducted further negotiations in Geneva and London. The Firestone Company accepted a reduction in the interest rate from 7 to 5 percent and agreed that the current expenses of government and the cost of the plan of assistance would have priority over the cost of servicing the Firestone loan. The Finance Corporation of America also agreed not to collect interest when Liberia's annual income remained below $500,000 a year. It promised to guarantee the salaries of the foreign advisers when these could not be met out of current revenues and agreed to make a $150,000 loan as initial capital.[6] These concessions would result in estimated annual savings to the Liberian government of about $62,000.[7] The Firestone Company's acceptance of modifications in its financial arrangements, however, was contingent on the strengthening of the league's plan of assistance. The Liberia Committee accepted eight out of twelve Firestone-proposed changes in the plan, demanded as "sufficient guarantees." Under these changes, the chief adviser's authority over the provincial commissioners would be strengthened, and a two-thirds majority rather than a unanimous vote of the League council would determine decisions on the plan's application.

Harvey Firestone now seemed to be moving swiftly toward the attainment of one of his major objectives, an American adviser; the State Department continued tacitly to support his stand while remaining avowedly neutral on the nationality question.[8] In early June, Lord Cecil spoke with General Winship. The general disapproved of too much American control, but he thought that the appointment of an American could be made under League auspices.[9] On June 23, 1933, J. P. Moffat optimistically reported, "The news from Liberia looks distinctly more hopeful with Winship actually succeeding in moderating somewhat Cecil's position."[10] "It looks now," he said, "as though a compromise would be made whereby an American should be selected as Chief Adviser, but responsible to and removable by the League." Cecil, the chairman of the Liberia Committee, spoke directly with Harvey Firestone Jr. on the subject and stressed the need for truly international action in the Liberian situation. The League of Nations diplomat reported, "Firestone seemed to recognize the force of this, and undertook that if the nationality of the Chief Adviser was American, he would consider whether it might not be possible to arrange that the Financial Adviser and the Military Commander should belong to other nations."[11]

A sticking point remained: Liberian objection. Barclay's regime remained adamantly opposed to an American adviser.[12] The Liberians did not want an American adviser, nor did they want strengthened league supervision over their internal affairs. Again the focus of negotiation shifted back to Monrovia. General Winship and Melville Mackenzie, the British representative on the Brunot commission, were dispatched to persuade Barclay that the plan devised was the best Liberia could hope for under the circumstances. Mackenzie had hopes of swaying Barclay to accept an American chief adviser on the condition that the president of the United States would nominate a non-American financial adviser.[13] The British Foreign Office also hoped to sweeten the pill for the Liberians by suggesting that Liberian acceptance of the League of Nations plan would result in official British recognition of the Barclay regime.[14] Lord Cecil, after some agonizing, reconciled himself to the idea of an American chief adviser, although he hoped to leave the question of the nationality of the adviser open in the Liberia Committee's report to the League council.[15]

Given its racial subtext, what was the African American response to the Liberian crisis? It differed considerably from both the response to Garvey's Liberian emigration program of the twenties and its reaction to the Italian invasion of Ethiopia in 1935. The UNIA sought and received large-scale black involvement in a movement of diasporic redemption. The Ethiopian crisis elicited a widespread black response to a broader international issue. The Liberian crisis, however, involved neither mass black involvement in a black movement nor mass black involvement in an international issue. The mass of Depression-weary African Americans were not perfervid in their defense of Liberian sovereignty. Few public demonstrations occurred, and the organization of ad hoc support groups remained a rarity. However, the organizational scope of the African American response to and defense of Liberian sovereignty was, paradoxically, much broader than that of Garvey's UNIA. Highly visible organizations like the NAACP made repeated and frequently successful attempts to influence foreign policy decisions. In this the tendency of some officials to view the Liberian crisis as a "black scandal" of peculiar concern to American blacks aided them.

After the U.S. election, a lull in African American activity on behalf of Liberia pervaded. Certainly the NAACP had other issues at hand. Some in the WILP remained focused on saving the Monrovia regime, however. After the League of Nation's end-of-year meetings, Dorothy Detzer and Anna Graves returned to the United States. In late January 1933, they both spoke to officials at the State Department. J. P. Moffat complained that Graves was "a combative old maid, extremely well versed in certain phases of the problem and well documented." He felt that "although her facts were pretty correct, she drew one wrong inference after another, steadily impugned the motives of the American Government and the Firestones and accepted as gospel truth everything that had been told her by Cecil, Madariaga, Grimes [and] Ligthart."[16]

After the interview, Graves then embarked on a tour of Southern black colleges. On February 3, she sent the NAACP a long and rather detailed explication of the Liberian situation, along with the request that the organization publish as much of it as possible. William Pickens of the NAACP urged caution; the organization might give an airing to Graves's views, but it could "not afford to *follow*" Graves. The white woman was a "damned untactful fool."[17] In June of 1933, Graves wrote Walter White from Geneva, urging immediate action on behalf of Liberia. The next month, she cabled to urge the NAACP to send a representative to Geneva while General Winship and the Firestone representatives were there.[18] In August, she again wrote to White, complaining that the NAACP had not answered her letters. "If," Graves wrote, "Liberia disheartened gives in and becomes a peon state — gives in because she had so little moral support — practically none, until this last minute from American Negroes — I think her fate will be partly the fault of the American Negroes' lukewarmness from December 1930 until July 1933."[19]

This prodding followed on the heels of Monrovia's own urgings. A few days earlier, secretary of state Grimes had predicted to Graves that

> if . . . the moral sentiment in the United States can be aroused, and the Negroes can be aroused from their apathy no doubt the Government [of the United States] can be induced to modify or, at least, postpone taking any action against us, and we should, even in the event of a postponement, work towards such conditions as to make a return to any plans that presently have been formed, impracticable.[20]

The WILPF's insistent prodding of the NAACP reflected its international focus and the strategies of the Barclay regime. An American civil rights organization could hardly have the same priorities. Yet the NAACP was not as somnolent as Graves maintained. When, in early June, Graves cabled her organization's Washington office to urge mobilization of black opinion, she received a response. Graves maintained that the Liberians did not want an American general adviser, and she wanted to pressure Washington into accepting the same position.[21] Dorothy Detzer relayed this message to Walter White, who, failing to reach Du Bois, cabled General Winship and Lord Cecil informing them that the "National Association for Advancement Colored People in name its 327 branches Negro and white membership of 100,000, vigorously urges upholding Liberian desire General Adviser shall not be nationality concessionaire."[22] White also sent a telegram to President Roosevelt, urging that his administration issue a statement "repudiating impression that American Government is upholding Firestone interests in Liberia."[23] In an effort to mobilize African American opinion, he sent copies of this communication to the leaders of the major black organizations. To insure coverage, White used William Stone, head of the Washington office of the Foreign Policy Association, to spread notice of the NAACP's actions on the Liberian front. Stone, in turn, was able to get Ludwell Denny of the Scripps-Howard papers to write a sympathetic editorial.[24] Denny believed that the chief adviser should be neither British nor French nor American. The following month, Du Bois weighed in with an article in *Foreign Affairs*, based, in part, on Anna Graves's memorandum. Unlike Denny, Du Bois held the idea of any foreign overseer for Liberia in suspicious regard. After all, the republic's chief fault was "to be black and poor in a rich, white world."[25] Sidney De La Rue, receiver of customs for Liberia during the King years and now receiver in Haiti, was stung by the article's accusation that under his administration, $156,000 had been squandered due to mismanagement. In a long exculpatory letter to Du Bois, the white official maintained that he had only worked for the good of Liberia and had not hoodwinked it in any way. Indeed, he maintained that "from the time the loan was consummated and the money released so purchases could be made, until the time I gave up my work, was less than six months."[26]

By the summer of 1933, when the League of Nations was debating the Liberia issue in London and Geneva, the battle lines on the Liberian issue had been drawn in the United States. The U.S. undersecretary of state noted that the State Department had the support of George Schuyler and "the approval of the more conservative negro elements, such as Dr. Moulton [Moton], President of Tuskegee, and several other prominent negroes such as Dr. Johnson of Fisk University, and Mr. [Lester] Walton."[27] The government was drawing criticism from a group of "aggressive negroes" and white anti-imperialists. Among the blacks were W. E. B. Du Bois of the National Association for the Advancement of Colored People, and Carl Murphy, the editor of the *Baltimore Afro-American*. Among the white anti-imperialists were the Foreign Policy Association and the Women's International League for Peace and Freedom. The WILPF saw itself as the vanguard of the anti-imperialist organizations. Indeed, it took on the mantle of *mater familias* within the diverse coalition opposed to intervention in Liberia.

On June 6, Detzer visited the State Department again and spoke with undersecretary (then acting secretary) William Phillips, who supposedly told her he would take no action on the chief advisership until, in her words, "he had given an opportunity to some of us who are opposing an American in that place, to discuss the matter after Winship returns."[28] On the same day, the Foreign Policy Association's William Stone lobbied J. P. Moffat as well. A month later, Detzer informed Graves that she "had hammered hard at Walter White to get a good colored delegation" to go with her for an interview with General Winship. White had turned to Du Bois, who was, unfortunately, unable to come up from Atlanta. Detzer bombarded the sextagenarian with telegrams, but to no avail. Eventually, she went to the meeting in the company of a white woman from Alabama. At the State Department, she forcefully denounced the League plan "because it represented a form of 'paternalism' which she felt would interfere with the free development of negro culture."[29]

Dorothy Detzer. Photo from Women's International League for Peace and Freedom.

Detzer gave Carl Murphy a report of her meeting with General Winship and asked that Murphy disseminate it, with the aim of creating "strong expressions of moral indignation."[30] After the meeting, the WILPF executive secretary also persuaded Ludwell Denny to write another Scripps-Howard editorial. Denny called Mordecai Johnson, president of Howard University, and stressed the need for African American support on the Liberian issue. Johnson contacted White and asked that the NAACP support Detzer and her group. The Washington-based university head was able to secure a meeting with William Phillips, the acting secretary of state.

On July 31, 1933, a group of prominent blacks and some members of the WILPF met Phillips at the State Department. The group included Mordecai Johnson, Du Bois, White, Detzer, Rayford Logan of the Association for the Study of Negro Life and History, Charles Wesley of Howard University's history department, and Emmett Scott, secretary of that university.[31] Also in attendance were Addie W. Hunton, chairperson of the WILPF's interracial commission, Archie Pinkett, secretary of the NAACP's Washington branch, and Addie W. Dickerson, president of the International Council of Women of the Darker Races. Mrs. Daniel Partridge, the white Alabamian, accompanied Detzer as a representative of the WILFP. Several days before the meeting, Wesley and Logan had drafted a statement on Liberia. They defended the Black Republic's repudiation of its debt and urged the creation of a supervisory commission that would be liberal in its approach and include a Liberian and an American black. They attacked a proposal that education in Liberia be completely turned over to missionary societies. The delegation maintained that African Americans would not be content until they had heard

Liberia's side of the controversy and said that the American black population stood solidly behind the maintenance of Liberian sovereignty.[32]

Undersecretary Phillips began the meeting with a brief outline of the United States's historical interest in Liberia, adding that as a great-nephew of Wendell Phillips, the nineteenth-century abolitionist, he took special interest in Liberia. Phillips indirectly blamed Liberia's present financial plight on the previous U.S. administration. While the United States supported legitimate interests in Liberia, he said, the Roosevelt administration would not sacrifice Liberia simply to appease American business.[33] Du Bois, acting as spokesman for the group, read his own prepared statement. The black elder statesman declared, "The darker world had become convinced that it is being used and exploited by Europe and America for the benefit and power and luxury of white folk and at the expense of poverty, and slavery for yellow, brown and black."[34] Du Bois warned that as greater numbers of blacks received university degrees, they were becoming more impatient than ever before with racism. Du Bois said blacks did not believe Washington wanted a new deal for black states and compared Haiti and Liberia. He asked that the League's plan of assistance not be rammed down the throats of the Liberians and urged that the proposed Liberian budget under the plan be amended to include funds for education. Du Bois also requested that the United States support the appointment of a chief adviser acceptable to Liberia, that no ultimatum be set on Liberia's acceptance of the plan, and that the United States officially recognize the Barclay regime.[35]

The selection of General Winship as American commissioner produced some sharp exchanges between Du Bois and Phillips and between Phillips, Johnson, and Detzer. Just before the delegation left, Du Bois suggested that it might have been better to send a black instead of a white Southerner. Phillips reportedly answered, "Yes, it might have been wiser."[36] But Rayford Logan reported that "when members of the delegation told him [Phillips] that Negroes are alarmed by Winship's present role in the negotiations because of his Southern antecedents, and attempted to point out how disastrous has been the policy of appointing Southern white men to similar posts — the lessons gained from Haiti and from the appointment of such men to command in colored regiments during the World War furnished glaring examples — the Acting Secretary remarked that 'we will not go into that.' "[37] Logan believed that although the delegation had not moved Phillips away from the appointment of an American chief adviser, there was at least hope that it had thwarted the selection of a Southerner. He felt that "to appoint to this post a man with the 'ideals' of the Southern gentleman of 1860, as Miss Dexter [*sic*] . . . so aptly described him, would bespeak either a crass ignorance or a determination to flout the earnest appeal of nearly fifteen million American and Liberian Negroes." After the delegation's visit, the State Department released to the press this account: "Mr. Phillips stated . . . that he would be glad to give careful consideration to the views of so large a group of friends of Liberia and that he would transmit them to Major General Blanton Winship, the present American representative on the League Committee, for his consideration and such suggestions to the Committee for alterations as might seem feasible."[38]

In reality, neither Phillips nor the members of the delegation left the interview entirely pleased with its outcome. Logan wrote that "the delegation derived little satisfaction from its audience. . . . In the last analysis, protection of American interests abroad is entrusted to American marines."[39] Detzer thought the conference might speed up processes already in motion; three days later she wrote to White, "I am told confidentially that they are worried inside the State Department about further publicity and agitation on this question of Liberia and are going to sign and seal the League plan as quickly as possible."[40] Inside the department, secretary of state Cordell Hull decided to seek the opinion of President Roosevelt on the Liberian matter. Moffat drew up the memorandum to Roosevelt, noting to himself, "There is no policy in the world that has not got its critics and personally I do not take the criticisms of either the radical negro groups, the pacifist groups or the professional anti-imperialists, such as Raymond Leslie Buell, too seriously."[41]

However dismissive Moffat might have been, these very groups and individuals continued in their activity and effectiveness. On the very day that the delegation met with Phillips, Buell wrote to Grimes, urging rejection of the League's plan. The political scientist advised that the chief adviser not be an American and that the loan moratorium should continue. Furthermore, Firestone should not participate in any new loan and its concession should be greatly reduced. He assured Grimes that the Roosevelt administration would not condone an invasion.[42] Publicly, Buell expressed his views in the August 16 issue of the *New Republic*. Privately, he asked Detzer to urge Grimes to reject the League of Nations plan without modifications. He cabled Graves in Geneva and told her to shore up Grimes's determination to refuse.

In early September of 1933, Walter White wrote to Buell, after the latter reported that the secretary of state was sticking to his previous position. "It was probably naive of me," White mused, "but I had hoped that the long interview we had with Phillips on July 31 might result in some change, however slight, on the part of the State Department."[43] Phillips himself reviewed the interview thusly: "The suggestions which I obtained from this conference are two in number: (1) The desirability of an allowance so that the state will not be deprived of a certain amount of education under the auspices of the state; (2) That if the Firestones could be induced to spread their loan over another group of bankers, the Department would be in a far stronger position in its efforts to see justice done in Liberia."[44] For his part, Phillips believed the United States had three alternatives: take control of Liberia, withdraw completely, or collaborate with the League of Nations. The undersecretary favored adoption of a League plan with a strong chief adviser, a slight readjustment downward of the Firestone contract, and the advance of new money by Firestone. "Perhaps I should also add," he wrote to Roosevelt, "that the Liberian plantation, which is from all accounts one of the best rubber producing units in existence, is our only major source of rubber independent of the Far East and hence a very important consideration in our national defense."[45]

The delegation's requests were not entirely in vain. The United States did push for more funds for education in the revised plan of assistance presented in the fall. Phillips also seriously considered ways of spreading the financing of the Firestone loan among various financial groups, thus lessening the rubber company's dominance. He discussed the matter with Winship, who suggested that the members of the delegation to Phillips might be sounded on their willingness to take on the loan through the purchase of Finance Corporation of America bonds.[46]

The critics of the State Department's Liberian policy had, as Detzer suspected, caused uneasiness in official circles. The August of 1933 saw Detzer in a flurry of activity; she strenuously pushed for the *New Republic* and the *Nation* to publish articles favorable to the Liberians. The lobbyist reminded Ernest Gruening and Oswald Garrison Villard of the *Nation* that they had been very active on the Haitian issue and could scarcely do less for Liberia. Moffat complained in his diary that he and his colleagues were "in a bit of a jam as the radical negro groups are accusing us of imperialism and have worried Hull by writing in the *New Republic* and *The Nation* that the permanent officials, the Department, without his knowledge and understanding, are continuing to destroy Liberia for the benefit of American vested interests."[47] Soon thereafter he reported that the critics were "continuing their attack on our Liberian policy . . . indicating that Mr. Hull is an honest man surrounded by the Machiavellian and sinister influences of 'the careers' who after all are nothing but tools of Wall Street and the vested interest and out of sympathy with the philosophy of the New Deal."[48]

In August of 1933, Winship and Mackenzie again set off for Liberia, and on August 25, they presented Barclay with a note containing the compromise plan intended to pull all of the parties into agreement. Barclay, however, continued to have reservations. In the face of this recalcitrance, Harvey Firestone agreed in September to countenance a non-American adviser if the League plan were accepted without modification. Winship, in Monrovia, was instructed "to see if in return for this concession, he could keep all the other powers firmly aligned against reopening negotiations."[49] But Liberia did not seem to be moving toward acceptance of the plan. Moffat of the State Department wrote of the "total bankruptcy" of the American policy vis-à-vis Liberia and felt that the United States was "now faced with the alternative of dropping Liberia or letting it fall of its own weight or probably be absorbed by England and France or else of modifying the League Plan virtually leaving the Firestones to one side."[50] The British consulate in Monrovia likewise viewed the prognosis as bleak and complained "that since the last return of Mr. Grimes from London and Geneva . . . the attitude of the Liberian Government has been decidedly unfriendly to all white residents and especially to this Legation."[51] This hostile attitude had "been accentuated by the failure of General Winship and Dr. Mackenzie to persuade the de facto President and his cabinet as to the advisability of accepting the last plan of assistance." The head of the British legation had recently been told "by Colonel Davis, the Aide de Camp to the President, that they feel that they have been 'let down by Lord Cecil.' I pointed out," he reminded them, "that in order to obtain concessions for Liberia, Lord Cecil was obliged to accept the condition demanded by the Finance Corporation."[52] But Barclay still had several major reservations to the League's plan, and they all revolved around the issue of Liberian sovereignty. After several years of haggling, the Liberia Committee was down to its last concessions to the Black Republic. In October of 1933, it adopted a report agreeing that the chief adviser should be neither a United States citizen nor a national of a state having territory contiguous to Liberia. It also agreed that the portion of the budget allotted for running the Liberian administration should be increased from $300,000 to $325,000, with the extra amount reserved for education. Monrovia was given until the next session of the League council to accept or reject the plan. Despite these concessions, Louis Grimes of Liberia protested that the arrangements arrived at in the autumn in Geneva differed from those agreed on in the summer in London.[53]

In the middle of October, continuing Liberian maneuvering to thrust aside the League jolted the U.S. State Department. The department received "a very disturbing telegram from Liberia indicating that the Liberians were preparing to reject the League Plan and then turn around and ask us to assume all adviserships."[54] When Winship and Briggs returned from Geneva in October, Moffat mused "whether or not to threaten Liberia into accepting the Plan."[55] "The advantages are obvious," he noted. "The disadvantages are that if we tell them that if they reject we will disinterest ourselves from them entirely, this may be taken as passive permission by the British and French to go in on their own." Winship and Briggs wanted to urge Barclay to accept the plan as a condition for continued American friendship; the State Department continued to hope that Monrovia would relent.[56] On November 19, the department issued a statement again reiterating its support for the League plan: "Should the present administration of Monrovia reject this opportunity, such action could only be construed as opposition to reforms the urgent desirability of which has been apparent for over three years, and as indifference to the welfare of the million and a half native people of Liberia."[57]

The Showdown

On January 12, 1934, the Liberian legislature accepted the plan of assistance subject to twelve major reservations diminishing the authority of the chief adviser and his foreign assistants. The Liberian reply came too late for the January meeting of the council, and the League then resolved to give Liberia until May to accept or reject the plan as presented in October. But the Liberian representative made it clear that his government would maintain its reservations. Harvey Firestone was very displeased. Moffat reported, "He is now hoping that the League will send an ultimatum threatening joint intervention on the ground that this is in accordance with President Roosevelt's policy."[58] Firestone, in fact, wanted the U.S. government to propose such action to the League. A few days later, Moffat telephoned Harvey Firestone Jr. and pointed out that the League of Nations was only empowered to impose sanctions and that mandates did not constitute joint affairs. A month later, Firestone Sr. appeared increasingly pessimistic about the future of his investment, fearing that the Liberians would next attack the plantation contract.[59] In his opinion, the only solution to the problem was armed intervention. In April, the Firestones had a conference with the new secretary of state, Cordell Hull, and came away thinking the new man favored strong action in Liberia.[60] On May 25, therefore, Harvey Firestone again asked for force to reinstate the fiscal officials.[61] But if external force was still not forthcoming, internal revolution might produce the same end. Factions opposed to Barclay grew more restive as the May deadline for Liberia's acceptance or rejection of the League plan approached. The American chargé wrote, "This growing pro-American faction is naturally looking to Firestone for support and this may prove a possible solution to the present impasse."[62] In February, the U.S. secretary of state met with a delegation of black missionaries concerning Liberia. Hull indicated his goodwill toward the Black Republic, but made evident his exasperation with the Barclay regime. This tact may have been designed to make the group think more positively of those elements inside Liberia inclined toward greater cooperation with the United States.[63] In early May of 1934, the State Department heard of a movement led by ex-presidents Howard and King to have the Liberian government accept the League plan with the request that the chief adviser be an American.[64] The black newspaperman Lester Walton (later to be American minister to Monrovia) wrote to Claude Barnett of the Associated Negro Press that Barclay was under great pressure and might resign rather than accept the League plan.[65] Ex-president Howard issued a public "warning," hinting that Barclay and his colleagues might best be advised to hand over the government to others.[66] The American chargé in Monrovia was instructed to tell the Liberians that the United States would not come to their aid in the event of a foreign invasion if the League plan were rejected. As a result

> They have for the first time become seriously worried and public opinion is running hard against the Administration. Arthur Barclay no longer wishes his nephew to remain President and the latter is apparently considering resignation. The petition requesting immediate acceptance of the Plan is being rapidly signed and should be presented on the 10th [of May]. Ex-President King has threatened Barclay that if he did not immediately accept the League Plan, he would fight and would organize to do so if necessary. . . . Ex-President Howard, the elder statesman of Liberian politics and former protector of Barclay, has now come out against him. I don't want to be unduly optimistic but it almost looks as though the ice jam has broken after all these months.[67]

In late May, after the Liberian rejection of the League plan, Harvey Firestone Sr. sought to use the rumors of an impending coup in Liberia to prompt the United States to forcible intervention. Harvey Firestone Jr. announced that enemies of the Barclay regime were ready to strike, but needed encouragement from the United States. Yet the State Department still did not favor force, and Moffat reminded the younger

Firestone that "to encourage a revolutionary body would be to incur a frightful responsibility in case it failed to work out."[68] Before the May showdown at the League, Liberian secretary of state Clarence Simpson took note of the U.S. State Department's hopes for an internal change in Liberia. "To my great disappointment," said Simpson, "I now discovered that the Americans, while increasing the official pressure on our Government in a last minute attempt to make us change our minds, were also seriously hoping that irresponsible elements claiming to be favorably inclined towards the 'Assistance' Plan would take over the Government as a result of what could only be a violent revolution." The secretary observed, "If anything, this revelation increased our determination to resist all pressure."[69]

The optimism of the State Department indeed proved premature. Eight days before either the plan's acceptance or rejection, Moffat reported, "the pressure on the [Liberian] Government was sagging off again as Barclay is spreading two rumors: one, that MacVeagh [the American chargé] was not accurately representing us and that he had not received confirmation [on the nature of the situation] from Lyon [the Liberian consul in Baltimore], and two, that the League was going to postpone consideration of the Liberian problem to a later session of the Council."[70] The British House of Lords had met in April of 1934 and condemned Liberia in the harshest of terms. Earl Stanhope, undersecretary of state for foreign affairs, strongly attacked the government's treatment of its indigenous population.[71] Lord Lugard had circulated a denunciation of the Barclay regime in which he proposed expulsion of Liberia from the League. "Suppose, your Lordships," wrote Lugard, "that the U.S. or any other State declined any longer to be flouted by Liberia and resorted to force, is there any Member of the League which would be prepared to champion the cause of misrule?"[72] In the House of Lords debate, Lugard presented a scheme for restricting Americo-Liberian authority to Monrovia and the coast. If this proved impracticable, he suggested the African state be expelled from the League.

When the League council finally met on May 18, 1934, the rapporteur from the Liberia Committee presented a report and resolution withdrawing the plan of assistance in view of the Liberian reservations. Anthony Eden asked for the expulsion of Liberia. In the British House of Lords, Earl Buxton concurred, arguing that the United States should now take responsibility for the country or that it should become a mandate.[73] Lord Cecil also said that expulsion might have to be considered. But this did not by any means present a clear option. In January of 1934, a British Foreign Office official had advised quite candidly, "It seems hardly open to us at this date to ask, or to expect, that the League should threaten anyone, even Liberia, with expulsion; and in that case our best policy seems to be to bring the dismal failure at Geneva to an end as soon as possible, or at least to disassociate ourselves as far as possible from it." Now that League assistance had been rejected, Britain could tell the Americans that Liberia was their concern ("the Americans are, after all, the last people who ought to sneer at the League for unwillingness to encroach upon sovereign rights)."[74] There existed some uneasiness at leaving the matter entirely up to the United States, but the consensus was that America would shoulder the responsibility.[75]

In April, at a private Geneva meeting attended by representatives of France, Poland, the United States, and Britain, it had been agreed that while the expulsion of Liberia was desirable, it would be difficult to get unanimity on this subject in the League council.[76] The League, as a body seeking to encourage the rule of law in international relations, was bound by its own legalisms. If Liberia, a sovereign state, would not accept the League's recommendations, the organization had no recourse but to abide by that decision. The Liberian situation mirrored the League's impotence in other international disputes. Legally, there existed no sanction applicable to Liberia. Even if sanctions could have been applied, it is doubtful the other members of the League would have united in carrying them out. And so, exasperated by Liberia's failure to meet its deadline, the League withdrew its proffered assistance on May 18, 1934.

The Winning Coalition

The Barclay regime had staved off the League, leaving the Firestone interests, various American missionary groups, and British humanitarians troubled. Partisans of the Monrovia government felt pleased. Dorothy Detzer was particularly ecstatic. In her campaign to save the Black Republic, the white woman had been indefatigable. She had gained an interview with the chairman of the House Foreign Affairs Committee and sent copies of the League's draft plan to several senators, including Robert LaFollette Jr., Edward Costigan, William Borah, and William King. She urged the legislators to pass her views on to the president; her central point was that no American should serve as chief adviser. In late August 1933, Detzer received a cable from Geneva saying that the British and the Americans had offered to recognize the Liberian administration if it would accept the compromise plan worked out by General Winship. She immediately confronted Ellis Briggs at the State Department and, after much sparring, Briggs showed her a joint note sent to the Liberians on the previous day by the British and American legations.[77]

Detzer despaired of the State Department and sought to reach the president directly. She approached a friend, Morris Ernst, as to the best way to reach the ear of Franklin D. Roosevelt. He told her that she should contact Felix Frankfurter, then a member of the Harvard law faculty. On August 30, she appealed to the future justice, asking him to intercede with Roosevelt on her behalf. In her memoirs, the denouement of the Liberian situation hinged on this appeal, which received the reply, "Your letter has been read by the highest authority."[78] As Detzer recalled, "Early in October, the press announced that the President had requested Secretary of State Hull 'to review the United States' Liberian policy.' And a few weeks later when the Council of the League met, the Council endorsed a greatly revised plan of assistance submitted to it by the Roosevelt Administration, and this plan Liberia promptly signed."[79] In actuality, Detzer was doubly mistaken. Liberia did not accept the League plan, and Roosevelt's response read, as transmitted through an aide, "Send for this lady, see her and explain how and where she is wrong."[80]

The Roosevelt administration did take a slightly new stance on the matter, however. In keeping with the new president's views, the State Department told Harvey Firestone in late September that the United States would not tacitly support his continued request for an American chief adviser.[81] On October 9, 1933, Blanton Winship announced that his government would support a non-American as chief adviser under a League plan of assistance. Detzer wrote to Roosevelt and secretary of state Hull to express her organization's satisfaction.[82] Walter White put out an NAACP press release in which he credited his organization with having made the United States yield. This constituted an obvious exaggeration. However, the civil rights organization had taken some initiatives on its own which doubtlessly had an impact in the black community. In the *Crisis,* Du Bois forged a defense of Liberia firmly rooted in racial solidarity. He informed his readers that he had asked the Liberians not to yield on questions of sovereignty. Du Bois advised, "Our business is to see in what respect the Liberians need help and the persons best able to give this information are the Liberians themselves."[83] White wrote Detzer and praised Rayford Logan for getting a defense of the Black Republic published in the *Southern Workman,* the Hampton Institute's "arch-reactionary" organ.[84]

As American policy began to shift, Detzer continued her campaign, convinced that she was a prime mover of official policy. In November of

1933, she lobbied to have the United States government back proposed Liberian amendments to the League plan. She met secretary of state Hull and attempted to gain support for changes proposed by Grimes in June. Detzer went beyond Grimes's reservation and proposed changes in the 1926 Firestone plantation agreement. The American secretary of state remained unmoved; he informed Detzer of his full support of the League's position.[85] In an effort to shore up Liberian support and to give overseas anti-imperialists a greater voice in the Liberian matter, the WILPF proposed that an American be among Liberia's representatives in Geneva.

At times, the organization's ardor outstripped even that of Secretary Grimes in Geneva. On one occasion, Anna Graves proposed to the Liberian that he more actively involve the NAACP in the struggle with the American government. She proposed that the organization have a representative in Liberia; the African official was wary of the plan.[86] To him, it smacked of organizing a black fifth column in the United States. He did promise to reimburse Graves for telegrams she sent on Liberia's behalf. In the autumn of 1933, Anna Graves unsuccessfully proposed herself. Later, in June of 1934, Dorothy Detzer proposed Raymond Buell or W. E. B. Du Bois. The political scientist was asked first and appeared flattered by the prospect.[87] The idea of being able to attend all League deliberations, not only those on Liberia, sounded attractive. Unfortunately, Buell was already involved in an investigative commission on Cuba and decided to decline. Du Bois was then asked. Detzer produced a highly flattering letter from Grimes, which called the professor "a leader of our race." The Liberian secretary of state believed that should Du Bois be appointed, "members of the race would be flattered, and, no doubt even those who are now lukewarm would be induced to rally more enthusiastically to the support of our cause." To have the grand old man of African American letters in Geneva would represent "an earnest of greater cooperation in the future between the African Negro and the American Negro."[88] It was a tempting prospect. Du Bois informed Grimes that he was concerned that he really be of use in bringing about a settlement in Akron and Washington.[89] The Liberian secretary of state and Detzer continued to talk of having Du Bois as a Liberian representative until August of 1934.

The times were not auspicious. It was a period of turmoil. The scholar broke with the NAACP in July of 1934 and gave up the editorship of the *Crisis*. Du Bois did not leave for Switzerland. He did, however, write to Detzer about the idea of his penning a book to counter recent Firestone propaganda. In November, he wrote Grimes to say that he very much wanted to answer a pro-Firestone book, James C. Young's *Liberia Re-*

discovered.[90] The elder statesman proposed that the Liberian government subsidize him. The Liberian secretary of state was interested, but wanted to know exactly how much the project would cost.[91] Detzer wrote to discourage this idea, and Du Bois then proposed the ingenious possibility of having "it done through some organization here to which Liberia might make an indirect contribution."[92] The scheme came to naught.

The WILPF encouraged the Liberian government to stonewall the League and, subsequently, to rely on the United States. This latter position reflected the belief that foreign policy under Roosevelt would diverge significantly from that of his predecessor. When the plan of assistance finally collapsed in May of 1934, Emily Balch wrote Detzer that the League and Great Britain were stymied and that "'they' now look to her [the United States] to do the job good and handsome."[93] Balch put forth the idea that her organization should organize a conference on Liberia similar to the one it had organized on Cuba. In June of 1934, Detzer told the State Department that the United States could now freely aid Liberia on its own.[94] But there were dissenters. In July, Anna Graves wrote to Du Bois from Rio de Janeiro that any such proposal was "arrant nonsense and really treason to Liberia."[95] Detzer was well meaning but naive, the kind of woman who "is very much flattered by just the kind of flattery which the young men in the State Department are trained to give to these women who think that they can change the leopard's spots." In an archly sexist observation, the doughty Graves wrote: "Perhaps at a dinner party for a few minutes she *does* influence them, but the lobby of the munition makers and the rubber interests is much stronger than any one's beaux yeux on the other side." Graves firmly opposed any American-sponsored plan. All that Liberia needed was "protection" from its colonial neighbors. She knew that Du Bois had been mentioned as a possible Liberian delegate to the League. Like a schoolmarm, she lectured the scholar on his proper role:

> I think your usefulness would be in defending Liberia against the insidious attacks of the British and French who are determined that she shall have so many stones thrown at her that she will be damned. (If one can damn with stones!) You will have John Harris and Lord Cecil and Lord Noel Buxton. Speak in London as publicly as possible. Liberia hasn't real orator speak for her in London. And if possible get your speech in the Manchester Guardian. It has been outrageously unfair to Liberia and I think that Firestone advertisements or the advertisements of some companies allied to Firestone and to other colonial interests have bought it. . . . But it is mad on the subject of showing up Hitler and [of having] his outrageous behavior to the Jews known to the world. Get some well known Jew to help you.[96]

The idea of Graves lecturing the sixty-six-year-old on his responsibilities smacks of both condescension and the quixotic. At the same time, it indicates both the Liberian regime's reach and its effectiveness. Graves sojourned in Rio de Janeiro, but she was not too far away to obtain a copy of Detzer's request that Du Bois serve as a representative to the League. Secretary Grimes kept her informed.

When the State Department talked of "radical Negro groups," they usually had in mind the NAACP and the WILPF. Some sporadic concern for Liberia manifested itself outside the inner circle of the NAACP and the WILPF. For example, on June 24, 1933, the Pennsylvania State Negro Council adopted a series of resolutions supporting Liberia's independence and urging revisions in the country's agreements with Firestone. The president of Cheyney State Teacher's College, Leslie P. Hill, sent the resolutions to secretary of state Cordell Hull and requested their publication. Hill also wrote to the NAACP, asking that it endorse his group's resolutions.[97] In December of 1933, the representatives of more than a dozen student groups belonging to the Universal Ethiopian Students Association met in Harlem. They noted the Roosevelt administration's anti-imperialistic statements. In light of these, they asked their government to condemn the past activities of Firestone in Liberia.[98]

Postures: Philanthropic and Missionary

In the summer of 1933, Liberian secretary of state Grimes wrote Walter White urging action on behalf of Liberia and warning that Henry West of the Colonization Society, Thomas Jesse Jones of the Phelps-Stokes Fund, and Bishop Campbell of the Protestant Episcopal Mission were "dancing attendance on Mr. Firestone."[99] In his July meeting at the State Department, Du Bois warned, "We have too often seen missionary enterprises as the handmaiden of capitalistic and imperialistic designs and we are sure that the Christian people of America will not wish to supplant Government education by Church education in Liberia any more than in the United States."[100] Some educational and proselytizing organizations saw the Liberian crisis as a golden opportunity to achieve their aims.

The close contact between the Firestone Company and some philanthropic groups did continue throughout the crisis of Liberian independence. On May 5, 1933, Thomas Jesse Jones met with the Firestones and reported them "very much perplexed."[101] The following day, Jones wrote to Dr. Robert Moton, Booker T. Washington's successor, inviting him to Washington to lobby for a stronger defense of U.S. interests in the Black Republic. On May 12, a delegation, including Moton, met with undersecretary of state Phillips to ask that the United States retain its dominant position in Liberia. Moffat described Moton as quite effective. "It was [,] I suppose, a case of atavism [*sic*], where the descendant of Wendell Phillips once again was touched by the appeal of the oppressed negro."[102]

The Federal Council of Churches in Christ in America also weighed in. It presented the State Department with a copy of a resolution urging an American chief adviser.[103] The council held that "the Government and people of the United States, have, we believe, a definite and unique contribution to make to the advancement of Liberia and Liberians, a contribution which has vital significance also for the whole continent of Africa."[104] Du Bois wrote Sidney Gulick from Spelman College in Atlanta saying that he "was exceedingly sorry that the Federal Council of Churches endorsed the Firestone plan which is apparently standing back of this gigantic effort to steal Liberia."[105] Several weeks later, Du Bois wrote to Bishop Francis McConnell of the Federal Council and told him that he had looked upon him as "one of the liberal leaders in America" and asked him to reconsider his group's position. Du Bois was most unhappy "to see again, that the Christian Church is acting as the handmaiden and forerunner of capitalistic exploitation and imperial domination of the black race."[106] Dorothy Detzer wrote Walter Van Kirk of the council that the resolution shocked her.[107] In September, Walter White wrote to Raymond Buell saying that he, Du Bois, and Detzer "had a long and somewhat acrimonious discussion with representatives of the Federal Council of the Churches of Christ." White and his colleagues found the churchmen "abysmally ignorant of recent developments."[108]

Black missionary groups were torn between the conflicting demands of racial solidarity and Christian uplift. George Schuyler, always the gadfly, saw them, in any case, as essentially worthless. Noting Liberian conditions, he charged:

> If these practices are so shocking and reprehensible and have been going on so long, one wonders why there has never been an outburst of protest from the missionaries who overrun the country. As a class they have sat serene and complacent and observed the forced labor of whole tribes on the government roads. They have stood with closed mouths and seen "boys" returned from Fernando Po who were unable to walk because of sleeping sickness and elephantiasis. They have never seen it to protest to the outer world about the debauchery of native women living as concubines in the homes of many of the leading Liberians. The spectacle of hundreds of little children enslaved as drudges in households has never aroused their pity to the point of protest. If they observed the socially harmful custom of pawning, they have kept it quietly to themselves.[109]

W. H. Matthews, resident bishop of the A.M.E. Zion Church in Liberia, retorted that missionaries had stood at the forefront of reform efforts. While there were "some weak-kneed, spineless" missionaries, the majority were God's agents of uplift. If mission work had not done much for Liberia, it was because of tepid support from African American churches. "I make this criticism [of them] . . . for being so stingy and faint-hearted about making liberal contributions, both of men and of money with which to help that field."[110] The editor of the *Voice of Missions,* the publication of the African Methodist Episcopal Church, reportedly informed Schuyler that "the missionary is not a professional reformer, a platform or newspaper denouncer of social or political ills." The journalist responded that the spreader of the gospel was either "a reformer or else he is merely a hypocritical advance agent for western imperialism."[111]

As in many such cases, Schuyler had overstated the case. Black churches were quite capable of protesting imperialism when the issue was clear as black and white. Some black churches, such as Harlem's Abyssinian Baptist, were outspoken against the American occupation of Haiti. The threatened white takeover of Liberia was capable of producing a similar response. Established organizations, working separately or in tandem, vigorously lobbied and petitioned on behalf of Liberia. Their leaders could claim to speak for millions of members. The National Baptist Convention (which could claim 3,196,623 members in 1931), the African Methodist Episcopal Church (545,814 members in 1931), and the African Methodist Episcopal Zion Church (456,813 members in 1931) all, at various times, spoke to American officialdom on behalf of Liberian sovereignty.[112] Black mission groups were poorer than their white compeers; the A.M.E. Church and the National Baptist Convention spent $330,000 on missions in the period 1923–33, in comparison with over $2,250,000 spent by white mission groups.[113] The A.M.E. Church had a large estate at its Mount Coffee mission, and the National Baptist Convention's station at Suehn constituted Liberia's biggest industrial training institution. The National Baptist Convention and the Lott Carey Baptist Foreign Mission Convention ran fourteen schools with a staff of thirty-four teachers. The A.M.E. Church operated six schools, in addition to Monrovia College.

In spite of their numbers, one writer has argued, "U.S. officials seemed to take very little notice of the missionaries in any case. When they worried about black reaction and responded to black demands, it was the aggressive NAACP and its perceived ability to arouse African-American voters that they took into consideration."[114] This probably makes for too sweeping a statement. Research in progress may indicate far more interconnections between black church folk and the power structure than previously supposed.[115] In any event, the black churches, which strenuously argued that Liberia remain open as a field for black missionary enterprise, represented a broad segment of the black population. They opposed the idea of white control as the price for the amelioration of Liberian problems. If forced to decide between "cleaning up" Liberian conditions through white agency or maintaining the sovereignty of the Black Republic, most black groups favored the latter.

A meeting of black missionary groups convened in Washington on February 7, 1934. The meeting was called by the foreign mission board secretaries of the four major African American denominations active in Liberia: Dr. L. L. Berry of the A.M.E. Church; Dr. J. E. East of the National Baptist Convention; Dr. H. T. Medford of the A.M.E. Church; and Dr. J. H. Randolph of the Lott Carey Baptist Convention. The clerics invited approximately fifty African American religious leaders and a few interested black laymen, including Emmett Scott, William Jones, and Lester Walton. A few very involved whites, such as Henry West, Harvey Firestone Jr., and Thomas Jesse Jones, also received invitations to address the group. Jones, the great white exponent of a firm American presence in Liberia, was reportedly confident that the gathering "was a really serious group which was thoroughly in accord with the policy of the United States regarding the present Liberian situation, and felt that they [the black missionaries] might be trusted to keep in line."[116] In a conference with Frederick Hibbard of the State Department, Jones expressed the view that the black missionaries should be allowed to follow their own lead, as the appearance of government interference might subject the department to criticism.[117]

Most of the whites present (including Jones and Harvey Firestone Jr.) urged the group to recommend Liberia's acceptance of the League of Nations plan. Two black clergymen, Reverend Walter Brooks, a Baptist pastor from Washington, and Bishop Matthews of the A.M.E. Zion Church, strongly disagreed.[118] To reconcile opposing views, a committee of concerned blacks, consisting of Matthews, Emmett Scott, Lester Walton, and the Reverend W. H. Jernagin, drew up a number of resolutions which the conference subsequently adopted. The missionary groups stated their support for Liberian independence and called for reconsideration of the League plan of assistance "in the light and spirit" of Monrovia's reservations. As might have been expected, they asked that missionary activity in Liberia "remain under the guidance of American influence."[119] One resolution also requested an American chief adviser. The resolutions were sent to the American secretary of state and transmitted to the Liberian government as well.

Bishop Matthews was particularly persistent in his efforts to have the State Department normalize relations with Liberia. The day before the conference, he met with William Phillips and strongly urged this course of action.[120] At the conference itself, he reiterated these views and attacked the United States for assailing Liberia on the slave trade issue but failing to castigate Spain. When labor conditions in Liberia came up, he was quick to draw a comparison with the treatment of black labor in Mississippi. Inside the State Department, J. P. Moffat took note of the conference and commented, "We are preparing ammunition to explain why it is impossible to recognize, in the present circumstances, and how lacking are any efforts of Barclay to take our wishes or recommendations into consideration."[121] It was Moffat's own feeling that not to have recognized Barclay had been a mistake, but "I do not see how it could be done while he is engaged in slapping us in the face." On February 14, 1934, Cordell Hull received a delegation of black missionaries, and Moffat prepared a short reply for the secretary to deliver, which Hull "embroidered on in a very humorous and understanding way, sending them away convinced of his good will toward Liberia in general, but his thorough annoyance toward the cavalier attitude of Barclay in particular."[122]

J. E. East of the National Baptist Convention was another black participant in the Washington meeting who expressed reservations about the course of action urged on black missionaries. On May 1, East wrote to the Advisory Committee on Education in Liberia and the board of trustees of the Booker T. Washington Institute in Liberia. Regretting that he could not attend these two bodies' joint meeting, he, nevertheless, wanted to give them a black point of view. In East's opinion, blacks almost unanimously opposed any move that would force Liberia to accept a plan of assistance. He stated that in spite of the array of evidence presented by the white delegates at the Washington meeting, many blacks were still unhappy about the conference's recommendations. He urged the holding of a broader conference in which various black groups (churches, fraternal organizations, educational institutions, and the press) would be better represented, and he said African American groups would attempt to take their appeals directly to President Roosevelt. "It is also proposed that we will have all of our associations and conventions, both large and small throughout the country . . . flood our State Department and White House with a suitable petition, urging that Liberia will not be forsaken now by our own Government for the sake of her 12,000,000 colored citizens." East proposed drawing in Harvey Firestone and urging him to use his influence. "He certainly would gain millions of friends and customers among our group for his products," observed the clergyman.[123]

East's letter had some impact. Writing of the meeting to which East had addressed his comments, Thomas Jesse Jones observed that the letter had convinced him of an important point: if white philanthropists tried to cajole blacks into pressuring Liberia to accept the League's plan of assistance, the attempt would probably backfire.[124] Later in May of 1934, Reverend East and other representatives of black missionary boards visited the State Department and lobbied for continued American interest in Liberia, regardless of the outcome at Geneva (in Moffat's view, "a series of rather nice sentimental appeals on behalf of the continued interest in Liberian welfare").[125] A little thereafter, the State Department had another meeting with East and his confreres, who asked that the United States undertake the entire supervision of the Liberian affair and, interestingly, appoint an American chief adviser.[126] The bishops of the African Methodist Episcopal Church met at the annual conference of the Foreign and Home Mission Board in June of 1934 and considered the Liberian matter. Again, they endorsed the formula of sovereignty with reform. The meeting maintained that Liberia should never be surrendered as a mandate to any European power; instead the United States, while respecting the sovereignty of the Liberian Republic, should provide a plan of assistance under American auspices.[127]

Although undersecretary Phillips refused to give assurances as to the future course of American policy, prominent blacks continued to ask the State Department to come to Liberia's assistance.[128] For instance, Bishop R. C. Ransom sent President Roosevelt an A.M.E. Board of Missions resolution that urged an American-controlled plan of assistance. Mary Fitz-Butler Waring, president of the National Association of Colored Women, sent a similar appeal. The president of the National Baptist Convention, Dr. L. K. Williams, cabled the Liberian president: "American Negroes intensely concerned in Liberia's future. Respectfully urge you ask American Government to provide plan of assistance."[129]

Settlement

As Firestone's influence waned in the face of a prevailing anti-interventionism, leaders of black opinion and white anti-imperialists faced little stiff opposition. Once it was obvious that there would be no American military intervention, even a certain congruence between the positions held by Firestone and those African American groups interested in the Liberian question developed. Neither Firestone nor the black groups wished to see a European mandate over Liberia. In the period following the withdrawal of the League plan, the rubber company and those blacks interested in keeping Liberia open to African Americans shared a common opposition to any real or supposed threat to impose such a mandate. Thus both black opinion and that of somewhat chastened American capital constituted powerful influences against a U.S. withdrawal from the Liberian imbroglio. In early 1933, secretary of state Stimson had reasoned that Liberia was not important enough to merit even the thought of invasion. A year later, the State Department lamented its inability to disassociate itself completely because of the insistent claims of black groups. Combined with the continuing demand for an "all-American" source of rubber, these claims constituted potent forces to contend with by the mid-thirties.

After the withdrawal of the League plan in May of 1934, the future course of Liberian events was uncertain. The day after the League dropped the plan, the American representative to the Liberia Committee announced to the British that his government would willingly cooperate in joint international action on the Liberian situation.[130] Ten days later, the British ambassador transmitted a letter to the American government which also promised cooperation "in any well-considered measures which the United States Government may consider appropriate to the occasion."[131] Liberian secretary of state Simpson went to Geneva in September because "we still feared that the question of 'assistance' might again be raised."[132]

In certain Liberian quarters, a more conciliatory attitude toward the Firestone Company became manifest. The Liberians had already shown unanticipated signs of willingness to mollify their creditor. In February of 1934, Monrovia unexpectedly paid Firestone $100,000 in monies due, and in July, the Monrovia *Weekly Mirror,* the voice of the True Whig Party, invited Harvey Firestone to Liberia.[133] The American chargé noted the article and thought it of interest because "Mr. Firestone is as anxious as Mr. Barclay to keep the British out of Liberia and for the moment, the loan, the moratorium and the Plantation Agreement have, with both these, assumed places of secondary importance as compared to their anxiety to maintain the independence of Liberia; the one for the sake of his cheap rubber supply outside British limitation agreements, and the other to save his presidential chair which he hopes to occupy for another seven years."[134] In July of 1934, the U.S. State Department sent Harry McBride, a former financial adviser to Liberia (in 1918), to undertake a special investigation of the republic.[135] In Monrovia, McBride reported that Barclay was drawing up his own plan of assistance.[136] In August of 1934, the Liberian president completed the three-year development plan. The legislature approved it in December, and in October, Barclay announced that two foreign specialists had already been hired.[137] McBride analyzed Barclay's plan and found it somewhat deficient in the scope and quality of the advisers. On his return to Washington, McBride concluded that the United States had two alternatives. It could "countenance a continuation of the present state of affairs, which is most unsatisfactory, which offers little hope of definite improvement in the future and which certainly leaves Liberia's foreign creditor [the Firestone interests] in a most unsatisfactory situation with no guarantee of any sort that payments upon the loan will ever be resumed" or it "could confront Liberia with a show of armed force either . . . alone or by some international combination as a lever to procure the acceptance of the provisions of the League Plan in its entirety." The latter alternative seemed "out of the question because of the present policy of the American Government in its foreign relations."[138]

Several days after McBride's return from Liberia, J. P. Moffat of the State Department called the Firestones to Washington. They would have to begin anew with the Liberians. Moffat said that "for better or worse the Administration would not use force." He declared optimistically that the period when the United States "intervened in small countries bending governments to their will, particularly on behalf of commercial interests, was definitely over." The Firestones indignantly replied that the government had a "direct responsibility" to uphold them, but they consented to think the matter over.[139] The formerly close collaboration between the Firestone Company and the State Department was increasingly subject to strain. The American chargé in Monrovia took a dim view of the rubber company's activities and communicated his feelings to Washington.[140] Reviewing a conversation between the chargé and Walter Hines of the rubber company, Moffat was forced to observe that the company man was not only callous in his view of the Liberian situation but had made "certain specific threats on behalf of the Firestones that if we do not do their bidding the Firestones will launch a press attack against the Administration and the Department which for advertising value would more than make up for the losses incurred in Liberia." Moffat mused, "The time may some day come when it will be useful to confront Mr. Firestone, Sr. with the expressed views of his agent."[141]

The Firestones did agree, in November of 1934, to come to a modus vivendi with the Barclay regime. The Dutch and the British had renewed their restrictions on rubber exports in April of that year, and with the increased cost of rubber, the company became more anxious to reach an agreement with the Liberians. In December of 1934, the Liberian legislature approved Barclay's three-year plan of internal reform and authorized him to renegotiate the 1927 loan. On January 1, 1935, the Liberians signed Supplementary Agreement Number One (supplementary to the 1926 loan agreement) between the government and the Finance Corporation of America and the National City Bank of New York. The new accord noted Liberia's development plan and provided that Liberia would not pay current interest on the Firestone loan when annual revenue fell below $450,000 — the "Basic Budget."[142] The basic budget included the salaries of the loan officials and advisers in addition to regular administrative expenses. Interest on the 1927 bonds was lowered from 7 to 5 percent until the end of 1942. Should the national revenue rise above $450,000, the surplus would be applied to pay current interest. If this sum were not sufficient, the balance of the yearly interest would be canceled. Income beyond what was necessary to pay the interest would apply to amortization as well as to the liquidation of the floating debt.[143]

The Liberian government promised to issue bonds worth $355,000 to clear up interest payments due as of January 1, 1935. At the end of three years (December 31, 1937) the provisions of the 1926 agreement would be automatically revised. Supplementary Agreement Number One's implementation was contingent on the repeal of the 1932 moratorium and other violations of the 1926 agreement. The Liberian legislature proceeded to do as it had promised. In March of 1935, Liberia and Firestone concluded a supplementary plantations agreement (Supplementary Plantations Agreement Number One). The new agreement enlarged the value of tax exemptions granted Firestone. Some Liberians complained that the value of these new tax exemptions much exceeded that of reducing the interest rate from 7 to 5 percent, but in return for the exemptions, the Firestone interests returned to Liberia canceled bonds to the value of $650,000.[144] Of this sum, $400,000 represented an advance on land rent, and $250,000 stood in connection with tax exemptions. The Firestone Plantation Company received the exclusive right to explore and mine minerals in the area of its lease, subject to a royalty of no more than 10 percent on valuable minerals. It also obtained the right to operate a radio communications system and its own airfields.

In May of 1935, President Franklin D. Roosevelt approved the granting of formal diplomatic recognition to the Barclay regime.[145] The following month, the Liberian legislature ratified the new agreements and repealed all repudiationist legislation. By the opening of 1936, the Barclay regime, so imperiled just a short time before, had weathered the storm. American capital had gained a new deal. But an internal storm still raged. Monrovia had outlasted its battle with the Firestone Company and the League. It remained to be seen whether it could outlive the battle with its own subjects.

The Question of Impact

An analysis of the Liberian crisis has convinced one observer that

> black Americans are likely to be most successful in influencing the foreign policy of their country when: (1) the area of the world is one in which they have manifested a traditional interest and with which they have had historical or long-standing sentimental ties, (2) the area is perceived by policy makers as lying outside of the sphere of significant American national interests, (3) the interests of other American groups in the area are minimal, (4) the question at issue can easily be dramatized in terms of traditional American values and foreign policy principles, (5) organizations exist within the black community which, as a result of continuous study of international developments, can readily articulate an Afro-American position and rally the black community in support of that position, and (6) Afro-Americans establish a tradition of injecting foreign policy issues in which they are concerned into political campaigns, especially on the congressional and presidential levels.[146]

The first and second of these points prove the most significant. African Americans held some influence in the Liberian crisis because it represented a "black issue" to many policy makers. From the start, much black opinion was poised against the Firestone Company's interventionist designs. These groups' lobbying efforts raise this question: what effect, if any, did they have on the actual course of American foreign policy? The view has been expressed that such activities, especially among blacks, were exiguous and had almost no effect on the outcome of policy. According to one analyst, "If Africa is of relatively small concern to the United States, it is surely also true that the Negro attitude in the United States toward Africa has only a marginal bearing on American policy there. To put it in crude terms, there is no reason to assume that anybody can deliver a sufficiently substantial Negro vote on African issues to affect the outcome of significant elections."[147]

Looking specifically at Liberia, another observer maintains that "Liberia's political independence was not saved because of any fear of the black vote or the protests of white liberals, although those factors sometimes influenced the timing of State Department actions (as did other domestic political considerations)." Instead, "the Department of State chose to subordinate the narrow interests of the Firestone Company and its demands for armed intervention to the expansion of American trade in Latin America."[148] It can be effectively argued that the United States was withdrawing from direct intervention in Latin America, its traditional sphere of influence, during the early 1930s and that this almost certainly precluded embarkation on a policy of armed intervention on another continent. Looking at overall U.S. policy during this period, one does detect a noticeable shift. Armed intervention for profit appeared an increasingly dubious proposition by the late 1920s. Americans had intervened in Latin America twenty-one times between 1898 and 1924 and yet had failed to firmly establish a hegemonic status quo. The Hoover administration defined a less belligerent policy.[149] Intervention in Liberia would have constituted both a turning away from this demarche and an economic error.

The NAACP and the WILPF as organizations espoused a vague liberal anti-imperialism. Beyond preserving Liberian independence, both had little or no plans for internal reform. What these groups did have, was educated memberships and access to some policy makers. However, it remains doubtful that Liberia constituted a major focus of interest for most blacks. It is significant that during the planning of the July 1933 NAACP/WILPF-sponsored meeting with the State Department invitations went out to William Stone, Charles Houston, Nannie Burroughs, Robert Moton, John Hope, Carl Murphy, and Claude Bennett. None of them attended. As Roy Wilkens noted, "The troubles of Liberia have never been a burning question to the Negro Americans, all intellectual sentimentalists to the contrary, because the colored people of this country have had too many pressing problems of their own literally upon their very doorsteps." The future NAACP executive secretary pointed out that "it is difficult for a people, as a mass, who have lynching, unemployment, starvation and peonage as daily companions to become excited over the sovereignty of a people 5,000 miles away."[150] To a small number of very vocal and visible Pan-Africanists, Liberia was important. While they and their allies did not set policy on Liberia, they helped to delimit it. In 1930, the State Department had rejected the idea of letting Liberia fend for itself. William Castle thought that "Negroes would be furious and would turn bitterly against the administration."[151] Around the same time, however, the State Department decided against calling in black leaders and outlining its Liberian policy to them. Ellis Briggs of the State Department said that since he was "inclined to believe, American negroes will oppose any monkeying with Liberia on the grounds that we are helping foreign imperialists to smother that scorbutic nation for whose birth we were, alas, responsible . . . little could be gained by taking them [i.e., African Americans] into our confidence in advance."[152] In his opinion, the government should take its own course of action "and let them yell."

If the Liberian crisis burst on the scene at a time when overt dollar diplomacy was falling into desuetude, it also came at a time of electoral shift. In 1920 and 1924, the twelve largest cities in the United States, taken together, elected a Republican majority. In 1928, they elected Democrats.[153] But, were black votes important in this shift? In terms of absolute numbers, no. In 1932, African Americans constituted less than 3 percent of the electorate. Also, two-thirds of blacks lived in areas in which their voting rights were restricted.[154] In 1932, three-fifths of voting African Americans voted for the Republican Party. The great shift to the Democratic Party did not really begin until the Congressional elections of 1934. The tide had turned by the second Roosevelt election.

How, then, do we account for the official skittishness over the Negro vote? Although the Northern, urban black vote may have been relatively small and not mobilized, it loomed large in the minds of certain State Department officials (especially William Castle). Militant blacks may have presented a specter to policy makers out of all proportion to their numbers, as was later the case with the Black Panthers and the Nation of Islam. One is reminded of an alarmist 1978 National Security Council report on "proposals for durable contacts between radical African leaders and leftist leaders of the U.S. black community."[155] The memorandum is replete with references to the possibility of widespread African American fifth-columnist activity in a situation in which there was little reason to suspect such activity would have any but the most marginal appeal.

In setting its own course, the State Department constantly looked back over its shoulder at "radical" black opinion. An emerging policy of nonintervention does not preclude the possibility that such opinion constituted a major influence in the handling of the Liberian situation.[156] The State Department was well aware of segments of the black public's scrutiny. In January of 1931, J. P. Moffat of the State Department expressed great concern about the publication of the report on the League's commission of inquiry: "The whole question is so dangerous from the point of view of party politics in the United States, including the negro vote, that it has to be handled with special care."[157] Due to undersecretary of state William Castle's great desire to keep black support for the Republican Party, the American chargé in Liberia, Henry Carter, wrote directly to President Hoover in 1930 with his request that the United States temporarily intervene. He went over Castle's head because he feared Castle would veto his ideas out of deference to black opinion.[158] In the autumn of 1932, secretary of state Henry Stimson heard from the NAACP that "we are sure that the negroes of the United States will vigorously resist . . . intervention not only because it will impose a great injustice upon the Republic of Liberia, but because it will be utterly inconsistent with the recent opposition expressed by the United

States to the intervention of Japan in Manchuria."[159] The secretary of state was warned that "if the Department does not change its attitude on a question of vital importance to colored voters in the United States we should not be able to avoid attributing its position to the hostility of the Hoover administration to the negro race." The warning appears to have had effect. When, in early 1933, Hoover said that if necessary he would go to extreme lengths, even naval force, to protect the Firestone Company's investment, secretary Stimson opposed him. According to Moffat, this was because "he can see, probably more clearly than the President, the howl this would produce in Europe and among our blacks in this country, and the ease with which it could be made to appear inconsistent with our Manchurian policy."[160] In February of 1933, Stimson pointed out to Harvey Firestone that armed intervention in Liberia would probably have severe repercussions among American blacks. And after it was decided to send General Winship to Monrovia, Moffat noted, "The trip will receive little space in the white press, but as the Negro papers will play it up big, it [has] to be drafted with meticulous care."[161]

The American government was well aware, therefore, that elements of black opinion not only rejected an American occupation of Liberia but also opposed the abandonment of Liberia to European powers. In the spring of 1934, Moffat said that in his view, Britain and France would not stand by indefinitely and see the Barclay regime defy them. Fighting between indigenous groups and the Monrovia government certainly gave them an opening for direct intervention, and it was very difficult for the United States to urge others to pursue a hands-off policy. However, because of "political and sentimental elements involved," the United States could not wash its hands of the Liberian affair.[162] A month later, Moffat became more explicit: "The Secretary is anxious to issue a press statement less with a view to influencing public opinion in Liberia than to influencing negro opinion in this country."[163] Undersecretary Phillips lamented, "Unfortunately the word was circulated not only in Liberia but in this country that Liberia's sovereignty was involved, and the fears of the colored population have been played upon.[164]

If, in fact, the State Department took cognizance of black opinion, the question of why remains. Many Pan-Africanists maintained that black opinion and voting power proved crucial vis-à-vis Liberia. In 1925, Du Bois had warned that if "the Firestone Plantations Company wishes it can repeat in Liberia all the hell that white imperialism has perpetrated heretofore in Africa and Asia. There is only one power that can in the slightest degree curb this and that is the black American with his vote."[165] Eight years later, George Schuyler wrote the NAACP, scoffing at its possible advocacy of a Scandinavian chief adviser. Schuyler pointed out "that there are no Negro voters in Scandinavia to bring pressure on either the governments of Norway or Sweden in case the man selected turns out to be a s.o.b."[166] In 1932, when the NAACP stated its strong rejection of a "dictatorial" chief adviser, the organization's stance alarmed the State Department, which feared that publication of this position would "raise the devil with the colored people," and lose the Hoover administration support among blacks.[167] Walter White of the NAACP wrote black sociologist E. Franklin Frazier on the same issue, noting that the United States had accepted a compromise text on the chief adviser's authority. "Fortunately," said White, "this matter arose just prior to what seems will be a very close election and at a time when the Administration is very much worried about the Negro vote being 'off the reservation.'"[168]

Harvey Firestone also attempted to use the issue of black votes as a lever to obtain policies favorable to his interests; unless the Liberian matter was taken away from consideration by the League, he claimed, the United States would not only lose its independent source of rubber but the Republican administration would also be "embarrassed with the negro race during the Presidential campaign of 1932."[169] Moffat, considering these arguments and counterarguments, complained of "the mental gymnastics of trying to carry two pails, one filled with negro votes and the other filled with Firestone campaign contributions."[170] In the autumn of 1932, Moffat predicted that Firestone would not push the administration on the Liberian issue until after the November 8 presidential election, when Hoover, if he won, would be under no compulsion to cultivate the black vote.[171]

When the Roosevelt administration came in, however, concern for black votes continued. In 1933, Dorothy Detzer felt that black electoral strength proved very important to the resolution of the whole matter. She told Anna Graves that this was true "particularly as Farley[172] is touring the South in order to try to gain southern votes because of the loss of the prohibition issue." She thought that if the Democrats alienated blacks at the same time, it would "be bad political strategy."[173] The following year, in the British House of Lords, Lord Frederick Lugard, colonialist par excellence, opined that African Americans were ignorant "regarding the true state of affairs in Liberia." He told his listeners, "We can understand and even sympathize with their desire to prove to the world that the Negro race is capable not only of self government but of governing a subject people." Charles S. Johnson's presence on the commission of inquiry should have convinced black American opinion of the deplorable conditions in Liberia. He warned African Americans that "so far from establishing the prestige of the Negro race in the eyes of the world by championing the cause of the Liberian oligarchy, they are seriously injuring it." Another peer, Lord Snell, took issue with Lord Lugard's belief that the United States would eventually take strong governmental action in Liberia, reminding his colleagues that "as practical politicians we should remember that there are 2,000,000 negro votes in the United States of America, and that therefore it is not easy to assume that that does not present a problem to the United States Government."[174]

A "Colored" Minister

Having seen how various black groups sought to influence the foreign policy apparatus from without, we still face the question of the role of blacks within that apparatus. In 1976, senator Frank Church remarked that "no agency in government, has less black influence than the State Department, and that's why we're in trouble in Africa."[175] Liberia made for one small exception. The ministership to Monrovia was a political appointment traditionally assigned to an African American. The office was a plum that fell to one of the black Republican or Democratic party faithful. During the Liberian crisis, the State Department frequently questioned the wisdom of this policy, arguing that any black in this office would be plagued by pressures which would hamper his efficiency. Chargé Clifton Wharton, the first African American to pass the Foreign Service examination (1924), was assigned to Monrovia in the 1920s, mainly because the State Department was at a loss as to where else to place him. Wharton remained largely confined to the "Negro circuit" of diplomatic assignments: Liberia, the Azores, the Canary Islands, and Madagascar. Later, looking back over his career, Wharton commented, "They couldn't care less; they didn't want me in the Department of State."[176] Even as Liberia and Firestone moved toward closure, black/white racial issues intruded. McBride thought that Liberia's confrontation with the League had increased Liberia's own race consciousness:

> President Barclay's lone stand against the League Plan has naturally brought him a certain amount of admiration among his faction. Up until his regime there was never in Liberia any pronounced "social problem." Liberia was a black man's country and no more was thought about it. Mr. Barclay, however, in rather violent attacks against white supervision has succeeded in kindling a certain amount of race hatred. His friends quite openly insist that they will never *give* white men any special rights of extra-constitutional authority in their government and say, "if they want it let them come and take it."[177]

A month after the United States officially recognized the Barclay regime, the American chargé in Monrovia wrote to McBride:

There can be no doubt that all the Liberians from Barclay down are genuinely pleased to have recognition. Barclay's reaction is, of course, easy to understand. It is a great personal triumph for him here and I suppose we can't blame him for a somewhat arrogant pride that he has brought the white colossus to his own terms. Both pride and vanity are well-developed qualities in his make up, as in fact they are with all Africans, but once that fact is recognized and accepted it should cause no difficulty. It simply means that no proposition, however simple, can be presented frontally. . . . Eugene O'Neal [sic], without ever having been to Liberia as far as I know, interpreted it perfectly in Emperor Jones.[178]

The case of Charles Mitchell, who received an appointment in 1930, demonstrated the problem of the ministership well. Mitchell, a former business manager of West Virginia State College, was sent to Monrovia in February of 1931. Being black certainly did not guarantee him smooth relations with the Barclay regime. During the early months of his tenure, Mitchell urged the State Department to recognize the regime, but Barclay, without that recognition, refused to accord the minister the status or cooperation he thought he deserved.[179] Relations between the two men became embittered, and when Liberia undertook its repudiationist measures, Mitchell strongly advocated American intervention, urging the United States to take control of the country and compel the lifting of the offending legislation.[180] Mitchell's tenure was not easy. The African American diplomat William Hunt, who arrived in 1931 and left the following year, was less than impressed by the African American minister:

The chief of the Mission had only arrived in Monrovia a few weeks before me, consequently, he was about as familiar with the Liberian situation as myself. This was my first experience with a Negro politician. He had no diplomatic training, and his duties at the time of my arrival seemed to be confined principally to coding and decoding messages to and from Washington relating to the "International Inquiry Commission" then under consideration by the League of Nations. A consummate sycophant, and notwithstanding my earnest effort to justify his much vaunted reputation as a great banker and financier, my brief service under him brought to the surface one of the most shallow and tiresome "hot air merchants" it has ever been my misfortune to know.[181]

In Washington, opinion of Mitchell was somewhat less than supportive. J. P. Moffat wrote in the summer of 1932 that the minister was "an extremely intelligent negro and a kindly one, perhaps too kindly."[182]

Unfortunately, Mitchell had "been double-crossed by Barclay and reluctantly admits that he sees no chance of development in Liberia unless some outside Power dominates the show." By January of 1933, Mitchell was "our poor negro Minister, who is bearing the brunt of Barclay's wrath and who is out-maneuvered about once a day by the latter's superior intelligence."[183] Moffat noted, "The Secretary could not forbear giving a good chuckle in appreciating the situation which our politics of requiring a darky Minister inevitably produce." In February of 1933, the president of Liberia demanded that Mitchell be recalled on the grounds that the minister "had overstepped the bounds of courtesy in writing personal letters to the President of Liberia which were so offensive that they could not be overlooked."[184] Mitchell was removed (he left on March 22, 1933) and replaced by the mission of Winship and Briggs.[185]

The question of a replacement naturally arose. The chargé in Monrovia wrote Moffat in September, urging to resist a black minister's appointment:

> In my opinion, while I do not doubt that many high class Negroes would like to be appointed Minister and Consul General here, their desire for the appointment is based primarily on the utter ignorance of conditions as they are, and I am convinced that they are not able to give, when here, the best that is in them; they cannot help being discouraged, and disgusted for that matter, at the flat failure of the Liberian Negroes to meet the standards of living, politics or learning that the American Negro now stands for. Also, I question that the Liberian feels or shows the respect due to the educated American Negro.[186]

In his view, the post "should be administered by a career white officer who has not had too much experience in the Far East, where questions of caste and color are predominant. [He] should be able to meet the principal Liberians in a friendly way, yet without familiarity or loss of caste." Almost two years later, with no minister yet appointed, a new chargé wrote the State Department, "Barclay has intimated that he would prefer this [i.e., a white envoy] and I feel that a sympathetic well-qualified white would be of greater use to both governments for the next year in formulating and launching Barclay's plan."[187] The Roosevelt administration stuck to the appointment policy of previous administrations. While chargés in Monrovia were debating the merits of a white man in the post, the man to be the next minister, Lester Walton, wrote to Claude Barnett of the Associated Negro Press, "You asked me in a previous letter about the State Department's attitude in sending to Liberia a white chargé d'affaires. When the time comes a Negro will be sent as U.S. Minister."[188]

Lester Walton.
Photo from Prints and
Photographs Department,
Moorland-Sprigarn
Research Center, Howard
University.

Walton provides an interesting case. In 1959, E. Franklin Frazier voiced the opinion that African American participation in the American Foreign Service apparatus would have little positive impact on Africa policy. In an extremely negative appraisal, he said, "Negroes lack any political philosophy except a narrow opportunism." Furthermore, he continued, "an increasing number of American Negroes may go to Africa as advisers and specialists, but they will go as Americans representing American interests, not African interests." He saw "evidence that middle class Negroes in such positions are deriving great satisfaction from what they regard as a new status and acceptance in American society."[189] Frazier's highly critical appraisal of blacks in the foreign policy apparatus highlights a point. The absolute number of blacks in the State Department is subsidiary to the perception of their role. Lester Walton's career as United States minister to Liberia amply demonstrates the ambiguities of a black man serving a white government on a black continent.

Lester Aglar Walton had been born in St. Louis in 1882 and obtained a high school education before going on to a long, varied career in journalism and, ultimately, diplomacy. Like another politician of the age, Al Smith, Walton also entered the world of show business. He began his journalistic career with the *St. Louis Star* and, by 1908, was manager and theatrical editor of the *New York Age*. As luck would have it, he married the publisher's daughter in 1912. The following year, Walton launched a movement, along with the Associated Press, for the capitalization of the word *Negro*. A year later, the newspaperman took a hiatus from journalism. He served as manager of Harlem's Lafayette Theater from 1914 to 1916 and from 1919 to 1921. He composed lyrics for songs, and during the First World War was a member of the Military Entertainment Service. The future diplomat stood out as a black Democrat and served as director of publicity for the Colored Division of the Democratic National Campaign Committee in 1924, 1928, and 1932. In the 1920s, he returned to journalism; from 1922 to 1931 Walton wrote for the *New York World*. When it collapsed in the Depression, he worked briefly for the *New York Herald Tribune* and then returned to the *New York Age*. The Depression found the sometimes impecunious Harlemite hopeful of political and economic change.

In July of 1933, Lester Walton informed Claude Barnett, "Confidentially, I heard from [James] Farley [chairman of the Democratic Party] this a.m., who did not speak of [the] collectorship but spoke of me being given consideration for [the] Liberian post when time comes."[190] Walton assured Barnett that "no Minister will be named for several months, what the brothers say notwithstanding."[191] In the following month, the would-be minister received a minatory note from Robert Vann, the editor of the *Pittsburgh Courier* and a man who had been appointed to the U.S. Attorney's Office. Vann confided: "I just left Mr. Farley . . . and I feel that I ought to drop you this note for your own protection. The ptronage [*sic*] from New York State will come through New York endorsements, and they must be regular."[192] By the beginning of the next year, Walton, back from a trip to Liberia, was still confident. "So far as [the] Department of State is concerned," he wrote Barnett, "I can confidentially say to you that I need not worry." The department was "not going to stand for any Tom, Dick or Harry going."[193] When, in the summer of 1935, the American chargé in Monrovia learned that Walton had achieved his ambition, he wrote Harry McBride, the special investigator on Liberian conditions:

> I am sorry you could not get a white man with all the qualifications but I appreciate the difficulties. In the face of them I don't think we could have gotten a better man than Walton. His friendship with Barclay, however, will be both an advantage and a detriment. As long as things go well he will be alright [*sic*] but in the matter of suggestion or advice he will be handicapped as no Negro, or at least no Negro here, willingly takes advice from another. They are born individualist in their own race. They will sometimes take advice from whites as no matter how much they dislike us they realize that we have had more experience and advantages. When the pressure comes Barclay will expect Walton to side with him as a member of his race and not

oppose him as a representative of the United States. Failure to agree with him will bring enmity as Barclay is emotional like all of them.[194]

Walton arrived in October of 1935. The British consulate in Monrovia described the new American minister as "a very agreeable and intelligent negro subject of America." It drew, however, an erroneous conclusion that Walton's appointment was unfortunate since "he has to protect American white interests here and there is always the possibility of a clash between the Firestone organization and the Government. . . . Mr. Walton's position would be very complicated by his race and colour."[195] In fact, Walton's economic opinions were not dictated by considerations of race and color; he saw the role of blacks in foreign policy as consistent with that of American economic interests. In 1933, he made his pro-business stance quite clear; invited by newspaper columnist Drew Pearson to meet with Dorothy Detzer, he expressed fear that Detzer might be of the same stamp as another WILPF member, Anna Graves, whom he had met in Geneva. "I grew tired of her wild talk and told her so far as the colored American was concerned, capital had done more for him than labor, which bars members of my race from trade unions."[196]

Walton had close ties to the pro-Firestone Phelps-Stokes Fund and had actively sought to become a pro-company propagandist. At the time of the investigation of 1930, Walton, then a journalist for the *New York Age,* was already receiving money from the Phelps-Stokes Fund through the Commission on Interracial Cooperation in Atlanta. Shortly after the stock market crash of 1929, the head of the commission wrote to Anson Phelps-Stokes of the Phelps-Stokes Fund praising Walton's usefulness.[197] But as the Depression deepened, the services of the black journalist seemed less essential. In early 1931, a representative of the fund wrote to Anson Phelps-Stokes complaining that although "during the past five or six years (or possibly seven years) the Interracial Commission has paid Mr. Walton a regular monthly salary of $83.33, I am not sure that Dr. [Will] Alexander [of the Interracial Commission] and his associates place the same value on Mr. Walton's services that we do."[198] Although he did not always present the views of the commission, Walton's articles on Liberia were seen as having a salutary effect on black public opinion. A month after the note, the philanthropist Phelps-Stokes wrote the commission, noting that the body had cut Walton's salary. The black journalist was described as "greatly distressed" at this and at "the uncertainty as to the future." Phelps-Stokes asked that the old salary be continued. He commented, "We do not, of course, however, make the continuance of our help to the Interracial Commission in any way dependent upon the employment of Mr. Walton. That would be manifestly improper."[199] Ten days later, the commission informed Phelps-Stokes that Walton receive pay for February and March. The commission also promised to speak with Dr. Moton of Tuskegee about Walton's future.[200]

During the uncertainty over his emoluments, Walton wrote to Phelps-Stokes outlining his plight. "On one or two occasions," he wrote, "I have suggested to Dr. [Thomas Jesse] Jones that the Fund pay me outright." Walton said Jones had advised him "that you [Phelps-Stokes] were unalterably opposed to such arrangements, as you did not want the fund to go on record as paying for publicity."[201] But, the embittered Walton wrote, "it should be kept in mind that all the time I devote to writing and releasing stories on Liberia or Hampton, etc., is distinct and separate from any financial arrangements with the New York *World* [one of the papers to which he supplied articles]."[202] Moreover, at great cost to himself, the journalist had defended the best interests of his race:

> A few weeks ago the President of the Dunbar National Bank expressed himself perturbed over Soviet Russia's program of seeking to stir up strife and discontent among colored Americans. It cannot be denied that an organized effort is being made to rally Negroes under the communistic banner and that the scheme is meeting with questionable success. Lynching, unemployment, discrimination against the Negro in labor unions and even in the North, are being effectively emphasized. Dr. Jones well knows that I believe in progress and want to see my race advance as fast as possible, but I believe this will come about by evolution rather than by revolution. To me it seems the height of folly for men in high places to sit in smug complacency without turning a hand to combat a sinister campaign of a nation to create discord and disloyalty among one-tenth of our country's population.[203]

During the hectic lame duck period of the Hoover administration, Walton became involved in the machinations to bring about a favorable outcome for the rubber baron. In late January, Thomas Jesse Jones wrote to Harvey Firestone Jr. and informed him that the advisory committee was very concerned about conditions in Liberia. Propaganda was needed. Jones proposed that Walton go to Washington from New York: "in his own way Mr. Walton should urge the State Department to action as regards publicity." Henry West would accompany the black journalist, who would have to return to New York quickly "to see Mr. George Foster Peabody who is very influential with the incoming administration." If Firestone approved the plan, Jones would advance Walton his traveling expenses.[204] In May of 1933, Walton wrote of his continuing efforts to present the Firestone cause to the black American public:

"While there [Washington] I had a talk with friends [presumably Firestone] relative to their getting a correspondent. They pointed out that if such a step were taken the identity of the correspondent would be discovered sooner or later with calamitous results to them."[205] In July of 1933, L. A. Roy of the Phelps-Stokes Fund noted that it would be excellent if funds could be found for some American black with the correct views to accompany a representative of the fund on a trip to Monrovia.[206] In the same month, Walton went to Liberia as a correspondent. He also visited Geneva. On his return to the United States, Walton embarked on a lecture tour and gave an essentially pro-Firestone view of the troubles with the Barclay regime. After his appointment as American representative to the Liberian government, Walton continued his intimate relations with the Phelps-Stokes Fund and kept its members abreast of Liberian developments. When in 1935 the Liberian cabinet received a salary increase, he told an officer of the fund that he hoped Harvey Firestone would not be "unduly pessimistic" about this action and felt the American capitalist would "be justly compensated for all that he has gone through."[207]

As minister, Walton, with some opportunism, seemed quite able to balance the conflicting forces around him. While remaining an intimate and hidden friend of the Firestone interests, he was also able to gain Barclay's confidence. In November of 1935, Walton wrote to Claude Barnett, "Confidentially the most cordial and confidential relations exist between President Barclay and me. By working together informally, you can do so much more than going through formal procedures."[208] However, five years later Walton expressed a much more jaundiced view of the Barclay regime, complaining that the Liberians would never accept advice unless it was delivered with a hand "of iron in the silken glove."[209]

Walton, who came to view himself as the black expert on Liberian affairs, clearly seems to have maneuvered successfully through the Liberian crisis on the basis of self-interest. As the Phelps-Stokes Fund's protégé, he assiduously sought to ingratiate himself with white philanthropic interests, who at certain times paid him, and with the Firestone Company. His position as a loyal Democrat stood him in good stead after the advent of the Roosevelt administration. His guiding principle during the crisis was self-advancement rather than adherence to any of the aims of the various black groups debating the Liberian issue. His success in attaining the ministership gave vivid proof of the rewards gained by tenacity. At the same time, his success highlights the ambiguities surrounding the role and allegiance of the black diplomat in Africa. Ironically, Walton, the maneuverer par excellence, was to end his stint in Liberia in disillusionment. He wrote to Du Bois, "There is a certain element here and in the United States which looks with some disfavor on my presence here as American Minister. [It is] the aim of certain Americans to bring about the appointment of a white man as chief of diplomatic mission in Liberia. Either that or a Negro who is willing to do their bidding."[210]

Walton and some of his predecessors in Monrovia represented no overall black consensus, or even constituency, on African affairs. They emerged from the infighting of American partisan politics, and they offered no substantive black input to American African policy. What input there was, came from a heterogeneous collection of "Race Men" motivated by the call of black solidarity.

7 Enterprise in Black and White

> Much of the black militant talk these days is actually in terms
> far closer to the doctrines of free enterprise than to those of the welfarist
> thirties — terms of "pride," "ownership," "private enterprise," "capital," "self-
> assurance," "self-respect." . . . What most of the militants are asking
> is not separation but to be included. . . . to have a share of
> the wealth and a piece of the action.
>
> — Richard Nixon

> It should be obvious that African Americans cannot fundamentally
> transform capitalist, patriarchal, racist America by themselves.
>
> — Cornel West

In 1999 a Millennium Summit of African Americans and Africans met in
Accra, Ghana. Unlike the Pan-Africanist congresses of the interwar period, the meeting pursued a very different focus:

> The theme of the Millennium Summit was "Business, Trade, and Invest-
> ment," expressed in the motto "Africa Can Compete." Indeed, it is in this
> area that the fifth Summit may have its biggest and most far-reaching im-
> pact. Thirteen African Heads of State and 5 Vice-Presidents, the United
> States Government delegation headed by the Secretary of Labor and includ-
> ing Assistant Secretaries of Commerce, Agriculture and Transportation and
> 281 corporations and businesses from America, Europe, Africa and India
> were involved in the fifth Summit. A major contribution toward maintain-
> ing the enabling environment needed for market economic and for the
> continued growth in business, trade and investment in Africa was achieved.[1]

Thomas Faulkner's vision of economic Pan-Africanism is here magni-
fied a hundredfold. African Americans, with their tremendous buying
power, should "give back" to the motherland and, at the same time,
make a profit. Perhaps the twenty-first century will see this dream ful-

filled. In the interwar years, because of its place in a colonized Africa, Liberia was touted as the *only* place for the unfolding of the black economic destiny. During the crisis of the 1930s, the Americo-Liberian elite, while discouraging schemes for massive immigration, continued to play on the theme of Liberia as a frontier of economic opportunity. For many blacks in the Diaspora, Liberia represented something more than a symbol of black self-rule — it was the one area where black enterprise might flourish.

At a fundamental level there existed, from the beginning, an inherent contradiction between the "self-improvement" aim of African American settlement in Liberia and the propaganda of African "redemption." If Africa was the land in which the blacks of the Americas would advance their economic position, it should have been obvious that such advancement did not necessarily ring consonant with the economic interests of the indigenes. Early in the Liberian scandal, a State Department official queried Thomas Faulkner: "I asked how he reconciled his attitude towards the conditions which he alleged existed in the Republic with his desire to raise capital for [Liberian development]." Faulkner's reply on this point remained vague and immediately involved him in generalities regarding his belief that the "American negro should be the salvation of the Black Republic."[2]

The career and political aspirations of a man like Thomas Faulkner amply demonstrated the difficulties the Liberian elite had in controlling the activities of emigrant black entrepreneurs. Faulkner believed the rhetoric of diasporic redemption. His business acumen had led him to political involvement. He had been mayor of Monrovia during World War I and had led the People's Party in the late 1920s. However, there was a "glass ceiling" he could not break. The established True Whig families were loath to give way before an interloper, even one who lived in Liberia for over forty years. Faulkner, a tragically Promethean figure, received little consistent overseas support. Reform efforts were belittled and dismissed, as was the idea of free and open elections. Speaking of Faulkner's complaints about the rigged election of 1927, Benjamin Nnamdi Azikiwe sneered, "it may be observed that his defeat for the presidency, coming so proximate with his mission to the United States in order to expose the economic and political shortcomings of that Republic, savours of disappointment."[3] There lies little truth in this characterization. Indeed, in the autumn of 1931, Faulkner attempted to form a united black front on an approach to a League mandate. He wrote Barclay that a member of the Liberian opposition had contacted Antoine Sottile in Geneva. Barclay did not reply. A week later, the businessman again wrote the Liberian president, announcing, "With the aboriginal populace and the labouring classes of Liberia at my back, I feel that not much can be done to retrieve Liberia's lost prestige before the world without the hearty cooperation of . . . the masses of Liberia."[4] To Barclay, he urged "the combining of all the forces of Liberia in one grand rally to save the future prestige of Liberia."[5] Except for Garveyites, Liberia remained synonymous with the True Whig Party for many in the Diaspora; the True Whig government *was* Liberia. Unfortunately, few outsiders demanded democratic reform as the price of their support. It was a tragically lost opportunity.

Commentators have said that given the contradictions in the stated aims of Liberian settlement, the nineteenth-century settlers could not be faulted if "though there was much talk of 'brotherhood' and 'uplifting the race' . . . the 'race men' from the U.S. actually had little scruple when it came to using whatever force and deception was necessary to deprive the natives of their land and resources."[6] The harassed settlers from the New World were only obeying the logic of settlement. Thereafter, the perpetuation of the view of Liberia as a land of opportunity ignored the conflicts inherent in the creation of a settler society. Black capitalism would demand black workers. The creation of the notion of a homogeneous black folk community could only partially paper over the potential antagonism between these two. To the Diaspora, Liberia held out the promise of transforming a dispersed and marginal black bourgeoisie into a national one. However, the promise remained largely chimerical. For one thing, American blacks possessed little capital. But the great failing of the proposed economic linkages, little realized at the time, was that black entrepreneurship in Liberia did not jibe with the ongoing policy aims of the Liberian elite. J. Gus Liebenow noted that this elite tended to discourage Liberian business and encouraged the entrance of foreign groups other than blacks at various levels of economic enterprise.[7] In the 1930s, Bishop Matthews of the A.M.E. Zion Church also remarked this, but dismissed its significance, asking African Americans, "How is it that the Jew and the Greek and the Italian have more business firms right in our own segregated communities than we have?"[8] The bishop failed to realize that in Liberia the small scale of black entrepreneurship could have reflected the conscious decisions of the ruling elite. Since nonblacks could not become citizens of the Black Republic, this created a situation, especially in terms of small retail trade, in which a mercantile minority (i.e., the Lebanese) could be allowed in at the sufferance of the ruling group and remain dependent on its goodwill. Although it was suggested in the 1930s that capital from America might prove the answer to the "Syrian Problem" (the Lebanese), the attitudes and long-range interests of the entrenched elite opposed the creation of a group of black entrepreneurs with citizenship rights and interests that might run counter to theirs.[9] Mandinka (Mandingo) merchants from neighboring Guinea were also encouraged to trade as temporary sojourners.

Ian Duffield, looking at West Africa and Afro-America in the interwar period, concluded that "by the late 1920s, Pan-Africanism based on produce-trading began to decline, initially signaled by the loss of faith in black American partners and their replacement by white Americans."[10] Duffield spoke particularly of British West Africa. But a close examination of the Liberian situation reveals that any such generalization for West Africa as a whole proves dangerous. In the twenties and thirties, economic Pan-Africanism (linking Liberia and the Diaspora) remained an important element in the thought of both African Americans and Liberians. For example, in late 1933, the Liberians proposed to send a commission to the United States to solicit financial and moral support from American blacks, as well as from white American corporations.[11] The major response to such appeals was bound to come not from the broad mass of African Americans, but from the black bourgeoisie. The individuals and organizations espousing the cause of Liberia came, for the most part, from the articulate and relatively more comfortable segments of the community. The Americo-Liberian elite which had rejected the proffered aid of Garvey and Garveyism in the 1920s, in the next decade, quite readily solicited the aid of some of Garvey's enemies.[12] Unlike Garvey, the would-be black coadjutors of the 1930s posed no threat of immediate inundation through emigration or of the destruction of the oligarchy's entrenched position. With the promise of an independent Liberia as a field for black economic exploitation, the support of some segments of this group of black strivers could be maintained. Although no actual upsurge of African American investment occurred in Liberia in the early 1930s (a time of general economic distress), those years witnessed a proliferation of schemes for and interest in African American participation in the Black Republic's economic development.

In 1931, William Edgenton, an African American who had lived in Liberia, wrote in the *Atlantean*:

> The Liberian Development Association which constitutes most of the Negro millionaires of America and the neighboring islands, with the greatest talents of modern development, has stretched out her hand to rescue her and offer the little republic aid in a cure for her economic and financial ailments — not to criticize or scandalize her present existence, but to convert the so-called slave ground of Liberia into a land of peace and plenty, where

the eastern and western Negroes will co-operate in all business lines, and her factory whistles will call the laboring natives instead of the Spanish steamers.[13]

In January of 1934, Dr. S. P. Radway of the Afro–West India Round Trip Association wrote to Edwin Barclay from Martinique and proposed "a mammouth [*sic*] Industrial Scheme" which would be "Auxiliary to the African Industries Company Ltd." of Monrovia. Radway argued that blacks in the West Indies had skills and capital which their colonial status did not allow them to develop. In answer to his own query, "*Where* then must we go?" he replied that Liberia provided the only hope. Perhaps remembering the Garvey debacle, he promised that proposed immigrants would constitute no burden to the state and would not upset the established order.[14] In the same month, a black man in Liberia's Montserrado County urged the president to prohibit the entry of white concessionaires and, instead, to embark on an extensive propaganda campaign in the Diaspora. Cash cropping should be begun on a massive scale, he advised, backed up by a fund of $40,000.[15] In the summer of 1934, a black prospector, J. T. Betts, informed Barclay that he was undertaking surveys in the hinterland, his efforts motivated by "racial interest in this Negro Republic."[16]

By far the most ambitious program to furnish black economic aid for Liberia partially resulted from the efforts of the Liberian consul general in Baltimore, Ernest Lyon. Lyon, an American and former minister to Liberia, assiduously cultivated African American moral and financial support, while opposing schemes for mass emigration.[17] Jones had had a long and varied career; he had contacts with groups as diverse as the Communist Party and the YMCA. In addition, he had served for eight years as executive secretary of the local branch of the National Urban League. In June of 1933, he informed the Liberian secretary of state that he was about to launch a campaign to counteract adverse comment in American newspapers. Lyon adopted the tack that Liberia's economic troubles were traceable to her participation in World War I and said that prominent African Americans were beginning to rally to her defense.

The consul general encouraged William Jones, whose paper, the *Baltimore Afro-American* had initially taken a very dim view of the slavery scandal, to take an active interest in the welfare of West Africa's only republic. In early October of 1933, Jones and two other colleagues visited the State Department and called on J. P. Moffat. The visitors said that their mission was to cement ties between the United States and Liberia. In November of 1933, Jones arrived in Monrovia as a goodwill delegate from the Save Liberia Movement, a group representing fifteen prominent African Americans.[18] Walter White had written him letters of introduction. The editor had come to the view that ties between Afro-America and Liberia must depend on more than sympathetic race feeling. In his view, economic self-interest would, in the future, bind both peoples together and provide a vent for American black capital. Money would be raised in the United States for Liberian development, and unemployed African American professionals would find employment in Liberia. Jones made contact with Thomas Faulkner and held discussions with the Liberian secretary of the treasury, who probably subsidized his trip.

Before the legislature and public groups, the newspaperman put forth a plan of financial and technical assistance. His program contained several parts: an educational campaign would be launched to generate interest in Liberian development; an annual development fund of approximately $1,000,000 would be raised; a Liberia-America trading and banking company would be established; fifty scholarships would be granted in the United States to young men and women pledged to do developmental work in Liberia; and "foundational aid" would be organized for farm development and educational work in Liberia.[19] Jones proposed to raise some of the money through direct appeal. Teachers and students might contribute small sums of money (a "Save Liberia" button could be given to every child who collected more than a dime).[20]

Jones also planned to appeal to fraternal organizations and churches. The money raised "would be regarded as kind of a subsidy, such for instance, as the colonial Governments have given to develop their large coast towns, harbors and roads, and would be used by the Liberian Government to do similar development." Money would also be raised by issuing bonds of a projected American Liberian Trading Company.[21] "Thousands of fathers and mothers of young boys could," Jones reasoned, "be induced to buy a $5, $10, or $25 bond for and in the name, perhaps of their children, which would mature 20 years from now just when their children would be in the prime of life." Such bonds would strengthen the links between black America and Liberia because they "would give such boys and girls a permanent interest in the development of the country." African American capital, in Jones's view, would counterpoise the forces ranged against the Black Republic. "Instead of the white dictators urged by the League of Nations, the [Liberian] legislature voted for a plan calling for colored advisors, an open door to immigration from the U.S.A, co-operative trade relations, and assistance for internal development."[22]

By early 1934, Jones had returned from Liberia and wanted a meeting with prominent blacks to draw up a program that would eventually be presented to President Roosevelt.[23] In January, Carl Murphy, the president of the *Afro-American,* announced a Washington meeting of prominent blacks to devise ways of alleviating Liberia's economic troubles. Later in the month, Jones, Willard W. Allen, Grand Master of the Black Masons, and Consul General Lyon met at the State Department and outlined a plan for saving Liberia. Subsequently, the *Afro-American* devised a long list of names of prominent blacks prepared to submit a program to the American president.[24]

Like many schemes for African American and Liberian cooperation, the Jones plan did not progress far beyond the planning stage. The State Department did not support the project, and many African Americans opposed it.[25] The *Pittsburgh Courier* attacked Jones's plan as "incredible philanthropy" in view of the social and economic hardship already endured by the African American population.[26] By August of 1934, Jones's ardor had obviously cooled considerably. When it was proposed that the editor aid in the formation of an "Americo-Liberian Society," Jones "seemed to be very timid about the idea because he did not know how it would be received by the leaders in the United States of America."[27] A year later, the journalist had obviously despaired of black capital being able to develop Liberia on its own. He hoped that the American Departments of Labor and Commerce might advocate trade with Monrovia and use Liberia as an opening through which to promote cotton trade in Africa.[28]

The political left vociferously attacked the Jones plan of 1933. Harry Haywood, a black communist, denounced the scheme as an attempt by the black bourgeoisie to serve as lackeys of American imperialism in Africa.[29] He denounced the program's class motives and lambasted it as a scheme to allow the black petite bourgeoisie to play a comprador role in Africa. Haywood argued that "this can be seen in the statements of one of its leaders, 'we are beating our hearts and souls trying to break through the thick wall of prejudice which bars us from the higher brackets of big industry here in America, when there is a virgin field which [we] can develop in Africa.'"[30] He maintained that the plan to protect an independent Liberia avoided mention of the role of U.S. capital in the Liberian economy. He questioned the underlying rationale of any program to bail out Liberia and concluded that the Jones plan's "propaganda was aimed largely at the ghetto petite bourgeoisie — themselves driven into poverty by the Depression."[31]

In addition, Haywood specifically condemned George Padmore for his supposed support of the Jones plan. According to his detractors within the Communist Party, it was Liberia which caused both Padmore's break with international communism and his espousal and elaboration of Pan-Africanism. Padmore faced criticism for allegedly failing to "recognize the fact that the condition of the two million natives in Liberia is not the same as the condition of the ruling stratum of the Americo-Liberians and that the natives must also fight against these black oppressors and imperialist lackeys."[32] He was expelled from the International Trade Union Committee of Negro Workers, for which he had formerly served as secretary. The new secretary denounced Padmore's supposed interest in the Jones plan and wrote that "the actions of Padmore could have but one result; to undermine the unity of Liberian workers in their struggles against exploitation and oppression by the Imperialists and the Americo-Liberian ruling class; to weaken the working class movement under the slogan of race unity instead of class unity, thereby strengthening the hands of the Imperialist oppressors and their Negro allies.[33]

The whole idea of Afro-America coming to the aid of the Americo-Liberian elite was excoriated in the Communist organ, the *Negro Worker,* which also deplored Padmore's supposed backsliding on the Liberian issue.[34] According to the paper, Padmore had "become one of the most zealous organizers of the Roosevelt-Jones 'Committee of Aid.'" The entire idea of defending the Black Republic was ridiculous. "Can the freedom of the native workers," asked the *Negro Worker,* "be purchased by raising five million dollars or any other large sum?" The paper asked, "Does freedom come through such a Utopian plan?" It answered, "As long as the higher strata of the native population can be bribed by the big corporations and landlords, it is child's play to think that the imperialist bandits will give one concession without it being forced from them by the mass struggles of the toiling population."[35]

In the acrimonious debate that followed Padmore's split with the party, it became clear that the Jones plan per se was not the cause of the Pan-Africanist's expulsion from the Communist ranks. Rather it was Padmore's espousal of racial solidarity across class lines (mixed with intraparty conflict) that resulted in the break. In late 1935, he attacked the Communist International for fabricating charges against him on the Liberian issue. "Why," he asked, "did the C.I. not accuse me of this years ago, for the last article I wrote on the Liberian question was in January, 1932, when I was still *persona grata.*"[36] The secretary and chief executive of the American Communist Party, Earl Browder, retorted that the real reason for Padmore's expulsion lay in his espousal of the notion of race war and his acceptance of Japan's role as the protector of East Asia against white imperialism.[37]

The Liberian crisis clearly shows that by the mid-1930s, Padmore's thinking followed a Pan-Africanist rather than a communist logic. Early in his career, he had held that the actions of the Americo-Liberian elite proved the fallacy of Garvey's belief in black entrepreneurs.[38] And in 1931, he attacked "the diplomacy of the white imperialists in using the Negro national reformist leaders—like Marcus Garvey . . . Dr. Du Bois . . . and others—as their agents in paving the way for increasing attacks upon the standard of life of the Negro masses."[39] However, by 1934 he could write to Du Bois that "Liberia has her faults, but since white politicians are no better than black ones, it is our duty to save the 'black baby' from the white wolves."[40] There is little proof that Padmore was the motive force behind the Jones plan (as the Communist Party seemed to allege), but the party was correct in thinking that he concerned himself more with preserving the integrity of the Black Republic than with overthrowing its oligarchy. Padmore attacked the party for its blindness to the fact that "Liberia is an economic colony of American imperialism, and as such it is the duty of American Communists to defend Liberia" despite that country's failings.[41] The Jones plan met with Padmore's approval because it promised to share up Africa's only republic.

The West Indian–born writer emerged as one of the leading enunciators of Pan-Africanism as an anticommunist alternative for the liberation of Africa. In his later work, *Pan-Africanism or Communism,* he bluntly stated that Pan-Africanism was "an independent political expression of Negro aspirations for complete national independence from white domination—Capitalist or Communist."[42] In 1938, the London-based International African Service Bureau, of which Padmore was chairman, wrote to Barclay through its treasurer T. Ras Makonnen:

This organization . . . takes a special interest in the condition and progress of the State of Liberia. . . . Those of us in the Western world follow its career jealously, because, although some of us may never have seen Africa, we know that equality for the Negroes in the Western world is inextricably bound with the emancipation for the African people. This organization has in the past and may, in the future, pass severe criticism on the condition of the Liberian people or on certain aspects of its Government, but we take this opportunity of assuring you, and the people whom you govern, that such criticisms are made in the interests of the Liberian people and of the Negro race as a whole. Whereas we stand for the complete emancipation of every part of Africa from European domination, we stand firmly for the national independence of the State of Liberia. Liberia is not an Imperialist State. We unhesitatingly condemn all whose criticisms have as their aim, direct or indirect, the bringing of Liberia into the orbit of the European dominion of

Africa. We urge and advocate the necessity of Africans and peoples of African descent, and all their allies and representatives, fighting, if necessary, with arms in hand, for the independence of Liberia.[43]

The Promise of Return

As I have argued, the 1930s saw a continued ambiguity in the relationship between the Liberian ruling elite and blacks in the Diaspora. The issue of emigration may give some evidence of this ambiguity. Although the Christy-Johnson commission had officially recommended African American emigration and the Brunot commission had expressed the "hope that some of these foreign [League of Nations] specialists may be recruited from among the representatives of the negro race," there was no torrent of African American movement to Liberia in the wake of the 1930 League investigation. Monrovia was suspicious of immigrants and required them to post a bond of $100.[44] This means closed the possibility of emigration to impecunious African Americans, who formed the vast majority of American blacks during the Depression.

Some African Americans managed to make it to Liberia in spite of immigration restrictions — only to find their dreams grossly betrayed. The most tragic case was that of John "Sweet Candy" Hall, "a lanky six-footer," who "never smiled much, nor did he beckon to little children or even glance . . . meaningfully at the bare-breasted virgins whose display was only to attract the 'Merican Man' so that their offspring would be automatically categorized as 'civilized.'"[45] Hall and his family immigrated in the twenties and started a small baking business with their meager savings. "Sweet Candy" Hall sold his baked goods from a stall in Monrovia, a stall periodically demolished by drunken members of the Liberian militia. The booth was this very petty capitalist's life. Exasperated after frequent complaints to the police, he took matters into his own hands. On May 10, 1927, he shot and killed several militiamen. Hall, a partisan of Thomas Faulkner, took refuge in the house of George Vanjah Dimmerson, a prominent member of the People's Party. Unable to dislodge him with gunfire, the police set the house ablaze:

> Whether "Sweet Candy" would afterwards be classed as a hero, or a martyr, or an outlaw did not matter anymore. . . . As the fire consumed the building and it was beyond anyone's capacity to rescue anything, the only escape that was being made was when the shells of "Sweet Candy's" guns exploded as the fire reached them. "Sweet Candy" himself made a dash for the adjoining kitchen. . . . Clearly and loudly everyone heard the echo of the last act of "Sweet Candy" when he pulled the trigger of the gun which ended his life.

The unforgiving fire equally consumed the body of "Sweet Candy" leaving only the remains of a roasted heart and a few parts gathered from the scattered pieces of his body.

The demanding public stressed that whatever was left of "Sweet Candy's" body should be put on display.[46]

African American opinion continued to be divided on the question of Liberian hospitality. Late in 1934, Claude Barnett, of the Associated Negro Press, expressed his misgivings: "We have helped to make Negro public opinion have confidence in the present [Barclay] administration in order that [the American] government might feel the pressure of aiding the Republic and yet there is considerable question of how much confidence we have in them."[47] Ten years before, W. E. B. Du Bois had attempted to silence such doubts by telling African Americans that "there is not a thing that American Negroes can tell Liberians about the needs of Liberians that Liberians do not know and have not discussed and desired for fifty years, and they are bitter when the descendants of slaves who meekly submitted to their slavery presume to ladle out loads of obvious advice to people who for a hundred tremendous years have dared to be free."[48] Yet complaints about the Black Republic continued to issue forth from various African Americans. In December of 1933, the *Pittsburgh Courier* published an account of the experiences of Mrs. Elizabeth McWillie, an African American emigrant who had returned in disgust to the United States. Mrs. McWillie claimed immigrants suffered extortion and that several groups from the West Indies had been left destitute. The woman reported that many immigrants from the United States were "so fed up on Liberia that they would kiss a Mississippi cracker if he could only get them away from there."[49] She criticized the delegation, led by Du Bois, which went to the State Department to plead Liberia's case and declared, "Lots of people in Liberia wonder why Du Bois keeps on talking about Liberia. He knows nothing about the country nor the conditions existing there." Claude Barnett received a letter, originally sent to Dr. L. K. Williams of the National Baptist Convention, in which the writer, an African American, said, "I have never in my life seen black people hate other black people as this Administration and the so called leading people in Liberia hate the American Negroes; they do not want any American Negroes out here in large numbers."[50]

Was there any substance to African American doubts as to the sincerity of the Americo-Liberian elite or did such fears simply result from the misadventures of a few disgruntled individuals? After the abortion of the UNIA's plans, the Liberian oligarchy was clearly wary of too great an

African American presence. In the aftermath of the failure of Garvey's scheme, the Liberian regime kept a lookout for further Garveyite attempts at settlement.[51] In 1934, Henry West of the American Colonization Society wrote that he "had looked forward to an all-Negro staff at Kakata [site of an educational institution], knowing that Dr. East, Dr. Jernigan and other of our colored friends, including Mr. Walton [of the *New York Age*], were desirous that this experiment should be tried," but he noted that the opposition of Kakata's Liberian advisers was "very emphatic."[52] In 1936, when Walton served as American minister in Monrovia, reports were received that a large group of African Americans wanted to emigrate. The minister and President Barclay agreed to issue a statement that welcomed skilled artisans but that also said, "as Liberia is autonomous, it has been compelled to take a definite position regarding the coming of organized groups, having as their object the making of the country the base of international antagonisms."[53] The message from Monrovia remained "send money, not people."

Plantation Life

The Firestone archives appear to remain closed to this investigator. What we do have is a mass of company publicity which spells out the official version of Firestone in Liberia. Well before the scandal of 1929, there had even been some hope that the spread of *white* American capitalism to Africa would benefit black America. Initially, Firestone seemed to promise a new dawn. In 1925, a writer in the *Chicago Defender* praised Harvey Firestone as a "great man with great wisdom" whose plantations would benefit not only Liberians but also African Americans. Black Americans, he believed, might find an outlet for their talents under the auspices of the company: "It is our chance. Let us be prepared for it when it comes."[54] The same year, another newspaper elaborated on such prospects:

> At the Census of 1920 only one colored man in the entire country gave his occupation as that of a forester; fifty reported themselves as architects; eighty as civil engineers and thirty-one as mechanical engineers . . . , due to the fact so few of our young men have taken up these professions, because of the difficulty of obtaining employment. It appears that the Firestone Company may be obliged to select a mixed, if not all-white administrative force to put over this great piece of constructive work in the black Republic, in whose progress all of us are greatly interested.[55]

The *Newport News Star* ran a story headlined "Firestone $100,000,000 Puts Republic of Liberia Definitely on Map of World: New Field Affords Outlet for Negroes, Skilled Artisans, Mechanics, Physicians, and Others to Be Taken to Liberia."[56] The following year, the *New York News* inaccurately claimed that Firestone was employing blacks in Liberia. In its enthusiasm, the paper falsely announced, "Firestone Carries 500 Students from Tuskegee — Hampton Group to Exploit Africa's Wealth."[57]

The question was, Did black colleges and universities really fit into Akron's plans for African development? In November of 1928, Harvey Firestone Jr. gave an interview to *Opportunity,* the Urban League's organ. The journal warned that "the Negro of America is apt to be skeptical of anything that even remotely suggests economic imperialism." Reflecting on the Congo atrocities, *Opportunity* commented on "the most vindictive and systematic cruelty ever recorded." Speaking of Liberia, the black journal showed itself hopeful: "This responsibility Mr. Firestone clearly recognizes — and the plans and methods which he outlines, if carried out, will insure a happy future for Liberia and will inaugurate a new era in economic expansion."[58] In the "authorized" interview, Firestone Jr. said,

> We find the Liberian native an excellent workman, naturally intelligent and quick to learn. Witness our carpenters, masons, mechanics, and automobile drivers — all of them trained in two years, and some of them, men who never performed skilled work before. Our men work without a contract of any kind and may come and go as they desire. Sometimes they travel 200 miles to join our forces. Then we assign groups from one section to land where they may build their own villages, at the company's expense. It is our wish to interfere with their habits and customs as little as possible. We believe that respect for their usual mode of life keeps them contented. But we are studying their manner of living and expect to develop a program of improvement adapted to Liberian customs.[59]

Firestone saw itself as the great white patron of an increasing tractable black stepchild. The company took up the "White Man's Burden" with alacrity. Harvey Firestone Jr., a frequent visitor to the republic, announced, "Our vast plantations in Liberia in a day's routine covers the widest range of activities, from tapping rubber trees to running a hospital and from operating a radio station to acting as peace-maker in native squabbles."[60] Firestone gave money to the Booker T. Washington Institute at Kakata and to a variety of missionary societies. The people were grateful: "In Liberia the natives have composed a song to Firestone in their own tongue as a mark of the esteem in which they hold our organization." They, like white Americans, were thankful for the superior product emerging from the Akron factory: "This fact is an increasing inspiration for us to produce tires which will measure up always to such an expression of confidence."[61]

A decade after its first exploratory mission, Firestone began the regular tapping of its trees and employed a 10,000-man workforce. Firestone spent $275,000 on the maintenance and construction of 125 miles of roads connected to its plantations and gave the Monrovia government $63,000 to improve the national road system. The big company in the little country also acquired the right to its own radio service, linking it to Akron and the world. Eventually, the plantations were divided up into divisions of from 1,500 to 2,500 acres. Each had a headquarters containing an office, a warehouse, and a collection station. The latter contained the tank in which the raw latex was stored and equipment for straining and weighing it. A white divisional superintendent, who usually had his house nearby and who drew on the assistance of Liberian clerks, oversaw the headquarters. Harvey Firestone Jr., the heir to the kingdom, described plantation life:

> The plantations are organized into units of four thousand acres and the operating force of each consists of an American supervisor and five hundred natives. The daily task of tapping begins at six in the morning and by two in the afternoon, when the eight-hour day is finished, the men are free to do whatever they please. At night they eat their heartiest meal of the day, consisting of rice, fish, wild game, vegetables and fruits, all of it highly seasoned with spicy peppers and rich oils. The energy of the men and women alike is boundless. After dinner they bring out the tom-toms and by the flickering light of blazing fires take part in weird rhythmic dances. With furious vigor and fanatical fervor, each dancer whirls about until it would seem that the breaking point of human endurance had been reached. Most fantastic of all these exhibitions is that of the "Devil Dancer," whose identity is carefully concealed behind a black wooden mask, grotesquely carved, and with countless strands of raffia grass flowing from his shoulders to his feet. For hours at a time he tirelessly performs his function of driving the evil spirits away.[62]

The rubber-tappers lived in satellite villages that eventually came to house the divisional store, African school, medical center, and repair shop. The company depended on migrant labor that usually served for periods of two years; one-third of them were Kpelle. An orthography of that language was published. Among the Kpelle, Mah, Dan, Loma, and Kissi wage labor produced significant change in formerly closed subsistence economies. By working on the plantations, long-isolated people like the Mah learned skills that they took back for the production of tree crops in their home areas. There, removed from the plantations, rice and other staple crop cultivation was integrated with tree crop harvesting and, in some cases, individuals were able to hire others to help in the work. Women's rolls changed, and a greater reliance on communal labor in the construction of granaries and in forest clearance emerged. Migration to work on the plantations became integrated into rites of passage and put within the context of traditional kinship organization. Among the Kru and Grebo, it provided yet another alternative to people already habituated to wage labor.

Firestone set up a trade school for "Natives" and collected hut taxes for the government. Indeed, Barclay authorized the creation of special judicial districts on Firestone property. These had Liberian justices of the peace operating with Firestone-built courts and jails. Harvey Firestone Jr. opined that justice was frequently a much simpler matter: "Confident that his wisdom is infallible and his judgments unerring, they take their personal problems to 'massa boss' and, in their disputes, call upon him to act as judge and jury. . . . No matter which way his verdict goes, they are completely satisfied."[63] Wage rates were kept low. By the end of the 1930s, members of the Americo-Liberian oligarchy were complaisant because some had become owners of their own rubber holdings. Higher wage rates benefited neither them nor the American rubber firm. For the latter, paternalism justified all.

Firestone provided housing and health care. The company initially built square houses on a rectangular grid pattern. Later, these were replaced by circular houses with close-by garden plots. The employer strictly maintained social control and frowned on the growing of the diet staple, rice, on the plantation. The isolation of plantation villages from subsistence farmland had serious consequences. Food production was discouraged in favor of emphasis on wagework in the concession sector. R. C. Porter, a Firestone manager, told town chiefs that no plantation employees should reside in their towns aside from clerks and overseers. One of the benefits of such segregation would be the workers' removal from any other labor obligations. Chiefs were also warned that they would be held responsible for disapproved behavior within their towns. Porter announced his intention of "driving all gamblers and loafers out of the country towns in our area."[64]

Firestone had its critics within and without Liberia. In a remarkable volte-face, Sidney De La Rue asked, in his exculpatory letter to Du Bois in July of 1933: "Do you remember Firestone's newspaper publicity — than he would establish model villages, schools, sanitation, etc., etc. — all sorts of modern social betterment. No one feels more discouraged than I do at the present situation."[65] Laborers' complaints about working conditions and company stores indicated that the company fell far short of the roseate image portrayed in its publicity. The Firestone-controlled United States Trading Company sold everything from safety pins to motorcycles. Furthermore, although the League investigation had ended the middleman role of the Liberian Labor Bureau, Firestone recruited through district commissioners, a situation rife with possibilities for abuse. This was especially true since the commissioners received one-half cent for each man per day. Paramount chiefs and clan chiefs also received remuneration. The Labor Bureau was left with the residual task of approving labor quotas requested by Firestone's different divisions. In early 1936, Barclay himself asked the secretary of the interior to look into conditions.[66] The company denied that it had sought to establish a monopoly over selling goods on its property. It asserted that the company had the right to license individual traders and to assign them specific places on its estates. It made no response to the general issue of continuing labor abuse.

In spite of Du Bois and others' early hopes for an integrated managerial staff on the Firestone Plantations, by the late 1930s, Firestone had its own white imperium in the Black Republic. There were white golf courses, white schools, and white churches. A handful of white males lived in some version of *Heart of Darkness* and *Our Town*. One white woman, based with her husband in Monrovia, wrote: "The world of Monrovia and that of the 'Little America' on the rubber plantations were different, and the road between was anathema to the foreigners at either end, but it was the price required of each for exchanging the provincialism of one community for that of another."[67] The beating of a Liberian driver by two white company employees near the start of Firestone's activities in the 1920s almost caused a riot and exacerbated Liberian suspicions of the rubber giant. A white Southerner, employed to pen a laudatory view of the Firestone enterprise, wrote: "Every member of the staff felt himself studied by hundreds of observant eyes." The natives admired whites, "but they probed them as well for those human weaknesses and foibles that mark men of all conditions." Superintendents had to be on guard: "By silent understanding everybody concerned knew that the white man in the black man's country had a position to maintain."[68] Men who dared to marry African women faced dismissal. Concubinage was not completely frowned on, however, at least in the opinion of one former employee: "Many white men take Mohammedan girls from the Mandingo tribe. The average Mandingo woman is sold from five pounds upward."[69] So strict was official company segregation that Liberian authorities could not gain admittance to company compounds without permission (a situation only changed by governmental act the year after Little Rock). On the issue of segregated schools, a company publication maintained: "Teaching of American and European children in the same schools and classes as the Liberian children is impracticable, owing to the language barrier and the very large differences in the children's ages, curricula, and cultural backgrounds. . . . for this reason alone, the classes could not be integrated."[70] A colonial encampment worthy of the British Raj existed within the economic enclave:

> Firestone has built a full-scale, nine-hole golf course and clubhouse in the Harbel Hills area, and another at Cavalla. Overlooking the Harbel golf course is the luxurious Firestone Guest House, where visiting Company officials and distinguished Liberians and foreigners are entertained, and all American and European employees and their families stay for a few days upon arriving and before leaving the plantations. A second, larger clubhouse for the American and Europeans staff is located elsewhere on the Harbel Plantation. Here, dances, supper parties, and other entertainments are held, sound movies are shown twice a week, and a circulating library is maintained. . . . Domestic servants are plentiful and each household usually has at least two to five — cooks, houseboys, laundrymen, children's nurses, and gardeners. . . . Domestic servants are invariably males, as Liberian fathers and husbands do not like their daughters and wives to work for others. Thus, it is a common sight on the plantations to see American and European babies being tenderly cared for by strapping young Liberian men.[71]

And here, for Afro-America, lay the rub. Perhaps unconsciously, *Opportunity* had remarked in 1928 that "the atmosphere of America reigns."[72] In the country club atmosphere of the encampment, social equality would have presented an omnipresent threat. In May of 1937, Du Bois wrote to Walton about the continuing color bar. He noted that he was "still deeply suspicious of the Firestone monopoly whose chief object is to make money." The scholar said: "Recently, however, I have heard that one . . . [black] clerk official has been employed." He asked the minister, "Is it true? I would like to know the facts."[73] The general color bar remained. Two years later in 1939, in *Black Folk: Then and Now,* Du Bois lambasted the rubber giant to such a degree that his publisher, Henry Holt, had deep concern about legal action from Akron.[74] Du Bois observed that "the difficulty still remains that the Firestone contract is unfair, but is backed by the American government."[75] The tire company Du Bois had once favored bestrode the Black Republic like a colossus. Rubber was king; it made up 70 percent of Liberia's exports.

By 1940, some 72,500 acres had been planted with rubber tress and 7,000 tons of latex were being produced from the 39,200 acres of mature trees. Liberia was now firmly on the map of colonial and semi-colonial raw material producers and could boast of having the largest latex-processing plant in the world. Garvey had seen his duel with Du Bois as one between white capital and black enterprise. White capital won hands down.

8 The Literary Mirror

It has always been assumed that the Black's only possible
aspiration would be to become "White" . . . a curiously loaded conundrum when one considers how many White multitudes found, and find,
themselves in Africa because they were bored with being White and hoped
to become Black, as it were, painlessly, and without laying down
what Kipling called "the White Man's Burden."

— James Baldwin

Fiction is not reportage, and even reportage (in the form of travel literature) does not constitute social analysis or even social reality. In spite of
the claims of cultural studies, any major event or epoch is too capacious
to be contained by any one subjective experience. What literature does
allow us to do is to feel what observers felt, to smell what they smelled,
and to see how they responded to events to which we, the readers, alone
know the denouement.

In 1930, Evelyn Waugh visited Ethiopia as a journalist covering the
coronation of Haile Selassie. Two years later, he published *Black Mischief,* an acerbic little book which burlesqued a mythical African state
caught between "Progress" and "Barbarism." A combination of Ethiopia, Zanzibar, and Ruritania, Waugh's Azania is threatened with a
League of Nations mandate as it lurches from crisis to crisis. Thirty
years after its publication, the author archly observed "that it seemed an
anachronism that any part of Africa should be independent of European
administration. History has not followed what then seemed its natural
course." Indeed. World War II and decolonization have made *Black
Mischief* a sadly dated and quaint minor oeuvre.[1]

We may wonder what would have resulted if Waugh had been sent to
Liberia instead of Ethiopia in 1930. Had he turned his gaze on the Black
Republic, no doubt his vision would have been as dyspeptic as his view
of the empire of the Negus. As it was, the Liberian slavery scandal did
inspire its own literature — at least two novels and two highly literate

travel accounts. The first two flowed from the pen of George Schuyler; the latter were the products of Graham Greene and his cousin Barbara Greene. In the works of Schuyler and the Greenes, Liberia is refracted through very different sets of lenses. Schuyler's outrage stands as the polar opposite of the weltschmerz of Catholic and upper middle-class Graham Greene.

The Cynic as Muckraker

Schuyler emerged as the great antagonist of the Liberian regime, a stance which began his long drift toward the lunatic right (he ended his days as a writer for the John Birch Society). Henry Louis Gates Jr. has observed that "Schuyler's position in the black intellectual community was one of critic from within. Schuyler constructed his intellectual role as that of a dissident, reserving his animus for his fellow black intellectuals, and cultivating critical skepticism as his calling."[2] The man who had been a liberal muckraker in the 1920s emerged after the Liberian crisis as a supreme cynic, especially concerning Pan-African appeals.

When the United States sent its note to Liberia, Schuyler was a thirty-four-year-old journalist with a colorful past. He was born in Providence, Rhode Island, and raised in Syracuse, New York, the scion of domestic servants. He quit high school at the age of seventeen and entered the army, which took him as far afield as Hawaii. Honorably discharged in 1919, he went through a series of odd jobs. In 1923, he became a writer for A. Philip Randolph's socialist *Messenger.* The following year, the *Pittsburgh Courier* hired him, a job he retained for the next forty-two years. During the Jazz Age, Schuyler became a protégé of H. L. Mencken and wrote several essays intended to deflate the pretensions of most of his peers. Among them were "The Negro-Art Hokum" and "Our Greatest Gift to America." In 1931, he published his first novel, *Black No More,* a science fiction fantasy in which the races in the United States eventually trade colors. The work reflects Schuyler's belief in assimilation and complete social equality. This view also found expression in such writings as his first nonfiction book, *Racial Intermarriage in the United States* (1929), and in his own racially exogamous marriage.

Schuyler became involved in Liberia in the wake of the League commission's investigation. When publisher George Putnam wanted a book on the slavery allegations, Arthur Spingarn of the NAACP recommended Schuyler. The journalist traveled to Monrovia via Liverpool and arrived in February of 1931. Traveling on the same ship was the newly appointed American minister to Monrovia, Charles Mitchell. Once in Monrovia,

Schuyler stayed at the American legation for a time and then set off on a tour of the hinterland. He persuaded the American minister to let the U.S. vice consul accompany him. With the assistance of the head of the Firestone plantations, he was able to obtain porters. He first set off by sea from Monrovia with "15 pounds of salt, a case of Scotch and two cases of trade gin, 100 pounds of leaf tobacco, a water filter, pots and pans, cheap cutlery for George [i.e., the vice consul] and me (the carriers ate with their hands), folding chairs, cots, medical supplies, folding bathtub and other paraphernalia, including a locked tin box full of British coins."[3] Schuyler spent three months in Liberia and interviewed indigenous people on their condition. He also contracted malaria.

After his return to the United States, Schuyler published a series of exposés on Liberian slavery in the *New York Evening Post,* the *Buffalo Express,* the *Philadelphia Public Ledger,* and the *Washington Post.* In the autumn, in his own paper, the *Pittsburgh Courier,* he wrote wrenchingly of the depredations of the Frontier Force and the political class's corruption. In essence, Schuyler publicly expressed what the more circumspect Charles S. Johnson privately knew.

Attack came soon. Race Men of various stripes took offence. Edwin Barclay said that Schuyler's writings constituted "a hodge-podge of all the legends that are told up and down the coast on Liberia and the Liberians, reinforced by the most recent 'revelations' of Christy and Johnson."[4] Missionaries were also upset by Schuyler's charges of forced labor and concubinage.[5] Walter White took exception to Schuyler's attacks on the Black Republic and tried to interest the *New York Evening Post* in an opposing article by an Episcopalian clergyman. White remarked, "it is interesting that Mr. Schuyler, a colored man, made charges against Liberia and that Mr. Hazzard [the clergyman] a white man, is coming to Liberia's defense."[6] Schuyler reacted to criticism with the same vehemence with which he attacked the Liberian elite. In the fall of 1931, he angrily wrote to White:

> Frankly I cannot see what the N.A.A.C.P. or the Urban League has to do with it. If anyone needs advancing in Liberia it is the natives who are systematically robbed and persecuted. Lastly, the only official delegate of Liberia at Geneva is a white man, Sottile, who I understand has never been to Liberia! The other two Liberians at Geneva, Morais and Brownell [indigenes], are fighting the present government and asking for foreign supervised elections.[7]

Later Schuyler wrote, "The N.A.A.C.P., the [*New York*] *Age* and almost all other Negroes want the U.S. government to end slavery and forced labor of Negroes in Mississippi, but they seem not so keen to end the slavery and forced labor of Negroes in Liberia."[8] The journalist argued that "in both instances local customs and prejudices are behind the atrocities, and local authorities will not or cannot alter them for the better." So in both cases outside intervention was called for. "The difference seems to be," Schuyler wrote, "that in Mississippi the whites are exploiting the blacks, while in Liberia the blacks are exploiting the blacks, just as blacks do in Haiti and Abyssinia." He charged that "the rabid 'race men' insist that black folk can do no wrong." He believed that "American supervision should last for at least 20 or 25 years until the Liberians are competent of administering the country, which clearly they are not at present."[9] Schuyler admitted that his views differed "from those of the majority of Afro-Americans." He retorted that "for that matter [so] do realistic views of almost everything. This divergence of view has never caused me to suffer from insomnia." In his view, Liberia's problems were of her own making since she had asked for the Firestone Company and the loan.[10] According to Schuyler, it was the "consensus among Americans in Liberia" that the United States undertake the Black Republic's "benevolent supervision."[11]

For African Americans, charges of African misrule can prove particular wrenching. In 1933, Schuyler wrote, "Arriving in Monrovia, the capital, enthusiastic over being at last in a country ruled by black men, he [the African American visitor] is shocked by the lack of common sanitation, the unpaved, rock-strewn, meandering, weed-grown, unlighted streets, the swarms of rats, and the general atmosphere of shiftlessness and decay."[12] This is a dangerous terrain; the observation of one discrete African situation becomes symbolic and symptomatic of the continent. More than half a century after Schuyler, the African American reporter Keith Richburg seems to be his new incarnation. Visiting Liberia for the first time in the early 1990s, he wrote: "If I was to find any country in Africa to which I would have some immediate connection, Liberia should have been it—a country founded by freed slaves." Instead of feeling kinship, Richburg, like Schuyler before him, was appalled. "But instead of encountering some long-lost soul mates," he lamented, "I found myself in the only English-speaking country in the world where I had to hire a translator, listening to dope-smoking soldiers in drag explaining how 'juju' can stop bullets from going into a man's chest."[13] Racial disappointment with "homecoming" becomes an overly generalized dismissal of the "dark continent." The average suburban Euro-American would probably feel no more comfortable in Northern Ireland or Kosovo than does the American "returnee" to Africa. The difference is that the white American is never called on to identify Northern Ireland or Kosovo as a totemic Europe.

Putnam published Schuyler's novel *Slaves Today* in 1931. A rather stilted *roman à clef*, the book reads like an amalgam of Chateaubriand's *Atala* and the slavery commission's report. The indigenes are noble while the Americo-Liberians are, with one notable exception, degenerate. The president of Liberia, Sidney Cooper Johnson, is a thinly disguised stand-in for Edwin Barclay: The president sets the plot in motion when he appoints a corrupt district commissioner to collect men and rice from a Gola village. The villain, Commissioner David Jackson, descends on the village of Takama, just as the hero, Zo, is marrying his beloved, Pameta. Unable to make the tribute, the head of the village is publicly whipped. A melee ensues in which villagers are shot. At this point, a central plot device comes into play; Pameta is kidnapped to satisfy the district commissioner's lust.

Reaching the district headquarters of Boloba, Zo finds Pameta imprisoned and tries to free her, but the lovers' escape is foiled and the commissioner has Zo whipped and jailed. The hero makes an abortive break for freedom and winds up being sent to Fernando Po. Betrayed on all sides, including by a coldhearted mulatta prostitute, he loses what little money he has. Malaria finally fells Zo, and he goes to the island hospital, a place filled with venereal disease, smallpox, and yellow fever. Finally, after serving a two-year stint on the island, he is freed. Unfortunately, his sufferings have not yet ended. He returns to Monrovia, where he is arrested for disturbing the peace. His meager savings are confiscated, and soldiers again kidnap him. After this travail, Zo finally makes good his escape.

While the saga of labor abuse has been evolving, Zo's beloved Pameta has become Jackson's concubine. In a situation redolent of the Old South, the unfortunate slave woman is both the object of her master's lust and of his wife's wrathful jealously. Jackson's wife, an Americo-Liberian woman with an American education, finds herself degraded by the web of domestic arrangements in which she is forced to exist. Gradually weakened by venereal disease, the unfortunate slave girl is raped by Jackson and cast out of the household. Zo finds Pameta in the road, and she dies in his arms. Revenge comes when Zo breaks into the commissioner's house and stabs him to death. The protagonist loses his own life in the process; a sentry shoots him. Having disposed of the noble young couple at the center of his novel, Schuyler hammers home a political point. In a rigged election, Sidney Cooper Johnson, Edwin Barclay's alter ego, defeats Tom Saunders, a reform-minded lawyer and tribune of the indigenous majority, whose character is based on that of Thomas Faulkner. Corruption triumphs; the administration continues, and the traffic in human flesh goes unabated.

A synopsis of *Slaves Today* gives some idea of what it is: a melodramatic exposé in which contemporary events serve as an armature for a denunciation of a specific issue — the slave trade. While Zo and Pameta suffer, their characters are not limned with any psychological depth. Schuyler offers some good descriptions of Gola life, but it basically serves as an ethnographic backdrop to the young lovers' tragedy. The writing is engaged; there is no time for Conradian musings on the general nature of human evil. David Jackson is evil; the reasons why he became that way or the ways in which this evil relates to what may be lurking in our own subconsciousness remain irrelevant. *Slaves Today* stands much closer to *Uncle Tom's Cabin* than it does to *Heart of Darkness*. H. L. Mencken, who had kind words for the novel, did stop to note that it was "too indignant to be altogether convincing."[14]

Addressing an audience encapsulated within the Old Dixie Narrative, Schuyler used the abolitionist images of the nineteenth century for effect. Driven home is the idea of slavery as the slave girl's sexual degradation and her mistress's humiliation. "Mrs. Jackson, like most of the aristocratic Liberian ladies, liked to pretend that her husband kept no concubines in their home, although she knew better."[15] This ignorance was feigned; the wives of big officials knew full well that they were only the chief wives in harems recruited from among their husbands' indigenous charges. "Nevertheless, Florence Jackson hated the institution, hated her position as head of the harem, and hated each and every one of the women though she knew they were not responsible for being there." Mrs. Jackson had graduated from an "American Negro college" and is the child of an impecunious but long established, Americo-Liberian family. Jackson marries her to further his presidential ambitions. Florence, like many a woman in the "Big House," is not happy:

> But despite her understanding appreciation of the merits of concubinage, Florence Jackson in her six months of married life was unable to reconcile herself completely to being nothing more than chief wife. She was an incurable romanticist, and there was no romance in such an existence. She often grew bitter about it all, and rather than risk another quarrel with her husband she took out her spite on the servants. She ruled her household like a martinet. On the slightest provocation she would go into paroxysms of rage, slapping and cuffing whoever happened to be in the immediate vicinity. The women feared her and she hated them.[16]

In his little Liberian novel, Schuyler transgressed; he ruptured a central construct of Pan-Africans — the unity of the black folk community. The NAACP's Mary White Covington wrote that "*Slaves Today* should make every American Negro who reads it cease to talk of the brutal white man. Brutality does not depend upon race but upon opportunity."[17] The *New York Evening Post* commented, "Mr. Schuyler's interest in satire is beginning to be engaged not merely by conflict between races or within a race but more largely human."[18] In some quarters, Schuyler provoked a storm. Benjamin Nnamdi Azikiwe, who was soon to write the highly defensive *Liberia in World Politics,* reposited that *Slaves Today* was "biased and superficial." The Nigerian would grant that "he [Schuyler] is sincere like all social reformers are, but a critic of colonial politics cannot be unilateral in the treatment of a subject that is of international importance."[19] Both the heaviest and briefest blows came from Du Bois. He indicated that the work was beneath contempt. Reviewing several books at once, he commented:

> The last book is George Schuyler's *Slaves Today.* We place this book last because we like it least. And frankly, we are sorry that George Schuyler wrote it. Schuyler is a militant, outspoken man, with the courage to stand up against surrounding convention. He has knocked and laughed at the foibles of his race and of white folk, without quibble or apology. But in all of his writings, save this, he stood upon the solid ground of personal knowledge. He knew America. Now suddenly, he rushes off on a trip to Africa and while he is still the keen investigator and truthful reporter, he misses his background. He does not realize the history of Liberia, and of present-day imperialism and industry in Africa. The story of forced labor in Liberia is not new. . . .
>
> Does this excuse Liberia? No, but it explains the situation and without that explanation Liberia cannot be understood. Here is a country, hemmed in as only a small, helpless group of internationally despised people can be. . . . There was only one thing that Liberia had left, and that was her native labor. She could not use it herself because she had no capital. She was beset by England, France and Spain to allow them to use it. . . . She was guilty but she was not nearly as guilty as Spain, Belgium, France and England. And to picture Liberia as a land of slaves, and say nothing about her background and surroundings, is both unfortunate and untrue. What Mr. Schuyler ought yet to do is to study Liberian history and the economics of West Africa. The men who have made Liberia, Roberts, Russwurm, Johnson, Barclay and others, are as fine a set of gifted and devoted human beings as ever worked at the problem of human uplift. They deserve recognition.[20]

So read the full-blown racial defense, the one to be repeated often in the next four years. Liberia was "guilty," but Liberia did not have agency. In a world dominated by white imperialism, an attack like Schuyler's constituted a diversion from the real enemy. The author of *Slaves Today* counterattacked; he called the venerable head of the Pan-African movement to task. The grand old man had placed himself "in the very vulnerable position of fervently defending the rascally Liberian governing class." The novelist ridiculed the "big shining limousines in which corpulent government officials bounce along over the rocky streets." Then Schuyler asked the big question: "Are we not to expect that Negro colonists who are so excessively religious and shout 'The Love of Liberty Brought Us Here' will be more human to their black native wards than would white colonists?" He lectured the professor: "Right is right and wrong is wrong Dr. Du Bois, regardless of the color of the individuals or groups involved." Then, the muckraker let go his Parthian shot: "Admiring you immensely as I do for your courage and tenacity in persistently championing the cause of colored peoples, I am sorry that you permitted your belligerent and commendable Negrophilism to warp your vision in the case of the Liberian racketeers."[21]

The Liberian slavery scandal marked perhaps the most significant turn in the road in Schuyler's quixotic migration to the right. Around the same time, George Padmore abandoned the notion of class struggle in favor of the defense of African elites at all costs. In Schuyler's case, his political reorientation led to an intellectual and political isolation, one in which he increasingly and ineffectively thrashed about. He published no other book until his autobiography in the 1970s. More immediately, he made an enemy of Du Bois, who opposed his employment by the NAACP. Du Bois was stung; indeed, he came to feel that Schuyler caused many of his ongoing problems. In late 1934, he wrote to Anna Graves of the WILPF that he felt unable to influence the NAACP on the Liberian matter because "Walter White . . . is definitely under the influence of George Schuyler." The journalist, since his attack on the Black Republic, had become a problem to the former editor of the *Crisis*; "Schuyler has been hired indirectly by White to attack me in various ways and consequently White feels under obligations to him."[22]

The issue was more than just a clash of personalities. Speaking of the idea of "Negro art," Schuyler believed that spirituals, the blues, and jazz were in no way written in any cultural atavism. He probably would have said the same thing of Du Bois's "Sorrow Songs." Such cultural items were "no more expressive or characteristic of the Negro race than the music and dancing of the Appalachian highlanders or the Dalmatian peasantry are expressive or characteristic of the Caucasian race." Schuyler would have vociferously disagreed with Henry Louis Gates's assertion that "African-American culture is an African culture with a difference as signified by the catalysts of English, Dutch, French, Portuguese, or Spanish languages and cultures, which informed the precise structures that each discrete New World Pan-African culture assumed."[23] Schuyler would have labeled this *hokum*. Simply, "the Aframerican is merely a lampblacked Anglo-Saxon. . . . Aside from his color, . . . your American Negro is just plain American."[24] Schuyler's radical assimilationism would only surface again at the very end of the twentieth century, and then only tentatively, in discussions of African American social/cultural isolation. While Schuyler, like so many other African American intellectuals, evaginated all over the ideological landscape — from socialism to the John Birch Society — his racial (or "nonracial") thinking proved truly radical. One commentator notes,

> In dissolving notions of culture based on color, Schuyler presents challenges to both African and white Americans. In a system which trains us to think in terms of black and white, Schuyler's rather radical proposal that "the words, 'Negro,' 'white,' 'Caucasian,' 'Nordic,' and 'Aryan' would have to be permanently taken out of circulation" if we are to begin solving the problem of racial discrimination, leaves us stripped of familiar tools which we have used to explain our situation for years. For Schuyler, an invocation of race is an invocation of race; we can hardly begin to dismantle this hegemony based on difference by continually insisting on that difference even though the use of "race" in terms of liberation may have a different emphasis that [*sic*] the use of race as an instrument of oppression. The only way to break the felt twoness of double consciousness is to smash the race-based hegemony that necessitates the cultural schizophrenia in African Americans. By insisting on authentic racial difference, we may be able to chip away at some aspects of hegemony, but we wind up reproducing it in other, unexpected ways.[25]

Schuyler's thought constituted the antithesis of Du Bois's "Conservation of Races." The journalist was acutely aware of the fragility of the racial concept, however constructed. The destiny of African Americans was not a castelike state for all of perpetuity. Their destiny was, ultimately, to be like everyone else; Du Bois's totemic Africa was unnecessary.

The War Tourists

Four years after Schuyler traveled to Liberia, the novelist Graham Greene and his cousin, Barbara, made a visit. The trip, which began as a vague suggestion after a wedding reception — a combination of "champagne and fate" — began as a lark. Greene was in his early thirties, his cousin, a socialite (later the Countess Strachwitz), in her early twenties. Graham Greene stood in marked contrast to Schuyler, the autodidact. The Englishman had been educated at Berkhamsted School, where his father was headmaster. He attended Balliol College, Oxford, and afterward worked for three years for the *Times* of London. Central to his writing and his sensibility was the fact that he converted to Roman Catholicism in 1926. By the time of his foray into Liberia, Greene was already the author of the critically acclaimed *Stamboul Train*. A year younger than Waugh, and a fellow convert to Roman Catholicism, Greene shared some of his compatriot's habits, if not attitudes.[26] Both Greene and Waugh traveled widely, publishing travel accounts and transforming their experiences into novels. An account of his visit to Ethiopia, *Remote People* (1931), preceded Waugh's *Black Mischief* (1932). Greene's finest work of fiction, *The Heart of the Matter*, grew out of his West African experience.[27]

Greene's *Journey without Maps*, the account of his Liberian sojourn, had a gestation of at least two years. By the early thirties, the author was familiar with the works of Joseph Conrad and André Gide. A biography of H. M. Stanley, written by the German Carl Jacob Wassermann, also greatly impressed him. He felt pulled toward the "dark continent." In the 1950s he mused, "Is it that the explorer has the same creative sickness as the writer . . . and that to fill in the map, as to fill in the character or features of a human being, requires the urge to surrender and self-destruction?"[28] West Africa proved attractive to Englishmen because it possessed those very aspects that inspired fear — "the mists, the mangrove swamps, the malaria, black water and yellow fever of the Coast." Perhaps significantly, just before his journey, Greene read *The Inner Journey* by Kurt Heuser. The protagonist flees the civilized and urbanized West in search of release from civilization and, possibly, the embrace of death.[29]

In spite of his interest in 1932, it took Greene two more years to get to Liberia. Departing London in January of 1935, the Greenes voyaged to the British colony of Sierra Leone. Both were to keep a record of their travels, although he remained unaware that she was writing anything (her account, *Land Benighted*, reissued as *Too Late to Turn Back*, was published two years after his). The Greenes pursued a far more extensive itinerary than that of Du Bois, Schuyler, or even Charles S. Johnson. The travelers went up the Sierra Leonean railroad through Bo to Pendembu, and then on by foot and hammock, crossing into Liberia at Bolahun. They then took a roundabout route through northwestern Liberia, hugging the border with French Guinea and visiting such towns as Zigita, Zorzor, Ganta, Tapee-Ta, and Bassa Town. The Greenes and their bearers reached the coast at Grand Bassa, where he abandoned his men, poor foreigners hundreds of miles from their homes and in the midst of peoples likely to relieve them of their earnings. The two Europeans returned to Monrovia by sea.

Whereas Schuyler burned with a white-hot fury, Graham Greene's tone throughout his peregrination remained subdued. Ironic detachment may be necessary for a certain type of travel writing; witness the works of Bruce Chatwin and V. S. Naipaul. The writer does not want to set down a gushing travelogue; at the same time, he or she wants to avoid the unsophisticated hectoring of the missionary (or the modern aid worker). The value of the place lay in its queer transmogrification of the quotidian. For Greene in the 1930s, Liberia provided a canvass on which to paint his mordant view of the general state of human nature. Early on in *Journey without Maps,* he hit on the "seediness" of the Liberian capital as a kind of hyperreality: "There seemed to be a seediness about the place you couldn't get to the same extent elsewhere, and seediness has a very deep appeal: even the seediness of civilization, of the sky-signs in Leicester Square, the 'tarts' in Bond Street, the smell of cooking greens off Tottenham Court Road, the motor salesman in Great Portland Street."[30] Waugh had struck a similar note in *Remote People* when he compared Addis Ababa to *Alice in Wonderland*; only in the fictional place could one find a "parallel for life in Addis Ababa . . . the peculiar flavour of galvanized and translated reality."[31] Interestingly, in 1935, Greene wrote a review of a documentary on Ethiopia, saying the film "leaves you with a vivid sense of something very old, very dusty, very cruel, but something dignified in its dirt and popular in its tyranny and perhaps more worth preserving than the bright slick streamlined civilization which threatens it."[32]

Some critics have detected in Graham Greene a literary wasteland — "Greeneland." This is "a mental landscape of boredom, failure, distrust, betrayal, and despair, reflected in a physical landscape of run-down city streets, squalid buildings, livid advertising signs, lonely bed-sitting rooms, torn curtains, dirty colors, stained beds covered with crumbs." In what we now call the Third World, Greene's vision expands. Beyond the West, he evokes "the soft decay of tropical buildings, the omnipresent vulture and other animal forms of *memento mori,* sick, diseased, hopeless, native inhabitants, impossible social and political conditions, Europeans sweating in unhappy exile from home."[33] Whereas Du Bois waxed eloquent about the noble qualities the "native" had to impart to "modern man," Greene sees both as involved in the same human dilemmas. His view is generally dyspeptic; human beings everywhere are sunk in the coils of the same problems. Schuyler's very noble Zo and Pameta have no place in Greene's view of the hinterland; the same can be said of *Slaves Today's* superdegenerate Americo-Liberians. To Greene, Liberia offered simply another view of the human condition.

Greene's Africa does not coincide with Du Bois's totemic Africa. It is also not Schuyler's Liberia awaiting uplift from the likes of Thomas

Faulkner. Greene tries to see himself in the Other, "like the images in a dream to stand for something of importance to myself."[34] At the same time, his whiteness encloses him. He noted, "Everywhere in the north I found myself welcomed because I was a white, because they hoped all the time that a white nation would take the country over." Greene alternately cajoles and bullies his "boys." They are his fellow humans, but not equals: "The character of a carrier is childlike. He enjoys the moment. He cannot connect cause and effect." The porters, for all of Greene's concern with the human condition, exist across a chasm. The writer can only bridge it with racial noblesse oblige: "He [the porter] is used to one meal in the day at evening, he lives on the edge of subsistence, and it would be a hard master who grudged him the unexpected pleasure of an extra meal."[35] Barbara Greene, seeking to explain her cousin and the natives, wrote, "Graham . . . from the beginning treated them exactly as if they were white men from our own country. He talked to them quite naturally and they liked him." In almost the next sentence, however, the most sentimental of paternalisms manifests itself. "After the day's trek they would like to lie round him, and joke and laugh, while he, like a benevolent father, would smile kindly upon them."[36]

Greene's "primitive" may not be a noble savage, but he or she remains unselfconscious. Both Greenes recorded an episode as they approached the coast near the end of their journey. Graham wrote, "A young girl hung around all day posturing with her thighs and hips, suggestively, like a tart. Naked to the waist, she was conscious of her nakedness; she knew that breasts had a significance to the white man they didn't have to the native."[37] Barbara observed the observer: "A young girl, an obvious little prostitute, hovered round and postured in front of Graham." The proof of "civilization" was there: "I felt that at some time she had been down to the coast and that she had known white men." The English-woman wrote that the girl was "over-optimistic, or she would have realised at once that my cousin was beyond noticing anything."[38]

Even before this, Graham Greene had been disquieted in the village of Greh. It is a "scrap of 'civilization.'" He opined that "sexual inversion is rare among the blacks, [but] a pair of naked homosexuals stood side by side all day with their arms locked and their hair plaited in ringlets staring at me."[39] Like the nineteenth-century traveler Sir Richard Burton, Greene liked his natives "raw." He wrote that he had "developed a bitter dislike of the very appearance of Bassa men, the large well-covered bodies, the round heads, the soft effeminate eyes." The curse was civilization, for "the Coast had corrupted them, had made them liars, swindlers, lazy, weak, completely undependable."[40]

It is in their assessment of the Americo-Liberian ruling group that

Schuyler and Greene most clearly diverge. One is all indignation; the other resignation. Describing the president of Liberia in *Slaves Today,* Schuyler writes, "President Johnson was a Liberian aristocrat. . . . Like most of his contemporaries, His Excellency was not of the material of his pioneer grandparents. . . . he won international fame for saying nothing adroitly. The long, involved sentences which characterized his diplomatic notes had caused the foreign ministers of great powers to scratch their heads in puzzlement and admiration. His state papers were always masterpieces because they could be interpreted in many ways, but they seldom contained anything definite."[41] Greene met the same man, and what the black American's account described as duplicity becomes charm: "Then the President came in; a middle-aged man called Barclay with curly greying hair in a thick dark suit, a pinned and pinched old school tie and a cheap striped shirt. Africa, lovely, vivid and composed, slipped away, and one was left with the West Indies, an affable manner, and rhetoric, lots of rhetoric." Both Greene and Schuyler observe the same phenomena; their difference lies in their distinct moral compasses. In a later serialized novel, *Black Empire,* Schuyler has Barclay violently overthrown by a black army from America. For Greene, "seediness" was inherent in the human condition. He would not disagree with Schuyler's assessment that Barclay was a racketeer, but racketeers were to be expected: "Liberian politics were like a crap game played with loaded dice." As a politician, Barclay partook of the politician's nature:

> He was a politician in the Tammany Hall manner, but I never saw any reason to change my opinion that he was something new on the Coast. He might be out to play his own game, but he was going to play it with unexampled vigour and the Republic would at least pick up some chips from his table. I asked him whether his authority was much the same as the American President's. He said it was more complete. "Once elected," he said, "and in charge of the machine" — words ran away with him; something candid and childlike and excited continually peeped through the politician's dignified phrases — "why then, I'm boss of the whole show."[42]

District commissioner Jackson in *Slaves Today* is a syphilitic brute who lives by extortion. Greene, too, writes of some bad official types. In one case he mentions district commissioner Reeves of Kolahun as a man who "belonged, psychologically, to the early nineteenth century, to the days of the slave trade." The writer paints a monster: "With his seal-grey skin, dark expressionless eyes, full deep red lips, dressed in a fez and a robe of native cloth, he gave an effect, more Oriental than Africa, of cruelty and sensuality; he was gross, impassive and corrupt."[43] This is as good an indictment as any found in Schuyler. Counterposed to this portrait, Greene placed good officials. For instance, he was greatly impressed by the district commissioner in Ganta who "had a reputation for fairness, honesty and efficiency."[44] Schuyler also found "good" officials; in his novel, a character named Rufus Henderson is presented as the type of reform-minded administrator who might have improved conditions. However, for the black journalist, the presence of such types did not change the essential rottenness of the regime; it was a case of a few good men in a dung heap.

While Schuyler, the black cynic of the Jazz Age, created a sentimental and melodramatic indictment, Greene, the deeply religious convert, gave a model of moral detachment. Before he left Britain, he had picked up a copy of the British *Blue Book* describing conditions in Liberia. The volume is replete with accounts of atrocities by the Frontier Force:

> After the outbreak of hostilities . . . operations against the disaffected tribes appear to have been conducted in a ruthless, callous and brutal manner with regard for the lives of innocent women and children, as will be apparent from the casualty figures which were supplied . . . by the dissident tribes. The number of women and children killed amounted to seventy-two as against sixty-nine men. The plantation town of Wolokri in the Sasstown interior was attacked at night when the inhabitants were asleep and totally unprepared. The soldiers crept into the banana plantations, which surround all native villages, and poured volleys into the huts. In the subsequent confusion and flight women and children were ruthlessly shot down and killed. One woman who had that day been delivered of twins was shot in her bed, and the infants perished in the flames when the village was fired by the troops. At this town 3 men, 14 women and 8 children met their death.[45]

After reviewing the account, Greene could only muse, "It really seemed as though you couldn't go deeper than that; the agony was piled on in the British Government Blue Book with a real effect of grandeur; the little injustices of Kenya became shoddy and suburban beside it."[46] In a world full of abuses, what was one to do?

Greene's ironic detachment becomes most obvious in his treatment of Colonel Elwood Davis, "The Dictator of Grand Bassa." Davis was a man accused in the international press of atrocities in the southern Liberian counties. When Greene met the man charged with burning villages and slaughtering their inhabitants, Greene felt, as he frequently did, charmed: "Even at a distance there was something attractive about the dictator of Grand Bassa. He had personality."[47] At times, the Englishman hovers between irony and credulity. Davis brought up the British report charging that he had burnt children alive. The colonel assured his British visitor, "There was no one who loved children more than he did.

He had pickaninnies of his own. . . . His enemies in Monrovia . . . had pretended to believe in these atrocities, and even his mother, back in America, had read about them."[48] Did Greene believe his interlocutor? It doesn't matter; the writer was entranced by the soldier, who "carried himself with a straight military swagger, . . . very well dressed in a tropical suit with a silk handkerchief stuck in the breast pocket."

During the Spanish Civil War, Ernest Hemingway called Nancy Cunard a "war tourist."[49] The term is equally applicable to Greene in the midst of the Liberian "native rebellions." As an observer he observes well, but he remains impassive. Writing of one of Davis's captives, he noted, "The old prisoner was a half-wit; I saw one of the warders beating him with his club to make him move to the tin basin in which he had to wash, but he didn't seem to feel the blows."[50] The Greenes' seeming imperturbability appears curious—and disturbing. Barbara observed the same scene and wrote of it in a very similar vein:

> I walked towards the prison, and studied it from every side. It was not pleasant. It was a small, dark hut, and out of the little windows gaunt and hungry faces were gaping. Men and women, tied by ropes to the bars across the windows, were staring out into the compound. Inside I could imagine it would be suffocatingly hot, a second black hole of Calcutta. A few of the prisoners were lying outside, tied by the leg to wooden posts, in the glowing heat, unable to get into the shade. They all wore the heavy, stupid expressions of animals, and when the warders beat them with clubs, they seemed hardly to feel the blows.[51]

The next day, when the Greenes met Davis, Barbara was awestruck. "No longer," she wrote, "could I think of him as a cold-blooded murderer of women and children. His personality was too colourful, his gestures were too theatrical." What impresses the Greenes is not the "banality of evil," but evil as vaguely amusing theater. Both Graham and Barbara lapse into a kind of moral obtuseness; Nick and Nora Charles have been set down in Africa without a moral compass. The impression is of two terribly blasé wayfarers, who, in spite of their sophistication, are constantly gulled by the local administration. One is reminded of Franco Zefirelli's depiction of English women abroad in *Tea with Mussolini*.[52] Perhaps an even better parallel would be the Duke and Duchess of Windsor waxing rhapsodic about the grey eyes of Attaturk and the deep blue of Hitler's. There is little malice, only an inability to see beneath the surface. Barbara was charmed:

> Graham sent a note over to Col. Davis asking for an interview. . . . I sat on the verandah and waited. After an hour it got dark and there was still no sign of Graham. I called for a lamp, and got out the stories of Saki and Somerset

Maugham, and tried to read . . . I was introduced to Col. Davis, and we shook hands.

"We want some whiskey," said Graham.

"I usually drink Ovaltine," the Dictator of Grand Bassa explained to me. "But just to-night——."

"Of course," I murmured.

He was a good-looking man, tall and straight, with a neat black-pointed beard. Unfortunately he had too many gold teeth, so that his flashing smile lost a good deal of its charm. . . . At the moment he was playing the part of the man of the world, and once again I felt my shorts were too short.[53]

In a telling vignette, Barbara Greene's cousin expressed his anxiety not to raise the issue of human rights with his Liberian hosts. Meeting a district commissioner whom he liked, Graham sought to reassure him: "He was courteous and reserved and it was hopeless to try to convince him that our journey had no political motive." Greene resolved to try anyway: "I felt our amicable expressions becoming shrill in the effort to convince . . . he was a man with such admirable qualities that one wanted to leave him with a good impression."[54]

Recently, writing of Hemingway's African novels, a critic has remarked "that a principled refusal to be sentimental actually stifles feeling and the explanation for feeling; then, in turn, that refusal becomes in itself sentimental." In Hemingway's case, he "is a great truth-telling writer, except when he becomes sentimental about truth telling and thus becomes untruthful."[55] Like, Hemingway, Greene believed that he presented the world, especially the non-West, as it was. "I assure you," he wrote, "that the dead child lay in the ditch in just that attitude. In the canal at Phat Diem the bodies stuck out of the water." He despaired of his critics, for "argument is useless. They won't believe the world they haven't noticed is like that."[56] This defense, if one may call it that, seems a bit thin. What the reader sometimes gets is no more than a picture postcard of misery interlaced with local color. Schuyler in the 1930s or Shawcross in *The Quality of Mercy*, describing the killing fields of Cambodia, exhibit many of the conditions found in Greeneland. But an important difference exists. Greene seems to conclude that the poor and the seedy shall always be with us. The novelist later opined, "There was the excitement of sin itself; excitement in guilt and fear, even in being unmasked . . . these elements were active in most good writing."[57] Greene's project cannot have any political outcome; it is not meant to. And, unlike André Gide in his 1928 *Voyage au Congo*, Greene's experience did not result in political engagement. The Englishman ends up in a position very similar to Du Bois's—to him, the cruelties of the regime represent the cruelties of tropical regimes everywhere. After their departure, an official of the

British legation wrote that the Greenes "were charmed by the President and the members of the Cabinet they met, but complained against one District Commissioner." The official continued, "I think they found conditions in Liberia so normal they were disappointed!"[58]

The Revenge Fantasy

As seen, Schuyler's position on the Liberian regime could never approximate Greene's laissez-faire stance. His position was unequivocal. In the foreword to *Slaves Today,* he became overtly political: "If this novel can help arouse enlightened world opinion against this brutalizing of the native population in a Negro republic, perhaps the conscience of civilized people will stop similar atrocities in native lands ruled by proud white nations that boast of their superior culture."[59] The year in which Greene published *Journey without Maps,* Schulyer began a serialized novel, *Black Empire.* Writing under the nom de plume Samuel I. Brooks, he published the work between 1936 and 1938. The first section appeared in the *Pittsburgh Courier* as the *Black Internationale* from November of 1936 to July of 1937. The second section, actually entitled *Black Empire,* was printed between October 1937 and April 1938.

Taken together, *Black Internationale* and *Black Empire* form a bizarre work. Indeed, it almost constitutes a Rorschach test for both the writer and the reader. In it, Schuyler rejects assimilation and puts forth a Manichaean world in which the Black World strikes back, pushing the White World almost to the point of collapse. It is a futuristic revenge fantasy in which brains rather than hustler rhetoric make Liberia the center of black world liberation. The stories are full of novelties: television, solar power, facsimile machines, hydroponics, atom smashers, euthanasia, and biological warfare. The works indeed adumbrate some of the horrors of World War II. In one chilling example, the Black Internationale gasses 15,000 whites locked in a theatre. Schuyler's work resembles a number of other fantastical works, whether literary or political. There are echoes of the early French serial film, *Fantômas.* The *Black Internationale* also brings to mind Dr. Marbuse and Sax Rohmer's Fu Manchu. There are even hints of the *Protocols of the Elders of Zion.* At its "secret confab" in the Catskills, a black mastermind and his minions plot world domination through manipulation of the stock market and the control of sectors of the produce trade. In one truly curious twist, Schuyler's fictional black conspiracy mirrors the way he imagined international communism operated in the 1940s: "To destroy modern civilization and institute the new slavery, they have schemed to use the American, West

Indian and African Negroes. . . . So much the better, they argue, if civil strife and wholesale destruction of these peoples result."[60]

A young black reporter, Carl Slater, Schuyler's alter ego, functions as the serial's narrator. The serial begins when the journalist in the novel sees a well-dressed black man in the company of a white woman. Slater follows the two and sees the man strangle the woman to death. Slater, the witness, is kidnapped at gunpoint, forced into a waiting car, and made to take a sleeping concoction. He awakens to find himself in a luxuriously appointed bedroom, where a curiously silent butler waits on him. After dressing, the reporter is taken into the presence of the murderer, Dr. Henry Belsidus. Belsidus is the evil genius of Schuyler's pot-boiler, a rich Harlem physician of mysterious origin whose practice is largely confined to rich white women. The doctor launches into exposition over breakfast: the murdered woman had failed in an assignment and had to be eliminated. She was a cog in his master plan—black domination of the world. Belsidus offers Slater a choice—join the doctor's operation or be killed. The narrator accepts.

Schuyler's position in his nationalist serials diametrically opposes his deconstruction of race in *Black No More*. In the twenties, he had argued for a multiplicity of black experience across the world. The *Black Internationale* and *Black Empire* reverse that. They are Pan-African, or, better yet, Pan-Melaninist concoctions in which black blood, however diluted, speaks. Class, language, religion, gender, and color sink into insignificance. Having painted Belsidus as a sometimes-fiend, he provides him with a partial justification in the form of racial payback: "Was there no end to this cruelty, this ruthlessness, this cold and calculating killing?" The reply is quick: "But then what omelet was ever made without breaking eggs? How had Africa been enslaved except through murder"?[61] Schuyler is schizoid in the serials; violence is extreme, but often deplored. The narrator, Carl Slater, is allowed the position of participant observer, alternatively fascinated and repelled by Belsidus. Throughout, the leader of the Black Internationale is described in pejorative terms; he is "sardonic," "ruthless," the "sinister physician."

Slater's first assignment is to serve as Belsidus's private secretary at a meeting of the Black Internationale (curiously set in the Catskills). At the opening of the meeting, three delegates are liquidated as spies. The remaining delegates then listen to their leader expound his views. Central to Belsidus's plans is the liberation of Africa from colonial rule. Subsequently, Slater learns that this is more than a pipe dream. The Black Internationale has secret farms and factories. Also, Belsidus has a network of burglars who bring tons of precious metals pouring into the coffers of the organization. The mastermind, ever mindful of the credulity of the masses, has created a new religion, the Church of Love, a heady mix of drugs, sex, and salvation. The narrator himself leads a chaste existence; he falls in love with the head of the Internationale's air force, the beautiful Patricia Givens. She, however, is ruthlessly dedicated to the cause and has no time for romance.

Schuyler, perhaps because of his army experience and extensive travel, knew of the divisions among white folk. Keenly aware of whiteness as a construction, he has his Belsidus character plot the destruction of white America by playing on its internal divisions. The Black Internationale retaliates against a lynching in Mississippi by bombing the town from the air. Once the deed is done, leaflets are dropped which proclaim the act the work of the Church of Rome. Although Givens and Slater are almost captured on their flight back to the North, they return safely. Belsidus is delighted at the growth of sectarian antipathy among the white Christian brethren. With America in turmoil, the hour for action arrives. Five thousand of Belsidus's legionnaires are sent to Freetown, Sierra Leone, the base for an invasion of Liberia. Monrovia is attacked and the government overthrown. The colonial powers are alarmed, but the new chief of state reassures them that little Liberia will not become a point d'appui for anticolonialist adventures. Of course, he is lying.

Discord is sewn between the various colonial powers. A Second World War breaks out.

> The war was growing more devastating by the hour. Every principal city in Europe had been bombed by one or the other of the belligerents, and in every case incendiary and gas bombs had been used. All restrictions were off and human brutality was revealed at its worst. Hospitals, churches, homes of non-combatants, all were blown to bits by the terribly destructive aerial attacks. Millions of armed men hurled themselves against the artillery, machine guns, liquid fire, tanks and bayonets of opposing armies. And as each report came in, the grin of Dr. Belsidus grew more diabolical.[62]

As the Europeans kill each other, the Black World strikes. Africa revolts and Europeans either flee or are killed. Two months of intensive fighting ensue. At the end of it, Africa is free. The new leader of the Black World proclaims the capital of a united Africa to be Kakata in the interior of Liberia.

Schuyler's serials on the Liberian theme reveal that he remained dead set against the Liberian oligarchy. The future of Africa lay with the indigenous chiefs — under the beneficent tutelage of the Black Internationale. Immigrants from the United States come "and most of them adjusted themselves to the new life. In every case they had paid their own money for passage to the new land of opportunity."[63] The *Black Internationale* and *Black Empire* represent, in many ways, Garveyite fantasies without Garvey. Garveyite themes run throughout the serials, even down to Belsidus's creation of a black-owned fleet with names like SS *Fred Douglass, Sojourner Truth, Phyllis Wheatley, Samory,* and *Bessie Coleman.*

Considering the fact that Schuyler considered himself an inveterate anti-Garveyite, his serial surprises. As early as 1923, the author was a member of the anti-Garvey Friends of Negro Freedom, a group intent on getting the Jamaican deported. In early 1923, Schuyler advised the Friends of Negro Freedom, "Don't let up on Brother Marcus lest more foolish Negroes be taken in by this sable Ponzi."[64] In the early 1920s, Schuyler described Garvey as "the Imperial Blizzard," "America's greatest buffoon," or "America's greatest collector of antiques."[65] The journalist's "Shafts and Darts" column in the *Messenger* delighted in attacking the UNIA with a constant stream of gutter humor. When the *Negro World* announced that "the Members of the UNIA Are the Strongest Negroes in the World," Schuyler sophomorically retorted, "Everyone who has ever been unfortunate enough to enter Liberty Hall when the great mass of Garveyites within were stirring with emotion, and the windows, as usual, were closed, will heartily agree with this statement."[66] In an extremely unkind commentary on Garvey's impending imprisonment, Schuyler played with the idea of a fictional publishing house putting out Marcus Garvey's *Atlanta or Leavenworth: Their Relative Merits as Havens of Rest.* In *Black No More,* Schuyler burlesqued Garvey as the racketeering hustler Santop Licorice. After the publication of *Slaves Today,* he was almost thrown off a podium in New York by irate UNIA members. Schuyler announced, "I did not then and do not now approve of the loud mouth, ignorant, inefficient manner in which Garvey went about the business."[67] In December of 1933, Garvey lambasted the journalist as "one of the most dangerous libelers of true American Negro character." Schuyler was a "circus monkey," who "with a little red coat and his evolved tail, and with a little rouge on his long lips . . . would be sure to remind his audiences of this illustrious prototype that swung from the branches of trees in the dense African forest."[68]

Like many black intellectuals of the time, Schuyler's political line was subject to meanderings. An assimilationist who often said that he believed in the unique destiny of African Americans, he could find, at times, a nub of truth in the Pan-African rationale. In 1929, with Garvey safely deported, Schuyler could summon up some praise for the fallen leader:

> Marcus Garvey has a vision. He sees plainly that everywhere in the Western and Eastern hemispheres the Negro, regardless of his religion or nationality, is being crushed under the heel of white imperialism and exploitation. Rap-

idly the population of the world is being aligned in two rival camps: white and black. The whites have arms, power, organization, wealth; the blacks have only their intelligence and their potential power. If they are to be saved, they must be organized so they can present united opposition to those who seek to continue their enslavement.[69]

In the *Black Internationale,* Schuyler refers to his problem with Garveyism. In his opinion, the UNIA favored talk over intelligence. Dr. Belsidus announces, "one of the great mistakes made by minority leaders in the past has been ballyhoo. Therefore we have established no newspapers or magazines, given no talks over the radio, staged no parades or demonstrations."[70] In Schuyler's fantasy, Belsidus is quietly clever where Garvey had only been loud. "Had Garvey been more diplomatic and less mouthy," the journalist believed, "he might have attained his objective in Liberia. As it was, he bragged about what he was going to do in Liberia and then squawked when the canny Liberians barred him and his movement."[71]

What are we to make of Schuyler's creation of Belsidus and his black nationalist fantasy? Assessing his own work, he remarked, "I have been greatly amused by the public enthusiasm for 'The Black Internationale,' which is hokum and hack work of the purest vein. I deliberately set out to crowd as much race chauvinism and sheer improbability into it as my fertile imagination could conjure." He added, "The result vindicates my low opinion of the human race."[72] Was the journalist by the late 1930s simply a cynical opportunist? Benjamin Lawson notes the difficulty of trying to divine exactly Schuyler's motivations:

> At times, even during the thirties, he seemed assimilationist, at other times, race conscious if not black nationalist. The divisions in Schuyler have created divisions in his critics between those who see him as a split personality and those who conclude his was a personality unified and defined by a quality like 'American-ness' — albeit hounded by other, spectral, selves. Simply taking Schuyler's statements at face value, for all these reasons, leads to a naive reading.[73]

Henry Louis Gates sees Schuyler as fragmented. He believes that the serials "teach us about Schuyler's complicated response to the pressures of ideological conformity among blacks — and the failure of most received ideological stances or political programs to account for this complexity."[74] Schuyler's ambiguity could betray something deeper, a more complex riff on Du Bois's double consciousness. Certainly, Schuyler was aware of the elder statesman's formulation: "One ever feels his two-ness — an American, a Negro."[75] Schuyler's "Negro" is itself divided, divided between the assimilationist and the Race Man. In the serials, writing under another name, the journalist allows himself to become a Super Race Man. His writing constitutes a direct repudiation of his previous public writings and stance. There is a Jekyll and Hyde quality to Schuyler; each side forms a true part of the other. The man who lauded his "blonde and shapely" white wife and praised "hybrid vigor" in his daughter Philippa, kept somewhere within him fantasies of sexual revenge and a cache of racial misogyny. Many states considered Schuyler's marriage illegal, and the portrayal of interracial marriage was banished from the cinema after the Motion Picture Code of 1934, along with that of homosexuality and drug addiction.[76]

Schuyler offers a transgressive and troubling treatment of interracial sex. It provides a leitmotiv for much of his writing. Already in *Slaves Today*, it causes the writer to muse that "there is a certain affinity between individuals of opposite colors. The fascination of the unknown is so alluring that mutual stimulation is inevitable." Zo, the hero, falls for the wiles of Marie, a *mulata* prostitute on Fernando Po. Schuyler wrote: "Zo was black and Marie was almost white. . . . Her particular weakness was for strong black men."[77] In the late 1930s serials, black sexual potency proves central to the plot. One of the secrets of Belsidus's success is that he has discovered the White Race's Achilles' heel—the white woman. The doctor's boudoir becomes the locus of racial revenge. Martha Gaskins, the novelettes' only continuing white character, is cut off from her own people and serves only as an object of use or abuse to Belsidus. She is the ultimate race traitor—her motives can never be noble, motivated as they are by an insatiable lust for the head of the Black Internationale. The closing lines of the serial reflect her isolation and her doom. Carl Slater observes her: "I looked down the front row to where Martha Gaskins sat, her blonde hair looking odd among those Negroes. She was twisting her tiny handkerchief in her hands, while a pair of tears coursed unnoticed down her cheek."[78] Schuyler's ending is less horrific than Waugh's in *Black Mischief*, in which a white female do-gooder is eaten by an African she is trying to help, but it proves no less mordant.

Black sexual potency is, in and of itself, the thread that links the disparate parts of the Black World. While Belsidus prefers to remain in the background, a surrogate, the Reverend Samson Binks, creates the Church of Love, designed to appeal to the black masses. Schuyler was aware that, in the wake of the collapse of Garveyism and with the advent of the Depression, many black "joiners" had become members of religious groups, such as Father Divine's Peace Mission movement, in an effort to find an anodyne to the pain of living in white America. Indeed, in 1936, a former Garveyite could write to the head of the UNIA and inform him that "Garveyism was the highest grace this so-called race had. . . . But to-day a greater than Garvey is here." The writer went on to say to Garvey, "you were regarded as the world's most fearless leader in this present civilization before the coming of FATHER DIVINE. . . . Please try HIM out as 23,000,000 of us did, you NEED HIM as all the World does."[79] One historian has noted that many writers particularly "noted women's participation in the movement only to emphasize women's fanaticism, ignorance or sensual longings for Father Divine."[80] Schuyler held a dim view of religion in general, and the Peace Mission's celibate but fanatical adherents did not appeal to him. Father Divine's movement owned dormitories, food stores, clothing stores, restaurants, and farms. In his serial, Schuyler goes the Peace Mission one better; it provides material benefits — clothing and groceries — as well as sex and drugs. The centerpiece of worship is a huge ithyphallic representation of the black man:

> "Gaze upon Him!" boomed the voice again. We all looked upward. The music had ceased now. Only the low chanting of the chorus relieved this awed silence. Now the great arms, which had been folded, slowly unfolded and stretched out full length. The great breast began to rise and fall. The huge eyes became luminous and the great head began slowly to nod up and down. It was awesome indeed. The singing ended. The eyes continued to blaze. The great head moved up and down. . . . Suddenly, a woman screamed. Then another, and then another. They were piteous agonizing screams, and a body fell to the tile floor.[81]

Like *Slaves Today,* but less obviously so, *Black Internationale* and *Black Empire* are political works arising out of the author's detestation of the Liberian regime. During the conquest of Monrovia, the Executive Mansion is besieged. Finally, after a furious gun battle, Edwin Barclay surrenders: "The last man to emerge with hands over his head and tears streaming from his eyes was the President of Liberia."[82] The Americo-Liberian is replaced by Belsidus, who speaks to a gathering of traditional chiefs, "Liberian people would not let you have guns, but I give them to you. Is it not so"? The new leader continues to harangue his audience, saying, "Liberian people would not let you have bullets, but I give them to you. Is it not so? Liberian people take food and wine from you, but I give you food and wine. Is it not so?"[83] During Schuyler's lifetime, this scenario remained simply a revenge fantasy. But three years after his death in 1977, the last Americo-Liberian president was executed in his bed.

9 The "Native Problem"

A few nights ago, a well-dressed
man from the Foreign Ministry. . .ordered a beer, and
proceeded to explain what happened here. . . .
All of Liberia's troubles. . .all the death
and misery, were the fault of the aborigines. . . .
A few days later one of Liberia's most
prominent lawyers begged to differ. "It was the settlers who,
in many ways, brought the destruction upon themselves."

—Tim Weiner, *The New York Times*,

September 3, 2003

Barclay, after having braved both the Firestone Company and the State Department, settled into his last term—one that he had extended to eight years instead of four. At the end of 1934, the president had gained the True Whig nomination for another term. He faced as his chief opponent the ever resourceful C. D. B. King. Politics make strange bedfellows. Thomas Faulkner let his People's Party followers join a splinter group of the True Whig Party organized by King. Still seeking to reform the system, Faulkner asked for outside help in monitoring the elections, but no help was forthcoming. In May of 1935, Barclay was elected by a vote of 311,569 to 7,784. Since the electorate numbered only 15,000, this constituted another truly astounding victory.[1] A pattern in Liberian politics was emerging; King unsuccessfully challenged his successor as Barclay was to unsuccessfully challenge his.

King, the man at the center of the slavery scandal, remained within the circle of oligarchic power, although excluded from its center. Graham Greene described him after his electoral combat with Barclay. The ex-president was tired. By engaging in the election, "he was complying with a custom; one could see that he would be glad to go back to bed."

King "had had a finer fling than most Liberian Presidents: banquets in Sierra Leone, royal salutes from the gunboat in the harbour, a reception at Buckingham Palace, a turn at the tables at Mont Carlo. . . . [He was] a black Cincinnatus back on his farm."[2] In retirement, King served for a time as a lawyer for Firestone. Decade after decade, the ex-president weathered the vicissitudes of political life. In 1955, fifteen years after the death of Marcus Garvey, he became Liberian delegate at the Bandung Conference, temporarily switching from West African oligarch to Third World spokesman.

Barclay devised his own plan of assistance to satisfy international opinion. An American was hired to train the Frontier Force, a Pole to advise on trade relations, and a Pole and a Hungarian to work on health and sanitation questions. Some African Americans hoped to play important roles in Liberian rehabilitation, but in the main, they did not receive encouragement. Emily Balch of the WILPF spoke to Melville Mackenzie on the subject. Later she wrote, "Dr. McKenzie says (as we always heard in Haiti) that the last thing they [the Liberians] themselves want is any American Negroes mixing in." Supposedly, the Liberians would "see in them a danger to their monopoly of governmental pie."[3] Raymond Buell did ask the Tuskegee director of extension work to recommend several agronomists to the Foreign Policy Association for referral to the Liberian government. Some years later, he opined that the eight "emergency" specialists hired in 1934 were no more than "international window-dressing."[4] The experts remained largely powerless and, at the end of their tenure in December of 1937, were let go. The economy did improve, however. In January of 1939, Walton wrote to Du Bois that the worst was over; the country had balanced its budget in spite of a decrease in revenue in 1938. The American minister thought the Barclay regime a great success, and if it received "the strong moral support of the United States," Liberia had less and less to fear.[5]

Barclay was firmly in the driver's seat. In his second inaugural address, he proved himself a master of Liberian rhetoric. Mistakes were admitted, reform promised:

> Liberia and Liberians in the past few years have had to pass through the crucible of both responsible and irresponsible criticism. This has thrown into high relief their real and fancied deficiencies. The severest self-analysis will not leave us unconvinced that some of that criticism was [deserved]. This experience will have been without benefit if it has not developed in us the courage to face realities. We should not, therefore, hesitate to shed that self-complacency with which we have been so strongly inhibited in the past, and secure such assistance and adopt such competently recommended

methods as will assure the strengthening of our National Institutions, the broadening of our social activities and the proper basing of the Nation's economic life.[6]

Barclay struck a note of guided democracy that would not have been found strange in the authoritarian regimes of the 1930s: Liberia's situation "not only implies that the people are willing to submit to the authority of that [national] leadership when exercised for the common welfare, but also imports that they are disposed to yield themselves to a disciplined cooperation with Government in all that tends to the public good whatever the individual or group sacrifices involved." Bolstered by his lengthened term, he seemed to paraphrase Mussolini's dictum, "the State is that Absolute before which all individuals and groups are relative." Barclay saw no hope for Liberia "unless the people generally give unreserved allegiance to a definite national Ideal and to a course of policy dominated and directed by a central Will."[7] Internationally, Liberia would follow a policy of laissez-faire. In his inaugural, Barclay proclaimed that the country would respect the territory of its neighbors. It would, in turn expect "reciprocal consideration." In a veiled reference to Firestone, he reminded his listeners, "it cannot be supposed that we will continue to submit to undue economic and political exploitation."

The Natives Are Restless

At the end of the Second World War, Raymond Buell warned that "unless something radical is done to narrow the gap between the governing oligarchy and the Liberian people it is not impossible that within twenty-five years fighting in Liberia will break out, as it has recently done in Java and Indo-China. Indeed, such fighting might already have broken out except for the presence of American troops in Liberia."[8] Thirty-five years after this prediction, the Liberian ancien régime was swept away. On April 12, 1980, William R. Tolbert, the last of the True Whig presidents, was executed in the Executive Mansion by a group of young soldiers. Members of the cabinet were stripped and shot on a nearby beach. Revolution brought neither democracy nor peace. The collapse of Americo-Liberian rule was followed by more than a decade of internecine violence. Tolbert's successor, Samuel K. Doe, ruled with declining effectiveness for a decade. When rebels killed him in 1990, Liberia plunged into a sanguinary civil war far more severe than the eruptions of the 1930s. The African American journalist Keith Richburg reported:

On a sticky hot November morning in 1992, I found myself . . . on the outskirts of Monrovia, the besieged capital of war-torn Liberia. I was interviewing soldiers from the Alligator Battalion, and the boys (none of them looked older than twenty-one) were passing around a particularly pungent marijuana cigarette while keeping a vigil here against incursions into the city from the surrounding swampland.

The battalion commander Captain Jungle Jabba, was dressed in an Operation Desert Storm T-shirt and gold-rimmed sunglasses. His deputy commander, distinguishable mostly by his tennis shoes and thick dreadlocks, identified himself as Captain Pepper-and-Salt—"because I will peppa' the enemy," he explained, waving his AK-47. And further down the road . . . the soldier inspecting cars was decked out in a flowing ash blond woman's wig, held down by a black plastic shower cap pinned on his head. At his side was a twelve-year-old boy named Abraham, who called himself a member of the "special forces" and claimed to have been fighting in Liberia's jungles since he was ten. Abraham wore camouflage pants and had two grenades fastened to his belt on either side.[9]

By the time a brief peace was restored in 1997, at least 150,000 of the country's 2.8 million people were dead, and 2 million were refugees within Liberia or abroad. As in the 1930s, calls for intervention emerged, but this time they came from human rights activists and the remnants of the democratic opposition. As in the 1930s, there was no intervention. Charles Taylor, a former warlord of indigenous and Americo-Liberian descent, won the election in 1997, after years of bloodily fighting off his rivals. As a popular Liberian street saying put it, "Same taxi, new driver." Change had been long in coming. When it came, it proved catastrophic.

Half a century after Elie Garcia's denunciation of the dominant elite, the latter was still in the driver's seat. In spite of the hopes of various segments of tribal Liberian society, post-1930 events did not soon end the dominance of the Americo-Liberian elite. Although there was some amelioration in the administration of the "Native policy," there still was one. Some Western-educated indigenes had looked on the year 1930 as the dawning of a new era in which the reins of power would be transferred to their hands. However, the Barclay regime (and with it, the Americo-Liberian elite) had managed to weather the storm presented by both internal and external opposition. No basic changes came in the 1930s. There was no radical redistribution of power inside the country and no imposition of externally fostered reforms. Barclay skillfully manipulated both the internal and the external situation. Cloaked with the legitimacy bequeathed him by the doctrine of national sovereignty, he steadfastly and successfully maintained that there could be no interference in the internal affairs of Liberia. By 1936, as chief executive of the one remaining independent state in Africa, he also drew on prevailing sentiments of racial solidarity and anti-imperialism abroad. By paradox, many foreign observers converted the crushing of "native" into a symbol of the triumph of Black Power.

After 1930, Liberia did attempt to appease world public opinion. As we have seen, the legislature enacted laws prohibiting labor export and the pawning of human beings. A public health service was created, and the hinterland administration underwent reorganization. However, the public relations value of such actions was largely negated by the news that the Monrovia government was forcibly attacking the Kru and Grebo for testifying before the League's commission of inquiry. The people of Sasstown, especially, resisted under the leadership of Kru chief Juah Nimley (Senyo Juah Nimene). This struggle gave rise to stories of a calculated policy of reprisal on the part of the Barclay regime. Resistance continued until 1936, when the "rebel chief" was captured and exiled.

Resistance in the 1930s: "Little Horrors"

In early 1930, Thomas Faulkner wrote to Sir Eric Drummond of the League of Nations and warned of "a bloody fight or a revolution," if the organization did not intervene.[10] The following year, League investigator Charles Brunot heard that the indigenous population would revolt if outside assistance was not forthcoming, and it was feared that, deprived of funds for ammunition, the Monrovia regime might topple.[11] The Liberian government and various foreign observers maintained that a "provocateur," one "John Stuart, alias Major Frank or Major Ford," went to Sasstown and announced that the authority of the Monrovia regime was all but defunct.[12] After Stuart departed from Sasstown, the district commissioner himself hurriedly abandoned his post, and from July 1930 until October of 1931, the town had no local representative of the central government. In order to resolve inter-Kru disputes and to assert the power of the Barclay regime, Colonel Elwood Davis was sent to the Kru Coast. He arrived in May but failed to establish his authority immediately.

Davis was a black American from Indianapolis, who had emigrated to Liberia around 1919 as part of what the British legation cryptically referred to as the "Zionist Mission." The same source animadverted, "He very soon turned into a fake medical officer, in which career he was supported by President King . . . [and] continued his careers as an imitation Public Health Officer and an imitation soldier under successive Administrations.[13] These strictures were probably misinformed.

Charles S. Johnson of the 1930 League commission reported that Davis had served against Mexico in Pershing's Tenth Cavalry and later as a troop trainer in World War I.[14] In spite of, or perhaps because of, his military experience, Davis proceeded cautiously on the Kru Coast. He waited ten weeks, writing letters to defiant tribes in hopes of avoiding a confrontation.

In July, at Pallipo in Liberian District No. 5, Davis found the people insubordinate, supposedly due to the propaganda spread by "Stuart."[15] There was also an outbreak of internal strife at Nana Kru. The feuding there only constituted a prelude to the violence which was to erupt in and around Sasstown in 1931. The reasons given for the violence are many and various. Initially, the trouble may have involved border disputes between Sasstown and Picaninny Cess.[16] Liberian garrisons in the two areas may have taken sides in the dispute and become involved in armed conflict. The Monrovia government, for its part, attributed the disturbances to the tyrannical practices of paramount chief Juah Nimley, who was invited to Monrovia and lectured on the conduct expected of him.

According to Monrovia, this was to no avail. On August 27, 1931, President Barclay wrote to Davis, telling him that the collector of the port and the customs guards at Sasstown had been driven away and asking him to go in and reimpose order. In November of 1931, actual fighting began between the Sasstown Kru and the Monrovia government. Davis had failed to meet with Nimley, who would accept neither messengers nor letters. A delegation of educated Kru sent by Barclay arrived in Sasstown to help mediate the dispute between their kinsmen and the government, an action which Nimley may have interpreted as a divisive ploy. While the delegation was holding a palaver with Davis and Nimley, the chief's men surrounded the conference hall. The knowledge that Nimley's men stood without, caused consternation within. According to the Liberian government, when Davis began to address the assemblage, "Major Grant [one of Davis's officers] stepped outside[,] returned and said to [the] Paramount Chief and the Council: 'Chief Nimley, you have informed us that you have no war with the Government, and we have come here with that assurance.'" The major then asked, "How is it that when I stepped outside, I observed several hundred of your men armed and in war dress, secreting themselves in ambush and behind trees and houses?"[17] At this point, the meeting broke up in disorder. Men fled outdoors and fighting began. The Liberian officials moved to New Sasstown (separated from Old Sasstown by a stream). Fighting continued for the whole of the first day and was resumed on the morning of the second, when Nimley's supporters withdrew. The town was burned, along with two nearby fishing villages. For the rest of the month, government troops carried out punitive operations against Sasstown's surrounding farms. Meanwhile, villages allied to Sasstown attacked villages loyal to the Monrovia government.[18] Near the end of December, Colonel Davis and Major Grant went to the capital to report on the situation. During their absence, Nimley's followers made an unsuccessful attack on New Sasstown, their only offensive of the war.

Juah Nimley's resistance to the Monrovia regime originated in his objection to the policies of the central government and was sustained by his fear that the government would treat him as it had the "rebels" of 1915–16. Early in 1934, he wrote Lord Cecil, chairman of the League of Nations's Liberia Committee, stating his fears: "It is most certain that we will be arrested like the Nana Kru Chiefs who are now in Custody at Sinoe, and in the end we may be killed like the 75 chiefs who were invited to a 'Peace Conference' at Sinoe but who were seized and executed in 1916."[19] Nimley feared that if he did not comply with the president's order to disarm, his refusal would be used as an excuse for further attacks on his people. While resisting, Juah Nimley continued to maintain his loyalty to the central government. In 1931, he expressed this to a special peace delegation from Monrovia:

> The rumor that has reached the Government that we do not want to pay taxes is false. We know that it is our duty to pay our hut taxes annually as same is for the upkeep and benefit of our land. . . . We do not really refuse to pay the taxes for the year 1931 but due to the financial depression throughout the world, produce, our chief supporter [*sic*], has no value and hence we could hardly get means to pay the taxes.[20]

In 1932, Juah Nimley complained to a British investigator that the government was deliberately spreading stories of his intransigence. He protested, "after the International Commission of Enquiry left Liberia there was no native man who said there is no Liberian Government. . . . What else can the native man do to show that he recognizes the Liberian Government? He pays taxes, he pays customs duties."[21]

The Sasstown troubles received much international publicity. Some quarters reported that the Frontier Force had butchered six hundred unarmed civilians.[22] The Kru managed to communicate their grievances to the world fairly effectively. In 1931, the American minister noted that he had received numerous complaints from various parts of Liberia, including the Kru Coast. "The legation is conscious of the fact," said the minister, "that some of the complaints coming to us may be exaggerated, yet it is believed that the attempted institution of reforms by the Government so far does not meet the requirements necessary to insure safety of life in districts where soldiers are stationed."[23]

The *West African Review* of January 1932 said that Barclay had demanded of a conference of Kru chiefs that they divulge the authors of an appeal for outside aid which read, "We appeal to the League of Nations through the United States and Great Britain for our protection, the protection of our lives, our wives and children, also for our continued survival, as we are being slaughtered and inhumanly treated in every instance now, and unless something is done, and that immediately, we are certain that we will not be able to survive very much longer under the inhuman treatment of this administration."[24] After the chiefs all denied knowledge of the document's authorship, Barclay supposedly had them sign a statement denying its allegations. In the following month, with widespread atrocities still being reported internationally, a group of Kru residents in New York appealed to the State Department for aid.[25]

In January of 1932, the British consul wrote the Foreign Office, "I receive disquieting reports concerning Kru war, indicating unabated serious warfare, destruction of towns, depredations and killing of natives."[26] The Barclay regime was reportedly encouraging civil strife and "establishing terror by hunting and exterminating Sasstown tribes." He urged "definite action if Kru tribes are to be saved from extermination or permanent disorganization." On January 30, the representatives of the American, British, and French governments told the Liberia Committee that Barclay's government was taking draconian measures against indigenes. On March 7, these governments protested what was reported as a calculated policy of atrocity.[27] The British, American, German, and French governments sent notes to their Liberian counterpart and asked that an investigator be sent to examine the situation in detail. The Liberians accepted the investigation, but expressed their doubts about foreigners' rights to interfere. Barclay told the British legation that his government had taken no reprisals. "Explicit assurance is [given], however," Barclay announced, "that no action will be taken against the Kru tribes concerned so long as they refrain from attacking neighbouring peaceful tribes and threatening foreign interests established under the protection of the Liberian Government."[28]

On March 14, 1932, the British vice consul was sent to the Kru Coast to report on conditions. A week later, Barclay sent his own commission, consisting of one American — Winthrop Travell, a loan official — and two Liberians — Reverend F. A. K. Russell, a Grebo, and J. F. Coleman, editor of the *Monrovia Weekly Mirror.* These inquires produced three individual reports (Travell submitted a minority report), published in Geneva in May of 1932. Even before their publication, the U.S. State Department was afraid they would "endeavor to whitewash the administration by laying the blame for the outrages upon the truculent behaviour of one of the tribes which 'had been misled' by the spreading of propaganda that the coming of [the] International Commission meant [the] end of Liberian Government authority."[29] The official Liberian reports did indeed attribute the troubles on the Kru Coast to the seditious activities of outside agitators and to the desire of the indigenous people not to pay tax. The latter charge was, no doubt, often true. But what looked like obduracy to Monrovia must have seemed a justified rejection of outside exploitation to many of the peoples of the Kru Coast.[30]

British vice consul D. D. Rydings's report proved more authoritative. He dismissed a rumor of genocide and calculated that forty-one villages had been burned and a total of 141 men, women, and children killed.[31] He concluded that before the outbreak of hostilities, Colonel Davis had acted with restraint, but that "after the outbreak of hostilities, operations against the disaffected tribes appear to have been conducted in a ruthless, callous and brutal manner without regard for the lives of innocent women and children as will be apparent from casualty figures which were supplied to me by the dissident tribes."[32]

In April of 1932, the U.S. representative to the League of Nations's Liberia Committee informed the State Department that according to British sources, grave abuses still occurred on the Kru Coast.[33] The following month, the League council, in agreement with the Liberian government, sent Melville Mackenzie, former member of the Brunot commission, to Liberia to investigate conditions further and, if possible, bring peace. The Liberians, although approving of the visit, complained that the tone of Mackenzie's commission was dictatorial: when he arrived on a British naval vessel, the Liberians were warned not to make reprisals against the indigenes.[34] On July 12, 1932, the League representative arranged a truce between the Monrovia government and the Kru and Grebo and between warring factions of the indigenous population. In September of 1932, Mackenzie reported to the League on his mission. Peacemaking had, for the time being, succeeded: the truce was to last one year and the people were to be allowed to return to their farms. Monrovia promised to inflict no reprisals. Mackenzie emphasized the temporary nature of the peace. It was urgent, in his opinion, that foreign administrators be appointed before the end of one year, since the disarmed population would find itself at the Frontier Force's mercy at the end of that period.[35]

On July 1, 1933, the Mackenzie truce expired, and in the last days of August, intratribal warfare broke out between the Fishtown and Nimeah sections of the Grebo, with twenty-eight Nimeah men reportedly killed.[36] Nevertheless, in his annual address in October, Barclay set forth a roseate official view of the internal situation: "The Secretary of the Interior reports a state of absolute political tranquility throughout the Republic, even in the district which was in a disturbed condition two years ago."[37] In the spring of 1934, Barclay undertook a tour of the Kru Coast. Former secretary of state Louis B. Grimes wrote to Lester Walton, telling him "that while the noble lords [i.e., the British House of Lords] were discussing the massacre of the tribesmen in Sasstown President Barclay was in Sasstown with his wife and other female relatives, and was being not only loyally and enthusiastically, but even affectionately received."[38] Barclay himself viewed his trip as proof of the high esteem in which the Kru populace held him.[39] According to the Liberian government, Kru friendly to the government supposedly offered to arrange a palaver between Barclay and Nimley, but Nimley refused. The president thought that "many of the followers of Juah Nimley were anxious to return to their homes on the beach, but were deterred from doing so by the wicked manner in which he enforces his orders that they should not submit."[40] The Sasstown leader was accused of executing members of his community who urged submission to the central authority. According to the government, "loyal" Kru could not understand "why, in accordance with the McKenzie [sic] . . . Settlement, they should be deprived of access to their plantations which are being profitably exploited by the rebellious portion of the tribe who, through Dr. McKenzie's [sic] arrangement, have access to the Coast while the loyal people lose the proceeds of their plantations."

Barclay attacked British stories of atrocities as mere inventions and announced that none of the three hundred chiefs he had spoken to in a council at Grand Cess had confirmed reports of bloodshed. As to the reports of harsh proceedings against the people of Sasstown, the president said that Liberian forces had taken offensive action against no one and that, instead, dissident Kru had attacked government forces out on patrol.[41] Barclay claimed that the canoes of dissident tribesmen had been seized "as a measure of precaution and given over to the loyal chief at Sasstown for safe-keeping." Barclay maintained that he had freed the suspect tribesmen on their giving assurance of their loyalty to the Monrovia regime. "That is," said the president, "all there was to this charge of atrocity alleged to have been committed by the Frontier Force against unarmed tribesmen."

Mackenzie strongly disagreed with Barclay's analysis of the Kru situation. He received information from an anonymous Swiss trader who said that conditions on the south Liberian coast were in a state of turmoil. According to the trader, the president, accompanied by troops and five hundred carriers, was met by such hostility that he had to ask for a British cargo steamer to stop at Sasstown and take him off to Monrovia. According to the anonymous source, "King Niminyio" of the Grebo had taken to the "Bush" to organize resistance. The Swiss informant predicted that when the Kru and Grebo realized that the League was not going to send administrators, a general uprising would ensue, beginning at Cape Palmas. "He [the Swiss] adds," Mackenzie assured a League official, "that the white residents will be in no danger at all, as the tribes have no quarrel with the whites, and indeed are only anxious to be administered by them, in view of their knowledge of conditions, particularly in Sierra Leone, where large numbers of them have worked on the ships."[42] The British consulate in Monrovia did not give much credence to Mackenzie's information. It did inform the Foreign Office, in October of 1934, that the people of Picaninny Cess had recently fought among themselves and that the Frontier Force had been sent in.[43]

In spite of Barclay's claims that conditions in Liberia were essentially normal, the American legation remained suspicious. "Although members and partisans of the administration," commented the chargé John MacVeagh, "maintain their denials that there have been any unusual disturbances on the Kru Coast, it has been admitted by the commanding officer of the Frontier Force to friends in Monrovia that the soldiers have been engaged against the tribesmen."[44] In March of 1934, the legation received word that soldiers led by Captain Henry Dennis, the brother of the secretary of the treasury, had in the previous month, without warning, attacked several villages and taken prisoners to Sasstown.[45] The American legation could give no comfort to Kru petitioners for protection and the charged noted, "one of the messengers, who was a very dignified old subchief or headman, thereupon burst into tears saying they would all be murdered if no outside assistance was forthcoming." The legation complained that the Monrovia government was arming tribe to fight tribe and predicted that fighting would soon erupt again.[46]

The failure of the League of Nations's plan of assistance in the spring of 1934 threw the plight of Liberia's indigenous population into high relief. Would anything be done? British foreign minister Sir John Simon was already deeply concerned about the whole matter. "We have, I understand," Simon wrote, "definite news . . . that the tribes whom Dr. Mackenzie disarmed (Heaven knows why) are in danger." Fearing adverse publicity, he urged that a strong note be sent to Liberia on the subject.[47] Simon wrote the British consul in Monrovia, asking that he get assurances that mistreatment of the indigenous population would end. "His Majesty's Government will not content themselves," he wrote, "with an empty denial."[48] The outcome of this pressure did not prove reassuring. On April 18, Earl Stanhope, undersecretary of state for foreign affairs, told the House of Lords that the British consulate had delivered a note to the Liberian secretary of state. "In his reply," Stanhope informed the Lords, "the Liberian Secretary of State stated that he had no knowledge that any such events were happening and that he denied that the assurances given in the Liberian Note [of 1932] had been disregarded; and he made rather impudent suggestions that the protest was made in regard to Liberian subjects and not in regard to British subjects, and therefore he did not quite see what cause we had for interference."[49]

At Geneva, the Liberian representative, M. de Bogerde, implied that Liberian electoral politics had probably influenced and biased the sources of Britain's information.[50] The Liberian secretary of state, Clarence Simpson, maintained that "since the British communication advanced no fresh evidence to substantiate the charges which had been categorically denied by the Liberian Government a year earlier, and since the situation in the Kru districts at the time was perfectly quiet and normal, the British communication seemed to have more relevance to the events taking place at Geneva than to those supposed to have taken place around Fishtown [in Grebo country]."[51]

Sir John Simon continued to urge some kind of action on the Kru question in spite of official Liberian denials of maladministration of "native" areas. The British Foreign Office informed the American government that it would take "any well-considered measures which the United States Government may consider appropriate to the occasion," for it "would be a dereliction of duty to civilization if the misgovernment of the native tribes by Liberia were to be allowed to continue."[52] American policy on the "Native question" was nebulous. In April of 1934, the American chargé in Monrovia advised that no action be taken until after the May session of the League (although he did recommend that an international police force be set up or that France and/or Britain should take the country on as a mandate).[53] In May, the British Foreign Office spoke to an American embassy official in London and suggested a division of responsibility: "The native tribes were our chief concern, while the negroes in Monrovia and the financial chaos were perhaps

America's business."[54] The British were not anxious to intervene, but neither did they wish to abandon Nimley to his fate. A Foreign Office official said that "it is abundantly clear that Chief Nimley counts still on the League and on us to mediate between him and the Government and I think it is up to us (and/or the League) to see that he gets no raw deal."[55] In November of 1934, the Foreign Office interviewed one of the American fiscal officers, P. J. Fitzsimmons, while he was in London, noting that he felt the United States did not want any responsibilities on the other side of the Atlantic and "realized that the Krus were our [Britain's] main interest and his advice was for us to get out of Liberia and take the Krus with us to Freetown [Sierra Leone], where they were wanted and would be useful."[56]

Exit Strategies

Humanitarian intervention soon becomes the victim of humanitarian fatigue and cost accounting. The later examples of Somalia and Haiti indicate the reluctance democracies may have in intervening where "national interests" are not obvious. And so it was that, after the collapse of the League plan and with the Firestone Company nearing a modus vivendi with the Barclay regime, the Kru had become an increasing embarrassment in some quarters. Sir John Simon, the British foreign minister, still concerned about the "Kru problem," informed his ambassador in Washington that the British and American legations should put pressure on Barclay and Nimley to come to some kind of settlement and that recognition of the Barclay regime would depend on such a settlement.[57] Four months later, the British complained that the American chargé had not received explicit instructions on the type of message to be sent to Nimley.[58] The British suspected that the United States was moving unilaterally toward recognition of the Liberian regime. They admitted that the Barclay regime might be trying to reform itself, but felt the settlement of the Kru difficulties key to recognition.[59]

The American legation's conception of how to effect such a settlement differed increasingly from that of the British. The American chargé complained that "due to some inexplicable confusion between Yapp [of the British consulate] and the Foreign Office, the latter felt that a joint suggestion to Barclay by us here would bring the protagonists together and Yapp was even instructed to proceed on that basis." The American felt that such a course would produce no results and prided himself on bringing his British counterpart around to his way of thinking. They agreed to send a Catholic priest with a message for Nimley (after getting the chief a safe conduct from the Liberian government).[60]

The British representative drafted a letter to Nimley that resembled the British advice given to the Kru during the 1915–16 uprising: "I deplore the continued absence of friendship between you and the Liberian Government and it would be well if you and your followers were to make your peace with that Government."[61] But the Liberian government, ever sensitive to interference in its internal affairs, raised objections to certain aspects of these peace preparations. Secretary of state Simpson rejected the British use of the terminology *peace palaver*. The solution of the Kru problem constituted an internal matter between the rulers and the ruled, and not a negotiation between equals. "The Liberian Government," Simpson noted, "would regard any doubt as to its *bona fides* in this matter as unwarranted."[62] Soon thereafter, the American chargé announced, "The [Liberian] Government intends to have no conference with Nimley which will properly settle the difficulties." The chargé concluded that it was perhaps best for the United States not to communicate with Nimley.[63]

Thus the United States, having sounded its alarm in 1929 about the condition of Liberia's indigenes, had by mid-1934 begun to wash its hands of them.[64] By 1936, the Sasstown insurgents had come to the conclusion that "the friendly Diplomatic [*sic*] relationship between the Government of Liberia, and that of the United States of America [is] tantamount to Firestone's personal interest and not that of the poor suffering Natives as theretofore."[65] The United States sent a letter to the British in April of 1935, inviting them to recognize the Barclay regime (which was repealing its anti-Firestone legislation).

In Monrovia, the American legation gave its view of the people they had supposedly originally intervened to help:

> The Kru tribe is one of the more intelligent of the native tribes, certainly more warlike and less tractable to government authority than many of the others. They are proud and their traditions as an organized tribe go back for centuries. They are satisfied with their tribal government and while intensely clannish and faithful to tribal law and tradition they have no feeling of brotherhood to other African tribes and certainly little, if any, patriotic feeling toward Liberia as a State and nation. They object to interference with tribal chiefs of their own choosing and see no reason why they should subject themselves to any other Negro, particularly one whose forebears came to Africa less than a century ago and who in consequence is an alien to them. White domination they can understand but their sense of government has not been sufficiently developed to accept domination by any other

black. Hence there will be friction for many years to come between this tribe and the Liberian Government.[66]

The American chargé maintained that the Kru were no more oppressed than any other indigenous people in Liberia. It was their greater sophistication that was responsible for their greater notoriety: "The fact is that as coastal people they have worked on ships for generations and being more intelligent than many of the tribes in the interior they are more vocal and use this opportunity to acquaint the world with their grievances."[67] Chargé Frederick Hibbard blamed the British for implanting the idea of external assistance in Nimley's head and thus encouraging his continued resistance. Hibbard complained, "That idea [i.e., outside assistance] is firmly fixed and how it got there doesn't matter much. I do not think the British entirely blameless for its presence but they make it evident now that they intend to do nothing to make it a reality so we must start from there." In Hibbard's view, the truce negotiated by Mackenzie had left more problems than it had solved. The chargé told Washington that the negotiator had "undoubtedly wanted to be the Chief Adviser under the League Plan." Although Mackenzie had denied promising Nimley the return of any League representative, Hibbard opined, "I am sure he felt that within a short time the Liberian problem would be effectively under the control of the League and that accordingly within the year's time limit he set there would be a white man on the scene to make final arrangements of the points at issue." Besides, even if Mackenzie had not had ulterior motives, he had failed to take into account the "native" mentality. Hibbard reminded the American investigator, Harry McBride, "You know from your own experience how easy it is for these people, with their vivid imaginations unaffected by fact, to construe or interpret any statement according to their wishes or ideas." The truce of 1932 had in reality weakened the chances for a real modus vivendi between all the parties concerned, because "it is not possible for a bush Negro to distinguish between the League of Nations and the British Government when the representative of the former is a subject of the latter, arriving on a British gun boat and accompanied by a British army officer on political service in Freetown who insisted on being kept thoroughly informed of all proceedings and even attended some of the palavers."[68]

The Americans lived in hope that the entire "Kru business" would blow over. Hibbard wrote, "The British . . . just as we, have many more vital preoccupations in their foreign policy and are glad to have someone show them a graceful exit from a situation which viewed from any other angle can only be settled by actual intervention." Very prematurely the official concluded, "they will therefore, be glad to follow us in assisting Barclay in his plan and in extending recognition."[69] To a certain extent, American hopes were justified. A British Foreign Office official wrote the embassy in Washington, "Now, to be perfectly frank, we are just as anxious as are the United States to be rid of the Liberian question, if only for a year or two."[70] However, before the whole issue could be ignored, the Kru question had to be resolved. Early in 1935, the British made the same point to the Americans: "As the United States Government are aware His Majesty's Government's main preoccupation in Liberia relates to the position of the Kru tribes, any agreement which might be reached must thus necessarily entail a return to the tribes of at least a reasonable proportion of their arms."[71] One member of the Foreign Office took the view "that we would look peculiarly foolish if, after all the interest we have displayed . . . in the trials and tribulations of the Krus, we were to renew official relations with the Liberian Government without having obtained any kind of guarantee that these unfortunate natives will no longer be persecuted by the Monrovian blacks."[72]

Where appeals to reason failed, the Americans hoped appeals to economic interest might succeed. The American chargé in Monrovia confided to McBride in Washington, "One powerful factor which may influence the British toward recognition . . . is the recent visit here of one of the managers of the [British] Consolidated African Selections Trust." Here was the economic lever the chargé hoped would consign the Kru question to oblivion. A British diamond mining concession in Liberia presumably would stifle British complaints about the conditions on the Kru Coast. "If Consolidated African Selections Trust," the chargé wrote, "thinks the concession is of sufficient value, and they appear to at present, they will put pressure on the British Government to regularize its relations with Liberia by recognition and the trade opportunity will outweigh any humanitarian feelings the British may have for the Krus, Lord Cecil and the Archbishop of Canterbury not withstanding."[73] Liberian secretary of state Louis Grimes wrote to Emily Balch of the WILPF that economic interests might well overcome humanitarian interference: "You may have read that recently gold, platinum and diamonds have been discovered in the Sierra Leone protectorate." Investment might well spill over into Liberia. Minerals were found in the Liberian district of Galahun, "which they [the British] voluntarily transferred to us . . . in 1909."[74]

The British Foreign Office was interested; an official noted in his minutes that an officer of the trust (a body supported by the Colonial Office) had pointed out the benefits to be gained from recognition.[75] Later the same official remarked that "there is no reason why British interests like the Consolidated African Trust should not play a leading role [in Liberia]," but "to do so . . . would mean the loss of our good name on the west coast of Africa, besides laying His Majesty's Government open to the most violent criticism in the country."[76] The British representative in Monrovia, a supporter of recognition, lamented, "Our trading interests are not developing here and unless the Consolidated African Selections Trust comes in I think the time is rapidly approaching when Liberia will be of little interest to us though I suppose it may be necessary to keep someone here for strategic interests or as it were 'a look-out' man."[77] He added that Britain's policy in Liberia had resulted in failure: "Nothing would please any of the three [the Americans, the Germans, the Dutch] more than to see us embroiled further — who else troubles about the Kru people besides ourselves . . . in my own mind, I am satisfied that the Krus are being left in peace and are suffering little or no hardship but that they're definite mischief-makers."

The question of British recognition hung in the balance. As long as the Sasstown Kru continued to resist, recognition seemed to promise embarrassment. After official American recognition of the Barclay regime in 1935, a Foreign Office official, weighing the pros and cons of recognition, complained, "It is in many ways a pity that our freedom of action should be hampered by our previous commitments in support of these troublesome tribes, but I submit that the arguments in favour of recognition do not at present outweigh those against such a course." The British were, indeed, wrestling with the problem of how to end the Barclay-Nimley impasse. One Foreign Office official mused, "Mr. Nimley is a sick man and it is possible that he may die before long. He is 62. His demise would of course from our point of view be a fortunate event."[78]

In the spring of 1935, the American chargé complained that the British had "a number of vociferous old ladies who ask embarrassing questions at odd times about the situation on that Coast; questions often based on erroneous information, some of which unfortunately has come from Foreign Office sources."[79] The British Anti-Slavery and Aborigines Protection Society did view Liberia as a prime case of all those evils it sought to eradicate. In 1931, Sir John Harris, the society's parliamentary secretary, pointed out with pride that Britain had opposed Liberia's entry into the League of Nations. According to Harris, the subsequent course of events had proven one great fiasco, and the Black Republic had demonstrated its complete unfitness to govern Liberia's indigenous peoples.[80] In 1934, the society decided to ask the Foreign Office whether papers could be published about the Liberian question and whether it was possible to send a delegation to speak with the American ambassador.[81] The Foreign Office did not favor this approach, but said that it would not stand in its way. The Foreign Office proposed that the society get in touch with the corresponding organization in the United States. Harris, however, visited the Foreign Office and indicated that he did not wish to work through the American philanthropic groups, but instead would approach the American Society of Friends. Early in 1935, Harris considered pushing the idea of a new commission of inquiry to explore allegations that those who had testified before the Christy commission in 1930 had since suffered mistreatment.[82]

But as the final phases of Nimley's resistance approached, even the humanitarians began to adopt a less strident tone on the issue of atrocities in Liberia. The International Bureau for the Protection of Native Races held its seventh biennial assembly in Geneva in September of 1935 and said Liberia had failed to abide by Article 23 of the Covenant of the League of Nations relative to "primitive populations" administered by members of the League. But later a report of the bureau noted that "the Liberian Government was able to master the situation, the disturbances having been most likely the last stages of a revolt undertaken by some tribes in their fight for their independence, or even for the establishment of a native Home Rule."[83] The bureau was willing to give the Barclay regime the benefit of the doubt. Its report spoke "of a work of reform begun by President Barclay, after peace was established, for a complete reorganization of the administration of his country, and the appointment of natives to high Government posts." The Anti-Slavery and Aborigines Protection Society was still dubious, recording that it did not give the report full credence. Yet, with the gradual isolation of Nimley, even the most ardent humanitarian had to fall into line. In the summer of 1936, Lord Cecil, who had previously been in accord with the Anti-Slavery Society, urged recognition based on the premise that if Liberia should lapse into future abuses, recognition might be withdrawn.[84]

With the failure of the League plan, the Sasstown rebels' hope for outside intervention dwindled and the evaluation of their plight became more pessimistic. In the summer of 1934, after the League's abandonment, they managed to cable directly to the League's secretary-general. They complained of Frontier Force provocations, saying that if they retaliated, the Liberian government "would tell the League that they are justified to attack us because we are wild uncontrollable people, when, in fact, most of us are seafaring and law abiding men who have traveled a good deal and we are not wild at all, as the Liberians have tried to represent us."[85] Their petitioner said that Lord Lugard, a member of the League mandates commission, could vouch for them as respectable seafaring folk.

In June, the Kru community of Accra, in the Gold Coast, appealed to the secretary-general, and in July a Kru petitioner wrote to British foreign minister Sir John Simon for aid.[86] "Your kind intervention has recalled memories," wrote the Kru, "of the old relationship which has long existed between the Kroos and the English-speaking world under which impression I have always believed that, although the League of Nations has the matter in hand, you English speaking nations whose Christian feeling from a moral point of view in the interest of humanity for the protection of the weak has made you the police of the civilized world, will not fail in an action against the intruder of your old friends as they entirely depend on you for help."[87] Other appeals from the Krus and their friends bombarded the League and the British and American governments.[88] Juah Nimley told Lord Cecil of the Liberia Committee in early1934 that "our hearts are broken since we heard that the Liberians have rejected the League's Plan."[89] Cecil gave the letter to the British government and replied, "I am afraid that I have no power to interfere in any way." Six months later, Nimley again appealed to Cecil and said that "disappointment and sorrow ran throughout the whole of Liberia when it was found out that President Barclay along with his first cousin, Mr. Grimes, had turned down the League's Plan which all of us wanted."[90] "We understand," said Nimley, "that the Liberian question has been handed over to the American Government, if this is true, we must humbly beg of your Lordship to use your influence with the American people and the League to prevent this [i.e., further reprisals]."

In February of 1935, the still unconquered chief appealed to the British in Monrovia, who ignored him. Nimley complained that "as the small guns and weapons I have in my possession have been taken from my hand by the League Councillors . . . that causes my little shaking in body and in natural spirit and even there is no way to escape . . . I shall be in torture together with my people and states."[91] Frantic appeals went out to British humanitarian and philanthropic interests in a last-ditch effort to spur British intervention. In May of 1936, Lady Kathleen Simon of the Anti-Slavery and Aborigines Protection Society received a letter from a Liberian stranded in Paris, who pleaded in awkward yet moving terms, "The present-day conditions in Liberia is as such that the situation is just as before in toto and the only solution to abolish the atrocities would be a collective security with [in] the frameworks of British Justice under Great Britain Mandatory Power, this I can assure you is the wishes of the people of Liberia and the only solution to save the Natives from the existing masscrition [massacre] throughout."[92]

By August of 1936, Nimley's position had become serious. A refugee from his camp, C. J. Julius, escaped to Accra and attempted to enlist humanitarian support for the chief who for over five years had defied the Monrovia regime.[93] In August, Julius appealed to the British Foreign Office; his message received a cold response. An official thought it, "to say the least . . . inconvenient that we should receive this petition from the Krus at a moment when . . . it has been decided that the time has come to recognize the Liberian government.[94] The British position was well known in Monrovia. Walton wrote the State Department, "the impression appears to be quite general that Great Britain now finds itself in an awkward spot on the Kru question." The African American diplomat thought that "if Chief Nimley comes to Monrovia, as he has been advised by my British colleague, the British Foreign Office will be in a position to announce that the Kru question has been settled."[95] On July 12, British consul Yapp reported that Barclay had been informed that all of the tribes supporting Nimley had surrendered and that the chief himself was in flight. Liberian secretary of state Simpson proudly announced a bloodless victory.[96] The Foreign Office quickly reconciled itself to this denouement of the Kru affair. Suspicion lingered that the crushing of the "revolt" had not been completely without bloodshed. "If blood *is* unfortunately shed in the process," said a British official, "I submit that this would give us no more right to protest than the civil war in Spain would entitle us to protest to Madrid against the measures taken against General Franco."[97]

On September 9, Nimley found himself in government hands and on October 6, the chief and two of his leaders arrived in Monrovia as prisoners. The three men were interviewed at the War Department and then sent to confinement at Monrovia's military camp. The following day, their great antagonist, Edwin Barclay himself, interviewed them for three hours. The British representative, who had long viewed Nimley as a diplomatic nuisance, had to confess, "Dressed in native costume he bore himself with much dignity as he marched through the town under escort. I am told that the crowd assembled to watch his progress was the largest ever seen in Monrovia and that he was the recipient of hearty cheers. Everyone was anxious to see the 'wonderful Nimley,' as he was called."[98] The British representative admired Barclay's tactics as much as he admired Nimley's bearing. Barclay's great strategy had been, in his eyes, the "encirclement plan," which made the women dissatisfied enough to desert the fighters. The consul warned the Foreign Office that the area might still prove troublesome in the future when the Liberian government got around to collecting taxes.[99]

Barclay magnanimously declared that Nimley, previously accused of being a butcher of his own people, had only been led astray by educated members of his tribe.[100] The chief and his two headmen, Santi and Parle

Weah, were sent to exile in Gbanga, Saniquelli, and Belle Yella, respectively. In 1937, the chief, leader of a five-year war, received permission to return to Sasstown as a common citizen, and he died shortly thereafter. Nimley, "wonderful Nimley," had seen defeat.

The "Civilized Element"

In his annual message of 1936, Barclay, in a clement mood, proclaimed, "It is clear Juah Nimley himself attempted to persuade his people from the course upon which they had determined and had been overborne by his advisers and particularly by the so-called 'civilized' element of the tribe."[101] From the outset, Barclay had been deeply suspicious of educated natives' efforts to maintain an independent political line. For instance, he regarded with much suspicion schooled Kru attempts at mediation in October of 1931. The special delegation sent to the Kru Coast under the leadership of Reverend D. W. Herman ran very much afoul of the chief executive. The group, among other things, asked for the recall of Colonel Elwood Davis. The delegation felt that the Kru did not actually want war and told Barclay that they would meet with the recalcitrants in early November. Barclay made a furious and swift reply to this offer: the delegation was not to temporize with the Kru of Sasstown, but to make them see the error of their ways.[102] They were severely warned not to undermine the administration's prestige or authority.[103] Herman was arrested for sedition, released, and rearrested in December of 1932 by executive order. By April of 1933, the clergyman and many of his colleagues found themselves back in jail. Herman and other Kru prisoners in the Sinoe jail complained "that since some of our people were killed in 1917 [sic] after the Kru Coast war, and now the Liberian Government is held responsible, they [i.e., the Sinoe authorities] will not put their hands on us but will starve us to death."[104]

According to Monrovia, the seditious propaganda of outside agitators had fueled the war on the south coast. In the spring of 1934, Barclay had already stated this rationale for the recurring violence there:

Dr. McKenzie [sic], in his report to the Government on his mission to Sasstown, attributed much of this unrest, more or less, to the civilized Krus who reside in Monrovia. He is quite correct in this because facts which are reported to the Government by certain foreign agents in Monrovia are absolutely unknown in the places to which they claim to refer. It is known that each tribe on the Kru Coast has a colony in Monrovia, and so it is possible for a man claiming to be a Dio or a Wissapo man, who, however, may never have been at Dio or Wissapo nor had any communication therefrom, to have communicated to the British Consul alleged facts [of atrocities] set out in his despatch.[105]

Although Barclay may have been unwilling to admit it, the issue on the coast was not "civilized" standards per se. It was competition. Well-traveled indigenes represented a potential threat to the oligarchy; they might become the leaders of discontent welcoming in foreign intervention. The solution was co-optation into the outer circle of the ruling elite or rigid political and economic exclusion. Many educated Kru and Grebo were taken into the power structure — after abandoning most of their ties with their untutored brethren. Indeed, in 1924, a completely assimilated Grebo, Henry Too Wesley, became vice president of the republic. Yet economic and social horizons remained limited by inertia, if not by malice. Illustrative is the case of one Grebo, who

> as a youth . . . had worked his way on a steamer to Germany as a purser's clerk; on his savings he had taken passage in steerage to Baltimore. Eventually he had found his way to Tuskegee Institute, where he remained four years. After his school years he had gone to Beloit, Wisconsin, and from there to Detroit, Michigan, where he worked in the Ford automobile plant. Finally under missionary auspices, he had returned to Liberia, bringing a sawmill with a capacity of 10,000 feet a day. In time the mill failed. The enterprising young Grebo had gone to work for Firestone at the Du Plantation, with Ohe Plenyano Welo, another returned native who had studied at Harvard and at the Union Theological Seminary. Because of his Grebo connection, Welo had been transferred to Cape Palmas. Difficulties had developed with the management and he had finally found himself out. Of native descent, he had taken advantage of a provision of the Firestone agreement to the effect that a native could claim a land reserve. He had thus secured 100 acres in Gyidetarbo adjoining the Firestone development. He now grew coffee, rice, cassava, cucumbers, okra, and onions, and made a fair living. But he was neither Liberian, native, nor American, nor was he able to exercise the prerogatives of a capitalist. He was simply "out." It was the plight of the self-reliant educated native who does not seek adjustment of his status in government employment.[106]

The majority of educated natives knew of their rulers' poverty. One political scientist pondered the resistance to the Monrovia government: "An ambivalent case was that of the Kru, who continued their resistance into the 1930s, yet were the most cash-minded group along the coast."[107] The case does not prove all that ambivalent. More traveled than the Americo-Liberians, with broader horizons and more earning power, some indigenes saw the settlers as the source of backwardness.

One observer reported, "A native man who had just returned to the town from the Gold Coast, after a three-year absence . . . standing, hands akimbo, observing a half erected concrete building at the edge of the native village." The man's "face was twisted into a heavy grimace of disgust. 'I'm a tradesman. I wear tan and white shoes and eat at a hotel in Lagos. They told me they were building a great tower here and collected £6.0.0 [*sic*]. I come back and see this thing.'" The inhabitant of Grand Cess, the observer reported, continued, "They call this thing the tower. If this wasn't my native land where my wife and child stay, I never come back. Look at the streets. They don't got none. No sewer. Nothing."[108]

During the crisis of the 1930s, a number of educated natives might have benefited from a change of the political order: Postmaster general Momolu Massaquoi (Vai); ex–vice president Henry Too Wesley (Grebo); F. W. M. Morais, a member of the national legislature (Grebo); Didwo Twe, ex-member of the legislature (Kru); justice F. E. Besylow (Vai); justice Abayomi Karnga (Congo); and Montserrado County attorney Doughba Carranda (Congo).[109] Massaquoi was one of the most prominent members of the group; he had been Liberian consul general in Hamburg and, on Samuel Ross's death in 1929, had received the appointment of postmaster general. (He was later accused of malfeasance by the government and fired.) Massaquoi was married to Gabriel Johnson's daughter and had been the principal financial supporter of the *Liberian Patriot*, a pro-Garvey newspaper published in Monrovia by George Marke. Before the scandal, the British consulate noted that Massaquoi was "related by marriage to the little group of influential Americo-Liberian families, and with great power amongst the Vai tribes, he may be the next President."[110] Edwin Barclay's intensified grip on the Liberian government after 1930 precluded any such possibility. In 1931, Al-Haj Massaquoi, Momolu's eldest son, wrote to Lady Kathleen Simon of the Anti-Slavery and Aborigines Protection Society to complain that indigenous persons had little or no access to the higher echelons of power.[111]

The Barclay regime saw Didwo Twe, an ex-member of the legislature, as the evil genius behind Kru resistance, while Twe viewed himself as the tribune of the people. As early as December of 1930, he had written to Charles S. Johnson, protesting raids on the Kru Coast.[112] In April of 1932, he wrote to the American minister saying he feared deportation because of his role in exposing abuse on the coast and because of his absolute refusal of co-optation by the Barclay government.[113] According to Twe, Barclay had made dire threats against "educated Africans." Twe claimed that "on the first of May 1931, in the presence of the Hon. M. Massaquoi, Rev. D. W. Harman [Herman], Mr. G. F. Sharpe, Chief

Kpade Boi, Dappe Togba and myself, President Barclay said to Paramount Chief Blogba Togba, . . . I will burn down the whole Kru Coast, if you don't stop talking about 'white man,' 'white man.' " Barclay, according to Twe, warned, "You take it from me as an order and send word and tell your people that I say there will be only two months of peace on the Coast and no more." When Twe attempted to interject, he was supposedly told, "You damned civilized natives who ought to be leading your people properly are misleading them."[114] In 1927, the American legation had made a careful compilation of the extant facts of Twe's life. He was

a member of the Settra Kroo Tribe, [and] was born in Monrovia. There is no record of the exact date of his birth but he appears to be about forty years of age. He started his education in Monrovia under Miss Mary Sharpe, an American missionary, and Doctor Paulus Moort. In 1900 he went to the United States for further education and remained there up to 1910. Congressman William W. Grout of Vermont helped Mr. Twe to obtain an education, and Mr. Twe attended St. Johnsbury Academy at St. Johnsbury, Vermont, and the Rhode Island State College of Kingston, Rhode Island. After the Congressman's death, Senator John T. Morgan of Alabama and Samuel Clemens became interested in Mr. Twe. It is very unfortunate that both Senator Morgan and Mr. Clemens died before Mr. Twe could finish his education. I have been told that Mr. Twe, while in America, contributed articles to the "American Journal of Psychology," edited by Doctor G. Stanley Hall and to "The Boston Transcript." Since 1910 he has been a district commissioner for a number of years on the Sierra Leone frontier and has assisted the Anglo-Liberian and Franco-Liberian boundary commissions. At present, he is assistant to Mr. Robert A. Farmer, American Engineer, in constructing a coast telephone system.[115]

After the first reverberations of the slavery crisis were felt, and with the increasing harassment of dissidents within Liberia, Twe fled to Sierra Leone in November of 1932, when the Liberian government issued a writ for his arrest on charges of sedition.[116] Late in 1934, Twe wrote to a friend in England, advocating armed revolution. He argued that it was certainly within the Kru's power, "but in order to . . . succeed fully . . . hold their independence intact till recognition, acceptance of the League's Plan and the arrival of white specialists, the Kru people ought to have at least 6 machine guns and 500 rifles with sufficient ammunition." According to the Kru nationalist, "This is now the only obstacle in the way to free a million people from oppression. . . . We hope the Lord could touch the hearts of some good men to come to the assistance of our people to bring about the establishment of the 'Kru

Republic,' which the people want."[117] The British consulate in Monrovia, which favored recognition of the Barclay regime, harshly condemned Twe's opinions, viewing him as "a thorough-paced scoundrel." Yapp of the consulate suggested that "if he disappeared . . . no one would be the worse off."[118]

By the autumn of 1934, Twe realized that the international community had almost completely dropped the Liberian matter. Nevertheless he suggested that if the great powers did decide to send out a caretaker, he, Twe, should accompany him. He wrote Lord Cecil that "England certainly has been very sincere throughout . . . and she really wants to relieve the oppressed people, but the League is no good at all."[119] Unfortunately for the Kru exile, Cecil replied, "I am afraid I see nothing that the British Government or I myself can do more to help at the present time."[120]

Twe also corresponded with Sir John Harris of the Anti-Slavery Protection Society, and in 1935, Harris sent Twe a letter via Graham Greene. The episode is curious, revealing, perhaps, the degree to which the fate of the Kru had become a sideshow. Greene, a future intelligence officer in Sierra Leone during World War II, had read all the reports of savage government reprisals. Early on, he seemed to envision himself as a fact finder. "If there was anything to hide in the Republic," Greene noted, "I wanted to surprise it."[121] Twe, whom he referred to in his published account as "Mr. D," was his contact in Freetown. Greene has left us a vignette of his cloak-and-dagger encounter with the Kru statesman:

> Mr. D. lived in Krutown. Krutown is one of the few parts of Freetown with any beauty. . . . The native huts still stand among the palm trees on the way to Lumley Beach, the women sitting outside with their long hanging breasts uncovered. Mr. D's house was in the only Europeanized street. A bare wooden stair led into a room with wooden walls on which were hung a few religious pictures in Oxford frames. There were four rickety chairs and an occasional table with a potted plant on it. Crudely painted Mothers of God bore the agony of the seven swords with indifference. Christ just above his head exposed a heart the colour of raw liver. Insects hopped about on the wooden floor and Mr. D gently instructed me how to reach the frontier.[122]

The Englishman was told that he would probably not be allowed to visit the Kru Coast, but that the visitor might book passage from Monrovia to Cape Palmas. If he followed this plan, he could say that he had changed his mind and disembark unexpectedly at Sinoe. From Sinoe, he could follow the beach to Nana Kru, where he could get guides to take him to the Kru resisters. "Mr. D" was especially concerned that the traveler visit "Bellivela" (Bella Yella), the camp for political prisoners. The Kru told his guest, "They'll have to invite you inside the camp for the night . . . and then you can poke around and see things." Greene did not follow this plan. Once in Liberia, he abandoned any thought of playing the Roger Casement role in the Liberian saga. The Englishman lost his nerve and avoided visiting Sinoe and Maryland altogether. Referring to his time in Freetown after meeting Twe, he wrote, "That night I dreamed of Mr D and the Customs at the border, a muddled irritating dream. . . . I had arrived at the Customs with all my bags and boxes and Mr D tied up in a bale. . . . I was afraid all that time that the Customs inspector would discover Mr D, that I would be fined for smuggling, and have to pay a heavy duty."[123] Dreams have power; Greene abandoned his mission.

By early 1936, Twe had lost his own resolve; he decided to come to terms with the Barclay regime. He returned unexpectedly to Monrovia from Freetown and asked for the protection of the British consulate. The Liberian secretary of the interior ordered Twe to leave the country, and the consulate informed him that it could not intervene. Barclay did receive Twe in audience and eventually gave permission for him to stay in Monrovia on condition that he refrain from political activity.[124]

Another regime critic pursued a similar trajectory. In August of 1931, Dr. F. W. M. Morais was sent to Europe to attend meetings of the League of Nations and to present the case of Liberia's indigenous majority. Lord Lugard, speaking to the House of Lords, mentioned that he was in touch with "an intelligent, educated native of Liberia, who states that he has been sent as a delegate by 24 tribal chiefs to represent their case in Europe."[125] The British consulate in Monrovia, however, appeared less than enthusiastic about Morais's abilities and commented that "he was at one time employed in the French colonial service in the Ivory Coast, but was ejected for fraud, for which he served a term of imprisonment."[126] Morais was accompanied to Europe by N. S. Brownell, a Grebo lawyer. While in Geneva, Morais said the majority population wanted proportional representation and "the introduction of civil service reforms, along with the development of an educational system under the supervision of the League of Nations." According to Morais, the indigenous people felt "that the country should not be mandated as foreshadowed in the foreign press, but that they should be given an opportunity to participate in the Government."[127]

In Maryland County, the Morais mission's activities were followed with avid interest. In October of 1931, the American minister in Monrovia heard that reprisals had been made against the Grebo chiefs and their people who had contributed to Morais's trip. Superintendent Harold Fredericks of Maryland remonstrated a native gathering thereof and was surprised at their unanimity. He queried them as to the motive for sending the men to Geneva. They responded, "To talk ground palaver." He asked for clarification and got a poetic, if politically pointed, reply: "When you are traveling on the beach, there is a small bird called 'Gbedabwe'; it keeps on running all the time — some time you will see it in front of you; and at other times in the rear of you. That little bird puts a parable saying that 'ground palaver is as long as the sea coast.' So the ground palaver that Dr. Morais has gone to talk is as long as the beach — nobody can relate it all."[128] The superintendent dismissed the meeting. Subsequently, Fredericks arrested a number of prominent people.[129]

Morais returned from Geneva in 1932 to much jubilation on the Kru Coast. Grebo opinion was gratified, but divided. Edwin Gahie Gyude Hodge, Charles S. Johnson's assistant in 1930, was a young firebrand. Johnson had been greatly impressed with his abilities. Contrasting him with the Americo-Liberian surveyor Victor Cooper, Johnson had observed, "The first [Cooper] is uncouth, mannerless and of a bumptious puerility, and Americo-Liberian; the latter suave, gracious, well-read, keenly intelligent and native, sticking at times in the evening to his native dress — the lappa."[130] In 1932, Hodge, who was to spend several spells in Barclay's prisons, disagreed with his mentor, Morais, on several points. "One of these," wrote Hodge, "was that he seemed fed up with the rule of the Americo-Liberians and wanted the country mandated to some foreign power who would teach these people how to govern [,] while on my part I felt that this country had been ruled by the Americo-Liberian for over a hundred years, and that it was time for the aborigines to rule it."[131] In any event, joy among the Grebo at Morais's return was short-lived. The doctor and several of his companions were arrested for sedition. In one of the few accounts from the indigenous side, Hodge recorded:

> They put us in the upper story of the house with a soldier at the entrance of the door to guard us. Later on that evening Dr. Morais had a severe fever and chill. I asked the soldier to call Major Grant of the LFF who was in charge. The Major came with some pills for Dr. Morais who was shivering all over. He took the pills from Major Grant and covered himself. When things were all quiet I told Dr. Morais that I wanted us to go home. He asked "How?" I said that I wanted to go and seize the gun from the soldier, knock him down and we could escape. He was horrified to hear me make that suggestion, so I let it at that. Of course Dr. Morais was a much older man than I was, and, having youth on my side, I could afford to venture things that he could not.[132]

Old and sick, Morais was deprived of his seat in the legislature and sentenced to fifteen years imprisonment at Bella Yella. A group of Grebo chiefs cabled a protest to the International Society for the Defense of Native Peoples in Geneva, which in turn informed the League of Nations. Monrovia was told to expect no consideration from the League barring the prisoners' release. By the time Barclay signed the order, four of Morais's fellows in confinement were dead of malnutrition and exposure. Morais's collaborator, Brownell, abandoned the fight and was made attorney general in the Barclay cabinet. The Liberian consul general in the United States, Walter F. Walker, exulted, "Mr. Brownell's delusions were of short duration. He early returned to Liberia, denounced the mischievousness of Mr. Morais, and settled down to repair whatever damage his temporary political insanity has caused."[133]

Morais himself also eventually abandoned his opposition.[134] In August of 1934, the champion of Grebo rights wrote to the superintendent of Maryland County offering his services as a peace negotiator:

As to the needed reforms suggested by the League growing out of complaints from Native Chiefs, and which I sponsored and defended at Geneva, I note with much satisfaction the introduction of such policies by the present administration calculated to render effective a complete change over from the regrettable past and that to the betterment of my people's interest, in support of which I have willingly volunteered my good offices toward an amicable but honorable settlement of this outstanding feud.[135]

Late in 1934, in an article in the *Monrovia Weekly Mirror,* Morais attempted to explain and exculpate his past conduct:

In 1927 I was elected as Representative of the Native element for the County of Maryland in the National Legislature, at a moment that Native policy in vogue and pursued by the extant administration was causing great hardship to my people; at the time the situation created was pregnant with revolution [,] of feeling and loss of confidence in the Government to whom they look and are still looking for protection. I raised my voice against the abuses [,] publishing a Minority Report which revolutionized the conscience of the world but without effective realization of my honest dreams.

In consequence of findings, suggestions and recommendations to the International Commission of Inquiry I was selected by my people the autochthons to go to Geneva and solicit the good offices of the League of Nations towards amelioration of conditions particularly amongst the Interior tribes. . . . [Later] whilst at Grand Cess I was arrested and sent to Belle Yallah; en route I suffered great discomfort, inconveniences and pain due to [a] recent surgical operation which physically incapacitated my undertaking such a journey. After a stay of six months, I was brought to Cape Palmas imprisoned and arranged [*sic*] for trial. Subsequently I sought an opportunity of settling down and studying at close range as to whether or not introduction of remarkable features then marked a radical change of policy in favour of the entire Native population. I have made the study and am now convinced that the sun is beginning to set on the regrettable past with its pensive memories; in my opinion if Mr. Barclay is maintained or continued in office as President we might look forward to the dawn of a new era when this Country should witness the advent of better days.[136]

Morais's subsequent attempt to negotiate with the Sasstown Kru proved far from successful. Juah Nimley at first refused to see him. Then the services of one Dr. Schneidenburger (described to the British consulate as "an old derelict German Jew who years ago went to South Africa as [a] gold-digger and was there sentenced to a term of hard labour") were procured, and Nimley was persuaded to receive Morais if the latter came in African dress.[137] When the meeting did take place, the paramount chief still insisted on waiting for word from the League of Nations. Early in 1935, Morais wrote in the *Weekly Mirror* that Nimley was justifiably afraid of making peace because of his memories of the 1916 events, but stated that he believed Barclay was making a sincere effort at a settlement.[138]

The Brothers Abroad

Overseas, even among African Americans, the cause championed by men like Morais found little consistent support.[139] In 1933, the black scholars Charles Wesley and Rayford Logan had written, "An antagonism has developed and has been intensified recently between a small governing class and a larger class of the governed who have taken less interest through the years in the changes in the Liberian administration." Having said this, they offered a paradoxical solution: "It seems imperative therefore to strengthen the Liberian government for the sake of its own maintenance."[140] To most Europeans and white Americans, the indigenous people of Liberia could not be trusted to establish anything so radical as "native home rule." In 1935, the American chargé made it clear that the troubles in Liberia had their origin in the nature of colonial rule: "The Liberian Government must weld this amorphous mass of indigenous natives into a homogeneous whole. . . . Hence they must exert pressure on the recalcitrant tribes."[141]

To many of the overseas black defenders of Liberia, the country represented the future toward which they believed Africa should move. Traditional Africa was loved, but only as an abstraction, and future glory was envisioned in terms of Western paradigms. Traditional Africa, that Africa subsumed under the rubric *Native,* could not be allowed to stand in the way of race fulfillment (the nurturing and maturation of progress in an African setting). In 1932, the NAACP issued a statement by a former educational adviser to Liberia, maintaining that "the fundamental difficulty in Liberia is a clash between the new and the old — a clash between [the] so-called ideals of western civilization and jungle customs and traditions . . . the jungle man practically lives on the wild fruits and animals of the forests and knows not how to do a day's work."[142] Some defenders of Liberia did, disingenuously, attribute to it the character of a culturally synthetic state, one merging itself with indigenous Africa: "The true mission of Liberia in Africa, according to one of its executives, is not in the establishing of a Negro State, based upon Western ideas, rather it is the attainment of a Negro nationality having its foundations rooted in African cultural institutions and modified by Western thoughts."[143] Yet despite such rhetorical flourishes, the defenders of Liberia had little to say about the faceless "native" creators of "African cultural institutions." Where indigenes were mentioned, they appeared only as the specters of "Kru militarism" or, in Du Bois's words, "the warlike native tribes."[144]

To "tribal" Liberians, however, the situation in the Black Republic presented a dilemma far more immediate than that confronting their brethren in the Diaspora. "I love Liberia and I think it has a right to exist as an independent Negro Republic and should never be placed under any kind of mandatory power," said the son of a Grebo chief at Fisk University in Tennessee, "but if Liberia continues to treat helpless individuals unfairly, as she does the Natives, just because they have no submarines and men-of-war or armies to defend them and battle against any unbearable power, she should be taken over by the League of Nations."[145] In the face of such sentiments, the supporters of the Monrovia regime could only reply with the charge of racial treason. Given the imperatives of ethnic solidarity, they insisted, specific abuses paled in significance. Native pleas for help, either to the League or to a white power, constituted a breach of the racial front. In an attack on F. W. M. Morais, Walter F. Walker, the Liberian consul in New York, argued that colonialists would use reports of conditions in Liberia as the opening wedge of imperialism: "This is an old trick practiced by dominant powers to break down racial solidarity and political understanding and to have people commit national hari-kari." Old Dixie was summoned up: "It was the orchestral accompaniment of American slavery to prevent uprisings among the slaves."[146] Azikiwe, Nigerian nationalist that he was, saw Morais's appeal to the League as a threat to the racial ideal embodied in Liberia:

The cause espoused by Dr. Morais is a worthy one, but his method of approach is rather crude, and it completely destroys the sincereness [sic] of his mission. No useful purpose can be served by a direct approach to the League of Nations because it is an international organization, and only political entities are recognizable before it as members. . . . It is therefore painful to see this great son of Grebo, who was ably commended by the Chief Justice of the Republic, and who occupies an important position to strengthen the link between the Government and the aborigines by his enlightened leadership, fall into a miasma of partisan politics.[147]

Very interestingly, Marcus Garvey was one of the few Pan-Africanists to take the part of the natives. In early 1934, he wrote in the *Blackman* that conditions for the indigenous majority were horrible. He said, "At the present time, it is said that they have more than a score of political prisoners locked up in a dirty jail almost starving and ready to die from that starvation, simply because they happened to have been opponents of the government in the discovery of the shocking slave traffic."[148] He was greatly disappointed, "because Liberia really has been regarded as the hope of the Negro race in the experiment of independent nationalism and self-government." The country held out promise, but remained badly administered. His own betrayal by C. D. B. King was, he noted, a sign of the rulers' greed and decadence. But there was hope. The situation was redeemable. The head of the UNIA strongly believed that "when the Statesmen of that country can make up their minds to give the Negroes within, and those without, a square deal, then we think the country will receive all the assistance necessary to send her forward, and there will be very little possibility of the continuance of such scandals as we are now hearing about."[149]

On the left, the Communist International attacked both the defenders of the Barclay regime and the idea of a League mandate. Communists urged an emphasis on the "workers' struggle." While still a member of the American Communist Party, George Padmore had, on behalf of the International Trade Union Committee of Negro Workers, exhorted the black workers of the world to rally to the defense of Liberia. Within the Black Republic, he urged the creation of trade unions among seamen. He asserted in the *Negro Worker,* "The very first task which stands before the workers, especially the seamen and dockers in the coast ports of Liberia, such as Monrovia, [and] Great Bassa, is to organize themselves into trade unions as the basis for the development of a broad mass anti-imperialist movement; for only in this way will the Liberian workers be able to defend their economic interests and carry on the struggle for improving their political and social conditions."[150] Another writer in the *Negro Worker* argued that a mandate for Liberia would solve nothing: "They [i.e., "the native masses"] realise that the problem which misgovernment and particularly the economic system, have created, demands drastic solution—a solution to consist not in mandating their country and therefore in intensifying exploitation, oppression and poverty, but a solution which must consist in and be based upon revolutionary activity of the natives themselves."[151]

Apparently neither Juah Nimley's resistance nor Didwo Twe's call for a "Native Republic" qualified. In May of 1935, the same writer concluded:

> Facts clearly indicate that objective factors are not wanting for the mobilization of the Liberian masses for decisive struggle, but that on the other hand, and very unfortunately[,] they do emphatically show the total absence of the necessary subjective factors: that unless the exploited masses gird their loins and wage a relentless struggle against their subjugators and oppressors, freedom is not forthcoming; that unless the labouring masses are organized and taught through systematic propaganda, education and political enlightenment to realise that freedom does not come as a gift, but must be fought for and unless the opportunist and treacherous National Reform Native Intellectuals are persistently and consistently exposed—the great cause of the struggle of liberation is doomed to fail.[152]

If the indigenous population did not figure prominently in the thought of those who defended Liberia out of racial solidarity, the Communist International paid them little more attention. The International Trade Union Committee of Negro Workers had a definition of *worker* which excluded the masses within the boundaries of Liberia. Seeing the paid workers of a few ports and the Firestone Plantations as the vanguard of revolution, the committee behaved as if revolt and resistance to the regime did not exist. It never dwelled on the issue of hut taxes and forced requisitions. The committee paradoxically called for revolution where there was none and ignored it where it had been ablaze for five years.

Peace

The 1930 investigation of Liberia and the subsequent international spotlighting of the Black Republic did have an impact on the government's Native policy. In addition to outlawing labor export and pawning, after

1930 the Liberian regime sought to curb other outrageous instances of abuse of the majority population. The Barclay administration prided itself on this new departure, and in the mid-thirties proclaimed, "It is a common expression of the natives to say, that 'under this present administration we are not compelled to carry on our heads soldiers, messengers and other subordinate officials; we are not compelled to leave our homes and go miles away to work roads.'"[153] The regime sought, on numerous occasions, to avoid provoking open conflict with its indigenous population. When, in September 1931, a group of "civilized" Maryland citizens petitioned the president for aid and ammunition for use against a suspected Grebo uprising, Barclay denied their petition and advised them not to take precipitate action against their neighbors.[154] In Maryland in the following year, Lieutenant Colonel W. V. S. Tubman (who later served as president from 1944 to 1971) reportedly allowed one of his men to burn a house in a Grebo town without provocation. A subordinate officer was reprimanded by a special court of inquiry.[155] In the same month, the county superintendent, Harold Fredericks, wrote to Barclay that "with Brownell and Morais instigating the Greboes to passive resistance and prominent Kroos at your end fomenting open defiance against Government authority, it behooves all administrative officials, especially those coming in contact with Natives, to avoid semblance of any policy which might accelerate an already grave situation, in other words, let sleeping dogs lie protem [sic]."[156] Three years later, Fredericks wrote the president that the old order was changing and that he hoped civil service reform would open careers to talent and benefit indigenous youth.[157]

But if the thirties saw an amelioration of Native policy, no drastic change in the Liberian social structure occurred. In July of 1936, as Juah Nimley's resistance neared collapse, Lester Walton wrote to Harry McBride at the State Department about conditions in the interior. A foreign expert had done an investigation and, noted the minister,

> The situation in the hinterland, so far as administration is concerned, is just what I expected. Mr. Saben has returned with a wealth of evidence against gross misrule on the part of District Commissioners: 104 villages were visited, two-thousand persons interviewed. Seventy-four villages were more or less depopulated, the natives having gone over to Sierra Leone because of the rank injustices committed by District Commissioners.
>
> Forced labor, vicious exploitation of the natives by Frontier Force, Unjust [sic] and excessive fines are some of the contributory factors to occasion resentment and dissatisfaction, impelling many natives to reluctantly settle in Sierra Leone. Mr. Saben believes not less than $50,000 yearly is exacted from natives in fines which does not find its way to Monrovia but to dis-

honest District Commissioner[s] and other sources, including paramount chiefs. This rough estimate of revenue loss by the Government, or to be more accurate, this disgraceful system of fining the natives for personal gain and forcing natives to work for nothing renders it difficult, and in many instances, impossible, for the Liberian Government to collect hut and other taxes. It should be remembered that Mr. Saben only visited the Western Province — the one from which the most sensational stories emanate about graft and misrule.[158]

The reform Native intellectuals — men like Twe and Morais — and the idea of a native republic received little support from any quarter. Yet it was here, perhaps, that the greatest possibility for change lay. Had native home rule been successful, the 1930s would have seen a significant shifting of elites. An indigenous, Western-educated elite with strong connections to the traditional rulers and political groupings could have come to the fore. The political structure of Liberia would have come to resemble that of many African states in the postcolonial period. It is evident that, in the thirties, the idea of a West African republic representing such a union of forces presented an anathema to a wide spectrum of outside opinion. Unfortunately, this attitude served to perpetuate a situation that eventuated in more than a decade of bloody civil war.

10 Fascism and New Zions

All the things that Hitler was to do so well later, Garvey was doing
in 1920 and 1921. He organized storm troopers, who marched,
uniformed in his parades, and kept order and gave
colour to his meetings.

—C. L. R. James

The Negro is an American citizen, but his thinking is often
more Negro than American. The white American may look with
subjective interest upon Munich, but the American Negro regards the
latest lynching as infinitely more important to him. The white American
may recoil with horror at the German barbarisms against the Jew. But
the American Negroes cries, "Hitler be damned, and the Jew too, what
about the Jim Crow here?" The Negro may evidence some momentary
excitation about Italy's rape of Ethiopia, but the dismemberment of
Czecko-Slovakia is the white man's business.

—Ralph Bunche

The struggle for Liberian independence was almost immediately succeeded by the loss of independence by Africa's only other independent
state. The Ethiopian crisis of the mid-1930s was the Liberian crisis writ
large, involving as it did political realignments that were to be crucial to
the Second World War. From the Wal Wal incident of 1934 to the
collapse of Ethiopian resistance in the spring of 1936, the attention of
much of the world was riveted on a crisis that shifted the European
balance of power as Hitler and Mussolini moved together and proved
the League's impotence.

As in the case of Liberia, Ethiopia became a symbol of Pan-Africanist aspirations and hope. Since the time of the Greeks, *Ethiopia* had served as a metonym for *Black Man's Land* and, in the eighteenth and nine-teenth centuries, the term was similarly used. The independent black church movement in South Africa took the name Ethiopianism, draw-ing its inspiration from the biblical prophesy, "Ethiopia shall stretch forth her hands unto God."[1] Blyden believed, "there is no people, except the Hebrews and other ancient inhabitants of Palestine, more frequently mentioned in the Scriptures of the Old and New Testaments than the Ethiopians, and there is no country more frequently referred to than Ethiopia; and that the record of no people, whether in sacred history or in ancient secular history, has less of the discreditable than the record of the Ethiopians."[2] The historic defeat of Italy in 1896 by the emergent Ethiopian state added to its glamour in the Diaspora. The Abyssinian polity headed by Menelik II (1889–1913) became the paladin of blacks throughout the world. The spell of an ancient but vague place was on the Diaspora. In 1916, John William Morris published his *The Ethio-pian's Place in History.* Ten years later, J. E. Blaychettai wrote *The Hidden Mystery of Ethiopia,* and in the same year Drusilla Dunjee Houston's *Wonderful Ethiopians of the Ancient Cushite Empire* appeared.[3] Later at Howard University, Leo Hansberry did yeoman work in tirelessly pop-ularizing the Ethiopian past. More recently, Henry Louis Gates Jr. has commented, "nowhere in the twelve African countries that I visited was I more consistently mistaken for an African than in the ancient country of Ethiopia, the second most populous in Africa."[4]

As in other cases, a dichotomy existed between Totem and the Place. The former was a conflation of biblical references, classical allusions to the culture of Meroe/Nubia on the Upper Nile, and the power of the metonym. John Sorenson notes in *Imagining Ethiopia:*

> "Ethiopia" can be understood as a historical fiction based on and main-tained by power. . . . Indeed, [it is possible to] argue that Ethiopia was created as a dependent colonial state that could serve the interests of Euro-pean powers. This has been a controversial intervention and, indeed, a threatening one to those who identify with Ethiopia as a long-unified state. In discussing Ethiopia as a created image, however, it is important to recog-nize that it was not simply an invention of Western power; the image of Ethiopia was constructed on the basis of an already-existing discourse of domination, that of the Amhara elite. This discourse proposed a particular version of history in which the boundaries of the contemporary state were

projected backwards into a distant historical period. The image of Ethiopia contained within this discourse is one of African grandeur, liberty, modernization, and stability.[5]

The governing elite ruling was very adept at creating a pedigree that both emphasized uniqueness and continuity. In the mid-1920s, a Western confidant of the emperor published a list of the rulers of Ethiopia that stretched back to 4470 B.C.[6] To many of its supporters in the Black World, mythic Ethiopia represented a regal past consonant with "Civilization," an anchor that challenged the notion of the unclothed and un-Christian "Native." The Nigerian Azikiwe wrote, "Ethiopia is the last vestige of black autocracy." The empire "represents the type of government which the forefathers of Africans established on this continent."[7] Jomo Kenyatta regarded the country as "the remaining relic of the greatness of an Africa that once was."[8] Erased from this vision were the Sidama, the Oromo, the Somali, the Boran, serfdom, raiding — and slavery.

In the wake of the abortion of the UNIA plan in Liberia, a number of blacks from the United States and the Caribbean sought to recreate their African Dream in Ethiopia. In November 1930, Ras Tafari was crowned emperor of Ethiopia, as Haile Selassie. In attendance was Arnold Josiah Ford, an immigrant to the United States from Barbados. In New York, he had assumed the leadership of a group of black Jews. Ford's group believed that the people of the Old Testament were black. The people of the Diaspora were their descendants or, more directly, descendants of the Falashas, the Jews of Ethiopia. Ford's movement rose out of the same ferment that had powered the UNIA. In the wake of the betrayal of Garvey's Liberian plan, the UNIA's anthem "Ode to Ethiopia" lived on. The secular and modernist Garveyite project became sacralized. Ford eventually organized six hundred members into the congregation Beth B'nai Abraham and its adjunct, the Aurienoth Club (Angel of light club). The latter collected membership fees with a view to encouraging migration to an overseas Zion. Ford's chance meeting with Tamrat Emanuel, a Falasha scholar invited to New York by the American Jewish League, plus a discussion with Ato Kantiba Gabrou, a member of a 1930 Ethiopian mission to the United States, spurred ideas of emigration. After Haile Selassie's coronation, Ford stayed on.[9] In 1931, Gabou told Ford that Haile Selassie had approved a grant of eight hundred acres near Lake Tana for African American settlement. Some sixty-six of Ford's followers eventually came to settle in Ethiopia. However, as in the past, the Place imposed impediments. Long-distance travel in the midst of the Depression was arduous and expensive. The outcome was redolent of the Chief Sam Gold Coast fiasco of twenty years before. By

1934, Ford was ill and some of his followers were embroiled in legal disputes for nonpayment of rents. Many of the black Jews returned to the United States.

Ford was not the only personage in the Diaspora seeking a home in Ethiopia. Another North American black, Emmett Jones, president of the Rising Sun Club of Philadelphia, wrote to Gabrou and was informed that the Tana region had been reserved for African American settlement. A black immigrant in Ethiopia, Daniel Alexander, received copious pro-emigration correspondence from the United States. One man, Lewis Livingstone wrote Alexander, "We [African Americans] have just what is needed for Africa." He also noted that an "Ethiopian Club" had organized an exhibition in Chicago. In New York, F. A. Cowan organized the Pioneers of Aethiopia. In 1931 he wrote to a correspondent in Nicaragua, "Aethiopia stretches out her hand for you, calling you to come. The possibilities are very unlimited." Ethiopia was that Promised Land that had for so long eluded the Diaspora: "Tradesmen and business are greatly in demand. The Pioneers offer you all the land that you can intelligently handle free, and tax free for seven years."[10] Plans included a Pioneer Lumber Company and a Pioneer Shoemaking Company. Indeed Cowan asserted that nearly one hundred men and women had already settled. Yet another movement in pursuit of an eastern Zion was the Pacific Movement of the Eastern World. Its head was St. Louis-based David D. Erwin. Erwin wrote Cordell Hull and announced that thousands of African Americans were anxious to leave for the Empire of Ethiopia.[11] Hattie Koffie, a woman who actually went to Ethiopia, returned in 1934 but continued to urge emigration. The white American government played a central role in her plan. Washington should buy the homes of American blacks at market prices so that they could buy land in Ethiopia. She further asked President Roosevelt and Secretary Hull to use their diplomatic influence to persuade the imperial government to subsidize the emigrants' travel.[12] Mittie Maud Lena Gordon, president of the Peace Movement of Greater Ethiopia, estimated that 400,000 African Americans would leave if provided assistance.[13] Events overtook her movement; by the time her organization was in high gear, Ethiopia had become absorbed into Italian East Africa. Independent Liberia was fixed as the cynosure of the Peace Movement of Greater Ethiopia's ambitions.

In 1930–31, the American consul in Ethiopia reported that approximately one hundred persons from the West Indies and the United States resided in the empire; he complained that they were "troublesome and often impecunious American negroes of whom the most objectionable appear to be British West Indian 'Garveyites' with American naturalization."[14] The consulate was afraid that the immigrants might appeal to it for money. One proposal in this situation was the idea that the State Department might "restrict or refuse" passports to blacks planning to travel to Ethiopia. Consul Addison Southard calculated that some recent arrivals at least were from New York and Cleveland. The United States government suspected that most immigrants were West Indians who had become naturalized to gain the benefits of a U.S. passport. The Americans also suspected that the British were deliberately delaying the issue of passports to persons they considered indigent. The State Department redoubled its efforts to check on the finances of any "colored" immigrants and disseminated information designed to discourage would-be emigrants.

The Fascist menace to Ethiopia after the opening of 1934 provoked an upsurge of Pan-Africanist activity across the black world.[15] Several excellent monographs have dealt in detail with the wider diasporic response to the Italo-Ethiopian War.[16] They raise a question: What was the interconnection, as in the case of Liberia, between Africa the totem and Africa the place? During the Italo-Ethiopian crisis, and for a generation thereafter, the two blurred. At the time, West Africans, West Indians, African Americans, and black Britons rallied to the cause, and support organizations rose, split, and fell. Established organizations, like Britain's League of Colored Peoples and the United States's NAACP, took up the cause. New organizations, many ephemeral, were formed specifically to confront Italian aggression. In London, Jomo Kenyatta and others organized the International African Friends of Abyssinia (IAFA). The West African Student Union (WASU) also became active in London, and West Africa was the site of numerous protests. In the United States, many of those formerly involved in the defense of Liberia threw themselves into defending Haile Selassie's empire. Willis Huggins, a New Yorker who had been considered for the post of educational adviser in Liberia, founded the very active Friends of Ethiopia. The Howard University historian W. Leo Hansberry established the Ethiopia Research Council, while Charles Houston, dean of the Howard Law School, served on the executive council of American Aid for Ethiopia. So great was the furor created by Italian aggression that it constituted one of the few instances in the mid-thirties on which Du Bois, Schuyler, and the NAACP all found themselves on the same side of a question. In March of 1935, the NAACP condemned Italian aggression to the U.S. State Department and the League. Walter White announced, "Italy, brazenly, has set fire under the powder keg of white arrogance and greed which seems destined to become an act of suicide for the so-called white world."[17] The *Crisis* published an article, "Ethiopia Awakes," in the summer of 1935 in which

Reuben Young, an African American who had spent a year in Ethiopia, urged African Americans to send technical experts. Centralization under the firm hand of Haile Selassie was what was needed.[18]

As in the case of Liberia, Ethiopia stretched forth her hands to the Diaspora. An emissary, Malaku Bayen, was able to encourage several well-known African Americans to volunteer for service in his homeland. Aviators John Charles Robinson and Hubert Julian went to the beleaguered African state. The physician John West also traveled to Ethiopia to serve. In Harlem, Captain Alfred L. King, leader of the remnant UNIA, spearheaded an intensive campaign to save Haile Selassie's empire. The most prominent organization taking up the cudgels in the United States was the Provisional Committee for the Defense of Ethiopia (PCDE). It drew support from the League of Struggle for Negro Rights (with communist assistance), the Improved and Benevolent Paternal Order of Elks, and the UNIA. In March of 1935, 3,000 people met in Adam Clayton Powell's Abyssinian Baptist Church to raise funds and send protests to the U.S. and Italian governments as well as the League. A coalition of groups that met in Chicago in July of 1935 brought together a group of strange bedfellows in support of the emperor's regime: communist organizations, Italian American anti-Fascists, representatives of churches, lodges, clubs, and the YMCA. August of 1935 saw a flurry of activity among various groups. On August 3, up to 25,000 people attended a meeting in Harlem to hear A. Philip Randolph, Adam Clayton Powell Jr., Roy Wilkins, and William Pickens speak for the PCDE. The group agreed to send Willis Huggins to Geneva to present a petition to the League.[19] The delegate to Geneva met with the Ethiopian minister to Great Britain, who asked the black American to return and raise funds and technical assistance. The outcome of these efforts was the founding of the Friends of Ethiopia, which had 106 branches by the end of 1935. The organization was linked to the Association for the Study of Negro Life and History and the redoubtable WILPF.

The latter organization had long been involved with Ethiopia and followed a course notable for its anticolonial fervor and ideological meanderings. The Women's International League for Peace and Freedom went from attacking slavery under the Ethiopian government to lobbying vociferously on its behalf. In 1930, Sir John Harris had approached the WILPF's international secretary in Geneva over the issue of forced labor in the mountain empire. In a situation echoic of Firestone in Liberia, Harris informed the WILPF that an American company, J. G. White, had been contracted by the government of Ras Tafari Makonnen (soon to be known as Haile Selassie) to build a dam and operate a mining concession. The Ethiopian government had allegedly offered the company slave labor, which the company had accepted. Dorothy Detzer went to the State Department, which assured her that an American concern would never use slave labor. In mid-August of 1930, Detzer met Gano Dunn, president of J. G. White, and queried him as to the company's labor practices. Detzer was told that the Ethiopian government "bitterly opposed" slavery; the institution had been abolished three years earlier. Detzer wrote of her deep skepticism: "I also realized that a decree made three years ago . . . did not abolish slavery any more than prohibition had stopped drinking in this country."[20] She demanded to know the wage rates and whether those wages were a standard the International Labor Organization would approve. Dunn noted that the company would do nothing to sully its reputation by paying substandard wages or using coerced labor. By April of 1931, Detzer was informed by one of her sources that the company had abandoned the project. By the spring of 1932, the plan seemed definitely over. However, the Tana Dam project surfaced again the following year, and the WILPF once again sprang into action. The organization questioned the State Department as to the employment of slave labor. The department referred the women's group to Gano Dunn's statement of 1930 promising not to use slave labor. The matter dropped and antislavery agitation, as well as the project, fell into desuetude.

By the mid-1930s, the question of human rights abuse in Haile Selassie's empire had definitely taken a backseat to anti-imperialism. William Phillips gives us a glimpse of the view from the other side of a State Department desk. Writing of a 1935 interview with a member of the WILP on the Ethiopian question, he confided to his diary:

A most annoying woman, asked me whether we are going to take any action in regard to the Italian-Ethiopian situation in view of the Kellogg Pact. She asked whether Ethiopia had made any appeal based on the Pact. I told her that Ethiopia had taken no action vis-à-vis the United States. I admitted probably unwisely, that I was giving the subject thought. After leaving my office apparently she telegraphed to her colleague in Geneva who represents the Women's International League for Peace and Freedom, advising her to urge the Government of Ethiopia to make an appeal to the United States, with especial reference to the Kellogg Pact and saying that the Government here was considering the matter very seriously. This shows how untrustworthy the woman is and I have been taught a good lesson. Never again will I have anything to do with her beyond the merest formalities.[21]

Between December 13, 1934, and May 20, 1935, the WILPF wrote to the League three times, demanding that it take action on the Italo-Ethiopian question.[22] In July of 1935, the affiliate organization in Geneva, the Union Mondiale des Femmes pour la Concorde Internationale, presented a petition to the League on behalf of thirty-one African American organizations. The Ethiopian empress made a worldwide appeal to women on a WILPF- sponsored radio program in September.[23] As in the case of Liberia, Ethiopia became "Africa," only more so. The issue of internal corruption and slavery, which had long troubled Ethiopia's relations with the outside world, had to be held in abeyance in the face of blatant Fascist aggression. Few people found a way of navigating a political path between the Scylla and Charybdis of feudalism and fascism. Indeed, at the time, it may have been impossible.

Nineteenth-century Ethiopia had spread southward under Menelik II, an expansion that led to land appropriation, taxation, and slave raiding in non-Amharic-speaking and non-Christian areas. Expansion was accompanied by ethnic chauvinism; the word *shankalla* (black) became a term of abuse, as did the word *barya* (slave).[24] Amharic settlement revolved around the military stockade (*katamma*), and a system similar to sharecropping (*neftenya-gabbar*) provided labor and tribute. After 1917, the regent Ras Tafari (later Haile Selassie, 1930–36 and 1941–74) tried to control the centrifugal forces within his "empire." Gradual emancipation was proclaimed a national goal in 1918, but the proclamation failed to appease Western abolitionists.[25]

In 1919, an Anglo-Ethiopian commission was ordered to the southwestern borders of Ethiopia to establish the boundary and investigate the problem of border incursions. The British members of the commission found considerable evidence of slave raiding by government officials and their retinues. The problem was acute along the borders with British colonial territory in the south, "the broad arc of territory extending from Borana in the southeast, to Lake Rudolph (and Toposa) in the southwest, and heading northward to the Wellega–Upper Nile Province frontier."[26] Ethiopian soldiers/settlers (*neftenya*) were unpaid and lived off the land, frequently retiring to Addis Ababa with slaves and other goods. The reports disturbed British officialdom, but authorities did not want the issue of slaving to disrupt Anglo-Ethiopian relations, especially with the prospect that British interest would be called on to build a dam of Lake Tana to control the waters of the Blue Nile. Ethiopian cooperation was also necessary if the flow of arms across the border into Sudan was to be interdicted.

In 1920, Sir John Harris lobbied in Geneva against the persistence of slavery in the postwar world. One of his chief targets was Ethiopia, where reports of slave raiding ran rampant. In 1922, sensational reports reached the British press. Evidence was produced to show that many of the slaves had come from the surrounding British territories and that many were reexported to the Arab peninsula. Harris, miffed by the dilatory nature of his government's response, got the New Zealand delegate to the League, Sir Arthur Steel Maitland, to bring the matter before the League assembly in September of 1922. The other Europeans with interests in Ethiopia, France and Italy, feared that British abolitionism might serve as a pretext for British takeover. Ethiopia gained admittance to the League in the following year, with British provisos that the country limit the arms traffic and inform the international organization on internal slavery.

The slavery question in Ethiopia remained an issue in the 1920s, just as it did in Liberia. In an effort to stave off adverse comment and further investigation, Ethiopia declared all children born after 1924 free. The central government also provided stiff penalties for slave trading and raiding. New regulations made it difficult to reclaim fugitive slaves, and slavery courts were established throughout the country. In addition, provisions were made for the care of freed slaves. Unfortunately, some slaving continued, and small numbers of slave children were still sent to Arabia and the Sudan. Social convention still upheld the institution. A sympathetic European wrote in 1927, "the Abyssinian maintains that the Bible contains no prohibition of slave-owning, and they point out that Moses commanded the Israelites to enslave their prisoners and make them work." An Ethiopian informant commented, "We were followers of the Mosaic religion before we became Christians . . . and we only did what Moses taught." No less a personage than Empress Zauditu wrote to the British, "the reason why some men were declared slaves was that certain nations were at war with us, and this had caused money to be spent which those nations had to repay by their labor."[27] In 1928–30, in an attempted revolt by Ras Gugsa Wale, estranged husband of Zauditu, northern rebels were put down with the help of southern Amharic leaders and their followers, many of whom had grown fat from the land and labor of indigenous Oromo, Sidama, or Somali. Slavery, central control, and "modernization" formed a heady brew and, in Ethiopia the place, could not help but produce continued tensions. By the late 1920s, the tempo of slaving slowed, due only in part to imperial rescripts flowing from Addis Ababa. Slaving also met increased slave resistance: "For those who chose to hold their ground, the acquisition of firearms permitted an active and convincing stance of deterrence. . . . Henceforth, the slaves taken from such sources would be prisoners of war, byproducts of period punitive expeditions rather than the steady yield of small-scale commercial ventures. By 1930, the increasing incidence of 'gabbar [tenant] stealing' only served to underscore the erratic nature of supply."[28]

When the Liberian scandal burst on the scene in 1929, the Ethiopian government took notice. Haile Selassie was installed as emperor in November of 1930 and proved incapable of compensating slave owners or of sending punitive expeditions to slaving areas. League action against Liberia may well have presaged action against the empire. One tactic to take with international opinion was to hire foreign advisers. In 1930, Ethiopia employed one Greek adviser, one German, two Swiss, one American, one Englishman, and two Frenchmen in its central administration. In 1932, the emperor received a delegation from the Anti-Slavery and Aborigines Protection Society. In August of the same year, in a preemptive strike, the emperor set up a Slavery Department under the direction of an Englishman. The League's Committee of Experts on Slavery (CES) looked into the matter and, after some jockeying among the colonial powers, published a report that, while critical, gave way to cautious optimism. The Committee of Experts suggested that slavery might be ended by noncoercive measures such as taxation, rewarding masters for manumitting slaves, and allowing slaves to work for their manumission. Little was achieved. The emperor's adviser on slavery and abolition resigned in 1933 on the grounds that antislavery measures were not being enforced. The "Third Annual Report on Slavery in Ethiopia," written by the British Minister in Addis Ababa, Sir Sidney Barton, for the period 1934–35, confirmed suspicions that little or nothing was being done. The emperor's Slavery Department had, "so far as can be judged," been reduced to a shadow of its former self. The judges of the Slavery Court faced popular opposition and a lack of support from local officials.[29]

The advent of the Fascist regime in 1922 had seen twists and turns in Rome's policies, all of them intended to get greater leverage in the Horn of Africa. Italy eventually supported Ethiopian membership in the League and, in 1928, concluded a treaty of friendship. In a move seen from the time of the Boer War to the recent conflict in Iraq, the decision for military action simultaneously disinterred the reports of nongovernmental human rights groups. The work of British and other antislavery groups became fodder for Italian propaganda. The Italian government, with the overt approval of the Catholic Church, emphasized the continuing need to eradicate slavery in "backward" Ethiopia. The scene had already been set. In 1929, Lady Kathleen Simon, in her book *Slavery*, had faulted both Liberia and Ethiopia for their toleration of slaving. In the latter case she wrote:

> During the consideration of slavery by the League of Nations, Signor Mussolini's Government drew the attention of Sir Eric Drummond to a raid on a slave caravan, which had taken place within the knowledge of Italian

officials. . . . The picture is drawn for us of a wretched gang of 150 slaves being driven to a coast port by brutalised slave-dealers, when suddenly a rival body swoops down upon the miserable caravan, and in the bloody fray which then takes place, some thirty of the wretched slaves, incapable of defending themselves, are killed and mutilated.[30]

At the time of the Italo-Ethiopian War, the Italian government strenuously attempted to remind the world that Ethiopia represented nothing more than a slave state. In 1935, Rome announced to the League:

The survival in Ethiopia of the system of slavery and the similar institution termed gebbar not only constitutes a horrible offence against civilization and an open breach of the obligations imposed by Article 23 of the Covenant of the League of Nations, but also represents a flagrant violation of the *special obligations* assumed by the Ethiopian Government at the time of its admission to the League. . . . If the Ethiopian Government had really been sincere in its intentions, it would have taken firmly and without delay the abolition of slavery, the slave trade and slave-raiding. . . . It will be noted that the Negus has never decreed the complete abolition of slavery, though that was the *sine qua non* of Ethiopia's admission to the League ten years previously; he has merely taken steps to have slaves placed under guardianship in some cases and to prohibit their sale . . . but he has never provided adequate means for the purpose.

That the measures taken by the Negus have all been utterly inadequate and illusory is proved by the fact that there are upwards of two million slaves in Ethiopia. Ethiopia . . . is the only Christian State now remaining in the world which recognizes the legality of the slave status.[31]

For many of the eventual defenders of Ethiopia, such charges seemed specious or irrelevant. Very few blacks, besides the expatriate chanteuse Josephine Baker, defended Italy's abolitionist mission. Indeed, Paul Robeson correctly observed, "There may be serious problems — slavery, for example — but Ethiopia could work out her own problems in time. There is no reason to believe that Italy can work them out for her."[32] Azikiwe mocked the pretensions "of some 'humanitarian' Italians who believe that slavery was rampant in Ethiopia and that it was imperative that the beneficent influences of Italian civilization should be carried into Ethiopia for the good of the world."[33] Du Bois opined that the attack formed part of "the program of the white world."[34] The charge of slavery was fatuous; Italy "accuses Ethiopia of savagery because she is not an industrialized state and because she still harbors the institution of domestic slavery, forgetting that the slavery that survives in Ethiopia has nothing in common with the exploitation of slaves through the slave trade or modern industrialism." In Harlem, the *Voice of Ethiopia* turned the charge against the invaders themselves: "What are we, the Sons of Freedom, going to do about the modern slavery? Will we suffer quietly this economic slavery? Will we suffer quietly the robbing and enslavement of Africa?" The challenge was thrown at African Americans: "Will we let Mussolini get away with his brigandage?"[35] One of the West African defenders of Ethiopia saw the slavery matter as largely immaterial. It constituted an internal matter; if Ethiopia was guilty "she should either give up trafficking in slaves and continue as a member of the League or cease forthwith to be a member. But there is no record that . . . Abyssinia ever, trafficked in slaves."[36] After the horrors of the twentieth century, how could Mussolini, with his poison gas and airplanes, claim any civilizing mission? George E. Moore, leader of the Gold Coast Aborigines' Rights Protection Society Deputation to England in 1934, rightly saw nothing but gross hypocrisy in Rome's claims:

To say nothing of the horrible murders and other hideous crimes daily perpetuated in so-called civilised Europe, we know of the atrocities perpetrated on the natives of the Belgium [*sic*] Congo by members of the civilized race, we know of the dastardly and barbarous acts done in the Great War, and we know of the deadly instruments of war being amassed for the destruction of human life by all the so-called civilised nations. Can anything be more barbarous? Then they talk of slavery in Abyssinia. There is much more slavery in the colonies under the government of the so-called civilized nations than you find in Abyssinia. In the colonies there is the tendency of the natives being autocratically ruled, ruthlessly exploited and politically and economically enslaved.[37]

According to one observer, "Sophisticated analyses of the complex factors which had caused the Italo-Ethiopian crisis were of little concern to the masses of black Americans."[38] As with much having to do with Pan-Africanism, reality often intruded inconveniently on wish fulfillment. Willis Huggins, a New York educator, met with an Ethiopian delegation in New York in 1930. He then spoke in Geneva on Haile Selassie's behalf in August of 1935 but was thoroughly disillusioned by early 1937. Huggins, going between Afro-America and the empire, accused the monarch of heading a rotten regime, of escaping to London with $10 million from the national treasury, and of disassociating himself from the anticolonialist struggle.[39] Like many were later to discover, the emperor was no progressive. Huggins was especially incensed by further imperial demands for money from the Black Diaspora. What was the money for? "How will Italy be ousted from Ethiopia? How could funds be distributed to the masses there in the face of Italian control?" The African American launched his most withering attack on the hierarchal nature of the Amharic ancien régime itself. How much "'relief' work," he asked, "was done for the masses by the 'nobility' before the Italians came?" Furthermore, "How many government supported public schools were there in Ethiopia under the old regime?" Simply put, the regime of Haile Selassie, in spite of the propaganda campaign to save it and the emperor's sangfroid at Geneva, did not deserve continued support. To Huggins, "The 'royal' parasites that have misruled the country in recent years turned over its inner control to foreign legations. . . . However, they were not dignified enough to prevent starving peasants from picking undigested grains of corn from the droppings of emaciated animals."[40] The emperor had become an irrelevancy: "The forlorn figure which mopes now in England is not 'His Majesty Haile Selassie I.' . . . This latter personality has 'gone with the wind' from Ethiopia and exists today only as a shell of the 'front' which he put up while the world was at his feet . . . feet which were sprouting wings for his ignominious flight."

What caused Huggins's volte-face? The answer perhaps lies in the vagaries of the delicate issue of racial classification and notions of racial and national solidarity. Alabama-born Huggins was a noted educationalist. In 1924, at the age of thirty-eight, he had been the first African American appointed to the New York School Department. He had received a Ph.D. in education from Fordham and held down two jobs; he served as a high school assistant principal and history teacher in two different schools. In addition, he was a Race Man who for a time held the post of president of the New York Association for the Study of Negro Life and History. Once in Ethiopia, the visitor became aware of much ambiguity on the part of the emperor and his court on the issue of race. In the parlance of another time, Huggins believed the emperor was afraid to "own his blackness" (at least in terms laid down in the U.S. census). The issue was confused. Indeed, as the historian Harold Marcus has pointed out in an article entitled "The Black Man Turned White," Europeans had, at least since the expansion of Abyssinia in the late nineteenth century, annexed the dominant ethnic group to the 'White Race.'"[41] Huggins had hit upon the conundrum posed by the construction of "race." Many white Americans, obsessed with enforcing hypodescent at home, seemed equally obsessed with denying "blackness" abroad. In 1919, prior to a visit of an Ethiopian mission to the United States, Addison Southard, then American vice-consul in Aden, opined that the visitors would be "darkskinned men with the hair and some the features of the negro, although the Abyssinian is not a negro."[42] While in the United States, the delegates were treated as "honorary whites" and one of the visitors asserted that Ethiopians were of the "darker race . . . but not like American Black men. We are treated like white men."[43] A decade later, Southard noted that the ruler, Empress Zauditu and others of her class "still are proud of their Semitic blood."[44] This Semitic blood did not stop the few Ethiopians in the United States from experiencing racial slights. However, it did encourage the white foreign policy establishment to shield visitors from Addis Ababa from the racial realities of the United States. Regarding a 1930 delegation, the state department was quite explicit. The planned head of the mission was advised to "don Ethiopian garb which would give him very much less the appearance of an American darky."[45] The African should "be placed in [the] hands of a White American who will use tact to prevent any demonstration by Harlem or Howard University."[46] For white America, it was Harvard, not Howard, that weighed in. In 1935 Carlton Coon of the Harvard anthropology department went to the Horn of Africa to determine the race of its inhabitants. Later he wrote,

> The least Negroid peoples of the highlands are the Ethiopians proper — who speak Amharic, Tigre, and Tigrinya — and the Gallas. The former are descended from southern Arabians who invaded Ethiopia during the first millennium B.C., and the latter from cattle people who entered the highlands from the west in the sixteenth century A.D. . . . Both are essentially Caucasoid in body build and facial features. Both vary in skin color from a light yellowish brown, in some cases almost yellow, to the various shades of brown that they themselves recognized and of which they are acutely conscious. None is black.[47]

In the 1930s some Ethiopians, such as Malaku Bayen, a member of the Young Ethiopia Movement, Aaj Workneh Martin, sometime ambassador to London, and Kantiba Gabrou, mayor of Gondar and diplomat, reached out to the African Diaspora. Others were more aloof. The elite faced a dilemma similar to that of its compeers in Monrovia. White capital was needed for development and white diplomatic support was essential to national independence. On the one hand, white involvement always carried within it the potential for economic and political penetration. This was plainly obvious in Mussolini's 1928 treaty of trade and friendship. On the other hand, recruitment of blacks from the Diaspora carried less political risks, but also brought in less capital. At the psychological level it also meant that a proud and class-ridden state was making common cause with the pariahs of the West. When Fascist propaganda taunted that a Jim Crow car would have to be put on the train to Geneva to accommodate the Negus and other Negroes, it struck a nerve.

Huggins noted the struggle of some white writers to show that "at least the 'Amharas' were 'Hymarite Arabs' utterly different from the so-called 'true African.' "[48] And Huggins was the latter. An early *New York Times* article described him as "Black in color as the proverbial 'ace of spades,' and having all the racial characteristics of the true African negro."[49] Huggins had made the arduous voyage to Ethiopia, but he had not found "Brothers Beyond the Sea." In 1937, he wrote, under the subtitle of "Ethiopians in a Racial Fog," of the mistakes made:

> Holding on to slavery, at this late date, and rejecting social civil and economic modernization, her luckless leaders kept her metamorphosed in the sheen of her ancient grandeur and in the shroud of the legend of her Christian primacy and, per force, expected a League of White Nations to fight for them against a white race. These leaders did not realize that white men no longer die for black men. . . . In reality, the recent leaders of Ethiopia are still in the racial fog. They still believe that they are of the white race, and so believing they doubly indict themselves. For, if they be of the white race, then in the nature of the oppression which they placed upon the blacks, they should have been disposed long, long ago. But they have not read history aright. They did not read between the lines of the pseudo-scientific verbiage which classed them as "white."[50]

Huggins found himself cast in a role similar to that of Schuyler on the Liberian question. In addition, he was accused of following the line taken by Garvey after the emperor had snubbed the UNIA leader in London. But the issue was deeper. Garvey, usually considered the least class-conscious of the nationalists, was quite capable of divining class in a color-coded world. As David Levering Lewis notes: "Despite his histrionics, Garvey was too intelligent not to see the limits of color in politics. He understood that the real problem in racial relations existed, . . . 'not because there is a difference between us in religion or in color, but because there is a difference between us in power.' "[51] At a time when many in the Diaspora lionized the emperor, the head of the UNIA saw the divisions *within* Ethiopia. On the surface, the emperor's lack of race consciousness troubled Garvey. "The Emperor of Abyssinia," he wrote, "allowed himself to be conquered, by playing white, by trusting to white advisers and by relying on white governments, including the white League of Nations."[52] Although he phrased his analysis in racial terms, he never fully accepted a posited black folk community in either Liberia or Ethiopia. Garvey raised a question about the emperor — "Why he kept the majority of his countrymen in serfdom and almost slavery is difficult to tell." According to the head of the UNIA, "They [i.e., the majority of Ethiopians] felt that they had a cause against the

Amharic white loving Emperor whose brutality to them [gave] Mussolini the cause to fool the world that he was bestowing a blessing upon the people of Abyssinia by freeing them."[53] In an expression very different from the unquestioning Pan-Africanism of others, he echoed his previous condemnation of the Liberian oligarchy:

> It was a piece of impertinence to suggest that black men should be held as slaves. We must admit that we glorified Haile Selassie when the war started, fought his battles to win international support, but we ever felt deep down in our hearts that he was a slave master. We had hoped that if Abyssinia had won that we would have forced the Government of Abyssinia to free the black[s] whom they held as slaves. We would have preferred this than seeing the country taken by Mussolini or any European power. . . . The future freedom of Abyssinia must be built upon the highest principles of democracy. That is why it is preferable for the Abyssinian Negroes and the Negroes of the world to work for the restoration and freedom of the country without the assistance of Haile Selassie, because at best he is but a slave master. The Negroes of the Western World whose forefathers suffered for three hundred under the terrors of slavery ought to be able to appreciate what freedom means. Surely they cannot feel justified in supporting any system that would hold their brothers in slavery in another country whilst they are enjoying the benefits of freedom elsewhere. The Africans who are free can also appreciate the position of slaves in Abyssinia. What right has the Emperor to keep slaves when all the democratic sections of the world were free, when men had the right to live, to develop, to expand, to enjoy all the benefits of human liberty[?][54]

In 1941, Haile Selassie returned to his throne with the aid of a British expeditionary force. He was to remain "King of Kings" for the next thirty years. Two days before Christmas 1941, Dr. Willis Huggins plunged to his death from the George Washington Bridge, leaving a note saying "Something is going to happen."[55]

Garvey had a modernist project, one that led him to lambaste the emperor. The crowning of Prince Tafari Makonnen as Haile Selassie in 1930 produced a very different outcome among some in Garvey's homeland. Rastafarianism expanded on Ethiopia as a Totem, a heroic backdrop to a diasporic dream. Like some nineteenth-century utopian socialists, the movement veered from the actively political to the religiously millennial. Early on, Paul Erlington called for free passage back to the motherland and social reform in Jamaica. For others, ancient and noble Africa became transformed into the home of a living god (Rastafari) who would solve the problem of diasporic existence by taking black folk back to the omphalos of the black world. The sources were various, but they all harkened back to a mythic Ethiopia. In 1935, L. F. C. Mantle appeared in Jamaica and claimed to have served with the British army in Palestine and to have visited Ethiopia and Tibet. He professed to be a rabbi, a faith healer, and a doctor of divinity. He disappeared, but left behind a core of esoteric lore linking all black people with Ethiopia and Ethiopia with the ancient Jews, who were black. Other leaders in Jamaica, such as Joseph Hibbert, Archibald Dunkley, Robert Hinds, and Leonard P. Howell, replaced the UNIA's focus with a heady mix of esoteric theology.[56] The link with Garveyism existed, but supernatural agency replaced the UNIA's cement, tractors, and motor corps.[57] The men given credit for sparking Rastafarianism all had, save for one, spent time abroad, knew of Garveyism, and finally sought refuge in a kind of recalcitrant quietism in which political action waited on the will of the divine. Hibbert, a master mason and a member of the Ancient Order of Ethiopia, founded the Ethiopian Coptic Church and used elements of the Ethiopic Bible as the basis of his theology.

Leonard Howell set himself up in the eastern parish, denied colonial authority, and told his followers not to pay taxes. In addition, he predicted that on August 1, 1934, the centenary of the enactment of abolition in the British Caribbean, Jamaicans would emigrate en masse to Africa. In December of 1933, Howell was arrested on charges of sedition and sentenced to two years incarceration. Dunkley and Hibbert were also arrested and imprisoned. Howell emerged from prison in 1935 and published a book, *The Promised Key,* a compilation of exhortatory arcana. After the defeat of Ethiopia, the movement continued — without a magical Middle Passage out of "Babylon." Around 1940, Howell set up a commune called Pinnacle near Kingston, in the hills of Saint Catherine. Instead of repatriation to a "Beloved Continent," the Pinnacle represented a return to the maroon past (or Howell's version of it). The men wore beards and dreadlocks and engaged in polygyny and cannabis smoking if they wanted to. Overleaping the all-too-concrete plans of the UNIA, the Rastafarians engaged in a "wilderness experience which became the 'bridge-burning act,' solidifying the movement around certain rites and practices with which they are now identified."[58]

A branch of the Ethiopian World Federation Inc. was established in Jamaica in 1938. Through it, some Rastafarians maintained a link with the putative mother/fatherland. When Haile Selassie visited Jamaica in 1960, many Rastafarians were audibly disappointed on seeing the short and sallow monarch emerge from his plane. Myth had met reality. The emperor died fifteen years later, but God lives on: "For Rastafarians . . . there existed and continues to exist only one perfect, immortal, omnipotent and omniscient Ras Tafari. . . . Therefore, any suggestion that he died is a demonstration of ignorance."[59] Myth conquered reality.

One may ask, how could the regime of Haile Selassie, which finally collapsed because of its indifference to African suffering, have emerged as the paladin of the suffering black world? By the time the empire fell apart in 1974, it was widely denounced as a decadent remnant of a bygone age, a government so out of touch with reality that it willingly saw thousands of its own subjects starve to death rather than admit its own incompetence. In the Polish journalist Ryszard Kapuscinski's *The Emperor,* a courtier, speaking as news of mass starvation spreads, says: "Here you can see, my friend, the irresponsibility of the press, which . . . praised our monarch for years and then suddenly, without any rhyme or reason, condemned him."[60] Looking closely at the emperor, we are left somewhere between the heroic image of the proud Ethiopian portrayed in Frank Capra's World War II propaganda film *Why We Fight* or the god of the Rastas and the little king in Waugh's *Black Mischief.* Haile Selassie may have meant well, but he remained within the constraints of his worldview and position. As in the case of the modernizing but feudally based regime of King Amanullah in Afghanistan, change proved to be, ultimately, unmanageable. Interestingly, before they both collapsed, the elites of Liberia and Ethiopia had become ideological allies. "Liberia found its own reflection in Ethiopia: Amhara dominance over other ethnic groups paralleled that of 'the Americo-Liberian minority [that] imposed its norms and institutions upon the . . . sixteen or more ethnic groups' in Liberia, employing 'all the mannerisms of an imperial power.' "[61]

Ethiopia's political liquidation helped increase Liberia's stock among some Pan-Africanists. In the mid-thirties, Ernest Lyon reminded Barclay that Liberia was the only black-ruled state in Africa. In his view Ethiopia was independent, "but Abyssinia is not Negro." Such sentiments were common.[62] In 1933, Lester Walton had met in Paris with the Liberian secretary of state, the Ethiopian minister to France, and a Haitian representative. Little concrete emerged from the meeting; Walton opined that the Ethiopian representative was "disinclined to enter into any cooperative movement (non-political) in the interest of the black people of the world."[63] When Italian invasion of Ethiopia seemed imminent in 1935, Walton bitterly remarked, "the representatives of Abyssinia in Geneva and France have always officially ignored representatives of Liberia and Haiti." The situation was ironic: "Abyssinians have been declaring they are not Negroes. Now they are appealing for Negro aid."[64] During the crisis, the Accra (Gold Coast) *African Morning Post* warned its readers that Liberia would follow Ethiopia as the next victim of European colonial aggrandizement.[65] In the summer of 1935, the British consulate in Monrovia said the Liberians were showing great interest in the fate of Haile Selassie. The consulate thought the Italian invasion would make the Liberians more jealous of their independence and, at the same time, more amenable to outside advice.[66] In the same summer, William Jones of the *Baltimore Afro-American* told his readers that it was "of deep significance . . . that just at this time when Abyssinia is the focus of world diplomatic relations, the United States Government steps in and announces recognition of the only other parcel of land not under colonial rule in that great country [*sic*]."[67] In 1936, as Ethiopia moved toward collapse, President Barclay vowed Liberia would "maintain her status as a Negro State in the age of imperialistic conquest."[68]

After the fall of Ethiopia, George Padmore's London-based International African Service Bureau informed Barclay, "Today [now] that Abyssinia has been made a subject State and the last of the ancient African Kingdoms is destroyed, Liberia becomes of special importance as a symbol of African independence."[69] Perhaps foreseeing the political demise of Ethiopia, Azikiwe had asserted that Liberia constituted the center of the Pan-African project: "German Kultur and Kulturkampf are possible in Germany; Japanism is realizable in Japan. If African Kulturkampf must be consummated — it is inevitable, despite all attempts to stifle national consciousness and self-determination — then the incubator for the hatching the egg of a great national awakening, toward the establishment of a black hegemony, is the Republic of Liberia."[70] The little polity remained the standard-bearer of the race.

Black Fascism?

Edward Said has recently criticized Bernard Lewis's work on the Middle East as long on generalizations and short on specifics. For example, Said quotes Lewis: "During the 1930s, Italy and then, far more, Germany offered new ideological and political models, with the added attraction of being opposed to the Western powers. These won widespread support, and even after their military defeat in World War II, they continued to serve as unavowed models in both ideology and statecraft." Said remarks: "Mercifully, since they are 'unavowed models,' one doesn't need to offer any proof of their existence as models."[71] Equally, in a fascinating and highly thought-provoking reading of Garveyism, Paul Gilroy finds that it was "fascist." He notes Garvey's attempted collaboration with white supremacists and his emphasis on race and regimentation. Indeed, Garvey did say in a 1937 interview, "Mussolini copied fascism from me, but the Negro reactionaries sabotaged it."[72] One can go even further; Garvey opined that the Jews had brought their troubles in Germany on "themselves in that their particular method of living is inconsistent with the broader human principles that make a people homogeneous. The Jews like money."[73] Gilroy comments that there are "two recurrent attributes of what I feel can be justifiably named fascism: brutalism and masculinism."[74] Of course, here one could be speaking of movements headed by Andrew Jackson, Paul Kruger, or Osama bin Laden. In a world long characterized by patriarchy and the more recent evolution of world wars, who is not a fascist, using these core attributes? The culture critic declares, "The recent bloody histories of authoritarian regimes in Iran, Greece, Latin America, Indo-China, and Africa all suggest that fascism is not productively grasped as Europe's own private and internal drama." Furthermore, "the capacity to perpetuate evil is not itself modern, but the metaphysics of modernity brought a special tone to it. The scale and power of the nation-state condition it."[75] Yet this catalogue leaves questions dangling — was it pre- or post-1979 Iran that was fascist?

We should avoid the temptation to make *fascism* simply a penumbra of meaning, an aesthetic reactionary chic forced backward onto a varied political reality, including both regimes of the right and the left, the authoritarian and the totalitarian, and the racist and nonracist. We should remember George Mosse's caveat: "To be sure, writing about self-representation has become popular among scholars of late, but when they address 'representation,' they are almost always concerned with loose psychological or textual associations, rather than with the specific historical context in which visual self-representation takes place."[76] It should be remembered that all fascistic regimes are authoritarian, but that not all authoritarian regimes are fascistic. Then there is the question of race and the state. In 1922, Garvey said that his movement was "determined to purify and standardize our race."[77] It is not to split hairs to ask if Mussolini's program in the same year was specifically "racial" or if he meant it when he asserted that the state was absolute, harmonizing capital and labor and, with its futurist dynamic, sweeping aside the sectarian differences of the past. Italian Fascism was not fully raced in its first decennium. The honorable C. D. B. King visited the Quirinal in 1927, and Gandhi followed five years later. For over a decade of its existence, "non-Aryans" occupied important positions in the Fascist colonial administration, the party apparatus, and the cabinet. We must ask if in the early 1920s fascism offered the ideological (or aesthetic) equivalent of the Anglo-Saxon Clubs or the Ku Klux Klan. Certainly some distinction must be drawn between both the style and the ideology of exponents of Herrenvolk Democracy and Giovanni Gentile or Roberto Michels.

Without a general theory of fascism, we run into pleonasms devoid of all explanatory meaning. We arrive, indeed, at that point described by Michel Foucault: "The non-analysis of fascism is one of the important political facts of the past thirty years. It enables fascism to be used as a floating signifier, whose function is essentially that of denunciation."[78] To compare Garveyism with fascism (or Fascism) compares to comparing the Nation of Islam and a generalized Islamic fundamentalism. Obviously, points of similarity exist, but, wrenched from its historical context, the comparison has little heuristic or analytical value.

The Garvey of the immediate post–World War I period operated in an ideological ambiance very different from that immediately preceding the Second World War. Orchestrated mass demonstrations do not, of themselves, fascism make. Indeed, monster parades can be organized to celebrate both Stakanovism and "Kraft durch Freude." Like Du Bois's, Garvey's political admiration could extend to a wide variety of regimes. During his career, the Jamaican expressed admiration for the British Empire, the Russian Revolution, and the Zionist Movement. While viewing Hitler as a German patriot, Garvey's political vocabulary never completely abandoned the words of twentieth-century liberalism. Unlike Italian or German fascism, Garveyism did not stridently repudiate democracy. When in 1937 Garvey denounced the Negus for betraying the race "when all the democratic sections of the world were free, when men had the right to live, to develop, to expand, to enjoy all the benefits of human liberty," we must assume some level of sincerity.[79] If not, we must assume only the most cynical of opportunisms.

Both Garvey and Du Bois were attracted to strong men, but this does not make either of them fascists. Both were eclectically looking at what a series of new and successful movements could do for their people. Du Bois visited Nazi Germany in 1936 under the sponsorship of the Oberlaender Trust. He traveled widely: "I have read German newspapers of all sorts and places; I have read books, listened to lectures, gone to operas, plays and movies, and watched a nation at work and play. I have talked with a half dozen officials."[80] His aim was to "study the way in which popular education for youth and adults in Germany has been made to minister to industrial organization and advance; and how this German experience can be applied so as to help in the reorganization of the American Negro industrial school, and the establishment of other social institutions."[81] The professor strongly condemned the regime's minority policies. Hitler's racial attitudes were abhorrent, especially "the frightful anti-Semitic propaganda." Racism was a plague. After leaving Germany, Du Bois opined, "there has been no tragedy in modern times equal in its awful effects to the fight on the Jews in Germany. It is an attack on civilization, comparable only to such horrors as the Spanish Inquisition and the African slave trade."[82] On the one hand, Du Bois could not ignore the porno-political ravings of Julius Streicher, "the most shameless, lying advocate of race hate in the world, not excluding Florida." On the other, Hitler's Germany offered a respite from the Negrophobia of his own *Heimat*. Du Bois informed the readers of the *Pittsburgh Courier*, "it would have been impossible for me to have spent a similarly long time in any part of the United States, without some, if not frequent cases of personal insult or discrimination."[83] The sojourner mused that perhaps only a dictatorship could have saved postwar Germany and that National Socialism was the "most astonishing sight in modern history." The regime's ideology was not wholly illogical and might form a bridge to true socialism: "The longer I looked at Hitler's Germany the more I realized that it was a socialistic state. It was copying the Soviet Union in innumerable ways."[84]

Du Bois showed greater enthusiasm for Germany's anti-Comintern ally, Japan, even in its most sorry and sanguinary actions. The professor's opinion of the Japanese was informed by his continuing belief in the dominance of the racial struggle in world affairs. In an article entitled "Inter-racial Implications of the Ethiopian Crisis: A Negro View," Du Bois saw the Italian invasion as the beginning of a generalized revolt of the colonized.

> Japan is regarded by all colored peoples as their logical leader, as the one non-white nation which has escaped forever the dominance and exploitation of the white world. No matter what Japan does or how she does it, excuse leaps to the lips of colored thinkers. Has she seized Korea, Formosa and Manchuria? Is she penetrating Mongolia and widening her power in China itself? She has simply done what England has done in Hong Kong and France in Annam, and what Russia, Germany and perhaps even the United States intended to do in China. She has used the same methods white Europe has used, military power and commercial exploitation. And yet in all her action there has been this vast difference: her program cannot be one based on race hate for the conquered, since racially these latter are one with the Japanese and are recognized as blood relatives. Their eventual assimilation, the accord of social equality to them, will present no real problem. White dominance under such circumstances would carry an intensification of racial differences. Conquest and exploitation are brute facts of the present era, yet if they must come, is it better that they come from members of your own or other races?[85]

In his seventh decade, Du Bois held to the notion that "the problem of the twentieth century is the problem of the color line." For him, as with his fellow racial thinkers on the other side of the line, the world was Dixie writ large. Visiting Shanghai in 1937, the black scholar remarked: "I saw last night a little white boy of perhaps four years order three Chinese out of his imperial way on the sidewalk . . . it looked quite like Mississippi."[86] The professor went on to wax rhapsodic about Japanese imperialism in Manchuria, where there was "no apparent discrimination between motherland and colony." The reason: "Because Japanese and Manchoukuans are so nearly related in race that there is nor can be no race prejudice." He reached a remarkable conclusion: "Ergo: no nation should rule a colony whose people they cannot conceive as Equals."[87] The problem lay not with imperialism per se; indeed, it might do much good if imposed by people of the same "race." The fact that Du Bois expressed these sentiments shortly before the "Rape of Nanking," in which the Japanese massacred over 200,000 Chinese civilians, is, to put it mildly, lamentable. The professor informed the black readers of the *Pittsburgh Courier*, "it was Japan's clear cue to persuade, cajole, and convince China. . . . But China sneered and taught her folk that Japanese were devils." What was Japan to do? It had done the necessary: "Japan fought China to save China from Europe and fought Europe through China and tried to wade in blood toward Asiatic freedom." Du Bois admonished his readers, "Negroes must think straight in this crisis."[88] The idea of wading "in blood toward Asiatic freedom" is to wade in the military euphemisms of the twentieth century. Du Bois adumbrates Lyndon Johnson in Vietnam by thirty years, but his thought no more fits within a general theory of fascism than does that of the bellicose Texan.

Both Du Bois and Garvey believed, for most of their lives, in the primacy of race. Garvey *was* an avowed racialist. Indeed, it is possible, without overfascination with trappings — jackboots and peeked caps — to see him as the mirror reflection of white racists. In a review of Scott Malcomson's work on American race formation, Orlando Patterson observes: "The greatest irony of America's separatist history, Malcomson argues, is the fact that 'the racial contest was over ideological or psychological materials that were remarkably similar and in many ways identical.' At all periods of American history, 'those preoccupied with racial destinies walked about in a forest of mirrors.'" In the sociologist's opinion then, it is "no wonder . . . that Marcus Garvey developed close friendships with white separatists and that today white separatists often simply borrow from the rhetoric of black separatists, as black separatist leaders had previously done with their 'defensive breastwork against whites?"[89] The continuing question is: How do we account for the long-term flirtation between Garvey and the radical fringe of American racism?

Greater Liberia

In *Juneteenth,* Ralph Ellison's posthumously published work, a virulently racist senator named Sunraider is murdered by a young black man and then comforted in dying by a pious Southern black preacher, Reverend Alonzo Hickman.[90] Again, fact is sometimes stranger than fiction. Marcus Garvey, the Great Black Man of the century, ended his career as a supporter of Senator Theodore Bilbo (1877–1947), the Great White Racist of the century. At first glance, the Mississippi legislator would seem the most unlikely of supporters for any form of black nationalism. In 1935, in his *Forerunners of American Fascism,* Raymond Swing felt that "if he were ten years younger, knowing the rabble throughout America to be not unlike the rabble of Mississippi, he might go out to rouse it. He is a portent.[91] Bilbo's brand of populism consisted of castigating the business and planter elites, while constantly appealing to poor white racism. In his fight to oppose blacks voting in primary elections, he said that he was "calling on every red-blooded American who believes in the superiority and integrity of the white race to get out and see that no nigger votes." He added: "And the best time to do it is the night before."[92] Bilbo had been a Baptist lay minister and a lawyer before devoting himself to politics. He became a state senator in 1907, lieutenant governor in 1912, and served two terms as governor (1916–20, 1928–32). In 1923, when Garvey's Liberian project still appeared viable, Bilbo mocked Mississippi state "senator T. G. McCallum's scheme to move negroes of the United States to darkest Africa," as "wonderful to contemplate, a fact to be devoutly wished for, but . . . an idle dream."[93] Seventeen years later, he was an ardent proponent of the formerly "idle dream." In the year of Garvey's death, he wrote, "some of my colleagues and other public men are afraid of the proposal for resettlement of American Negroes in Africa . . . they regard it as fantastic, too visionary, too big a job." Bilbo had become convinced that "it would certainly be cheaper and better to care for them in that way [i.e., emigration] than to let them stay in the United States and keep them indefinitely on the relief rolls."[94] Obsessed by the specter of interracial sex, Bilbo saw black emigration as the final solution to his American dilemma, as expressed in his book, published the year of his death, *Take Your Choice: Separation or Mongrelization.*[95] He characterized the work as "an honest attempt to conserve and protect and perpetuate my own white race and white civilization, and at the same time impress especially the black and yellow races with the fact that they must join in an effort to protect the integrity of their own race, blood, and civilization."[96]

In the early thirties, Bilbo became aware of the Peace Movement of Ethiopia, an emigrationist organization headed by a former UNIA member, Mittie Maude Lena Gordon. The Louisiana-born Gordon had been a delegate to the 1929 UNIA convention in Jamaica. She founded her single-issue lobbying movement in Chicago in December of 1932. Its aim was federal "repatriation" of African Americans to Liberia. The movement reasoning was that the cost of establishing African Americans in West Africa would be less than the price of welfare in the United States. In 1933, the Peace Movement sent a petition with over 400,000 signatures to President Roosevelt for help with its project. The petition was a *cri de coeur* to Pharaoh:

> Whereas the distress of the unemployed is most severely felt by such of the uneducated American Negroes who abhor alms, both public and private, in any guise; and whereas the removal of half million of the poorest from a competitive labor market, at this time, would tend to relieve to that extent the condition and improve the opportunities of the remainder, we, the subjoined signatories, Americans citizens of African extraction, individually and collectively, join in respectfully petitioning the President to consider our proposal, confident that his conclusions will be for the best interests of our families and of the community at large. We are of the so-called North, most of us having been driven from a cruel and avowedly intolerant South to the cities and towns of the Middle West, without a just opportunity to earn a livelihood in our abject new state. . . . Hungry, cold and miserable, the pursuit of life, liberty, and happiness in America appears futile. Given an opportunity in our own ancestral Africa, the knowledge of farming and simple farm machinery and implements which we have acquired here would enable us to carve a frugal but decent livelihood out of the virgin soil and favorable climate of Liberia, or such other well-disposed country where the Federal Government, in its wisdom, might acquire a footing for us.
>
> We respectfully ask that the President graciously have this matter investigated now, with a view to fulfilling the expressed desires of Abraham Lincoln in this respect. We are a liability now, and any cost of this project, no matter how great, would still, we sincerely believe, be a sound investment for the American people.[97]

The petition was shunted to the State Department and then relegated to the Division of Western European Affairs. The division felt that African American emigration was a dead issue. Mistakenly, Bilbo believed that representatives of Gordon's group had visited Liberia, where Edwin Barclay had guaranteed them large territories. "Formal announcement," Bilbo said, "has been made by President Barclay that millions of acres of land in Liberia are now ready and waiting to be settled by American Negoes [*sic*]."[98] Minister Walton noted, "A Mr. Jones, an American missionary . . . is said to have been the one who gave Bilbo the idea when he was in the United States last year. An erroneous impression was created that he was some kind of representative of the Liberian Government."[99] The Liberian booster was a former black Mississippian who had emigrated in 1902 after graduating from Jackson College. Later he returned to the United States and studied at Meharry Medical College. Back in Liberia, he combined preaching, teaching, dentistry, and medicine. He was Bilbo's man on the scene. The senator exulted "A titan, a man among men in Liberia, is this Dr. Jones!"[100]

The Peace Movement of Greater Ethiopia was not the only group that approached Bilbo. In 1938, Ramon A. Martinez, a law graduate from the University of Puerto Rico and a Detroit attorney, put forth a plan for the voluntary emigration of African Americans to British and French territories adjacent to Liberia. Twelve million blacks could go to this "Greater Liberia" on land ceded in return for cancellation of the colonial powers' war debt. Martinez, the leader of the Negro Nationalist Movement, trumpeted that such a bold move would "meet the war-debt situation, solve our domestic race problem, create overseas a vast source of supply for rubber and other raw materials of the tropics and bring into being a market for American manufactures."[101] Eventually, in various pieces of legislation, Bilbo was to ask for the settlement of war debts due the United States, for the creation of a colonization bureau, and for assisted emigration to lands acquired for that purpose.

In spite of newer emigrationist voices, Bilbo was impressed by Garvey, who was "the most conspicuous [*sic*] of all the organizers of his race." Garvey had "definitely succeeded in establishing the fact that there is an overmastering impulse, a divine afflatus among the masses of Negroes in the United States for a country of their own and a government administered by themselves."[102] Garvey responded. The Eighth International Convention of the UNIA met in Toronto in August of 1938 and passed a unanimous vote in support of Bilbo's stance. Garvey wrote to Bilbo, "it is not necessary to comment on the vital importance of your motion, in that it strikes at the very future of the race in as far as its nationalistic aspirations are concerned."[103] The senator replied that he was "happy to know that your organization will give me fullest cooperation in the program that I am trying to project for the benefit of the Negroes in the United States."[104] Garveyites in various cities sent letters and delegations to the Mississippian. Mass meetings were organized and, by April of

1939, the UNIA had collected 50,000 signatures in support of emigration. From New York, Carlos Cooks, the president of the UNIA Advance Division, wrote the Southern legislator, "our speaking staff is anxious, eager, and ready to swing into action."[105] Bilbo attempted to fund a speaking tour for the group, while Garvey in England named a committee to pressure Washington. Garveyites in Cleveland, Philadelphia, and New York grouped themselves into a Lobby Committee on [the] Greater Liberia Act.

After a flurry of activity and anticipation, Bilbo introduced his repatriation bill (Senate Bill 2231) to the Senate on April 24, 1939. Claude Barnett went to a Peace Movement meeting a few days before the bill was submitted and said that President Gordon excoriated "big n . . . s' ministers and newspapermen." She gave "both Garvey and the NAACP the deuce in her talks."[106] On the day the bill was introduced, its black supporters packed the senate gallery. Barnett wrote Walton in Monrovia, "the Peace of Ethiopia folk made a trek to Washington . . . they are a crude, ignorant lot, reminding one of the early Garvey days."[107] *Time Magazine* seemed bemused by Gordon: "Last week some 300 of her followers, who mostly are on Relief (as is she), arrived in Washington by truck and car, so fagged that they could hardly drag themselves up the Capitol steps to hear their friend from Mississippi." The leader of the Peace Movement was described as "a portly mulatto" who "raises her cream-coffee arms [and] shouts to her audiences, 'There's amalgamation for you! See what it does to us.'"[108] Gordon had written Bilbo, "We highly approve your opposition to the mixture of the two races; for we, likewise, detest the same thing." Her movement stood for the average black woman and man: "We are Negroes who represent the industrial masses, farmers, and men of skill, and in the land of our forefathers we will not only make a living for ourselves but will be free from race prejudice and discrimination."[109]

The Greater Liberia Act called for the subsidized and voluntary emigration of African Americans to the Black Republic. The senator foresaw the exodus of from 5 to 8 million African Americans over a period of fifteen to twenty-five years. The plan would favor persons in their reproductive years; the hope of the sponsor was that those who remained would die off. Garvey said of the bill: "The Senator's desire for carrying out the purpose of his Bill may not be as idealistic as Negroes may want, but that is not the point to be considered."[110] What was important was "the opportunity of the Negro to establish himself and there is no doubt that this Bill offers such an opportunity." Garvey wholeheartedly supported the bill and attacked those members of the "Negro press" who opposed it. He maintained that certain of the senator's comments on race in previous years proved irrelevant in the present case. It was the bill that mattered. Bilbo's effort constituted "one that no Negro can make in America at the present time, because he [i.e., the Negro] lacks the necessary influence in the Senate."[111]

Garvey effusively praised Bilbo and his fellow segregationist, Earnest Sevier Cox. "These two white men," he wrote, "have done wonderfully well for the Negro and should not be forgotten." Cox dedicated a book, *Let My People Go,* to Garvey and communicated with many UNIA branches. In 1932, he lobbied for an emigration resolution in the Virginia state legislature. The proposal died in committee. In 1934, Cox made contact with Mittie Gordon. Curiously, the white racist became the national representative of the Peace Movement of Ethiopia two years later. The semi-moribund American Colonization Society was contacted in an effort to get its sponsorship. The group also endeavored to obtain the endorsement of Edwin Barclay. As in the case of the failed Garvey scheme, they received mixed signals. The Peace Movement sent two representatives, David Logan and Joseph Rockmore, to Liberia in 1938. Lester Walton opined that, "President Barclay does not take seriously the expressed hopes of the PME that financial support will be received from the United States."[112] The two emissaries spent one month in Liberia and were frequently in the company of Thomas Faulkner, who persisted in his dreams of immigration and uplift. Barclay acted to dampen the effects of any emigration proposal by demanding that all immigrants have proof of at least $1,000 in assets. Cox, acting as the white patron of Peace Movement activities, eventually got the Virginia legislature to petition Congress for federal aid to emigration. Later, Cox expressed his thanks to the state governor on behalf of the Peace Movement, the National Union of People of African Descent, the Universal Negro Improvement Association, and a group of black Virginians.[113]

Perhaps the most notorious of Garvey's white racist supporters was Thomas Dixon, whose novel *The Clansman* had made it to the screen as *Birth of a Nation* in 1915. In 1939, Dixon published *The Flaming Sword,* a racist phantasmagoria centered on the specter of black sexuality. In the novel, the protagonist bequeaths $10 million for the establishment of a Marcus Garvey Colonization Society for the voluntary emigration of African Americans.[114] The title came from a line by Du Bois: "Across this path stands the South with flaming sword." Garvey expressed himself "very much interested in Mr. Dixon's new work and more so when he has stated that his desire is to work on behalf of the repatriation of Negroes to Africa."[115]

Garvey was not the first black leader to attempt to reach a modus vivendi with Southern racists. Booker T. Washington had attempted to do so in the late nineteenth century. His successor, Robert Moton, voiced the opinion that "the white man of the South loves the Negro."[116] Radical segregationists could, theoretically, be attracted to the idea of a black-free America. However, most whites would not opt for such radical solutions; Jim Crow did its work well enough. The African American position was to be perpetually neither in nor out. In 1914, the year in which Garvey began the UNIA in Jamaica, Theodore Roosevelt attempted to avoid this perpetual nonsolution. The ex-president contemplated the alternatives in facing the "Negro Question": extermination, segregation, or amalgamation. Extermination had reduced the indigenous population, but was no longer morally acceptable. Speaking through a nameless South American interlocutor, Roosevelt opened the taboo subject of social equality. He claimed to have spoken to a Brazilian statesman, "himself of pure white blood," who assured him that segregation was no fit resolution: "Slavery was an intolerable method of solving the problem, and had to be abolished. But the problem itself remained in the presence of the Negro." The South American further noted blacks would "remain a menacing element in your [North American] civilization, permanent, and perhaps even after a while a growing element." In Brazil, the situation was quite to the contrary; the black was being absorbed into the dominant society. Segregation and amalgamation were both fraught with danger, but the nameless interviewee proclaimed that the Brazilian solution would "in the long run, from the national standpoint, prove less disadvantageous and dangerous than the one you of the United States have chosen."[117] Roosevelt had broached and obliquely approved what most Americans would have avoided at all costs — interracial sex.

Garvey would have viewed such musings as utopian or immoral or both. In his view, blacks could *never* be integrated into white society on the basis of *complete* equality. They formed an exogenous body in the social and political life of a white man's country. Inclusion would only produce a bastardized chaos. Addressing the white majority, he said: "No real race loving white man wants to destroy the purity of his race, and no real Negro, conscious of himself, wants to die, hence there is room for an understanding, and an adjustment. And that is just what we seek."[118] Garvey believed that in seventy to eighty years, race relations in the United States would have worsened. Indeed, "the problem of the twentieth century" would extend well beyond it. To the Jamaican, competition from immigrants would pauperize blacks and increase racial hostility. In his weltanschauung, informed by late nineteenth-century social Darwinism, a group had to protect itself or die. "Power," Garvey said, "is the only argument that satisfies man. Except the individual, the race or the nation has power that is exclusive, it means that the individual, race or nation will be bound by the will of the other who possesses this great qualification."[119] In Garvey's worldview, the proximity of two races, black and white, must engender conflict, eventuating in the elimination of the weaker.

Such thought was not heterodox. Indeed, it represented an outlook common to most Americans: color determined both class and power; the history of the world was the history of universal pigmentocracy. Popular racial theorists like Madison Grant and Lothrop Stoddard stood far closer to Garvey than any integrationist could ever do. Indeed, Garvey's views and those of a man like Stoddard were congruent. For instance, Stoddard insistently warned of the dangers against white world supremacy facing the white race after the bloodletting of the Great War. In *The Rising Tide of Color,* published in 1920, he divided the planet into blocks based on color : "Black Man's Land," "Red Man's Land," "White Man's Land," "Brown Man's Land," and "Yellow Man's Land."[120] Race was all; history was a war of colors, race against race. Phenotype trumped both class and climate. The "White Race" was a world minority engaged in a titanic battle with all the others, especially the "Yellow," for world domination. Africa was up for grabs; the "Brown Race," represented by Arabs and their affines, was, in Stoddard's schema, attempting to gain control of the continent through the spread of Islam.

A. James Gregor, discussing "Fascism, Marxism, and Race" very helpfully points out that racial thinking "is a 'natural' product of the intense emotion associated with the nationalism of deprived and humiliated peoples. That reactive nationalists have a tendency to invoke an enduring biological basis for their nationalism is evidenced by the history of contemporary revolutionary thought."[121] Garvey's 1922 meeting with Edward Clarke of the Ku Klux Klan constituted an attempt to come to terms with what he perceived as the complementary nature of white racism. He said of the meeting: "I was speaking to a man who was brutally a white man, and I was speaking to him as a man who was brutally a Negro."[122] If race is essential and racial antipathy natural, this appears to be a realistic stance. But Garvey misread the signals. Varieties of racist thought exist; Garvey did not adequately take the measure of his white interlocutors. Using Kwame Appiah's typology, we may divine that Garvey was a racialist among racialists.[123] The philosopher differentiates *extrinsic racism* from *intrinsic racism*:

One such doctrine we might call *extrinsic racism:* extrinsic racists make moral distinctions between members of different races because they believe that the racial essence entails certain morally relevant qualities. The basis for the extrinsic racists' discrimination between people is their belief that members of different races differ in respects that *warrant* the differential treatment. . . . Evidence that there are no such differences in morally relevant characteristics . . . should thus lead people out of their racism if it is purely extrinsic. As we know, such evidence often fails to change an extrinsic racist's attitudes substantially. . . . But at this point — if the racist is sincere — what we have is no longer a false doctrine but a cognitive incapacity. . . . *intrinsic racists,* on my definition, are people who differentiate morally between members of different races, because they believe that each race has a different moral status, quite independent of the moral characteristics entailed by its racial essence. Just as, for example, many people assume that the bare fact that they are biologically related to another person — a brother, an aunt, a cousin — gives them a moral interest in that person, so an intrinsic racist holds that the bare fact of being of the same race is a reason for preferring one person to another.[124]

I would argue that Garvey was, in this typology, an extrinsic racist confronting the intrinsic racism of white America. While white theorists, like Lothrop Stoddard, spoke of "White World Supremacy," Garvey spoke of "Africa for the African," a less magniloquent phrase that left room for each race to flourish in its particular God-given locale. Like the fictional Belsidus, he did not aim to establish black world supremacy, but to smash the exploitative hegemony of the white world. The leader of the UNIA saw a multicolored and multipowered world in which each color was left to rule itself. Amalgamation and assimilation would never work; the modus vivendi existed by abandoning the idea of a modus vivendi. To Garvey, Diaspora itself resulted in this ongoing state of tension and disequilibrium. Even, the embourgeoisement of a segment of the black population would not provide a final solution to the "Negro Question." In the Garveyite analysis, the greater (and darker) part of the race would be left to struggle even more intensely against pauperization and marginalization. Segregation was a halfway house on the road to race war. As in the case of European anti-Semitism, racial proscription would cut a bloody swath, obliterating lines of class, gender, and age. A few months before Hitler unleashed his blitzkrieg, Garvey wrote that the African American "is confronted with a civilised man as an opponent who is thoughtful to the point of silence. What this man aims to do with him is only known to the man himself, but past experience and the attitude of the races to which the individual belongs, are sufficient to suggest to any thoughtful man what his intentions are." And then the warning: "Any sensible man would make it his business to see that he is not outdone, and today the American Negro faces his most dangerous period at this point."[125]

Marcus Garvey was an authoritarian who believed in mass mobilization to advance a program of racially based nationalism. In this he bears some resemblance to his Zionist contemporary Vladimir Jabotinsky (1880–1940). What appeared to be pessimistic emigrationism promised a definitive answer to the conundrum of African American existence. Blacks in North America formed a minority surrounded by enemies in perpetuity. The only permanent refuge came from emigration. Rent strikes, unionization, cooperative buying, and the establishment of small businesses did not address the central problem of national minority status. Electoral politics, while not entirely dismissed, could provide no permanent solutions. As with Theodore Herzl and his Zionist colleagues, coalition politics in situ could only provide palliatives. In the mid-1930s, as violence flared between Jews and Palestinians, Garvey expressed both his admiration of Zionism and his ambivalence toward Jews: "The Jews are getting it in the neck in Palestine. The Arabs are not sparing them. The whole world is sorry for the Jews."[126]

As early as January of 1934, Garvey had given his impression of the new National Socialist state. Its development was ominous: "Germany [wants] revenge — a revenge that will almost cause the eternal vendetta. The only thing we are doubtful about is, in what form or shape this revenge will come upon us as a civilization." Teutonic vengeance had to be watched: "The Negro, like everybody else, therefore, should be ready for eventualities if it is not hoped that we be a German or a Japanese world."[127] As fascism spread, so did uneasiness among other black thinkers, not all Garveyites. By the late 1930s, emigrationism, usually seen as a relic of the nineteenth century, resurfaced as a nightmare within a nightmare. Worldwide economic depression and state-sponsored ideologies of biological racial superiority created a climate that made some wonder how secure the American black really was. For many African Americans, the hope held out by the Great Migration had proven a chimera. The Peace Movement's petition of 1933 had made this clear; the racial proscription of the South had been succeeded by the unemployment and cold of the North. Others also revived the emigrationist question. Magistrate Myles A. Paige, judge of special sessions in New York, spoke to a YMCA group and pointed out that blacks had been outstripped in job competition. If things did not improve and blacks gain entry into the industrial workforce, he reportedly said, "we're going to get our passage back."[128] Elmer A. Carter, a member of the New York State Unemployment Insurance Appeal Board, was concerned that the country would have thirteen million or more permanently unemployed in the future. In a situation of "last hired and first fired," African Americans were especially vulnerable. Their position as the group with the greatest percentage of persons on relief did not bode well. Emigration might prove to be an answer.[129] In 1937, Arthur Schomburg mused: "I am becoming very doubtful of the Negro finding a place for himself in the next quarter of a century. . . . We will either be relegated to the level of the sidewalk or back to Africa in the spirit of the philosophy of Marcus Garvey."[130] The year before, Ralph Bunche had said, "Should America develop its own brand of Fascism, which presumably would be an intensification of much that now exists in the South, both the Negro and the Jew would provide handy scapegoats." A fascist future for America would prove devastating for African Americans. Commenting on an article on the United States in a German periodical, Bunche noted that the author believed, "The Negro must be refused citizenship and protecting legislation by the removal of the Fourteenth and Fifteenth Amendments from the Constitution. Thus each state, and particularly the South will be free to deal with its own little race problem in any way it sees fit . . . a plan of emigration whereby Negroes would be systematically shipped out of the country . . . [would] be adopted."[131] Although Du Bois spent most of the 1920s castigating Garvey's African plans, his faith in the African American's permanent place in the United States wavered. Events in Europe troubled him. In 1940, the professor observed the possible need for the "eventual emigration" by "some considerable part" of the black population. The African American, like the Jew, might be "pushed out of his . . . fatherland."[132]

Reacting directly to the *Kristallnacht*, Garvey set forth one of his last briefs for emigration:

> Recently the whole world has had an exposition of what has happened to the Jew in Germany. The Jew has been a part of German civilization for centuries. He was uppermost in the intellectual, industrial and financial groups, but in the midst of all this comes Hitler with his programme from time to time of eliminating from the State all Jewish inhabitants and their contributions and developing a pro-German State. . . . Taking the example of what has happened in Germany is another proof of what is to happen to the Negro in America, being a minority of the great population. The economic situation in America is bound to reach a point where determined action will be taken and when this time comes the Negro, irrespective of his cry for help, will as a minority, get the club in his neck and there will be no world sympathy for him, even as the Jews has had some kind of sympathy expressed by other nations.[133]

Mass emigration never materialized, nor did a race war. In spite of support from a handful of fringe segregationists, assisted black emigration always remained a dead letter. White America took no interest. In

Ralph Johnson Bunche with globe. Photo from Prints and Photographs Department, Moorland-Sprigarn Research Center, Howard University.

spite of rampant racism and segregation in both the South and the North, black expatriation found little white support. The ideology of white supremacy, impregnated with the idea of the intrinsic inferiority of the "Negro," had become so deeply ingrained in American culture that any assertion of "Negro nationalism" seemed, ipso facto, subversive. A white supremacist like Lothrop Stoddard could never sanction black independence: "Such progress as certain negro groups have made has been due to external pressure and has never long outlived that pressure's removal, for the negro, when left to himself, as in Haiti and Liberia, rapidly reverts to his ancestral ways."[134] In a more mundane example of racist praxis, hooded white men in Jacksonville, Florida, had attacked a UNIA ship in early 1925. They resented the ship's symbolism; after boarding, they threatened to throw the white captain overboard for "working for niggers."[135] Race was the defining point in white "American" self-identity. At some level, perhaps subconsciously, the majority had become aware of the necessity of the black Other. Many racists were concerned that blacks remain in the South; migration and emigration were the least of their priorities. Blacks were, for most of the first half of the twentieth century, still essential to Southern agriculture. In many instances, economic necessity demanded that labor be kept "in its place," not lost.

The sincerity of Bilbo's support seems suspect, especially his proposal that Eleanor Roosevelt be named "Queen of Greater Liberia." The politician had shown little or no interest in the UNIA in its heyday when he served as governor of Mississippi. It is hard to believe the man who quipped that the ancestors of American blacks had gone into the jungle to "cut up some fried nigger steak for breakfast," really had faith in Africa or its peoples.[136] Segregationist flirtation with emigrationism may have been no more than a tactic to embarrass white liberal opinion by exposing a powerful dark countercurrent in the "colored" community. An offshoot of the tact would obviously be division among African Americans themselves. Dixon's 1939 novel attacked "the junta fighting for intermarriage" and heaped abuse on, among others, the communists James W. Ford and Earl Browder, as well as Du Bois, James Weldon Johnson, A. Philip Randolph, Claude McKay, Carl Van Vechten, J. E. Spingarn, and Moorfield Story. Bilbo noted, "the Negroes are divided on the subject of repatriation. There is a right wing, and there is a left wing."[137] He believed he had the support of the former. The petition of the Peace Movement of Greater Ethiopia had, in his opinion, made this clear: "We are simple-minded, sincere, law-abiding workers who have maintained traditions of simple honesty, industry and frugality, as much from choice as from necessity. Few of us have education, but we have learned not to heed the blandishments of self-seeking politicians, imposters, and the unworthy and the undesirable products of a hectic civilization that is foreign to our nature."[138] Bilbo's aim may have not been repatriation, but to expose the fragile basis on which Northern integrationism was built. The Greater Liberia Bill survived Garvey. It had two readings in the Senate and was buried in the Committee on Foreign Relations. In 1946, Bilbo threatened to revive his bill, but died before he could do so. Except for his quixotic advocacy, expatriation of African Americans has never received much national support. No truly important twentieth-century conservative paladin ever emerged to champion total segregation through expatriation. Indeed, among the racial mainstream, the endeavor remained as ever: "Keep the Negro in his place."

The Death of Black Emigrationism

At the 1995 Million Man March, Minister Louis Farrakhan invoked the senator Theodore Bilbo as the embodiment of white supremacy.[139] But times have changed. Whereas Garvey's legions had marched for national self-determination, Farrakhan's million assembled for "atonement." Garvey's modernist project had collapsed and was succeeded by a plethora of "nationalist" movements that eschewed nationalism. As Daryl

Scott notes: "Treating blacks as a nation and various black movements as nationalism stretches the definition beyond parameters used by most students of nationalism. Except for colonizationists, few black Americans have imagined their people as a distinct political community with a desire for self-governance." Indeed, "Short of these traditional criteria, the case for black nationhood and nationalism rests on efforts of blacks to gain social and cultural autonomy and political representation within political communities dominated by whites."[140]

By the late 1940s, Du Bois ardently supported Zionism in Palestine. Black emigrationism had, meanwhile, retreated to the fringes of the African American political spectrum. Stephen Howe is incorrect when he says, "the ideologies of political Zionism and Pan-African or Afro-centric assertion, despite (or perhaps in part because of) their substantial shared ancestry, have long been opposed."[141] From Blyden through Du Bois to Bunche there was support for a Jewish state. Over time, however, the idea of redemption through settlement lost its appeal. Anticolonialism shifted the focus to the rights of indigenes and Herzl's project could not but help appear Eurocentric.

African Americans face the question: What do we put in place of what most of the world calls "nationalism?" The writer/activist Ron Bush calls for "revolution." But what is its content? We are told: "I do not use 'revolution' in the traditional or Leninist sense of the seizure of power by a revolutionary party, which then presumably operates the state on behalf of the working class and popular classes. By revolution I mean profound *social transformation* that not only redistributes power but democratizes it; empowers ordinary people to participate in and help determine the affairs of state, economy, and to society." Such transformation would challenge "the law of value that impels all production to center ultimately on the profit motive; establishes a cooperative commonwealth in which production for human needs takes priority over production for exchange."[142] This reads like a manifesto from the Democratic Party's left rather than a call for the political self-assertion of the African American people in opposition to the confines of the 1787 constitution. If racism is endemic and essential to the American political fabric, Bush's social transformation is no more than a pious hope. Black nationalism becomes no more than a militant protest movement asking/demanding more of the goods of North American society. It becomes what Bush accuses some of his black colleagues of—— "much of their focus has been on exhortation, often substituting inspiring rhetorical militance [*sic*] for substantive programs and strategies for destroying the power white capitalist hegemony and domination."[143]

The idea of social transformation within the political system does make perfect sense if one believes that the majority of Americans are, at some level, immune to the extreme intrinsic racism that runs the gamut of peoples as diverse as the Serbs and the Hutu. One would have to trust that much of the bloodshed attendant on the movement of the United States westward was an aberration. Given the increasing use of the term *Black Holocaust,* the politically meliorist content of what remains of black nationalism jars with its fervid rhetoric. If one believes that the minority is surrounded by a truly genocidal majority, waiting for *them* (i.e., the majority) to undergo a social transformation may prove a long, if not futile, enterprise. It may even be bizarrely myopic, if not suicidal . . . *if* one accepts the premise. Since Garvey, an independent state as the solution has receded in black discourse. The Forty-Ninth State Movement foundered. The Republic of New Africa created a cultural enclave and little else. The Nation of Islam still calls for the creation of a political entity, but its creation is not central to its political message. Groups that do threaten the political order, rather than demanding change within that order, are proscribed, whether they be the Black Panther Party or the Puerto Rican Frente de Liberación Nacional.[144]

The caste model of U.S. race relations, so popular in the 1930s, may explain much more than the often misused term *nationalist.* African Americans constitute an endogamous and largely segregated minority within American society. They seek neither the end to endogamy nor what is vaguely perceived as "assimilation." What used to be called social equality is no longer a topic for serious political discussion. What is important is access to employment and equal treatment before the law. African American politics resembles not so much contemporary nationalisms as it does caste politics in present-day India, where "the growing political power and independence of the lowest castes, generally referred to as 'scheduled castes' is being felt across the country. They are voting in greater proportions than ever before."[145] India had affirmative action before the United States and has wholeheartedly endorsed what some Americans call quotas. But, let us be quite clear. Caste entitlement, in India or in the United States, does not abolish caste. More jobs for untouchables (*dalits*) does not abolish untouchability. Long ago, Pierre van den Berghe pointed out that the presence of clearly demarcated "races" in a society presupposed the existence of racism.[146]

Race remained and remains a central fact in American political life, but it did not spawn a full-blown minority nationalism or a race war. Ralph Bunche noted that world conflict did not revolve around the somewhat outdated scenarios painted by white supremacists, like Stoddard, or those Pan-Africanists who saw the world as an endless repetition of the

Old Dixie Narrative. In 1940, the political scientist observed: "As winter approaches and fighting on a large scale becomes impossible in already war-torn Europe, Africa obliges by offering a milder climate in which the white men of Europe may continue to murder each other at will under the full glare of the African sun."[147]

Postscript:
Africa and Human Rights

And this, alas, is the response of today's dictators and tyrants

when they are told: open up your prisons, release your hostages.

They respond: Can you tell a cat to stop mousing? I shall die

with a slave in my stockade.

— Wole Soyinka

Garvey's last gambit, the Greater Liberia Bill, did not succeed. How-ever, in 1940, the year of his death, forces were set in motion that did result in several thousand blacks being sent to Liberia by the federal government. The Barclay regime continued its very comfortable modus vivendi with white America. As the Second World War loomed, the U.S. government approached Pan American World Airways to construct landing strips in Liberia, a development full of meaning for the future. The airline turned to Firestone, which built an airfield near the main plantation at Harbel. After the outbreak of war, Liberia became a vital link in the air routes to North Africa, the Near East, and the Soviet Union. African American troops were sent, and 600 planes a month made the run from the United States. Money poured in, with the Amer-ican dollar replacing the pound sterling as the national currency. Road systems and a deep water harbor were surveyed. In early 1943, Franklin D. Roosevelt visited Liberia and in turn received visitors Barclay and president-elect William V. S. Tubman. The former pariah regime, once accused of slave dealing and rampant violence, had returned to its place as America's "best friend" on the African continent.

Among the defenders of the Black Republic during its crises, some now found themselves rewarded, some cast adrift. Dorothy Detzer was given the Liberian Order of African Redemption and continued to pur-sue her ardent anti-imperialism into the era of the cold war. Du Bois complained in 1941 that he had long been promised the order, but never received it. He wrote to Walton that he would like, "as a matter of justice, to have the Order which was at one time given me." The professor observed: "I should never of my own initiative ask for the decoration but it rather goes against my grain to have been unfairly deprived of it."[1] Walton forwarded the decoration from Barclay to Atlanta. Nnamdi Azikiwe, future president of Nigeria and one of the most vociferous of the academic defenders of Liberia, made for a somewhat different case. Publicly, Monrovia passionately praised his propaganda efforts. Its private sentiments were something else. In 1936, Azikiwe, while working as a journalist in Accra, Gold Coast, asked for the position of local Liberian consul. The Liberian secretary of state warned Barclay of the Nigerian's "unveiled denunciation of British colonial policy." He noted that Azikiwe "and a number of the contributors to his journal are reported in Authoritative circles as agents of Russia and consequently capable of arousing bolshevism." The incumbent consul was a Briton employed by the Elder Dempster shipping line and was on excellent terms with the colonial administration.[2] The white man kept the job.

A more pathetic case was that of Antoine Sottile, the Italian lawyer who represented Liberia before the League at the beginning of the scandal. As a Jew, Sottile was affected by Mussolini's 1938 racial laws. Desperate, he appealed to his former employers for the protection of Liberian citizenship. In September of 1938, he wrote to Barclay, pleading "Will you do me the honour to reappoint [me] LIBERIAN CONSUL Honoraire?" The diplomatist promised "I shall be Your OBEDIENT SERVANT WITHOUT ANY SALARY OR EXPENSES. I shall work for your interests." He promised to forget the salary already owed him and begged Barclay to "NOT REFUSE MY FRIENDLY AND RESPECTFUL OFFER." Searching for a way to justify his continued usefulness, he put forth the argument that the League was more important than ever because of the Czech crisis. In December, Sottile pleaded again and noted that his previous letter had gone unanswered. Adding to the gravity of his situation was the fact that he, as Liberian delegate, had voted against Italy in 1935 during the Ethiopian crisis.[3] Unfortunately, the former "Liberian" diplomat was swept up in the maelstrom leading to the Second World War. He survived, but with a burning animus toward the government which had so cavalierly left him to his own devices. Subsequently, other defenders of the Black Republic were to feel the same way.

Monrovia's most prominent white liberal supporter, Raymond Leslie Buell, died at the early age of fifty beset by doubts. In 1947, on the centenary of Liberian independence, a posthumous work was published in which the political scientist questioned the fitness to rule of the very oligarchy he had done so much to prop up.[4] Buell's support for the Monrovia regime in the thirties had turned to dire predictions of revolution by the mid-forties. The defender of the True Whig oligarchy had awakened, as from a dream, to find himself the advocate for an inbred group of grafters. The political scientist had come full circle. Americo-Liberians, however, tended to "resent bitterly the criticisms and also resent delving into the past. Some of them even go so far as to accuse me of being a Firestone agent—proof of a short memory!"[5] Sounding like George Schuyler ten years earlier, Buell wrote,

> The oligarchy attempts not only to govern itself but also the vast Native majority in the hinterland. Unlike more modern oligarchies, the Liberian Government has lacked the vitality necessary even for material development. Liberia had no hotels; no medical profession; no teachers' college or other secondary educational institutions as good as those in neighboring British colonies; no censuses not even a culture of its own. It lacks adequate roads into the interior (it has no railway) and modern harbors on the coast. It has too few able men at the top and a rate of illiteracy for the population as a whole of probably 95 per cent. Liberia has been too poor even to maintain a diplomatic mission in Washington—unlike Haiti and Ethiopia. It is a country in a comatose situation, crying out for economic, political, and cultural development. Despite its survival for nearly a hundred years, Liberia remains a sick country, perhaps the sickest part of Africa. Unless this sickness is soon cured, racial chauvinists will say, if unjustly, that the Negro everywhere is incapable of self-government.[6]

Buell reported, "the American Negro consultants have sympathized with the criticisms advanced against Liberia, and tend to regard conditions in that country as a reflection on the Negro as a whole."[7] In 1941, an African American writer, Dr. George W. Brown, wrote a scathing history of the Black Republic. Published by the press of the Association for the Study of Negro Life and History, Brown's work maintained that "extortions, bribes, petty grafting, court and legal corruption, flagrant abuses against the persons and property of individuals by soldiers or minor officials, misappropriation of funds, and 'selling out the country' continue to revive the unsavory charges made within and against the Republic."[8] Other black opinions began to question the entrance of Barclay into the American embrace. During Barclay and Tubman's 1943 trip, African American newspapers showed themselves less than awed. The *Baltimore Afro-American* commented adversely on president-elect Tubman and carried the caption, "Salary $30,000; Native Wages 25 Cents a Day."[9] The *Chicago Defender* was equally critical. It characterized Barclay's speech to the U.S. Senate as "painful stupidity."[10]

In 1944, Padmore attempted to portray the Barclay-Firestone collaboration as unwilling victimization. In the Black Republic, the U.S. military was "further tightening . . . the grip of international finance."[11] In

Padmore's reading, the Liberian government had no agency. Other commentators were not so forgiving. The oligarchy had to be confronted. The following year, Eslanda Goode Robeson, the wife of Paul Robeson, denounced the authorities' shortcomings: "Considering the high purpose for which this black colony was founded, and the brave democratic principles upon which this now so-called republic is supposed to rest, the backwardness, poverty and lack of franchise among the subject Liberian people as against the wealth and official corruption among the ruling Americo-Liberian citizens makes a shameful picture — a disgrace to the 'Republic' and to the United States which sponsors it."[12]

Progressive white opinion had also soured on Liberia. In 1943, Arthur Hayman and Harold Preece published a work which accused the Barclay government and Firestone of bringing the "worst forms of modern industrial exploitation to Liberia . . . at the expense of thousands of black peasants who were uprooted from their fields to make way for the rubber plantations."[13] Hayman was a former Firestone engineer with great sympathy for Liberia's indigenous majority. He hoped that postwar anticolonialism would free not only British West Africa but would also be the death knell of the Americo-Liberian ruling clique. Hayman and Preece reflected back on the issue of slavery: "Twelve years after the palace revolution [i.e., the fall of King], the Barclay regime cannot say truthfully that it has abolished slavery. . . . There is only one field in which the . . . administration can point to any . . . accomplishments — collecting taxes." The idea of the president of Liberia having any part in a democratic postwar world seemed farcical; "President Barclay no more dares walk down the streets of Monrovia or into a country village unescorted than does Pierre Laval in Paris."[14] The State Department, which had refused to recognize the Barclay government for five years, was quick to jump to its defense. When Hayman and Preece published an article based on their book, Henry Villard, head of the African division, attacked the authors. Liberia was, in the official's opinion, "a most successful experiment in self-government by colored people."[15] The American foreign policy apparatus had come full circle.

A Pan-African response to the crisis of Liberian independence had been partly responsible for shoring up its independence. Marcus Garvey never visited Liberia, the place that was to be the locus of his plan for black redemption. In 1940, he died in relative obscurity in London. In the same year, W. E. B. Du Bois published his intellectual autobiography, *Dusk of Dawn,* and reflected on his visit of a decade and a half before. He never returned to the country. Both men left behind legacies, some apparent at the time, others not. Du Bois continued his ideologi-

President Edwin Barclay, President of the Republic of Liberia, signs the University guest book, May 26, 1943. (l. to r.) President Mordecai W. Johnson (Howard University), President-Elect William V. S. Tubman (Liberia), President Edwin Barclay, General Benjamin O. Davis (U.S. Army).

cal odyssey. As Sterling Stuckey notes: "It was fitting that Du Bois, by the time of the Manchester conference [1945], no longer thought New World blacks would lead a movement for African liberation." This realization "represented a culminating point in fifty years as a Pan-Africanist in which he had consolidated and gone beyond much of earlier nationalist thought."[16] By the 1960s, both Du Bois and Garvey were recognized as the greatest of twentieth-century diasporic heroes, although they still appealed to different audiences.

The Collapse of the Ancien Régime

Both Garvey and Du Bois had encountered the Liberian oligarchy, and it outlived them both. However, it did not survive the twentieth century. The Barclay administration arrogated increased powers to the presidency, a tendency amplified during the subsequent tenure of William V. S. Tubman (1944–71). Sedition laws imposed during the 1930s identified dissent with external subversion, and Barclay was able to solidify his position by exploiting fears of destabilization. The crisis of the thirties constituted a challenge-and-response situation in which the Liberian executive reacted by strengthening its power. In 1955, Barclay found himself in opposition to the "dictatorial" policies of his successor, opposition crushed by the strengthened presidency that Barclay had himself helped inaugurate.[17]

The great claim of the Tubman regime was that it initiated a "unification policy" which finally brought the majority of Liberia's people into national life. In 1944, twenty years after Du Bois's visit, the franchise was extended to all adult males who paid the hut tax. Tubman was also a master at encouraging the enclave economy begun with Firestone, while, at the same time, avoiding overt political domination. Tubman did not attempt to oust foreign capital. He assiduously cultivated increased foreign investment, with iron mining, after 1945, supplanting rubber as the major field of foreign investment and profit. Christopher Clapham has noted that the "economic relationship with foreign corporations leads easily to the assumption that these corporations must play a large part in government" since "the government and the corporations have a common interest in maintaining a source of wealth from which both profit."[18]

The long-lived Tubman regime was succeeded by a short-lived one. In 1934, at the age of twenty-one, future president William R. Tolbert Jr. effusively praised the chief executive in his valedictory address at Liberia College. In "Education as Related to Civic Progress," he described Barclay as a man with "supreme" interest in the people and as one whose mind was "elevated to most lofty plains." The administration was opposed by a "vulgar rabble" which occupied the "lower rungs of the [social] ladder." Education, under the right leadership, would lead the state forward, Tolbert declared. "Education is the adapter which will make the nomadic spirit of freedom of self reliance compatible with cooperation, wealth and security of Civilization." All, even the untutored, could see the value of education; an educated individual would work for the "advancement of his brother, the well-being of his race, the prosperity of the nation and the confederation of the world."[19] As Graham Greene had commented of Barclay, "rhetoric, lots of rhetoric."[20] Thirty-six years later, Tolbert lay disemboweled in the Executive Mansion, and for the first time a "Native" ruled. Warning signs had appeared before the collapse. Riots over an increase in the price of rice in 1979 had adumbrated growing mass discontent. Tolbert's elaborate hosting of the meeting of the Organization of African Unity had displayed his own grandiosity and the irrelevance of the proceedings to the great majority of Liberians.

What is significant about the collapse of the old Liberian order is its bloody aftermath. The "little horrors" reported in 1932 pale in comparison with the kaleidoscopic violence unleashed by the 1980 coup. Four years after the takeover, the government killed students and faculty at the University of Liberia. The following year witnessed revenge and ethnic killings as a result of a threatened invasion of the country in November of 1985. Further murders were committed when soldiers entered United Nations premises and attacked civilians. Death squads also entered private homes and eliminated supposed opponents. In 1989, the regime of Samuel Doe began to topple, and a year later he himself was killed in a bizarrely videotaped execution that began with the cutting off of the president's ears and then proceeded to other appendages. At one point, at least three rebel movements contested for power. Ethnic killing and ethnic cleansing proceeded as members of the Krahn, Gio, Mandingo, and Congo groups were set on by their enemies. Atrocities abounded:

> Some describe the pain of seeing a spouse or child die because of malnutrition or the unavailability of medical care. Others tell of seeing their girlfriends, wives, daughters, or sisters raped and killed. One young man reported being forced to kill his own fiancée. Weeping uncontrollably, he followed orders to execute the person he loved most because he knew the alternative for her would be a much more painful and prolonged death. A common tale from the war is that soldiers would make a wager as to the sex of an unborn child and then cut upon the pregnant woman's stomach to settle the bet. Less dramatic, but nevertheless an atrocity of war, men tell of being beaten and then forced to "thank" their torturers for the needed discipline. Frequently such victims were required to sing songs while being abused.[21]

After more than a decade of violence, Charles Taylor won the election in 1997. A man of partially Americo-Liberian background, he operated in an ambience in which he represented a whole new constellation of ethnic and generational forces. Taylor had emerged as the warlord of warlords. One of his contributions to the fighting had been the large-scale use of child soldiers. James Kormon, a Liberian trained in advanced developmental studies in Britain, observed:

> Uneducated young men were easily manipulated. Many of the atrocities of the war were committed by unenlightened young kids who were easily recruited and controlled by the warlords. The warlords further degraded the minds of the youth by providing drugs that completely clouded their ability to think. Thus, kids would advance directly into a hail of bullets or would walk irrationally toward heavily armed opponents. These child soldiers were easily fooled. For example, by placing a string around the children's

necks the leaders led them to believe that they could not die. The most fearful sight I ever saw in my life was the behavior of uneducated kids at Prince Johnson's base. Those children were drinking human blood from a gallon bottle. The worst part was that they were in a happy mood; they were jubilant because they believed they now were gun proof.[22]

One of the most fascinating and, at the same time, repellent slogans to emerge from the killing fields of Liberia is, "He Kill My Ma, He Kill My Pa: I Will Vote for Him!" The new president promised that since he was the man who had made the mess, he was the man to fix it. The cry also expresses the world turned upside down. In a world dominated by family, hierarchy, and a traditional ideology justifying gerontocracy, youth—exposed to the weaponry and the action movie fantasies of the West—were able to imagine that they had seized power. Violence was symbolic of a kind of sanguinary children's crusade: "Saying 'Pappy, you are too frisky,' young soldiers would demand the shoes or shirt of men who they once would have obeyed almost instinctively."[23] Cars and other property were taken, and elders were made to do demeaning tasks, such as pumping gasoline. The violence which swept Liberia in the 1990s has not abated; across the border, in Sierra Leone, the pattern is repeating itself, with the added horror of wholesale amputations of the limbs of civilians.

President Taylor stayed abreast of events in the smaller neighboring country and is even reported to support one of the more sanguinary groups. Jesse Jackson has tried to mediate between the Sierra Leonean factions, but his efforts brought no peace. Indeed, it raises the question of whether appeals to pan-ethnic unity in such situations are any more valuable in West Africa than they are in Northern Ireland or the southern Balkans. By August 2003, Taylor had gone into exile.

In 1960, twenty years after Garvey's death and three years before his own, W. E. B. Du Bois, longest-lived of the Pan-Africanists, went into honorable exile in Ghana. Thirty-seven years after his foray into Liberia, Du Bois returned to the mother continent. Image met reality: The Pan-Africa of the congresses and the petitions met the Africa of the post-colonial rulers. It was a symbolic homecoming, but

Adu Boahen, a Ghanaian aristocrat and one of Africa's leading historians, was always unpersuaded of the goodness of the fit of Du Bois and Kwame Nkrumah [the leader of Ghana]. Boahen believed that Nkrumah's real spiritual mentor was not W. E. B. Du Bois but Marcus Garvey, that the Ghanaian president "reached out for Du Bois out of reverence and because he was the lone survivor—but Garvey was the source." One need only register the significance of the red, black, and green colors of the national flag, centered by a black star, to realize the powerful influence of Garvey, suggested Boahen. The chemistry of the two men [Du Bois and Nkrumah], of the African sage and the continental liberator, never fully mixed. Insecure, unevenly educated, increasingly autocratic, criticized as too favorable to expatriate black Americans by his own advisers, and engulfed by a ubiquitous corruption he soon altogether ceased trying to contain, the Osaygefo (redeemer) was inwardly never comfortable with his incorruptible, imported icon.[24]

The conjuncture certainly raises difficult questions. Recently a Nigerian writer has said, "Du Bois and all those who participated in the Pan-African Congress movement exalted Africa and declared a strong commitment to the articulation and defense of black/African interests." He continues, "One area of success was Liberia. Paradoxically, it was American intervention and involvement . . . that ultimately saved Liberia from suffering the fate of other African countries."[25] What does "success" mean? Was political independence the only aim? Was the aim the simple expulsion of the colonialists, or the creation of new and just ways of molding congeries of people into states with a modicum of social justice?

The Liberian situation of the 1930s adumbrated later developments. Could things have developed differently? Hypotheticals are always risky, and counterfactual history is exactly that. At the end of the Second World War, several voices pointed out that a great anticolonial struggle was about to begin and that Liberia stood on the wrong side of it. Looking back at all the conferences and lobbying of the interwar period, one has the feeling that if the bulk of Pan-Africanists had been as interested in reform as in independence, the outcome would have differed. Universal suffrage, proportional representation, and monitored elections do not seem all that radical in retrospect. Even though Thomas Faulkner's appeals found little overseas support, the case of Jean-Bertrand Aristide of Haiti demonstrates that now, at least for some in the Diaspora, the quality of a government is as important as its existence. A lesson learned tardily still makes for a lesson learned.

Afro-America and Africa

The Liberian crisis brings up a continuing issue: on what pretext can an assumed racist America intervene in black countries? In Haiti in 1915, the United States asserted that it needed to maintain order. By the time of the Liberian scandal, American policy makers were aware of the contradictions arising from armed intervention to "save" black Africans on the other side of the ocean. Nonintervention also fit within the larger framework of American policy, which, up until the 1960s, preferred to consider Africa a strictly European sphere of influence.

The Liberian crisis united a group of African American spokesmen against the threat of direct American intervention in Africa. But the crisis demonstrates certain ambiguities in the relationship between African Americans and their government. Some leaders, like Du Bois for a time, considered that the reconstruction of Liberia should be put in non-American (and, supposedly, nonracist) hands. Other black leaders sought to encourage their own government to display an "enlightened" interest in Africa. The question of what role the American government should play vis-à-vis the external black world surfaced during the Liberian crisis, but it did not find clarification. The issue remains — should African Americans encourage and serve their government in Africa or should they discourage the active participation there of a government that until recently has been clearly racist?

We must recognize that the type of issue confronted is of paramount importance. In issues clearly black and white — that is, black versus white — the formation of a consensus comes fairly easily. In 1967, Stokely Carmichael (later Kwame Touré) said, "The best protection for Africa today is African-Americans inside the United States because when we start to move against South Africa, if the United States dares to come into this continent, the African-Americans will burn that country down to the ground."[26] His language engages in hyperbole, but the fear has long been present that blacks might prove to be a break on American policy. In the same year, Rupert Emerson observed, "The most vital and unique concern of the United States with Africa derives from the existence of the 10 percent of the American population which . . . traces its ancestry to Africa."[27] Two years later, C. Eric Lincoln said, "As the American Negro grows more politically powerful, and as its [*sic*] identification with the struggles of emergent Africa and Asia is strengthened by the mutual recognition of one common problem — color — the Negro minority is destined to become an important counterweight to the traditional racial tone which has in the past characterized our foreign policy."[28]

Africa — "Mother Africa," "The Beloved Continent," "The Motherland" — signifies different things to different people. The totemic Africa of the old Pan-African imagination remains free of the firsthand engagement of a man like Blyden. It is possible to love Africa without knowing Africans. By 1957, only 1 percent of African Americans, in contrast to 6 percent of whites, could name as many as five African territories;

70 percent of blacks, compared with 55 percent of whites, could not name any at all.[29] In a 1990 study of African American leaders, 47 percent of those queried felt that "very few black Americans feel any real close connection to Africa."[30] At the same time, more than 90 percent of those interviewed believed "black political leaders have a special obligation to influence U.S. foreign policy on behalf of Africa." There is ambiguity. Less than a quarter of respondents mentioned "more focus on Africa" when asked to recommend one major shift in U.S. foreign policy. The majority agreed that African Americans should be more concerned about Africa than any other area; 41 percent disagreed.

The fear that the rhetoric of Pan-Africanism might translate into action prevailed in certain quarters. In 1962, a number of civil right leaders had already formed the American Negro Leadership Conference on Africa (ANCLA). Three years later, two members of the National Security Council wrote that the Johnson administration was "quite concerned over the prospect of an imminent Negro leadership conference to set up an organization to influence U.S. policy on Africa."[31] In a 1978 National Security Council memorandum, policy makers considered the consequences of an alliance between African states opposed to apartheid and African American activists opposed to United States policy on South Africa: "These factors taken together may provide a basis for joint actions of a concrete nature by the African nationalist movement and the U.S. black community." The National Security Council feared "attempts to establish a permanent black lobby in Congress including activist leftist radical groups and black legislators; the re-emergence of pan-African ideals; resumption of protest marches recalling the days of Martin Luther King; renewal of the extremist national idea of establishing an 'African Republic' on American soil." Ominously, the memo suggested that "leftist radical elements of the black community could resume extremist actions in the style of the defunct Black Panther Party."[32] The emergence by the early 1980s of TransAfrica, an antiapartheid black lobbying group, was, no doubt, the very kind of development feared. Perhaps even more troubling to those wishing to maintain the status quo in South Africa was the passage of the Comprehensive Anti-Apartheid Act of 1986, which followed intensive lobbying.

For African Americans, the truly difficult task is determining what policies should be adopted toward the present myriad of black-ruled countries. Here, as seen in the Liberian case, race alone can provide no clear-cut guidelines. Divisions on what policies to pursue are likely to mirror the internal ideological divisions of the black community. Michael Clough has noted, "while there is significant black support for increased aid to Africa, there is no consensus on who should receive that aid and for what purposes."[33] When an African trade bill went before the U.S. Congress in the summer of 1999, African American opinion stood divided on whether to support or oppose its provisions. Tony Smith, commenting in 2000, noticed

> African American leaders are preoccupied most by domestic economic and political concerns, for assimilation is not assured. Funds are short (and often derived from sources outside the community). There is no strong external state or clear foreign enemy to encourage ethnic cohesion with respect to foreign affairs. Their membership rolls involve smaller proportions of the community. And their organizations lack interlocking directorships and depend instead on strong (and therefore often competitive) personalities.[34]

Recently, the economist George Ayittey has issued a severe critique of African American involvement in postcolonial Africa, citing it as "more of a hindrance than help." He claims that American blacks are incapable of seeing oppression as more than an issue of white versus black. "As such," he writes, "they have no difficulty condemning the architects of apartheid in South Africa with as much venom as they would the tyrannical regimes elsewhere in Africa."[35] The social scientist also sees an element of vicarious enjoyment in the American view of Africa, arguing that "it is . . . gratifying when black Americans come upon black African presidents — living proof that blacks are capable of running a country." The Cameroonian sociologist, Axelle Kabou, suggests that negritude (and by extension Afrocentric glorification of the African past) has only bolstered indigenous dictatorships in the name of a specious authenticity.[36]

This criticism is too broad. Divisions on what policies to pursue are likely to mirror the internal ideological divisions inside the black community. The latter is not, nor has it ever been, monolithic. In the mid-1990s, Louis Farrakhan and Senator Carole Mosely-Braun both visited brutal Nigerian dictator Sani Abacha. At the same time, one should remember that Randall Robinson of TransAfrica had already denounced the regime. Lobbying, newspapers ads, and demonstrations in front of the Nigerian embassy were all employed to draw attention to the issue. Reverend Joseph Lowery of the Southern Christian Leadership Conference acknowledged, "I think it would be inconsistent for us to express concern about repression and tyranny by the white dictators in South Africa and ignore the same thing in black Africa."[37] Randall Robinson announced, "We shall oppose the Nigerian government with as much tenacity as we opposed the [former white] South African government, with as much tenacity as we opposed the military regime in

Haiti."[38] The lobbyist saw this stance as "a high-water mark in maturity in the black community." Given the signal work done by the African American community in support of the democratically elected Aristide government in Haiti, it becomes obvious that for some interested in foreign policy, the days of blanket support for "big men" have passed. In the first year of the new century, Robinson went further in commenting on "Daniel Arap Moi, who has run his country [Kenya] with a corrupt and abusive hand for more than twenty years." Robinson notes, "Mr. Moi, seventy-five, has held on to power by accommodating graft, opposing multiparty democracy, and fomenting ethnic tension."[39] We have come a long way from Du Bois's uncritical adulation of C. D. B. King or Carol Mosley-Braun's moral myopia vis-à-vis Sani Abacha.

Envoi: Slaves Today

Recently, David Brion Davis has raised an interesting point:

> The twentieth century has clearly witnessed more slavery than all the preceding centuries combined. I have in mind not only the tens of millions of men, women, and children who were subjected to state servitude by Nazi Germany, Communist Russia, Communist China and smaller totalitarian states. Or the Southern blacks in chain gangs and the coerced migratory farm workers. In a sense, the multinational Atlantic Slave System can be seen as the first stepping stone toward the multinational corporations that today employ millions of virtual slaves in various construction and production projects in Asia, Africa, and Latin America.[40]

This stands in direct contradiction to the Old Dixie Narrative, which sees "Negro chattel slavery" as sui generis. For instance, in 1917, Du Bois wrote as if slavery had ended in the 1860s and it was now time for the West to make recompense by creating a great "Negro" state out of the former Belgian Congo and what had been German Africa.[41] Africa had never been given the opportunity to develop because "Liberia and Haiti were never given a sincere chance and were from first to last harassed, as only modern capitalism can harass little and hated nations." Du Bois saw African slavery as a past event, inextricably connected with the rise and fall of Atlantic slaving. African slavery had resulted from wholly exogenous forces and it had ended.

Today in the United States, slavery, both historical and contemporary, has become a political football. On the right, a polemicist like Dinesh D'Souza can, using the facts of the past, cobble together an argument concerning the present, which only serves to obfuscate issues. He asks,

"What do Americans [i.e., white Americans] today owe blacks because of slavery?" He answers, "probably nothing."[42] An answer as arch as the question would be: *Reparations*. At the other end of the spectrum we find an increasing tendency to reify North American slavery; slavery in Dixie becomes the nil plus ultra of human suffering. We arrive at a horror without parallel. The problem with this approach is that it leads to a perverse sacralization. The Old Dixie Narrative takes on the quality of the crucifix of the inquisitor's wall; the greatest crime has already been committed. Memory cannot serve as a goad to search out similar events. There can be no similar events; indeed, to search for them would be to desecrate and disrespect the past. In the United States, the "debate" on slavery remains rooted in the past. It also remains highly presentist; the discussion of slavery mainly reflects present-day discussions of race relations. Sometimes marvelously naïve results ensue. For example, Steven Spielberg's 1997 film *Amistad* was endlessly discussed in terms of the state of race in the United States at the end of the 1990s. A conversation on the Latin slave trade never intruded. It would have been a grave embarrassment, as would have been the fact that both the "cargo" and the crew of the schooner would have qualified for affirmative action. In current constructions of slavery, contemporary interethnic relations provide the parameters for what will and what will not be examined.

As said at the outset, Africa to many signifies as the home of the black race, the symbolic antipode of Europe, the home of the white. To many observers, the Black Man's Land had failed utterly. In an outburst of postcolonial ire, Doris Lessing finds independent Zimbabwe a nightmare: "[Robert] Mugabe is now widely execrated and rightly, but blame for him began late. Nothing is more astonishing than the silence about him for so many years among liberals and well-wishers — the politically correct." She scolds, "A man may yet get away with murder, if he is black."[43] Such sentiments verge on white racism. In the last five centuries, black men (and women) have gotten away with precious little. And to sugarcoat the pre-independence regime of Rhodesia as one of paternalistic white farmers and grateful black workers is to turn history on its head. However, the broader issue of regime failure remains. The last decade of the twentieth century saw civil war in Liberia, Sierra Leone, Sudan, Rwanda, Somalia, Ethiopia, and the Congo. Famine and the AIDS pandemic stalked the continent.

If the image were not bad enough, slavery persisted or had a recrudescence. At century's end, there were an estimated 27 million slaves in the world, many of them on the black continent.[44] In Sudan, Mauritania, Ghana, Benin, and Gabon, various types of bound labor continue, much of it involving women and children. Looking at contemporary Africa,

Nigerian Nobel laureate, Wole Soyinka, warns, "Excuses for the current war against democracy on the African continent are becoming rampant from a variety of apologists. . . . Today, we shamefacedly admit that a practice of centuries — slavery — constitutes a blot on our humanity, one that we wish we could expunge from the pages of human history."[45]

What are we to do? Some denounce abuses. Joseph Cotton, a contemporary African American critic of slavery in Mauritania, echoes Schuyler's comments of half a century earlier: "Slavery is slavery and is wrong — no matter who engages in it."[46] He complains that the overall reaction of his community "confirmed my suspicion that many African Americans' professed (and often new-found) love for and pride in Africa and their African heritage is a fantasy." According to the newspaperman, "So many are so mired in the African past that they overlook the realities of the African present." Furthermore, he "concluded that most African-Americans have never really come to hate the institution of slavery for its own sake. They only hate what it has done to African-Americans as a subgroup within the African Diaspora, and they turn a deaf ear to instances of slavery that do not directly affect them or their families."[47]

Accusation without the wide diffusion of information remains fruitless. The world that the slaveholders made and the Old Dixie Narrative that it created are not easily displaced. Slavery in Africa is an embarrassment. An implicit question will always be, "Is the news from Africa good for African Americans?" Herein lies the need for moral sensitivity and ethical education. In 1934, the archimperialist Lord Frederick Lugard chided, "The Negro community in the United States appears to be misinformed . . . far from establishing the prestige of the Negro race in the eyes of the world by championing the cause of the Liberian oligarchy, they are seriously injuring it."[48] Should one day Bishop Desmond Tutu, Nelson Mandela, and Wole Soyinka unite in a condemnation of slavery and other forms of social oppression on the mother continent, certain of Africa's defenders in the Diaspora would feel more than discomforted. Luckily, the increasing black criticism of the oppression and misrule of certain African regimes gives a hopeful sign. Indeed, in September of 1999, Susan Rice, an African American and United States undersecretary of state for African affairs, rigorously denounced one African country, Sudan, for specifically condoning the practice of slavery, along with a series of other human rights abuses.[49] The following May, Congresspersons Eleanor Holmes Norton, Donald Payne, and a host of other dignitaries met on Capitol Hill to launch a concerted campaign to sanction companies doing business with Sudan (especially an oil company).

This book has been a cautionary tale. Seventy years ago, one African state was accused of grave human rights abuses. The regime was saved, only to collapse of its own rot half a century later. The question of corruption and labor abuse had been delayed, not banished. The dilemma remains. Criticism of an independent African state gives aid and comfort to enemies of the race; ignoring human rights abuse means denying the suffering of millions of the race. On all grounds — but above all on moral grounds — we must rise to the challenge. As Martin Luther King Jr. said, "The greatest sin of our time is not the few who have destroyed, but the vast majority who had sat idly by."[50]

Notes

Introduction

1   Azikiwe, *Liberia in World Politics,* 208, citing the editorial page of the *Brooklyn Citizen* of January 11, 1931.
2   Smith, "Negro Self-Government," 736.
3   Skinner, *African Americans and U.S. Policy,* 10.
4   Stuckey, *Slave Culture,* 3.
5   The so-called melting pot has been discredited since the time of D. P. Moynihan and Nathan Glazer's *Beyond the Melting Pot* (Cambridge, Mass.: MIT Press, 1963) was published more than a generation ago.
6   Howard W. French, "The Atlantic Slave Trade: On Both Sides, Reason for Remorse," *New York Times,* April 5, 1998.
7   "Slavery's Past, Paved Over or Forgotten," *New York Times,* July 15, 2003.
8   French, "The Atlantic Slave Trade."
9   Snelgrave, *New Account of Some Parts of Guinea,* 158, 160.
10 Maulana Karenga, *Introduction to Black Studies* (Los Angeles: University of Sankore Press, 1993), 117.
11 D'Souza, *End of Racism,* 73.
12 Lewis H. Latham, "The Black Man's Burden," *Harper's,* June 1977, 16.
13 D'Souza, *The End of Racism,* 74, citing Zora Neale Hurston, *Dust Tracks on a Road* (1942 Philadelphia: Lippincott, 1971).
14 Richard Wright, *Black Power,* 121.
15 "Television Focuses on Africa's Human History," *New York Times,* October 24, 1999. The article reviews Henry Louis Gates's documentary/travelogue *Wonders of the African World.*
16 Gates, *Wonders of the African World,* 196–97. For further reading, see John Thornton, *Africa and Africans in the Making of the Atlantic World, 1480–1680* (Cambridge: Cambridge University Press, 1992).
17 See Lawler, *Soldiers of Misfortune.* Indeed, thousands of Ashkenazim did die at the hands of their Polish, Ukrainian, and Baltic neighbors. And, strangely, the Germans killed a far greater percentage of their European Jewish captives than they did of their North and West African prisoners of war.
18 Pearl-Alice Marsh, "Open Letter to Contributors" (newsletter), African Policy Information Center (APIC), Washington, D.C., July 1998.
19 Henry S. Wilson, *Origins of West African Nationalism,* 94, citing Edward W. Blyden, "Our Origin: Dangers and Duties," annual address before mayor and Common Council of Monrovia, National Independence Day, July 26, 1865.

20 *Three Negro Classics,* 37.

21 Essien-Udom, *Black Nationalism,* 149 n. 27.

22 Richburg, *Out of Africa,* xvii–xviii.

23 Elkins, *Slavery.*

24 Patterson, *Slavery and Social Death,* 1–14.

25 Toni Morrison commented: "Some historians told me 200 million died. The smallest number I got from anybody was 60 million." "The Pain of Being Black" *Time,* May 22, 1989, 120.

26 Ibid.

27 Henry Louis Gates Jr. and Cornel West, *The Future of the Race* (New York: Vintage Books, 1997), 73.

28 David Brion Davis, "Looking at Slavery from Broader Perspectives," *American Historical Review* 105, 2 (2000): 457.28.

29 Eric Williams, *Capitalism and Slavery* (London: Andre Deutch, 1964), 7.

30 Patterson, *Slavery and Social Death,* vii.

31 Qtd. in Rodney, *How Europe Underdeveloped Africa,* 100.

32 Kolchin, "Big Picture," 468.

1 Confronting the Motherland

1 Rath, "Echo and Narcissus," 490.

2 Rich and Wallerstein, *Africa: Tradition and Change,* 451, citing John Henrik Clarke, ed., *Malcolm X: The Man and His Times* (New York: Macmillan, 1969).

3 Du Bois, "The Conservation of Races," *W. E. B. Du Bois: A Reader,* 23.

4 Ibid., 24.

5 W. E. B. Du Bois, "The Social Equality of Whites and Blacks," *Crisis,* November 1920, 16. The reaction of the administration of Warren G. Harding, as well as that of the Universal Negro Improvement Association is described in detail in David Levering Lewis's *W. E. B. DuBois: The Fight for Equality,* 76.

6 Lewis, *W. E. B. DuBois: The Fight for Equality,* 38–39.

7 Ibid., 28, citing W. E. B. Du Bois, *The Souls of Black Folk* (New York: Knopf, 1903).

8 Ibid., 24.

9 Moses, *Afrotopia,* 11, citing Vernon Williams Jr., *Rethinking Race: Franz Boas and His Contemporaries* (Lexington: University of Kentucky Press, 1996).

10 Du Bois, *Dusk of Dawn,* qtd. in Du Bois, *W. E. B. Du Bois: A Reader,* 655.

11 Elombe Brath, "Marcus Garvey: The First African Internationalist," *Caribe* 9, 1 (1987): 21.

12 Tony Martin, "Marcus Garvey: His Cumulative Impact," *Caribe* 9, 1 (1987): 4.

13 James, *Holding Aloft the Banner,* 187–88; Padmore, *Pan-Africanism or Communism,* 138.

14 Stein, *World of Marcus Garvey,* 277.

15 Hill, "The First England Years and After," 47, citing Marcus Garvey, "The British West Indies in the Mirror of Civilization: History Making by Colonial Negroes." For the full text, see Garvey Papers, I, 1826–August 1919: 27–33.

16 Ibid., citing "Universal Negro Improvement Association: Address Delivered by the President at the Annual Meeting," *Daily Gleaner,* August 26, 1915.

17 Bennett, *Before the Mayflower,* 344.

18 Hill, "The First England Years and After," 60.

19 Essien-Udom, *Black Nationalism,* 21.

20 Kahn, "Political Ideology of Marcus Garvey," 124.

21 Qtd. in Rupert Lewis, *Marcus Garvey: Anti-Colonial Champion,* 109. On Garvey in Cuba in 1921, see *El Heraldo de Cuba,* March 4, 1921.

22 Garvey, *Philosophy and Opinions,* 270.

23 Cronon, *Black Moses,* 206.

24 Sinner, *African Americans and U.S. Policy,* 442, citing Du Bois, *Crisis,* January 1921.

25 Qtd. in Gaines, *Uplifting the Race,* 240.

26 Skinner, *African Americans and U.S. Policy,* 472, citing J. Edgar Hoover to John B. Cunningham, August 10, 1922, in Hill, *Marcus Garvey Papers,* vol. 4.

27 Gaines, *Uplifting the Race,* 242.

28 Cronon, *Black Moses,* 206.

29 See Burkett, *Garveyism as a Religious Movement,* 1.

30 The leader of the association proclaimed that, while the deity was interested in his creatures' spiritual well-being, "man's physical body is for his own protection, is for his own purpose." The race must fight its battles in the material world, "and not blame God and Christ for the things that happen to us in the physical." Garvey, *Philosophy and Opinions,* 1:32.

31 Qtd. in Padmore, *Pan-Africanism or Communism,* 13.

32 Skinner, *African Americans and U.S. Policy,* 481, citing Du Bois to Hughes, January 5, 1923, in Du Bois, *Correspondence.*

33 Charles S. Johnson, *Bitter Canaan,* 85.

34 Hargreaves, "African Colonization in the Nineteenth Century: Liberia and Sierra Leone," 65, citing G. W. Ellis Jr., in *Liberia,* no. 26 (February, 1905). See also H. H. Johnston, *Liberia* (London: Hutchinson, 1906), 1:602–3.

35 Draper, *Rediscovery of Black Nationalism,* 24, citing Carter G. Woodson, ed., *The Mind of the Negro as Reflected in Letters Written during the Crisis, 1800–1860* (Washington, D.C.: Association for the Study of Negro Life and History, 1926).

36 Ibid., 23.

37 Blyden, "Call of Providence to the Descendants of Africa in America."

38 Qtd. in Brath, "Marcus Garvey," 15–16.

39 Hill, "Black Zionism," 41, citing the *Negro World,* February 1, 1919. See also Hill, *Marcus Garvey Papers,* 1:356.

40 Hill, *Marcus Garvey Papers,* 7:917. This is an essay originally published in the *Blackman,* entitled "Bill Introduced into United States Senate Aiming

at Carrying out the Idea of the UNIA, A Greater Government for the Negroes of the World in Africa, June 1939."

41 Hill, *Marcus Garvey Papers,* 7:686, editorials by Marcus Garvey in the *Blackman,* July–August 1936.

42 David Brion Davis, "Jews and Blacks in America," *New York Review of Books,* December 2, 1999, 58.

43 Ibid.

44 Martin, *Race First,* 244, citing Robert Minor in the *Daily Worker,* August 18, 1924.

45 Eisenberg and Miller, "The Negro Leader as a Marginal Man," 193–95.

46 See Leo Spitzer, *The Creoles of Sierra Leone* (Madison: University of Wisconsin Press, 1974), 162–64.

47 Redkey, *Black Exodus,* 291.

48 Fierce, *Pan-African Idea in the United States,* 145, citing *Liberia Bulletin,* February 1904.

49 Americo-Liberian Industrial Company folder, Lester Walton Papers, box 8, file 1.

50 Qtd. in I. K. Sundiata, "The On-to-Africa Movement," *Journal of Negro History* 61, 4 (1976): 395.

51 Fierce, *Pan-African Idea in the United States,* 151, citing Booker T. Washington to Theodore Roosevelt, March 21, 1908.

52 Ibid., 165, citing the *Tuskegee Student,* June 20, 1908.

53 Martin, *Race First,* 123, citing the *Negro World,* May 8, 1920.

54 Qtd. in Stein, *World of Marcus Garvey,* 117.

55 Hill, *Marcus Garvey Papers,* 113 (in forthcoming volume), article in the *Liberian News,* Monrovia, August 1924, enclosure in C. A. Wall to U.S. Secretary of State, August 8, 1924.

56 Cronon, *Black Moses,* 130.

57 Martin, *Race First,* 124, citing "Interview with the Acting President of Liberia. By the Commissioners of the Universal Negro Improvement Association, Tuesday, March 22, 1921," USNA RC 59, 882.001.

58 Martin, *Race First,* 132, citing memorandum of Charles H. Hughes to President, n.d.

59 Weisbord, "Marcus Garvey, Pan-Negoist," 419–29.

60 Hill, *Marcus Garvey Papers,* 9:227, excerpt from draft memorandum by John Cooper Wiley, Division of Western European Affairs, ca. September 1921.

61 Hill, *Marcus Garvey Papers,* 9:89, R. Pêtre, French chargé d'affaires, Monrovia, to Aristole Briand, November 22, 1921.

62 Hill, *Marcus Garvey Papers,* 9:706, Georges Bouet, French chargé d'affaires, Monrovia, to Martial-Henri Merlin, December 15, 1922.

63 Hill, *Marcus Garvey Papers* (in a forthcoming volume), enclosure, Georges Bouet to governor-general of French West Africa, July 24, 1923.

64 Hill, *Marcus Garvey Papers* (in a forthcoming volume), Georges Bouet to French Minister of Foreign Affairs, July 4, 1924.

65 Hill, *Marcus Garvey Papers* (in a forthcoming volume), citing Great Britain, Public Records Office, Colonial Office (PRO, CO) 532/289, Septem-

ber 5, 1925, footnote 1 to Francis O'Meara to British Secretary of State for Foreign Affairs, August 8, 1924.

66 Qtd. in Redkey, *Black Exodus,* 20.

67 Qtd. in Stein, *World of Marcus Garvey,* 122.

68 Garvey, *Philosophy and Opinions,* 2:399.

69 See Liebenow, *Liberia.*

70 Hill, *Marcus Garvey Papers* (in a forthcoming volume), enclosure in the *Liberian News,* August, 1924, Sidney De La Rue to William Castle, August 24, 1923, United States National Archives (USNA) RG 59, file 882.51/657.

71 Martin, *Race First,* 133, citing *Negro World,* March 28, 1925.

72 Qtd. In Charles S. Johnson, *Bitter Canaan,* 160.

73 Ibid.

74 Martin, *Race First,* 122, citing C. G. Contee, "The Worley Report on the Pan-African Congress of 1919," *Journal of Negro History* 57 (1970).

75 Ibid., citing *New York Age,* September 20, 1919.

76 Ibid.

77 Ibid., citing "Unrest among the Negroes," October 7, 1919, USNA, RG 28, box 53, unarranged 398, and Contee, "Worley Report."

78 Memorandum, Division of European Affairs, September 25, 1919, USNA, RG 59, 882.00/630.

79 Memorandum, Third Assistant Secretary, Department of State, regarding Messrs. Emmett Scott, Louis Cobb, and William Lewis, November 24, 1919, USNA, RG 59, 882.00/630.

80 Martin, *Race First,* 125, citing the *Crisis,* June 1921.

81 Ibid., 122, citing Edwin Barclay, "Minutes of Meeting, March 22, 1921."

82 Interview by UNIA commissioners with Edwin Barclay, March 22, 1921, footnote 11, De La Rue to William Castle, August 24, 1923, DNA, RG 59, 882.51/657.

83 Weisbord, "Marcus Garvey, Pan-Negoist," 425, citing speech by Governor of Sierra Leone, January 22, 1925.

84 C. D. B. King, "Address at the Grammar School, Freetown, Sierra Leone, 1925," Liberian National Archives.

85 Memorandum by John H. MacVeagh, April 25, 1934, USNA, RG 59, 882.01 FC/829.

86 Lyon to Simpson, July 1934, State Department file, Liberian National Archives.

87 Charles Morrow Wilson, *Liberia,* 35.

88 Cruse, *Crisis of the Negro Intellectual,* 124.

89 Draper, *Rediscovery of Black Nationalism,* 56.

90 Stein, *World of Marcus Garvey,* 277.

91 Ibid., 255.

92 Ibid., 221.

93 A. F. Elmes, "Garvey and Garveyism: An Estimate," in *Marcus Garvey and the Vision of Africa,* ed. John Henrik Clarke (New York: Random House, 1974), 123. The text was originally published in *Opportunity,* May 1925.

94   Stein, *World of Marcus Garvey,* 222.
95   Crouch, *All-American Skin Game,* 43.
96   Appiah, *In My Father's House,* 5.
97   Ibid.
98   Ibid., 6–7.
99   Malcolm X, *By Any Means Necessary* (New York: Pathfinder, 1970), 120.
100 Kahn, "The Political Ideology of Marcus Garvey," *Marcus Garvey,* 135.
101 Qtd. in David Jenkins, *Black Zion,* 120.
102 Daryl Scott, "The Primordial South: White Nationalism in the American South since 1865," forthcoming. See William L. Van Deburg, *New Day in Babylon: The Black Power Movement and American Culture, 1965–1975* (Chicago: University of Chicago Press, 1992).

2 The Black Zion

1   Melville Herskovitz, "The Significance of West Africa for Negro Research, *Journal of Negro History* 21, 1 (January, 1936), 15.
2   Skinner, *African Americans and U.S. Policy,* 432, citing "Report by Special Agent 800, New York City, 21 July 1920," in Hill, *Marcus Garvey Papers,* vol. 2.
3   Hill, *Marcus Garvey Papers,* 2:412, Report of UNIA meeting, Liberty Hall, July 11, 1920.
4   Ibid., 9:69, Cyril Henry to O. M. Thompson, July 1, 1921.
5   Ibid.
6   Du Bois, "Little Portraits of Africa: The Place, the People," *Crisis,* April 1924, qtd. in Du Bois, *A Reader,* 669.
7   Sibley and Westermann, *Liberia, Old and New,* 162.
8   Greene, *Journey without Maps,* 80.
9   See Warren L. Azevedo, "Tribe and Chiefdom on the Windward Coast."
10   Ibid.
11   Bell I. Wiley, ed., *Slaves No More: Letters from Liberia, 1833–1869* (Lexington: University of Kentucky Press, 1980), 28.
12   Ellis, *Negro Culture in West Africa,* 74.
13   Pate, *Amistad,* 192–93.
14   Yoder, "He Kill My Ma," 55–56.
15   Charles S. Johnson, *Bitter Canaan,* 89.
16   Svend E. Holsoe, "Slavery and Economic Response among the Vai (Liberia and Sierra Leone)," in Miers and Kopytoff, *Slavery in Africa,* 295–303.
17   British Consul Errol MacDonell to Principle Secretary of State for Foreign Affairs, November 27, 1903, Foreign Office (hereafter cited as FO) 47/36.
18   See Caroline Bledsoe, *Women and Marriage in Kpelle Society* (Stanford, Calif.: Stanford University Press, 1980).
19   John Fulton, "The Kpelle Traditional Political System," *Liberia Studies Journal* 1, 1 (1968): 3.
20   Yoder, "He Kill My Ma," sec. "Tension Concealed by Social Order," 44.

21 J. F. Johnson, ed., *Proceedings of the General Anti-Slavery Convention,* 260; testimony of Rev. John Clarke.

22 Meillassoux, "Essai d'interprétation."

23 Rey, "L'esclavage linager."

24 Ronald W. Davis, *Ethnohistorical Studies on the Kru Coast,* 57, citing Thomas Ludlam, "An Account of the Kroomen on the Coast of Africa," *African Repository* 1 (1825–26).

25 Nevinson, *A Modern Slavery,* 16.

26 Donner, *Hinterland Liberia,* 123.

27 Warren d'Azevedo, *The Gola of Liberia* (Human Relations Area Files, 1972), 1:122.

28 Donner, *Hinterland Liberia,* 278.

29 Stewart, *Liberia,* 77–78.

30 Henry S. Wilson, *Origins of West African Nationalism,* 114, citing Alexander Crummell, "Our National Mistakes and the Remedy for Them," annual address before the Common Council and citizens of Monrovia, 1870, in Crummell, *Africa and America* (New York: Negro Universities Press, 1891).

31 Ibid.

32 Burrowes, "The Americo-Liberian Ruling Class," 30.

33 Ibid., 50.

34 Maurice Delafosse, "Un état nègre: La république de Liberia," *Bulletin du Comité de l'Afrique Française, Renseignments Coloniaux* 9 (1900): 174–75.

35 Strong, *The African Republic of Liberia and the Belgian Congo,* 1:37, 46.

36 Akpan, "Liberia and the Universal Negro Improvement Association," 111.

37 Gershoni, *Black Colonialism,* 64, citing Worley to Johnson, September 17, 1921, Records of the Department of State Relating to Internal Affairs of Liberia, 1910–1929.

38 Qtd. in Charles S. Johnson, *Bitter Canaan,* 197.

39 Qtd. in ibid., 218.

40 Garvey, *Philosophy and Opinions,* 2:374.

41 Ibid., 2:377.

42 See Jane Martin, "'Krumen down the Coast': Liberian Migrants on the West African Coast in the Nineteenth Century," working paper, Boston University African Studies Center, 1982.

43 Akpan, "The African Policy of the Liberian Settlers," 268, citing the *Lagos Weekly Record,* July 2, 1910.

44 The Liberian regime has used a variety of currencies during its history. In the nineteenth century, there was a shortage of specie, and a variety of currencies circulated; prices were quoted in both English and American currency. Until the early 1930s, the only bank in Monrovia was the Bank of British West Africa. When that bank withdrew, its place was taken by an American bank with connections to Firestone interests. Since 1943, Liberia has used American currency, which remains interchangeable with Liberian specie (at present there is no Liberian paper currency).

45 Haliburton, *Prophet Harris,* 23.

46 Ibid., citing "Father Stauffer's Journal."
47 Qtd. in Jenkins, *Black Zion,* 85.
48 Qtd. in Richardson, *Liberia's Past and Present,* 181.
49 Blyden, *Selected Letters,* 492.
50 Haliburton, *Prophet Harris,* 25, citing Ernest Lyon to the Secretary of State, April 1910, USNA RG 59, 882.00/367.
51 Ibid., citing *African League* 10, 12 (1909).
52 Ibid., 68, citing Casely Hayford, *William Waddy Harris: The West African Reformer and His Message* (London: C.M. Phillips, 1915), 9.
53 The elder Ross was a man who, on several occasions, had felt confident enough to challenge the national executive. He had served as a judge, county superintendent (thrice), senator, and vice president of the republic from 1896 to 1899. He died in the latter year, but Samuel continued his father's political tradition.
54 Charles S. Johnson, *Bitter Canaan,* 250, and Charles S. Johnson Papers, unpublished manuscript copy.
55 As early as 1896, Ross, already a prominent member of the Americo-Liberian, attempted to use an interethnic dispute on the Kru Coast to coerce money and belongings from a group near Blue Barre.
56 Jones, "The Struggle for Political and Cultural Unification," 232, citing Dispatch from the United States Legation, Monrovia, Liberia, January 1913, USNA, RG 59, 882.00/525.
57 Ibid., 232.
58 Ronald W. Davis, *Ethnohistorical Studies,* 56, citing Scholfield to the U.S. Secretary of the Navy, November 30, 1915, USNA.
59 Jones, "The Struggle for Political and Cultural Unification," 239. See British Consul General to the Kru of Sinoe, December 11, 1915, USNA, RG 59, 822.001. The reply to the Kru was sent in care of C. D. B. King, Liberian Secretary of State.
60 Memorandum from Kru on the revolt of 1915, transcribed September 12, 1930, Charles S. Johnson Papers, box 88.
61 Ibid.
62 Qtd. in Jones, "The Struggle for Political and Cultural Unification," 240.
63 Du Bois, "Little Portraits of Africa: The Place, the People," *The Crisis,* April 1924 qtd. in Du Bois, *A Reader,* 668.
64 Skinner, *African Americans and U.S. Policy,* 492, citing Du Bois, *Dusk of Dawn.*
65 Qtd. in Chalk, "Du Bois and Garvey," 141.
66 Qtd. in Skinner, *African Americans and U.S. Policy,* 497 n. 106.
67 Qtd. in ibid., 497 n. 107.
68 Du Bois, *Dusk of Dawn,* 117.
69 Ibid., 127.
70 Ibid., 125.
71 David Levering Lewis, *W. E. B. Du Bois,* 120.
72 Du Bois, *Dusk of Dawn,* 127.
73 Charles S. Johnson, *Bitter Canaan,* 216.
74 Du Bois, *A Reader,* 688.

75 Charles S. Johnson, *Bitter Canaan,* 212.
76 Taylor, "The Involvement of Black Americans," 62, citing memorandum by Castle of conversation with Du Bois, March 26, 1924; Chalk, "Du Bois and Garvey," 137.
77 Charles S. Johnson, *Bitter Canaan,* 85.
78 Stein, *World of Marcus Garvey,* 51, citing the *Crisis,* December 1918–January 1919.
79 Martin, *Race First,* 301, citing *Negro World,* January 26, 1924, reprinting editorial from *Gold Coast Leader,* December 1, 1923.
80 Garvey, *Philosophy and Opinions,* 2:397–98.
81 Ibid., 1:72.
82 Hill, *Marcus Garvey Papers,* 9:144, Madarikan Deniyi to the *Richmond Planet,* January 29, 1921.
83 Ibid., 651, pamphlet by M. Mokete Manoedi, New York, c. July 1922, enclosure in Manoedi to Winston S. Churchill, September 30, 1922.
84 Qtd. in Garvey, *Philosophy and Opinions,* 2:399–400.
85 Martin, *Race First,* 127, citing *Liberian News,* August 10, 1924.
86 Marcus Garvey to C. D. B. King, December 5, 1923, USNA, RG 59, file 143, 882.511/16.
87 Garvey, *Philosophy and Opinions,* 2:397. See Stein, *World of Marcus Garvey,* 212.

3 Abuse

1 The author served as president of the Liberian Studies Association in 1981.
2 Garvey, *Philosophy and Opinions,* 2:397.
3 Ibid.
4 Reeve, *Black Republic,* 122.
5 Unzueta, *Geografía histórica,* 199.
6 League of Nations Secretariat, *Report,* 36. Averaging at least six hundred workers per year, the figure should be higher; for a period of thirteen years the total should be significantly higher (c. 7,800).
7 H. Markham Cook to General Missionary Committee, June 10, 1915, Methodist Missionary Society, Primitive Methodist Mission, Fernando Po, box 3.
8 Unzueta, *Geografía histórica,* 199.
9 Richard C. Bundy to Secretary of State, February 9, 1919, USNA, RG 59, 882.504/6 (microfilm M613, location 10–14–5, roll 14).
10 Ibid.
11 Charles S. Johnson, *Bitter Canaan,* 163.
12 Report on leading personalities in Liberia, including additions received in the Foreign Office up to January 30, 1930, PRO, FO, 371/14658.
13 League of Nations Secretariat, *Report,* 36–38.
14 The Wedabo and the Po River people perhaps represent a fishmen-bushmen dichotomy. The Po were Kru who had migrated down the coast,

probably before the Wedabo people had settled inland of them. The Wedabo are thought to be related to the Kru above Grand Cess, but their language contains many Grebo words. The Wedabo held a corridor to the sea, but their farming country, with its capital, Soloken, was one or two days journey into the interior. See League of Nations Secretariat, *Report,* 19.

15 Ibid.

16 Charles S. Johnson, *Bitter Canaan,* 5

17 Meanwhile the commissioner, without asking the chiefs who was guilty, caught seven Wedabo men as probable culprits in the incident.

18 Charles S. Johnson, *Bitter Canaan,* 21. This was done, and supposedly the men were put to work on Yancy's private farm at Webblo.

19 Ibid., 9.

20 Ibid., 22.

21 During World War I, the Monrovia government imposed an annual hut tax on "uncivilized" peoples. By 1922, the amount collected from this source reached $151,213,70, or one-third of gross government revenue. Akpan, "Black Imperialism," 230.

22 Ibid.,17.

23 Ross to Barclay, radiogram, c. October 6, 1927, Charles S. Johnson Papers, box 88, file 5.

24 League of Nations Secretariat, *Report,* 17. The influences were thought to include president C. D. B. King.

25 Ibid.

26 A. C. Reeve to Consul-General, Loanda Luanda, July 4, 1920, PRO, FO, 371/5562. Criminal offenses were supposedly punished with excessive cruelty, and police brutality allegedly ran rampant. In 1921, Britain launched an investigation into these conditions when a Sierra Leonean, Kaba-Limba, was severely flogged after being accused of robbing the house of the widow of a prominent planter. The flogging caused the acting British vice consul to lodge a protest, and the affair eventually reached the ambassadorial level; in August of 1921, a protest was staged in Madrid. In 1922, another case arose when Tommy Timini, a Sierra Leonean recruited in Liberia, was not paid and complained to the Liberian vice consul on Fernando Po. Timini was an employee of the black planter Joseph Dougan, and the British vice consul noted that he "was surprised to hear from the Curador Spanish labor officer himself that Mr. Dougan is anything but the gentlest of masters. He is at the present 'under going' a fine for ill-treatment to boys" (A. C. Reeve to A. S. Paterson, June 6, 1922, PRO, FO, 371/8465).

27 Buell, *Native Problem,* 2:780.

28 Akpan, "Liberia and the Universal Negro Improvement Association," 121. J. Chaudhuri notes that customs revenue in 1923–24 was a little over $392,000; in 1913, the customs revenue had been $486,395.72. See Chaudhuri, "British Policy," 210.

29 Buell, *Native Problem,* 2:781, citing *Agricultural World,* February 1925.

30 Lewis May, British Vice-Consul, Santa Isabel to Foreign Office, July 18, 1925, PRO, FO, 371/11100.

31 Ibid.

32 Buell, *Native Problem,* 2:782.

33 Consul-General Rule, Monrovia, to Foreign Office, December 23, 1927, PRO, FO, 371/12758.

34 Barclay to George Johns, March 20, 1928, U.S. Department of State, Records Relating to the Affairs of Liberia, 1910–1929, microfilm roll 14. U.S. Department of State, Records Relating to the Affairs of Liberia, 1910–1929, are hereafter cited as DSRRAL.

35 Mr. Barleycorn was interviewed by the author in Santa Isabel (now Malabo) on March 2, 1970.

36 Barclay to Johns, March 20, 1928, DSRRAL, microfilm roll 14.

37 League of Nations Secretariat, *Report,* 109.

38 Ibid., 36. The members of Ross's group included Thomas F. C. Pelham, Robert W. Draper, E. C. W. King, I. C. Johnston, M. A. Bracewell, and C. L. Cooper. Pelham and Draper were Ross's sons-in-law. Two of the members of the group were female clerks.

39 Barclay and Barclay were attorneys for Thodomiro Avendano, president of the syndicate. Witnesses were J. Douglas, E. A. Monger, and J. V. O. Howard. League of Nations Secretariat, *Report,* 109.

40 Ibid., 36.

41 Wharton to Department of State, October 22, 1929, DSRRAL, microfilm roll 14.

42 Charles S. Johnson, *Bitter Canaan,* 136.

43 W. T. Francis, U.S. Consul to Liberia, to Secretary of State, June 2, 1928, USNA, RG 59, 882.66/1. Woermann was shipping Kru laborers to South West Africa (Walvis Bay) as stevedores with two-year contracts (Monroe Phelps to Secretary of State, April 10, 1929, USNA, RG 59, 882.5048/21).

44 Wharton to Castle, November 29, 1929, DSRRAL, microfilm roll 14.

45 Diary of Charles S. Johnson, Johnson Papers, May 12, 1930, 110.

46 Mitchell, "America's Liberian Policy," 241.

47 League of Nations Secretariat, *Report,* 42–43.

48 Ibid., 41.

49 Ibid., 36.

50 As late as 1936, two observers maintained, "Spanish ships are still calling at Liberian ports and are taking contract labourers to the Spanish colony." Akpan, "African Policy," 488, quoting H. J. Grenwell and Roland Wild, *Unknown Liberia* (London: Hutchinson, 1936).

51 League of Nations Secretariat, *Report,* 41.

52 Ibid., 44.

53 Ibid., 45.

54 McBride Memorandum (Washington), October 3, 1934, Annexed Memorandum of the Government of Liberia on the Kru Situation, USNA, RG 59, 882.10 FC/915.

55 Schuyler, "Wide 'Slavery,'" 1.

56 Ibid.

57 Du Bois, review of *Slaves Today,* by George S. Schuyler, in *Book Reviews,* 161–62. The original review appeared in the *Crisis* in February 1932.

58 Hochschild, "Leopold's Congo," B4.
59 Lindqvist, *Exterminate All the Brutes,* 160.
60 John Gunther, *Inside Africa* (New York: Harper, 1955), 656. In Hochschild's words, "between 1880 and 1920, according to the best demographic estimates today, the population of the Congo was slashed in half: from roughly 20 million to 10 million people. (Some writers cite even higher numbers: in the *Origins of Totalitarianism,* Hannah Arendt used a figure of 12 million deaths.)" Hochschild, "Leopold's Congo," B4.
61 Miers and Roberts, *End of Slavery in Africa,* 45.
62 Hochschild, "Leopold's Congo," B4.
63 Hodges and Newitt, *Sâo Tomé and Príncipe,* 38.
64 Ibid.
65 Curtin et al., *African History,* 462–63.
66 Rich and Wallerstein, *Africa: Tradition and Change,* 279, citing Geoffrey Gorer, *Africa Dances* (London, 1934).
67 Cooper, *From Slaves to Squatters,* 63.

4 Investigation of an Investigation

1 League of Nations Secretariat, Report, 36.
2 Sibley and Westermann, *Liberia, Old and New,* 303.
3 Padmore, *American Imperialism,* 29, citing African World, October 5, 1929.
4 See Steve Love and David Giffels, Wheels of Fortune: The Story of Firestone Rubber (Akron, Ohio: University of Akron Press, 1999), 112–13.
5 Qtd. in Brandes, Herbert Hoover, 117, citing James C. Lawrence, The World's Struggle with Rubber (New York: Harper, 1931).
6 Padmore, *American Imperialism,* 18, citing Firestone Non-Skid, December 1925.
7 Qtd. in Azikiwe, "In Defense of Liberia," 32.
8 For Firestone's projection of his labor needs, see Mower, "The Republic of Liberia," 3, citing Harvey S. Firestone Sr., "We Must Grow Our Own Rubber," Country Gentleman, April 1926.
9 Du Bois, "Liberia, the League, and the United States," 695.
10 Schmokel, "United States and the Crisis," 307.
11 Berg, "Development of a Labor Force," 407.
12 Akpan, "African Policy," 447.
13 Daniel, *Shadow of Slavery,* 132.
14 Azikiwe, "In Defense of Liberia," 40.
15 Nearing, *Black America,* 32, citing Hugh M. Dorsey, "As to the Negro in Georgia."
16 Ibid.
17 Oshinsky, *Worse than Slavery,* n.p., citing Frank Sanborn, keynote address to "Ninth Atlanta Conference on Negro Crime," 1904.
18 Ibid., citing Hasting Hart, report to Russell Sage Foundation, 1929.
19 Ibid., citing L. G. Shrivers, "A History of the Mississippi Penitentiary," 1930.

20 Ibid., citing David Cohn, Where I Was Born and Raised (Boston: Houghton Mifflin, 1935).{AU: Pls. add place and publisher in parens}

21 Ibid., citing Proceedings of the Annual Congress of the American Prison Association (Indianapolis: W.B. Burford, 1919).

22 William Hemphill, engineer, qtd. in Barry, *Rising Tide,* 122.

23 Ibid., 320.

24 Ibid., 329.

25 Oscar R. Williams, "Making of a Black Conservative," 178, citing "Labor Conditions Affecting the Negro along the Mississippi River," Investigation #2, December 1932, NAACP Papers.

26 Ibid., 177, citing "NAACP Levee Camp Investigators Jailed and Threatened in Mississippi," NAACP press release, 1933, NAACP Papers.

27 Padmore, *American Imperialism,* 45.

28 Verill, Porto Rico, 309.

29 Plummer, "Afro-American Response," 130, citing John B. Russell, "Marine Looks Back on Haiti," typescript in the United States Marine Corps Historical Museum, Personal Papers Collection, Washington, D.C.

30 Rayford W. Logan, Haiti and the Dominican Republic (New York: Oxford University Press, 1968), 126, citing Robert Lansing to J. H. Oliver, January 30, 1918.

31 H. M. to William Phillips, October 31, 1918, USNA, RG 59, decimal file, 838.00/1547.

32 Burks, *Land of Checkerboard Families,* 18.

33 Plummer, "Afro-American Response," 130.

34 See Brian Weinstein and Aaron Segal, Haiti: Political Failures, Cultural Successes (New York: Praeger, 1984).

35 James Weldon Johnson, "Self-Determination in Haiti," Nation 111 (1920): 265.

36 Ibid.

37 The Assistant Secretary to Marcus Garvey, September 22, 1920, NAACP Papers.

38 Hill, *Marcus Garvey Papers,* 1:359, U.S. Postal Censorship, enclosure, New York, January 16, 1919; Eliezer Cadet to H. Dorsinville, Port-au-Prince, Haiti.

39 Qtd. in Plummer, "Afro-American Response," 138.

40 Hill, *Marcus Garvey Papers,* 4: 1053, Convention Reports, September 1, 1922; Mr. Garvey on Membership Loan System, September 1, 1922.

41 Plummer, "Afro-American Response," 137, citing the *Messenger,* August 1921.

42 Ross, "Black Americans and Haiti," 385. Walter White to Stenio Vincent, October 4, 1933, NAACP Papers, box c-329.

43 Stanfield, introductory essay to Charles S. Johnson, *Bitter Canaan,* x.

44 Ibid.

45 Taylor, "Involvement of Black Americans," 61, citing Bundy to Secretary of State, August 21, 1920 and October 20, 1920, USNA, RG 59, 88.51/1169 and 882.5048.

46 W. T. Francis to William Castle, January 16, 1828, USNA, RG 59 882.5048/1.

47 Henry Carter (?) to William Castle, January 16, 1928, USNA, RG 59 (microfilm M613, location 10–14–5, roll 5).

48 Schmokel, "United States and the Crisis," 307.

49 Garvey, *Philosophy and Opinions,* 2:409.

50 Ibid., 2:410.

51 Qtd. in Martin, *Race First,* 136.

52 W.E. B. Du Bois to the Editor, Chicago's Daily Worker, August 28, 1924, Du Bois Papers, microfilm reel 13, frame 391. The original Du Bois Papers are at the University of Massachusetts at Amherst.

53 W. E. B. Du Bois to N. Azikiwe, November 11, 1932, Du Bois Papers, microfilm reel 36.

54 Stein, *World of Marcus Garvey,* 214.

55 David Levering Lewis, *W. E. B. DuBois,* 127.

56 Ibid., citing Herbert Aptheker, ed., *The Correspondence of W. E. B. Du Bois,* vol. 1 (Amherst: University of Massachusetts Press, 1973).

57 Du Bois to Secretary of State, March 24, 1924, USNA, RG 59, 882.00/739 (microfilm M613, location 10–14–5, roll 14).

58 Du Bois, "Liberia, the League, and the United States," 684. Earlier in the century, Du Bois had hoped the Belgian or German colonial governments would let African Americans become the economic leaders in their colonies. See Rudwick, W. E. B. Du Bois, 210.

59 Chalk, "Du Bois and Garvey," 141, citing W. E. B. Du Bois, "A Second Journey to Pan-Africa," New Republic, December 7, 1921.

60 Chalk, "Anatomy of an Investment," 20, citing Castle to Harrison, July 1, 1924, USNA, RG 59, 882.6176 F51/1. De La Rue is also reported to have urged that the replacement for American consul Solomon Hood be a white man. If Hood remained in the United States (where he was visiting temporarily), it was argued that he could be very influential in creating support for Firestone among the black population.

61 The first agreement provided for the lease of an old British-owned rubber plantation at Mount Barclay (where Firestone would be able to conduct feasibility studies). The second granted the right to lease up to 1 million acres for a period of fifty years. Harbor improvements were included in the Third Draft Accord. Firestone would improve the port of Monrovia with aid contributed by the Liberian government.

62 Chalk, "Anatomy of an Investment, 18.

63 Ibid., 19–20, citing C. R. Russell to Castle, June 22, 1924, USNA, RG 59, 882.616 F51/2.

64 According to a later report of the interview, De La Rue sought to impress on Firestone that "he should not expect to have any control over the country or over the loan." The receiver "explained that this must be a banker's loan and that the control would be exercised by an advisor nominated by the Government . . ., the State Department would not approve of Firestone going into Liberia without a loan, that the Department had accepted 'his policy as its policy' and that a loan would have to be made." Ibid., 21, citing Tredwell to Harrison, January 15, 1925, USNA, RG 59, 882.6176F.

65 Buell, *Liberia,* 30.

66 Ibid.

67 This loan to repay a loan in reality increased Liberia's financial burden. The interest rate was raised from 5 to 7 percent, and the life of the loan was extended from 1952 to 1966. Only part of the loan was ever issued; in large part it paid off the loan of 1912 and the internal floating debt. Liberia could make no refunding loan without the consent of an American financial adviser; the Finance Corporation of America had an option on any new loan. In 1952, Liberia actually managed to repay its loan ahead of schedule. See Taylor, Firestone Operations, 57.

68 Later this very financial bureaucracy was realized to be a burden. Advisers' salaries and service charges amounted to a fixed charge of nearly $270,000 a year. This constituted 20 percent of Liberian revenues in 1928 and approximately half of those revenues in 1931. Like previous loans, the Finance Corporation's was unproductive; more than 90 percent of the $2,500,000 advanced paid off existing debts.

69 Chalk, "Anatomy of an Investment," 22–23, citing a memorandum by Leland Harrison, July 8, 1924, in U.S. Department of State, Foreign Relations of the United States, 1925, 2:379–82. This annual title hereafter cited as *USFR.*

70 Chalk, "United States and the International Struggle," 90.

71 Chalk, "Anatomy of an Investment," 25, citing Roger Tredwell to Leland Harrison, January, 1925, USNA, RG 59, 882.6176 F51/70; Tredwell to Harrison, January 11, 1925, USNA, RG 59, 882.6176 F51/72. Receiver De La Rue, in his eagerness to get a banker's loan, had already approached the British and the French about the project. The French chargé in Monrovia looked forward to the building of a railway across Liberia to the French territory in the north. See Tredwell to Harrison, January 1, 1925, USNA, RG 59, 882.6176 F51/70.

72 Chalk, "Anatomy of an Investment," 26, citing Tredwell to Harrison, January 1, 1925, USNA, RG 59, 882.6176 F51/70. Tredwell, the Foreign Service inspector, greatly disapproved of the position taken by the receivership on the loan question. He described his tour of inspection in Liberia as "one of the most disagreeable experiences of my whole career and I shall be glad when it is finished." See Tredwell to Harrison, January 11, 1925, USNA, RG 59, 882.6176 F51/72; Tredwell to Harrison, January 1, 1925, USNA, RG 59, 882.6176 F51/70.

73 Chalk, "Anatomy of an Investment," 27, citing Castle to De La Rue, March 13, 1925, USNA, RG 59, 882.6176 F51/82.

74 Buell, Liberia, 31. In November of 1929, the American chargé in Monrovia reported that a German trader had been approached by a Liberian in an effort to obtain laborers from Firestone's Du plantations for transport to Fernando Po. See Chargé d'Affaires (Monrovia) to State Department, November -, 1929, Charles S. Johnson Papers, box 89, file 6. Earlier in the same year, the American minister had informed the State Department of an attempt to have a British employee of Firestone procure labor for Fernando Po. David Ross, an adopted son of Samuel Ross, admitted to

the League of Nations commission of inquiry that he had carried gin, tobacco, and rice to the No. 7 Firestone plantation in an effort to lure away labor. Certain workers did leave and go to Monrovia, but when they learned that they were to be sent to Fernando Po, some escaped. One African policeman supposedly sent his brother to Ross for four shillings. See League of Nations Secretariat, Report, 42. Wage rates were also an issue between Firestone and its competitors for labor. It was reported that "they, certain Americo-Liberians, solicited Mr. Firestone confidentially, it seems, not to pay wages in excess of twenty-five cents a day or the rubber work would rob their private farms of labor." Young, Liberia Rediscovered, 43. It was also reported that "in the beginning common laborers were paid 2 to 4 shillings per day, but the government objected saying that Liberian farmers were protesting on grounds that high wages took away their labor." George W. Brown, Economic History of Liberia, 206, citing George Schuyler, "Is Liberia a Slave State?" *New York Evening Post,* July 2, 1931.

75 Qtd. in Buell, *Liberia,* 31.

76 Chalk, "Anatomy of an Investment," 30, citing USFR, 1926, 2:568–70.

77 Ibid.

78 Knoll, "Firestone's Labor Policy," 50, citing D. A. Ross and C. A. Myers to Harvey S. Firestone Sr., April 8, 1927, Firestone Papers, in the possession of Dr. Svend Holsoe, Department of Anthropology, University of Delaware.

79 Ibid., citing Anthony J. Nimely, The Liberian Bureaucracy: An Analysis and Evaluation of the Environment, Structure, and Functions (Washington, D.C.: University Press of America, 1977).

80 Ibid., 55, citing Harvey S. Firestone Jr., diary entry, February 2, 1928, USNA microfilm 613, roll 27.

81 Ibid., 54, citing Firestone Manager to Rt. Hon. Arthur Henderson, M.P., December 13, 1929, enclosure in Charles S. Johnson to U.S. Assistant Secretary of State, October 1, 1930, Charles S. Johnson Papers.

82 Anderson, Liberia, 134.

83 Long before the Firestone investment, an American minister to Liberia had spotted the potential for American use of the existing labor force. In 1912, the minister prepared a report on the subject. See Richard Bundy to Secretary of State, November 20, 1912, USNA, RG 59, 82.5048 (microfilm M613, location 10–14–5, roll 14).

84 Sidney De La Rue, "Annual Report of the General Receiver of Customs and Financial Adviser to the Republic of Liberia for the Fiscal Year 1925–26," 1927–28, DSRRAL, microfilm roll 30.

85 Buell, *Native Problem,* 2:834–35.

86 Clifton R. Wharton to Castle, March 3, 1927, DSRRAL, microfilm roll 30.

87 Clipping from the Liberian Express and Agricultural World, November–December 1928, enclosure in William Francis to Department of State, March 22, 1929, DSRRAL, microfilm roll 14.

88 Report on Firestone Plantations, "Bo Zieko Fahtow," DSRRAL, microfilm roll 31.

89　This information was supplied to the U.S. State Department by the chargé in Monrovia. Wharton to Secretary of State, September 8, 1929, DSRRAL, microfilm roll 14.

90　League of Nations Secretariat, Report, 79.

91　John Loomis to Henry Carter, May 10, 1929, DSRRAL, microfilm roll 27. It was added, "The number of laborers shipped is not the question but the demoralizing influence it has upon officials and the further effect of driving natives across the frontiers to other countries."

92　"Memorandum: International Labor Conference at Geneva," May 20, 1929; "American Interest Therein" (State Department memorandum?), Charles S. Johnson Papers, box 88, file 6.

93　Department of State Memorandum, June 13, 1929, on preliminary summary of Report on Slavery by American minister at Monrovia, DSRRAL, microfilm roll 14.

94　Qtd. in Buell, *Native Problem,* 2:831. See also Lloyd Beecher, "State Department and Liberia," 139, citing memorandum of interview with Barclay, Washington, D.C., August 24, 1925, USNA, RG 59, 882.617 F51/125.

95　Azikiwe, *Liberia in World Politics,* 206, citing U.S. Press Release No. 67, 21–22; and League Document No. CL 3.1931 VI. Azikiwe also refers to U.S. Press Release No. 68, 28.

96　Buell, *Native Problem,* 2:831.

97　Schmokel, "United States and the Crisis," 308.

98　Buell, *Native Problem,* 2:831.

99　Ibid., 2:833.

100　Ibid., 2:847. Buell may have overstated the diplomatic role of the United States in this regard. The United States had traditionally supported the integrity of Liberia in its boundary disputes with its European neighbors. During the Firestone negotiations, the United States may have been doing no more than displaying its traditional solicitude for the Black Republic. William Castle of the State Department did inform Liberian secretary of state Barclay that the French were playing a "disreputable political game" in claiming a certain territory on the border between French Guinea and Liberia. For a discussion of the boundary dispute in the context of the Firestone negotiations, see Beecher, "State Department and Liberia," 148, citing G. H. M. to Castle, Washington, D.C., August 13, 1924, USNA, RG 59, 751.8215/191; Carter to Castle, Washington, D.C., August 13, 1925, USNA, RG 59, 751.8215/209; Castle interview with Barclay, August 24, 1925, USNA, RG 59, 882.6176 F51/125; Kellogg to American Embassy in Paris, Washington, D.C., October 28, 1925, USNA, RG 59, 751.8215/212; Myron Herrick, Ambassador to France, to Secretary of State, Paris, November 13, 1925, USNA, RG 59, 751.8215/219. See also Forderhase, "Plans That Failed," 61. The King regime may have used the "French menace" to cow internal opposition to the Firestone concession, arguing that by anchoring American investment in Liberia, the republic was saving itself. Thirty years after the Firestone negotiations, president William Tubman justified the granting of the concession on the grounds of national security: "One of the main reasons why the terms of the loan were accepted was political rather than economic. Border incidents and boundary disputes thereafter ceased." Qtd. in Taylor, Firestone Operations, x.

101 Division of Western European Affairs Memorandum to William Castle, June 6, 1927, USNA, RG 59, 882.00/766 (microfilm M613, location 10–14–5, roll 14). Professor G. Wilson of the Bureau of International Research, Harvard University and Radcliffe College, sent the chapter dealing with Liberia in Buell's book, *The Native Problem in Africa*, to the State Department.

102 Ibid. Labor discontent with Firestone also resulted from pay practices. The pay began with a shilling a day at both the Du and Cavalla plantations. On the advice of the white staff at the latter plantation, pay was changed to one pound per month and food. The laborers complained, and the new pay system was abandoned.

103 Castle (Department of State) to William T. Francis (Monrovia), June 21, 1928, DSRRAL, microfilm roll 14.

104 Chief Clerk to President (Monroe Phelps?) to Commissioner David S. Carter, January 20, 1930, Liberian National Archives.

105 League of Nations Secretariat, Report, 79.

106 Castle to American Legation, Monrovia, August 18, 1928, DSRRAL, microfilm roll 14.

107 Kellogg to American Consul, Geneva, July 28, 1928, DSRRAL, microfilm roll 14. An American magazine, *Outlook*, dismissed Junod's activities and quoted Harvey Firestone Sr., as saying, "As the Firestone Company controls only one million acres in Liberia and there are forty-two million acres of land available, it is obvious that no such scheme peonage and land confiscation is contemplated." "No Rubber Peonage," 607.

108 C. D. B. King to Department of State, August 30, 1928, DSRRAL, microfilm roll 14.

109 Francis to Department of State, August 28, 1929, DSRRAL, microfilm roll 14.

110 Castle to American Legation, Monrovia, August 29, 1928, DSRRAL, microfilm roll 14.

111 Carter (Department of State) to Harvey S. Firestone Jr., August 29, 1928, DSRRAL, microfilm roll 14.

112 Qtd. in Francis to Castle, March 22, 1924, DSRRAL, microfilm roll 14.

113 Department of State Memorandum of the Press Conference, August 30, 1928, USNA, RG 59, 882.5048/12 (microfilm M613, location 10–14–5, roll 14).

114 Chalk, "Anatomy of an Investment," 27, citing Castle to De La Rue, February 25, 1925, USNA, RG 59, 882.6176 F51/81; Castle to De La Rue, March 13, 1925, USNA, RG 59, 882.6176 F51/82.

115 Hill, *Marcus Garvey Papers*, 9:264, Marcus Garvey to Sir Eric Drummond, Secretary General, League of Nations, Geneva, September 11, 1928.

116 Francis to Castle, March 22, 1924, DSRRAL, microfilm roll 14.

117 Castle to Undersecretary of State, April 25, 1929, USNA, RG 59, 882.5048/22 (microfilm M613, location 10–14–5, roll 14).

118 Castle to Patton, May 3, 1929, USNA, RG 59, 882.00/787 (microfilm M613, location 10–14–5, roll 14). Phelps-Stokes had written to Castle on April 29, informing him of Patton's report.

119 Castle to Secretary of State, May 24, 1929, USNA, RG 59, 882.5048/54 (microfilm M613, location 10–14–5, roll 14).

120 Qtd. in Richardson, *Liberia's Past and Present*, 411.

121 Wharton (Monrovia) to Secretary of State, August 1, 1929, DSRRAL, microfilm roll 14.

122 Taylor, "Involvement of Black Americans," 62, citing Stimson to Wharton, July 22, 1929.

123 Wharton to Department of State, September 21, 1929, DSRRAL, microfilm roll 14.

124 Francis to Department of State, supplemental memorandum, May 4, 1929, DSRRAL, microfilm roll 14. After the Liberian government expressed a willingness to appoint a commission for the investigation of the slavery allegations, the department expressed the fear "that the Liberian Government will attempt to entangle the Firestone Plantations Company in order to save its own face" (Clifton Wharton to Secretary of State, July 30, 1929, DSRRAL, microfilm roll 14).

125 Department of State, Division of West European Affairs, Memorandum to Castle, July 30, 1929, DSRRAL, microfilm roll 14.

126 Memorandum (Henry Carter), "Suggestions as to Policy during My Absence on Leave," September 4, 1929, USNA, RG 59, 882.5049/214.

127 Raymond Bixler, *The Foreign Policy of the United States in Liberia* (New York: Pageant Press, 1957), 87.

128 Ibid., citing Minister at Monrovia to Department of State, March 8, 1929, USNA, RG 59, 882.617 F51/272.

129 Ibid., citing Secretary of the Treasury of Liberia to Supervisor of Customs, April 4, 1929, USNA, RG 59, 892.51/2005.

130 Chargé (?) (Monrovia) to Department of State, October 21, 1921, enclosing: "A Few Articles Refused Publication by the Editors of the Newspapers," Albert Porte, Crozierville, Liberia, September, 1929, Charles S. Johnson Papers, box 89, file 5.

131 B. M. Robinson to Harvey Firestone Jr., December 23, 1929, Charles S. Johnson Papers, box 88, file 6.

132 Ibid.

133 Department of State (J.P.M.) to Charles S. Johnson, Mr. Mariner, and Mr. Gilbert, January 3, 1930, Charles S. Johnson Papers, box 89, file 5.

134 Gabriel L. Dennis, "Annual Report of the Secretary of the Treasury, R. L. for Treasury Operations" (Monrovia, 1933), Claude Barnett Papers, Liberia, 1925–45. The report covers the period January 1 to September 30, 1930.

135 John Stanfield, introductory essay to Charles S. Johnson, *Bitter Canaan*, xxxv–xxxvi, citing memorandum of December 16, 1929 (U.S. State Department).

136 Ibid., xxxvi.

137 Padmore, "Workers Defend Liberia," 7.

138 Stimson to Hoover, October 24, 1929, DSRRAL, microfilm roll 14.

139 Castle to Trevor Arnett, November 26, 1929, DSRRAL, microfilm roll 14.

140 Stanfield, introductory essay to Charles S. Johnson, Bitter Canaan, xxvi, citing Emmett Scott to Henry Stimson, 15 November 1929, Liberia Record Group (LRG), USNA.

141 Ibid., xxvii, citing Clifton Wharton to Secretary of State, 16 September 1929, LRG, USNA.

142 Ibid., citing Message to State Department official, 31 October 1929. LRG, USNA. One official noted: "The only thing in the file concerning Dr. Scott's connection with negotiations for the 1921 loan was a letter complaining of the lack of attention received by Mr. King and his party while in the United States. It is well known, however, that Charles Lewis, a Boston lawyer, presented a claim for $50 a day for work in connection with loan negotiations. Lewis is a great friend of Scott and they both worked together on the loan negotiations, but I have never heard that Scott presented any claim for services." According to Stanfield, Scott had been connected with Garveyism in the early twenties, a fact that would have made him less than welcome in Monrovia. This is doubtful. As early as 1919, Scott, in the employ of the War Department, had warned Garvey against agitation. See Stein, *World of Marcus Garvey,* 186, citing Minister at Monrovia to Department of State, march 9, 1929, USNA, RG 59, 332.617 F51/272.

143 Stanfield, introductory essay to Charles S. Johnson, *Bitter Canaan,* xxx, citing Assistant Secretary of State to Henry Carter, November 18, 1929, LRG, USNA.

144 Ibid.

145 Ibid., citing J. P. Moffat to William Castle, 18 December 1929.

146 See Yenser, *Who's Who.* Also see Gilpin, "Charles S. Johnson." Charles S. Johnson died in 1956.

147 Matthew William Dunne, "Next Steps: Charles S. Johnson and Southern Liberalism," *Journal of Negro History* 73, 1 (1998): 2.

148 J. P. Moffat Papers, *Diplomatic Journal,* vol. 29, 1930–1931, Bcrnc, February 11, 1930.

149 Stanfield, introductory essay to Charles S. Johnson, *Bitter Canaan,* xxxi, citing Trevor Arnett to William Castle, December 18, 1929.

150 Ibid., citing Jackson Davis to William Castle, December 4, 1929, LRG, USNA.

151 Matheus, a professor of languages, was one of the minor lights of the Harlem Renaissance. He was born in West Virginia in 1887 and was educated at Western Reserve, Columbia, Chicago, and the Sorbonne. In 1925, he won the Opportunity short story contest with a work entitled "Fog." The following year, he won first prize for the personal experience section, second prize in the drama section, and honorable mention in the poetry and short story sections. Matheus's travels took him to Haiti and Cuba, as well as Liberia. Brown, Davis, and Lee, *Negro Caravan,* 65.

152 J. P. Moffat Papers, *Diplomatic Journal,* vol. 29, 1930–31, Berne, February 12, 1930.
153 League of Nations Secretariat, Report, 6.
154 Stanfield, introductory essay to Charles S. Johnson, *Bitter Canaan,* xliii. See Charles S. Johnson, African Diary, Johnson Papers, April 1930, n.p.
155 Charles S. Johnson Papers, African Diary, April 25, 1930, 89.
156 Ibid.
157 League of Nations Secretariat, Report, 6.
158 "Bitter Canaan," 250, Charles S. Johnson Papers, untitled manuscript of *Bitter Canaan.*
159 Schuyler, "Wide 'Slavery,'" 1. In July of 1929, the King administration consisted of King (president), Edwin Barclay (secretary of state), Samuel G. Harmon (treasury secretary), Louis A. Grimes (attorney general), Samuel Ross (postmaster general), James W. Cooper (interior secretary), B.W. Payne (public instruction secretary), and John L. Morris (public works secretary). Supposedly, King, Barclay, Ross, and Morris were widely known to be connected with the labor trade.
160 Monrovia Legation Report on Leading Personalities, December 21, 1930, FO, 371/1456. King was the son of a West Indian immigrant. He was educated in Sierra Leone and had served as attorney general and secretary of state.
161 Akpan, "African Policy," 464; Azikiwe, *Liberia in World Politics,* 212.
162 Akpan, "African Policy," citing Reber to Secretary of State, Monrovia, October 9, 1930, USNA, RG 59, 882.00/856.
163 Grimes to King, July 31, 1930, Grimes Papers, Miscellaneous Pamphlets and Documents, Monrovia, Liberia, part 1, roll 2.
164 Ford to Henderson, December 12, 1930, in Great Britain, *Papers Concerning Affairs in Liberia.*
165 Chalk, "Anatomy of an Investment," 29, citing Carter to Castle, June 7, 1926, USNA, RG 59, 882.6176 F51/177.
166 Clifton Wharton, Chargé d'Affaires, Monrovia, to Secretary of State, July 30, 1929, DSRRAL, microfilm roll 14.
167 Charles S. Johnson, *Bitter Canaan,* 149.
168 Report on Leading Personalities in Liberia, January 30, 1930, PRO, FO 371/14658 042862, J333/333/24.
169 Charles S. Johnson, *Bitter Canaan,* 162.
170 Joseph Johnson to Secretary of State, September 1, 1929, DSRRAL, microfilm roll 6.
171 Division of Western European Affairs memorandum, unsigned, 1929, DSRRAL, microfilm roll 6. For an article critical of slavery in Liberia and praising Faulkner, see Caroline Singer, *New York Times,* January 19, 1930.
172 Mariner, Firestone Jr., and Briggs, Conversation, "Conditions in Liberia," November 5, 1930, USNA, RG 59, 882.00/857.
173 Akpan, "African Policy," 447, citing Henry Stimson Memorandum, May 2, 1930, USNA, RG 59, 882.W/882.
174 Report on Leading Personalities in Liberia, including Additions Re-

ceived in the Foreign Office up to January 30, 1930 (Monrovia, December 21, 1930), PRO FO, 371/14658.

175 Ibid.

176 Mitchell, "America's Liberian Policy," 258, citing USFR, 1930, 3:379.

177 Hunt, "From Cabin to Consulate," n.p.

5 Dollar Diplomacy

1 George Schuyler, "View and Reviews," *Pittsburgh Courier,* August 15, 1931, qtd. in Mckinley, "When Black is Right," 239.

2 Paul Johnson, "Colonialism's Back — and Not a Moment Too Soon," *New York Times Magazine,* April 18, 1993, 22.

3 Ibid.

4 Ibid., 44.

5 Niall Ferguson, "British Imperialism Revisited: The Costs and Benefits of 'Anglobalization'," in "The British Empire and Globalization: A Forum," *Historically Speaking: Journal of the Historical Society* 4, 4 (2003), online journal: www.bu.edu/historic/hs/april03.html.

6 Niall Ferguson, "The Empire Slinks Back," *New York Times Magazine* (April 27, 2003): 54.

7 Memorandum, Castle to Stimson, September 18, 1930, USNA, RG 59, 882.00/846.

8 Memorandum (Henry Carter), "Suggestions as to Policy during My Absence on Leave," September 4, 1929, USNA, RG 59, 882.5048/214.

9 Carter to Stimson, May 3, 1930, USFR, 1930, 3:396 (USNA, RG5 9, 882.51/2093).

10 Stimson to Carter, May 19, 1930, USFR, 1930, 3:396 (USNA, RG 59, 882.51/2093).

11 Carter to Stimson, May 12, 1930, USFR, 1930, 3:396 (USNA, RG 59, 882.51/2093).

12 Moffat to P. Gilbert (Geneva), April 29, 1930, USNA, RG 59, 882.00/820.

13 Castle to Stimson, September 18, 1930, USNA, RG 59, 882.00/820.

14 Chalk, "The United States and the International Struggle," 183, citing Stimson, Memorandum of an interview with Harvey Firestone, December 10, 1930, USFR, 1930.

15 Ibid., citing Ellis O. Briggs, Memorandum, December 27, 1930, USFR, 1930.

16 Ibid., citing Stimson, Memorandum of an interview with President Hoover, January 3, 1931, USFR, 1930. On January 26, Stimson had a meeting with senator William E. Borah of Idaho in which he, among other things, outlined the alternatives for American policy in Liberia.

17 "Regeneration of Liberia," 38.

18 Taylor, "Involvement of Black Americans," 72, citing Alain Locke, "Slavery in the Modern Manner, *Survey,* March 1, 1931.

19 Ibid., 72, citing Rayford W. Logan, "The International Status of the Negro," *Journal of Negro History* 18, 1 (1933): 33–36.

20 Ibid., citing *Crisis,* November 1932.
21 National Baptist Convention (the Revs. W. F. Graham, W. H. Jernagin, J. C. Jackson, Mrs. S. W. Layten, the Rev. J. E. East) to Stimson, March 4, 1931, Phelps-Stokes Fund Archives, box 47, S-4 (4).
22 Lady Kathleen Simon, *Slavery* (London: Hodder and Stoughton, 1929), appendix 1, 269.
23 Lester A. Walton to Adolph Fischer, February 28, 1940, Lester Walton Papers, box 11, file 1.
24 Inikori, "Slaves or Serfs," 67.
25 Ibid., 68.
26 Ibid., 66.
27 Marvin Harris, *Patterns of Race in the Americas* (New York: Walker, 1964).
28 Miers and Roberts, *End of Slavery in Africa,* 5.
29 Lovejoy, *Transformations in Slavery,* 13.
30 Orlando Patterson, *Slavery and Social Death* (Cambridge, Mass.: Harvard, 1982).
31 The case of Marie Louise de Orleans, rejected in her new Spanish home and probably eventually poisoned, comes to mind, as does the case of Catherine of Bragança, the largely ignored queen of England. Both women were the subjects of popular riots, and both failed to produce issue.
32 Suzanne Miers and Richard Roberts, *The End of Slavery in Africa* (Madison: University of Wisconsin Press, 1988), 52, citing Margot Lovett, "From Wives to Slaves: Changing Perceptions of Tonga Women within the Context of Twentieth-Century Male Labor Migration from Nyasaland, 1903–1953," paper presented at the Twentieth Annual Meeting of the African Studies Association, Madison, Wisconsin, 1986.
33 Miers and Kopytoff, *Slavery in Africa,* 7.
34 Rattray, *Ashanti Law and Constitution,* 38.
35 Ibid., 43.
36 Qtd. in ibid., 94.
37 Azikiwe, "In Defense of Liberia," 44.
38 "House of the Free," *New Statesman,* January 17, 1931, 429.
39 Associated Negro Press News Release, January 28, 1931, Claude Barnett Papers, box 188.
40 Azikiwe, *Liberia in World Politics,* 173–74, citing Otto Rothfield, "Liberia and the League of Nations," *Crisis,* April 1931.
41 Gonzalo Sanz Casas, "Politica colonia y organización del trabajo en la isla de Fernando Póo, 1880–1930," (Ph.D. diss., University of Barcelona, 1983), 247, citing "Información instruida para depurar hechos denunciados en la Direccion general de Marruccos y Colonias sobre la reculta de braceros," 1931, Archivo General de la Administración Civil del Estado (henceforth cited as AGACE), carpeta 136.
42 Ibid., 246. Carpeta 22 sobre esclavitud en Liberia, Presidencia del Consejo de Ministros, Direccion General de Marruecos y Colonias, Seccion de Colonias, Madrid, 25 julio 1932, Antonio Canovas al Ministerio de Estado, AGACE, Seccion Africa-G, caja 132.

43 "Coloured Labour in Fernando Po as the Result of a Visit Made August 29–September 1, 1936," enclosure no. 1. to Mr. Yapp's dispatch no. 72 from Monrovia, 15, 1936, PRO, FO 458/127.

44 Greenwall and Wild, *Unknown Liberia*, 1.

45 Chalk, "Anatomy of an Investment," 20, citing C. R. Bussell to W. R. Castle Jr., June 22, 1924, USNA, RG 59, 882.6176 F51/2; De La Rue to Castle, December 21, 1924, USNA, RG 59, 882.6176 F51/79. De La Rue was not on good terms with the American minister to Liberia, an African American, Solomon Porter Hood. Of Hood, De La Rue wrote, "Hood could have gotten filled up with race hatred while he was back in the United States. It took him nearly a year to forget he was black the time he first came out" (qtd. in Chalk, "Anatomy of an Investment," 24).

46 Howard to Mc Bride, September 11, 1934, USNA RG 59, 862.01. FC/9221/2.

47 Buell, "Reconstruction of Liberia," 123.

48 Ibid., citing League of Nations, Memorandum of the Government of Liberia on the Report of the Experts, c/Liberia/13, April 29, 1932.

49 Ibid. The British lent the Liberian government a medical expert, and the Barclay government appointed a Hungarian, Dr. Fusyek, director of sanitation. In 1932, Buell wrote that no authentic cases of yellow fever had been reported since 1929.

50 The bank was eventually replaced by the Bank of Monrovia, Inc., a Firestone subsidiary.

51 Brunot had been governor of the Ivory Coast and was later to serve as governor of the Cameroons. Suret-Canale, *French Colonialism in Tropical Africa*, 315, 456.

52 The 1931 League of Nations investigators also sought a revamping of the Liberian legal system. The chief legal adviser was to become president of the Liberian circuit court. The jury system was to be temporarily discontinued, in the apparent belief that this would strengthen the faith of foreign capital in Liberian justice. The eight administrators were to have wide-ranging powers in cases involving indigenous people. It was proposed that this include the power to exact summary penalties for petty offenses. Liberian juries were to continue to exercise authority in coastal areas. For the cost estimate of the total plan, see Beecher, "State Department and Liberia," 182.

53 Buell, "Reconstruction of Liberia," 130. See League of Nations, minutes of the 10th Meeting of the Liberia Committee, January 29, 1931, c/Liberia/10. Reporting in May of 1932, the Liberia Committee stated that it would not recommend a new loan to a country "already so encumbered" as Liberia (Buell, 131).

54 The Western Province would have included all of present-day Lofa County and part of Bomi Territory. The Central Province would have included what are now Bong and Nimba Counties, and the Eastern Province would have included present-day Grand Gedeh County and parts of Maryland County.

55 It was left unclear whether the powers of the financial adviser were to be

those set down in the 1926 loan contract or whether they were to be more wide-ranging.

56 Chalk, "United States and the International Struggle," 186, citing Ellis Briggs, Memorandum, May 17, 1932, USFR, 1932, 2:726–27; P. Gilbert (Consul at Geneva) to H. L. Stimson, May 26, 1932, USFR, 1932, 2:732.

57 Ibid., citing H. L. Stimson to P. Gilbert, January 13, 1932, USFR, 1932, 2:687–89.

58 J. P. Moffat Papers, Diplomatic Journal, vol. 29, 1930–31, Berne, February 12, 1930.

59 Statement made by Dr. Juris A. Sottile at the 62nd session of the Council of the League of Nations, Public meeting, January 22, 1931, Louis B. Grimes Papers, Liberia/League of Nations Papers, part 2, roll 1.

60 Padmore, *Memoirs of a Liberian Ambassador,* 37.

61 Qtd. in Stanfield's introduction to Johnson, *Bitter Canaan,* xxi.

62 Simon, *Slavery,* 90, citing League of Nations Temporary Slavery Commission C. 426. M. 157.1925, 6:25.

63 Qtd. in Richardson, *Liberia's Past and Present,* 154.

64 De Madariaga, *Americans,* 14.

65 Buell, "Reconstruction of Liberia," 129, citing League of Nations, Minutes of the 6th and 10th Sessions, January 1932.

66 Ibid., 130.

67 Buell, citing League of Nations, Memorandum of the Government of Liberia on the Report of the Experts, c/Liberia/13, April 29, 1932.

68 Ibid., citing League of Nations, Letter of August 8, 1931, communicated to the Council, May 19, 1932, c.476.1932. VII, c/Liberia/31.

69 Ibid., citing League of Nations, Memorandum of the Government of Liberia on the Report of the Experts, c/Liberia/13, April 29.

70 Chalk, "The United States and the International Struggle," 187, citing Mitchell to Stimson, May 26, 1932, USFR, 1932, 2:732.

71 Ibid., 188, citing Stimson to Mitchell, June 8, 1932, USFR, 1932, 2:738–40.

72 Ibid.

73 Ibid.

74 Ibid. Stimson instructed Mitchell to keep these directives secret. The British consulate in Monrovia got wind of Stimson's move, although it thought that Liberia was being urged to completely abandon the League of Nations and opt for American assistance. According to an informant, Barclay had been willing to follow such a course if Liberian sovereignty remained protected. The consulate was told that the cabinet had refused the idea of an American adviser. C. Graham to Secretary of State for Foreign Affairs, July 20, 1932 with secret enclosure, FO, Consulate-General, Monrovia, microfilm roll 1. For a chronology of the American attempts to get an American chief adviser, see Confidential Memorandum on Mitchell-Barclay negotiation, June 1932, Liberian National Archives.

75 Chalk, "The United States and the International Struggle," 189, citing Mitchell to Stimson, June 24, 1932, USFR, 1932, 2:742–43.

76 Ibid., 190, citing Mitchell to Stimson, June 24, 1932, USFR, 1932, 2:742–

43; and Castle, Memorandum to British Embassy, August 27, 1932, *USFR*, 1932, 11, 748–49.

77 Diary of J. P. Moffat, September 23, 1932; diary of J. P. Moffat, September 21, 1932, J. P. Moffat Papers, 1932, vol. 2.

78 Chalk, "The United States and the International Struggle," 190. See Ellis Briggs to Osborne (British chargé in Washington), August 31, 1932, *USFR*, 1932, 2:750–51; H. Wilson (American Minister in Switzerland) to Stimson, September 22, 1932, *USFR*, 1932, 2:756–57; Stimson to Gilbert, September 21, 1932, *USFR*, 1932, 2:754.

79 Chalk, "The United States and the International Struggle," 190, citing diary of J. P. Moffat, September 26 and 28, 1932.

80 Chalk, "The United States and the International Struggle," 191, citing Stimson to Gibson, September 25, 1932, *USFR*, 1932, 2:750–59. The following day it was reported that a Firestone representative "was quite delighted" with a message from the secretary to the League (Diary of J. P. Moffat, September 26, 1932). The department feared that its instructions to the American member of the Liberia Committee would have the opposite effect when they became known. The American member was told to accept a formula whereby if the chief adviser were accused by the Liberians of countervailing the constitution, the matter would be referred to the Council of the League of Nations. While the issue was pending, Liberia would continue to carry out the orders of the chief adviser.

81 Qtd. in Buell, "Reconstruction of Liberia," 129. Buell was dubious about this figure.

82 "Report of the Experts Designated by the Committee of the Council of the League of Nations Appointed to Study the Problem Raised by the Liberian Government's Request for Assistance," in Great Britain, *Papers Concerning Affairs in Liberia,* annex to appendix 1, 64.

83 See Great Britain, *Papers Concerning Affairs in Liberia,* annex to appendix 1, 64, citing League of Nations, Draft Plan of Assistance, c/Liberia/16, May 14, 1932.

84 Diary of Charles S. Johnson, March 27, 1930, Charles S. Johnson Papers.

85 Suret-Canale, *French Colonialism in Tropical Africa,* 315.

86 Buell, "Reconstruction of Liberia," 130, citing League of Nations, Minutes of the 8th Meeting, Committee of the Council, January 25, 1932, c/Liberia/6. Ligthart had already expressed these sentiments to British legations in Monrovia (Constantine Graham to Foreign Office, July 8, 1931, FO, Consulate-General, Monrovia, microfilm roll 1).

87 "Report of the Experts Designated by the Committee of the Council of the League," Great Britain, *Papers Concerning Affairs in Liberia,* annex to appendix 1, 64.

88 Buell, "Reconstruction of Liberia," 131, citing League of Nations, *Official Journal,* March 1932.

89 Ibid., 134, citing League of Nations, *Official Journal,* March 1932.

90 Ibid., citing League of Nations, Minutes of the 11th Meeting, January 30, 1932.

91 Diary of J. P. Moffat, August 20, 1932, Moffat Papers. A month later,

the Harvey Firestones, Sr. and Jr., visited the State Department and announced that they wanted the nationality of the chief adviser to be discussed at Geneva. Stimson was forced to choose between antagonizing either "the Liberal and League elements" or Firestone. He chose not to antagonize Firestone, and the American representative to the Liberia Committee was instructed to bring up the matter (diary of J. P. Moffat, September 20, 1932).

92 The company sent a representative (Walter Howe) to Washington, who asked that the department delay publicity on the plan until he had had a chance to change Firestone's refusal to negotiate (ibid., October 6, 1932). The next day, Moffat complained that "the Firestones having been given an inch i.e., concessions in the League of Nations plan are now demanding an ell and want us to pull more chestnuts out of the fire for them" (ibid., October 7, 1932).

93 Chalk, "The United States and the International Struggle," 193, citing diary of J. P. Moffat, October 8, 1932.

94 Ibid., citing Castle to Firestone, October 10, 1932, USFR, 1932, 2:771–73.

95 Ibid., 194. At the end of the meeting, Firestone sent a telegram to Geneva saying he was willing to cooperate. See also Stimson to Gilbert, October 11, 1932, USFR, 1932, 2:773.

96 Ibid., 195, citing Stimson to Gilbert, October 13, 1932, USFR, 1932, 2:774–75; Finance Corporation of America to Castle, October 26, 1932, USFR, 1932, 2:776.

97 The repudiation was seen as solidifying the relations between the State Department and Firestone. "It offers the company," wrote Moffat, "the most admirable means of escape from negotiating further with the League Committee at Geneva." Chalk, "The United States and the International Struggle," 197, citing diary of J. P. Moffat, December 19, 1932.

98 Padmore, *Memoirs of a Liberian Ambassador,* 42.

99 Chalk, "The United States and the International Struggle," 197, citing diary of J. P. Moffat, December 28, 1932.

100 White to William Steen, March 20, 1931, NAACP Papers, G-220. White thanked Steen, a State Department employee, for "the valuable report on slavery in Liberia." Steen had previously supplied the NAACP with information on Haiti.

101 Ibid. See White to Dantes Bellegrade, March 24, 1932, Records of the National Association for the Advancement of Colored People, Library of Congress, Washington, D.C. G-220.

102 Stanfield, introductory essay to Charles S. Johnson, *Bitter Canaan,* xlv, citing Johnson to Du Bois, March 10, 1930, LRG, USNA.

103 Johnson to White, September 30, 1932, NAACP Papers, G-220.

104 Frazier to White, October 1, 1932, NAACP Papers, G-220.

105 Castle to White, October 17, 1932, NAACP Papers, G-220. On October 11, White had written to Johnson, and they agreed that at least one black should sit on the Advisory Committee of Experts. White passed this information on to Stimson. White to Johnson, October 11, 1932, NAACP Papers, G-220.

106 White to Grimes, October 11, 1932, NAACP Papers, G-220.

107 White to Grimes, October 11, 1932, NAACP Papers, G-220.

108 White to Grimes, June 8, 1933, NAACP Papers, G-221.

109 For example, in 1919, Mary Church Terrell, longtime president of National Association of Colored Women, addressed an international meeting in Zurich as a delegate from the WILPF. Terrell's sporadic participation was supplemented by the others. In 1924, James Weldon Johnson spoke to a WILPF summer school in Chicago. He presented a program with the title "The Race Problem and Peace." In 1926, the WILPF's national board sought ways to attract black organizations and individuals to its summer programs. By 1928, there existed an interracial committee under the direction of Addie Hunton, an African American activist and the wife of the African American leftist academic Alphaeus Hutton. The WILPF member Mildred Scott Olmsted was especially active in outreach to black churches, Boy Scout troops, schools, and other organizations. At the group's annual meeting in April of 1929, the director of policy presented a statement condemning racial and ethnic prejudice. The WILPF's involvement with Liberia followed several other international forays. For instance, the organization had sent a delegation to examine U.S. imperialism in Haiti in 1926. The trip produced a book, *Occupied Haiti,* two chapters of which were written by the two members of the organization's Haitian committee. From 1930 to 1933, the WILPF also acted in a watchdog capacity vis-à-vis a plan by an American company to build a dam in Ethiopia with what some alleged was slave labor.

110 Qtd. in Foster, *Women and the Warriors,* 173 n. 39.

111 Detzer, *Appointment on the Hill,* 124. Detzer herself, while in Geneva, spoke with Cecil on the question of the chief adviser's nationality.

112 Ross, "Black Americans and Haiti," 107.

113 Ibid., 108, L. A. Grimes to Anna M. Graves, February 5, 1932; Anna Melissa Graves Papers, 1919–1953, DG015, Swarthmore College Peace Collection, Swarthmore, Pennsylvania, drawer 4, box 17.

114 Ibid., Grimes to Anna M. Graves, July 15, 1932, Graves Papers, drawer 4, box 17.

115 Ibid.; Maud Miles to White, September 26, 1932, NAACP Papers, G-220. On September 27, the NAACP sent a telegram of protest to Stimson. In early 1933, Graves sent Walter White a long memorandum on the background of the Liberian scandal. White sent the document to Buell for comment. It was the political scientist's view that the memorandum was in large part accurate but too specific in its allegations to be substantiated.

116 Ross, "Black Americans and Haiti," 115, citing *Herald Tribune* (New York), September 28, 1932.

117 Ibid., 118, citing Walter White to Edward Barclay, September 27, 1932, NAACP Papers, G-220.

118 Ibid., 123, citing Grimes to Walter White, October 7, 1932, NAACP Papers, G-220.

119 Ibid., citing Statement of Dr. W. E. B. Du Bois in *To Colored Voters—*

Franklin D. Roosevelt: A Leader in Progressive Democracy, pamphlet (New York: The National Colored Citizens Roosevelt Committee, 1932), 14.

120   Taylor, "Involvement of Black Americans," 77; Memorandum by Ellis O. Briggs of a Conversation between Briggs, East, and Jernagin, March 14, 1932, USNA, RG 59, 882.01 FC/226.

121   Memorandum by Briggs of a Conversation with Jernagin, September 2, 1932, USNA, RG 59, 882.01 FC/348. The letter delivered by Jernagin and his colleagues came from the executive secretaries of the Lott Carey Baptist Mission Society and the Foreign Mission Boards of the National Baptist Convention, the A.M.E. Church, and the A.M.E. Zion Church.

122   Stimson to E. H. Coit, September 9, 1932, Phelps-Stokes Fund Archives, box 47, S-4 to S-8. Coit had written to Stimson on September 1, 1932.

123   The committee included the following organizations: the American Colonization Society (Washington, D.C.), the New York State Colonization Society, the Boston Trustees of Donations, the Phelps-Stokes Fund, the Trustees of the Booker T. Washington Agricultural and Industrial Institute, the National Council of the Protestant Episcopal Church, the Board of Foreign Missions of the Methodist Episcopal Church, the Board of Foreign Missions of the United Lutheran Church in America, and the Foreign Mission Board of the National Baptist Convention.

124   The white educationalist dominated "Negro education" in the period 1913–46 and inherited Booker T. Washington's position of patronage in matters of black education. He toured Africa in the early 1920s with two Phelps-Stokes commissions and emerged as an expert on colonial education. Jones had first visited Liberia in 1920 and had received a negative impression of the place. In 1928, he delivered a rebuttal to Raymond Buell's Williamstown address attacking Firestone.

125   Thomas Jesse Jones, "Tentative Views on Liberian Affairs," August 31, 1931, Phelps-Stokes Archives, box 47, S-4(4).

126   Diary of J. P. Moffat, August 19, 1932.

127   Chalk, "The United States and the International Struggle," 197, citing diary of J. P. Moffat, December 28, 1932.

128   Chalk, "The United States and the International Struggle," 198, citing diary of Henry L. Stimson, January 17 and 21, 1933. The Stimson Diary is available in the Special Collections of Sterling Library, Yale University, New Haven, Connecticut.

129   William Appleman Williams, *The Tragedy of American Diplomacy* (New York: Delta, 1972), 131–32.

130   Chalk, "The United States and the International Struggle," 198.

131   Ibid. Stimson did, however, agree to support Firestone's determination not to alter his agreements with Liberia until the moratorium was lifted. Memorandum, "The Action of the League of Nations with Regards to Liberia," December 24, 1932, FO, 371/17039. The memorandum was drawn up to help the secretary of state for foreign affairs get an overview of the Liberian situation.

132   Stimson to Lord Robert Cecil, January 23, 1922, PRO, FO 371/17039.

133   M. Peterson to E. H. Carr (Geneva), January 24, 1933, FO, 371/17039.

134 Chalk, "The United States and the International Struggle," 201, citing Cecil to Stimson, January 25, 1933, USFR, 1933, 2:884–85.

135 Ibid., citing J. P. Moffat, Memorandum, January 26, 1933, USFR, 1933, 2:886; diary of J. P. Moffat, January 26, 1933.

136 Stimson was greatly disappointed and viewed the cable as a "discouraging example of League politics and impotency." Chalk, "The United States and the International Struggle," 201, citing Stimson to Gilbert, USFR, 1933, 2:887–88; diary of Henry L. Stimson, February 1, 1933, Special Collections of Sterling Library, Yale University, New Haven, Connecticut.

137 Chalk, "The United States and the International Struggle," 199.

138 Chalk, "The United States and the International Struggle," 199, citing diary of J. P. Moffat, January 21, 22, and 23, 1933.

139 Diary of J. P. Moffat, January 26, 1933, Houghton Library, Harvard University, MS Am 1407, Series 2, Diplomatic journals and other papers, vols, 30–36, Washington, 1931–34.

140 Henry Litchfield West, *Liberian Crisis,* 33. He also felt that Liberia would "either go along in its own way until it finally disintegrates upon the sands of national bankruptcy or else some nation will lay a heavy hand upon it."

141 Diary of J. P. Moffat, January 2, 1933.

142 Foreign Office Minute by Wallinger on A. Fletcher (British Library of Information, New York) to R. Leeper (Foreign Office), May 19, 1933, enclosing pamphlet by Henry West, *The Liberian Crisis,* FO, 371/17041. It was added that the British chargé d'affaires in Monrovia described West "as a 'voluble and self-important old gentleman,' but thought Mr. Jesse Jones less objectionable."

143 Briggs to Moffat, February 28, 1933, Moffat Papers, vol. 2, 1933, A–F personal file.

144 Memorandum on Liberian Situation, February 10, 1933?, Phelps-Stokes Archives, box 47 (S4–3).

145 Diary of J. P. Moffat, March 3, 1933.

146 Diary of J. P. Moffat, February 2, 1933.

147 Chalk, "The United States and the International Struggle," 202, citing diary of Henry L. Stimson, February 3, 1933.

148 Chalk, "The United States and the International Struggle," 203, citing Gilbert to H. L. Stimson, February 7, 1933, in *United States Foreign Relations* 2: 899–900; Moffat Diary, February 7, 1933.

149 Chalk, "The United States and the International Struggle," 204, citing Moffat Diary, February 7, 1933; Stimson Diary, February 7, 1933.

150 Diary of J. P. Moffat, February 7, 1933.

151 This was a function somewhat misunderstood by Harvey Firestone Jr., who came to Washington and expressed the wish that the general negotiate a completely new contract between his finance corporation and the Liberian government. Diary of J. P. Moffat, April 6, 1933.

152 Sir John Simon to Routh, March 18, 1933, FO, 371/17040.

153 Foreign Office Minute by Wallinger, May 31, 1933, on Report by Routh

to Foreign Office, May 12, 1933, enclosing Lyle's proposals to Liberia, May 3, 1933, FO, 371/17041.

6 A New Deal for Liberia

1 Tony Smith, *America's Mission: The United States and the Worldwide Struggle for Democracy in the Twentieth Century* (Princeton, N.J.: Princeton University Press, 1994), citing Julius W. Pratt, *Cordel Hull, 1933–1944* (New York: Cooper Square, 1964), 162.

2 Ibid., citing Samuel I. Rosenman, ed., *The Public Papers and Addresses of Franklin D. Roosevelt* (New York: Random House, 1938–50), 2:130, 544ff.

3 Buell, "New Deal and Liberia," 19.

4 The British information agency in New York took note of Buell's article and sent London a news comment which took cognizance of Liberia's wider significance. Buell had raised the question of "whether the State Department is at present equipped to carry out in our foreign policy the political philosophy which dominates the Roosevelt administration elsewhere. In its first real test the State Department is found tenaciously supporting the Firestone concession, which violates every principle of the New Deal." British Library of Information New York to News Department British Foreign Office, August 18, 1933, enclosing clipping, FO, 371/17043.

5 Hallgren, "Liberia in Shackles," 185.

6 Buell, Liberia, 39.

7 C. von Renthe-Fink to Foreign Office, June 28, 1933, transmitting Report of the Liberian Committee to the Council adopted on June 27, 1933, FO, 371/17041.

8 In June of 1933, Winship had written the department and asked that he be allowed to state that the United States would accept a satisfactory neutral. The department quashed the suggestion in an effort "to abstain from breaking with the Firestones." Diary of J. P. Moffat, June 19, 1933.

9 The secretary general would write to the American government and ask whether there were any Americans suitable for the post of chief adviser. After the nomination of one or two, the secretary-general could pick the most suitable candidate. United Kingdom Delegation (Geneva) to Foreign Office, June 2, 1933, enclosing in no. 1 note by Cecil on conversation with Winship, FO, 371/1704.

10 Diary of J. P. Moffat, June 23, 1933.

11 Cecil to von Renthe-Fink, June 30, 1933, FO, 371/17042.

12 Telegram from Routh (Monrovia) to Foreign Office, June 6, 1933, FO, 371/17041.

13 Foreign Office Memorandum (M. Peterson), July 1, 1933, FO, 371/17042.

14 Ibid. See also Osborne (Washington) to Foreign Office, August 19, 1933, FO, 371/1703.

15 Raymond Buell to Cecil, August 4, 1933; Cecil to Buell, August 14, 1933, Papers of Viscount Cecil, ADD 51168. Buell sent Cecil the proofs of an article he had written to be published in the *New Republic.* Ibid., September 9, 1933.

16 Diary of J. P. Moffat, September 23 and 24, 1933.

17 Diary of J. P. Moffat, January 23, 1933. Graves claimed that Harvey Firestone Jr.'s conversion to Buchmanism (Moral Rearmament) was a publicity stunt. She also supported Liberia's financial moratorium.

18 Ross, "Black Americans and Haiti, Liberia," 131, citing Anna Graves to Walter White or William Pickens, February 3, 1933; memo from "Dean" William Pickens, February 25, 1933, NAACP Papers, G-220.

19 Graves (Geneva) to White, July 19, 1933, NAACP Papers, G-221.

20 Ross, "Black Americans and Haiti, Liberia," 136, citing L. A. Grimes to Anna Graves, August 5, 1933, Graves Papers, drawer 4, box 17.

21 Ibid, 137, citing cable of Anna Graves, as quoted in telegram of Dorothy Detzer to Walter White, June 6, 1933, NAACP Papers, G-220.

22 Ibid., 138, citing cables of Walter White to Lord Cecil and General Winship, as quoted in letter of Walter White to W. E. B. Du Bois, June 7, 1933, NAACP Papers, G-220.

23 Ibid., citing telegram of Walter White to President Franklin D. Roosevelt, June 7, 1933, NAACP Papers, G-220.

24 Ibid., 139; see *New York World-Telegram,* June 14, 1933.

25 Du Bois, "Liberia, the League, and the United States," 695.

26 Sidney De La Rue to W. E. B. Du Bois, July 7, 1933, Du Bois Papers, microfilm reel 39.

27 Phillips to Roosevelt, August 16, 1933, USNA, RG 59, 882.01 FC/620a.

28 Detzer to White, June 8, 1933, NAACP Papers, G-220.

29 Ross, "Black Americans, Haiti, Liberia," 143, citing Memorandum of Conversation between Gen. Winship and Miss Dorothy Detzer, July 17, 1933, USNA, RG 59, 882.01,

30 Ross, "Black Americans and Haiti, Liberia," 143, citing Dorothy Detzer to Anna Graves, July 18, 1933, NAACP Papers, G-221.

31 Other members of the group were Addle W. Dickerson, president of the International Council of Women of Darker Races; Addle W. Hunton, chairman of the board, Interracial Commission, WILPF; Archie Pinket, secretary of the Washington branch of the NAACP; Mrs. Daniel Partridge Jr., secretary of the Washington branch WILPF; Nannie Burroughs of the National Association of Colored Women; and Charles H. Houston of the National Bar Association. These were unable to attend. White to Wilkins, August 2, 1933, NAACP Papers, G-221. Those who declined to attend were Claude Barnett of the Associated Negro Press, Carl Murphy of the *Baltimore Afro-American,* Dr. Robert Moton of Tuskegee, and John Hope.

32 Mordecai Johnson to White, July 27, 1933, NAACP Papers, G-221. There was a difference of opinion on some issues. Some members of the delegation wanted an American chief adviser, while others wanted a European (preferably a Scandinavian).

33 Qtd. in Forderhase, "Plans That Failed," 140.

34 Ibid., citing copy of speech delivered by Du Bois, July 31, 1933, USNA, RG, 882.01 FC/61 1/2.
35 Statement of Du Bois at State Department, July 31, 1933, NAACP Papers, G-221.
36 Press Release, August 4, 1933, NAACP Papers, G-221.
37 Logan, "Liberia's Dilemma," 360.
38 State Department Press Release, July 31, 1933, NAACP Papers, G-221.
39 Logan, "Liberia's Dilemma," 361.
40 Detzer to White, August 3, 1933, NAACP Papers, G-221. White was out of town, so the letter was given to Du Bois.
41 Diary of J. P. Moffat, August 15, 1933.
42 Ross, "Black Americans and Haiti, Liberia," 147, citing Raymond L. Buell to L. A. Grimes, July 31, 1933, NAACP Papers.
43 White to Buell, September 8, 1933, NAACP Papers, G-221.
44 Memorandum of conversation between William Phillips (Undersecretary of State) and Delegation Opposing United States Policy in Liberia, July 31, 1933, USNA, RG 59, 882.01 FC/612 1/2.
45 Phillips to Franklin Roosevelt, August 16, 1933, USNA, RG 59, 882.01 FC/620a.
46 Taylor, "Involvement of Black Americans," 76. See Phillips to Winship, August 2, 1933, USNA, RG 59, 882.01 FC/612A; Winship to Secretary of State, August 5, 1933, USNA, RG 59, 882.01 FC/614; Winship to Secretary of State, August 8, 1933, USNA, RG 59882.01 FC/617; Secretary of State Hull to Winship, August 7, 1933, USNA, RG 59, 882.01 FC/614.
47 Chalk, "The United States and the International Struggle," 206.
48 Diary of J. P. Moffat, September 8, 1933, Moffat Papers. He added that "They were particularly mean to Bill Phillips." Phillips to Franklin Roosevelt, August 16, 933 USNA, RG 59, 882.01 FC/620a.
49 Diary of J. P. Moffat, September 23 and 24, 1933.
50 Ibid., September 9, 1933.
51 Routh to Foreign Office, September 18, 1933, FO, 371/17043.
52 Ibid.
53 League of Nations, Committee of the Council appointed to examine the problem raised by the Liberian government's request for assistance, minutes of the thirty-first meeting, Geneva, October 9, 1933, c/Liberia/31 (1), 12, FO, 371/17044.
54 Diary of J. P. Moffat, October 16, 1933. Moffat wrote, "We had at once to get off a telegram ruling this out as our good faith might be seriously challenged. We got it off just in time to reach General Winship who is leaving Europe tomorrow morning and authorized him to bring the contents of the incoming and outgoing telegrams to Cecil's attention."
55 Ibid., October 30, 1933.
56 Ibid., November 1, 1933.
57 Buell, *Liberia*, 40, citing U.S. Department of State, *Liberia: Documents Relating to the Plan of Assistance Proposed by the League of Nations* (1933).
58 Diary of J. P. Moffat, January 17, 1934.
59 Ibid., February 24, 1934.

60   Ibid., April 26, 1934.

61   Ibid., May 25, 1934. In April, the French ordered a gunboat to Monrovia to protest a diplomatic incident. See Diary of J. P. Moffat, April 20, 1934.

62   MacVeagh to Secretary of State, February 5, 1934, USNA, RG 59, 882.01 FC/791. A year before, Moffat had reported receiving "a memorandum from the British Embassy which Osborne, who delivered it, termed 'rather nasty.'" This was accompanied by "the gratuitous oral statement that according to their agents in Monrovia, the Americans in Liberia were deliberately endeavoring to produce a condition which would force American intervention." Diary of J. P. Moffat, February 11 and 12, 1933. See also ibid., May 8, 1934.

63   Diary of J. P. Moffat, February 14, 1934.

64   Ibid., May 8, 1934.

65   Walton to Barnett, May 10, 1934, Claude Barnett Papers, Lester Walton file, box 187, 1925–1937.

66   D. C. Howard, "A Warning," Monrovia, May 5, 1934, Albert Porte Papers, microfilm, Northwestern University Library, Evanston, Ill., roll 1, Personal Papers and Documents.

67   Diary of J. P. Moffat, May 9, 1934.

68   Chalk, "United States and the International Struggle," 209, citing diary of J. P. Moffat, May 8, 9, 18, 21, 25, and June 14, 1934; Gilbert to Hull, USFR, 1934, 2:797–98. See also diary of J. P. Moffat, July 20, 1932.

69   Simpson, *Memoirs,* 187. Simpson was born in Royesville in 1896 and had started his political career as a customs official. Later, he became acting postmaster general and speaker of the Liberian House of Representatives. He served as secretary-general of the True Whig Party from 1930 to 1944. He took over the office of secretary of state from Grimes in late 1933 and visited Geneva in September of 1934. In 1944, Simpson became vice president. Juah Nimley, the leader of the Kru people of Sasstown, described Simpson as "one of the principal men used by Ross to decoy men to be sent to Fernando Po by misrepresenting to them their real destination. In some cases the men were really kidnapped . . . he is therefore one of the men who should have been prosecuted for slave dealing according to the Christy-Johnson commission's recommendation." Juah Nimley Sopon Nabwe, secretary to Cecil, August 6, 1934, Papers of Viscount Cecil, ADD 51101.

70   Diary of J. P. Moffat, May 10, 1934. Moffat said, "In order to block up both of those holes, we prepared a statement for the Secretary to hand to Lyon."

71   Great Britain, *Parliamentary Debates* (Lords) vol. 91 (1934), 753.

72   Lugard to Stanhope, April 16, 1934, FO, 371/18041.

73   Great Britain, *Parliamentary Debates* (Lords) vol. 91 (1934), 747–48.

74   Consul Patterson (Geneva) to Foreign Office, January 17, 1934, Minute by Peterson, January 19, 1934, FO, 371/18040.

75   See Foreign Office Minute (Sir John Simon), March 15, 1934, FO, 371/18040; Foreign Office Minute, Liberian situation, March 21, 1934, FO, 371/18040.

76 R. C. Stevenson (Geneva) to Peterson, April 11, 1934, FO, 371/18040.

77 United Kingdom Delegation to the League of Nations to the Foreign Office, May 19, 1934, FO, 371/18040.

78 Detzer, *Appointment on the Hill,* 136. A British foreign office telegram to the Monrovia consulate on August 23 said, "You make it clear that provided this opportunity is taken, the League plan accepted and an amnesty thereafter granted to all political prisoners now detained by the Liberian Government, His Majesty's Government will be prepared to recognize and enter into full diplomatic relations with the existing Liberian Administration." The United States adopted a similar course. Sir John Simon to Routh (Monrovia), August 23, 1933, in Great Britain, *Papers Concerning Affairs in Liberia,* 11.

79 Ibid., 135. Morris Ernst was the man who supposedly suggested Detzer contact Frankfurter.

80 Memorandum for the Secretary of State, September 26, 1933, USNA, RG 59, 882.01 FC/709.

81 Taylor, "Involvement of Black Americans," 76. See memorandum of conversation with Harvey Firestone Jr., September 21, 1933, USNA, RG 59, 882.01 FC/663. White of the NAACP suspected such a shift and asked a State Department messenger to attempt to obtain a copy of the document on the subject. White to Steen, October 2, 1933, NAACP Papers, G-221.

82 Ross, "Black Americans and Haiti, Liberia," 163, citing Dorothy Detzer to the President and the Secretary of State, October 10, 1933, USNA, RG 59, 882.01, Foreign Control/677.

83 Ibid., 156, citing the *Crisis,* November 1933, 262.

84 Ibid.,155, citing Walter White to Dorothy Detzer, September 30, 1933, NAACP Papers, G-221.

85 Ibid., 165, citing Cordell Hull to Dorothy Detzer, November 4, 1933, NAACP Papers, G-221.

86 Ibid.,141, citing L. A. Grimes to Anna Graves, July 16, 1933, Anna Melissa Graves Papers, 1919–1953, DG 015, Swarthmore College Peace Collection, Swarthmore, Pennsylvania, drawer 4, box 17.

87 Ibid., 191, citing Raymond L. Buell to Dorothy Detzer, June 20, 1934, Detzer Papers, 1913–1981, DG 086, box 2, Swarthmore College Peace Collection, Swarthmore, Pennsylvania.

88 Ibid., 192, citing Dorothy Detzer to W. E. B. Du Bois, June 27, 1934, Detzer Papers, box 2.

89 Ross, "Black Americans and Haiti, Liberia," 192, citing L. A. Grimes to Dorothy Detzer, August 6, 1934, WILPF Papers, box 17.

90 Young, *Liberia Rediscovered.*

91 W. E. B. Du Bois to L. A. Grimes, November 19, 1934; L. A. Grimes to W. E. B. Du Bois, December 12, 1934, in Du Bois, *Correspondence,* 17–18.

92 W. E. B. Du Bois to L. A. Grimes, December 4, 1934, in ibid., 29.

93 Ross, "Black Americans and Haiti and Liberia," 186, citing Emily G. Balch to Dorothy Detzer, May 25, 1934, Dorothy Detzer Papers, 1913–1981, DG 086, box 2, Swarthmore College Peace Collection, Swarthmore, Pennsylvania.

94 Ibid., citing Frederick P. Hibbard, June 29, 1934, USNA, RG 59, 882.01, Foreign Control/841-2/3.

95 Anna Graves to W. E. B. Du Bois, July 17, 1934, Du Bois Papers, microfilm reel 42 1934.

96 Ibid.

97 Ross, "Black Americans and Haiti, Liberia," 141, citing Pennsylvania State Negro Council to NAACP, June 6, 1933, NAACP Papers, G-220.

98 Ross, "Black Americans and Haiti, Liberia," 174, citing Universal Ethiopian Students Association to W. G. Phillips, January 3, 1934, USNA, RG 59, 882.01, Foreign Control/761.

99 Ross, "Black Americans and Haiti, Liberia." Grimes to White, July 18, 1933, NAACP Papers, G-221.

100 Statement of W. E. B. Du Bois at State Department, July 31, 1933, NAACP Papers, G-221.

101 Jones to Moton, May 6, 1933, Phelps-Stokes Fund Archives, box 47, S-4 (4).

102 Diary of J. P. Moffat, March 12, 1933. In July, certain white and black missionary interests met with Winship. See Confidential Memorandum on Informal Conference with General Blanton Winship on July 24, 1933 (report dated August 3, 1933), Claude Barnett Papers, Lester Walton file, 1927–1935. The report was written by L. A. Roy, assistant secretary of the Advisory Committee of the Booker T. Washington Institute (Kakata, Liberia). Also present were Ellis Briggs, A. B. Parson, and J. E. East. Moton was the most prominent African American to support Firestone positions on Liberia. He was no stranger to the concerns of the Black Republic. During the First World War, he had urged the American government to grant the five-million-dollar loan to Liberia. In 1920, a white philanthropist, Olivia Phelps Stokes, named Moton coadministrator of a $50,000 trust fund. An outgrowth of this endowment was the Booker Washington Agricultural and Industrial Institute in Kakata, Liberia. Moton's work with the school involved him with the Advisory Committee on Education. Given Tuskegee's long involvement with white philanthropy, Moton's position is not hard to understand.

103 Samuel Cavert to Phillips, May 29, 1933, USNA, RG 59, 882.01 A/101/2.

104 Qtd. in Young, *Liberia Rediscovered*, 92.

105 W. E. B. Du Bois to Sidney Gulick, July 15, 1933, Du Bois Papers, microfilm reel 39.

106 W. E. B. Du Bois to Bishop Francis F. McConnell, August 4, 1933, Du Bois Papers, microfilm reel 39.

107 Detzer to Van Kirk, June 24, 1933, NAACP Papers, G-220.

108 White to Buell, September 8, 1933. Later Detzer spoke to Van Kirk, who appeared sympathetic. Detzer to White, September 16, 1933, NAACP Papers, G-221.

109 George Schuyler, "Missionaries 'Wink' at Conditions in Liberia," *Pittsburgh Courier,* October 17, 1931.

110 W. H. Mathews, "Schuyler Too Severe on the Missionaries in his Liberia Reports." *Pittsburgh Courier,* July 25, 1931.

111 George Schuyler, "Views and Reviews," *Pittsburgh Courier,* August 22, 1931.

112 Work, *Negro Year Book,* 262.

113 Ross, "Black Americans and Haiti, Liberia," 187, citing Roy to Winship, February 28, 1933, Phelps-Stokes Fund Archives.

114 Normandy, "African Americans and U.S. Policy," 222.

115 The scholar and diplomat Elliott Skinner is planning a forthcoming volume on African Americans and U.S. foreign policy from the end of the UNIA's program through the period of the Second World War.

116 Memorandum (Hibbard) on conversation with T. J. Jones, January 31, 1934, USNA, RG 59, 882.01 FC/791 1/2.

117 Ibid. The Phelps-Stokes Fund Archives do contain a "Proposed Statement for Liberian Meeting: Tentative Resolutions." Part of the resolutions read, "We are emphatically convinced that the sovereignty of Liberia can be saved only by the immediate and sincere acceptance of the League Plan of Assistance by the Republic of Liberia." Phelps-Stokes Fund Archives, box 47, S-5.

118 Taylor, "Involvement of Black Americans," 79, citing J. E. East and H. T. Medford to Secretary of State Hull, February 9, 1934, USNA, RG 59, 882.01 FC/905. See also *Baltimore Afro-American,* February 17, 1934, 21, and Kuyper, "Liberia," 99–100. Present at the meeting were the foreign mission boards of the National Baptist Convention of America, the New England Baptist Missionary Convention, the Lott Carey Baptist Convention, African Methodist Episcopal Zion and African Methodist Episcopal churches, the Methodist Episcopal, Lutheran, Protestant Episcopal and Presbyterian churches, and Friends of Liberia. Also present were Lester Walton of the *New York Age,* William Jones, Henry West, Thomas J. Jones, and Harvey Firestone Jr. Judge Frederick C. Fisher, an expert on the legal phases of the Liberian situation, was present, as well as George A. Kuyper, editor of the *Southern Workman* of Hampton Institute.

119 Ibid., citing *Baltimore Afro-American,* February 17, 1934; and East and Medford to Secretary of State Hull, February 9, 1934, USNA, RG 59, 882.01 FC/905.

120 Ibid. See Memorandum of conversation between William Phillips and Bishop Matthews on February 6, 1934, and February 16, 1934, USNA, RG 59, 882.01/33.

121 Moffat to Phillips, February 9, 1934, J. P. Moffat Papers, Personal Correspondence, vol. 7: N-Z, 1934.

122 Diary of J. P. Moffat, February 14, 1934. See also Memorandum on Hull meeting with Organization of Foreign Missions on February 14, 1934, USNA, RG 59, 882.01 FC/904.

123 J. E. East of the National Baptist Convention to the Advisory Committee on Education in Liberia and the Board of Trustees of the Booker T. Washington Institute in Liberia, May 1, 1934, Phelps-Stokes Fund Archives, box 47, S-4 (4).

124 Jones to West, May 8, 1934, Phelps-Stokes Fund Archives, box 47, S-4 (3).

125 Taylor, "Involvement of Black Americans," 80. See Memorandum by

Hibbard of conversation with East and attachments, May 16, 1934, USNA, I7EG59, 882.01 FC/825. See also *Baltimore Afro-American,* May 19, 1934, and Diary of J. P. Moffat, May 16, 1934.

126 Memorandum (Hibbard) of conversation with Foreign Mission secretaries, May 21, 1934, USNA, RG 59, 882.01 FC/825. Present were East; Dr. J. Harry Randolph, treasurer; the Reverend E. L. Harrison; Dr. G. O. Bullock; the Reverend J. L. F. Holloman; and Dr. John R. Hawkins, representing the Reverend L. L. Berry. The memorandum also contains a clipping from the *Baltimore Afro-American* of May 19, 1934: "U.S. Aid Sought If Liberia and League Differ."

127 Young, *Liberia Rediscovered,* 127.

128 Taylor, "Involvement of Black Americans," 88. See R. R. Moton to Franklin Roosevelt, June 23, 1934, USNA, RG 59, 882.01 FC/841 2/3.

129 Ross, "Black Americans and Haiti, Liberia," 188, citing *New York Age,* June 23, 1934. From time to time, covert collaboration between the Liberian government and elements of the African American community was proposed. During the crisis of the 1930s, Emmett Scott of Howard University kept alive the hope that a modus vivendi might be worked out with Firestone. He, particularly, appeared perfect for the role of a go-between. When he visited Liberia in 1908, he had acquired a godson, Emmett Lafayette Harmon, a nephew of secretary of state Grimes. Harmon worked for a while as an employee of the Liberian treasury and, in September 1932, arrived in the United States to attend Howard University. The following year, Scott, already deeply committed to finding a way out of the Liberian impasse, began searching for a way to bring Akron and Monrovia together. Early in September 1933, a relative of Harmon's arrived in New York, supposedly sent by the Liberian secretary of state with the approval of President Barclay. The messenger asked Harmon to find someone who could serve as a contact with Firestone. The Barclay administration wanted to know whether the rubber baron would accept a special envoy from Liberia. Harmon recommended his godfather as the man to sound out the tire company. Scott spoke to Harvey S. Firestone Jr. on September 7, 1933, and sent him a confidential memorandum prepared by Harmon. Harmon wrote Grimes that Scott had opened contacts with the American company and had obtained certain promises from them. The Liberian legislature authorized the sending of a delegation to Akron several months later. Later still, Harmon offered himself as a special delegate to visit Monrovia on behalf of the Advisory Committee on Education in Liberia. The Liberian's stated aim was to encourage a private understanding between the Liberian government, the United States government, and the Firestone Company. Little was achieved; Scott was wary of the efforts of his godson to act as a conduit. Indeed, the university official privately questioned the veracity of his ward "with regard to many of the matters he discusses." Ross, "Black Americans and Haiti, Liberia," 173, citing Emmett Scott to Walter F. Walker, June 27, 1934, Scott, series 2, box 87 (from the Moorland-Spingarn Research Center, Howard University).

130 United Kingdom Delegation to The League of Nations to the Foreign Office, May 19, 1934, FO, 371/18040

131 Buell, *Liberia,* 41. See Great Britain, *Papers Concerning Affairs in Liberia,* 52. See also Sir R. Lindsay (Washington) to Foreign Office, June 12, 1934, FO, 371/18041.

132 Simpson, *Memoirs,* 190.

133 Clipping from *Weekly Mirror* (Monrovia), July 6, 1934, Phelps-Stokes Fund Archives, box 47, S-5.

134 MacVeagh to Secretary of State, July 24, 1934, USNA, RG 52, 882.01 FC/886.

135 A British Foreign Office official saw the visit as "a temporizing move" and failed to see what new information McBride could unearth in light of all the previous missions. Osborne Washington to Foreign Office, July 23, 1934, Foreign Office Minutes by Wallinger, FO, 371/18042.

136 The State Department gave Barclay a free hand, although Firestone Jr. complained that Barclay was making political capital out of McBride's visit and that the Liberians were preparing to annul the plantations contract.

137 Buell, *Liberia,* 41.

138 McBride Memorandum, "Conditions and Recommendations on Liberia," October 3, 1934, USNA, RG 59, 882.01 FC/915.

139 Chalk, "United States and the International Struggle," 211, citing diary of J. P. Moffat, October 5, 1934.

140 MacVeagh Memorandum, "The Liberian Problem," June 11, 1934, USNA, RG 59, 882.01 FC/851.

141 Memorandum to Secretary of State, August 23, 1934, J. P. Moffat Papers, Memoranda, 1934–1935, vol. 23.

142 Buell, *Liberia,* 42.

143 Ibid., 42–43. On December 31, 1934, the floating debt stood at $650,000.

144 Ibid., 43.

145 Franklin Roosevelt, Memorandum for the Secretary of State, May 29, 1935, USNA, RG 59, 882.01/48.

146 Taylor, "Involvement of Black Americans," 88.

147 Rupert Emerson, "Race in Africa," 167.

148 Chalk, "United States and the International Struggle," 213.

149 The practice of sending special emissaries to iron out disputes was more frequently resorted to, and by 1931, the United States was planning to withdraw from Nicaragua and had refused to intervene in the Cuban revolution of 1929–30.

150 Ross, "Black Americans and Haiti, Liberia," 386, citing the *Crisis,* November 1934, 332.

151 Taylor, "Involvement of Black Americans," 84, citing memorandum, Castle to Stimson, September 18, 1930, USNA, RG 59, 882.00/846.

152 Ibid., citing memorandum, Briggs to Marriner, n.d., USNA, RG 59 882.01 FC/908.

153 Beecher, "State Department and Liberia," 120.

154 Nancy J. Weiss, *Farewell to the Party of Lincoln: Black Politics in the Age of FDR* (Princeton, N.J.: Princeton University Press, 1983), 21–26.

155 National Security Council Interdepartmental Group for Africa, Study in Response to Presidential Security Review Memorandum 1 NSC-46: Black Africa and the U.S. Black Movement (photocopy supplied by Wallace Short, Howard University).

156 When the League withdrew its plan of assistance, a Foreign Office official spoke to a member of the American embassy staff in London and inquired whether the argument that the United States would take some responsibility in Liberia because of the American black population was valid. In Conversation between Butterworth (American embassy) and Peterson (Foreign Office), May 4, 1934, FO, 371/18041, Peterson "said that this argument black interest was of a nature which made it perhaps easier and more suitable. I utilize in conversation rather than to put it down on paper." The American said that "as a Southerner he paid little attention to his negro fellow citizens and therefore to any argument based upon their presence in the United States."

157 J. P. Moffat Papers, Diplomatic Journal, vol. 29, 1930–31, Berne.

158 Beecher, "State Department and Liberia," 168.

159 White to Du Bois to Stimson, September 27, 1932, USNA, RG 5C, 882.01 FC/377.

160 Diary of J. P. Moffat, January 21, 1933.

161 Chalk, "United States and the International Struggle," 205, citing diary of J. P. Moffat, February 27, 1933.

162 Diary of J. P. Moffat, April 18, 1934; see also November 11, 1934.

163 Ibid., May 21, 1934.

164 Phillips, Memorandum of conversation with the Liberian Consul-General, May 24, 1934, USNA, RG 59, 882.51 A/225.

165 Du Bois, "Liberia and Rubber," 684.

166 Schuyler to White, June 17, 1933, NAACP Papers, G-220.

167 Taylor, "Involvement of Black Americans," 73–74. See Memorandum, Department of State, October 13, 1932, USNA, RG 59, 882.01 FC 410.

168 White to Frazier, October 4, 1932, NAACP Papers, G-220.

169 Qtd. in Chalk, "United States and the International Struggle," 192.

170 Diary of J. P. Moffat, October 11, 1932.

171 Chalk, "United States and the International Struggle," 192, citing diary of J. P. Moffat, September 26 and 28, 1932.

172 James Farley, Democratic National Chairman.

173 Detzer to Graves, July 18, 1933, NAACP Papers, G-221.

174 Great Britain, *Parliamentary Debates* (Lords), 5th series, vol. 91, 737.

175 Qtd. in Kornegay, "Africa and Presidential Politics," 8. Church was speaking to an April 1976 caucus of black Democrats in Charlotte, North Carolina.

176 Qtd. in Michael Krenn, *Black Diplomacy,* 24–25. Wharton eventually broke out of the circuit at the end of the 1940s and served as ambassador to Norway.

177 McBride memorandum, "Conditions and Recommendations on Liberia," October 3, 1934, USNA, RG 59, 882.01 FC/915.

178 Hibbard to McBride, July 17, 1935, USNA, RG 59, 882.01 FC/951 1/2.

179 Beecher, "State Department and Liberia," 179, 181.

180 Ibid., citing Mitchell to Secretary of State, January 20, 1933, USNA, RG 59, 882.01 FC/467; and January 25, 1933, USNA, RG 59, 882.01 FC/479.

181 Hunt, "From Cabin to Consulate," 213. Hunt was born in Tennessee in 1869 and educated at Groton Academy and Williams College in Massachusetts. In 1898, he became secretary to judge Mifflin W. Gibbs, U.S. consul to Madagascar. Three years later, Hunt himself became consul. In 1904, he married the ardent Pan-Africanist, Ida Gibbs, the daughter of his former patron. In 1906, he was transferred to St. Etienne, France, as U.S. consul. From there, he and his wife played an important role in the preparations for Du Bois's 1919 Pan-African Congress. In 1927, Hunt was transferred to Guadeloupe as U.S. consul, and three years later was moved to the Azores. He was transferred to Liberia as secretary of the legation in 1931 and retired the following year. Hunt died in Washington, D.C., nineteen years later. The William Hunt Papers are deposited at the Mooreland-Spingarn Library of Howard University, Washington, D.C.

182 Diary of J. P. Moffat, August 31, 1932.

183 Ibid., January 31, 1933.

184 Qtd. in Taylor, "Involvement of Black Americans," 74. See memorandum of conversation between Castle and Liberian Consul-General Ernest Lyon, February 11, 1933, USNA, RG 59, 882.01 FC/526.

185 Ibid. See Stimson to Mitchell, February 21, 1933, USNA, RG 59, 882.01, Winship Mission/10. See also Routh (Monrovia) to Foreign Office, January 6, 1933, FO, 371/17044.

186 McCeney Werlirch (Monrovia) to Moffat, September 17, 1933, J. P. Moffat Papers, vol. 4, 1933, 1–2.

187 Hibbard to Secretary of State, cable, June 6, 1935, USNA, RG 59, 882.01 FC/95 I.

188 Walton to Barnett, July 1, 1933, Claude Barnett Papers, Lester Walton file, 1927–1935. In January of 1933, Barnett had written to Barclay, asking him his racial preferences in ministers. Barnett to Barclay, January 19, 1933, Claude Barnett Papers, Associated Negro Press and World News Service, Business Dealings, Liberia. In May, Walton strongly remonstrated with Barnett for mentioning him in connection with the Liberian post. Walton to Barnett, May 20, 1933, Claude Barnett Papers.

189 E. Franklin Frazier, "Potential American Negro Contributions to African Social Development," in *Africa from the Point of View of American Negro Scholars,* ed. John A. Davis (Paris: Présence Africaine, 1959), 268, 277.

190 Walton to Barnett, July 21, 1933, Claude Barnett Papers, Lester Walton file, 1927–1935.

191 Ibid. Barnett and Walton followed the appointments being given to black Democrats with great interest in the first months of the Roosevelt administration. On July 11, 1933, Barnett wrote to Walton, "Well Bob Robert Vann, appointed to the U.S. Attorney General's office seems to have landed. He states the job is the biggest appointment ever given a Negro."

192 Robert L. Vann to Lester Walton, June 10, 1933, Lester Walton Papers, box 8, file 3.

193 Walton to Barnett, January 9, 1934, Barnett Papers, Lester Walton file, 1927–1935.

194 Hibbard to McBride, July 17, 1935, USNA, RG 59, 882.01 FC/951 I/2.

195 Walton to Barnett, January 9, 1934, Claude Barnett Papers, Lester Walton file, 1927–1935.

196 Walton to Drew Pearson, November 17, 1933, USNA, RG 59, 882.00/966? (misfiled).

197 Will Alexander to Phelps-Stokes, November 7, 1929, Phelps-Stokes Fund Archives, box 33, K-6.

198 L. A. Roy to Phelps-Stokes, February 7, 1931, Phelps-Stokes Fund Archives, box 33, K-6.

199 Phelps-Stokes to Alexander, February 9, 1931, Phelps-Stokes Fund Archives, box 33, K-6.

200 Alexander to Phelps-Stokes, February 19, 1931, Phelps-Stokes Fund Archives, box 33, K-26.

201 Walton to Phelps-Stokes, February 14, 1931, Phelps-Stokes Fund Archives, box 33, K-26.

202 Ibid.

203 Ibid. Walton obviously needed money. Jones and a Mr. Peabody attempted to get him work at the *New York Times*.

204 Thomas Jesse Jones to Harvey S. Firestone Jr., January 23, 1933, Lester Walton Papers, box 8, file 3.

205 Walton to Barnett, May 17, 1933, Claude Barnett Papers, Lester Walton file, 1927–1935.

206 Roy to Jones (Monrovia), May 17, 1933, Phelps-Stokes Fund Archives, box 7A, A-22 (lc).

207 Walton to Jones, October 4, 1935, Phelps-Stokes Fund Archives, box 38, K-26.

208 Walton to Barnett, November 26, 1935, Claude Barnett Papers, Lester Walton file, 1927–1935.

209 Beecher, "State Department and Liberia," 221; Walton to Secretary of State, Monrovia, May 28, 1941, USNA, RG 59, 882.00/1151.

210 Krenn, *Black Diplomacy,* 24, citing Lester Walton to W. E. B. Du Bois, September 8, 1945, Du Bois Papers, microfilm reel 58, frames 163–64.

7 Enterprise in Black and White

1 Available at www.summit.asylee.com/about.cfm.

2 Memorandum of conversation with Thomas J. R. Faulkner, August 14, 1930, USNA, RG 59, 882.00/841.

3 Azikiwe, *Liberia in World Politics,* 184.

4 Memorandum of conversation with Thomas J. R. Faulkner, August 14, 1930, USNA, RG 59, 882.00/841.

5   C. Abayomi Cassell Papers, roll 9; see Thomas J. R. Faulkner, *The Voice of the People* (Monrovia) 1, 2 (October, 1931).

6   Obatala, "Liberia," 17.

7   Liebenow, *Liberia,* 92.

8   Qtd. in Lyon to Secretary of State (Monrovia), June 20, 1933, Liberian National Archives.

9   For a discussion of the so-called Syrian Problem and capital from the United States, see the article by "Zephyrus" in the *Liberian Crisis* special issue of July 1935, entitled, "If Not an Agreement with America, Why Not a Liberian-American Agreement?" Liberian National Archives.

10 Ian Duffield, "Pan-Africanism," 611.

11 William Phillips to Legation (Monrovia), December 29, 1933, USNA, RG 59, 882.01 FC/753. The State Department said it could not take any official cognizance of such a commission.

12 During his sojourn in 1924, Du Bois had secretly planned a company venture with resident black diplomat Solomon Hood. Lillie Mae Hubbard, the consular clerk, communicated with Du Bois on his return home about gold and coffee consignments through "The Bopopoti," the name selected for the venture. After his departure for the United States, she wrote the professor that she had "not forgotten the "Bopopoti" Corporation and I hope President King's reply is favorable one to your letter." That aim was to "help introduce American trade." Du Bois Papers, microfilm reel 13, frame 814.

13 William Edgenton, "As to Liberian Slavery," *Atlantean,* November 1931, 11, Barnett Papers, Firestone Rubber Company file, 1925–1953. Edgenton had been in Liberia in 1918 and, in all, had spent five years there. Later he lived in Kansas City, Missouri.

14 J. Edmund Jones (Acting Secretary of State) to Barclay, January 6, 1934, enclosing Proclamation of Dr. S. P. Radway of the Afro-West India Round Trip Association, Liberian National Archives.

15 Richard N. Bedell to Barclay, January 2, 1934, Liberian National Archives.

16 J. T. Betts to Edwin Barclay, July 20, 1934, Liberian National Archives.

17 Werlich (Monrovia) to Hull, November 23, 1933, enclosing William Jones to Gabriel L. Dennis, Secretary of the Treasury, "A Memorandum of Co-Operation between Liberia and America," USNA, RG 59, 882.01.

18 Werlich (Monrovia) to Hull, November 23, 1933, enclosing William Jones to Gabriel L. Dennis, Secretary of the Treasury, "A Memorandum of Co-Operation between Liberia and America," USNA, RG 59, 882.01.

19 Ibid.

20 On leaving Liberia, Jones was optimistic. Noting the relative prosperity of Freetown, he wrote of the good prospects of a certain European trader and his African wife: "Some possibilities of trade expansion in Liberia are exemplified in the successful wholesale and retail establishment conducted by H. Genet here." "Women in Freetown, Africa, Want Silk Hose Now," *Baltimore Afro-American,* December 9, 1933, USNA, RG 59, 882.01 A/15.

21 William Jones, "Liberian Legislature Puts Future up to U.S.," *Baltimore*

Afro-American, December 2, 1933, USNA, RG 59, 882.01 A15. In early 1934, Carl Murphy, president of the *Afro-American,* notified Walter White of the NAACP that Jones had returned and wanted a meeting of black leaders to draw up a program for Liberia for presentation to Roosevelt (Murphy to Walter White, January 19, 1934, NAACP Papers, C-335).

22 Murphy to White, January 19, 1934, NAACP Papers, C-335. For Jones's promotion of his scheme, see *Baltimore Afro-American,* December 23, 1933, 1; December 30, 1933, 1; January 20, 1934, 17; February 10, 1934, 5; March 3, 1933, 5; March 10, 1934, 5; March 17, 1934, 5; April 7, 1934, 5; and June 23, 1934, 4 (cited by Taylor, "Involvement of Black Americans," 70).

23 Taylor, "Involvement of Black Americans," 80. Among those listed as supporting the Jones plan were Carl Murphy, Charles S. Johnson, Oscar De Priest, C. C. Spaulding, Emmett Scott, Charles H. Wesley, Rayford Logan, W. E. B. Du Bois, Mary McLeod Bethune, Carter G. Woodson, Channing H. Tobias, P. Bernard Young, Walter White, Eugene K. Jones, the Reverend J. H. Jernagin, Daisy C. Lampkin, Charlotte Hawkins Brown, William L. Patterson, E. Washington Rhodes, Hellen Allen Boys, John W. Davis, and Bishop W. Sampson Brooks.

24 White members of the proposed committee included Raymond Leslie Buell and Henry L. West.

25 For the State Department reaction, see Memorandum by Phillips of conversation with Ernest Lyon, W. W. Allen, and W. N. Jones, January 12, 1934, USNA, RG 59, 882.01 FC/767. Also see Memorandum (Hibbard) on conversation with T. J. Jones, January 31, 1934, USNA, RG 59, 882.01 FC/791 1/2.

26 Taylor, "Involvement of Black Americans," 80. See *Pittsburgh Courier,* February 3, 1934, 10.

27 Walter F. Walker (Consul, New York) to R. S. L. Bright (Executive Mansion, Monrovia), June 29, 1935, enclosing William Jones's column, "Day by Day," *Baltimore Afro-American,* n.d., Liberian National Archives.

28 Taylor, "Involvement of Black Americans," 80. See *Baltimore Afro-American,* August 4, 1934, 4.

29 "The Struggle for the Independence of Liberia," *Negro Worker,* June 1934, 12. Haywood, "Eighth Convention." For an abbreviated discussion of the Jones plan, see Haywood, *Black Bolshevik,* 428.

30 Haywood, "Eighth Convention."

31 "Struggle for the Independence of Liberia," 14.

32 Charles Woodson, "Expulsion of George Padmore from the Revolutionary Movement," *Negro Worker,* June 1934, 14–15.

33 "Struggle for the Independence of Liberia," 12.

34 "A Betrayer of the Negro Liberation Struggle," *Negro Worker,* July 1934, 9.

35 Ibid.

36 George Padmore, "An Open Letter to Earl Browder," *Crisis,* October 1935, 302. Padmore counterattacked by charging that the Negro Trade Union Committee had been abolished on orders from the Soviets, who were seeking to appease the British Foreign Office.

37 James R. Hooker, *Black Revolutionary,* 22.

38 Padmore, "Workers Defend Liberia," 7.

39 Ibid.

40 Hooker, *Black Revolutionary,* citing Padmore to Du Bois, February 17, 1934.

41 Padmore, "Open Letter," 302.

42 Padmore, *Pan-Africanism or Communism,* 148.

43 T. Ras Makonnen for the International African Service Bureau to Edwin Barclay, April 20, 1938, Liberian National Archives. Others associated with the IASB were I. Wallace-Johnson, C. L. R. James, Jomo Kenyatta, and B. N. Azikiwe. For a discussion of the rule and impact of the organization, see J. Ayodele Langley, *Pan-Africanism and Nationalism,* 337–46.

44 Great Britain, *Papers Concerning Affairs in Liberia,* annex to appendix 1, "Report of the Experts Designated by the Committee of the Council of the League of Nations: Final Observations," 80.

45 J. R. Hooker, *Black Revolutionary: George Padmore's Path from Communism to Pan-Africanism* (London: Pall Mall, 1967), 22, citing *New Leader* (September 13, 1941).

46 Ibid.,18.

47 Barnett to Jones, December 19, 1934, Phelps-Stokes Fund Archives, box 37, K-8.

48 Azikiwe, *Liberia in World Politics,* 353, citing W. E. B. Du Bois, "Sensitive Liberia," *Crisis,* May 1924. Also see "United States Envoy," *Crisis,* February 1924, 151.

49 "Woman Scores 'Backwardness' of Liberians," *Pittsburgh Courier,* December 9, 1933, USNA, RG 59, 882.00/997. Mrs. McWillie was a hairdresser who had returned to America with her husband, Herman. She said the Liberian authorities had feared her exposure of conditions and had attempted to detain her in Liberia.

50 Barnett to Walton, October 18, 1934, Claude Barnett Papers, Lester Walton file, 1927–1935.

51 See Wharton (Monrovia) to Secretary of State, August 1, 1929, DSRRAL, microfilm roll 14.

52 West to T. J. Jones, September 27, 1934, Phelps-Stokes Fund Archives, box 47, S4 (3).

53 Walton (via Firestone communications) to T. J. Jones, May 6, 1936, Phelps-Stokes Fund Archives, box 38, K-6. The message was sent to Jones, but was addressed to the Liberian consul in New York to be passed on to the press.

54 Bodie, "Images of Africa," 189, citing the *Chicago Defender,* November 7, 1925.

55 Anonymous news clipping, 1925, Claude Barnett Papers, Firestone Rubber Company file, 1925–1953.

56 *Newport News Star,* October 22, 1925, Claude Barnett Papers, Firestone Rubber Company file, 1925–1953.

57 *New York News,* February 13, 1926, Claude Barnett Papers, Firestone Rubber Company file, 1925–1953.

58 Editorials, *Opportunity,* November 1928, 325.

59 James C. Young, "Liberia and Its Future," 328.

60 Firestone, *Romance and Drama,* 124.

61 Ibid., 125.

62 Ibid., 124.

63 Ibid., 130.

64 Knoll, "Firestone's Labor Policy," 61, citing R. C. Porter to Senior Overseers and Clerks, November 21, 1929, Firestone Archives (Private Collection of Svend Holsoe, Philadelphia, Penn.).

65 Sidney De La Rue to W. E. B. Du Bois, July 7, 1933, Du Bois Papers, microfilm 13–16–16.

66 Knoll, "Firestone's Labor Policy," 64, citing excerpts from Memorandum of Meeting with President Barclay prepared by F. C. Fisher, February 20, 1936, Firestone Archives (Holsoe).

67 Furbay, *Top Hats and Tom-Toms,* 190.

68 Young, *Liberia Rediscovered,* 67–68.

69 Arthur Hayman and Harold Preece, *Lighting Up Liberia* (New York: Creative Age Press, 1943), 171.

70 Qtd. in Taylor, *Firestone Operations in Liberia,* 76.

71 Ibid., 81–82.

72 James C. Young, "Liberia and Its Future," 329.

73 W. E. B. Du Bois to Lester Walton, May 26, 1937, in Du Bois, *Correspondence,* 144–45.

74 David Levering Lewis, *W. E. B. DuBois,* 456.

75 Du Bois, *Black Folk: Then and Now,* 2.

8 The Literary Mirror

1 Waugh, *Black Mischief.*

2 Gates, "A Fragmented Man," 42.

3 Schuyler, *Black and Conservative,* 182.

4 Qtd. in Azikiwe, "In Defense of Liberia," 45. Answers to Schuyler's criticisms may be found in *New York Evening Post,* July 1, 1931; *Negro World,* July 18, 25, August 1,8, 1931; also *New York News and Harlem Home Journal,* July 18, 1931.

5 Schuyler, "Slaves Today–Missionaries 'Wink' at Conditions in Liberia," *Pittsburgh Courier,* October 17, 1931, reprinted in Hill and Kilson, *Apropos of Africa,* 345.

6 Memorandum from White to Royal Davis, July 14, 1931, NAACP Papers, C-335.

7 Schuyler to White, October 20, 1931, NAACP Papers, C-335. Schuyler was very annoyed about the letter of one Roger Baldwin, who disagreed with him on the whole Liberian matter.

8 George Schuyler, "Views and Reviews," *Pittsburgh Courier,* October 8, 1932 (enclosure), USNA, RG 59, 882.01 FC/407.

9 Ibid.

10 George Schuyler, *Pittsburgh Courier*, October 12, 1932, NAACP Papers, G-220.

11 Koren, "Liberia, the League, and the United States," 247, citing Schuyler, "Uncle Sam's Black Step-Child."

12 Schuyler, "Uncle Sam's Black Step-Child," 147.

13 Richburg, *Out of America*, 135.

14 Qtd. in Oscar R. Williams, "Making of a Black Conservative," 156.

15 Schuyler, *Slaves Today*, 227.

16 Ibid., 230.

17 Mary White Covington, "Book Chat," review of *Slaves Today*, by George Schuyler, *Pittsburgh Courier*, February 6, 1932.

18 Oscar Williams, "The Making of a Black Conservative," citing Vincent McHugh, "Dark Slaves of Liberia," review of *Slaves Today*, by George Schuyler, *New York Evening Post*.

19 Qtd. in Oscar R. Williams, "Making of a Black Conservative," 156.

20 W. E. B. Du Bois, review of *Slaves Today*, by George S. Schuyler, *Crisis*, February 1932, in Du Bois, *Book Reviews*, 161–62.

21 Harry M. Williams, "When Black Is Right," 235, citing George S. Schuyler to W. E. B. Du Bois, January 27, 1932, Du Bois Papers.

22 W. E. B. Du Bois to Anna Graves, November 17,1934, in Du Bois, *Correspondence*, 27.

23 Henry Louis Gates Jr., *The Signifying Monkey: A Theory of African American Literary Criticism* (New York: Oxford, 1988), 4.

24 George S. Schuyler, "The Negro-Art Hokum," *Nation*, June 16, 1926, 662.

25 Favor, "Building Black," 218.

26 W. J. West, *Quest for Graham Greene*, 65.

27 Graham Greene, *The Heart of the Matter* (New York: Viking Press, 1948). Evelyn Waugh, *Remote People* (London: Duckworth, 1931). Evelyn Waugh, *Black Mischief* (New York: Farrar and Rhinehart, 1932).

28 Sherry, *Life of Graham Greene*, 1: 562, citing Graham Greene, "Books in General," *New Statesman and Nation*, June 21, 1952.

29 Ibid., citing Greene, "Books in General," 564.

30 Graham Greene, *Journey without Maps*, 19.

31 David Lodge, "Waugh's Comic Waste Land," *New York Review of Books*, July 15, 1999, 31.

32 Sherry, *Life of Graham Greene*, 565, citing *Spectator*, July 5, 1935.

33 Porteous, *Landscapes of the Mind*, 108.

34 Graham Greene, *Journey without Maps*, 21.

35 Ibid., 116.

36 Barbara Greene, *Too Late to Turn Back*, 68.

37 Graham Greene, *Journey without Maps*, 215.

38 Paul Theroux, preface to Barbara Greene, *Too Late to Turn Back*, xxxi.

39 Graham Greene, *Journey without Maps*, 195.

40 Ibid.

41 Schuyler, *Slaves Today*, 12.

42 Graham Greene, *Journey without Maps*, 195.

43 Ibid., 85.

44 Ibid., 172.

45 Great Britain, *Papers Concerning Affairs in Liberia,* 27.

46 Graham Greene, *Journey without Maps,* 18.

47 Ibid.

48 Ibid.

49 Chisholm, *Nancy Cunard,* 244.

50 Graham Greene, *Journey without Maps,*201.

51 Barbara Greene, *Too Late to Turn Back,* 159.

52 *Tea with Mussolini* (1999) was based on Zefirelli's upbringing in Florence in the 1930s, a period in which some British expatriates were gulled by the order, interspersed with theatrical display, characterizing the Fascist regime.

53 Barbara Greene, *Too Late to Turn Back,* 161.

54 Graham Greene, *Journey without Maps,* 172.

55 James Wood, "The Lion King," review of *True at First Light,* by Ernest Hemingway, and *Hemingway: The Final Years,* by Michael Reynolds, *New York Times Book Review,* July 11, 1999, 15.

56 Qtd. in Porteous, *Landscapes of the Mind,* 108.

57 Qtd. in Richard Eder, "Our Man in Capri," review of *Greene on Capri: A Memoir,* by Shirley Hazard, *New York Times Book Review,* February 20, 2000, 13.

58 Great Britain, *Papers Concerning Affairs in Liberia,* 27.

59 Schuyler, *Slaves Today,* 6.

60 Harry M. Williams, "When Black is Right," 140, citing George S. Schuyler, *The Communist Conspiracy against the Negroes* (New York: Catholic Information Society, 1947).

61 Schuyler, *Black Empire,* 190.

62 Ibid., 137.

63 Ibid., 123.

64 Schuyler to the Editor, *Messenger,* March 1923, 86.

65 Williams, "When Black is Right," 158. Schuyler, "Shafts and Darts," *Messenger,* September 1923, November 1923, and February 1924.

66 Schuyler, "Shafts and Darts," *Messenger,* December 1923, 922–23.

67 "Schuyler Arouses Ire of Africans at Mass Meeting," *Pittsburgh Courier,* August 15, 1931.

68 Qtd. in Robert A. Hill, ed., *The Black Man* (Millwood, N.Y.: Kraus, Thomson, 1975), 4. Also see *Interstate Tattler,* August 23, 1929.

69 Schuyler, *Black Empire,* 275, citing *Interstate Tattler,* August 23, 1929.

70 Ibid., 88.

71 Ibid., 275, citing *Pittsburgh Courier,* November 18, 1933.

72 Robert A. Hill and R. Kent Rasmussen, afterword to Schuyler, *Black Empire,* 260, citing Schuyler to Prattis, April 4, 1937, P. L. Prattis Papers, Moorland-Spingarn Research Center, Howard University Library, Washington D.C.

73 Lawson, "A 1930s African-American View of Liberia," 258. See Ann Rayson, "George Schuyler: Paradox among 'Assimilationist' Writers," *Black American Literature Forum* 12, 3 (1978): 102–6.; Gates, "A Fragmented

Man," 31, 42–43; and James O. Young, *Black Writers of the Thirties* (Baton Rouge: Louisiana State University Press, 1973).

74 Gates, "A Fragmented Man," 42–43.

75 Du Bois, *The Souls of Black Folk,* in *Three Negro Class,* 215.

76 Sadly, the marriage followed the trajectory predicted for it by most of the enemies of "miscegenation." Schuyler's daughter grew into a maladjusted young adult and then became involved in a sordid sex scandal. A year after Philippa Schuyler's death in Vietnam in 1967, Schuyler's wife, Josephine, committed suicide. See Talalay, *Composition in Black and White.*

77 Schuyler, *Slaves Today,* 184.

78 Ibid., 238.

79 Beryl Satter, "Marcus Garvey, Father Divine," 43, citing a letter written by C. C. Austin.

80 Ibid., 46.

81 Schuyler, *Black Empire,* 61.

82 Ibid., 107.

83 Ibid.

9 The "Native Problem"

1 Ross, "Black Americans and Haiti, Liberia," 195.

2 Graham Greene, *Journey without Maps,* 242.

3 Ross, "Black Americans and Haiti, Liberia," 188, citing memorandum of Emily G. Balch, June 14, 1934, Detzer Papers, box 2, Swarthmore College.

4 Buell, *Liberia,* 42.

5 Lester Walton to W. E. B. Du Bois, January 14, 1939, in Du Bois, *Correspondence,* 183.

6 Edwin Barclay, Second Inaugural, January 6, 1936, in *The Inaugural Addresses of the Presidents of Liberia,* ed. Joseph Saye Guannu (Hicksville, N.Y.: Exposition Press, 1980), 300.

7 Ibid.

8 Buell, *Liberia,* v.

9 Richburg, *Out of America,* 134.

10 Qtd. in "Forced Labor in Liberia," 130.

11 Buell, "Reconstruction of Liberia," 133, citing League of Nations, Minutes of the 7th meeting, Committee of the Council, January 26, 1932.

12 Mitchell to Secretary of State, May 3, 1932, enclosing D. D. Rydings Report of April 15, 1932, USNA, RG 59, 882.01/966. Also see Report by Mr. W. A. Travell, Chairman of the Liberian Government's Special Commission to Sasstown, April 21, 1932 (Monrovia), Louis B. Grimes Papers, Liberia/League of Nations Papers, part 2, roll 2.

13 Yapp (Monrovia) to Sir John Simon, February 20, 1935, FO, 371/19235.

14 Diary of Charles Johnson, March 30, 1930, Charles S. Johnson Papers. Johnson also said that Davis had served in the Medical Department under Carranza (presumably with the Mexican army).

15 McBride Memorandum, October 3, 1934, USNA, RG 59, 882.01 FC/915; see annexed Memorandum of the Government of Liberia on the Kru Situation. Davis also found that Frontier Force soldiers had made unjust demands on the local people.

16 Davis, *Ethnohistorical Studies,* 114. Davis says, "It is claimed that Jehiupo was on the verge of famine, whereupon the Liberian commander ordered that the inhabitants of the towns be given certain areas then being cultivated by the Gbeta settlers at Sobobo."

17 McBride Memorandum, October 3, 1934, USNA, RG 59, 882.01 FC/915; see annexed Memorandum of the Government of Liberia on the Kru Situation. According to Jones ("Struggle for Political and Cultural Unification," 258), Nimley was not present at the meeting.

18 Bolloh, Dio, and Wissepo Kru groups burned the principal towns of the Niffu and Sobo groups which had remained loyal to the government. See Rydings Report of April 15, 1932, 18–20, qtd. in Mitchell to the Secretary of State, May 3, 1932, USNA, RG 59, 882.01/966.

19 Qtd. in ibid.

20 Mitchell to Stimson, November 27, 1931, enclosing "Complaint of the Sasstown Tribe Made before the Special Delegation Sent to Kru Coast by the President of Liberia to Make Peace," USNA, RG 59, 882.00/910.

21 Rydings Report, Statement Made by Paramount Chief Juah Nimley of the Sasstown Tribe, USNA, RG 59, 882.00/966.

22 See Buell, "Reconstruction of Liberia," 127.

23 Mitchell to Secretary of State, December 28, 1931, enclosing copy of a complaint of Chief Yourfee; copy of a complaint from the Gola section; copy of a complaint from the Kru Coast District, USNA, RG 59, 882.915. See also Mitchell to Stimson, November 5, 1931, USNA, RG 59, 882.00/899.

24 Mitchell to Secretary of State, January 22, 1932, enclosing clipping from West Africa Review for January, 1932, USNA, RG 59, 882.00/932.

25 Thorgues Sie et al. to Stimson, February 8, 1932, USNA, RG 59, 882.00/920.

26 Mr. Graham to Sir John Simon (telegram), January 27, 1932, in Great Britain, *Papers Concerning Affairs in Liberia.*

27 Buell, "Reconstruction of Liberia," 127.

28 Graham to Simon, telegram, March 9, 1932, enclosing Barclay to Graham, March 8, 1932, Great Britain, *Papers Concerning Affairs in Liberia,* no. 8.

29 Ibid.

30 For the report of Barclay's commission to the Kru Coast, see Mitchell to Secretary of State, March 21, 1932, USNA, RG 59, 882.00/941.

31 Mitchell to Secretary of State, May 3, 1932, enclosing Rydings Report, April 15, 1932, 23, USNA, RG 59, 882.00/966. Rydings had an unauthorized meeting with Nimley.

32 Ibid.

33 Samuel Reber (Geneva) to Stimson, April 20, 1932, USNA, RG 59, 882.00/949.

34 Grimes to Graham, June 16, 1932, Cecil Papers, ADD 51100.

35 "Chronological Survey," in Great Britain, *Papers Concerning Affairs in Liberia,* 4.

36 Werlich to Secretary of State, September 18, 1935, USNA, RG 59, 882.00/ 991.

37 Extract from the Annual Message of President Barclay delivered before the Liberian Legislature on October 25, 1933, FO, 371/18041.

38 Walton to Phillips, September 14, 1934, enclosing Grimes to Walton, August 21, 1934, USNA, RG 59, 882.00/1024.

39 McBride Memorandum (Washington), October 3, 1934, annexed letter, Barclay (Sasstown) to Secretary of State (Monrovia), May 5, 1934, USNA, RG 59, 882.01 FC/915.

40 Ibid.

41 Ibid.

42 Frank Walter (League of Nations) to William Stang, December 3, 1934, transmitting letter from Mackenzie, November 9, 1934, FO, 371/18043.

43 Yapp (Monrovia) to Foreign Office, October 23, 1934, FO, 371/18043. It was also reported that the Mano people had been driven back from the Bassa country and flogged by troops.

44 MacVeagh to Hull, April 30, 1934, USNA, RG 59, 882.00/1018. The situation on the Kru Coast was only part of the problem. MacVeagh reported in his letter that "two Dutchmen employed by the Holland Syndicate, who have been prospecting for the past few months in the bush back of Bassa, have told their chief that they were horrified at the way the natives were treated by the District Commissioners who took from them of their rice and left them barely enough to live on."

45 Ibid.

46 MacVeagh to Hull, April 17, 1934, USNA, RG 59, 882.00/1010.

47 Foreign Office Minute (Sir John Simon), March 15, 1934, FO, 371/ 18040. Simon wanted much stronger action than most of the functionaries in the Foreign Office had hitherto envisaged. An anonymous minute spoke of Simon's "sending eventually one of H. M. ships to Liberia — after the May 1934 meeting."

48 Sir John Simon to Routh (Monrovia), telegram, March 16, 1934, in Great Britain, *Papers Concerning Affairs in Liberia,* no. 16.

49 Great Britain, *Parliamentary Debates* vol. 91, 754–55.

50 Seventy-ninth Session of the Council of the League of Nations, Extract form Final Minutes of the 4th Meeting, Public, Held on May 18 1934, Geneva, in Great Britain, *Papers Concerning Affairs in Liberia,* no. 19.

51 Simpson, *Memoirs,* 87.

52 Sir John Simon to Lindsay, May 29, 1934, in Great Britain, *Papers Concerning Affairs in Liberia,* 20.

53 MacVeagh to Hull, April 17, 1934, USNA, RG 59, 882.00/1010.

54 Memorandum of conversation between Butterworth (third secretary of the U.S. embassy) and Peterson, May 4, 1934, FO, 371/1804. The American chargé in Monrovia was suspicious of British intentions and mentioned the fact that his opposite number had alluded to the sending of a naval vessel (MacVeagh to Secretary of State, March 5, 1934, USNA, RG 59, 882.00/1007). See also Routh to Foreign Office, April 19, 1934, FO, 371/18041.

55 Yapp to Foreign Office, October 23, 1934 (Minute by Wallinger), FO, 371/18043.

56 Fitzsimmons to Thompson, November-, 1934 (Minute of meeting between Wallinger, Thompson, and Fitzsimmons, November 28, 1934), FO, 371/18043.

57 Sir John Simon to Lindsay, December 18, 1934, FO, 371/18043.

58 Ibid.

59 Lindsay (Washington) to Foreign Office, April 4, 1935, FO, 371/19232.

60 Hibbard to McBride, April 19, 1935, USNA, RG 59, 882.01 FC/945 1/2.

61 Hibbard to McBride, May 4, 1935, enclosing Yapp to Paramount Chief Nimley of Old Sasstown, April 213, 1935, USNA, RG 59, 882.00/1030 1/2.

62 Ibid., enclosing Yapp to Simpson (Liberian Department of State), April 20, 1935, and Simpson to Yapp, May 1, 1935, USNA, RG 59, 882.00/1030 1/2.

63 Ibid.

64 Yapp to Foreign Office, October 22, 1934, press clipping from *West African Review,* October, 1934, FO, 371/18043.

65 De Long to Lady Simon, May 18, 1936, enclosing Chieftains Council of Assembly (Sasstown hinterland), "An Appeal," March 15, 1936, British Anti-Slavery and Aborigines Protection Society Papers, London.

66 Hibbard to McBride, April 19, 1935, USNA, RG 59 882.01 FC/945.

67 Ibid. Hibbard added that these grievances were "often more fancied than real, but the vivid African imagination makes them into a horrible and terrifying picture."

68 Ibid.

69 Hibbard to Harry (McBride?), April 19, 1935, USNA, RG 59, 882.01 FC/945 1/2.

70 G. H. Thompson (Foreign Office) to A. H. Wiggin (Washington embassy), December 31, 1934, FO, Consulate-General, Monrovia, microfilm roll 2.

71 Lindsay (British embassy, Washington) to Hull, January 17, 1935, USNA, RG 59, 882.01 FC/937. See J. P. Moffat Papers, Memoranda, 1934–35, vol. 23.

72 Yapp to Foreign Office, May 13, 1935, Situation in Liberia, Minute by Thompson, May 14, 1935, FO 371/19233.

73 Hibbard to McBride, May 4, 1935, USNA, RG 59, 882.00/1030 1/2.

74 Walton to Phillips, September 14, 1934, enclosing L. A. Grimes to Emily S. Balch, July 23, 1934, USNA, RG 59, 882.00/1024. See also Hibbard to Secretary of State, September 16, 1935, USNA, RG 59 711.82/47 and 841.6367.

75 Minute by Thompson of Foreign Office on Yapp (Monrovia) to Foreign Office, April 30, 1935, FO, 371/19233.

76 Minute (August 23, 1935) by Thompson on Yapp (on leave in England) to Thompson, August 16, 1935, FO, 371/19233.

77 Yapp to R. I. Campbell (Foreign Office), March 3, 1936, FO, 371/20213.

78 Lindsay (Washington) to Foreign Office, n.d., Minute by W. R. Rich, FO, 371/19233.

79 Hibbard to McBride, April 19, 1935, FO, 882.01 FC/945 1/2.

80 John H. Harris, "Liberian Slavery: The Essentials," reprinted from *Contemporary Review*, March 1931, British Anti-Slavery and Aborigines Protection Society Papers, London.

81 Sir John Harris (Anti-Slavery and Aborigines Protection Society) to Ronald (Foreign Office), June 15, 1934, FO, 371/18041.

82 Harris to A. Cartwright to Harris, February 8, 1935; Harris to Epstein (League of Nations Union), February 13, 1935, British Anti-Slavery and Aborigines Protection Society Papers, Oxford, no. 6490.

83 *Anti-Slavery Reporter and Aborigines Friend* 25, 4, fifth series (1936).

84 Cecil to Anthony Eden, August 31, 1936, FO, 377/2013.

85 S. Reber (Geneva) to Secretary of State, April 13, 1934, USNA, RG 59, 882.00/1011.

86 "In Re the Petition of the Kroo Community of Accra on Behalf of Their Chiefs . . . and Kinsfolk of the Republic of Liberia . . . to the Secretary-General of the Council of the League of Nations, June 23, 1934," Cecil Papers, ADD 51130.

87 J. Royal (?) to Sir John Simon, July 13, 1934, FO, 371/18042.

88 F. O. Hefty (Bureau International pour la Défense des Indigènes) to Simon, July 3, 1934, FO, 371/18041. Yapp to Foreign Office, September 3, 1934, FO, 371/18042; Frank Walters (League of Nations) to William Strong, Foreign Office, n.d., FO, 371/18043.

89 Juah Nimley (Sonpon Nabwe, secretary) to Cecil, February 28, 1934, Cecil Papers, ADD 51101.

90 Juah Nimley (Sonpon Nabwe, secretary) to Cecil, August 6, 1934, ADD 51101.

91 Yapp to Foreign Office, transmitting copy of letter from Nimley, February 13, 1935, FO, 371/19232.

92 W. E. De Lang (Paris) to Lady Simon, May 13, 1936, Anti-Slavery and Aborigines Protection Society Papers, London.

93 Morgan to the Archbishop of Canterbury, containing a copy of C. J. Julius to D. Twe, June 13, 1936, FO, 371/20213.

94 Minute by I. M. Pink on C. J. Julius to A. Eden (received August 25, 1936), FO, 371/2013. A similar petition was received from J. T. Nelson on September 7.

95 Lester Walton to United States State Department, report on conditions in Liberia, 1936, Lester Walton Papers, box 6, file 6.

96 Yapp to Foreign Office, July 12, 1936, FO, 371/2012.

97 Minute by I. M. Pink on Private Secretary Colonial Office to Foreign Office, August 11, 1936, FO, 371/2013.

98 Yapp to Eden, October 29, 1936, FO, 371/20213.

99 Ibid.

100 Wharton, telegram, to Secretary of State, October 29, 1936, USNA, RG 59, 882.00/1044.

101 Yapp to Foreign Office, November 6, 1936 (transmits copies of the Annual Message of the President of Liberia delivered before the legislature on October 28, 1936), FO, 371/2013.

102 Mitchell to Stimson, November 27, 1931, enclosing D. W. Herman, Chairman, Special Delegation (to Kru Coast), to Barclay, October 26, 1931, USNA, RG 59, 882.00/910.

103 McBride Memorandum, October 3, 1934, annexed Memorandum of the Government of Liberia on the Kru Situation, USNA, RG 59, 882.01 FC/915.

104 Kru Prisoners in Sinoe Jail to J. R. Sorbor (Sierra Leone), April 19, 1933, Phelps-Stokes Fund Archives, box 47, S-5. Sorbor had escaped from Monrovia.

105 McBride Memorandum (Washington), October 3, 1934, USNA, RG 59, 882.01 FC/915.

106 Charles S. Johnson, *Bitter Canaan,* 221.

107 Liebenow, *Liberia,* 33.

108 Qtd. in Charles S. Johnson, *Bitter Canaan,* 210.

109 Akpan, "African Policy," 469. P. G. Wolo was another prominent indigenous dissident.

110 Report on Leading Personalities in Liberia, including additions received in the Foreign Office up to January 30, 1930, G. Rule (Monrovia) to Foreign Office, December 21, 1930, FO, 37 I/14658. The consulate further noted of Massaquoi: "About 45 years of age (1927). An educated Vai Chief of considerable intelligence, but unscrupulous and thoroughly dishonest, as several English firms have reason to know. Unfavorably known to the authorities in Sierra Leone. An intriguer with political aspirations. Believed to have been concerned in the abortive attempt to overthrow the Government in January 1927."

111 Al-Haj Massaquoi to Lady Simon, October 3, 1931, British Anti-Slavery and Aborigines Protection Society Papers, London. Massaquoi was at University College in Dublin and requested financial assistance from Lady Simon to continue his studies.

112 Twe to Johnson, December 1, 1930, Charles S. Johnson Papers, box 88, file 13.

113 Mitchell to Stimson, April 28, 1932, enclosing Twe to Mitchell, April 22, 1932, USNA, RG 59, 882.00/965. See also Yapp to Simon, February 20, 1935, FO, 371/19235.

114 Mitchell to Stimson, April 28, 1932, enclosing Twe to Mitchell, April 22, 1932, USNA, RG 59, 882.00/965.

115 Clifton R. Wharton, Chargé d'Affaires ad interim, to Secretary of State, January 28, 927, USNA, RG 59, 882.00/762 (microfilm M613, location 10–14–5).

116 MacVeagh, Chargé d'Affaires ad interim, to Secretary of State, March 5, 1934, and Faulkner to MacVeagh, February 28, 1934, USNA, RG 59, 882.00/1006.

117 Epstein (League of Nations Union) to Wallinger, October 4, 1934, enclosing two letters from Twe to Mrs. Florence Morgan in England, FO, 371/18042. The letter of September 10, 1934, advocated an uprising.

118 Yapp to Thompson, January 8, 1935, FO, 371/19232.

119 Twe to Cecil, October 8, 1934, Cecil Papers, ADD 51101.

120 Cecil to Twe, October 22, 1934, Cecil Papers, ADD 51101.

121 Graham Greene, *Journey without Maps,* 45.

122 Ibid., 46.

123 Ibid., 48.

124 Yapp to Foreign Office, January 26, 1936, FO, 371/20213. In May of 1936, it was reported that since his return, Twe had continued to give aid and encouragement to rebels (I. Whisant to E. Barclay, August 29, 1936, Liberian National Archives).

125 Great Britain, *Parliamentary Debates* vol. 91, 926.

126 Yapp to Foreign Office, February 20, 1935, FO, 371/19235.

127 Azikiwe, *Liberia in World Politics,* 337.

128 Edwin Gahie Gyude Hodge, unpublished autobiography.

129 Mitchell to Stimpson, November 5, 1931, enclosing Faulkner to Mitchell, October 22, 1931, USNA, RG 59, 822.00/899. The men arrested included "Dr. Sie, a Graduate of Chicago, of Grebo tribe, influential among his people. W. T. Sancea, a Liberian influential among the natives, strong supporter of Dr. Morais, influential among the natives and was elected by them for representative in the recent election."

130 Stanfield introduction to Johnson, *Bitter Canaan,* vi.

131 Hodge unpublished autobiography, ch. 54.

132 Ibid.

133 Hayman, *Lighting Up Liberia,* 16, citing *Crisis,* November 1934.

134 In the spring of 1934, Morais appeared still to be championing those rights. See F. O. Hefty (International Office for the Protection of Native Races, Geneva) to Department of State, July 17, 1934, enclosing letter from Morais to Henri A. Junod, May 9, 1934, USNA, RG 59, 822.01 FC/870. In Liberia, Morais said the letter was not written by him (Harold Fredericks to Morais, July 7, 1934, Liberian National Archives).

135 League of Nations (C.460.M197. 1934 VII), October 12, 1934, annex: Morais to Fredericks, Superintendent, Maryland County, August 21, 1934, FO, 371/18043.

136 Yapp to Wallinger, February 4, 1935, enclosing F. W. M. Morais, "My Role to the Life," *The Weekly Mirror* (Monrovia), December 21, 1934, 5, FO, 371/19232.

137 Yapp to Foreign Office, October 23, 1934, FO, 371/18043.

138 Yapp to Wallinger, February 4, 1935, enclosing copy of *The Weekly Mirror* (Monrovia), January 4, 1934, 4, FO, 371/19232.

139 Hibbard to McBride, April 19, 1935, USNA, RG 59, 882.01 FC/945 1/2.

140 Mordecai Johnson to W. White, July 27, 1933, enclosing statement on Liberia by Charles Wesley and Rayford Logan, NAACP Papers, G-221.

141 Hibbard to McBride, April 19, 1935, USNA, RG 59, 882.01 FC/945 1/2.

142 White to Stimson, October 1, 1932, enclosing NAACP press release by Howard Oxley, USNA, RG 59, 882.01 FC/383.

143 Azikiwe, *Liberia in World Politics,* 398.

144 Qtd. in Chalk, "Du Bois and Garvey," 2.

145 Azikiwe, *Liberia in World Politics,* 338 n.1, citing the *Baltimore Afro-American,* August 20, 1932.

146 Walker, "Did the Liberian Natives Speak," 340. See W. F. N. Morais, "Liberia Natives Tell Their Story."

147 Azikiwe, *Liberia in World Politics*, 337.

148 Marcus Garvey, "The World as It Is," *Blackman*, January 1934, 12.

149 Ibid.

150 Padmore, "Workers Defend Liberia," 10, Claude Barnett Papers, Liberian News Releases, Miscellaneous, 1925–1950. To Padmore, the struggle among Liberian politicians was a useless game in which rival imperialisms moved politicians back and forth at will. The competition between Faulkner and King had been nothing more than an epiphenomenon of the clash of British and American imperialism: "The chief source the British Bank of West Africa from which King and his party got their funds to control the Government having been removed King was unable to put up any struggle against the opposition. The pro-American black politicians having ousted King immediately elected a provisional president to office in the person of Arthur Barkeley [*sic*], the very same faker who had served on the slavery commission on behalf of Liberia. The very first act of Barkeley [*sic*] in reward for the spoils of office was to issue permission to the Firestone Rubber Company to establish a bank in Monrovia in place of the defunct British establishment."

Thus, within a period of a few weeks a 'bloodless revolution' took place in Liberia, in which the pro-American forces defeated their British opponents.

151 M. Nelson, "Liberia and Imperialism," *Negro Worker*, July 1934, 19.

152 M. Nelson, "The Situation in Liberia," *Negro Worker*, May 1935, 24. See Isaac Wallace-Johnson, "Liberia Ahoy," *Liberian Patriot* (Monrovia), August 10, 1935, enclosed in Whittall (Monrovia) to Pink (Foreign Office), August 23, 1935, FO, 371/19234.

153 True Whig Party Memorandum, "The Significance of the Last Presidential Election," 1935?, Liberian National Archives.

154 Special Committee of Citizens, Maryland County, to Barclay, September 8, 1931, Liberian National Archives.

155 G. Brewer (Harper) to Barclay, April 10, 1932, Liberian National Archives.

156 Fredericks to Barclay, April 26, 1932, Liberian National Archives.

157 Fredericks to Barclay, May 20, 1935, Liberian National Archives.

158 Lester Walton to Harry McBride, July 27, 1936, Lester Walton Papers, box 8, file 6.

10 Fascism and New Zions

1 Psalm 68, verse 31.

2 Blyden, *Christianity*, 152; "Philip and the Eunuch," discourse delivered in the United States in 1882.

3 Howe, *Afrocentrism*, 35.

4 Gates, *Wonders of the African World*, 67.

5   Sorenson, *Imaging Ethiopia*, 19.

6   Rey, *In the Country of the Blue Nile*, 263–65.

7   Benjamin Nnamdi Azikiwe, *Renascent Africa* (New York: Negro Universities Press, 469), 164.

8   Esedebe, *Pan-Africanism*, 115, citing *Labour Monthly*, September 1935.

9   In 1931 Ford married one of the immigrants to Ethiopia, Mignon Innis. They had two sons, Abiya and Yosef. Abiya Ford now teaches communications at Howard University in Washington, D.C.

10 Harris, *African-American Reactions to War in Ethiopia, 1936–41*, citing USNA, RG 59, 884.55/2, Pioneers of Aethiopia, December 5, 1931.

11 Ibid., citing USNA, RG 59, 884.52/9, David D. Erwin to Cordel Hull, September 3, 1935.

12 Ibid., citing USNA, RG 59, FW 765.84/552, Hattie Edwards Koffie to President Roosevelt, January 22, 1936, Hattie Edwards Koffie to Minister of Foreign Affairs, Washington, D.C., July 15, 1935.

13 Ibid, citing USNA, RG, 884.51/10, M. L. Gordon to the White House, December 23, 1995.

14 Harris, *African-American Reactions*, 14–15, citing Addison Southard to Secretary of State, November 2, 1931, 884.55/7; Report of Migratory Movement in Ethiopia, 884.55/20; Addison E. Southard to Secretary of State, October 7, 1931, FW 884.55/3; Scott, "Rabbi Arnold Ford's Back-to-Africa Movement."

15 Much of this activity has been extensively researched. See Plummer, *Rising Wind*, 40–81.

16 Asante, *Pan-African Protest*; William Scott, *Sons of Sheba's Race*; and Harris, *African-American Reactions*.

17 Scott, 132, citing Walter White, *Amsterdam News*, October 5, 1935.

18 Reuben S. Young, "Ethiopia Awakens," 262–63.

19 Plummer, *Rising Wind*, 44, citing Mary R. Sawyer, "The Fraternal Council of Negro Churches, 1934–1964," *Church History* 59 (1990). The Fraternal Council of Negro Churches, an umbrella organization, met in Cleveland and decried the aggression, noting that "while by sympathy, principle, and ideals we are Americans to the core, we cannot be deaf to the cry that comes from a menaced nation in the land of our fathers' fathers." On August 18, 1935, a biracial Committee for Ethiopia held a day of prayer observed by 3,000 churches in the Caribbean and the United States.

20 Qtd. in Foster, *Women and the Warriors*, 170.

21 Diary of William Phillips, May 15, 1935, William Phillips Papers.

22 Plummer, *Rising Wind*, 40.

23 Ibid., 40.

24 Sorenson, *Imagining Ethiopia*, 28, citing Margery Perham, *The Government of Ethiopia* (London: Faber, 1969).

25 Marcus, *History of Ethiopia*, 120. Marcus says: "Slaves were manumitted to take their place alongside subsistence agriculturalists as sharecroppers in Ethiopia's developing market economy. This natural process occurred when criticism of Ethiopia's social system developed overseas. It was difficult for Europeans to appreciate that capitalism in Ethiopia was defeating

slavery when they saw an apparently thriving institution. As Ethiopia's best public relations man, Tafari claimed that his edict of 1918 banning the slave trade was a turn toward ultimate abolition. He patiently explained that he would have to educate his countrymen to see slavery as a social problem, since the government was trying to destroy a historic institution that many believed benefited both slave and owner. The process leading to liberation would be long and difficult, and the final stages had to be linked to economic growth in order to absorb the energies and talents of the hundreds of thousands of freedmen. Westerners, however, wanted quick action, and so the edict of 1918 won few friends in Europe."

26 Hickey, "Ethiopia and Great Britain," 3.

27 Rey, *In the Country of the Blue Nile*, 217.

28 Hickey, "Ethiopia and Great Britain," 42–43. He writes: "In time, slave raiding also became a more costly undertaking, both in terms of incurred risks and forgone opportunities. The development of the neftenya-gabbar system tied tenancy had already placed a considerable portion of southern Ethiopia beyond the pale of 'legitimate' slaving activity. Furthermore, the amalgam of indigenous groupings referred to as shankalla, the usual victims of these assaults, were no longer the easy targets they had been at the outset of the occupation. A certain minority of these peoples avoided enslavement through defensive migration, either to a 'protected' agricultural zone of the southwest, or across the Sudanese border. . . . By posting a battery of scouts, and dispersing into cover in advance of the slavers' arrival, the inhabitants of remote villages were able to significantly reduce the likelihood of capture. The depopulation often perceived by contemporary observers was more a product of outmigration and tactical retreat than an accurate indication of mortality and captivity rates."

See Jack Strauder, *The Majangir: Ecology and Society of a Southwestern Ethiopian People* (Cambridge: Cambridge University Press, 1971).

29 Asante, *Pan-African Protest*, 65, citing Third Annual Report on Slavery in Ethiopia, 10 August 1936, FO 371/20185.

30 Simon, *Slavery*, 20.

31 League of Nations, "Abstracts from the Memorandum of the Italian Government," 1399–400.

32 *New York Herald Tribune*, January 12, 1936.

33 Azikiwe, *Renascent Africa*, 221.

34 Du Bois, "Inter-racial Implications," 88–89.

35 Ottley, *"New World A-Coming,"* 111.

36 Asante, *Pan-African Protest*, 113, citing C. B. R. Wright, "The Italo-Ethiopian Dispute and International Law: An Open Letter to My Countrymen and Members of the Negro Race," *Sierra Leone Daily Mail*, October 12, 1935. Also, see the same source on the subject on October 10, 11, 15, and 17, 1935.

37 Ibid., 64, citing accession number 75.64, Aborigines Protection Society Papers.

38 William R. Scott, "Black Nationalism and the Italo-Ethiopian Conflict," 123.

39 Plummer, *Rising Wind,* 55, citing Willis N. Huggins, "Dr. Huggins Sums Up Ethiopian Situation," ANP release, Jan. 5, 1937, Claude Barnett Papers; *Chicago Defender,* February 13, 1937.

40 Willis N. Huggins, *Chicago Defender,* February 13, 1937.

41 Harold Marcus, "The Black Man Turned White: European Attitudes towards Ethiopians, 1850–1900," *Achiv Orientalni* 39 (1971): 156–66.

42 Harris, *African-American Reactions to War in Ethiopia,* 1936–41, citing USNA, RG 59, 033.8411, Addison E. Southard to Secretary of State, May 1, 1919.

43 Ibid., 5, citing the *Chicago Defender,* July 12, 1919.

44 Ibid., 8, citing USNA, RG 59, 884.4016, Negroes/1, July 30, 1930.

45 Ibid., 10, citing U033.841/80, Southard to Murray, September 18, 1931; *New York Times,* August 14, 1930.

46 Ibid., citing USNA, RG 59, 033.8411, List of Papers, Visits of Abyssinian Officials to U.S., 1930–39.

47 Carleton Coon (with E. E. Hunt), *The Living Races of Man* (New York: Knopf, 1965), 120. Coon's conclusions were based on his unpublished "Contribution to the Study of the Physical Anthropology of the Ethiopians and Somalis" (1935).

48 Huggins, and Jackson, *Introduction to African Civilizations,* 85.

49 "Booker T. Washington's Logical Successor," *New York Times,* February 19, 1911.

50 Huggins, and Jackson, *Introduction to African Civilizations,* 49–50.

51 David Levering Lewis, *W. E. B. DuBois,* 152.

52 Clarke, *Marcus Garvey and the Vision of Africa,* 363, citing *Blackman Magazine,* August 1936.

53 Hill, *Marcus Garvey Papers,* 7:740, editorial by Marcus Garvey in the *Blackman,* March–April 1937.

54 Ibid., 741.

55 "Negro Educator Is Found Drowned," *New York Times,* July 19, 1941. The body went missing from December to July.

56 Howell was the oldest of ten children and was born in rural Jamaica in the Bull Head Mountain district of upper Clarenden. In 1896, he served in the West India Regiment in the Ashanti Wars. In 1918, Howell became a cook in the United States Army transport service and was later granted U.S. citizenship. He worked construction in New York, where he was exposed to the UNIA's Pan-Africanism and the communism of George Padmore. In the mid-1930s, Howell's book, *The Promised Key* was published and contained much material from Robert Athlyi Rogers's book *Holy Piby* (1924) and the *Royal Parchment Scroll of Black Supremacy* of Reverend Fitz Balintine Pettersburgh (1926). Howell published his own book under the pseudonym Gangunguru Maragh, Hindi for "teacher of famed wisdom." His religious beliefs were an interesting mixture of Jamaica folk belief and a variety of esoteric beliefs he had been exposed to during his travels. In 1960, Howell, after claiming the godhead for himself, was committed to a Kingston mental facility. Joseph Hibbert migrated to Costa Rica at an early age, where he joined a Masonic Lodge, the Ancient Order of

Ethiopia. Dunkly was a seaman with the United Fruit Company. Like Howell, Dunkley and Hibbert returned to Jamaica between 1931 and 1932. Roanne Edward, "Early Rastafarian Leaders," *Microsoft Encarta Africana*.

57 Some maintained that Garvey himself had pointed the way when he supposedly declared, "Look to Africa when a Black king shall be crowned, for the day of deliverance is near." Nelson, "Rastafarians and Ethiopianism," 73, citing M. G. Smith, Roy Augier, and Rex Nettleford, *The Rastafari Movement in Kingston, Jamaica* (Kingston: University of the West Indies, Department of Extra-Mural Studies, 1988).

58 Ibid., citing Leonard E. Barrett Sr.

59 Nelson, "Rastafarians and Ethiopianism," 83.

60 Kapuscinski, *Emperor,* 109–10.

61 Sorenson, *Imagining Ethiopia,* 36, citing Liebenow, *African Politics,* 20.

62 Lyon to Barclay, June 20, 1933, Liberian National Archives.

63 Ross, "Black Americans and Haiti, Liberia," 364, citing Lester Walton to Claude Barnett, June 26, 1935, Claude Barnett Papers, "Africa-Liberia-Lester Walton, Dec. 34–Dec. 37."

64 Ibid.

65 *Weekly Mirror* (Monrovia), March 6, 1936, enclosing article from *African Morning Post* (Accra), Liberian National Archives.

66 L. H. Whittall (Monrovia), March 6, 1936, enclosing article from *African Morning Post* (Accra), Liberian National Archives.

67 Walter F. Walker (Consul, New York) to R. S. L. Bright (Executive Mansion, Monrovia), June 29, 1935 (enclosing article by William Jones), Liberian National Archives.

68 "Free Liberia," *Literary Digest,* August 8, 1936, 14.

69 T. Ras Makonnen for the International African Service Bureau to Edwin Barclay, April 20, 1938, Liberian National Archives.

70 Azikiwe, *Liberia in World Politics,* 395.

71 Said, "Impossible Histories," 72.

72 Gilroy, *Against Race,* 232, citing J. A. Rogers, *World's Great Men of Color* (New York: J. A. Rogers, 1947). Garvey made his comment to Rogers in London. Also see Martin, *Race First,* 66.

73 Hill, *Marcus Garvey Papers,* 7: 686, editorials by Marcus Garvey in the *Blackman,* July–August 1936.

74 Gilroy, *Against Race,* 234.

75 Ibid., 237.

76 Mosse, *Fascist Revolution,* xi.

77 Gilroy, *Against Race,* 233, citing Marcus Garvey, "The Ideals of Two Races," in *Philosophy and Opinions,* 2:338.

78 Gilroy, *Against Race,* 137, citing Michel Foucault.

79 Hill, *Marcus Garvey Papers,* 8:741.

80 Sollors, "Du Bois in Nazi Germany," 213, citing the *Pittsburgh Courier,* December 5, 1936.

81 Ibid., 208–9, citing memorandum to the Board of Directors of the Oberlaender Trust, February 8, 1935, Du Bois Papers, 46/260.

82   *Ibid.,* citing the *Pittsburgh Courier,* December 19, 1936.

83   Ibid., citing the *Pittsburgh Courier,* December 5, 1936.

84   David Levering Lewis, *W. E. B. DuBois,* 402, citing "Russia and America,"
     Du Bois Papers, Amherst.

85   Du Bois, "Inter-racial Implications," 88–89.

86   *Pittsburgh Courier,* February 27, 1937, in Du Bois, *A Reader.*

87   Ibid., 84.

88   David Levering Lewis, *W. E. B. DuBois,* 419, citing , inter alia, Du Bois,
     "Forum of Fact and Opinion," *Pittsburgh Courier,* March 13, 1937. For an
     overview of these matters, see Gallicchio, *African American Encounter.* For
     an account of the events at Nanking, see Honda, *Nanjing Massacre.* For a
     number of black leaders, hope lay in the East. As early as the end of World
     War I, Garvey had warned that "the next war will be between the Negroes
     and the whites unless our demands for justice are recognized. . . . With
     Japan to fight with us, we can win such a war." Garvey's movement
     attracted attention in Japan. In 1921, retired Japanese army general Kojiro
     Sato wrote his *Japanese American War Fantasy,* in which the Empire of the
     Chrysanthemum Throne invaded the United States with the collaboration
     of the UNIA. Three years later, in a nonfiction work, Mitsukawa Kametaro
     wrote *The Negro Problem,* in which he praised Garvey and saw African
     Americans as a fifth column in the event of hostilities with the United
     States. When war with Japan did finally break out in the 1940s, a number
     of black nationalists were arrested on suspicion of favoring a Japanese
     victory. Among them were Elijah Muhammad of the Nation of Islam,
     Mittie Maud Lena Gordon of the Peace Movement of Ethiopia, the Rev-
     erend Ethelbert A. Broaster of the International Reassemble of the
     Church of Freedom League Inc. (a black Hebrew congregation), and
     Bishop David D. Erwin and General Butler, leaders of the Pacific Move-
     ment of the Eastern World. See Ernest Allen, Jr., "When Japan was
     'Champion of the Darker Races': Satokata Takahashi and the Flowering of
     Black Messianic Nationalism," *The Black Scholar* 24, 1 (1993), 23–46.

     One did not have to be a black nationalist to admire Japan as a "colored"
     power. For prominent personalities as diverse as James Weldon Johnson,
     Walter White, William Pickens, and George Schuyler, Japan was the pal-
     adin of the "darker races." Du Bois, like many other molders of black
     public opinion, was courted by Prince Hikada Yasuichi, who had arrived
     in the United States in 1920. Hikada was a conduit for Japanese informa-
     tion about the American "Negro problem," as well as a speaker before
     various African American groups. In 1936, he proved instrumental in
     arranging a tour of Japan by Du Bois.

89   Patterson, "America's Worst Idea," 15.

90   Ralph Ellison, *Juneteenth* (New York: Random House, 1999).

91   Swing, *Forerunners of American Fascism,* 119.

92   Hill, *Marcus Garvey Papers,* 7:819, Thomas W. Harvey, Chairman, Second
     Regional Conference Committee to Theodore Bilbo, February 1938.

93   Martin, *Race First,* 349, citing Thurston E. Doler, "Theodore G. Bilbo's
     Rhetoric of Racial Relations" (Ph.D. diss., University of Oregon, 1968).

94 Theodore G. Bilbo, "An African Home for Our Negroes," *Living Age* 358, 4451 (June 1940), 327.

95 Theodore Bilbo, *Take Your Choice: Separation or Mongrelization,* (Poplarville, Miss.: Dream House Publishing Company, 1947).

96 Ibid., i.

97 Bilbo, "An African Home for Our Negroes," 328.

98 Ibid, 330.

99 Walton to Barnett, January 14, Barnett papers, box 188.

100 Bilbo, "An African Home for Our Negroes," 330.

101 A. Wigfall Green, *The Man Bilbo* (Baton Rouge: Louisiana State University Press, 1963), 100, citing *New York Times,* February 18, 1938.

102 Martin, *Race First,* 349, citing Bilbo, *Take Your Choice.*

103 Hill, *Marcus Garvey Papers,* 7:884, Marcus Garvey to Sen. Theodore G. Bilbo, August 13, 1938.

104 Ibid., 7:884 n. 2.

105 Hill, *Marcus Garvey Papers,* 7:925, Carlos Cooks, President, UNIA Advance Division, to Sen. Theodore G. Bilbo, October 3, 1939.

106 Barnett to Walton, April 18, 1939, Barnett Papers, box 188.

107 Claude Barnett to Lester Walton, April 29, 1939, Lester Walton Papers, box 9.

108 "Mr. Bilbo's Affatus," *Time Magazine* 38, 19 (May 8, 1939), 14.

109 Bilbo, "An African Home for Our Negroes," 328.

110 Martin, *Race First,* 351, citing the *Blackman,* November 1938.

111 Hill, *Marcus Garvey Papers,* 7:920, essay in the *Blackman,* "Bill Introduced into United States Senate Aiming at Carrying out the Ideal of the U.N.I.A.: A Greater Government for the Negroes of the World in Africa."

112 Ibid., 7:822 n. 3, Charles Watkins, President, Peace Movement of Ethiopia, . . . to Senator Theodore Bilbo, March 1938, citing Lester A. Walton to the Secretary of State, January 14, 1939, USNA, RG 59, 882.5211.

113 Martin, *Race First,* 352, citing the *Richmond Times–Dispatch,* January 27, 1940; Cox to Governor James H. Price, December 29, 1939, UNIA Central Division (New York) files, box 8, d. 10.

114 Ibid., 354; see Thomas Dixon, *The Flaming Sword* (Atlanta: Monarch Publishing, 1939).

115 Hill, *Marcus Garvey Papers,* 7:893, Marcus Garvey to Earnest S. Cox, October 6, 1938.

116 Qtd. in Barry, *Rising Tide,* 380.

117 Theodore Roosevelt, "Brazil and the Negro," *Outlook,* February 21, 1914, 410–11.

118 Garvey, *Philosophy and Opinions,* 2:2.

119 Brath, "Marcus Garvey," 17.

120 Stoddard, *Rising Tide of Color.*

121 Gregor, *Faces of Janus,* 158.

122 Martin, *Race First,* 346, citing *Negro World,* July 15, 1922.

123 Appiah, *In My Father's House,* 13. Appiah notes that "racialism is not, in itself, a doctrine that must be dangerous. . . . Provided positive moral

qualities are distributed across the races, each can be respected." Few can maintain such a lofty stance, and Appiah notes that racialists all too often fall into the trap of making invidious comparisons based on race and using these as a basis for differential treatment.

124 Ibid., 13–15.

125 Hill, "Black Zionism," 52, citing Hill, *Marcus Garvey Papers*, 3:16.

126 Hill, *Marcus Garvey Papers*, 7:686, editorials by Marcus Garvey in the *Blackman*, July–August 1936.

127 Marcus Garvey, "Germany Puzzles the World," *Blackman*, January 1934, 13.

128 Bilbo, "An African Home for Our Negroes," 329.

129 Ibid.

130 James, *Holding Aloft*, 211, citing Schomburg to Dabney, August 19, 1937, Schomburg Papers, reel 7.

131 Ralph Bunche, *A World View of Race* (Washington, D.C.: The Associates in Negro Folk Education, 1936), 93–94.

132 Du Bois, *Dusk of Dawn*, 197–200, 306. By the late 1940s Du Bois had emerged as a very strong supporter of Zionism. In a strange paradox, he and his assistant, Hugh Smythe, lobbied the resistant Liberian delegation to the United Nations to support the creation of Israel. David Levering Lewis, *W. E. B. DuBois*, 534. See Du Bois, "The Case of the Jews," *Chicago Star*, May 8, 1948.

133 Hill, *Marcus Garvey Papers*, 7:918, "Bill Introduced into United States Senate Aiming at Carrying out the Ideal of the U.N.I.A.: A Greater Government for the Negroes of the World in Africa," the *Blackman*, June 1939.

134 Stoddard, *Rising Tide of Color*, 100.

135 Stein, *World of Marcus Garvey*, 251.

136 Green, *The Man Bilbo*, 124.

137 Bilbo, "An African Home for Our Negro," 327.

138 Ibid.

139 Barry, *Rising Tide*, 128.

140 Daryl Scott, "The Primodial South: White Nationalism in the American South since 1865," unpublished manuscript, 15. See William L. Van Deburg, *New Day in Babylon: The Black Power Movement and American Culture, 1965–1975* (Chicago: University of Chicago, 1992).

141 Howe, *Afrocentrism*, 202.

142 Ron Bush, *We Are Not What We Seem: Black Nationalism and Class Struggle in the American Century* (New York: New York University Press, 1999), 35.

143 Ibid., 233.

144 See Venator Santiago, "Other Nationalists." Indeed, if we compare the career of the Puerto Rican nationalist Pedro Albizu Campos (1891–1965) and most black nationalists, we can see the boundaries of political protest. Albizu Campos entered Atlanta Federal Penitentiary a decade after Garvey on charges of sedition. He was to spend most of the rest of his life in prison. Interestingly, it was the Georgian Blanton Winship,

governor of Puerto Rico from 1934–39, who sent him there. Unlike most African American groups, he sought no reform under the terms of the American constitution. Material goods from Uncle Sam and a greater access to emigration to the mainland seemed like irrelevancies. For the record, Albizu Campos (who attended Harvard as a "Negro") and his Nationalist Party killed far more white policemen than either the UNIA or the Nation of Islam.

145 V. T. Rahsegkar. Dalit: *The Black Untouchables of India* (Atlanta: Clarity Press, 1995); Gurharpal Sing, *Ethnic Conflict in India* (New York: St. Martin's, 2000); Vijay Prashad, *Untouchable Freedom* (New Delhi: Oxford, 2000).

146 See Pierre van der Berghe, *Race and Racism* (New York: Wiley, 1976).

147 Ralph Bunche, "Africa and the Current World Conflict," in *Ralph J. Bunche: Selected Speeches and Writings,* ed. Charles P. Henry (Ann Arbor: University of Michigan Press, 1995), 144. Bunche acknowledged that Africans, too, would be caught up in this initially fratricidal war on their continent.

Postscript

1 W. E. B. Du Bois to Lester Walton, July 8, 1941, in Du Bois, *Correspondence,* 286.

2 Clarence Simpson to Edwin Barclay, August 21, 1936, Liberian National Archives, Treasury 1935–1936.

3 Dr. Antoine Sottile to Edwin Barclay, September 18, 1938; and December 24, 1938, Liberian National Archives, Presidential file. Sottile had not always had a smooth relationship with his employers. In July of 1933, L. A. Grimes had complained that Sottile had blundered. The jurist was the publisher of the *International Law Review.* Yugoslavia had contributed to the cost of the publication, but stopped when Belgrade felt that it was being criticized in its pages. Grimes felt that Liberia would lose the support of the Little Entente Powers. L. A. Grimes to Edwin Barclay, July 12, 1933, Liberian National Archives, Presidential file.

4 This is the already frequently quoted Buell, *Liberia: A Century of Survival.*

5 Ibid., vi.

6 Ibid., 2.

7 Ibid., 6.

8 Brown, *Economic History of Liberia,* 213–14.

9 Buell, *Liberia,* 68, citing *Baltimore Afro-American,* June 19, 1943.

10 Ibid., citing *Chicago Defender,* June 5, 1943.

11 Penny Von Eschen, *Race against Empire,* 39, citing George Padmore, "Padmore Sees Wall St. Invasion of Liberia," *Chicago Defender,* November 18, 1944.

12 Robeson, *African Journey,* 28.

13 Hayman and Preece, *Lighting Up Liberia,* 69.

14 Ibid., 274.

15 Von Eschen, *Race against Empire,* 201, citing Harry McAlpin, "Engineer's Attack on Liberia Policy Draws Fire of U.S. State Department," *Chicago Defender,* January 23, 1943. The image of the country was not helped by Elizabeth Dearmin Furbay's 1946 *Top Hats and Tom-Toms,* a work so severely critical of Liberia that it was banned in the country.

16 Stuckey, *Slave Culture,* 297.

17 See Wreh, *Love of Liberty,* chap. 8.

18 Clapham, *Liberia and Sierra Leone,* 105.

19 William Tolbert Jr., "Education as Related to Civic Progress," valedictory address, Liberia College, April 1934 (Monrovia: Printed by Authority, 1934).

20 Graham Greene, *Journey without Maps,* 195.

21 Yoder, "He Kill My Ma," 42.

22 Ibid., interview with James Korman; Monrovia, April 28, 1999.

23 Ibid., 51, citing interview with Samuel Z. Boakai, Buchanan, May 1999.

24 David Levering Lewis, *W. E. B. DuBois,* 687, citing "But Garvey Was the Source," interview with Adu Boahen, August 20, 1986.

25 Adekele, *Un-African Americans,* 138.

26 Edmundson, "Africa and the African Diaspora," 11, citing Stokely Carmichael (Kwame Toure), interview with the *Sunday News* (Dar es Salaam), November 5, 1967.

27 Michael Clough, *U.S. Policy toward Africa and the End of the Cold War* (New York: Council on Foreign Relations, 1992), 29, citing Rupert Emerson, *Africa and U.S. Policy* (Englewood Cliffs, N.J.: Prentice Hall, 1967).

28 C. Eric Lincoln, "The Race Problem and International Relations," in Shepherd, *Racial Influences on American Foreign Policy,* 57.

29 Shain, *Marketing the American Creed,* 136, citing Alfred O. Hero Jr., "American Negroes and U. S. Foreign Policy: 1937–1967," *Journal of Conflict Resolution* 13, 2 (1969).

30 Clough, *U.S. Policy,* 32, citing Joint Center for Political Studies, "Africa in the Minds and Deeds of African American Leaders," draft report to the Rockefeller Foundation, May 14, 1990.

31 Ibid., citing Memo to McGeorge Bundy from R. W. Komer and Rick Haynes, March 30, 1964, National Security Council files, Lyndon Baines Johnson Presidential Library, University of Texas at Austin.

32 National Security Council, Interdepartmental Group for Africa: Study in Response to Presidential Security Review Memorandum INSC-46, Black Africa and the U.S. Black Movement, March 17, 1978, supplied by Wallace Short, Howard University.

33 Clough, *U.S. Policy,* 34.

34 Tony Smith, *Foreign Attachments,* 116.

35 Ayittey, *Africa in Chaos,* 287.

36 Howard French, "An Ignorance of Africa as Vast as the Continent," *New York Times,* November 20, 1994, citing Axelle Kabou, *Et si l'Afrique refusait le développement* (What If Africa Refused Development?) (Paris: L'Harmattan, 1991).

37 Ayittey, *Africa in Chaos,* 287, citing *Washington Post,* March 14, 1995.
38 Ibid., citing *Washington Post,* March 1, 1995.
39 Robinson, *Debt,* 114.
40 David Brion Davis, "Looking at Slavery from Broader Perspectives," *American Historical Review* 105, 2 (2000), 466.
41 Du Bois, "The Negro's Fatherland," *Survey,* November 10, 1917, in Du Bois, *A Reader,* 652.
42 D'Souza, *End of Racism,* 113.
43 Doris Lessing, "The Jewel of Africa," *The New York Review of Books* 1, 6 (April 10, 2003), 6.
44 Bales, *Disposable People* (Berkeley, CA, 1999), 9.
45 Wole Soyinka, "Cultural Relativism and Absolute Rights, Sakarov Lecture, Brandeis University, March 31, 1998.
46 Samuel Cotton, *Silent Terror: A Journey into Contemporary African Slavery* (New York: Harlem River Press, 1998), 149.
47 Ibid., 149.
48 Lord Lugard, *Hansard,* Debate of the House of Lords, April 23, 1934, Great Britain, *Parliamentary Debates* vol. 90–94, 1933–34.
49 Susan Rice and David Scheffer, "Sudan Must End Its Brutal War against Civilians," *Herald Tribune,* September 1, 1999.
50 Qtd. in Nate Hentoff, "Anybody Care about Black Slaves?" *Village Voice,* August 20, 1998, 20.

Select Bibliography

Primary Sources

Archival Sources, Manuscript Collections, and Public Documents

Barnett, Claude. Papers. Boxes 187, 188. Chicago Historical Society. Chicago, Ill.

British Anti-slavery and Aborigines Protection Society Archives. London, U.K.

British Anti-slavery and Aborigines Protection Society Papers. Rhodes House, Oxford University. Oxford, U.K.

Cassell, C. Abayomi. Papers. Available on microfilm, Northwestern University Library. Evanston, Ill.

Cecil, Viscount. Papers of Viscount Cecil of Chelwood. British Museum, add 51071–204. London, U.K.

Du Bois, W. E. B. Papers. Available on microfilm, 89 reels. Library of Congress. Washington, D.C.

Great Britain. *Papers Concerning Affairs in Liberia, December 1930–May 1934.* Cmd. 4614 (1934). London: His Majesty's Stationery Office, 1934.

Great Britain. *Parliamentary Debates,* House of Lords, 5th ser., vols. 71, 83, 91.

Grimes, Louis B. Papers. Available on microfilm. Northwestern University Library. Evanston, Ill.

Johnson, Charles S. Papers. Fisk University Library. Nashville, Tenn.

League of Nations Secretariat. *Report of the Liberian Commission of Enquiry.* C.658.M272, June 1930.

Liberian National Archives Monrovia, Liberia.

Methodist Missionary Society Archives. London, U.K.

Moffat, J. Pierrepont. Papers. MSAm 1407, series 2, diplomatic journals and other papers, vols. 30–36, Washington, 1931–34. Houghton Library, Harvard University. Cambridge, Mass.

National Association for the Advancement of Colored People. Records. Library of Congress. Washington, D.C.

Phelps-Stokes Fund Archives. New York, N.Y.

Phillips, William. Papers. MSAm 2232, series 2, undersecretary of state, 1933–36. Houghton Library, Harvard University. Cambridge, Mass.

Porte, Albert. Papers. Available on microfilm. Northwestern University Library. Evanston, Ill.

Public Record Office, British Foreign Office. 72/1626.

Public Record Office, British Foreign Office. 367/16, 17, 61. London Foreign
    Office. 47/36. Liberia Foreign Office. 371.
Public Record Office, British Foreign Office. 368/1632.
Public Record Office, British Foreign Office. 458. Correspondence between
    the Foreign Office and the British Consulate-General in Monrovia.
Public Record Office, British Foreign Office. 458/104–458/127.
    Correspondence from the Consulate-General, Monrovia, Liberia. Available
    on microfilm, Northwestern University Library, Evanston, Ill.
Simon, Lady Kathleen. Papers. Manuscripts. British Empire S25. Rhodes
    House, Oxford University. Oxford, U.K.
U.S. Department of State. *Foreign Relations of the United States, 1910–1941.*
    Washington: U.S. Government Printing Office.
U.S. National Archives, Department of State. Washington, D.C. Records of
    the Department of State Relating to the Affairs of Liberia, 1910–1929.
U.S. National Archives, Department of State. Washington, D.C. Records of
    the Department of State Relating to the Internal Affairs of Liberia, 1910–
    1941. Available on microfilm, Northwestern University Library. Evanston,
    Ill.
U.S. Office of Coordinator of Information, Research, and Analysis Branch,
    Department of State, Office of Intelligence Research. Washington, D.C.
    Interview with Firestone Company, March 3, 1942.
Walton, Lester A. Papers. Boxes 8, 9, 10, 11, 14. Schomburg Center for
    Research in Black Culture. New York Public Library. New York, N.Y.

Secondary Sources

Newspapers and Serials

Amsterdam News (c.1920–30)
Baltimore Afro-American (c.1920–30)
Blackman (1934)
Chicago Defender (c.1920–30)
Crisis (c.1911–40)
Messenger (c.1922–23)
Negro Worker (c.1925–35)
Negro World (c.1920–27)
New York Times (c.1920–40)
Pittsburgh Courier (c.1929–40)

Books and Pamphlets

Adamson, Judith. *Graham Greene: The Dangerous Edge: Where Art and Politics
    Meet.* New York: St. Martin's, 1990.
Adekele, Tunde. *Un-African Americans: Nineteenth-Century Black Nationalists
    and the Civilizing Mission.* Lexington: University Press of Kentucky, 1998.

Anderson, Robert Earle. *Liberia: America's African Friend.* Chapel Hill: University of North Carolina Press, 1952.

Appiah, Kwame Anthony. *In My Father's House: Africa in the Philosophy of Culture.* New York: Oxford University Press, 1992.

Asante, S. K. B. *Pan-African Protest: West Africa and the Italo-Ethiopian Crisis, 1934–1941.* London: Longman, 1977.

Ayittey, George B. N. *Africa in Chaos.* New York: St. Martin's, 1998.

Azikiwe, Nnamdi. *Liberia in World Politics.* London: Stockwell, 1934.

Bales, Kevin. *Disposable People: New Slavery in the Global Economy.* Berkeley: University of California Press, 1999.

Barry, John M. *Rising Tide: The Great Mississippi Flood of 1927 and How It Changed America.* New York: Simon and Schuster, 1997.

Behrens, Christine. *Les Kroumen de la côté occidentale d'Afrique.* Talence, France: Domaine Universaire de Bordeaux, 1974.

Bell, Bernard W., Emily Grosholz, and James B. Stewart, eds. *W.E.B. Du Bois on Race and Culture: Philosophy, Politics, and Culture.* New York: Routledge, 1996.

Bennett, Lerone. *Before the Mayflower: A History of Black America.* 1969. Chicago: Johnson Publishing, 1987.

Blyden, Edward W. *Christianity, Islam, and the Negro Race.* 1887. Edinburgh: University of Edinburgh Press, 1967.

———. *Selected Letters of Edward Wilmot Blyden.* Ed. Hollis R. Lynch. Millwood, N.Y.: KTO, 1978.

Boley, G. E. Saigbe. *Liberia: The Rise and Fall of the First Republic.* New York: Macmillan, 1983.

Brandes, Joseph. *Herbert Hoover and Economic Diplomacy: Department of Commerce Policy, 1921–1928.* Pittsburgh, Pa.: University of Pittsburgh Press, 1962.

Bravo, Carbonel, Juan. *Fernando Po y el Muni: Sus misterios y riquezas: su colonización.* Madrid: Imprenta de Alrededor del Mundo, 1917.

Brawley, Benjamin. *A Social History of the American Negro: Being a History of the Negro Problem in the United States, Including a History and Study of the Republic of Liberia.* 1921. New York: Macmillan, 1970.

Brooks, George E., Jr. *The Kru Mariner in the Nineteenth Century: An Historical Compendium.* Newark, Del.: Liberian Studies Association in America, 1972.

Brown, George W. *The Economic History of Liberia.* Washington, D.C.: Associated Publishers, 1941.

Brown, Sterling A., Arthur P. Davis, and Ulysses Lee, eds. *The Negro Caravan: Writings by American Negroes.* 1941. Salem, N.H.: Oyer, 1991.

Buell, Raymond Leslie. *Liberia: A Century of Survival, 1847–1947.* Philadelphia: University of Pennsylvania Press, 1947.

———. *The Native Problem in Africa.* 2 vols. New York: Macmillan, 1928.

Burkett, Randall K. *Garveyism as a Religious Movement: The Institutionalization of a Black Civil Religion.* Metuchen, N.J.: Scarecrow, 1978.

Burks, Arthur J. *Land of Checkerboard Families.* New York: Coward-McCann, 1932.

Bush, Rod. *We Are Not What We Seem: Black Nationalism and Class Struggle in the American Century.* New York: New York University Press, 1999.

Campbell, Horace. *Rasta and Resistance: From Marcus Garvey to Walter Rodney.* Trenton, N.J.: Africa World Press, 1987.

Campbell, Penelope. *Maryland in Africa: The Maryland State Colonization Society, 1831–1857.* Urbana: University of Illinois Press, 1971.

Chireau, Yvonne, and Nathaniel Deutsch, eds. *Black Zion: African American Religious Encounters with Judaism.* New York: Oxford University Press, 2000.

Chisholm, Anne. *Nancy Cunard.* New York: Knopf, 1979.

Clapham, Christopher. *Liberia and Sierra Leone: An Essay in Comparative Politics.* New York: Cambridge University Press, 1976.

Clarke, John Henrik. *Africans at the Crossroads: Notes for an African World Revolution.* Trenton, N.J.: Africa World Press, 1991.

Clower, Robert W., et al. *Growth without Development: An Economic Survey of Liberia.* Evanston, Ill.: Northwestern University Press, 1966.

Cooper, Frederick. *From Slaves to Squatters: Plantation Labor and Agriculture in Zanzibar and Coastal Kenya, 1890–1925.* New Haven, Conn.: Yale University Press, 1980.

Cronon, E. David. *Black Moses: The Story of Marcus Garvey and the Universal Negro Improvement Association.* Madison: University of Wisconsin Press, 1969.

Crouch, Stanley. *The All-American Skin Game; or, the Decoy of Race: The Long and the Short of It, 1990–1994.* New York: Pantheon, 1995.

Cruse, Harold. *The Crisis of the Negro Intellectual.* New York: Morrow, 1967.

Curtin, Philip, et al. *African History: From Earliest Times to Independence.* New York: Longman, 1995.

Daniel, Pete. *The Shadow of Slavery: Peonage in the South, 1901–1969.* Urbana: University of Illinois Press, 1972.

Davis, David Brion. *Slavery and Human Progress.* New York: Oxford University Press, 1984.

Davis, Ronald W. *Ethnohistorical Studies on the Kru Coast.* Newark, Del.: Liberian Studies Association in America, 1976.

De La Rue, Sidney. *Land of the Pepper Bird: Liberia.* New York: Putnam, 1930.

Derrick, Jonathan. *Africa's Slaves Today.* London: Schocken, 1975.

Detzer, Dorothy. *Appointment on the Hill.* New York: Henry Holt, 1948.

Diawara, Manthia. *In Search of Africa.* Cambridge, Mass.: Harvard University Press, 1998.

Donner, Etta. *Hinterland Liberia.* Trans. Winifred M. Deans. London: Blackie, 1939.

Draper, Theodore. *The Rediscovery of Black Nationalism.* New York: Viking, 1970.

D'Souza, Dinesh. *The End of Racism: Principles for a Multiracial Society.* New York: Free Press, 1995.

Du Bois, W. E. B. *Black Folk: Then and Now: An Essay in the History and Sociology of the Negro Race.* New York: Henry Holt, 1939.

——. *Book Reviews by W. E. B. Du Bois.* Ed. Herbert Aptheker. Millwood, N.Y.: KTO, 1977.

——. *The Correspondence of W. E. B. Du Bois.* Vol. 2, *Selections, 1934–1944.* Ed. Herbert Aptheker. Amherst: University of Massachusetts Press, 1997.

——. *Dusk of Dawn: An Essay toward an Autobiography of a Race Concept.* 1940. New Brunswick, N.J.: Transaction, 1984.

——. *W. E. B. Du Bois: A Reader.* Ed. David Levering Lewis. New York: Henry Holt, 1995.

Dunn, D. Elwood, and Svend E. Holsoe. *Historical Dictionary of Liberia.* Metuchen, N.J.: Scarecrow, 1985.

Elkins, Stanley M. *Slavery: A Problem in American Institutional and Intellectual Life.* Chicago: University of Chicago Press, 1976.

Ellis, George. *Negro Culture in West Africa: A Social Study of the Negro Group of Vai-Speaking People, with Its Own Invented Alphabet and Written Language Shown in Two Charts and Six Engravings of Vai Script, Twenty-Six Illustrations of Their Arts and Life, Fifty Folklore Stories, One Hundred and Fourteen Proverbs, and One Map.* New York: Neale, 1914.

Eltis, David. *Economic Growth and the Ending of the Transatlantic Slave Trade.* New York: Oxford University Press, 1987.

Esedebe, P. Olisanwuche. *Pan-Africanism: The Idea and Movement, 1776–1963.* Washington, D.C.: Howard University Press, 1982.

Essien-Udom, E. U. *Black Nationalism: A Search for an Identity in America.* New York: Dell, 1969.

Fanon, Frantz. *Black Skin, White Masks.* Trans. Charles Lam Markmann. New York: Grove, 1967.

Fax, Elton C. *Garvey: The Story of a Pioneer Black Nationalist.* New York: Dodd, Mead, 1972.

Fierce, Milfred C. *The Pan-African Idea in the United States, 1900–1919: African-American Interest in Africa and Interaction with West Africa.* New York: Garland, 1993.

Firestone, Harvey S., Jr. *The Romance and Drama of the Rubber Industry.* Akron, Ohio: The Firestone Tire and Rubber Company, 1932.

Firestone Plantations Company. *Liberia and Firestone: The Development of a Rubber Industry: A Story of Friendship and Progress.* Akron, Ohio: The Firestone Tire and Rubber Company, 1956.

Fleming, G. James, and Christian Burckel, eds. *Who's Who in Colored America.* 7th ed. Yonkers-on-Hudson, N.Y.: Christian E. Burckel, 1950.

Foster, Carrie A. *The Women and the Warriors: The U.S. Section of the Women's International League for Peace and Freedom, 1915–1946.* Syracuse, N.Y.: Syracuse University Press, 1995.

Fraenkel, Merran. *Tribe and Class in Monrovia.* London: Oxford University Press for the International African Institute, 1964.

Franklin, V. P., et al., eds. *African Americans and Jews in the Twentieth Century: Studies in Convergence and Conflict.* Columbia: University of Missouri Press, 1998.

Furbay, Elizabeth Dearmin. *Top Hats and Tom-Toms.* London, J. Gifford, 1946.

Gaines, Kevin K. *Uplifting the Race: Black Leadership, Politics, and Culture in the Twentieth Century.* Chapel Hill: University of North Carolina Press, 1996.

Gallicchio, Marc. *The African American Encounter with Japan and China: Black Internationalism in Asia, 1895–1945*. Chapel Hill: University of North Carolina Press, 2000.

Gates, Henry Louis, Jr. *Wonders of the African World*. New York: Knopf, 1999.

Garvey, Marcus. *The Marcus Garvey and Universal Negro Improvement Association Papers.*Vol. 1, *1826–August 1919*. Ed. Robert A. Hill. Berkeley: University of California Press, 1983.

——. *The Marcus Garvey and Universal Negro Improvement Association Papers.* Vol. 2, *27 August 1919–31 August 1920*. Ed. Robert A. Hill. Berkeley: University of California Press, 1983.

——. *The Marcus Garvey and Universal Negro Improvement Association Papers.* Vol. 3, *September 1920–August 1921*. Ed. Robert A. Hill. Berkeley: University of California Press, 1983.

——. *The Marcus Garvey and Universal Negro Improvement Association Papers.* Vol. 4, *September 1921–September 1922*. Ed. Robert A. Hill. Berkeley: University of California Press, 1983.

——. *The Marcus Garvey and Universal Negro Improvement Association Papers.* Vol. 5, *September 1922–August 1924*. Ed. Robert A. Hill. Berkeley: University of California Press, 1983.

——. *The Marcus Garvey and Universal Negro Improvement Association Papers.* Vol. 6, *September 1924–December 1927*. Ed. Robert A. Hill. Berkeley: University of California Press, 1983.

——. *The Marcus Garvey and Universal Negro Improvement Association Papers.* Vol. 7, *November 1927–August 1940*. Ed. Robert A. Hill. Berkeley: University of California Press, 1983.

——. *The Marcus Garvey and Universal Negro Improvement Association Papers.* Vol. 9, *Africa for the Africans, 1921–1922*. Ed. Robert A. Hill. Berkeley: University of California Press, 1983.

——. *Philosophy and Opinions of Marcus Garvey; or, Africa for the Africans*. 1923. Ed. Amy Jacques-Garvey. New York: Atheneum, 1986.

Geiss, Imanuel. *The Pan-African Movement*. Trans. Ann Keep. New York: Africana Publishing Company, 1974.

Gershoni, Yekutiel. *Black Colonialism: The Americo-Liberian Scrabble for the Hinterland*. Boulder, Colo.: Westview, 1985.

Gide, André. *Travels in the Congo*. 1928. Trans. Dorothy Bussy. Berkeley: University of California Press, 1962.

Gilroy, Paul. *Against Race: Imagining Political Culture beyond the Color Line*. Cambridge, Mass.: Belknap, 2000.

——. *The Black Atlantic: Modernity and Double Consciousness*. Cambridge, Mass.: Harvard University Press, 1993.

Glaude, Eddie S. *Is It Nation Time? Contemporary Essays on Black Power and Black Nationalism*. Chicago: University of Chicago Press, 2002.

Gomez, Michael A. *Exchanging Our Country Marks: The Transformation of African Identities in the Colonial and Antebellum South*. Chapel Hill: University of North Carolina Press, 1998.

Green, A. Wigfall. *The Man Bilbo*. Baton Rouge: Louisiana State University, 1986.

Greene, Barbara. *Too Late to Turn Back*. 1938. London: Settle Bendall, 1981.

Greene, Graham. *The Heart of the Matter*. New York: Viking Press, 1948.

———. *Journey without Maps*. 1936. New York: Penguin, 1980.

Greenwall, Harry James, and Roland Wild. *Unknown Liberia*. London: Hutchinson, 1936.

Gregor, A. James. *The Faces of Janus: Marxism and Fascism in the Twentieth Century*. New Haven, Conn.: Yale University Press, 2000.

Haliburton, Gordon MacKay. *The Prophet Harris: A Study of an African Prophet and His Mass-Movement in the Ivory Coast and the Gold Coast, 1913–1915*. New York: Oxford University Press, 1973.

Harris, Joseph E. *African-American Reactions to War in Ethiopia, 1936–1941*. Baton Rouge: Louisiana State University Press, 1994.

Haywood, Harry. *Black Bolshevik: Autobiography of an Afro-American Communist*. Chicago: Liberator Press, 1978.

Hill, Adelaide Cromwell, and Martin Kilson, eds. *Apropos of Africa: Sentiments of Negro American Leaders on Africa from the 1800s to the 1950s*. London: Cass, 1969.

Hill, Polly. *The Migrant Cocoa-Farmers of Southern Ghana: A Study in Rural Capitalism*. Cambridge: Cambridge University Press, 1963.

Hochschild, Adam. *King Leopold's Ghost: A Story of Greed, Terror, and Heroism in Colonial Africa*. New York: Houghton Mifflin, 1998.

Hodges, Tony and Malyn Newitt. *São Tomé and Príncipe: From Plantation to Microstate*. Boulder, Colo.: Westview, 1988.

Holloway, Jonathan Scott. *Confronting the Veil: Abram Harris, Jr., E. Franklin Frazier, and Ralph Bunche, 1919–1941*. Chapel Hill: University of North Carolina Press, 2002.

Holloway, Joseph E. *Liberian Diplomacy in Africa: A Study of Inter-African Relations*. Washington, D.C.: University Press of America, 1981.

Honda, Katsuichi. *The Nanjing Massacre: A Japanese Journalist Confronts Japan's National Shame*. Ed. Frank Gibney. Trans. Karen Sandness. Armonk, N.Y.: M. E. Sharpe, 1999.

Hooker, James R. *Black Revolutionary: George Padmore's Path from Communism to Pan-Africanism*. London: Pall Mall, 1967.

Hopkins, A. G. *An Economic History of West Africa*. New York: Columbia University Press, 1973.

Howe, Stephen. *Afrocentrism: Mythical Past and Imagined Homelands*. New York: Verso, 1998.

Huggins, Willis N., and John G. Jackson. *Introduction to African Civilizations: With Main Currents in Ethiopian History*. 1937. New York: Negro University Press, 1969.

James, Winston. *Holding Aloft the Banner of Ethiopia: Caribbean Radicalism in Early Twentieth-Century America*. New York: Verso, 1998.

Jenkins, David. *Black Zion: Africa Imagined and Real as Seen by Contemporary Blacks*. New York: Harcourt Brace Jovanovich, 1975.

Johnson, Charles S. *Bitter Canaan: The Story of the Negro Republic*. New Brunswick, N.J.: Transaction, 1987.

Johnson, J. F., ed. *Proceedings of the General Anti-Slavery Convention.* London: John Snow, 1843.

July, Robert W. *A History of the African People.* New York: Scribner, 1970.

Kapuscinski, Ryszard. *The Emperor: Downfall of an Autocrat.* Trans. William R. Brand and Katarzyna Mroczkowska-Brand. New York: Harcourt Brace Jovanovich, 1983.

Klitgaard, Robert. *Tropical Gangsters: One Man's Experience with Development and Decadence in Deepest Africa.* New York: Basic Books, 1990.

Krenn, Michael L. *Black Diplomacy: African Americans and the State Department, 1945–1969.* Armonk, N.Y.: M.E. Sharpe, 1999.

——, ed. *Race and U.S. Foreign Policy from 1900 through World War I.* New York: Garland, 1998.

Langley, J. Ayodele. *Pan-Africanism and Nationalism in West Africa, 1900–1945: A Study in Ideology and Social Classes.* Oxford: Clarendon, 1973.

Lawler, Nancy Ellen. *Soldiers of Misfortune: Ivoirien Tirailleurs of World War Two.* Athens: Ohio University Press, 1992.

Lemelle, Sidney J., and Robin D. G. Kelley. *Imaging Home: Class, Culture, and Nationalism in the African Diaspora.* New York: Verso, 1994.

Lewis, David Levering. *W. E. B. DuBois: The Fight for Equality and the American Century, 1919–1963.* New York: Henry Holt, 2000.

Lewis, Rupert. *Marcus Garvey: Anti-Colonial Champion.* Trenton, N.J.: Africa World Press, 1988.

Lewis, Rupert, and Maureen Warner-Lewis, eds. *Garvey: Africa, Europe, the Americas.* 1951. Trenton, N.J.: Africa World Press, 1994.

Liberia. *Handbook of Liberia.* Monrovia: Published by Authority, 1940.

Liebenow, J. Gus. *Liberia: The Evolution of Privilege.* Ithaca, N.Y.: Cornell University Press, 1969.

Lief, Alfred. *The Firestone Story: A History of the Firestone Tire and Rubber Company.* New York: Whittlesey House, 1951.

Lindqvist, Sven. *Exterminate All the Brutes: One Man's Odyssey into the Heart of Darkness and the Origins of European Genocide.* New York: New Press, 1996.

Lovejoy, Paul E. *Transformations in Slavery: A History of Slavery in Africa.* New York: Cambridge University Press, 1983.

Lowenkopf, Martin. *Politics in Liberia: The Conservative Road to Development.* Stanford, Calif.: Hoover Institution Press, 1976.

Madariaga, Salvador de. *Americans.* London: Oxford University Press, 1930.

Mantero, Francisco. *Portuguese Planters and British Humanitarians: The Case for S. Thome.* Lisbon: Redaç' de Reforma, 1911.

Marcus, Harold G. *A History of Ethiopia.* Berkeley: University of California Press, 1994.

Marinelli, Lawrence A. *The New Liberia: A Historical and Political Survey.* New York: Praeger, 1964.

Markakis, John, and Ayele, Nega. *Class and Revolution in Ethiopia.* Nottingham, U.K.: Spokesman, 1978.

Martin, Tony. *Race First: The Ideological and Organizational Struggles of Marcus Garvey and the Universal Negro Improvement Association.* Dover, Mass.: Majority Press, 1986.

Mazrui, Ali A., and Mazrui, Alamin M. *The Power of Babel: Language and Governance in the African Experience.* Chicago: University of Chicago Press, 1998.

McCartney, John T. *Black Power Ideologies: An Essay in African-American Political Thought.* Philadelphia: Temple University Press, 1992.

McKinley, Edward H. *The Lure of Africa: American Interests in Tropical Africa, 1919–1939.* Indianapolis: Bobbs-Merrill, 1974.

Miers, Suzanne, and Igor Kopytoff, eds. *Slavery in Africa: Historical and Anthropological Perspectives.* Madison: University of Wisconsin Press, 1977.

Miers, Suzanne, and Richard Roberts, eds. *The End of Slavery in Africa.* Madison: University of Wisconsin Press, 1988.

Mixer, Knowlton. *Porto Rico.* New York: Macmillan, 1926.

Morel, E. D. *E. D. Morel's History of the Congo Reform Movement.* Eds. William R. Louis and Jean Stengers. Oxford: Clarendon, 1968.

Moreno-Moreno, José A. *Reseña histórica de la presencia de España en el Golfo de Guinea.* Madrid: Consejo Superior de Investigaciones Científicas, Instituto de Estudios Africanos, 1952.

Morgan, Chester M. *Redneck Liberal: Theodore G. Bilbo and the New Deal.* Baton Rouge: Louisiana State University Press, 1986.

Moses, Wilson Jeremiah. *Afrotopia: The Roots of African American Popular History.* New York: Cambridge University Press, 1998.

Mosse, George L. *The Fascist Revolution: Towards a General Theory of Fascism.* New York: H. Fertis, 1999.

Nearing, Scott. *Black America.* New York: Schocken, 1969.

Nevinson, H. W. *A Modern Slavery.* London: Harper, 1906.

Oshinsky, David M. *Worse Than Slavery: Parchman Farm and the Ordeal of Jim Crow Justice.* New York: Free Press, 1996.

Ottley, Roi. *"New World A-Coming": Inside Black America.* Boston: Houghton Mifflin, 1943.

Padmore, George. *American Imperialism Enslaves Liberia.* Moscow: Centrizdat, 1931.

——. *Pan-Africanism or Communism? The Coming Struggle for Africa.* London: Dobson, 1956.

Padmore, George Arthur. *The Memoirs of a Liberian Ambassador: George Arthur Padmore.* Lewiston, N.Y.: Edwin Mellen, 1996.

Pate, Alex. *Amistad.* New York: Penguin, 1997.

Plummer, Brenda Gayle. *Rising Wind: Black Americans and U.S. Foreign Affairs, 1935–1960.* Chapel Hill: University of North Carolina Press, 1996.

Porteous, J. Douglas. *Landscapes of the Mind: Worlds of Sense and Metaphor.* Toronto: University of Toronto Press, 1990.

Radell, Karen Marguerite. *Affirmation in a Moral Wasteland: A Comparison of Ford Madox Ford and Graham Greene.* New York: Peter Lang, 1987.

Ramos-Izquierdo y Vivar, Luis. *Descripción geográfica gobierno, administración y colonizacón de las colonias españolas del Golfo de Guniea.* Madrid: Imprenta de Felipe Pefia Cruz, 1912.

Rampersad, Arnold. *The Art and Imagination of W. E. B. Du Bois.* Cambridge, Mass.: Harvard University Press, 1976.

Rattray, R. S. *Ashanti Law and Constitution.* Oxford: Clarendon, 1969.

Redkey, Edwin S. *Black Exodus: Black Nationalist and Back-to-Africa Movements, 1890–1910.* New Haven, Conn.: Yale University Press, 1969.

Reeve, Henry F. *The Black Republic: Liberia, Its Political and Social Conditions To-day.* London: Witherby, 1923.

Reid, Ira De Augustine. *The Negro Immigrant: His Background, Characteristics and Social Adjustment, 1899–1937.* New York: Columbia University Press, 1939.

Rey, Charles Fernand. *In the Country of the Blue Nile.* London: Duckworth, 1927.

Rich, Evelyn Jones, and Immanuel Wallerstein, eds. *Africa: Tradition and Change.* New York: Random House, 1972.

Richardson, Nathaniel R. *Liberia's Past and Present.* London: Diplomatic Press, 1959.

Richburg, Keith B. *Out of America: A Black Man Confronts Africa.* New York: Basic Books, 1997.

Robeson, Eslanda Goode. *African Journey.* 1945. Westport, Conn.: Greenwood, 1972.

Robinson, Randall. *The Debt: What America Owes to Blacks.* New York: Dutton, 2000.

Rodney, Walter. *How Europe Underdeveloped Africa.* London. Bogle-L'Ouverture, 1972.

Rodriguez, Richard. *Brown: The Last Discovery of America.* New York: Viking, 2002.

Rudwick, Elliott M. *W. E. B. Du Bois: Propagandist of the Negro Protest.* New York: Atheneum, 1968.

Saha, Santosh C. *Culture in Liberia: An Afrocentric View of the Cultural Interaction between the Indigenous Liberians and the Americo-Liberians.* Lewiston, N.Y.: Edwin Mellen, 1998.

Sawyer, Amos. *The Emergence of Autocracy in Liberia.* San Francisco: Institute for Contemporary Studies, 1992.

Sawyer, Roger. *Slavery in the Twentieth Century.* London: Routledge and Kegan Paul, 1986.

Schuyler, George S. *Black and Conservative: The Autobiography of George S. Schuyler.* New Rochelle, N.Y.: Arlington House, 1966.

——. *Black Empire.* Ed. Robert A. Hill and R. Kent Rasmussen. Boston: Northeastern University Press, 1991.

——. *Slaves Today: A Story of Liberia.* New York: Brewer, Warren, and Putnam, 1931.

Scott, William R. *The Sons of Sheba's Race: African-Americans and the Italo-Ethiopian War, 1935–1941.* Bloomington: Indiana University Press, 1993.

Shain, Yossi. *Marketing the American Creed Abroad: Diasporas in the U.S. and Their Homelands.* New York: Cambridge University Press, 1999.

Shepherd, George W., Jr., ed. *Racial Influences on American Foreign Policy.* New York: Basic Books, 1970.

Sherry, Norman. *The Life of Graham Greene.* Vol. 1, *1904–1939.* New York: Viking, 1989.

Sibley, James L., and D. Westermann. *Liberia, Old and New: A Study of Its Social and Economic Background with Possibilities of Development*. Garden City, N.Y.: Doubleday, Doran, 1928.

Silén, Juan Angel. *Pedro Albizu Campos*. Río Piedras: Editorial Antillana, 1976.

Simon, Kathleen. *Slavery*. 1929. New York: Negro Universities Press, 1969.

Simpson, Clarence. *The Memoirs of C. L. Simpson*. London: Diplomatic Press, 1961.

Skinner, Elliott P. *African Americans and U.S. Policy toward Africa, 1850–1924: In Defense of Black Nationality*. Washington, D.C.: Howard University Press, 1992.

———, ed. *Beyond Constructive Engagement: United States Foreign Policy toward Africa*. New York: Paragon House, 1986.

Smith, Anthony D. *National Identity*. Reno: University of Nevada Press, 1991.

Smith, Robert A. *The American Foreign Policy in Liberia*. Monrovia: Providence Publications, 1972.

Smith, Tony. America's Mission: *The United States and the Worldwide Struggle for Democracy in the Twentieth Century*. Princeton: Princeton University Press, 1994.

———. *Foreign Attachments: The Power of Ethnic Groups in the Making of American Foreign Policy*. Cambridge, Mass: Harvard University Press, 2000.

Snelgrave, William. *A New Account of Some Parts of Guinea and the Slave-Trade*. 1734. London: Frank Cass and Company, 1971.

Solomon, Mark I. *The Cry Was Unity: Communists and African Americans, 1917–36*. Jackson: University Press of Mississippi, 1998.

Sorenson, John. *Imagining Ethiopia: Struggle for History and Identity in the Horn of Africa*. New Brunswick, N.J.: Rutgers University Press, 1993.

Stein, Judith. *The World of Marcus Garvey: Race and Class in Modern Society*. Baton Rouge: Louisiana State University Press, 1986.

Stewart, Thomas McCants. *Liberia: The Americo-African Republic*. New York: Edward O. Jenkins' Sons, 1886.

Stoddard, Lothrop. *The Rising Tide of Color against White World-Supremacy*. New York: Scribner, 1920.

Strong, Richard P., ed. *The African Republic of Liberia and the Belgian Congo*. 2 vols. Cambridge, Mass.: Harvard University Press, 1930.

Stuckey, Sterling. *Slave Culture: Nationalist Theory and the Foundations of Black America*. New York: Oxford University Press, 1987.

Suret-Canale, Jean. *French Colonialism in Tropical Africa, 1900–1945*. Trans. Till Gottheiner. London: Hurst, 1971.

Swing, Raymond. *Forerunners of American Fascism*. 1935. Freeport, N.Y.: Books for Libraries, 1969.

Talalay, Kathryn. *Composition in Black and White: The Life of Philippa Schuyler*. New York: Oxford University Press, 1995.

Taylor, Wayne Chatfield. *The Firestone Operations in Liberia*. Washington, D.C.: National Planning Association, 1956.

Terán, Manuel de. *Síntesis geográfica de Fernando Póo*. Madrid: Instituto de Estudios Africanos, 1962.

Thomas, Hugh. *The Slave Trade: The Story of the Atlantic Slave Trade, 1440–1870.* New York: Simon and Schuster, 1997.

Three Negro Classics: Up From Slavery/Booker T. Washington; The Souls of Black Folk/William E. B. Du Bois; The Autobiography of an Ex-Colored Man/James Weldon Johnson. New York: Avon, 1965.

Unzueta, Abelardo de. *Geografía histórica de la Isla de Fernando Póo.* Madrid: Consejo Superior de Investigaciones Científicas, Instituto de Estudios Africanos, 1947.

Van Deburg, William L., ed. *Modern Black Nationalism: From Marcus Garvey to Louis Farrakhan.* New York: New York University Press, 1997.

Verrill, A. Hyatt. *Porto Rico Past and Present and San Domingo of Today.* New York: Dodd, Mead, 1914.

Vincent, Theodore G. *Black Power and the Garvey Movement.* Berkeley, Calif.: Ramparts, 1971.

Von Eschen, Penny M. *Race against Empire: Black Americans and Anticolonialism, 1937–1957.* Ithaca, N.Y.: Cornell University Press, 1997.

Von Gnielinski, Stefan, ed. *Liberia in Maps.* London: University of London Press, 1972.

Walker, Clarence Earl. *Deromanticizing Black History: Critical Essays and Reappraisals.* Knoxville: University of Tennessee Press, 1991.

Waugh, Evelyn. *Black Mischief.* 1932. New York: Penguin, 1938.

———. *Remote People.* London: Duckworth, 1931.

Weisbord, Robert G. *Ebony Kinship: Africa, Africans, and the Afro-American.* Westport, Conn.: Greenwood, 1973.

Wellard, James. *Lost Worlds of Africa.* New York: Dutton, 1967.

West, Henry Litchfield. *The Liberian Crisis.* Washington, D.C.: American Colonization Society, 1933.

West, W. J. *The Quest for Graham Greene.* London: Wiedenfeld and Nicolson, 1997.

Wilks, Ivor. *Asante in the Nineteenth Century: The Structure and Evolution of a Political Order.* New York: Cambridge University Press, 1975.

Williams, Walter B., and Maude W. Williams. *Adventures with the Krus in West Africa.* New York: Vantage, 1955.

Williams, William Appleman. *The Tragedy of American Diplomacy.* New York: Delta, 1972.

Wilson, Charles Morrow. *Liberia.* New York: William Sloane, 1947.

Wilson, Henry S. *Origins of West African Nationalism.* London: Macmillan, 1969.

Wilson, Walter. *Forced Labor in the United States.* New York: International Publishers, 1933.

Wintz, Cary, ed. *African-American Political Thought, 1890–1930: Washington, Du Bois, Garvey, and Randolph.* Armonk, N.Y.: M. E. Sharpe, 1996.

Woodson, Carter G. *The African Background Outlined; or, Handbook for the Study of the Negro.* Washington, D.C.: Association for the Study of Negro Life and History, 1936.

Work, Monroe N., ed. *The Negro Year Book, 1931–1932.* Tuskegee, Ala.: Negro Year Book Publishing, 1931.

Wreh, Tuan. *The Love of Liberty: The Rule of President William V. S. Tubman in Liberia, 1944–1971.* London: Hurst, 1976.

Wright, Richard. *Black Power: A Record of Reactions in a Land of Pathos.* New York: Harper, 1954.

Wright, W. D. *Black Intellectuals, Black Cognition, and a Black Aesthetic.* Westport, Conn.: Praeger, 1997.

Yancy, Ernest Jerome. *Historic Lights of Liberia Yesterday and Today.* 3d ed. Tel Aviv: Around the World Publishing House, 1967.

———. *The Recent Liberian Crisis and Its Causes.* Buffalo, N.Y.: Buffalo Liberian Research Society, 1934.

Yenser, Thomas, ed. *Who's Who in Colored America.* 6th ed. New York: Thomas Yenser, 1944.

Young, James C. *Liberia Rediscovered.* Garden City, N.Y.: Doubleday, Doran, 1934.

Articles and Essays

Adams, Edward C. L. "Gullah Joe (The Story of an African Slave)." In *Tales of the Congaree,* ed. Robert G. O'Meally. Chapel Hill: University of North Carolina Press, 1987.

Adeleke, Tunde. "Black Americans and Africa: A Critique of the Pan-African and Identity Paradigms." *The International Journal of African Historical Studies* 32, 3 (1998): 505–36.

Akpan, M. B. "Black Imperialism: Americo-Liberian Rule over the African Peoples of Liberia, 1841–1964." *The Canadian Journal of African Studies* 7, 2 (1973): 217–36.

———. "Liberia and the Universal Negro Improvement Association: The Background to the Abortion of Garvey's Scheme for African Colonization." *Journal of African History* 14, 1 (1973): 105–27.

Allen, J. "When Japan Was 'Champion of the Darker Races': Satokata Takahashi and the Flowering of Black Messianic Nationalism." *Black Scholar* 24, 1 (1994): 23–46.

Azevedo, Warren L. "Tribe and Chiefdom on the Windward Coast." *Liberian Studies Journal* 14, 2 (1989): 90–116.

Azikiwe, Benjamin Nnamdi. "In Defense of Liberia." *Journal of Negro History* 17, 1 (1932): 30–50.

———. "Liberia and World Diplomacy." *Southern Workman,* May 1932, 229–32.

———. "Liberia Declares a Moratorium." *Southern Workman,* June 1933, 276–80.

Barclay, Edwin. "The Case of Liberia." *Crisis,* February 1934, 40–42.

Benson, W. "After Liberia." *Political Quarterly* 2, 2 (1931): 257–66.

Berg, Elliot. "The Development of a Labor Force in Sub-Saharan Africa." *Economic Development and Cultural Change* 13, 4.1 (1965): 394–412.

Bilbo, Theodore G. "An African Home for Our Negroes." *Living Age* 358, 4451 (June 1940): 327–35.

Blakey, Michael L. "Race, Nationalism, and the Afrocentric Past." In *Making Alternative Histories: The Practice of Archaeology and History in Non-Western Settings,* ed. Peter R. Schmidt and Thomas C. Patterson. Santa Fe, N.M.: School of American Research Press, 1995.

Blyden, Edward Wilmot. "The Call of Providence to the Descendants of Africa in America." In *Negro Social and Political Thought, 1850–1920: Representative Texts,* ed. Howard Brotz. New York: Basic Books, 1966.

Brath, Elombe. "Marcus Garvey: The First African Internationalist." *Caribe* 9, 1 (1987): 11–23.

Bravo Carbonel, Juan. "Possibilidades económicas de la Guinea Espaniola." *Boletín de la Sociedad Geográfica Nacional* 73, 8 (1933): 524–47.

Browder, Earl. "Earl Browder Replies." *Crisis,* December 1935, 372.

Buell, Raymond Leslie. "The Liberian Paradox." *Virginia Quarterly Review* 7 (1931): 161–75.

———. "Mr. Firestone's Liberia." *Nation,* May 2, 1928, 521–24.

———. "The New Deal and Liberia." *New Republic,* August 16,1933, 17–19.

———. "The Reconstruction of Liberia." *Foreign Policy Reports* 8 (1932): 120–24.

Burrowes, Carl Patrick. *The Americo-Liberian Ruling Class and Other Myths: A Critique in the Liberian Context.* Occasional paper, Temple University, Department of African-American Studies, 1989.

Buxton, Charles R. "Improvement in Liberia." *Crisis,* March 1935, 92.

Cassell, Nathaniel H. B. "Liberia Defended by a Liberian." *Current History* 35 (1931): 880–82.

Chalk, Frank. "The Anatomy of an Investment: Firestone's 1927 Loan to Liberia." *Canadian Journal of African Studies* 1, 1 (1967): 12–32.

———. "Du Bois and Garvey Confront Liberia: Two Incidents of the Coolidge Years." *Canadian Journal of African Studies* 1, 2 (1967): 135–42.

Chrisman, Robert. "Aspects of Pan-Africanism." *Black Scholar* 4, 10 (1973): 2–8.

Christy, Cuthbert. "Liberia in 1930, with Discussion." *Geographical Journal* 75 (1931): 515–40.

"Clearing up the Liberian Mess." *Christian Century,* February 4, 1931, 156.

Crichlow, Cyril A. "What I Know about Liberia." *Crusader,* December 1921, 20–23.

Davis, David Brion. "Looking at Slavery from Broader Perspectives." "American Historical Review Forum: Crossing Slavery's Boundaries." *American Historical Review* 105, 2 (2000): 452–66.

Drake, St. Clair. "Negro Americans and Africa Interest." In *The American Negro Reference Book,* ed. John P. Davis. Englewood Cliffs, N.J.: Prentice-Hall, 1966.

Du Bois, W. E. B. "Again, Liberia." *Crisis,* October 1933, 236.

———. "Inter-racial Implications of the Ethiopian Crisis: A Negro View." *Foreign Affairs* 14, 1, (1935): 88–92.

———. "Liberia and Rubber." *New Republic,* November 18, 1925, 326–29.

———. "Liberia, the League, and the United States." *Foreign Affairs* 11, 4 (1933): 682–95.

———. "Pan-Africa and New Racial Philosophy." *Crisis,* November 1933, 247–62.

———. "Postscript — From a Traveller." *Crisis,* December 1932, 387–88.

———. "Postscript — Liberia." *Crisis,* March 1931, 102.

———. "Stand Fast, Liberia." *Crisis,* November 1933, 260–61.

Duffield, Ian. "Pan-Africanism: Rational and Irrational." Review of *The Pan-African Movement,* by Imanuel Geiss. *Journal of African History* 18, 4 (1977): 597–620.

Edmundson, Locksley. "Africa and the African Diaspora: The Years Ahead." In *Africa in World Affairs: The Next Thirty Years,* ed. Ali A. Mazrui and Hasu H. Patel. New York: Third Press, 1973.

Eisenberg, Bernard, and Kelly Miller. "The Negro Leader as a Marginal Man." *Journal of Negro History* 45, 3 (1960): 190–95.

Emerson, Rupert. "Race in Africa: United States Foreign Policy." In *Racial Influences on American Foreign Policy,* ed. George W. Shepherd Jr. New York: Basic Books, 1970.

Ferguson, Niall. "British Imperialism Revisited: The Costs and Benefits of 'Anglobization.' " "The British Empire and Globalization: A Forum." *Historically Speaking, Journal of the Historical Society* 4, 4 (2003). Online: www.bu.edu/historic/hs/april03.html.

———. "The Empire Slinks Back." *New York Times Magazine,* April 27, 2003, sec. 6, 54–57.

Flemming, Walter. "Deportation and Colonization: An Attempted Solution to the Race Problem." In *Studies in Southern History and Politics: Inscribed to William Archibald Dunning, Ph.D., Ll.D., Lieber Professor of History and Political Philosophy in Columbia University by His Former Pupils, the Authors.* New York: Columbia University Press, 1914.

"Forced Labor in Liberia." *The Nation,* February 26, 1930, 256.

Fraenkel, Merran. "Social Change on the Kru Coast of Liberia." *Africa* 26 (1966): 154–72.

Frazier, E. Franklin. "Potential American Negro Contributions to African Social Development." In *Africa from the Point of View of American Negro Scholars,* ed. John A. Davis. Paris: Présence Africaine, 1958.

Gates, Henry Louis, Jr. "A Fragmented Man: George Schuyler and the Claims of Race." *New York Times Book Review,* September 20, 1992, 31, 42–43.

Gbadezesin, Segren. "Kinship of the Dispossessed: Du Bois, Nkrumah, and the Foundations of Pan-Africanism." In *W. E. B. Du Bois on Race and Culture: Philosophy, Politics, and Poetics,* ed. Bernard W. Bell, Emily Grosholz, and James B. Stewart. New York: Routledge, 1996.

Gilpin, Patrick J. "Charles S. Johnson: Scholar and Educator." *Negro History Bulletin* 39, 3 (1976): 544–48.

Guttierez-Sobral, José. "The Outlook at Fernando Po." *West Africa* 11, 1 (1901): 334–36.

Hallgren, Mauritz A. "Liberia in Shackles." *Nation,* August 16, 1933, 185–88.

Hanchard, Michael. "Afromodernity: Race, Diaspora, and Transnational Identity." *Northwestern University Program of African Studies Newsletter* 8, 2 (1998): 2.

Hargreaves, J. D. "African Colonization in the Nineteenth Century: Liberia and Sierra Leone." In *Boston University Papers in African History*. Vol. 1. Boston: Boston University Press, 1964.

Harlan, Louis R. "Booker T. Washington and the White Man's Burden." *American Historical Review* 71 (1960).

Hayden, Thomas. "A Description of the 1970 Grand Cess Bo." *Liberian Studies Journal* 4, 2 (1971–72): 183–88.

Herskovits, Melville. "The Significance of West Africa for Negro Research." *Journal of Negro History* 21, 1 (1936): 15–30.

Hill, Robert. "Black Zionism, Marcus Garvey, and the Jewish Question." In *African Americans and Jews in the Twentieth Century: Studies in Convergence and Conflict,* ed. V. P. Franklin et al. Columbia: University of Missouri Press, 1998.

———. "The First England Years and After, 1912–1916." In *Marcus Garvey and the Vision of Africa,* ed. John Henrik Clarke. New York: Random House, 1974.

———. "Jews and the Enigma of the Pan-African Congress of 1919." In *Jews in Black Perspectives: A Dialogue,* ed. Joseph R. Washington Jr. Rutherford, N.J.: Fairleigh Dickinson University Press, 1984.

Hlophe, Stephen. "The Significance of Barth and Geertz' Model of Ethnicity in the Analysis of Nationalism in Liberia." *Canadian Journal of African Studies* 7, 2 (1973): 237–56.

Hochschild, Adam. "Leopold's Congo: A Holocaust We Have Yet to Comprehend." *Chronicle of Higher Education,* May 12, 2000, 134–36.

Holt, Thomas C. "The Political Uses of Alienation: W. E. B. Du Bois on Politics, Race, and Culture, 1903–1940." *American Quarterly* 42, 2 (1990): 301–23.

Hooker, J. R. "The Negro American Press and Africa in the Nineteen Thirties." *Canadian Journal of African Studies* 1, 1 (1967): 43–50.

Hudson, J. Blaine. "The African Diaspora and the 'Black Atlantic': An African American Perspective." *Negro History Bulletin* 60, 4 (1997): 7–14.

Inikori, Joseph E. "Slavery in Africa and the Transatlantic Slave Trade." In *The African Diaspora,* ed. Alusine Jalloh and Stephen E. Maizlish. College Station: Texas A & M University Press, 1996.

———. "Slaves or Serfs? A Comparative Study of Slavery and Serfdom in Europe and Europe." In *The African Diaspora: African Origins and New World Identities,* ed. Isidore Okpewho, Carole Boyce Davies, and Ali A. Mazrui. Bloomington: Indiana University Press, 1999.

Issacs, Harold R. "The American Negro and Africa: Some Notes." *Phylon* 20, 3 (1959): 219–33.

Ivy, James W. "A Negro's View of Liberia." Letter to the editor. *Nation,* December 6, 1933, 653.

Kahn, Robert. "The Political Ideology of Marcus Garvey." *Midwest Quarterly* 24, 2 (1983): 117–37.

Kaplan, Robert. "The Coming Anarchy." *Atlantic Monthly,* February 1994, 44–82.

Knoll, Arthur J. "Firestone's Labor Policy, 1924–1939." *Liberian Studies Journal* 16, 2 (1991): 49–73.

Kolchin, Peter. "The Big Picture: A Comment on David Brian Davis's 'Looking at Slavery from Broader Perspectives.'" *American Historical Review* 105, 2 (2000): 467–71.

Koren, William. "Liberia, the League, and the United States." *Foreign Policy Reports* 10, 1 (1934): 239–48.

Kornegay, Francis. "Africa and Presidential Politics." *Africa Report* 21, 4 (1976): 7–20.

Kuyper, George Adrian. "Liberia and the League of Nations." *Southern Workman,* April 1934, 112–17.

Langley, Jabez Ayodele. "Garveyism and African Nationalism." *Race* 6, 2 (1969): 157–72.

Lapham, Lewis H. "The Black Man's Burden." *Harper's,* June 1977, 15–18.

Lawson, Benjamin. "A 1930s African-American View of Liberia: George S. Schuyler." *Liberian Studies Journal* 20, 2 (1995): 247–62.

League of Nations. "Abstracts from the Memorandum of the Italian Government to the League of Nations." *Official Journal* 13 (1935): 1355–1416.

Lessing, Doris. "The Jewel of Africa." *The New York Review of Books* 1, 6 (April 10, 2003), 6–10.

"Liberia." *Opportunity,* November 1928, 324–25.

"Liberia." *Southern Workman,* April 1934, 99–100.

"The Liberian Commission." *Opportunity,* January 1931, 6.

"Liberian Slavery." *Spectator,* January 3, 1931, 68–69.

Logan, Rayford. "The American Negro's View of Africa." In *Africa Seen by American Negroes,* ed. John A. Davis. Paris: Présence Africaine, 1958.

———. "The International Status of the Negro." *Journal of Negro History* 18, 1 (1933), 33–36.

———. "Liberia's Dilemma." *Southern Workman,* September 1933, 357–63.

Martin, Tony. "Marcus Garvey: His Cumulative Impact." *Caribe* 9, 1 (1987): 1–6.

———. "The Pan-Africanism of W. E. B. Du Bois." In *W. E. B. Du Bois on Race and Culture: Philosophy, Politics, and Poetics,* ed. Bernard W. Bell, Emily Grosholz, and James B. Stewart. New York: Routledge, 1996.

Mazrui, Ali A. "Pan-Africianism: From Poetry to Power." *Issue* 23, 1 (1995): 35–38.

Meillassoux, Claude. "Essai d'interpretation du phénomène économique dans les societés traditionelles d'autosubsistence." *Cahiers d'études africaines* 7 (1961): 38–67.

Miller, Joseph C. "History and Africa/Africa and History." *American Historical Review* 104, 1 (1999): 1–32.

Morais, W. M. "Liberian Natives Tell Their Story." *Crisis,* September 1934, 272–73.

Moses, Wilson J. "Culture, Civilization, and Decline of the West." In *W. E. B. Du Bois on Race and Culture: Philosophy, Politics, and Poetics,* ed. Bernard W. Bell, Emily Grosholz, and James B. Stewart. New York: Routledge, 1996.

Mower, J. H. "The Republic of Liberia." *Journal of Negro History* 32, 3 (1947): 265–306.

"Mr. Bilbo's Afflatus." *Time Magazine* 38, 19 (May 8, 1939): 14–15.

Nelson, Gersham. "Rastafarians and Ethiopia." In *Imagining Home: Class, Culture, and Nationalism in the African Diaspora,* ed. Sidney J. Lemelle and Robin D. G. Kelley. New York: Verso, 1994.

Normandy, Elizabeth. "African-Americans and U.S. Policy towards Liberia, 1929–1935." *Liberian Studies Journal* 17, 2 (1993): 203–30.

"No Rubber Peonage." *Outlook,* August 8, 1928, 607.

Obatala, J. K. "Liberia: The Meaning of Dual Citizenship." *Black Scholar* 4, 10 (1973): 16–19.

Padgett, J. A. "Ministers to Liberia and Their Diplomacy." *Journal of Negro History* 22, 3 (1937): 50–92.

Padmore, George. "Forced Labor in Africa." *Labor Monthly,* April 1937, 237–47.

———. "Hands Off Liberia." *Negro Worker,* October–November 1931, 10.

———. "An Open Letter to Earl Browder." *Crisis,* October 1935, 302–15.

———. "Workers Defend Liberia." *Negro Worker,* October–November 1931, 10.

Patterson, Orlando. "America's Worst Idea." Review of *One Drop of Blood: The American Misadventure of Race,* by Scott L. Malcomson. *New York Times Book Review,* October 22, 2000, sec. 7, p. 15.

Plummer, Brenda Gayle. "The Afro-American Response to the Occupation of Haiti, 1915–1934." *Phylon* 43, 2 (1982): 125–43.

"Proceedings of the Annual Meeting of the Association for the Study of Negro Life and History Held in New York City, November 8–12, 1931." *Journal of Negro History* 17, 1 (1932): 1–7.

Rath, Richard C. "Echo and Narcissus: The Afrocentric Pragmatism of W. E. B. Du Bois." *Journal of American History* 84, 2 (1997): 461–95.

"The Regeneration of Liberia." *Opportunity,* February 1931, 38.

Renner, G. T. "Liberia: Where America Meets Africa." *Home Geographic Monthly* 1 (April 1932): 31–36.

Rey, Pierre-Phillippe. "L'esclavage linager chez les Tsangui, les Punu et les Kuni du Congo-Brazzaville: Sa place dans le système d'ensemble des rapports de production." In *L'esclavage en Afrique précoloniale,* ed. Claude Meillassoux. Paris: François Maspero, 1975.

Rogers, Ben F. "William E. B. Du Bois, Marcus Garvey, and Pan-Africa." *Journal of Negro History* 40, 2 (1955): 154–65.

Roosevelt, Theodore. "Brazil and the Negro." *Outlook,* February 21, 1914, 410–11.

Said, Edward. "Impossible Histories: Why the Many Islams Cannot Be Simplified." *Harpers,* July 2002, 69–74.

Satter, Beryl. "Marcus Garvey, Father Divine, and the Politics of Race Differences and Race Neutrality." *American Quarterly* 48, 1 (1996): 43–65.

Schmokel, Wolfe. "The United States and the Crisis of Liberian Independence." *Boston University Papers on Africa* 1, 1 (1966).

Schuyler, George. "More about Liberia." Letter to the editor. *Crisis,* December 1934, 375–76.

———. "Uncle Sam's Black Step-Child." *American Mercury,* June 1933, 147–56.

———. "Wide 'Slavery' Persisting in Liberia, Post Reveals." *New York Evening Post,* June 29, 1931, 1.

Scott, Rebecca. "Small-Scale Dynamics of Large-Scale Processes." *American Historical Review* 105, 2 (2000): 472–79.

Scott, William R. "Black Nationalism and the Italo-Ethiopian Conflict, 1934–1936." *Journal of Negro History* 63, 2 (1978): 188–34.

Sherman, Mary A. "Some Liberian Intellectuals in the Nineteenth Century." *Liberian Studies Journal* 6, 2 (1975): 162–76.

"Slavery and Forced Labor in Liberia." *International Labor Review* 23 (1931): 533–47.

"Slavery in Liberia." *Economist,* January 17, 1931, 105–6.

Smith, Rennie. "Negro Self-Government at a Crisis in Liberia." *Current History* 35 (1931): 732–36.

Sollors, Werner. "W. E. B. Du Bois in Nazi Germany, 1936." *Amerikastudien: German Association for American Studies Quarterly* 44, 2 (1999): 206–22.

Sullivan, Mary Jo. Review of *Ethnohistorical Studies on the Kru Coast,* by Ronald Davis. *Journal of African History* 19, 2 (1978): 280–82.

Sundiata, Ibrahim. "Didwo Twe: Liberian Opposition and Hinterland Policy in the Twentieth Century." "Grass Roots Leadership in Colonial West Africa," *Tarikh* 7, 1 (1981): 47–56.

Taylor, Arnold. "The Involvement of Black Americans in the [Liberian] Forced Labor Controversy, 1929–1935." In *Proceedings of the Conference on Afro-Americans and Africans: Historical and Political Linkages, Held June 13–14, 1974, Washington, D.C., at Howard University.* Washington, D.C.: Howard University Press, 1974.

Taylor, R. R. "Looking over Liberia." *Southern Workman,* March 1930, 122–31.

Tonkin, Elizabeth. Review of *Ethnohistorical Studies on the Kru Coast,* by Ronald Davis. *International Journal of African Historical Studies* 10, 3 (1977): 533–35.

Walker, Walter F. "Did the Liberian Natives Speak?" *Crisis,* November 1934, 340.

Walton, Lester. "Liberia's New Industrial Development." *Current History* 31, (1929): 108–14.

"War in Liberia: Kru King Captured as Beaten Tribesmen Die in Jungle." *Literary Digest,* November 7, 1936, 15–16.

Weisbord, Robert G. "Marcus Garvey, Pan-Negroist: The View from Whitehall." *Race* 11, 4 (1970): 419–29.

Young, James C. "Liberia and Its Future." *Opportunity,* November 1928, 327–31.

Young, Reuben S. "Ethiopia Awakens." *Crisis,* August 1936, 262–63, 283.

Papers, Interviews, Unpublished Manuscripts, Dissertations, and Theses

Akpan, M. B. "The African Policy of the Liberian Settlers, 1841–1932: A Study of the 'Native' Policy of a Non-colonial Power in Africa." Ph.D. diss., Ibadan University, 1968.

Barleycorn, Edward. Interview by the author. Santa Isabel (now Malabo), Republic of Equatorial Guinea, March 2, 1970.

Beecher, Lloyd N. "The State Department and Liberia, 1908–1941: A Heterogeneous Record." Ph.D. diss., University of Georgia, 1971.

Bodie, Charles A. "The Images of Africa in the Black American Press, 1890–1930." Ph.D. diss., Indiana University, 1975.

Breitborde, L. B. "Some Linguistic Evidence in the Study of Kru Ethnolinguistic Affiliation." Paper presented at the ninth annual conference of the Liberian Studies Association, Macomb, Ill., April 1977.

Chalk, Frank. "The United States and the International Struggle for Rubber, 1914–1941." Ph.D. diss., University of Wisconsin, 1970.

Chaudhuri, Jyotirmoy P. "British Policy towards Liberia, 1912–1939." Ph.D. diss., University of Birmingham, 1975.

Coger, Dalvan. "Black American Immigration to Liberia, 1900–1930." Paper presented at the eighth annual conference of the Liberian Studies Association, Bloomington, Ind., March 1976.

Cole, Johnnetta Betsch. "Traditional and Wage-Earning Labor among Tribal Liberians." Ph.D. diss., Northwestern University, 1967.

Cole, Robert Eugene. "The Liberian Elite as a Barrier to Economic Development." Ph.D. diss., Northwestern University, 1967.

Favor, J. Martin. "Building Black: Constructions of Multiple African American Subject Positions in Novels by James Weldon Johnson, Jean Toomer, Nella Larsen, and George Schuyler." Ph.D. diss., University of Michigan, 1993.

Forderhase, Nancy. "The Plans That Failed: The United States and Liberia, 1920–1935." Ph.D. diss., University of Missouri, 1971.

Guannu, Joseph. "Liberia and the League of Nations." Ph.D. diss., Fordham University, 1972.

Haywood, Harry. "Eighth Convention: Description of Eighth Convention of the Communist Party of the United States, Cleveland, Ohio, April 2–8, 1934." Chapter 13 of unpublished autobiographical manuscript draft, c. 1975.

Hickey, Dennis. "Ethiopia and Great Britain: Political Conflict in the Southern Borderlands, 1916–1935." Ph.D. diss., Northwestern University, 1984.

Hodge, Edwin Gahie Gyude. Chapters 48 and 54 of unpublished autobiography, c. 1995.

Holsoe, Svend E. "Liberians: Americans and Africana." Paper presented at the Annual Liberian Studies Association, Newark, Delaware, November 1995.

Hunt, William A. "From Cabin to Consulate: The Autobiography of William H. Hunt." Unpublished manuscript. Ed. Harold T. Pinkett. Typescript in the possession of Mrs. Phyllis Gibbs Fauntleroy, Washington, D.C.

Johnson, Charles. "Bitter Canaan: The Story of Liberia," Johnson Papers, Department of Social Science, Fisk University, 1930.

Jones, Hanna Abeodu Bowen. "The Struggle for Political and Cultural Unification in Liberia, 1847–1930." Ph.D. diss., Northwestern University, 1962.

Klein, Martin A. "Slavery and the French Conquest of the Sahara." Paper presented at the annual meeting of the African Studies Association, Orlando, Florida, 1995.

Martin, Jane Jackson. "The Dual Legacy: Government Authority and Mission Influence among the Glebo of Eastern Liberia, 1834–1910." Ph.D. diss., Boston University, 1968.

Mayson, Dew Tuan-Wleh, and Amos Sawyer. "Capitalism and the Struggle of the Working Class in Liberia." Paper presented at the meeting of the Liberian Research Association, Buchanan, Liberia, June 23, 1978.

McCann, James. "The Political Economy of Rural Rebellion in Ethiopia: Northern Resistance to Imperial Expansion, 1928–1935." Working paper, African Studies Center, Boston University, 1984.

Mitchell, John Payne. "America's Liberian Policy." Master's thesis, University of Chicago, 1955.

Norris, Parthenia. "The United States and Liberia: The Slavery Crisis, 1929–1935." Ph.D. diss., Indiana University, 1961.

Ross, Rodney. "Black Americans and Haiti, Liberia, the Virgin Islands, and Ethiopia, 1929–1936." Ph.D. diss., University of Chicago, 1975.

Sullivan, Mary Jo. "Sinoe Settler Politics in the Late Nineteenth Century." Paper presented at the tenth annual conference of the Liberian Studies Association, Boston, April 1978.

Tonkin, Elizabeth. "Producers in Jlao [Sasstown]." Paper presented in absentia at the ninth annual conference of the Liberian Studies Association, Macomb, Ill., April 1977.

Venator Santiago, Charles R. "The Other Nationalists: Marcus Garvey and Pedro Albizu Campos." Master's thesis, University of Massachusetts, 1996.

Williams, Harry M. "When Black Is Right: The Life and Writings of George S. Schuyler." Ph.D. diss., Brown University, 1988.

Williams, Oscar R. "The Making of a Black Conservative: George S. Schuyler." Ph.D. diss., Ohio State University, 1997.

Yancy, Jerome. "The Recent Liberian Crisis and Its Causes." An Address delivered at Buffalo, New York, August 12 and 14, 1934, under Auspices of the Buffalo Liberian Research Society. Wilberforce, Ohio, 1934.

Yoder, John C. "He Kill My Ma, He Kill My Pa, I Will Vote for Him: A Study of Civic Values and State Failure in Liberia." Unpublished manuscript, 2001.

Index

Partridge, Mrs. Daniel, Jr., 176
Patterson, Orlando, 7, 9, 147, 308
Patton, Robert W., 123, 164–65
Pawning, 55–58, 123, 132–35, 147, 189, 283
Payne, Donald, 339
Peabody, George Foster, 208
Peace Movement of Ethiopia, 289, 309–12, 317, 320
Pearson, Drew, 207
Pennsylvania State Negro Council, 188
People's Party, 38, 136–38, 212, 220, 252
Pêtre, R., 35–36
Phelps-Stokes, Anson, 123, 207
Phelps-Stokes Fund, 131, 164, 167, 188, 207, 209
Philadelphia Public Ledger, 231
Philanthropic organizations, 209, 269, 270
Philippines, 126
Phillips, J. C., 135
Phillips, Ulrich B., 7
Phillips, Wendell, 177, 189
Phillips, William, 175–79, 192–93, 200, 292
Picaninny Cess, 70, 257, 262
Pickens, William, 21, 173, 291
Pinkett, Archie, 176
Pittsburgh Courier, 206, 217, 221, 230, 231, 245, 307–8
Poland, 149, 184, 253
Po River people, 83–84
Poro, 52, 53, 59
Porte, Albert, 125
Porter, R. C., 225
Poston, Robert L., 32, 33
Powell, Reverend Adam Clayton, Jr., 291
Protestant Episcopal Mission, 188

Quakers, black, 24

Race men, 210, 212, 231, 249–50, 298
Racism and race consciousness, 76, 98, 150, 156, 173, 210, 237, 304–5, 307, 315–17, 334–35, 338; African, 202, 300; American, 101–4, 144, 177, 308–21; Liberian, 162–63
Radway, S. P., 215
Randolph, A. Phillip, 21, 42, 106, 230, 320
Randolph, Dr. J. H., 191
Ransom, Bishop R. C., 193
Ras Tafari. *See* Haile Selassie
Rastafarians and Rastafarianism, 301–2
Reform plan. *See* League of Nations, Liberian reform plan of
Republican National Committee, 166–67
Republican Party, 199
Revenues, government, 62, 66, 88, 148, 150, 159, 195, 253, 284–85
Rice, Susan, 339
Richburg, Keith, 7, 232, 254–55
Río Muni, 80
Road-building. *See* Labor, Liberian
Robeson, Eslanda Goode, 328
Robeson, Paul, 296, 328
Robinson, John Charles, 291
Roosevelt, Eleanor, 320
Roosevelt, Franklin D., 163, 165, 168, 174, 178, 181, 185, 192–93, 196, 199, 217, 289, 310, 325; administration of, 139, 170–71, 176, 178, 185–86, 201, 204, 209
Roosevelt, Theodore, 30–31, 314
Ross, D. A., 110, 114, 116
Ross family, 37
Ross, J. J., 69
Ross, Samuel Alford, 69–70, 85–87, 89–94, 97, 134, 274
Roy, L. A., 208
Rubber industry, 194–95, 201, 223–24, 227–28. *See also* Britain, rubber interests of; Firestone Rubber Company
Russell, F. A. K., 259
Russia, Soviet, 208, 306–7, 325–26, 337
Rydings, D. D., 260

Stuart, John, 256–57
"Syrian Problem," 213

Taxation, 93, 148; on coffee, 89; exemptions for Firestone, 196; indigenous population and, 62–63, 70, 80, 225, 330; on laborers, 66, 80, 85, 96. *See also* Revenues, government
Taylor, Charles, 255, 331–32
Togba, Blogba, 275
Togba, Dappe, 275
Togba, Samuel, 92
Tolbert, William R., Jr., 254, 330
Touré, Kwame, 334
Trade, 214, 253, 336; European, 84
TransAfrica, 335, 336
Travell, Winthrop, 259–60
True Whig Party, 37, 60, 83, 103, 124, 136–38, 194, 212, 252, 254, 326–27
Tubman family, 37
Tubman, William V. S., 83–84, 135, 284, 325, 327, 329–30
Turner, Bishop Henry McNeal, 7, 28
Tuskegee Institute, 31, 106, 175, 208, 223, 253, 273
Twe, Didwo, 274–77, 283, 285

United States: adviser, proposed, 153; dealings with Firestone, 108–14; foreign policy of, 119, 205; Garvey Pan-Africanism and, 15–23, 108, 123; League of Nations and, 171; Liberian labor and, 97, 100, 104, 108; racial considerations and, 100–104; relations with Liberia of, 102, 107; support of Liberia, 30. *See also* African Americans, foreign policy role of; State Department, U.S.
Universal Ethiopian Students Association, 188
Universal Negro Improvement Association, 1, 15–21, 25, 31, 32, 35, 39, 42, 49, 64, 68, 75, 77, 79–80, 96, 106, 108, 110, 122, 124,
132, 173, 221, 248–50, 288, 291, 300, 302, 282, 310–16, 319, 320

Vai people, 52, 54–59, 61, 63, 148, 274
Van Kirk, Walter, 189
Villard, Henry, 328
Villard, Oswald Garrison, 179

Walker, Walter F., 279, 281
Walton, Lester, 175, 182, 191, 204–10, 222, 227, 253, 261, 271, 284, 303, 311–13, 325–25
Washington, Booker T., 7, 12, 17, 27, 30, 188, 313–14
Washington Post, 231
Watson, District Commissioner, 135
Watson family, 37
Waugh, Evelyn, 229, 238, 303
Weah, Parle, 271–72
Wedabo people, 83–85
Weekly Mirror, 194
Wesley, Charles, 130, 176, 280
Wesley, Henry Too, 273, 274
West, Cornel, 8, 211
West, Henry, 129, 165, 167, 188, 191, 208, 222
West Africa, 28, 98, 132, 148, 235, 332; U.S. policy toward, 97, 111, 214, 310. *See also* Africa
West African Review, 252, 259
West African Student Union, 290
West Indies, 11, 17, 76, 241; emigration from, 18, 75, 289 90
Wharton, Clifton, 128–29, 202
White, Walter, 107, 144, 162–63, 173–76, 178, 185, 188–89, 201, 216, 231, 236, 290
Williams, L. K., 193, 221
Williamstown Institute of Politics, 121
Wilkins, Roy, 103, 198, 291
Winship, Blanton, 169, 171–72, 174–75, 178–81, 184–85, 200, 204
Wissipo (Wissapo), people of, 272–73
Woermann Line, 90

IBRAHIM SUNDIATA is a Professor of History and African and Afro-American Studies at Brandeis University. His books include *From Slaving to Neoslavery: The Bight of Biafra and Fernando Po in the Era of Abolition* (1996), *Equatorial Guinea: Colonialism, State Terror, and the Search for Stability* (1990), and *Black Scandal: America and the Liberian Labor Crisis, 1929–1936* (1980).